MW00989808

TRADE POLICY AND GENDER EQUALITY

Trade policies create both 'winners' and 'losers', as some actors stand to benefit and others are left behind. More often than not, it has been women who have borne the negative impacts of international trade policy and it is thus imperative that future trade policy is negotiated and implemented with an eye towards women empowerment. This collection presents an innovative, systematic evaluation of the debate relating to international trade law, policy and gender equality. It analyses the role of WTO as a trade policy setter, current debates and possibilities for gender-inclusive trade agreements and other emerging topics such as e-commerce and gender-responsive standards. With a range of interdisciplinary contributions, contributions from diverse authors and national and regional case studies, this collection offers a comprehensive, up-to-date analysis of the intersections between trade law and gender, and is vital to ensuring that both men and women 'win' from trade policy in the future. This title is also available as Open Access on Cambridge Core.

Amrita Bahri is Associate Professor of International Trade Law at Instituto Tecnológico Autónomo de México (ITAM) and Co-chair Professor for the WTO Chair Program (Mexico). Bahri has published in the areas of international trade law, WTO dispute settlement, regional trade and gender justice. She serves on the Editorial Board of the *Journal of International Economic Law* and *Journal of Law, Market & Innovation*. She has been appointed by the European Commission to chair the Expert Panel Proceedings on Trade and Sustainable Development and she is an Advisory Board Member of the Center on Inclusive Trade and Development at Georgetown University.

Dorotea López is Director and Associate Professor at the Institute of International Studies of the University of Chile. Prior to joining the university, she served in the Chilean Directorate of International Economic Affairs, the Mexican Economy Secretariat and the Bank of Mexico. Her main research areas are trade policy and trade in services. She holds the Chilean WTO Chair and is part of the Chilean Foreign Policy Forum.

Jan Yves Remy is Director of the Shridath Ramphal Centre for International Trade Law, Policy and Services (SRC) at the University of the West Indies, Cave Hill Campus, Barbados. She is also the WTO Chair holder for the University of the West Indies, has been nominated as a panelist on two WTO disputes and has been included on the list of arbitrators under EU and UK FTA dispute settlement mechanisms. She serves on a number of boards, including as Board Member of Caribbean Women in Trade and the Executive Committee for TradeLab.

Trade Policy and Gender Equality

Edited by

AMRITA BAHRI

Instituto Tecnológico Autónomo de México

DOROTEA LÓPEZ

University of Chile

JAN YVES REMY

The University of the West Indies

Shaftesbury Road, Cambridge CB2 8EA, United Kingdom

One Liberty Plaza, 20th Floor, New York, NY 10006, USA

477 Williamstown Road, Port Melbourne, VIC 3207, Australia

314–321, 3rd Floor, Plot 3, Splendor Forum, Jasola District Centre, New Delhi – 110025, India

103 Penang Road, #05-06/07, Visioncrest Commercial, Singapore 238467

Cambridge University Press is part of Cambridge University Press & Assessment, a department of the University of Cambridge.

We share the University's mission to contribute to society through the pursuit of education, learning and research at the highest international levels of excellence.

www.cambridge.org
Information on this title: www.cambridge.org/9781009363709

DOI: 10.1017/9781009363716

When citing this work, please include a reference to the DOI 10.1017/9781009363716

First published 2023

A catalogue record for this publication is available from the British Library.

A Cataloging-in-Publication data record for this book is available from the Library of Congress

ISBN 978-1-009-36370-9 Hardback

Contents

Contributors

Renata Vargas Amaral is an experienced international trade lawyer, with an extensive and proven record of successful engagement at the World Trade Organization (WTO), bilateral and regional trade negotiations, domestic trade policy and market access. Over the course of her fifteen-year career, she has advised governments and private stakeholders on international trade matters, with a focus on WTO law. She currently serves as Adjunct Professor at the American University Washington College of Law, where she co-directs the certificate programme on WTO and US Trade Law and Policy. Dr Amaral is a Senior Consultant, the Vice-Chair of the ABCI Institute – a non-profit organization of international trade scholars headquartered in Washington, DC, and the founder of Women Inside Trade, a non-profit international organization that aims to contribute to the empowerment of women through its global network of professionals, specialized training and leadership development. She holds a PhD from Maastricht University (Netherlands) and the title of Doctor of Laws (sum cum laude) from the Federal University of Santa Carina – UFSC (Brazil), a LLM in international business law from Complutense University of Madrid (Spain), and a LLB from USFC. She is a frequent public speaker, and has published a book and several papers.

Amrita Bahri is Associate Professor of International Trade Law at Instituto Tecnológico Autónomo de México (ITAM) and Co-chair Professor for the WTO Chairs Programme (Mexico). Amrita has published in the areas of international trade law, WTO dispute settlement, public–private partnership for capacity-building in emerging economies, regional trade and gender justice. She serves on the Editorial Board of the *Journal of International Economic Law* (JIEL) and the *Journal of Law, Market & Innovation* (JLMI). Amrita has been appointed by the European Commission to the pool of candidates to chair the Expert Panel Proceedings on Trade and Sustainable

Development. She also serves on the Advisory Board of the Center on Inclusive Trade and Development at Georgetown University. Working with the International Trade Centre's team, Amrita has designed the very first framework to measure the gender responsiveness of free trade agreements. She explains this framework in ITC's policy paper titled 'Mainstreaming Gender in Free Trade Agreements'.

Tonni Brodber is the Representative of the UN Women Multi-Country Office – Caribbean. Prior to her appointment in August 2020, Ms Brodber served as Deputy Representative from 2015 to 2020 with the MCO Caribbean. Before this, she was the Team Leader for the Advancing Gender Justice in the Pacific programme with the UN Women Fiji Multi-Country Office. Ms Brodber served as the Gender Specialist for the United Nations Development Programme in South Africa, as well as briefly with the UN Women South Africa Multi-Country Office and established what is now the UN Women Country Office in Haiti. Her work experience also includes lecturing in International Relations and Development Studies at Yanshan University in China, and directing and co-producing, a film on Haiti.

Javiera Cáceres Bustamante is an instructor professor at the Institute of International Studies of the University of Chile. She holds a BA in English Literature and Linguistics from the Pontifical Catholic University of Chile and a MA in International Strategy and Trade Policy from the University of Chile. She has been a consultant for the World Bank, Interamerican Development Bank, Economic Commission for Latin America and the Caribbean (ECLAC), and the Chilean Under-Secretariat of International Economic Affairs on international trade and trade policy issues. Her main research interests are gender and trade, intellectual property, and trade policy.

Lillyana Sophia Daza Jaller currently works in the International Trade Unit of the World Bank, where she advises developing countries on regulatory issues related to digital trade. Prior to joining the World Bank, she served as Law Clerk at the Office of the United States Trade Representative in Washington, DC. Her experience also includes working as a Summer Associate at BMJ Consultores Associados, where she collaborated with research, writing, and lobbying efforts for World Trade Organization disputes on behalf of Brazil. Lillyana received her Juris Doctor from the American University Washington College of Law as well as a Certification of Information Privacy Professional from the International Association of Privacy Professionals. She volunteers on a pro bono basis for Catholic Charities Immigration Legal Services in order to use her legal skills in the service of others.

Anoush der Boghossian is the WTO Gender Policy Adviser and the Head of Trade and Gender in the WTO. She was appointed as the WTO's first trade and gender expert by former Director-General Roberto Azevêdo in 2017. She is one of the co-authors of the WTO/World Bank report on 'Women and Trade' and has published many articles and working papers on trade and gender. With four other experts, she organized and delivered a panel at Society of International Economic Law (SIEL) 2021 Milan Global Conference on 'Mainstreaming Gender in Trade and Investment Agreements: Best Practice Examples and the Missing Elements'. Anoush is a senior staff member of the WTO with fifteen years' experience in the Organization. Prior to her current responsibilities, she worked as the French-language spokesperson of the WTO, as the press officer to the former Director-General Pascal Lamy and to the former Deputy Director-General Valentine Rugwabiza. She also served the WTO as the NGO Liaison Officer and managed the WTO Public Forum for four years. Anoush began her career at the WTO in 2006 after acquiring ten years of professional experience in the private sector, in Brussels, working on EU policies as a public relations specialist. Among her educational achievements, she holds a Master's in European and International Law and a Master's in Communications. Among her personal achievements, she is a member of the 'Confrérie des Chevaliers du Tastevin', Chateau Clos de Vougeot (Burgundy, France) and she is an experienced diver.

Judit Fabian's work centres upon the idea of democratic global economic governance, which she is developing under the framework of inclusive global institutionalism. Her research has led to numerous academic and policy contributions in Canada and internationally, including presentations, authorship, and engagement with governments, arms-length organizations, and intergovernmental organizations. She co-authored the most downloaded Centre for International Governance Innovation (CIGI) paper of 2017, concerning the modernization of the North American Free Trade Agreement (NAFTA). She has also published on the question of preferential trade agreements versus multilateralism (2020) and is a proud contributor to the *Handbook on Gender, Diversity and Federalism* (2020) with a chapter on global governance. Judit is currently a fellow at the Canadian Global Affairs Institute, a visiting researcher at the Graduate School of Public and International Affairs, University of Ottawa, and is a member of the core group of the recently formed Gender Research Hub of the World Trade Organization (Switzerland). She completed a post-doctoral appointment at the School of Public Policy, University of Calgary, earned her PhD in political science at Carleton University, and her MA in political studies from Queen's University.

Vineet Hegde is a doctoral researcher at the Leuven Centre for Global Governance Studies, KU Leuven, Belgium. He is a teaching assistant in the Law of the WTO at the Faculty of Law and Criminology, KU Leuven, and also coaches the university's teams for the John H. Jackson Moot Court Competition. Vineet manages the Oxford Reports on International Trade Law Decisions, and supervises master theses on international economic law at the university. He has previously worked with the Government of India. Vineet holds an LLM from Georgetown University Law Center. He has published in the areas of international trade law in journals such as *Journal of International Economic Law* and the *Cambridge International Law Journal*.

Katrin Kuhlmann is Visiting Professor of Law at Georgetown University Law Center and the President and Founder of the New Markets Lab, a non-profit law and development centre. She is also a Senior Associate with the Global Food Security Program of the Center for Strategic and International Studies (CSIS), and serves as a member of the Trade Advisory Committee on Africa of the Office of the United States Trade Representative (USTR) and the Bretton Woods Committee. Her work and research focus on trade and development and comparative economic law, and she has developed a methodology for the design and implementation of inclusive trade rules. She was previously Lecturer in Law at Harvard Law School and the Yeutter Visiting Professor of Law at the University of Nebraska College of Law, Clayton Yeutter Institute of International Trade and Finance. Earlier in her career, she served as a trade negotiator at USTR and a lawyer at two international law firms, and she has held senior positions with several non-profit organizations and think tanks, including the Aspen Institute and German Marshall Fund. She holds degrees from Harvard Law School and Creighton University and was the recipient of a Fulbright scholarship to study international economics.

Dorotea López is Director and Associate Professor at the Institute of International Studies of the University of Chile. She holds a BA in Economics from Instituto Tecnológico Autónomo de México (ITAM), Mexico, an MPhil in Economics from Cambridge University and a PhD in Social Science from the University of Chile. Prior to joining the university she served in the Chilean Directorate of International Economic Affairs, the Mexican Economy Secretariat, and the Bank of Mexico. Her main research areas are trade policy and trade in services. She holds the Chilean WTO Chair and is part of the Chilean Foreign Policy Forum.

Mia Mikic is a trade economist with a keen interest in sustainable development and with a proven track record and experience in academia and international civil service. She is a board member of the Friends of Multilateralism Group and an Advisor at Large for the Asia-Pacific Research and Training Network on Trade (ARTNeT), an open network of research and academic institutions and think tanks in the Asia-Pacific region. She is also Visiting Fellow at the Institute for Euro-Asian Studies, the Faculty of Economics and Business, University of Zagreb, and a Research Fellow at the Waikato Management School, University of Waikato, New Zealand. Previously, she was Director for the Trade, Investment and Innovation Division in United Nations ESCAP (2017–2021), and has performed other functions in the UN (2005–2017). She was also Head of the Department of Economic Theory, Professor of International Economics and Director of Economic and Business International Programme at the University of Zagreb (2001–2005) following various other positions (1978–1988).

Felipe Muñoz Navia is Associate Professor at the Institute of International Studies of the University of Chile and Invited Researcher at Fudan Development Institute, China. He holds a BA in Economics and MA in International Studies, both from the University of Chile, and is PhD Fellow at Maastricht University, The Netherlands. His main research areas are trade policy and international economics, with particular emphasis on Latin America. He has participated in various research projects, including the WTO Chairs Programme and UNCTAD's Virtual Institute, and acted as a consultant for the World Bank, Interamerican Development Bank, Economic Commission for Latin America and the Caribbean (ECLAC), Japan External Trade Organization (JETRO) and the Chilean Under-Secretariat of International Economic Affairs, amongst others.

Marie-France Paquet has been the Chief Economist and Director General, Trade Analysis Bureau, at Global Affairs Canada since September 2017. As Chief Economist, she leads a team of analysts in reporting and advising on international trade, investment and economic issues. Current economic research and analysis projects include the impact of trade agreements on labour and gender, the determinants of export for SMEs, the impact of the Trade Commissioner Services on Canadian exporters' performance, or the impact of foreign direct investment on the economy, the vulnerability of Canadian supply chains, and the impact of COVID-19 on trade. Dr Paquet received her PhD in Econometrics from Université Laval jointly with Université Paris I Panthéon-Sorbonne.

Michelle Parkouda is Manager, Research at the Standards Council of Canada (SCC). She is responsible for leading research to demonstrate the economic and social value of standardization. She co-leads the gender strategy at SCC and is heading a project team at the United Nations Economic Commission for Europe drafting guidance on developing gender-responsive standards. Michelle has published research on the topics of gender, diversity, and trade. She has a PhD in Social Psychology from McGill University.

Jan Yves Remy is Director of the Shridath Ramphal Centre for International Trade Law, Policy and Services (SRC) at the University of the West Indies, Cave Hill Campus, Barbados, where she lectures in the SRC's flagship Master's in International Trade Policy Programme and conducts research on trade law, WTO reform, gender and trade, dispute settlement regimes, regional integration, climate change and e-commerce Her doctoral thesis focused on the role of the Caribbean Court of Justice in promoting Caribbean regional integration. She is also the WTO Chair for the University of the West Indies (Cave Hill Campus, Barbados), has been nominated as a panellist on two WTO disputes, and has been included on the list of arbitrators under EU and UK FTA dispute settlement mechanisms. She serves on a number of boards, including as Board Member of the Interim Board for Caribbean Women in Trade, as well as on the Executive Committee for TradeLab.

Maria V. Sokolova is an international trade expert with specialization in monetary aspects of trade integration, regionalism, and gender, currently at the International Institute in Geneva. She has experience in various international organizations, academia, and the private sector, and her empirical research has been published in peer-reviewed journals. She holds a PhD in International Economics and Law from the Graduate Institute, MSc from the University of St Andrews, and BSc from Russian Economic Academy. As a member of the Trade Experettes, Maria is an advocate for women's representation and empowerment in trade policy.

Amalie Giødesen Thystrup is Head of Section with the Danish Energy Agency. In the role of project manager, she is part of the team tasked with bringing the world's first energy islands to life. She was a post-doctoral researcher at the University of Copenhagen, Faculty of Law. Amalie holds a PhD from the University of Copenhagen (2018), awarded for a dissertation on trade in services. She has been a visiting scholar at Columbia Law School, Columbia Center on Sustainable Investment (CCSI), the WTO, and the Graduate Institute (IHEID), and she has been a stagiaire with the EU's

Mission to the WTO. Amalie has practised law in Denmark, and is admitted to the Bar in New York. She holds Master's degrees in Law from Benjamin N. Cardozo School of Law, NY (2012), and the University of Copenhagen (2011). Her scientific focus spans international trade law, sustainability, trade and gender, services, FDI, transport, and e-commerce.

Pieter Van Vaerenbergh is a trade and customs lawyer at Fieldfisher Brussels. He is also a teaching assistant in EU law at the Institute for European Law of KU Leuven and a lecturer at the Europa-Institut, Saarland University. Previously, Pieter was a research associate and PhD candidate at Saarland University, where his research and teaching activities focused on EU trade defence, sustainable trade law, and international dispute resolution. His work has appeared in, inter alia, the *Journal of World Trade* and the *Journal of International Arbitration*. Pieter also serves as an editorial board member of the *Zeitschrift for Europarechtliche Studien* (ZEuS) and coaches the Vis Moot team of Saarland University. Pieter graduated in law from Ghent University and obtained an LLM degree in International and European Law from the Europa-Institut, Saarland University. During his studies, he also interned at the European Court of Justice and the OECD.

Georgina Wainwright-Kemdirim is a senior official at Global Affairs Canada. She serves as lead negotiator of Canada's inclusive trade chapters in trade agreements, including Trade and Gender, and leads on the implementation of those in-force chapters. She was Canada's lead negotiator for the new Global Trade and Gender Arrangement recently signed by Canada and its Inclusive Trade Action Group partners – New Zealand and Chile. She is also Canada's Gender Focal Point for trade policy and negotiations and developed Canada's new approach for applying a comprehensive Gender-Based Analysis Plus (GBA Plus) to trade negotiations and final agreements.

Gabrielle White is a senior trade policy analyst currently working for the Government of Canada, where she leads a standards secretariat for the Department of Natural Resources. She previously worked as a programme manager for the Standards Council of Canada (SCC), where her work focused on standards and conformance, and oversaw SCC's input on the standardization components of Canada's FTAs and regulatory cooperation. In addition to her work in trade policy, Gabrielle is responsible for spearheading SCC's gender and standardization strategy, and continues to lead key initiatives in this area. She holds a Master's in Sociology.

Matthew Wilson is the Chief of Special Projects at the International Trade Centre. He has held various roles including Chief of Staff at the ITC, Senior

Adviser to the WTO Director General, Deputy Aid for Trade Coordinator at the WTO, and Trade and Human Rights negotiator for the Government of Barbados. He was the first 'Friend of the Chair' for the special and differential treatment negotiations of the Trade Facilitation Agreement. He holds degrees in Psychology, International Relations, and Development Studies, and is a Chevening Scholar. He is an innovation, diversity, and inclusion champion at the ITC.

Simonetta Zarrilli is Chief of the Trade, Gender and Development Programme of the United Nations Conference on Trade and Development (UNCTAD), a programme she has been leading since 2010. An experienced trade analyst with a long and successful career at the UN, Simonetta has worked on many trade issues, including preferential trade schemes; health, environment, and energy services; trade and biotechnology and renewable energies. She has carried out numerous analytical, intergovernmental, and technical cooperation activities on these issues, and has authored and coordinated many publications. Ms Zarrilli holds a postgraduate degree in European Studies from the College of Europe, Bruges (Belgium) and a degree in Law from the University of Siena (Italy). She is fluent in English, French, Spanish, and Portuguese, apart from her native Italian.

Foreword

Women play strategic roles in societal advancements and economic growth. They are essential partners in any country's journey towards increased economic, social, environmental and cultural sustainability. Trade can be key to strengthening women's role as economic actors, and therefore their engagement in trade is crucial. This engagement can be promoted by trade policy, though policy measures in other fields are necessary to make equal opportunities in trade a reality.

Women are not on the same footing as men in many areas, including when it comes to accessing the opportunities created by trade. Gender inequality is a long, widespread and stubborn form of inequality. It will now take more than 130 years to close the gender gap globally, and in 2022, a woman still had only three-quarters of the rights of a man. Evidence shows that women constitute 38 per cent of the global formal workforce, and they are paid, on average, only 77 per cent of what men earn worldwide. Recent studies show that the gender wage gap persists in export-oriented industries, even if women earn more compared to domestic-oriented industries. Additionally, only one out of five exporting companies is women-led. The uneven distribution of unpaid care work between men and women is inhibiting many women from achieving their full potential as economic agents, including in trade. Too many women are still working and trading in the informal sector, making them vulnerable to the economic, social and physical risks attached to it. There are too few women in leadership positions, especially in trade. In the WTO only 36 per cent of ambassadors are women and about 30 per cent of ministers in charge of WTO affairs are women.

This reality, however, can be changed and made anew. Trade can open a door to women's employment, offering decent work and economic independence. Trade can make the difference by lifting women out of poverty, provided they get a voice and that accompanying policies are in place.

In addition to the traditional barriers women face in trade, growing political instability, health crises and climate change are disproportionately and negatively impacting women's livelihoods and prospects.

That is why we need this book. It looks at trade and gender from a holistic perspective, approaching the issue from historical and negotiation angles. It also focuses on innovative and forward-looking trade initiatives and policies adopted regionally and nationally. Lastly, it puts a rare emphasis on the most vulnerable women in the world, those living in Least-Developed Countries. This volume is not about proving the links between trade policy and gender equality. They were clearly established a decade ago. In fact, this book is more than a book. It is a trade policy tool providing ideas to decision makers on how to make sure that trade truly delivers for all.

Dr Ngozi Okonjo-Iweala
Director-General of the World Trade Organization

Rebeca Grynspan
Secretary-General of the United Nations Conference on Trade and Development

Pamela Coke-Hamilton
Executive Director of the International Trade Centre

Acknowledgements

This book is the product of many who persevered over many months to see it to its successful conclusion. First, we would like to thank the authors of this volume for their valuable contributions, without which the global perspective represented would not have been possible. We would also like to thank Vineet Hegde and Pieter Van Vaerenbergh for their excellent assistance with editing and formatting the manuscript. Our heartfelt thanks to the WTO Director-General Dr Ngozi Okonjo-Iweala for her global leadership on women's empowerment issues, generally, and her unequivocal support, in particular, for this project. We express gratitude to her and to the other heads of Geneva-based trade organizations – UNCTAD and ITC – for contributing to this book's Foreword. We acknowledge, with warmth, the continuous support provided by our respective universities – the University of the West Indies, Cave Hill Campus, the University of Chile, and the Instituto Tecnológico Autónomo de México (ITAM, Mexico) – and the financing generously offered by the WTO Chairs Programme, the WTO Trade and Gender Unit and the University of Chile. Through that funding, we have been able to publish this book as an open-access resource and thereby guarantee that it can be widely disseminated and shared. Finally, we note that, as WTO Chairs of the Americas, we would not have been able to collaborate on this project without the platform provided through the WTO Chairs Programme and the WTO Secretariat team servicing it.

Abbreviations

50MAWS	50 Million African Women Speak Platform
AB	Appellate Body
ABAC	APEC Business Advisory Council
ACWL	Advisory Center on WTO Law
AFAWA	Affirmative Finance Action for Women in Africa
AfCFTA	African Continental Free Trade Area
AI	artificial intelligence
ANZCERTA	Australia–New Zealand Closer Economic Agreement
AoA	Agreement on Agriculture
APEC	Asia-Pacific Economic Cooperation
ASCC	APEC Study Centers Consortium
ASEAN	Association of Southeast Asian Nations
ASELA	Association of Entrepreneurs of Latin America
AU	African Union
BIT	bilateral investment treaties
BPfA	Beijing Platform for Action
BPO	business process outsourcing
BRICS	Brazil, Russia, India, China and South Africa
CAFRA	Caribbean Association Feminist Research and Action
CARICOM	Caribbean Community
CCFTA	Chile–Canada Free Trade Agreement
CEDAW	Convention on the Elimination of All Forms of Discrimination Against Women
CEO	Chief Executive Officer
CETA	Comprehensive and Economic Trade Agreement
CGE	computable general equilibrium
CIDA	Canadian International Development Agency

CIFTA	Canada–Israel Free Trade Agreement
COMESA	Common Market for Eastern and Southern Africa
CORFO	Chilean Economic Development Agency
CPTPP	Comprehensive and Progressive Agreement for Trans-Pacific Partnership
CSO	civil society organizations
CUSFTA	Canada–US Free Trade Agreement
CUSMA	Canada–United States–Mexico Agreement
DAWN	Decade for Women and Development Alternatives with Women for a New Era
DEPA	Digital Economy Partnership Agreement
DG	Director-General
DIRECON	General Directorate of International Economic Relations
DR	domestic regulation
DSM	dispute settlement mechanism
DSU	dispute settlement understanding
EAC	East African Community
EASSI	East African Sub-Regional Support Initiative
ECA	Economic Commission for Africa
ECCAS	Economic Community of Central African States
ECE	Economic Commission for Europe
ECLAC	UN Economic Commission for Latin America and the Caribbean
ECOSOC	Economic and Social Council
ECOWAS	Economic Community of West African States
EEZs	Exclusive Economic Zones
EIA	Economic Impact Assessment
EIF	Enhanced Integrated Framework
EPZ	Export Processing Zone
ESCAP	Economic and Social Commission for Asia and the Pacific
FAO	Food and Agriculture Organization
FDI	foreign direct investment
FTA	free trade agreement
FTAA	Free Trade Agreement of Americas
GAC	Global Affairs Canada
GATS	General Agreement on Trade in Services
GATT	General Agreement on Tariffs and Trade
GBA Plus or GBA+	Gender-Based Analysis Plus

GDP	gross domestic product
GSP	Generalized System of Preferences
GTAGA	Global Trade and Gender Arrangement
GTAP	Global Trade Analysis Project
GTG	Gender Technical Working Group
GVCs	global value chains
HIPC	heavily indebted poor countries
IADB	Inter-American Development Bank
IBRD	International Bank for Reconstruction and Development
ICRW	International Centre for Research on Women
ICSID	International Centre for Settlement of Investment Disputes
ICT	information and communications technology
ICTSD	International Centre for Trade and Sustainable Development
IDA	International Development Association
IEC	International Electrotechnical Commission
IEO	Independent Evaluation Office
IFC	International Finance Corporation
IGC	International Gender Champions
IIA	International Investment Agreements
ILO	International Labour Organization
ILRI	International Livestock Research Institute
IMF	International Monetary Fund
INGO	international non-governmental organizations
IO	international organizations
IPR	intellectual property rights
ISO	International Organization for Standardization
IT	information technology
ITAG	Inclusive Trade Action Group
ITC	International Trade Centre
ITTC	Institute for Training and Technical Cooperation
ITU	International Telecommunications Union
IWA	International Workshop Agreement
IWG	Informal Working Group
JSAG	Joint Strategic Advisory Group
JSI	Joint Statement Initiative
LAC	Latin America and the Caribbean
LDC	least-developed country

MAI	Multilateral Agreement on Investment
MC1	1st Ministerial Conference
MC11	11th WTO Ministerial Conference
MC12	12th WTO Ministerial Conference
MFN	Most Favoured Nation
MIGA	Multilateral Investment Guarantee Agency
MNE	multinational enterprises
MSME	micro, small and medium-sized enterprises
NAC	National Action Committee on the Status of Women
NAFTA	North American Free Trade Agreement
NGO	non-governmental organization
NTM	non-tariff measures
OACPS	Organisation of African, Caribbean and Pacific States
OCT	overseas countries and territories
ODA	Official Development Assistance
OECD	Organisation for Economic Co-operation and Development
PAS	publicly available specification
PPE	personal protective equipment
PPfFS	Policy Partnership for Food Security
PRGF	Poverty Reduction and Growth Facility
PRSP	Poverty Reduction Strategy Papers
PTA	preferential trade agreements
R&D	research and development
REC	regional economic communities
RMAAM	Women's Ministers and High Official Meeting of Mercosur
RMALC	Mexican Action Network on Free Trade
RMG	ready-made garment
RTA	regional trade agreement
S&DT	special and differential treatment
SADC	Southern African Development Community
SCC	Standards Council of Canada
SCM	subsidies and countervailing measures
SDG	Sustainable Development Goals
SEZ	Special Economic Zones
SIA	Sustainability Impact Analysis
SIDS	small island developing states
SME	small and medium-sized enterprises
SPS	Sanitary and Phytosanitary Measures

STDF	Standards and Trade Development Facility
STEM	science, technology, engineering and mathematics
STR	Simplified Trade Regimes
TBT	technical barriers to trade
TFA	Trade Facilitation Agreement
TFEU	Treaty on the Functioning of the European Union
TiSA	Trade in Services Agreement
TPRM	Trade Policy Review Mechanism
TRIPS	Trade Related Aspects of Intellectual Property Rights
TRTA	trade-related technical assistance
TTIP	Transatlantic Trade and Investment Partnership
UN	United Nations
UN-FfD	United Nations Conference on Financing for Development
UNCLOS	United Nations Convention on the Law of the Sea
UNCTAD	United Nations Conference on Trade and Development
UNDP	United Nations Development Programme
UNECE	United Nations Economic Commission for Europe
UNGA	United Nations General Assembly
UNWTO	United Nations World Tourism Organization
UPS	United Parcel Service
USAID	United States Agency for International Development
USMCA	United States–Mexico–Canada Agreement
VCLT	Vienna Convention on the Law of Treaties
WAEN	Women's Alternative Economic Network
WAND	Women and Development Unit
WBG	World Bank Group
WEF	World Economic Forum
WIPO	World Intellectual Property Organization
WLN	Women Leaders Network
WP.6	Working Party on Regulatory Cooperation and Standardization Policies
WPDR	Working Party on Domestic Regulation
WTO	World Trade Organization

1

Introduction

AMRITA BAHRI, DOROTEA LÓPEZ AND JAN YVES REMY

1.1 INTRODUCTORY REMARKS

With the narrowing space between international trade and domestic policy, the topic of women's empowerment[1] is increasingly becoming part of mainstream discussions in global governance circles. Indeed, renewed attention is now being paid to how international trade policies may impact gender equality.[2] Recently, multiple studies have demonstrated that trade policy is not gender-neutral.[3] Trade policies create both 'losers' and 'winners', as they benefit some and leave others behind.[4] The distributional outcomes of trade can vary between women and men, since they play different roles in society,

[1] In this book, we use the term '"women's empowerment" to refer to the process of increasing women's access to control over the strategic life choices that affect them and access to the opportunities that allow them fully to realize their capacities. Women's empowerment as an economic, political and sociocultural process challenges the system of sexual stratification that has resulted in women's subordination and marginalization in order to improve women's quality of life'. *See* Yin-Zu Chen and Hiromi Tanaka, 'Women's Empowerment' in Alex C. Michalos (ed.) *Encyclopaedia of Quality of Life and Well-Being Research* (Springer 2014).

[2] Gender equality denotes 'women having the same opportunities in life as men, including access to resources, opportunities and the ability to participate in the public sphere'. *See* Markéta von Hagen, 'Trade and Gender – Exploring a Reciprocal Relationship: Approaches to Mitigate and Measure Gender-Related Trade Impacts' (2014) *Deutsche Gesellschaft für Internationale Zusammenarbeit* <www.oecd.org/dac/gender-development/GIZ_Trade%20and%20Gender_Exploring%20a%20reciprocal%20relationship.pdf> accessed 8 May 2022.

[3] WTO, 'Women and Trade: The Role of Trade in Promoting Gender Equality' (July 2020) <www.wto.org/english/res_e/publications_e/women_trade_pub2807_e.htm> accessed 8 May 2022; OECD, 'Trade and Gender: A Framework of Analysis' (2012) OECD Trade Policy Papers <www.oecd.org/publications/trade-and-gender-6db59d80-en.htm> accessed 8 May 2022.

[4] Anthea Roberts and Nicolas Lamp, *Six Faces of Globalization: Who Wins, Who Loses, and Why It Matters* (Harvard University Press 2022).

markets, and the economy, and they enjoy different opportunities.[5] Hence, if trade policies are designed without taking into account their impact on gender powers and opportunities, these policies can magnify the existing gender gaps.[6]

Various international organizations, think tanks and countries are now turning their focus to developing a better understanding of the trade and gender nexus and how gender can be integrated into trade policies. In 2017, 118 members and observers of the World Trade Organization (WTO) agreed to a joint declaration enhancing women's empowerment in international trade.[7] This was a landmark initiative by WTO members in which they acknowledged the high degree of interconnectedness between trade and gender, and the need to have inclusive trade policies that are geared toward women's empowerment. An informal group on trade and gender was subsequently established at the WTO in 2020 to increase advocacy on women's issues and their participation in global trade.[8] These developments are aligned with and complement the other international legal instruments, such as the 1979 United Nations (UN) Convention on the Elimination of all Forms of Discrimination against Women (CEDAW).[9]

These recent developments reaffirm the intention and willingness of the WTO, as the largest trade organization, to engage in making trade more

5 Marzia Fontana and Cristina Paciello, 'Gender Dimensions of Agricultural and Rural Employment: Differentiated Pathways out of Poverty' (FAO, IFAD and ILO 2010) <www.ilo.org/employment/Whatwedo/Publications/WCMS_150558/lang–en/index.htm> accessed 8 May 2022; Marzia Fontana, 'Gender Justice in Trade Policy – The Gender Effects of Economic Partnership Agreements' (*One World Action*, 2009) <https://oneworldaction.org.uk/GendJustTrad.pdf> accessed 8 May 2022.

6 Gender refers to 'the social attributes and opportunities associated with being male and female and the relationships between women and men, and girls and boys, as well as the relations between women and those between men. These attributes, opportunities and relationships are socially constructed and are learned through socialization processes'. *See* UN Women, 'Concepts and Definitions' <www.un.org/womenwatch/osagi/conceptsandefinitions.htm> accessed 8 May 2022.

7 By 2020, 127 WTO members had signed the Buenos Aires Declaration, 'Buenos Aires Joint Declaration on Trade and Women's Economic Empowerment' 2017. For more details on WTO initiatives, *see* Anoush der Boghossian, 'Gender-Responsive WTO: Trade Rules and Policies Work for Women' (Chapter 2 in this book); Mia Mikic, 'Advances in Feminizing WTO' (Chapter 3 in this book). For discussions on why the WTO may not be a suitable forum to address gender equality, *see* Judit Fabian, 'Global Economic Governance and Women: Why Is the WTO a Difficult Case for Women's Representation' (Chapter 4 in this book).

8 WTO, 'Informal Working Group on Trade and Gender' <www.wto.org/english/tratop_e/womenandtrade_e/iwg_trade_gender_e.htm> accessed 8 May 2022.

9 Convention on the Elimination of All Forms of Discrimination against Women, Adopted and opened for signature, ratification and accession by United Nations General Assembly, Resolution 34/180 (18 December 1979).

inclusive. And for many, it is a development that is already too late in coming. To date, the WTO rulebook remains gender-blind, in the sense that it does not contain a single explicit provision that relates to gender equality.[10] Moreover, scholars have observed that the WTO makes a difficult case for the representation of women and their interests, as its multilateral framework is perhaps not ready to take on this additional issue over and above the 'legacy' and traditional issues lingering on the negotiation waiting list (such as agriculture, fisheries and services).[11] Even among the newer issues being debated for inclusion – such as digital trade, e-commerce, labour and intellectual property – gender-related issues still face some resistance. This demonstrates that, despite the many strides that have been made to advance gender issues at the multilateral level, questions remain about the suitability of the WTO as a forum to lead the démarche on gender and international trade.

Nevertheless, recent trends have shown a promising role for regional trade agreements (RTAs) – regional, bilateral, free or preferential – in advancing gender equality. A new generation of free trade agreements (FTAs) is increasingly incorporating provisions and chapters on trade and gender equality.[12] In addition, explicit gender-related provisions are finding their way into bilateral investment treaties (BITs) and non-reciprocal preferential trade access schemes.[13] Currently, of all trade agreements in force, more than 20 per cent have an explicit gender-related provision.[14] Even though we are yet to see concrete evidence of benefits that gender mainstreaming in trade agreements can have, more and more countries are embracing this approach.[15]

[10] Der Boghossian (Chapter 2 in this book). The author rebuts this claim.

[11] *See* Fabian (Chapter 4 in this book).

[12] For details, *see* Katrin Kuhlmann, 'Gender Approaches in Regional Trade Agreements and a Possible Gender Protocol under the African Continental Free Trade Area: A Comparative Assessment' (Chapter 10 in this book); Tonni Brodber and Jan Yves Remy, 'Leave No Woman Behind: Towards a More Holistic Gender and Trade Policy in CARICOM' (Chapter 11 in this book); Javiera Cáraces Bustamante and Felipe Muñoz Navia, 'South America's Leadership in Gender Mainstreaming in Trade Agreements' (Chapter 12 in this book).

[13] For details, *see* Renata Amaral and Lillyana Sophia Daza Jaller, 'Mainstreaming Gender in Investment Treaties and Its Prevailing Trends: The Actions of MNEs in the Americas' (Chapter 9 in this book).

[14] José-Antonio Monteiro, 'The Evolution of Gender-Related Provisions in Regional Trade Agreements' (2021) WTO Staff Working Paper ERSD-2021-8 <www.wto.org/english/res_e/reser_e/ersd202108_e.htm> accessed 8 May 2022; Amrita Bahri, 'Mainstreaming Gender in Free Trade Agreements' (*ITC*, 2020) <https://intracen.org/resources/publications/mainstreaming-gender-in-free-trade-agreements> accessed 8 May 2022.

[15] For details, *see* Cáraces Bustamante and Muñoz Navia (Chapter 12 in this book); Amrita Bahri, 'Gender Mainstreaming in Trade Agreements: Best Practice Examples and Challenges in the Asia Pacific' (Chapter 13 in this book); Marie-France Paquet and Georgina Wainwright-Kemdirim, 'Crafting Canada's Gender-Responsive Trade Policy' (Chapter 14 in this book).

While this represents some progress, almost no FTA so far contemplates how gender-related commitments can be implemented or enforced. Most legal provisions included in trade agreements so far have been drafted in the spirit of best-endeavour cooperation. Our review of the current FTAs with gender-related provisions illustrates some diversity. Some FTAs have included a whole chapter with a number of provisions on trade and gender, but no enforceable and binding legal obligations. In fact, in most agreements, gender-related provisions are drafted with non-mandatory verbs and 'soft' permissive grammatical constructions. On the other hand, a handful of countries have drafted such provisions with legally binding expressions. Other FTAs have just one gender-explicit provision, but that provision creates a legally binding obligation. Moreover, whereas several agreements are completely silent or merely make a single mention of expressions relating to gender equality, others include more than forty gender-explicit expressions in the main body of text. The topics addressed in gender-related provisions also vary from one region to another, as some regions have included provisions on social and healthcare concerns of women, and others have covered purely economic and market-oriented interests.[16]

There is also a significant variation in the level of understanding, readiness and appetite among countries to discuss and negotiate gender-related concerns in the trade policy context. On one hand, various countries, especially some in the North and South Americas, are leading gender-mainstreaming efforts.[17] On the other hand, many countries – particularly those in the Asia-Pacific and the Caribbean – are yet to take their very first step in this regard.[18] Moreover, the onset and prolonged setback of the COVID-19 pandemic have also altered countries' willingness to work on gender equality concerns, particularly within the context of their trade policy agenda. At the same time, this health pandemic could roll back the limited gains made over the past few decades in respect of women's empowerment as it has put women employees, entrepreneurs and consumers at the frontline of disproportionate pandemic-inflicted losses.[19]

[16] Bahri, 'Mainstreaming Gender in Free Trade Agreements'.

[17] For details, *see* Kuhlmann (Chapter 10 in this book); Brodber and Remy (Chapter 11 in this book); Cáraces Bustamante and Muñoz Navia (Chapter 12 in this book); Bahri (Chapter 13 in this book); Paquet and Wainwright-Kemdirim (Chapter 14 in this book).

[18] Bahri, 'Mainstreaming Gender in Free Trade Agreements'.

[19] Titan Alon, Matthias Doepke, Jane Olmstead-Rumsey and Michèle Tertilt, 'The Impact of COVID-19 on Gender Equality' (2020) NBER Working Paper No. 26947 <www.nber.org/papers/w26947> accessed 8 May 2022; UNFPA, 'COVID-19: A Gender Lens, Technical Brief

Against this backdrop, it becomes pertinent to study the interlinkages between trade policies and gender equality in a scholastic manner. Heeding this call and the 'gap' in the literature, the editors of this book – the Chairs of the WTO Programme from Mexico, Chile and Barbados – have come together to coordinate and interrogate the intersection between trade policy and gender equality. The research presented in this book addresses – and seeks to answer – a number of extant questions that have been raised by trade policymakers, negotiators, researchers and practitioners that, to date, remain unanswered: What role should the WTO play in facilitating or building an inclusive trade environment that works for the benefit of all, including women? Should gender-responsive provisions be included in trade policy instruments? Do such instruments really assist in reducing the barriers that women face, such as lack of access to finance and food security, digital divide, gender-blind standards of goods and services and pandemic-inflicted challenges? How are countries incorporating such provisions in their agreements, in what forms and with what scope? What makes an agreement gender-responsive, and how can countries increase the gender-responsiveness of their trade agreements? What are the associated risks and problems with taking on board gender-related commitments in trade agreements? What tools and methodologies do countries have for testing the potential of trade agreements in this respect? What options are available to developing and Least Developed Countries (LDCs) to increase their negotiating capacity and understanding of trade and gender issues? And finally, what role can investment treaties play in this respect as foreign investment can be an important lever for both women's empowerment and economic growth?

1.2 TRADE AND GENDER: CONCEPTUAL UNDERPINNINGS

There are two different yet complementary approaches to promoting policies that increase women's empowerment: bottom-up and top-down. The bottom-up approach calls for efforts to alter national laws, procedures and institutions, culture and social norms at the domestic level to reduce barriers that impede women's empowerment. The top-down approach calls for employing international law to incentivize changes at the domestic level. Using the top-down approach, multilateral as well as bilateral trade policies can be employed to reduce the barriers to women's empowerment as they could trigger changes in

Protecting Sexual and Reproductive Health and Rights, and Promoting Gender Equality' (March 2020) <www.unfpa.org/resources/covid-19-gender-lens> accessed 8 May 2022.

domestic laws and policies, societal setup and in the workplace and economic sectors.

The focus on the nexus between international trade and sustainable development predates the establishment of the WTO. One of the first acknowledgements of the interrelationship between gender and commerce can be traced back to the Treaty on the Functioning of the European Union (TFEU).[20] In 1995, the WTO's Marrakesh Agreement enshrined the objective of sustainable development in its very preamble.[21] A quarter-century later, the discussion in policy circles has evolved dramatically, and the term 'sustainable development' has become far better understood and accepted as a concept that relates to trade interests. The Addis Ababa Agenda of Action[22] builds a clear network between international trade and gender. It reads as follows: 'Recognizing the critical role of women as producers and traders, we will address their specific challenges in order to facilitate women's equal and active participation in domestic, regional and international trade.'[23] The UN General Assembly has called upon the WTO, the World Bank Group (WBG) and other international and regional bodies to support government initiatives and develop complementary programmes to help countries achieve full implementation of the Beijing Declaration and Platform for Action to protect women's rights.[24] The 2030 Agenda for Sustainable Development recognizes international trade as an engine for inclusive and sustainable economic growth, and an important means to achieve the UN's 2030 Sustainable Development Goals (SDG). Goal 5 explicitly sets out to achieve gender equality and empowerment of all women and girls.[25]

Various studies have shown that trade impacts women and men differently and that the specific nature of that impact is highly dependent on the structure and the development of each country, industry and/or sector. While trade

[20] Art. 157, Consolidated versions of the Treaty on European Union and the Treaty on the Functioning of the European Union (TFEU) [2016] OJ C202/1.

[21] Preamble, WTO Agreement: Marrakesh Agreement Establishing the World Trade Organization, 15 April 1994, 1867 UNTS 154, 33 ILM 1144 (WTO Agreement).

[22] UN, 'Third International Conference on Financing for Development (FfD3)' (13–16 July 2015) <www.un.org/esa/ffd/ffd3/conference.html> accessed 8 May 2022.

[23] UNGA, 'Addis Ababa Action Agenda of the Third International Conference on Financing for Development (Addis Ababa Action Agenda)', A/Res/69/313 (2015), para. 90.

[24] UN Women, 'On the 25th Anniversary of Landmark Beijing Declaration on Women's Rights, UN Women Calls for Accelerating Its Unfinished Business' (4 September 2020) <www.unwomen.org/en/news/stories/2020/9/press-release-25th-anniversary-of-the-beijing-declaration-on-womens-rights> accessed 8 May 2022.

[25] UNGA, 'Transforming Our World: The 2030 Agenda for Sustainable Development', A/RES/70/1 (21 October 2015) <www.refworld.org/docid/57b6e3e44.html> accessed 8 May 2022.

liberalization and agreements can have a negative impact on women, trade policies can equally benefit women as employees, entrepreneurs and consumers and hence can strengthen women's empowerment. The factors that mediate and influence the effect include resource endowments, labour market institutions, systems of property rights and other socio-economic characteristics.[26]

Possible differential impacts on men and women resulting from trade openness and trade agreements can further exacerbate existing gender inequalities.[27] Women tend to be more affected by the negative effects of trade liberalization and face more barriers than men when it comes to taking advantage of the opportunities offered by trade. This is mainly because of gender biases in education and training, wage inequalities and gender inequalities in the distribution of resources, as well as unequal access to productive inputs such as credit, land and technology.[28]

Trade agreements can disrupt economic sectors where women are mostly involved as employees or entrepreneurs, thereby depriving them of employment and business opportunities.[29] They can increase gender wage gaps and create poorer working conditions for women in developing countries. Pressure generated by trade liberalization can lead to volatile employment, rising need for flexible workers, poor working conditions, low wages and unemployment in certain sectors.[30] Empirical data has also shown that the overall gender wage gap remains large in countries where there has been a rapid growth in exports that rely on female labour.[31] Due to trade liberalization, female workers and producers are more likely to contribute to the unskilled labour force in export-oriented industries and remain concentrated in low-skilled activities, with little chance to access high-value-added jobs that remain

26 Marzia Fontana, 'The Gender Effects of Trade Liberalisation in Developing Countries: A Review of Literature' (Institute of Development Studies 2009) <www.ids.ac.uk/publications/the-gender-effects-of-trade-liberalization-in-developing-countries-a-review-of-the-literature/> accessed 8 May 2022.

27 For details, *see* der Boghossian (Chapter 2 in this book).

28 UNCTAD, 'Mainstreaming Gender in Trade Policy, Note by the UNCTAD Secretariat', TD/B/C.I/EM.2/2/Rev.1 (2009) <www.unctad.org/en/docs/ciem2d2_en.pdf> accessed 8 May 2022.

29 Karen Melanson, 'An Examination of the Gendered Effects of Trade Liberalisation' (2005) 2 (1) *Policy Perspectives* 10–17. Melanson explains how trade liberalization can lead to decrease in care work.

30 Remco Oostendorp, 'Globalization and the Gender Wage Gap' (2009) 23(1) *World Bank Economic Review* 141–161

31 For the case of North America, *see* Philip Sauvé and Hosny Zoabi, 'International Trade, the Gender Wage Gap and Female Labor Force Participation' (2014) 111(C) *Journal of Development Economics* 17–33.

male-dominated. This phenomenon, also known as the 'feminization of labour' refers to both an increase in female employment (typically in labour-intensive, low-value-added, low-wage activities) and a worsening of their working conditions and wages.[32]

Studies have shown that over the past decade, the number of women working in export-dependent firms has visibly increased; yet there are still fewer women working in export-dependent jobs than men.[33] Moreover, women generally work in sectors that are less engaged in trade.[34] Increasing their engagement in trade can therefore help women work better and for more competitive salaries.[35] Moreover, evidence shows that trade can help women move from the informal into the formal economy, offering better working conditions and access to various benefits.[36] In sectors with high levels of exports, women workers are more likely to be formally employed in a job with better benefits, training and security. World Bank and WTO studies have shown that women workers are less likely to work informally if they work in sectors that trade more or are more integrated into global value chains.[37] Hence, foreign trade can increase women's wages, as firms that export pay more and offer better working conditions than the firms that do not export.

Trade is also an agent of diversity: diversity of markets, clients, products and services. Therefore, presence in the international markets can help women entrepreneurs to use trade as an engine for business expansion and as a tool to

[32] Guy Standing, 'Global Feminization through Flexible Labour (1989) 17(7) *World Development* 1077–1095; Guy Standing, 'Global Feminization through Flexible Labour: A Theme Revisited' (1999) 27(3) *World Development* 583–602.

[33] Jayati Ghosh, 'Globalization, Export-Oriented Employment for Women and Social Policy: A Case Study of India' (2002) 30(11) *Social Scientist* 17–60.

[34] Across all OECD countries, women are much less likely than men to work in manufacturing, a highly traded sector. On average, only 30 per cent of the manufacturing workforce is made up of women. *See* OECD, 'Trade and Gender: A Framework of Analysis' (March 2021) 11–12 <www.oecd.org/publications/trade-and-gender-6db59d80-en.htm> accessed 8 May 2022.

[35] Many studies have found that an exporter wage premium exists – that exporters pay higher wages than non-exporters. *See*, for instance, Esther Ann Bøler, Beata Javorcik and Karen Helene Ulltveit-Moe, 'Working across Time Zones: Exporters and the Gender Wage Gap' (2018) 111(C) *Journal of International Economics* 122–133; Zornitsa Kutlina-Dimitrova, José M. Rueda-Cantuche, Antonio F. Amores and Victoria Román, 'How Important Are EU Exports for Jobs in the EU?' (EU Chief Economist Note November 2018) <https://ideas.repec.org/p/ris/dgtcen/2018_004.html> accessed 8 May 2022.

[36] Informal workers are defined as workers who neither benefit from a social security scheme nor have a working contract.

[37] World Bank and WTO, 'Women and Trade: The Role of Trade in Promoting Gender Equality' (30 July 2020) <https://openknowledge.worldbank.org/handle/10986/34140> accessed 8 May 2022.

mitigate the impact of occasional economic downturns.[38] Moreover, existing and future trade agreements between countries can increase trade flows and hence lead to more business opportunities for all, including women.[39] Trade liberalization fosters international competition and market access opportunities, and it increases the need to increase the business size and upgrade technologically.[40] Trade liberalization has led to the introduction of new technologies that can benefit women-owned businesses.

Use of new technology (such as blockchain-based applications) and online platforms to engage in e-commerce can provide to women's businesses a relatively easy and inexpensive way of allowing small businesses to enter foreign markets and of expanding their businesses. However, technology can also become the 'Achilles' heel' of the trade digitalization era as it can widen the digital divide between women and men. According to the International Institute of Rural Reconstruction, digitalization represents a challenge hardly overcome, especially for rural women in various regions, including in Africa.[41] There is therefore a need to enhance women's access and participation in digital learning, infrastructure, financing and trade. The growing trend of digital trade and e-commerce needs to be accompanied by supporting policies and training for women as the gendered digital divide continues to persist and even thrive in the current pandemic-triggered conditions.

At the household level, trade liberalization can impact women as consumers. By lowering prices of goods women generally purchase and thereby increasing their real incomes, trade can impact women consumers in lower-income quintiles.[42] Hence, trade liberalizing reforms can impact consumers by lowering prices and providing access to a wider variety of goods and services.[43] This is in line with the conventional wisdom, which suggests that trade lowers prices through greater competition and trade liberalization lowers

[38] ILO, 'Women and Men in the Informal Economy: A Statistical Picture' (2018) <www.ilo.org/wcmsp5/groups/public/—dgreports/—dcomm/documents/publication/wcms_626831.pdf> accessed 8 May 2022.

[39] For details, *see* der Boghossian (Chapter 2 in this book).

[40] UNCTAD, 'Mainstreaming Gender in Trade Policy', TD/B/C.I/EM.2/2/Rev.1 (19 March 2019).

[41] IIRR, 'Building Back Best: Strengthening Rural Women's Resilience Amid the COVID-19 Pandemic' (March 2021) <https://iirr.org/building-back-best-strengthening-rural-womens-resilience-amid-the-covid-19-pandemic/> accessed 8 May 2022.

[42] OECD, 'Trade and Gender: A Framework of Analysis' (March 2021) 22 <www.oecd.org/publications/trade-and-gender-6db59d80-en.htm#:~:text=A%20framework%20is%20proposed%20for,country%20support%20women's%20economic%20empowerment> accessed 8 May 2022.

[43] C. Broda and D. E. Weinstein, 'Globalization and the Gains from Variety' (2006) 121(2) *Quarterly Journal of Economics* 541–485.

barriers to trade (including non-tariff and tariff barriers), which then further lowers prices of goods for final consumers. However, studies have shown that tariff and non-tariff barriers are generally higher on most essential goods such as food staples, clothing and footwear.[44]

Trade liberalization can also have a negative impact on women as consumers and carers, as it leads to reduced import tariffs and government revenues. The reduction in import tariffs can negatively impact a government's revenue in the short term, forcing that government to reduce or withdraw the provision of social services that are otherwise subsidized or financed by that country's government. In some cases, this might lead to the privatization of certain social services that are relevant for women, increasing the cost of such social services and hence making them less affordable. This challenge has worsened during the pandemic, mainly for developing countries with resource constraints and limited fiscal space, as the pandemic-triggered needs have further limited governments' ability to make budgetary allocations to support schemes. On the other hand, it is also possible to argue that increased trade and associated growth can generate increased tax revenues for countries. If that happens, government budgets can be reinvested in sectors that predominantly benefit women and bring about large fiscal multipliers, such as in education, healthcare or social protection.

This discussion shows how trade policies need to be developed within the context of relations between and within economies, groups and genders. Incorporating the gender perspective into trade policies can therefore lead to designing and implementing policies that maximize opportunities, facilitate the integration of women into more dynamic economic sectors, mitigate gender disparities, and enable women's empowerment and well-being. Creating explicit linkages between trade policy and larger goals like gender equality and women's economic empowerment may help trade become a vehicle for long-term inclusive development. Effective regulation of international trade and full, effective participation of women can advance economic growth, sustainable development and women's economic empowerment. Yet, because trade is not gender-neutral, it is important for trade policymakers to engage in the negotiation and implementation of trade agreements with a gendered lens. The sheer interplay between trade and gender equality calls for the application of a gender lens to trade policies

[44] Alan V. Deardorff and Robert M. Stern, 'Measurement of Non-Tariff Barriers' (1997) OECD Working Paper No. 179 <www.oecd-ilibrary.org/docserver/568705648470.pdf?expires=1655752963&id=id&accname=guest&checksum=E8E491E03C3B460002DACE6A08B4D75B> accessed 8 May 2022.

and instruments.[45] But what does it mean to apply such a lens to mainstream gender in a trade policy context?

Gender mainstreaming is defined as 'the (re)organization, improvement, development, and evaluation of policy processes so that a gender equality perspective is incorporated in all policies at all levels at all stages, by the actors normally involved in policy-making'.[46] Gender mainstreaming in trade policies and agreements requires the application of a gender lens in the negotiation and formulation of trade policies; applying a gender lens entails the inclusion of gender-related concerns in the drafting and implementation of trade policies and agreements. The process of mainstreaming affirms a country's understanding, awareness or political will to reduce gender inequality through trade policies and agreements. The term 'gender responsiveness' is also used extensively in this book. It refers to a process that assesses how sensitive, informed or committed the provisions of a trade agreement are to issues relating to gender equality. In other words, the manner and extent to which an agreement mainstreams gender-equality considerations define how responsive that agreement is to gender-equality concerns.[47]

1.3 AIM AND STRUCTURE

This book examines how economic policies – primarily trade, and to some extent investment – might be adapted to address women's interests more effectively. It offers descriptive accounts and analyses on whether trade (and investment) agreements can further women's empowerment, how such instruments might be negotiated with a gender lens, what different options countries have to mainstream gender-equality concerns in their future trade agreements, what the mainstreaming experiences in different regions have been so far, and the constraints faced in doing the same. More specifically, this book enables its readers to gain knowledge and insights on the issues covered and in particular the following:

45 This discussion is inspired by UNCTAD's course on trade and gender linkages: the gender impact of technological upgrading in agriculture; WTO, 'Gender Aware Trade Policy: A Springboard for Women's Economic Empowerment' 4 <www.wto.org/english/news_e/news17_e/dgra_21jun17_e.pdf> accessed 8 May 2022.

46 Mieke Verloo, 'Reflections on the Concept and Practice of the Council of Europe Approach to Gender Mainstreaming and Gender Equality' (2005) 12(3) *Social Politics: International Studies in Gender, State & Society* 344–365.

47 These definitions initially proposed by the author in Amrita Bahri, 'Measuring the Gender-Responsiveness of Free Trade Agreements: Using a Self-Evaluation Maturity Framework' (2019) 14(11/12) *Global Trade and Customs Journal* 517–527. For details, *see* Kuhlmann (Chapter 10 in this book).

- an objective discussion on the role and potential of the WTO's multilateral trading system to create an inclusive trade environment, whether the WTO is gender-blind or gender-responsive as an organization, and reasons why it might present a difficult case for the representation of women and their interests in the global economic governance framework;[48]
- a deep understanding of the relationship between trade, investment and gender, with a focus on the role of women in the economy, and how gender-responsive and gender-inclusive trade and investment agreements can be instrumental for international cooperation and trade liberalization that can be made to work for everyone including women;[49]
- an overview of how substantive areas of trade policy can be put into the service of advancing inclusive trade, as various chapters examine areas including women and trade in services, digital trade, gender gap in standardization, access to resources such as finance, and inclusive regulation of food security and agriculture;[50]
- regional analysis of trade negotiations and concluded trade agreements in different regions including North and South America, the Caribbean, Asia-Pacific and Africa, including an overview of the strengths of their gender mainstreaming approaches and the hurdles and obstacles to trade negotiations and trade policy with respect to these regions;[51]
- reflections on emerging and significant issues that are expected to change the landscape of trade negotiations and consideration of gender interests in future policy-making, such as regulations on e-commerce and domestic regulation of services (including in the form of joint statement initiatives and declarations), the increasing need for women's representation in trade negotiations, the continuing impact of the pandemic and

[48] For details, *see* der Boghossian (Chapter 2 in this book); Mikic (Chapter 3 in this book); Fabian (Chapter 4 in this book).

[49] For details, *see* Simonetta Zarrilli, 'Women in the LDCs: How to Build Forward Differently for Them' (Chapter 5 in this book); Amaral and Daza Jaller (Chapter 9 in this book).

[50] For details, *see* Zarrilli (Chapter 5 in this book); Amalie Giødesen Thystrup, 'Gender-Inclusive Governance for e-Commerce, Digital Trade and Trade in Services: A Look at Domestic Regulation' (Chapter 6 in this book); Gabrielle White and Michelle Parkouda, 'The Importance of Gender-Responsive Standards for Trade Policy' (Chapter 8 in this book).

[51] For details, *see* Kuhlmann (Chapter 10 in this book); Brodber and Remy (Chapter 11 in this book); Cáraces Bustamante and Muñoz Navia (Chapter 12 in this book); Bahri (Chapter 13 in this book); Paquet and Wainwright-Kemdirim (Chapter 14 in this book).

the strategies being employed to deal with this impact, and the participation of LDCs in the creation of trade policies with a gender lens.[52]

To achieve the above-stated objectives, the book is divided into three parts.

The first part is titled 'The WTO and Gender Equality' and focuses on how the WTO could naturally lead this process, given its expertise in global rulemaking on trade issues and the institutional role that it can play in advancing the trade and gender agenda. It not only looks at the WTO as a trade policy setter, but zooms in on the WTO as an international organization. The chapters included in this part offer supporting arguments and critiques on whether the WTO can play a role in making trade policies work for women. The authors in these chapters offer reflections on how the WTO may advance gender equality, and also explore why the organization might still not be the appropriate arena for furthering the agenda of gender equality in the context of trade policies.

Chapter 2 by Anoush der Boghossian discusses how the WTO has evolved from a gender-blind organization to first a gender-aware and then a gender-responsive organization; in doing so, the chapter looks at its various mandates, agreements and objectives. Preparing a case for how trade policies can help, the chapter attempts to link human rights and women's economic empowerment with trade law to illustrate how the current WTO agreements can support gender equality and hence be the drivers of inclusive economic growth.

Chapter 3 by Mia Mikic takes account of the advances made so far in feminizing the WTO, and how the new problems and uncertainties brought by the prolonged pandemic may make it difficult to navigate the long-awaited reforms and actions. In doing so, the chapter assesses the degree to which the ongoing negotiations of trade rules on joint statement initiatives – on investment facilitation, e-commerce, services domestic regulation and Micro, Small and Medium-Sized Enterprises (MSMSEs) have taken a gender lens. The chapter also provides reflections on the need to increase women's representation in decision-making and trade policy positions and the dire need to break the glass ceilings that women in trade generally face.

Chapter 4 by Judit Fabian suggests why the WTO may not be the right place to explore gender solutions and the constraints that organization has in respect of furthering the agenda of gender equality. The main purpose of the

[52] For details, *see* Zarrilli (Chapter 5 in this book); Thystrup (Chapter 6 in this book); Maria Sokolova and Matthew Wilson, 'Setting Up the Table Right: Women's Representation Meets Women's Inclusion in Trade Negotiations' (Chapter 7 in this book).

chapter is to analyse why the WTO has proven such a great challenge for the representation of women and women's interests, with the author offering six supporting reasons that relate to politics, diplomacy, international law and the nature of the WTO's rulebook.

The second part is titled 'Current Issues in Gender Equality and Trade Policies' and covers current and emerging issues related to trade and gender, in substantive terms as well as in terms of the negotiation process. Ranging from cross-cutting gender provisions and chapters to specific topics such as e-commerce and gender-responsive standards, this part highlights where the current debates and possibilities for gender-inclusive trade agreements are located. It offers a lot of food for thought on various emerging and little-researched areas relating to trade, investment and women, such as women and e-commerce, negotiation capacity and least-developed countries, gender-responsive standards, multinational enterprises and their interaction with foreign investment and women, and what some investment treaties have to offer in respect of gender mainstreaming.

Chapter 5 by Simonetta Zarrilli provides an assessment of what women need, the barriers they face especially in a post-pandemic environment, and what has been provided to them in the LDCs so far. To do so, it discusses why women in LDCs face higher obstacles that hamper their capacity to fully benefit from international trade, and how these barriers are magnified by persistent and acute development challenges found in LDCs in the female-intensive sectors of agriculture, in artisanal and small-scale mining, in the Export Processing Zones (EPZ) and in tourism. The author proposes several support measures that would help women benefit more from their participation in these sectors, especially in a pandemic-like situation, and then assesses the measures that have been put in place by the LDCs through rescue packages.

Chapter 6 by Amalie Giødesen Thystrup examines e-commerce from a gender perspective and the provision on gender equality in the WTO Joint Statement Initiative on Services Domestic Regulation. With the Joint Statement Initiatives on Services Domestic Regulation and e-commerce seeking to include provisions on women's empowerment, the policy landscape of this intersection has developed, calling for further research and analysis. The author seeks to create new knowledge that is actionable for policymakers and stakeholders on gender divides in e-commerce, digital trade and trade in services, and what policy interventions are necessary to create multi-level dedicated gender-inclusive governance that is required at this unique time for trade digitization and formulation of new policy instruments.

Chapter 7 by Maria Sokolova and Matthew Wilson looks at women's representation in multilateral trade negotiations within the context of the overall goal of achieving more gender-sensitive outcomes in trade policy. The authors explain how the expansion of the scope and complexity of trade negotiations have created a negotiation capacity gap between developing and developed countries, and how such rising complications have impacted the structure of negotiating teams and the attributes of persons engaged in trade negotiations. This chapter also clarifies that there is a significant distinction between having women participating in trade negotiations and having the interests of women reflected in trade negotiation outcomes, and how they may not necessarily go hand in hand. The authors make a strong case for setting up the future negotiation tables in the right way and increasing women's representation in trade negotiations and policy-making.

Chapter 8 by Gabrielle White and Michelle Parkouda seeks to break the myth that *standards are gender-neutral*. The chapter shows that standards are more effective at protecting men compared to women, an important insight given that standards form the building blocks of how products, processes and services are designed and made to be interoperable. The authors explore the interconnected nature of gender, standards and trade to argue that the lack of gender-responsiveness of standards has a negative impact on the safety and well-being of women. They offer reflections on the importance of improving the gender-responsiveness of standards for creating a more inclusive trade environment and the role that trade policies can play in this respect.

Chapter 9 by Renata Amaral and Lillyana Sophia Daza Jaller adds a much-needed discussion on gender mainstreaming in investment treaties and how inclusion of gender provisions in investment treaties can be a successful strategy on overcoming gender inequality. In doing so, the authors rightly identify the role of multinational enterprises (MNEs) in leading the foreign investment process and the opportunity for MNEs to be the drivers of reducing the existing gender gap. The authors employ a pragmatic approach, as they provide various examples of actions and policies adopted by MNEs in the Americas towards promoting more opportunities for women.

The third part – 'Regional Approaches' – includes country and/or region-specific case studies on different trade and gender mainstreaming approaches. The book provides analysis of the trade negotiation experience and obstacles faced in negotiating trade policies with a gender lens in different regions including North and South America, the Caribbean, Asia-Pacific and Africa. With this regional analysis, readers can gain deep and insider insights into the factors that have led these regions and countries to define their approach in trade negotiations and their motivations behind taking onboard gender concerns in their trade policies and agreements. It also provides reflections on the trends employed so far in this respect and the constraints that have impeded such gender mainstreaming efforts. The chapters included in this part add a necessary dimension to this discussion, as they present policymakers with a range of options on strategies that have been employed so far, what remains undone in this respect, and the risks future negotiators need to consider if women's interests are not advanced and the challenges to be considered if they are advanced using trade policy instruments.

Chapter 10 by Katrin Kuhlmann presents a comparative assessment of approaches for evaluating and categorizing gender and trade approaches in RTAs. These include a focus on gender-responsiveness and incorporation of international and domestic legal design innovations and options for 'inclusive law and regulation' (with particular examples from African regional and domestic law) in order to use RTAs to address concrete challenges facing women. The chapter shines a light on how gender provisions could be shaped, reframed and better implemented in practice, with particular implications for the African Continental Free Trade Area (AfCFTA) and its gender-focused protocol which is currently in negotiation.

Chapter 11 by Tonni Brodber and Jan Yves Remy provides reflections on the presence (or lack thereof) of a Caribbean feminist agenda in international trade discussions and negotiations, as the authors examine the development of gender equality/feminism in the Caribbean and its intersections with foreign trade. Assessing the Caribbean Community's experience, the chapter provides discussions on the challenges Caribbean policymakers face in mainstreaming gender in trade policies and initiatives, and makes recommendations on how the Caribbean should mainstream gender and approach trade and gender in the future.

Chapter 12 by Javiera Cáraces Bustamante and Felipe Muñoz Navia shows how several countries in South America have pioneered gender mainstreaming in trade agreements. With a review of gender provisions in South American bilateral trade agreements and in the region's integration processes (Pacific Alliance and Mercosur), this chapter demonstrates how South America has advanced gender-sensitive trade policy-making which has now expanded to other regions. The discussions show that in addition to incorporating gender provisions that their developed partners have included in their trade agreements, South American countries have also demonstrated their ability to innovate and design gender-sensible trade regulations with practices that are quite unique to this region.

Chapter 13 by Amrita Bahri turns the focus to the Asia-Pacific region, providing a comprehensive account and assessment of gender-related provisions included in the existing trade agreements negotiated by countries in the Asia-Pacific. In doing so, the chapter considers the extent to which gender concerns are mainstreamed in these agreements, and examines the reasons that impede such mainstreaming efforts in the region. Interestingly, the chapter finds that most of the agreements negotiated by countries in Asia-Pacific are gender-blind, as they do not contain any gender-related or gender-considerate provisions, and the ones that do contain gender-related provisions do not include commitments relating to women's economic interests or economic empowerment as such provisions mainly relate to their personal welfare concerns.

Chapter 14 by Marie-France Paquet and Georgina Wainwright-Kemdirim presents Canada's experience in applying a gender lens in the negotiation and implementation of trade agreements. The authors of this chapter clarify the importance of understanding the effects of trade on people, and they engage in explaining Canada's new analytical approach. This can help in gathering data on the trade effects, which can guide the crafting of coherent gender-responsive and inclusive trade policies. The chapter examines, using practical examples, how Canada has employed its analytical approach and the observed benefits and limitations of this approach.

1.4 BENEFITS TO READERS

Given the significance of the subject matter in the field, this book is an invaluable source for academics, researchers, students, policymakers and the private sector at this critical time and beyond.

Academics and researchers: This book is a point of reference for scholars and researchers engaged in trade and gender. Researchers studying the impact of gender on trade policy and trade agreements, as well as scholars who are seeking to engage in trade and gender, will find the most topical issues concerning international trade and gender in this book. Moreover, it provides scholars with abundant food for thought on the major challenges in this field and how best to deal with them. This book also provides a great menu of research options and ideas for future research, including doctoral research topics.

Students: A growing number of universities are now offering courses on trade and sustainable development or more broadly on trade and development. These courses have now started to develop a module focused on trade and gender. Moreover, some universities and international organizations are offering standalone courses on trade and gender. The necessity to adopt a gender-sensitive approach in legal education emerges from the highest value and normative standards of modern international law. Currently, there is no textbook that provides a comprehensive review and assessment of international trade and gender in light of the most modern policy approaches and the most recently concluded and negotiated trade agreements. This book can become a useful teaching and learning resource at universities and organizations that are offering relevant courses.

Trade negotiators and policymakers: This book is beneficial for policymakers who are contemplating and negotiating new trade rules and trade agreements in response to recent developments in trade, investment and gender. With a multitude of trade and investment negotiations ongoing and an increasing demand for attention to non-economic issues on the verge of trade and investment cooperation, this book presents a unique tool for negotiators and policymakers to address the topic of gender. It provides timely contributions and guidance for policymakers to prepare, revise and negotiate new norms to make trade and investment more inclusive. Moreover, the book provides a literary basis for training government officials and trade negotiators across the globe on trade and gender.

Business stakeholders: As businesses begin to consider their corporate social responsibilities, this book is perfectly suited to those making corporate decisions to increase productivity in a sustainable manner and seeking to encourage creative thinking and innovation. The promotion of gender equality in businesses can also have a direct impact on the economic empowerment of women and female entrepreneurship. The findings presented in this book can help businesses gain an understanding of how they can engage in, and contribute to, the formulation of trade policy in their respective countries to ensure that trade works for and benefits everyone, especially women.

PART I

The WTO and Gender Equality

2

Gender-Responsive WTO

*Making Trade Rules and Policies Work for Women**

ANOUSH DER BOGHOSSIAN

ABSTRACT

A gender-responsive trade policy can lift obstacles faced by women in trade through, for instance, financial and non-financial incentives, or by providing access to trade-related infrastructure, especially in rural areas. Trade policies can create new opportunities for women entrepreneurs and female farmers, and for women to enter the workforce, in export sectors. In light of these opportunities, the chapter seeks to explore how capabilities for women can be expanded and enforced in global trade. Among other things, the research will delve into the ability of trade agreements to contribute to gender equality. Specifically, the chapter analyses these issues from the institutional aspect of the World Trade Organization (WTO) and its role in designing gender-inclusive trade policies and monitoring such policies through the Trade Policy Review Mechanism (TPRM).

* DISCLAIMER: This chapter represents the opinions of an individual staff member and is the product of professional research. It is not meant to represent the position or opinion of the WTO or its Members, nor the official position of any staff members of the WTO. It focuses on outlining current policy trends adopted by WTO members with regard to trade and gender. This analysis is based on information provided by WTO through their Trade Policy Review (TPR), the WTO Aid for Trade Monitoring and Evaluation Exercises, their notification of their Free Trade agreements FTAs) and Regional Trade Agreements (RTAs) to the WTO. This chapter also looks at some provisions of WTO Agreements with gender lens. In no way does it provide an interpretation of these rules and decisions. It simply provides a gender perspective on how trade rules and policies could support women, and how WTO members have actually been using them and translating them into their national trade policies, as reported in their TPRs.

2.1 INTRODUCTION

Empowering women can be the most rewarding action any government can take.[1] This resonates in the words of Rosine Bekoin, a cocoa producer from Ivory Coast: 'I used to think I had to wear a wrap, have a baby on my back and cook for my husband. I used to beg him for money. Now we make a budget together and I'm afraid of nothing because I know how to manage my money. I am stronger. I am a leader of many people now and know I can do things on my own.'[2]

The more women grow economically, the more societies and economies grow. Trade can foster their empowerment by advancing gender equality through the development and implementation of gender-responsive trade policies[3] as well as by implementing WTO agreements using a gendered lens.[4] Trade rules can impact women positively only if they are implemented to respond to the specific roles and needs of women in society and in the economy.

The WTO and its members support women's economic empowerment through various endeavours, including the Informal Working Group (IWG) on Trade and Gender established by the WTO in September 2020. Through the IWG, trade and gender related issues have been institutionalised at the organisation.

However, before achieving this institutionalisation, the WTO had evolved from a gender-blind[5] institution to a gender-aware[6] one in only five years.

[1] IMF, *Pursuing Women's Economic Empowerment* (IMF 2018) <www.imf.org/en/Publications/Policy-Papers/Issues/2018/05/31/pp053118pursuing-womens-economic-empowerment> accessed 8 May 2022; UNECOSOC, 'Meeting Coverage of the 63rd Commission on the Status of Women', WOM/2175 (13 March 2019) <www.un.org/press/en/2019/wom2175.doc.htm> accessed 8 May 2022.

[2] Jez Fredenburgh, 'The "Invisible" Women at the Heart of the Chocolate Industry' (BBC n.d.) <www.bbc.com/future/bespoke/follow-the-food/the-invisible-women-farmers-of-ivory-coast.html> accessed 8 May 2022.

[3] Anoush der Boghossian, 'Trade Policies Supporting Women's Economic Empowerment: Trends in WTO Members' (2019) WTO Staff Working Paper ERSD-2019-07 <www.wto.org/english/res_e/reser_e/ersd201907_e.pdf> accessed 8 May 2022.

[4] Global Alliance for Trade Facilitation, 'WTO's Trade Facilitation Agreement through a Gender Lens' (2020) <www.tradefacilitation.org/content/uploads/2020/05/2020-tfa-through-a-gender-lens-final.pdf> accessed 8 May 2022.

[5] 'Gender blindness' is defined as the 'failure to recognise that the roles and responsibilities of women/girls and men/boys are ascribed to, or imposed upon, them in specific social, cultural, economic and political contexts'. *See* EIGE, 'Gender Blindness' <https://eige.europa.eu/thesaurus/terms/1157> accessed 8 May 2022.

[6] 'Gender awareness' is defined as the 'ability to view society from the perspective of gender roles and understand how this has affected women's needs in comparison to the needs of men'. *See* EIGE, 'Gender Awareness' <https://eige.europa.eu/thesaurus/terms/1147> accessed 8 May 2022.

Following the General Agreement on Tariffs and Trade (GATT) and with the establishment of the WTO in 1995, trade rules did not integrate gender issues, making the WTO gender blind. Until 2016–2017, gender was not considered a part of the WTO mandate. This led the organisation to exclude the issue from all its discussions, operations, and negotiations, although WTO members have mentioned trade and gender measures in their trade policy review reports in the last decades. No research was conducted on this issue,[7] and no member of staff in the WTO Secretariat was working on it. There were no dedicated fora within the WTO. However, this changed in September 2020 with the establishment of the IWG on Trade and Gender.[8]

In 2017, a total of 118 WTO members and observers launched an informal declaration in the margins of the 11th Ministerial Conference in Buenos Aires. Members chose the informal path and used it with the purpose of integrating gender issues into the WTO, a discussion which was non-existent at the time. The same year, and as part of the negotiations on Services Domestic Regulation, Canada introduced the first gender-equality language in a WTO negotiating document. On 2 December 2021, sixty-seven members adopted the Services Domestic Regulation[9] and for the first time added a gender-equality provision to a WTO plurilateral agreement. This provision prohibits gender discrimination when authorising the supply of a service.

This chapter is structured as follows. Section 2.2 underscores the importance of women in trade and establishes that women are key drivers of economic and sustainable growth, and that trade can support this role. Section 2.3 explores how the WTO evolved from a gender-blind organisation to a gender-aware one, looking at its various mandates and the objectives of the WTO rules. Section 2.4 analyses whether the WTO has truly transformed into a gender-aware international organisation. Section 2.5 looks at how trade policy can expand and enforce the capabilities for women in global trade, and how it can create decent working conditions for women. Section 2.6 analyses the issue from a legal perspective and explores the link between human rights, women's economic empowerment, and trade law. Section 2.7 provides

7 Between 1995 and 2016, only one WTO Staff Working Paper was published on trade and gender. *See* Hildegunn Kyvik Nordås, 'Is Trade Liberalization a Window of Opportunity for Women?' (2003) WTO Staff Working Paper ERSD-2003-03 <www.wto.org/english/res_e/reser_e/ersd200303_e.htm> accessed 8 May 2022.

8 *See* Judit Fabian, 'Global Economic Governance and Women: Why Is the WTO a Difficult Case for Women's Representation?' (Chapter 4 in this book).

9 WTO, 'Declaration on the Conclusion of Negotiations on Services Domestic Regulation', WT/L/1129 (2 December 2021).

concluding remarks. In essence, the chapter will link human rights, women's economic empowerment, and trade law and explore how WTO agreements can support gender equality.

2.2 WOMEN ARE KEY DRIVERS OF ECONOMIC GROWTH

Women constitute a global economic force. The more they are involved, the more economies grow: increasing women's participation in the labour market to the same level as men's could raise some countries' gross domestic product (GDP) by up to 34 per cent,[10] and closing the gender gap could increase countries' GDP by an average of 35 per cent.[11] This analysis from the International Monetary Fund (IMF) has been confirmed in many countries. For instance, in Egypt, women represent 50 per cent of the population; many of them are educated, but they only constitute 24 per cent of the workforce. If women were better integrated into the economy, Egypt's GDP could increase by 30 per cent.[12] Similarly, in Peru, the correlation between higher per capita income and better gender equality has been noted since 2000. As Peru has increased its per capita income, gender inequality has decreased, as measured by the gender inequality index.[13] The massive entry of Peruvian women into the world of labour, largely due to a shift in the role of women in society, has been an important driver of growth as well as of economic and human development.[14] More recently, according to the United Nations Development Programme (UNDP), limiting women's employment could

[10] Katrin Elborgh-Woytek, Monique Newiak, Kalpana Kochhar, Stefania Fabrizio, Kangni Kpodar, Philippe Wingender, Benedict Clements, and Gerd Schwartz, 'Women, Work, and the Economy: Macroeconomic Gains from Gender Equity' (2013) IMF Staff Discussion Note SDN/13/10, fn 6 <www.imf.org/external/pubs/ft/sdn/2013/sdn1310.pdf> accessed 8 May 2022.

[11] Raquel Fernández, Asel Isakova, Francesco Luna, and Barbara Rambousek, 'Gender Equality and Inclusive Growth' (2021) IMF Working Paper WP/21/59 <www.imf.org/en/Publications/WP/Issues/2021/03/03/Gender-Equality-and-Inclusive-Growth-50147> accessed 8 May 2022.

[12] Presentation by Abla Abdel Latif, PhD, Executive Director and Director of Research of the Egyptian Center for Economic Studies (ECES) at the International Women Entrepreneurs Summit in September 2018 organised by SAWDF (South Asian Women Development Forum). *See* SAWDF, 'International Women Entrepreneurs Summit 2018' <https://sawdf.org/portfolio-item/international-women-entrepreneurs-summit-2018/> accessed 8 May 2022.

[13] Statement by the WTO Ambassador of Peru at the meeting of the Informal Working Group on Trade and Gender. *See* WTO, 'Informal Working Group on Trade and Gender' (26 February 2021) <www.wto.org/english/tratop_e/womenandtrade_e/iwg_trade_gender_e.htm> accessed 8 May 2022.

[14] Ibid.

reduce Afghanistan's GDP by an additional 5 per cent and would constitute an immediate economic loss of up to USD 1 billion.[15]

Women's contribution to the economy also impacts job creation, economic diversification, innovation, entrepreneurship, poverty reduction, and development. Even if they own or lead micro and small businesses, women entrepreneurs create jobs, for themselves and often for other women. According to a WTO survey on women entrepreneurs' knowledge gap on trade, in South Asia, East Africa, and Latin America, 57 per cent of workers employed by micro companies owned and led by women are female.[16] Also, according to the survey, 50 per cent of women entrepreneurs were motivated to develop their businesses to create jobs for others and 41 per cent of women created their businesses in order to be their own bosses.[17]

Women tend to be more involved in the services sector, thus fostering diversification. In low- and lower-middle-income countries, women make up about 40 per cent of workers in the services sector and in upper-middle- and high-income countries, they represent almost 70 per cent of the services sector workforce.[18] Some countries have included women's economic empowerment in their new economic diversification strategies, recognising women's key role in the economy. In particular, Saudi Arabia has undertaken ninety major human rights reforms over the past few years and women's empowerment constitutes a large share of these reforms, focusing on promoting female employment and women's political rights.[19] As a result, over the last four years, the rate of female unemployment in Saudi Arabia has

[15] UNDP, 'Afghanistan Socio-Economic Outlook 2021–2022: Averting a Basic Needs Crisis' (1 December 2021) <www.undp.org/publications/afghanistan-socio-economic-outlook-2021-2022-averting-basic-needs-crisis> accessed 8 May 2022.

[16] WTO, 'Assessing Women Entrepreneurs' Knowledge Gap on Trade in East Africa, South Asia, and Latin America' (unpublished survey 2019–2020. On file with author). More than 800 women entrepreneurs were surveyed in Latin America, South Asia, and East Africa between 2019 and 2020.

[17] Ibid.

[18] World Bank and WTO, 'Women and Trade: The Role of Trade in Promoting Gender Equality' (2020) <www.wto.org/english/res_e/booksp_e/women_trade_pub2807_e.pdf> accessed 8 May 2022.

[19] Presentation of Saudi Arabia at the 23 June 2021 meeting of the Informal Working Group on Trade and Gender of the WTO on Vision 2030. *See* Permanent Mission of the Kingdom of Saudi Arabia to the WTO, 'Vision 2030, an Economic Diversification Strategy and Women's Economic Empowerment' (23 June 2021) <www.wto.org/english/tratop_e/womenandtrade_e/230621_saudi_arabia.pdf> accessed 8 May 2022; *see also* Kingdom of Saudi Arabia, 'Vision 2030, an Economic Diversification Strategy and Women's Economic Empowerment' <www.vision2030.gov.sa> accessed 8 May 2022.

decreased by 13.9 per cent[20] due to the engagement of the female workforce.[21]

Women can drive innovation. Globally, female entrepreneurs are 5 per cent more likely than men to be innovative.[22] Also, when trained in new technologies, they tend to use them more than men to manage their businesses.[23] In Europe, 15 per cent of innovative start-ups are founded or co-founded by women.[24]

Women also contribute to poverty reduction as most women reinvest their income in their families. For instance, according to a survey by the WTO, in South Asia, East Africa, and Latin America, women reinvest their disposable incomes first in their business, second in their household expenses such as rent, food, education, and health, and third in the overall family income.[25]

Women entrepreneurs are the backbone of any economy. They represent approximately 30–37 per cent (8–10 million) of all micro, small, and medium-sized enterprises (MSMEs) in emerging markets.[26] In Brazil, Russia, India, China, and South Africa (BRICS), on average, women represent 25 per cent of business owners.[27] In Nigeria, women represent 41 per cent of micro-business

[20] In 2021, women represented about 30 per cent of the total Saudi workforce in the private sector. General Authority for Statistics (GASTAT), Kingdom of Saudi Arabia, Labor Market Statistics Q4 of 2021. *See* General Authority for Statistics (Saudi Arabia), 'Saudi Unemployment at 11.0%, Overall Unemployment at 6.9% in Q4/2021' (2021) <www.stats.gov.sa/sites/default/files/LMS%20Q042021E.pdf> accessed 8 May 2022.

[21] From 9 per cent in July 2020 to 7.4 per cent in January 2021. Kingdom of Saudi Arabia, 'Vision 2030' (n 19).

[22] Global Entrepreneurship Monitor, 'GEM Global Report 2016/17' (GERA 2017) <www.gemconsortium.org/report/gem-2016-2017-global-report> accessed 8 May 2022.

[23] ADB, '2019 Asian Development Bank Annual Report' (ADB 2019) <www.adb.org/sites/default/files/institutional-document/650011/adb-annual-report-2019.pdf> accessed 8 May 2022.

[24] European Innovation Council, 'EU Launches Women TechEU Pilot to Put Women at the Forefront of Deep Tech' (13 July 2021) <https://eic.ec.europa.eu/news/eu-launches-women-techeu-pilot-put-women-forefront-deep-tech-2021-07-13_en> accessed 8 May 2022.

[25] WTO survey, 'Assessing Women Entrepreneurs' Knowledge Gap on Trade in East Africa, South Asia, and Latin America (2019–2020)' (unpublished. On file with author).

[26] IFC, 'IFC Annual Report 2010: Where Innovation Meets Impact' (IFC/World Bank 2010) <www.ifc.org/wps/wcm/connect/16494d0c-77b8-474a-bafd-f8f8a928ff8c/AR2010_English.pdf?MOD=AJPERES&CVID=iYNAdVZ> accessed 8 May 2022.

[27] WTO average count on current and available data from the Sixth Economic Census released by the Indian Ministry of Statistics and Programme Implementation (January 2013–April 2014), Mastercard Index of Women Entrepreneurs Report 2018, and from the Second Eurasian Women Forum, September 2018. *See* Government of India, 'All India Report of Sixth Economic Consensus' (2016) <https://msme.gov.in/sites/default/files/All%20India%20Report%20of%20Sixth%20Economic%20Census.pdf> accessed 8 May 2022; MasterCard, 'Mastercard Index of Women Entrepreneurs (MIWE) 2018' (2018) <https://newsroom.mastercard.com/wp-content/uploads/2018/03/MIWE_2018_Final_Report.pdf> accessed 8 May 2022.

owners, with 23 million female entrepreneurs operating in the country. Nigeria has one of the highest female entrepreneurship rates globally.[28]

2.3 IS THE WTO REALLY GENDER BLIND?

Six hundred-odd pages of the WTO rulebook that governs international trade is gender neutral. Some would say that it is gender blind.[29] The WTO agreements make no explicit mention of terms such as 'gender', 'gender equality', or 'men and women'. Despite this silence, one cannot assume that the WTO is entirely gender blind. In fact, it has an implicit legal base and an explicit mandate to work on gender equality in trade. This is discussed in the following sections.

2.3.1 *An Implicit Legal Basis: The Objectives of the GATT and WTO*

The Preamble of the GATT provides that trade should be 'conducted with a view to raising standards of living, ensuring full employment and a large and steadily growing volume of real income'.[30] Similarly, the preamble of the Marrakesh Agreement establishing the WTO (WTO Agreement) stipulates that trade should be 'conducted with a view to raising standards of living, ensuring full employment and a large and steadily growing volume of real income ... while allowing for the optimal use of the world's resources in accordance with the objective of sustainable development'.[31]

The concept of sustainable development was described in the 1987 Brundtland Commission Report as 'development that meets the needs of the present without compromising the ability of future generations to meet their own needs'.[32] The Report further adds that '[p]overty is not only an evil in itself, but sustainable development requires meeting the basic needs of all and extending to all the opportunity to fulfil their aspirations for a better life. A world in which poverty is endemic will always be prone to ecological and other catastrophes'.[33] According to the United Nations (UN), sustainable

[28] PwC Nigeria, 'Impact of Women on Nigeria's Economy' (PwC 12 March 2020) <www.pwc.com/ng/en/publications/impact-of-women-on-nigerias-economy.html> accessed 8 May 2022.

[29] EIGE', Gender Blindness' (n 5).

[30] First recital, Preamble, General Agreement on Tariffs and Trade 1994, 15 April 1994, 1867 UNTS. 187, 33 ILM 1153 (GATT 1994).

[31] First recital, Preamble, Marrakesh Agreement Establishing the World Trade Organization, 15 April 1994, 1867 UNTS 154, 33 ILM 1144 (Marrakesh Agreement or WTO Agreement).

[32] World Commission on the Environment and Development, 'Our Common Future' (1987) (Brundtland Report), Section 3 'Sustainable Development' Article 27.

[33] Ibid.

development includes notions of inclusivity and resilience. To be achieved, inclusive and equitable economic growth, social inclusion, and environmental protection would need to be combined.[34] Some mistakenly interpret sustainable development as merely linked to the protection of the environment, but, as described above, it is a combination of issues that makes for sustainable development.

These definitions put women at the centre of sustainable development and directly link the WTO's sustainable development objectives to women's economic empowerment, giving the WTO an implicit legal basis to work on trade and gender. However, until 2016, the WTO never took the opportunity to connect gender equality with trade.

2.3.2 *An Explicit Legal Basis: The Aid for Trade Initiative and the WTO Technical Assistance Plans*

Gender equality has been part of Aid for Trade since its inception. The Aid for Trade initiative was created at the Hong Kong Ministerial Conference in 2005.[35] In 2006, the Aid for Trade Task Force composed of WTO members was set up to operationalise the initiative and frame its objectives.

The final report of the Task Force, released in July 2006 and presented to the General Council, provides that 'Aid for trade should be rendered in a coherent manner taking full account . . . of the gender perspective and of the overall goal of sustainable development'.[36] The report stipulates that donors and partner countries jointly commit to the 'harmonization of efforts on cross-cutting issues, such as gender equality'.[37] In fact, it provides an explicit and broad mandate for gender equality to be included in the Aid for Trade initiative.

Gender is thus an inherent part of Aid for Trade, with the IWG on Trade and Gender recognising its essential role in women's economic empowerment by establishing it as one of its four work pillars.[38]

[34] UN, 'The UN Sustainable Agenda' <www.un.org/sustainabledevelopment/development-agenda/#:~:text=Sustainable%20development%20has%20been%20defined,to%20meet%20their%20own%20needs> accessed 8 May 2022.

[35] WTO, 'Hong Kong Ministerial Declaration', WT/MIN(05)/DEC (22 December 2005) para. 57.

[36] Aid for Trade Task Force, 'Recommendations of the Task Force on Aid for Trade', WT/AFT/1 (27 July 2006), Section F.2 Guiding Principles.

[37] Ibid para. 42.

[38] WTO, 'Interim Report Following the Buenos Aires Joint Declaration on Trade and Women's Economic Empowerment', WT/L/1095/Rev.1 (25 September 2020).

In addition, the Biennial Technical Assistance and Training Plan 2018–2019 gave the mandate to the WTO Secretariat to develop a training module on trade and gender for WTO members and government officials.[39] The subsequent Biennial Technical Assistance and Training Plan 2020–2021 further confirms the integration of gender into the WTO training programmes.[40]

It is interesting to note that whereas trade and gender is a plurilateral issue in the WTO, the WTO Technical Assistance Plans are adopted multilaterally within the WTO Committee on Trade and Development by all WTO members. This shows a further institutionalisation of the issue in the WTO.

2.4 HAS THE WTO TRANSFORMED INTO A GENDER-AWARE ORGANISATION?

The issue of gender was first introduced into the WTO in 2016 due to the influence of non-state actors and the political impetus of former WTO Director-General Roberto Azevêdo.

WTO members formalised their relationships with non-governmental organisations (NGOs) when they established the organization.[41] Article V:2 of the WTO Agreement gives a legal basis for relations with NGOs and provides that 'the General Council may make appropriate arrangements for consultations and cooperation with non-governmental organizations concerned with matters related to those of the WTO'. In 1996, the General Council adopted the Guidelines for Arrangements on Relations with Non-Governmental Organizations, framing this cooperation.[42] The Guidelines describe NGOs as 'a valuable resource' that 'can contribute to the accuracy and richness of the public debate'.[43] Over the years, NGOs have influenced the agenda of the WTO. The introduction of the issues of cotton or fisheries subsidies in the WTO is a typical example of such influence. NGOs have also supported the WTO in integrating trade and gender into its work.

39 WTO, 'Biennial Technical Assistance and Training Plan, Revision 2018–19', WT/COMTD/W/227/Rev.1 (23 October 2017), Section 3.3.1. The plan provided that 'Trade-Related Technical Assistance (TRTA) is a core function of the WTO'. It stipulates that the purpose of the WTO trade-related technical assistance is 'to enhance human and institutional capacity to take full advantage of the rules-based Multilateral Trading System'. It also gives the WTO Secretariat the mandate to set up and conduct a training module on trade and gender.

40 WTO, 'Biennial Technical Assistance and Training Plan, Revision 2020–2021', WT/COMTD/W/248/Rev.1 (1 November 2019).

41 Article V:2, Marrakesh Agreement.

42 WTO, 'Guidelines for Arrangements on Relations with Non-governmental Organizations', WT/L/162 (23 July 1996).

43 Ibid.

In 2015, the NGO Women at the Table, working on 'structural barriers faced by women and preventing them from benefiting the world's economic, political and social development', created the International Gender Champions network (IGC) in collaboration with then US Ambassador and UN Director-General in Geneva.[44] The IGC is a 'collaborative network of senior female & male decision-makers who drive systems change' and today includes more than 300 international 'gender champions', including the Secretary-General of the UN, the heads of most international organisations, NGOs, ambassadors, and leaders in the private sector.[45] In order to focus its work, the IGC is organised in various thematic groups. The IGC Trade Impact Group was formed with the aim of pushing the integration of gender issues in the WTO. The Trade Impact Group is itself composed of some WTO members (developed and developing), the WTO, and other international organisations, as well as NGOs. It was created in 2017, the year of the WTO's 11th Ministerial Conference (MC11). Taking this opportunity, the group drafted a declaration to be launched at MC11. This informal instrument was eventually presented unofficially at the margins of MC11 in December 2017 and endorsed by 118 WTO members and observers. The informal path was chosen because of the sensitivity of the issue for some members and because it was not supported at the multilateral level. In fact, the Buenos Aires Declaration[46] is a simple 'PDF' document without the WTO logo or any specific official WTO symbol.[47] Despite this informality, it served as a platform to introduce discussions on gender into the WTO through thematic workshops organised by the organisation, and its members and external stakeholders. After two years of discussions and exploration of the issue, members decided to institutionalise it in the WTO, by establishing the IWG on Trade and Gender on 23 September 2020.[48]

Through their work within the IWG on Trade and Gender, WTO members committed to make trade work better for women and be more inclusive. They ran successful rounds of thematic discussions introducing

[44] *See* Women at the Table, 'Home' <www.womenatthetable.net/> accessed 8 May 2022.

[45] *See* International Gender Champions, 'About' <https://genderchampions.com/about#:~:text=The%20International%20Gender%20Champions%20> accessed 8 May 2022.

[46] WTO, 'Joint Declaration on Trade and Women's Economic Empowerment on the Occasion of the WTO Ministerial Conference in Buenos Aires in December 2017' <www.wto.org/english/thewto_e/minist_e/mc11_e/genderdeclarationmc11_e.pdf> accessed 8 May 2022.

[47] Document symbols are used to formalise a document and attribute it to a WTO body or committee and to WTO members multilaterally, plurilaterally, or individually. It formalises decisions and various types of communications between WTO members.

[48] WTO, 'Interim Report Following the Buenos Aires Joint Declaration on Trade and Women's Economic Empowerment', WT/L/1095/Rev.1 (25 September 2020).

the issue of trade and gender equality in the WTO for the first time. They designed and implemented the first work plan in the WTO on trade and gender based on four pillars: gender-responsive policy making; a gender lens applied to the WTO; research and analytical work; and Aid for Trade. They supported the introduction of gender-equality language in plurilateral trade negotiations.[49] Moreover, they further strengthened WTO members' experience and expertise in inclusive policy making.[50] They have, in sum, institutionalised gender issues in the WTO.

In June 2022, during the WTO's 12th Ministerial Conference (MC12), members negotiated and adopted a paragraph in the MC12 Outcome document[51] recognising the importance of women's economic empowerment and the work of the WTO on this issue, at the multilateral level. That means gender issues are now considered a part of the WTO work as a whole. Also, the Co-Chairs of the IWG on Trade and Gender released a joint statement[52] acknowledging that the WTO's work on trade and gender is in line with its objectives, as stipulated in its Preamble, and recognising the achievements made since the MC11 by WTO members as a basis for future work. In addition to the Interim Report establishing the IWG Group on Trade and Gender and Aid for Trade, these texts give WTO members an additional and stronger legal basis to work on trade and gender.

In parallel to this process, former WTO Director-General Roberto Azevêdo, who became an International Gender Champion in 2016, made a commitment to gender equality in trade and in the WTO Secretariat. In June 2017, he appointed the first WTO Trade and Gender Focal Point to lead this work in the organisation, who, in October 2017, launched the first WTO Trade and Gender Action 2017–2019 focusing on four key objectives: facilitating WTO members' work on trade and gender; conducting research; delivering training on trade and gender for government officials and raising awareness on the trade and gender nexus. The WTO is currently working on the basis of its second Action Plan 2021–2026.

The WTO gender focus was therefore built in an unusual way: from total informality to institutionalisation and driven by one NGO.

49 Declaration on the Conclusion of Negotiations on Services Domestic Regulation, WT/L/1129, 2 December 2021.

50 Progress Report on WTO members and observers technical work on women's economic empowerment (INF/TGE/R/1), 9 November 2021.

51 MC12 Outcome document, Paragraph 13 of WT/MIN(22)/24 – WT/L/1135, 17 June 2022

52 The Statement on Inclusive Trade and Gender Equality from the Co-Chairs of the Informal Working Group on Trade and Gender (WT/MIN(22)/7).

2.5 HOW CAN TRADE POLICIES HELP?

2.5.1 *A Gender-Responsive Trade Policy Can Lift Obstacles Faced by Women in Trade*

WTO members have mostly focused their gender-related trade policies on eighteen different categories of policy interventions.[53] In practice, many WTO members have focused their gender-related trade policies on providing financial and non-financial incentives to the private sector and women-owned/led MSMEs, lifting financial and procedural obstacles.

Access to finance is one of the keys to women entrepreneurs integrating into international trade. Without finance, women entrepreneurs cannot trade.[54] Lack of finance hinders their ability to cover trade-related costs such as specialised IT systems, skilled staff in customs procedures, standards compliance, packaging, trade agents, and trade finance.

Financial incentives set up by governments in the area of trade are therefore essential. In many cases, governments have established special quotas for women-owned companies to secure their access to such incentives.[55] Others have established specific 'women's funds' to provide affordable finance to women-owned companies or start-up enterprises led by women.[56] Through

[53] (1) Trade exports in the circular economy in support of women's economic activity and livelihood; (2) Data collection leading to informed policies; (3) Assessing the impact of trade, trade policies, and trade agreements on women; (4) Promoting female entrepreneurship; (5) Fostering women's participation in the economy; (6) Combating the impacts of COVID-19 on women; (7) Female leadership institutions and decision-making; (8) Gender chapters and provisions in free trade agreements and regional trade agreements; (9) Applying gender lens to trade and WTO; (10) Development aid and Aid for Trade targeting women; (11) Standards and gender; (12) Capacity building; (13) Financial and non-financial incentives to the private sector and women-owned/led MSMEs; (14) Agriculture and fisheries; (15) Government procurement; (16) standards; (17) Services; and (18) Trade strategies.

[54] Alisa DiCaprio, Ying Yao, and Rebecca Simms, 'Women and Trade: Gender's Impact on Trade Finance and Fintech' (2017) ADBI Working Paper Series No. 797 <www.adb.org/sites/default/files/publication/389186/adbi-wp797.pdf> accessed 8 May 2022; Hanan Morsy, 'Access to Finance: Why Aren't Women Leaning In?' (IMF – *Finance & Development Magazine* March 2020) <www.imf.org/external/pubs/ft/fandd/2020/03/pdf/africa-gender-gap-access-to-finance-morsy.pdf> accessed 8 May 2022; Hanan Morsy, 'Access to Finance – Mind the Gender Gap' (2017) EBRD Working Paper No. 202 <www.ebrd.com/publications/working-papers/access-to-finance> accessed 8 May 2022.

[55] WTO, 'Trade Policy Review – Pakistan', WT/TPR/S/311 (17 February 2015); WTO, 'Trade Policy Review – The Maldives – Minutes of the Meeting', WT/TPR/M/332/Add.1 (7 June 2016) 37.

[56] WTO, 'Trade Policy Review – Report by the Secretariat – Southern African Customs Union', WT/TPR/S/324 (30 September 2015) 356.

these support programmes, governments aim at facilitating access to credit for women's business activities, provide rural women with opportunities to access value chains, and help women to compete in regional and international markets. These incentives often take the form of credit guarantees, securities, grants, loans, or subsidised financing. Those financial schemes are often accompanied with other types of assistance for women small-scale entrepreneurs, such as with marketing or training in business management.[57]

Other incentives are non-financial and can take the form of simplified industrial or business licence processes for MSMEs and female entrepreneurs, preventing women from facing approval delays motivated by gender-biased behaviours,[58] as these constitute an additional trade cost for women. Non-financial incentives also include skills training on business and financial management aiming at building women's capacity to export and expand in regional and international markets.[59] Government could also go as far as setting up an online platform for businesswomen to market their products and support their access to international markets.[60]

Moreover, Aid for Trade can lift infrastructure obstacles faced by women especially in rural areas. While the Aid for Trade Initiative helps governments to build their trade capacity, access global markets, and increase their exports, it can also support women's economic empowerment by lifting some of the obstacles they are facing, especially with regard to trade-related infrastructure.

Lack of access to electricity can prevent female entrepreneurs or farmers from expanding their businesses, especially in rural areas. Faced with such problems, some resort to generators which increases their trade costs even further.[61] Aid for Trade has been addressing this issue, especially regarding women's needs through the creation and improvement of infrastructure. For example, Canada, an Aid for Trade donor, supports Burkina Faso in electrifying its rural areas, using solar energy. The project targets the development of businesswomen, the increase of production, the improvement of processing and storage options in specific sectors, such as onion production, and chicken

[57] WTO, 'Trade Policy Review – Report by the Secretariat – India', WT/TPR/S/313 (28 April 2015) 161–162.
[58] WTO, 'Trade Policy Review – Report by Egypt', WT/TPR/G/367 (16 January 2018) 7.
[59] WTO, 'Trade Policy Review – Report by the United States', WT/TPR/G/350 (14 November 2016) 24.
[60] WTO, 'Trade Policy Review – Separate Customs Territory of Taiwan, Pehghu, Kinmen and Matsu – Minutes of the Meeting', WT/TPR/M/377/Add.1 (28 January 2019).
[61] Interviews conducted by WTO trade and gender focal point with Women entrepreneurs from South Asia (December 2020). On file with author.

and fish livestock farming, which are female-led sectors. Women's groups were also involved in the project to ensure that it fits their needs.[62]

However, these types of projects are still rare. Donors and partner countries have been gradually and continuously integrating gender into their Aid for Trade objectives. In 2022, 92 per cent of developing countries and 90 per cent of donors (both bilateral and multilateral) have integrated women's economic empowerment as a priority in their national or regional development plans and objectives or trade-related development aid.[63] Both groups are therefore at a par, similarly to 2019, as revealed by the Aid for Trade Monitoring and Evaluation (M&E) Exercise in 2019.[64] Aid for Trade funding is also aligned with developing countries' priorities and objectives on women's economic empowerment, contrary to the last decade, when there was a clear disconnect between these objectives and the programmes with regard to gender. For example, when identifying constraints faced by women, four out of the six top obstacles are commonly acknowledged by both donors and recipients of Aid for Trade. These four aligned constraints are: access to finance, informal employment, access to digital services, and poor access to information.[65]

2.5.2 *A Gender-Responsive Trade Policy Can Create New Opportunities for Women*

Some WTO members have created specific opportunities for women entrepreneurs through their trade policies. Government procurement policies can support women entrepreneurs. In fact, government procurement represents around 15 per cent of GDP in most economies and women entrepreneurs are underrepresented in this market[66] as only 1 per cent participate in it. To increase market access to government procurement opportunities for women's businesses, some governments have set up preference schemes for women

62 Marianne Musumeci and Kaori Miyamoto, 'Strengthening the Gender Dimension of Aid for Trade in the Least Developed Countries' (Enhanced Integrated Framework 25 June 2019) <https://trade4devnews.enhancedif.org/en/news/strengthening-gender-dimension-aid-trade-least-developed-countries> accessed 8 May 2022.

63 Aid for Trade Global Review, *Empowering Connected, Sustainable Trade*, Chapter 4, <www.wto.org/english/res_e/booksp_e/aid4trade22_e.pdf> accessed 28 September 2022.

64 Anoush der Boghossian, 'Women's Economic Empowerment: An Inherent Part of Aid for Trade' (2019) WTO Staff Working Paper ERSD-2019-08 <www.wto.org/english/res_e/reser_e/ersd201908_e.htm> accessed 8 May 2022.

65 Aid for Trade Global Review, *Empowering Connected, Sustainable Trade* (n 63).

66 WTO, 'Workshop on Enhancing the Participation of Women Entrepreneurs and Traders in Government Procurement' (25 June 2018) <www.wto.org/english/tratop_e/womenandtrade_e/programme_workshop_e.htm> accessed 8 May 2022.

entrepreneurs. The quota allocation is on average about 20 per cent, and sometimes focuses on rural women. However, some of these quotas often include other vulnerable groups such as young or disabled people. Other countries generally prohibit gender-based discrimination in their government procurement laws when contracts are allocated. Some give preference to companies that implement gender equality or wage equality policies.[67]

Governments could use the work conducted by the International Standards Organisation (ISO) on defining women-owned companies internationally to foster women entrepreneurs' participation in their government procurement markets.[68]

Trade policies can also create opportunities for women to enter the workforce. Most WTO members include women's economic empowerment and their integration in the job market as a key priority in their national trade, investment, economic, and development strategies. They often highlight the means needed to achieve this goal. In Nigeria, for instance, the government fostered women's participation in the construction sector, where a labour shortage was identified.[69] Similarly, in Zambia, women were encouraged to work in the male-dominated mining sector.[70] Some policies target reduction in the number of women leaving the workforce because of childbirth;[71] others look at improving women's working environment or increasing female

[67] WTO, 'Trade Policy Review – Report by Paraguay', WT/TPR/G/360 (2 August 2017) 20, 21; WTO, 'Trade Policy Review – Report by Guyana', WT/TPR/G/320 (28 July 2016) 3; WTO, 'Trade Policy Review – Report by the Gambia', WT/TPR/G/365, (21 November 2017) 6, 9, 13; WTO, 'Trade Policy Review – Report by the Secretariat – Southern African Customs Union' (n 56); WTO, 'Trade Policy Review – Report by Iceland' WT/TPR/G/361 (30 August 2017) 7, 8; *see also* WTO, 'Trade Policy Review – Report by Mozambique', WT/TPR/G/354, 7 (29 March 2017); *see also* WTO, 'Trade Policy Review – Report by Chile', WT/TPR/G/315/Rev.1 (7 October 2015) 17, 18; *see also* der Boghossian, 'Women's Economic Empowerment' (n 64).

[68] ISO, 'IWA 34:2021, Women's Entrepreneurship – Key Definitions and General Criteria' <www.iso.org/standard/79585.html> accessed 8 May 2022.

[69] WTO, 'Trade Policy Review – Report by Nigeria', WT/TPR/G/356 (7 May 2017) 11.

[70] Lusaka Times, 'Mines Are Battling to Attract Skilled and Experienced People – Chamber of Mines' (23 June 2017) <www.lusakatimes.com/2017/06/23/mines-battling-attract-skilled-experienced-people-chamber-mines/> accessed 8 May 2022; Dale Benton, 'Global Mining Industry Suffering a Major Skills Shortage Problem, Chamber of Mines Finds' (*Mining* 17 May 2022) <https://miningglobal.com/supply-chain-and-operations/global-mining-industry-suffering-major-skills-shortage-problem-chamber-mines-finds> accessed 8 May 2022; WTO, 'Trade Policy Review – Zambia – Minutes of the Meeting', WT/TPR/M/340/Add.1 (19 September 2016) 18; Fitsum Weldegiorgis, Lynda Lawson, and Hannelore Verbrugge, 'Women in Artisanal and Small-Scale Mining: Challenges and Opportunities for Greater Participation' (IISD 12 May 2018) <www.iisd.org/publications/report/women-artisanal-and-small-scale-mining-challenges-and-opportunities-greater> accessed 8 May 2022.

[71] WTO, 'Trade Policy Review – Report by Japan', WT/TPR/G/310 (9 and 11 March 2015) 15.

leadership.[72] Some members added trade objectives targeted to women's economic empowerment, by tackling low skills in trade and addressing the restricted access of women entrepreneurs to export opportunities.[73] Sometimes, the objective of women's economic empowerment is indirectly underlined by focusing on trade strategies in specific sectors where women work, such as tourism and fisheries. Often, national entrepreneurship strategies focus on specifically supporting women entrepreneurs and small businesses, including companies owned and led by women. These plans also associate greater economic opportunities for women with private sector development.

Trade policies can create export opportunities for women through training. Women entrepreneurs face a knowledge gap in trade rules and proceedings. In South Asia, Latin America, and East Africa, only 50 per cent of women entrepreneurs received training on trade generally, and only 35 per cent received training on trade regulations and customs procedures.[74] Some members have set up capacity-building programmes for female farmers to understand the Sanitary and Phytosanitary (SPS) requirements and be able to comply with them while exporting their products.[75] Through such training and policies, not only can women export their products, but they can also diversify their productions, from commodities to value-added products and gain new markets. Hence, trade can help them in scaling up their businesses through economic diversification. One example is female mango producers, who were trained by the Enhanced Integrated Framework (EIF), as they were not only able to export their raw products by complying with SPS requirements, but were also able to produce value-added products such as mango juice, jam, and dried mangoes.[76] In 2018, the Gambia reported as part of its Trade Policy Review that its policies were focusing on 'providing access to

[72] Ibid; WTO, 'Trade Policy Review – Report by United Arab Emirates', WT/TPR/G/338 (27 April 2016).

[73] Der Boghossian, 'Women's Economic Empowerment' (n 64).

[74] WTO, 'Assessing Women Entrepreneurs' Knowledge Gap on Trade in East Africa, South Asia, and Latin America' (unpublished survey 2019–2020. On file with author). More than 800 women entrepreneurs were surveyed in Latin America, South Asia, and East Africa between 2019 and 2020.

[75] WTO, 'Trade Policy Review – Report by the Gambia' (n 67).

[76] EIF, 'Delivering Change in Mali: Investing in Women and Beyond' (*Trade for Development News EIF* October 2016) <https://enhancedif.org/en/publication/2016-10/delivering-change-mali-investing-women-and-beyond> accessed 8 May 2022, link no longer active; see also Mike Knowles, 'Mali Mango Project Is "Bearing Fruit"', 2 June 2017 <www.fruitnet.com/eurofruit/mali-mango-project-is-bearing-fruit/172388.article> accessed 19 May 2023.

both local and global value chains to producers with special focus on meeting the required quality and sanitary and phytosanitary standards'.[77]

2.5.3 *A Gender-Responsive Trade Policy Can Balance the Scale in Favour of Women by Reducing Gender Discrimination*

Some trade policies have had the result of socially empowering women. Within the trade policy review in 2015,[78] and in order to foster women's participation in its workforce, Japan announced the opening of its services sector to foreign housekeepers 'with a view to promoting women's participation in society, meeting their need for assistance for housework, and encouraging medium- to long-term economic growth'.[79] As a direct consequence, Japan has transformed unpaid care and domestic work into paid work.

In its procurement policy, the Swiss government has conditioned the allocation of contracts by only selecting companies that have an internal wage equality policy.[80] The government also conducted investigations to ascertain whether these internal policies were actually implemented. In 2018, following over 100 controls that were conducted, half of the companies reviewed were found to engage in no discrimination and 12.5 per cent were in violation of their own wage-equality policies.[81] In fact, following these investigations, half of the companies at fault reviewed the implementation of their policies, resulting in an increase of their female workers' wages.

Some trade policies that do not primarily target women's economic empowerment have resulted in better working conditions for female employees, and even better social laws based on gender equality. For instance, in the Philippines, the Information and Communication Technology (ICT) and Business Process Outsourcing (BPO) sectors are booming. According to the Philippines Statistics Authority, more than 55 per cent of workers in the BPO sector are women, working in medical transcription industries, data processing, and call centre activities.[82] This export services sector benefited

77 WTO, 'Trade Policy Review – Report by the Gambia' (n 67) 13.

78 WTO, 'Trade Policy Review – Japan – Minutes of the Meeting, Addendum', WT/TPR/M/310/Add.1 (9 and 11 March 2015) 122.

79 Ibid.

80 Patric Aeberhard at the WTO Workshop. See WTO, 'Workshop on Enhancing the Participation of Women Entrepreneurs and Traders in Government Procurement' (n 66).

81 Ibid.

82 WTO, 'Trade Policy Review – The Philippines – Minutes of the Meeting, Addendum', WT/TPR/M/368/Add.1 (28 May 2018) 114.

from the government's favourable trade policy (for instance, IT buildings were declared vertical economic zones). In the past, the Philippines' labour laws prohibited women from working night shifts and in 2011, and because the BPO sector contributes greatly to the national economy and as female BPO employees were dealing with customers located in different time zones, the government abolished the prohibition and added new requirements for companies, such as sleeping/resting quarters, mandatory transport services for women doing night work, catering in particular to those with children, spaces for nursing mothers allowing them no less than 40 minutes of lactation breaks, and the inclusion of breastfeeding programmes as part of the companies' development plans.[83]

2.6 APPLYING A GENDERED LENS TO TRADE LAW: THE LINK BETWEEN HUMAN RIGHTS, WOMEN'S ECONOMIC EMPOWERMENT AND TRADE LAW

This section examines the links between human rights, women's empowerment, and trade law, and demonstrates how WTO rules can have a real impact on women's lives. It will focus on two examples that demonstrate this link and also show that some of the WTO rules are grounded in women's reality, even if it was not the initial intention of the negotiators of these rules.

The first example relates to the WTO's Agreement on Agriculture.[84] WTO agreements can support women's economic empowerment in agriculture and consequently strengthen food security. Women are the guardians of food security. They play a critical role in agriculture not only as subsistence farmers, but also as farm workers in export crops, suppliers, and/or vendors to informal food markets, and cross-border food traders. They are therefore key players in the domestic/local food supply chain but also in regional/international value chains.

On average, women represent 42 per cent of the agricultural labour force in developing countries.[85] In the Southern Africa Development Community (SADC) region, according to the SADC Food Nutrition Security Strategy 2015–2025, women contribute to 60 per cent of total food production and

[83] Ibid.

[84] Agreement on Agriculture, 15 April 1994, Marrakesh Agreement Establishing the World Trade Organization, Annex 1A, 1867 UNTS 410 (Not reproduced in ILM).

[85] ILO, 'World Employment Social Outlook – Trends for Women 2017' (2017) <www.ilo.org/wcmsp5/groups/public/—dgreports/—inst/documents/publication/wcms_557245.pdf> accessed 8 May 2022.

perform more than 70 per cent of agricultural work.[86] In developed countries (upper and middle income countries), female farmers represent less than 20 per cent of the female workforce.[87] In the European Union, according to Eurostat, the number of women in agriculture has grown and women manage about 30 per cent of European farms (96 per cent of farms are family run). In some other European countries, this number is close to 50 per cent.[88]

Female informal cross-border traders play a key role in food security, as they mostly trade essential food products. In the SADC region, they contribute up to USD 20 billion annually to the region's trade.[89] Through their export activities, they bring their products to places where food is scarce. In West Africa, informal cross-border traders in food products represent about 30 per cent of the regional trade.[90]

Women represent two-thirds of the world's 600 million poor livestock keepers and, according to the International Livestock Research Institute (ILRI),[91] in most developing countries, more than 80 per cent of livestock products are sold in informal food markets, when alternative food sources do not exist for consumers.

Despite their essential role in agriculture, female farmers remain underpaid or even unpaid informal workers, they are excluded from training

86 SADC, 'Food and Nutrition Security Strategy 2015–2025' (2014) 13 <www.resakss.org/sites/default/files/SADC%202014%20Food%20and%20Nutrition%20Security%20Strategy%202015%20-%202025.pdf> accessed 8 May 2022.

87 ILO, 'Employment in Agriculture, Female (% of Female Employment) (Modelled ILO Estimate)' (29 January 2021) <https://data.worldbank.org/indicator/SL.AGR.EMPL.FE.ZS> accessed 8 May 2022.

88 Eurostat, 'Farm Indicators by Agricultural Area, Type of Farm, Standard Output, Sex and Age of the Manager and NUTS 2 Regions' (22 February 2021) <https://ec.europa.eu/eurostat/databrowser/view/EF_M_FARMANG__custom_636393/bookmark/table?lang=en&bookmarkId=f146257b-e328–43b7-b338–48c769ab000f> accessed 8 May 2022; Also cited in a European Parliament study. *See* Ramona Franić and Tihana Kovačiček, 'The Professional Status of Rural Women in the EU' (2019) Study requested by the European Parliament FEMM Committee <www.europarl.europa.eu/RegData/etudes/STUD/2019/608868/IPOL_STU(2019)608868_EN.pdf> accessed 8 May 2022.

89 Southern Africa Trust, 'The Experiences and Challenges of Women in the SADC Region: The Case of Trade and Agriculture Sectors' (January 2018) <https://media.africaportal.org/documents/Experiences_and_challenges_of_women_in_SADC.pdf> accessed 8 May 2022.

90 Antoine Bouet, Kathrun Pace, and Joseph W Glauber, 'Informal Cross-Border Trade in Africa: How Much? Why? And What Impact?' (2018) FPRI Discussion Paper <www.ifpri.org/publication/informal-cross-border-trade-africa-how-much-why-and-what-impact> accessed 8 May 2022.

91 International Livestock Research Institute, 'Why Women Are Essential in Livestock Development – and Why Livestock Are Essential in Women's Lives' <www.ilri.org/knowledge/stories/why-women-are-essential-livestock-development-and-why-livestock-are-essential> accessed 8 May 2022.

opportunities, and their access to resources and land ownership is impeded, contrary to men.[92] Women do not have the same advantages as men in agriculture. Inter alia, they lack access to reproductive resources and inputs. In Guatemala, for instance, they lack access to seeds.

One relevant provision in the WTO Agreement on Agriculture,[93] Article 6.2, if applied with a gender lens, can support female farmers in accessing these essential resources. Article 6.2, otherwise known as the 'development box', provides flexibility to developing countries to give their poor farmers input subsidies. According to the UN Food and Agriculture Organization (FAO), if women had access to reproductive resources to the same level as men, they would increase their production by 20–30 per cent.[94] Understanding the key role women play in food security, giving them this opportunity would strengthen the fundamental right to food. In 2016, to respond to emergency situations, the Gambia used this flexibility and provided bags of fertiliser to female farmers.[95]

The second example is the WTO Trade Facilitation Agreement (TFA) as it can support poverty reduction through training and by fostering women entrepreneurs' exports. If applied with a gender lens, the TFA could indirectly support women's skills development, thus contributing to poverty reduction.

The TFA helps WTO members to digitalise their customs procedures.[96] Such a commitment would allow women entrepreneurs to reduce their trade-related costs by avoiding face-to-face interactions with potential gender-biased customs officials that would delay processing their export permits. A 2012 United States Agency for International Development (USAID) survey showed that Indian women wait, on average, 37 per cent longer than men to see the same customs official when trading at the border.[97] As a consequence of these delays, women often compensate for their losses by imposing higher prices on

92 World Bank, 'Breaking the "Grass Ceiling": Empowering Women Farmers' (6 March 2018) <www.worldbank.org/en/news/feature/2018/03/06/breaking-the-grass-ceiling-empowering-women-farmers> accessed 8 May 2022.

93 The Marrakesh Agreement establishing the World Trade Organization and its Annexes (December 2017) 1–550.

94 FAO, 'The State of Food and Agriculture 2010–2011' (2011) <www.fao.org/3/i2050e/i2050e.pdf> accessed 8 May 2022.

95 WTO, 'Trade Policy Review, Report by the Gambia' (n 67) 54.

96 Agreement on Trade Facilitation (2017) Articles 7, 10 and 12. *See* WTO, 'Agreement on Trade Facilitation' <www.wto.org/english/docs_e/legal_e/tfa-nov14_e.htm> accessed 8 May 2022.

97 USAID, 'Women in Cross-Border Agricultural Trade' (2012) USAID Policy Brief No. 4 <www.agrilinks.org/sites/default/files/resource/files/EAT_PolicyBrief_WomenCrossBorderAgTrade_Oct2012_FINAL.pdf> accessed 8 May 2022.

their goods and thus increasing their wage gaps. In an ideal world, such a provision would have the desired effect of simplifying and helping women entrepreneurs through the maze of red tape and gender discrimination.

Using online processes could support them and prevent face-to-face interactions, as filling in a form online is less time-consuming than meeting customs officials in person in an office that can be located far from their homes. But the gendered digital divide still persists. In 2019, the proportion of women using the internet globally was 48 per cent compared to 58 per cent of men.[98] Also, when women have access to technology, it is often outdated. In addition, women face a general knowledge gap on trade rules and do not know where to find the trade-related information. Hence, to make the trade facilitation provisions fully work for women, it is important for governments to set up training programmes to enhance women's IT skills and their knowledge of trade rules. The TFA combined with adequate policies would have a multiplier effect by allowing women to be trained and to enhance their skills, thus reducing the trade costs they face and leading to poverty reduction.

There is another provision in the TFA that can support women. The *de minimis* provision is actually grounded in the reality of women entrepreneurs as they tend to run smaller businesses as compared to male entrepreneurs. Article 7.8.2(d) of the TFA establishes 'a *de minimis* shipment value of dutiable amount for which customs duties and taxes will not be collected'.

Various international agreements, such as the Revised Kyoto Convention by the World Customs Organization, incorporate this provision to facilitate trade.[99] It is currently also considered by WTO members in their negotiations on e-commerce in support of small businesses. In fact, this provision would be useful for women entrepreneurs engaged in exports, who are often trading small parcels given the nature of their businesses. For instance, many women entrepreneurs work in the garment and handicraft sectors, and women dominate the handicraft sector. In India alone, this sector employs more than 7 million people, most of whom are disadvantaged women.[100] More globally,

98 ITU, 'Bridging the Gender Divide' (July 2021) <www.itu.int/en/mediacentre/backgrounders/Pages/bridging-the-gender-divide.aspx> accessed 8 May 2022.

99 The International Convention on the simplification and harmonization of Customs procedures (as amended) (WCO 2008) (Revised Kyoto Convention) Article 4.13 <www.wcoomd.org/en/topics/facilitation/instrument-and-tools/conventions/pf_revised_kyoto_conv/kyoto_new/gach4.aspx> accessed 8 May 2022.

100 Business Standard, 'Indian Textile & Handicrafts Industry Is the Largest Employment Generator after Agri: Ajay Tamta' (*Business Standard* 9 November 2017) <www.business-standard.com/article/news-cm/indian-textile-handicrafts-industry-is-the-largest-employment-generator-after-agri-ajay-tamta-117110900180_1.html> accessed 8 May 2022.

87 per cent of sellers on Etsy – an international e-commerce platform that sells handicraft and vintage products – are women.[101] The platform connects 2.1 million sellers with 39.4 million buyers.[102] In this sector, dealing with small parcels is a daily task. Also, many women entrepreneurs, while formally established, trade informally. They call it the 'suitcase export'. They export small amounts of their goods to their networks abroad, mostly to friends and family, who sell their products for them. This sort of trade may grow in the context of the COVID-19 pandemic and its aftermath as the global small parcels market is expected to more than double from 103 billion parcels in 2019 to between 220 and 262 billion parcels by 2026.[103]

Lastly, women entrepreneurs mostly own or lead micro-businesses. The WTO Regional Surveys 2019–2020 data shows that 46.3 per cent of them have fewer than ten employees and 27 per cent between eleven and thirty employees.[104] Looking at bigger firms, only 4.6 per cent of women entrepreneurs employ between 51 and 100 staff and less than 5 per cent of businesswomen employ more than 100 workers. Only 3.3 per cent of women entrepreneurs own companies with more than 100 employees. This is also the case in developed countries. For instance, in Canada, 92.7 per cent of women-owned firms employ fewer than twenty staff members.[105]

2.7 CONCLUSION

After improving her skills as a cocoa farmer, Rosine Bekoin said: 'When I started the programme, I was shy. I did not believe in myself or that I could do anything impactful. The school built my confidence. I had to revalue myself as a woman . . . to see myself with equal rights as men . . . I keep telling my daughters that education will be what sees them through in life and

[101] Etsy, 'Celebrating Creative Entrepreneurship around the Globe' (Etsy Global Seller Census Report 2019' (2019) <https://extfiles.etsy.com/advocacy/Etsy_GlobalSellerCensus_4.2019.pdf> accessed 8 May 2022.

[102] Etsy, 'Unlocking Opportunity – Annual Report 2018' (2018) <http://s23.q4cdn.com/775204224/files/doc_downloads/2018-Annual-Report-(1).pdf> accessed 8 May 2022.

[103] Cathy Morrow Roberson, 'Global Parcel Volumes Expected to Double by 2026 on e-Commerce Boom' (2020) *Journal of Commerce* <www.joc.com/international-logistics/global-parcel-volumes-expected-double-2026-e-commerce-boom_20201012.html> accessed 8 May 2022.

[104] WTO, 'Assessing Women Entrepreneurs' Knowledge Gap on Trade in East Africa, South Asia, and Latin America' (n 16).

[105] Women Entrepreneurship Knowledge Hub, 'The State of Women's Entrepreneurship in Canada 2021' (June 2021) <https://wekh.ca/research/the-state-of-womens-entrepreneurship-in-canada-2021/> accessed 8 May 2022.

offers them true independence.'[106] For the last ten years, Rosine has been cultivating a small plot, yielding two crops annually. The next adventure for her is to build a factory, creating jobs for others and lifting her community.

Empowering women is a risk-free endeavour. As described in this chapter, women give back, either as work and income providers, often for other women, or as caretakers of their families and communities.

Trade is central to women's empowerment, not just as an agent of economic development but also as a provider of economic opportunities. Trade policy, instruments, and rules are linked to other issues and policies that are crucial for women's economic and social growth, such as infrastructure, education and capacity building, entrepreneurship, transport and mobility, workplace environment and safety. As seen in the chapter, trade policies can influence positive social development for women.

Sustainable development is at the centre of economic priorities, today more than ever before, and governments have realised that women are part of the answer, as they evolve from simply acknowledging it to taking action. Similarly, as this chapter has shown, the WTO is changing and is now working towards making trade work for women.

[106] Fair Trade Africa, 'I Am Back as a Woman' (4 September 2020) <https://fairtradeafrica.net/i-am-coming-back-as-a-woman/> accessed 8 May 2022.

3

Advances in Feminizing the WTO

MIA MIKIC

ABSTRACT

The years 2020 and 2021 will go down in history as the time when the COVID-19 pandemic caused the deepest recession of the century and killed and sickened many millions of people. Yet trade geeks might remember those years as the period during which gigantic advances were made in women's leadership and influence on trade policies and trade systems. A woman took the helm of the World Trade Organization (WTO) and the United Nations Conference on Trade and Development for the first time and a woman was once again appointed to lead the International Trade Centre. Also remarkably, after a slow start, a WTO Informal Working Group (IWG) on Trade and Gender was finally established in late 2020 (as the next step from the Joint Declaration on Trade and Women's Economic Empowerment of 2017). This chapter leans and builds on the author's previous work and provides an update on the IWG's work and the engagement of WTO members (Friends of Gender) interested in contributing to that work. Based on limited information available, the chapter gauges how much of the IWG's work programme has permeated into general WTO operations. In other words, it assesses (based on a text search) the degree to which the ongoing negotiations of trade rules/structural discussions on joint statement initiatives – investment facilitation, e-commerce, and micro, small, and medium enterprises – have taken a gendered lens. It also reports on the advances achieved in mainstreaming gender in the WTO Secretariat and membership representation in the WTO.

3.1 INTRODUCTION

If this book were a Twitter thread, then this chapter on 'Advances in Feminizing the WTO' could simply read: 'For the first time since its establishment, the WTO is put under the leadership of a woman.' It might continue: 'Starting in 2021, all three global institutions responsible for trade are led by women' (ending with an appropriate emoji 🙋♀).

However, there is much more to be said about the advances (or lack thereof) in work on recognizing the complex linkages between trade and gender, and this deserves a book chapter. This chapter was drafted while the WTO members, the Secretariat, and many interested parties, were readying themselves for the WTO MC12 planned to be held from 30 November to 3 December 2021 in Geneva, Switzerland.[1] Twenty-five years ago, during the 1st Ministerial Conference (MC1) held in Singapore, WTO members debated about, inter alia, the rationale for introducing (core) labour standards into the body of the multilateral rules governed by the (then) newly established WTO. While the Ministers dismissed such proposals,[2] the UN Economic and Social Commission for Asia and the Pacific (ESCAP) report (1996), dedicated to concerns related to the agenda of MC1, included a discussion on the impacts of trade liberalization on women.[3] In fact, the recommendations were rather broader, encompassing: (a) further study to ensure that liberalization policies did not exacerbate existing gender inequalities; (b) systematic and periodic gender-impact assessments of liberalization policies at the sectoral, national, and international levels; (c) further study of

[1] The 12th Ministerial Conference was originally scheduled to be hosted by the Government of Kazakhstan in its capital Nur-Sultan in 2021, but was postponed due to the COVID-19 pandemic. The MC12 finally took place in June 2022 at the WTO in Geneva, Switzerland, and was chaired by Timur Suleimenov, First Deputy Chief of Staff of the President of Kazakhstan. The outcomes (known as the Geneva package) and other relevant materials are available at WTO, 'Twelfth Ministerial Conference' <www.wto.org/english/thewto_e/minist_e/mc12_e/mc12_e.htm#outcomes> accessed 13 September 2022.

[2] The Ministerial Declaration stated: '4. We renew our commitment to the observance of internationally recognized core labour standards. The International Labour Organization (ILO) is the competent body to set and deal with these standards, and we affirm our support for its work in promoting them. We believe that economic growth and development fostered by increased trade and further trade liberalization contribute to the promotion of these standards. We reject the use of labour standards for protectionist purposes, and agree that the comparative advantage of countries, particularly low-wage developing countries, must in no way be put into question. In this regard, we note that the WTO and ILO Secretariats will continue their existing collaboration.' WTO, 'Singapore Ministerial Declaration', WT/MIN(96)/DEC (18 December 1996). The brief prepared for the press at the time pulled together pros and cons about the inclusion of labour standards, including forced labour, under the auspices of the WTO. *See* WTO, 'Trade and Labour Standards' <www.wto.org/english/thewto_e/minist_e/min96_e/labstand.htm> accessed 8 May 2022.

[3] UN ESCAP, 'Economic and Social Commission for Asia and the Pacific: Annual Report, 2 May 1995–24 April 1996', E/1996/36 E/ESCAP/1044 (Economic and Social Council Official Records 1996).

existing gender inequalities on trade and investment policies; (d) enabling policymakers to raise these issues within the context of the WTO and other policy-making institutions; (e) setting up a committee within the WTO to examine all the issues from a gender perspective (and incorporating women's voices on the setting up of WTO agendas); and (f) commitment of sufficient financing to a global gender equity fund).[4] It is thus only fitting that a quarter-century and eleven ministerial conferences later, the Ministers, once they meet, will have an opportunity to deliberate and finally adopt an ambitious and progressive WTO work programme on Trade for Women. The opportunity that was, after all, missed.

This chapter takes the recommendations by Mikic and Sharma on the steps towards feminizing the WTO and examines if any work associated with these recommendations has indeed occurred and in what form.[5] As a visual aid, the plan and summary of the chapter's content is given in Table 3.1. The recommendations refer to five areas, each covered in one section of the chapter. Section 3.2 provides an update on the IWG's work and the engagements of the WTO members contributing to that work (known as the Friends of Gender). Section 3.3, based on the limited information available,[6] gauges how much of the IWG's work programme has permeated into overall WTO operations as well as into the members' other approaches to trade liberalization. In other words, it assesses to what degree the ongoing negotiations of trade rules/structural discussions on joint statement initiatives (that is, investment facilitation, e-commerce, and MSMEs) have a gender lens. Section 3.4 offers information on the novel work of the Secretariat (as well as other organizations and partners, and in some cases members), improving the evidence and tools necessary to make informed decisions or to make better impact assessments. Section 3.5 comments briefly on the capacity-building work emerging in the Secretariat based on the announcement of a new strategy for the period from 2021 to 2026. Section 3.6 circles back to the role of women in leading trade and trade policy work through reviewing the advancement of women into leadership and

4 Nilufer Cagatay, 'Asian and Pacific Developing Economies and the First WTO Ministerial Conference: Issues of Concern' (1996) 22 *Studies in Trade and Investment* 323–334.

5 Mia Mikic and Vanika Sharma, 'Feminizing WTO 2.0' in Simon J. Evenett and Richard Baldwin (eds) *Revitalising Multilateralism: Pragmatic Ideas for the New WTO Director-General* (Centre for Economic Policy Research Press 2020).

6 As noted earlier, the chapter was drafted prior to the public release of most of the documents being prepared for the MC12 originally planned for December 2021. After the postponement of the MC12, several of the negotiated texts and reference papers were made available to the public. Any discovery of the application of the gender lens in these documents was added in the process of editing of this chapter.

TABLE 3.1 *Advancing from WTO 1.0 to WTO 2.0*

WTO 1.0 (Work programme 2020)	WTO2.0 (Feminized and modernized)	Actions taken in 2021 or expected to be taken at or after MC12
Raising awareness on links between trade and women	Full cognizance and acceptance of this new area of work through WTO IWG on Women and Trade (and working towards implementing the Declaration)	1. Final Work Plan for Implementing Activities under IWG on Trade and Gender adopted (2021). Withdrawn from the MC12 Agenda 2. Schedule of activities adopted, and six meetings held by end of October 2021 3. Draft proposal for the MC12 outcome document (led by the Friends of Gender) with recommendations on inclusion of Trade and Gender in the regular work programme was withdrawn from the MC12 Agenda
Facilitating WTO members' actions on trade and women	Binding and enforceable language in RTAs and WTO agreements Targeted trade assistance programmes and Aid for Trade	A preview of available negotiated text for MC12 which may contain gender provisions/clauses or imply impact: 1. Fisheries subsidies 2. Domestic regulation in services 3. Joint Statement Initiative – Micro, Small and Medium-Sized Enterprises 4. Joint Statement Initiative- Investment facilitation Developments in regional agreements and arrangements: 1. Global Trade and Gender Arrangement (GTAGA) 2. Bilateral and other free trade agreements (FTAs) Aid for Trade delivery programme
Generating new data on trade and women	Mandatory impact assessment and differentiated data collection	1. Database of gender-responsive trade policies implemented by WTO members made available after MC12[a] 2. New WTO Trade Cost Index 3. Research by the Secretariat and partners including a proposed Gender Research Hub made available after the MC12[b]

(continued)

TABLE 3.1 (*continued*)

WTO 1.0 (Work programme 2020)	WTO2.0 (Feminized and modernized)	Actions taken in 2021 or expected to be taken at or after MC12
Providing trainings to government officials and women entrepreneurs	Provisions on technical assistance specifically on enhancing women's role in trade, trade negotiations and policy-making	1. IWG announced a new capacity-building strategy which integrates gender elements 2. IWG announced the availability of trade policy tools to assist members to integrate gender into the policies[c]
Gender mainstreaming in WTO (Secretariat and membership representation)	Women ascending to leadership and decision-making	1. Woman appointed as Director-General (DG), and two women as Deputy-DGs (50 per cent) 2. Six divisional directors are women (35.3 per cent) 3. General Council and reporting bodies – five women are chairs (33.3 per cent) 4. TNC and committees – three women are chairs (33.3 per cent) 5. Council in goods – five women are chairs (35.7 per cent) 6. Council on services – zero 7. Council on plurilaterals – one woman chair (50 per cent) 8. Ambassadors – forty members (24.4 per cent) and four observers (16 per cent) are women

Source: Adopted and expanded from table 1 in Mikic and Sharma, 'Feminizing WTO 2.0' (n 6) 180.

[a] For the database on gender provisions in RTAs, *see* WTO, 'Database on Gender Provisions in RTAs' <www.wto.org/english/tratop_e/womenandtrade_e/gender_responsive_trade_agreement_db_e.htm> accessed 13 September 2022.

[b] For the Gender Research Hub information, including the research database on trade and gender, *see* WTO, 'Research Database on Trade and Gender' <www.wto.org/english/tratop_e/womenandtrade_e/research_database_women_trade_e.htm> accessed 13 September 2022.

[c] According to the WTO Secretariat's statement, this trade policy tool package will include (a) An extensive questionnaire that members could use (fully or partially) to integrate a full chapter into their trade policy reports or to assess how gender has been integrated into their trade policies; (b) A checklist derived from the questionnaire that can be used for the same purpose; (c) A guidebook to support members in this exercise; (d) Indicators that can help members understand how trade rules can be implemented with a gender lens. The first set of indicators will be developed for the Trade Facilitation Agreement. This package is complementary to the ITC's SheTrades Policy Outlook. As the tool is not publicly available at the time of finalizing this chapter, it is not possible to provide further comments on it. *See* WTO, 'WTO Secretariat Talking Points' (16 July 2021) <www.wto.org/english/tratop_e/womenandtrade_e/16july21/statement_from_wto_secretariat.pdf> accessed 8 May 2022.

decision-making positions in the WTO Secretariat and among the members' representatives in the WTO. Section 3.7 concludes.

The first two columns of Table 3.1 were presented by Mikic and Sharma as the pre- and post-feminization reform states of the WTO. The first column – WTO 1.0 – reflects what has been described as a gender-blind trade system that existed when the Buenos Aires declaration was adopted, but not fit to tackle the contemporary challenges to trade, not least because of not providing for women in trade. The second column – WTO 2.0 – describes the attributes of the trade rules system after the ambitious Buenos Aires declaration and other developments. WTO 2.0 by no means indicates that no further advances concerning the feminization of the WTO should be needed or expected. Nevertheless, WTO 2.0 would already be an advanced environment in which women would benefit from trade and contribute to trade policymaking more than at present. The third column of Table 3.1 lists the actions already taken in preparation for MC12, such as drafted and pre-negotiated statements, declarations, and other documents, and the decisions that need to be taken at MC12 to move the work forward.

It is obvious from Table 3.1, and more explicitly discussed by Mikic and Sharma, that the approach to the analysis of trade and gender issues in the context of the WTO needs to look at the organization from two perspectives: (1) as an international organization, and (2) as a set of various trade rules which form a so-called multilateral trading system. Trade and gender discussion related to the WTO as an international organization boils down to the following: (1) implementation of the mandates from the membership (i.e., Declaration on promoting women's empowerment); (2) delivery of technical assistance/capacity building for its members to improve formulation and implementation of gender-responsive trade policies and market-opening instruments; (3) generation and delivery of data, tools, and analysis relevant for evidence-based policy-making of members; and (4) finally, improving the gender composition of staff in the organization so as to enable the promotion of women into leadership positions (as well as to support members in this regard) and to promote gender equality. Looking at Table 3.1, rows 1, 3, 4, and 5 include initiatives and actions addressing trade and gender issues from the perspective of the WTO as an organization. When looking at the WTO as a set of rules for trade policies, which, in turn, determine how these policies impact women,[7] the focus is on how the gender lens is used when negotiating multilateral and plurilateral trade rules (Table 3.1, row 2).

7 Literature about how trade impacts women is not new at all. A sample of newer texts includes OECD, 'Trade and Gender: A Framework Analysis' (2021) <www.oecd.org/trade/topics/trade-and-gender/> accessed 8 May 2022; World Bank and WTO, 'Women and Trade: The Role of

3.2 LET'S MAKE IT FORMAL

It was almost three years after the 11th Ministerial Conference (MC11) in 2017 delivered the Buenos Aires Declaration on Trade and Women's Economic Empowerment calling for greater inclusion of women in trade and trade policy-making that there was any action.[8] Initially supported by 118 members and observers, this number has risen to 127 as of September 2022, which still leaves about one-third of members and observers sitting on the fence, including India, South Africa, and the United States.

It took an initiative by Botswana and Iceland to put together an IWG on Trade and Gender, which was inaugurated in September 2020 in a virtual meeting as per the new pandemic norm.[9] After a meeting in late 2020, the first regular (and again virtual) meeting of the IWG was in February 2021 and it resulted in adoption of the Schedule of Activities in 2021 (January–July) and a Draft Work Plan, which was soon revised into the Final Work Plan.[10] The two initial co-chairs were joined by El Salvador in April 2021 and the IWG continued working with the Friends of Gender (comprising nineteen members and observers, four international organizations and the Secretariat) towards a strong delivery for the MC12. Throughout still pandemic-affected 2021, the IWG had six meetings by the end of October, with another scheduled for 24 November. The work of the group evolved around the four

Trade in Promoting Gender Equality' (2020) <www.wto.org/english/res_e/booksp_e/women_trade_pub2807_e.pdf> accessed 8 May 2022; Bilge Erten and Pinar Keskin, 'Trade-Offs? The Impact of WTO Accession on Intimate Partner Violence in Cambodia' (2021) *Review of Economics and Statistics* 1–40; CIGI, 'Reshaping Trade through Women's Economic Empowerment – Special Report' (2018) <www.cigionline.org/sites/default/files/documents/Women%20and%20Trade.pdf> accessed 8 May 2022; and the one of the older ones, UNCTAD, 'Trade and Gender: Opportunities and Challenges for Developing Countries', UNCTAD/EDM/2004/2 (23 May 2004). This chapter does not expand into the discussion of impacts of trade on women.

8 WTO, 'Buenos Aires Declaration on Women and Trade Outlines Actions to Empower Women' <www.wto.org/english/news_e/news17_e/mc11_12dec17_e.htm> accessed 8 May 2022.

9 Botswana and Iceland also co-chair the International Gender Champions Trade Impact Group. *See* WTO, Informal Working Group on Trade and Gender <www.wto.org/english/tratop_e/womenandtrade_e/iwg_trade_gender_e.htm> accessed 8 May 2022. El Salvador joined as the third co-chair in April 2021. The IWG is open to all WTO members and observers seeking to intensify efforts to increase women's participation in global commerce.

10 WTO, 'Final Work Plan for Implementing Activities under the Informal Working Group on Trade and Gender', INF/TGE/W/1/Rev.2 (29 March 2021).

pillars stipulated in the Buenos Aires Declaration, and meetings were planned to feature members' experiences (best practices) in promoting women's economic empowerment, the most relevant recent research by the Secretariat and its partners, to discuss delivery of the Aid for Trade activities and efforts to clarify the meaning of the 'gender lens' and how it applies to the work of the WTO.[11]

After an active year, at the first anniversary meeting in September 2021, the IWG announced the draft MC12 outcome document containing recommendations for WTO members to continue work on increasing women's participation in international trade. The intention of this document was to convince members to include 'women's economic empowerment issues into the *regular work* of WTO bodies, improve the impact of Aid for Trade on women by mainstreaming gender considerations into programmes and strategies, increase data collection, and coordinate research'.[12] Unfortunately, due to the complex geopolitical situation resulting from the Russian invasion of Ukraine, this proposal never reached the MC12 Agenda. It was replaced with a rather unambitious '[s]tatement on inclusive trade and gender equality from the co-chairs of the Informal Working Group on Trade and Gender – Twelfth WTO Ministerial Conference'.[13] Instead of producing formalized work on Trade and Gender in the WTO and giving a boost to potential conversion from its current plurilateral mode to a multilateral one,[14] one paragraph almost at the end of the MC12 Outcome Document referred to, inter alia, work on trade and gender.

Nevertheless, members in the Friends of Gender and the co-chairs of the IWG ought to be commended for their initiative in turning the Buenos Aires Declaration that had lain dormant into an active work plan pre-MC12 as well as on the achievements in the aftermath of the MC12.

[11] For more information on the meetings agendas and participation by members and other agencies or partner institutions, *see* WTO, 'Meetings of the Informal Working Group' <www.wto.org/english/tratop_e/womenandtrade_e/iwg_trade_gender_e.htm#meetings> accessed 8 May 2022.

[12] WTO, 'Trade and Gender Informal Working Group Co-chairs Present Draft Outcome Document for MC12' (*WTO News* 23 September 2021) <www.wto.org/english/news_e/news21_e/women_23sep21_e.htm> accessed 8 May 2022 (emphasis added).

[13] WTO, 'Statement on the Inclusive Trade and Gender Equality from the Co-Chairs of the Informal Working Group on Trade and Gender', WT/MIN(22)/7 (12 June 2022).

[14] *See* commentaries by Caroline Dommen, 'WTO Advances Gender Agenda Amidst Calls for Broader Gender Lens' (IISD 2021) <https://sdg.iisd.org/news/wto-advances-gender-agenda-amidst-calls-for-broader-gender-lens/> accessed 8 May 2022, on the pros and cons of making the Trade and Gender work horizontal across the WTO and CSIS (2021) on the WTO IWG on Trade and Gender.

3.3 ENFORCEABLE (OR ANY?) PROVISIONS TOWARDS WOMEN'S ECONOMIC EMPOWERMENT

Admittedly, not all WTO members are keen to see the use of a gender perspective when deciding on their trade policies. There is a rich literature on how trade and trade policies may impact women in their roles as consumers, entrepreneurs, workers, or taxpayers, from both export and import (import competition) perspectives.[15] This literature explains the mechanisms through which trade impacts women's welfare (well-being) and not only their economic prosperity. It is important that policymakers (including officials in the relevant ministries and parliamentarians) understand these mechanisms as they are most often responsible for providing the negotiating mandate to negotiators who then must follow it in multilateral or other levels of negotiation.[16] Not to be forgotten, trade reforms that countries undertake on their own (so-called unilateral policies) often have the strongest impact on economic actors, including women.

As we saw, the proposals and requests to consider a gender lens when setting either trade-restricting or trade-expanding policies date many years back. However, our focus here is to identify if there was any 'leakage' from the Buenos Aires Declaration and the establishment of the IWG with its work plan into the texts that members were considering for negotiation and adoption at the MC12. Even a few days before the new date of the MC12, only a limited number of documents were publicly available as most of the

[15] Most of the relevant readings are summarized and referenced in, inter alia: Jane Korinek, Evdokia Moïsé, and Jakob Tange, 'Trade and Gender: A Framework of Analysis' (2021) OECD Trade Policy Papers No. 246 <https://doi.org/10.1787/6db59d80-en> accessed 8 May 2022; Ben Shepherd and Susan Stone, 'Trade and Women' (2017) ADBI Working Paper Series No. 648 <www.adb.org/sites/default/files/publication/224666/adbi-wp648.pdf> accessed 8 May 2022; Anh-Nga Tran-Nguyen and Americo Beviglia Zampetti (eds), *Trade and Gender: Opportunities and Challenges for Developing Countries* (UNCTAD 2004); World Bank and WTO, 'Women and Trade' (n 8).

[16] In this context it is relevant to mention findings of new research on the role of women leaders in starting or supporting trade wars. Contrary to the widespread beliefs on what women's aptitude would be towards trade conflict, 'the empirical results in this paper (obtained from a panel data of 49 importers and 102 trade partners over a 21-year period from 1998 to 2018 show that countries headed by women are not less likely to launch trade conflicts'. However, the paper demonstrates that 'women parliamentarians continue to exhibit a moderating effect on propensity of formal trade conflict initiations indicating that the level of office alters women's response to international policy issues'. *See* Neha B. Upadhayay, 'Are Only Men Fighting Trade Wars? Empirical Evidence from the Temporary Trade Barriers (TTB) Data' (2020) ERUDITE Working Papers 2020 <https://erudite.univ-paris-est.fr/fileadmin/public/ERUDITE/erudwp/ERU-03-20-nu.pdf> accessed 8 May 2022.

negotiating texts were still 'open for negotiations'. As a default option, a conversation with experts and 'insiders' was used to inform (considering confidentiality) on the existing gaps. Furthermore, in December 2021, several documents were released enabling us to check whether or not they remain 'gender-blind'.[17]

Table 3.2 combines agenda items of the MC12 (including those that were expected but in the end were dropped for geopolitical reasons) with an assessment of to what extent a gender lens is present.

The content of Table 3.2 does not invoke optimism that the WTO members will be embracing the recommendations on including strong and enforceable women's economic empowerment provisions in the WTO agreements any time in the near future. There is, of course, a continued risk that any new type of provisions able to impact trade flows might be abused as a new form of protectionism (e.g., green and environmental provisions, labour, health, and, indeed, gender). The danger of using these in a discriminatory fashion is much greater in the absence of any international rules to guide (and constrain as necessary) the behaviour of policymakers.

Furthermore, there is evidence that members have moved on with creative approaches to opening the markets to keep trade and investment going albeit outside the multilateral space. Some pursued these alternative rules (typically regional or bilateral, rarely unilateral), arguing that the multilateral route is not effective. Examples include so-called deep preferential trade agreements or sectoral agreements covering digital trade, known as digital economy partnership agreements (DEPAs).[18] Cynics would argue that it was because the non-most-favoured-nation (MFN) route allowed for more selective discrimination.[19] Notwithstanding, the same creativity should be used when it comes to promoting women's economic empowerment through trade

[17] The list of documents released is available on the WTO website, *see* WTO, 'Ministerial Conferences: Twelfth WTO Ministerial Conference – Documents' <www.wto.org/english/thewto_e/minist_e/mc12_e/documents_e.htm> accessed 8 May 2022.

[18] Recent examples of deep agreements are the Comprehensive and Progressive Trans-Pacific Partnership (CPTPP), Regional Comprehensive Economic Partnership (RCEP) and of DEPAs, Chile, New Zealand and Singapore deal. More about these in ESCAP (2021). *See* UN ESCAP, 'Asia-Pacific Trade and Investment Trends 2021–2022: Preferential Trade Agreements in Asia and the Pacific, United Nations, Bangkok' (2020) <www.unescap.org/sites/default/d8files/knowledge-products/APTIT_PTA_20212022.pdf> accessed 8 May 2022.

[19] This goes a long way back, to the rich literature on regional trade agreements being both stepping stones and stumbling blocks for multilateral non-discriminative trade. Phase 1 of the US–China agreement might be a concrete example, *see* Asako Ueno, 'Erosion of the Non-discrimination Principle through Waves of Preferential Trade Agreements: A. Warning from the Sutherland. Report' (REITI n.d.) <www.rieti.go.jp/en/columns/a01_0163.html> accessed 8 May 2022.

TABLE 3.2 *A delivery of the MC12 on women's empowerment provisions*

MC-12 Package of decisions and declarations	
Areaa	Women's empowerment provisions – if and how gender was mentioned
Trade and women (dropped from the agenda)	If the prepared Joint Ministerial Declaration On the Advancement of Gender Equality and Women's Economic Empowerment Within Trade 12th WTO Ministerial Conference (WT/MIN(21) 4 dated 10 November 2021)[b] was included, the outcome would have meant a confirmation of the IWG work programme and a push for concrete deliverables at the 13th Ministerial Conference
The MC12 outcome document	'13. We recognize women's economic empowerment and the contribution of MSMEs to inclusive and sustainable economic growth, acknowledge their different context, challenges and capabilities in countries at different stages of development, and we take note of the WTO, UNCTAD and ITC's work on these issues' This paragraph includes a footnote which reads: 'These are general messages on cross-cutting issues that do not change the rights or obligations of WTO Members (and do not relate to any Joint Statement Initiatives)'
'Trade and health' was adopted as the Ministerial Declaration on the WTO Response to the COVID-19 Pandemic and Preparedness for Future Pandemics and the Ministerial Decision on the Trade Related Aspects of Intellectual Property Rights (TRIPS) Agreement	No reference has been made despite the disproportional impact the pandemic has had on women
Agreement on fisheries subsidies	Despite the great significance of this Agreement for the United Nations Sustainable Development Goals and the Agreement's innovative transparency and notification requirements, the text remains silent with respect to the impact on or role of women in this area
Agriculture negotiation boiled down to adopting the Ministerial Declaration on the Emergency Response to Food Insecurity and the Ministerial Decision on World Food Programme Food Purchases Exemption from Export Prohibitions or Restrictions	As foreshadowed by the text entitled Committee on Agriculture in Special Session – Report by the Chairperson, H. E. Ms Gloria Abraham Peralta, to the Trade Negotiation Committee 19 November 2021 (TN/AG/50 dated 23 November 2021),[c] the adopted declaration also did not include any reference to women, their empowerment, or impacts on their well-being in area of agriculture trade (opening) or food emergency
Decision on E-Commerce Moratorium and Work Programme	No reference to gender or women's economic empowerment

A Smooth Transition Package in Favour of Members Graduating from the LDC Category	No reference to gender or women's economic empowerment has been made
Services domestic regulation	The Declaration on the Conclusion of Negotiations on Services Domestic regulation (WT/L/1129 dated 2 December 2021) and the Joint Initiative On Services Domestic Regulation – Reference Paper on Services Domestic Regulation (INF/SDR/2 dated 26 November 2021)[d] brought for the first time into the WTO rules a direct reference to women by including a provision prohibiting an exclusion of measures which discriminate against women. Below is the extract from the Reference Paper: Development of Measures: '22. If a Member adopts or maintains measures relating to the authorization for the supply of a service, the Member shall ensure that: (a) such measures are based on objective and transparent criteria (17) (b) the procedures are impartial, and that the procedures are adequate for applicants to demonstrate whether they meet the requirements if such requirements exist (c) the procedures do not in themselves unjustifiably prevent the fulfilment of requirements and (d) such measures do not discriminate between men and women (18)' And footnote 18: 'Differential treatment that is reasonable and objective, and aims to achieve a legitimate purpose, and adoption by Members of temporary special measures aimed at accelerating de facto equality between men and women, shall not be considered discrimination for the purposes of this provision'
Not discussed or adopted at the MC-12	
Joint Statement Initiative: MSMEs	Based on the Declaration on MSMEs released on 6 October 2021[e] Main text does not contain any reference to gender or women. However, in Annex I 'Recommendation on the collection and maintenance of MSME-related information', Point 3 in the appended Checklist refers to: 'Available statistics (overall or by sector) on MSME ownership by diverse groups (e.g., women, youth, etc.)'

(*continued*)

TABLE 3.2 (*continued*)

MC-12 Package of decisions and declarations	
	Several places in other annexes to this declaration miss the opportunity to include a clause/reference to women/gender, especially in the annex on trade finance and cross-border payments
Joint Statement Initiative: e-commerce	Draft text not available for public access
Joint Statement Initiative: Investment facilitation	*Draft text is not available for public access* and the chair's summaries do not provide sufficient details
Other ongoing WTO initiatives worth monitoring for possible direct inclusion to provisions related to women's empowerment through trade	
Clean cooking, women, and energy	Might be mentioned in declaration but nothing enforceable
Women and intellectual property (IP)	Continuing the theme of IP and innovation which has regularly featured on the Agreement on Trade-Related Aspects of Intellectual Property Rights (TRIPS) Council's agenda since 2012, Australia, the European Union, Japan, Switzerland, Chinese Taipei, the United Kingdom, and the United States proposed a discussion on 'Women and Intellectual Property' (IP/C/W/685), an initiative also co-sponsored by Chile and Canada Members engaged in a discussion about specific programmes for assisting or promoting women's participation in the IP system, and on measures that have proven useful for supporting women entrepreneurs in participating in the IP system. They also exchanged experiences on how to raise women entrepreneurs' awareness of the benefits of IP for their business activity, on the main challenges and specific barriers found for women entrepreneurs, and on economic sectors where women are particularly active and could benefit from the IP system

Source: Author's own, based on review of available documents and communication with experts.

[a] WTO, 'Twelfth Ministerial Conference' <www.wto.org/english/thewto_e/minist_e/mc12_e/mc12_e.htm#outcomes> accessed 13 September 2022.

[b] WTO, 'Joint Ministerial Declaration on the Advancement of Gender Equality and Women's Economic Empowerment Within Trade 12th WTO Ministerial Conference', WT/MIN21/4 (10 November 2021).

[c] WTO, 'Committee on Agriculture in Special Session – Report by the Chairperson, HE Ms Gloria Abraham Peralta to the Trade Negotiations Committee', TN/AG/50 (23 November 2021).

[d] WTO, 'Declaration on the Conclusion of Negotiations on Services Domestic Regulation', WT/L/1129 (2 December 2021).

[e] WTO, 'Informal Working Group on MSMEs, Declaration on Micro, Small and Medium-Sized Enterprises (MSMEs)', INF/MSME/4/Rev.2 (6 October 2021).

agreements. There were some very promising alternative arrangements and agreements that can work easily at the MFN level and can support modernization of the multilateral trade system. These include deep regional trade agreements with separate chapters (provisions) on driving women's economic empowerment through trade. Examples include most of the recent bilateral FTAs of Canada but also the plurilateral GTAGA, signed initially by New Zealand, Chile, and Canada and now joined by Mexico.[20] This is not a trade agreement, but a cooperation arrangement where countries can exchange lessons on both domestic policies and trade policies.[21] Readers interested in more details on this topic can refer to several other chapters in this volume which address trade and gender at the level of regional and bilateral trade and investment agreements in more detail than is possible in this chapter.[22]

3.4 IMPACT, IMPACT, IMPACT

An impact assessment has become an integral process of trade policy-making. No policy change – including trade-restricting/expanding policies at any level – should be passed to an implementation phase without prior scrutiny and *ex ante* impact assessment. Referencing the European Union's mandatory *ex ante* or *ex post* impact assessment of proposed agreements of grant of preferences, Mikic and Sharma proposed that an 'efficient strategy for the inclusion of a gender lens approach in trade agreements could be the inclusion of a mandatory impact assessment of proposed agreements wherein if an agreement does not contribute to women's economic empowerment, it would

[20] Global Trade and Gender Arrangement, 4 August 2020 <www.international.gc.ca/trade-commerce/inclusive_trade-commerce_inclusif/itag-gaci/arrangement.aspx?lang=eng> accessed 8 May 2022.

[21] *See* more details at New Zealand Foreign Affairs and Trade, 'Inclusive Trade Action Group (ITAG)' <www.mfat.govt.nz/kr/trade/nz-trade-policy/inclusive-trade-action-group-itag/> accessed 8 May 2022; Government of Canada, 'Minister Ng Promotes Benefits of Global Trade and Gender Arrangement at OECD' (9 June 2021) <www.canada.ca/en/global-affairs/news/2021/06/minister-ng-promotes-benefits-of-global-trade-and-gender-arrangement-at-oecd.html> accessed 8 May 2022; OECD, 'How Trade Can Support Women's Economic Empowerment Global Trade and Gender Arrangement (GTAGA): An Innovative Initiative to Support Women's Economic Empowerment through Trade' (9 June 2021) <www.oecd.org/trade/events/trade-women-economic-empowerment/> accessed 8 May 2022.

[22] Renata Amaral and Lillyana Sophia Daza Jaller, 'Mainstreaming Gender in Investment Treaties and Its Prevailing Trends: The Actions of MNEs in the Americas' (Chapter 9 in this book); Amrita Bahri, 'Gender Mainstreaming in Trade Agreements: Best Practice Examples and Challenges in the Asia Pacific' (Chapter 13 in this book).

not pass the "RTA transparency mechanism" review'.[23] This will be a step ahead of what the Buenos Aires Declaration proposed in terms of collection and sharing of better quality data, which will be able to be mined for deeper insights into the impacts of trade on women as well as how women may impact trade.[24]

As with some other instances where data availability takes the blame for lack of transparency or weak analytical work, most often an absence of solid gender-impact assessment of trade policy changes is explained by lack of data. As a member-driven institution, the WTO also falls into this mould of waiting for the members to supply data (which potentially might produce results not working in the interest of these members). The only solution is for the Secretariat to dedicate some of its own (very capable) human resources and in partnership with other international institutions, think tanks, and other actors and produce data and analysis necessary for gender-responsive policy-making. The first nudge for the Secretariat to move in this direction came with the Global Financial Crisis and calls for better monitoring of the use of discriminatory trade policies to which the Secretariat responded by producing six-monthly monitoring reports for G20 countries, responsible for the lavish share of global trade.[25] The COVID-19 pandemic was another strong impetus for the Secretariat to 'get out there', collect data, and provide members with evidence on how the pandemic impacted their trade (and more) as well as how the organization of global trade might have been impacting the members' capacity to respond to the pandemic. The Secretariat has responded to this challenge, and many members have been better informed and their decisions positively affected by the information and research available to all at the dedicated pages on 'COVID-19' and 'Trade'.[26]

[23] Mikic and Sharma, 'Feminizing WTO 2.0' (n 6). In the spirit of the GATT Art. XXIV, under which trade agreements resulting in harm to third countries should be assessed as not compliant with the rules, agreements which harm, or do not contribute positively to, women's economic empowerment, should be declared as not in keeping with the spirit (if not letter) of the WTO agreements.

[24] In addition to the WTO, 'Twelfth Ministerial Conference' (n 1), *see* also Oonagh E. Fitzgerald, 'Modernizing the World Trade Organization' (CIGI 2020) <www.cigionline.org/articles/modernizing-world-trade-organization/> accessed 8 May 2022; World Bank and WTO, 'Women and Trade' (n 8) chapters 2 and 3; or Susan Joekes, 'A Primer on Gender and Trade' <www.genderandtrade.com/_files/ugd/c947e9_a7141ac8ff644bff8bcd006731b9fa7c.pdf> accessed 8 May 2022.

[25] The latest report was issued on 28 October 2021: WTO, 'Report on G20 Trade Measures' (28 October 2021) <www.wto.org/english/news_e/news21_e/report_trdev_nov21_e.pdf> accessed 8 May 2022.

[26] WTO, 'COVID-19 and World Trade' <www.wto.org/english/tratop_e/covid19_e/covid19_e.htm> accessed 8 May 2022.

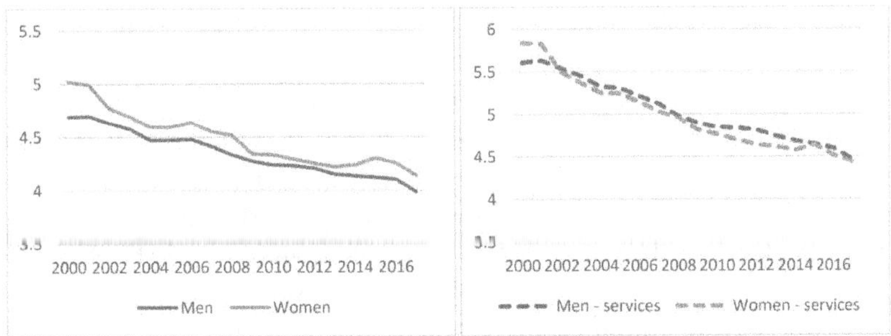

FIGURE 3.1 Global export cost index by gender.
Source: WTO, 'WTO Trade Cost Index: Evolution, Incidence and Determinants, Background Note' (24 March 2021) 5, figure 16.

Similarly, the Secretariat made progress in terms of collection of data and production of research, helping better policy-making. First, it produced a new Trade Cost Index, which provides more insights into determinants of trade costs and their burden with respect to different income groups and most importantly women and men separately.[27] This new methodology allows trade costs to be tracked for eighteen years for over forty countries.[28] Figure 3.1, reproduced from the Secretariat's note,[29] shows that women have been burdened with higher trade costs throughout the observation period.

As indicated in Table 3.1, the Secretariat announced that it will provide another novel database collating all gender-responsive trade policies implemented by WTO members. This database is sourced by information from members' trade policy reports and independent research produced by the Secretariat and other agencies. It also includes the gender provisions contained in various trade agreements that members have concluded.[30]

[27] The database is available from the WTO Trade Cost Index website under Economic Agents category. *See* WTO Trade Cost Index, 'Who Faces Higher Trade Costs? Trade Costs by Gender' <http://tradecosts.wto.org/categories.html> accessed 8 May 2022.

[28] Stela Rubinova and Medhi Sebti, 'The WTO Trade Cost Index and Its Determinants' (2021) WTO Staff Working Paper ERSD-2021-6 <www.wto.org/english/res_e/reser_e/ersd202106_e.pdf> accessed 8 May 2022.

[29] WTO, 'WTO Trade Cost Index: Evolution, Incidence and Determinants, Background Note' (March 2021) <http://tradecosts.wto.org/docs/Trade_Cost_Index_Background_Note_24-03-2021.pdf> accessed 8 May 2022.

[30] Additionally, some earlier work by the Secretariat staff provides useful insights. *See*, for example, Anoush der Boghossian, 'Women's Economic Empowerment: An Inherent Part of Aid for Trade' (2019) WTO Staff Working Paper ERSD-2019-08 <www.wto.org/english/res_e/reser_e/ersd201908_e.pdf> accessed 8 May 2022.

In 2021, the WTO launched the WTO Gender Research Hub to enhance collaboration and exchange among researchers and analysts working on the linkages between trade and gender. The Hub will also serve as a platform for dialogue between researchers and the IWG. The main participants in the Hub are the Organisation for Economic Co-operation and Development (OECD), the UNCTAD, the International Monetary Fund (IMF), the World Bank Group (WBG), the ITC, the UN Economic Commission for Latin America and the Caribbean (ECLAC), three holders of the WTO Chairs Programme (Chile, Mexico, and South Africa), and individual academics.[31]

3.5 FIRST, TEACH A WOMAN …

The WTO has been providing trade-related technical assistance (TRTA) to its members (and other stakeholders) since its establishment – expanding it from what was available during the era of General Agreement on Tariffs and Trade (GATT). Increasingly, the focus of the assistance has moved from negotiation to implementation, building capacity for trade policy-making and transparency. In support of Trade for Women, TRTA will also need revamping. According to the Secretariat's note on the new training strategy for 2021–2026,[32] the programme will combine tools to support WTO members, providing them access to concrete solutions for integrating gender into trade policies and for implementation of trade rules with a gender lens. It comprises a multi-pronged approach offering a regular course on trade and gender; training for the delegates in Geneva; online training; and national-level activities upon request.

In addition to the training on trade and gender linkages, which aims for gender-balanced participation, there is a need to enhance the capacity of women as negotiators, policymakers, policy influencers, and traders. As already noted by Mikic and Sharma, additional efforts should be made to close the knowledge gap for women working in trade.[33] As was exposed through the pandemic, lack of digital literacy for business (not to mention access to digital infrastructure) has undermined the capacity of millions of

[31] The first activity of this Hub was organized during the WTO Public Forum 2021. *See* WTO Conference Services, 'From Gender Research to Action for a Post COVID-19 Resilient World' (YouTube 29 September 2021) <www.youtube.com/watch?v=hLHW27FyVdo> accessed 8 May 2022.

[32] Anoush der Boghossian, 'WTO Technical Assistance on Trade and Gender: New Strategy 2021–2026' (WTO 2021) <www.wto.org/english/tratop_e/womenandtrade_e/16july21/item_3.4.d._wto_secretariat.pdf> accessed 8 May 2022.

[33] Mikic and Sharma, 'Feminizing WTO 2.0' (n 6).

women to cope with the pandemic-initiated crisis and caused further social and economic inequalities.[34] At the same time, the unpreparedness of national regulations to absorb the move to digital trade, online payments, and digitalization in general, made the situation in many developing countries hit by the triple crises of 2020 even worse. A crisis such as the world has been experiencing since January 2020 proves how important it is to have access to physical and natural capital to address external and internal shocks, but also, most importantly, to human capital. If we neglect improving the skills and knowledge of (about) half of human potential, we risk not being able to respond to these challenges. We are talking about 50 per cent of the population on average being women, so we must have at least such a ratio when we create human capital, in trade and in all other fields.

3.6 NO MORE GLASS CEILINGS FOR WOMEN IN TRADE?

There is a rich body of literature on the establishment of the international organization to govern trade, from the drafting of the 1948 Havana Charter to the 1994 Marrakesh Agreement and more which are not the subject matter of this chapter. However, very often – if not always – when Secretariat staff talk about the WTO, they categorize it as 'the member-driven organization', implying the existence of (possibly significant) limitations on the independent work of the Secretariat (this has been more recently and intensively discussed in the context of the role of WTO in the pandemic).[35] While these constraints impact appointments at the highest level of management (as documented by the appointment of the current Director-General), the author of this chapter

[34] The ITU reports that more than 50 per cent of the world's women are offline. This is more pronounced in developing countries, where the internet penetration rate for adult women is 41 per cent, compared to 53 per cent for men. For more details, *see* Alexandra Tyers-Chowdhury and Gerda Binder, 'What We Know about the Gender Digital Divide for Girls: A Literature Review' (UNICEF Gender and Innovation Evidence Briefs 2021) <www.unicef.org/eap/media/8311/file/What%20we%20know%20about%20the%20gender%20digital%20divide%20for%20girls:%20A%20literature%20review.pdf> accessed 8 May 2022; *see also* Kate Gromova, Reyn Anderson, and Garima Gupta, 'Opening a Global Conversation about the Gender Digital Divide' (World Bank 4 November 2021) <https://blogs.worldbank.org/digital-development/opening-global-conversation-about-gender-digital-divide> accessed 8 May 2022; ITC, 'Delivering on the Buenos Aires Declaration on Trade and Women's Economic Empowerment' (2020) <www.wto.org/english/tratop_e/womenandtrade_e/tig_rpt_dec20_e.pdf> accessed 8 May 2022.

[35] See, for example, in Alan Wm. Wolff, 'WTO 2025: Constructing an Executive Branch', PIIE Working Paper 22-8, May 2022 <www.piie.com/sites/default/files/documents/wp22-8.pdf> accessed 22 April 2023.

holds that these constraints do not apply to the recruitment of divisional directors and other staff in the Secretariat.[36]

In the absence of newer gender-differentiated statistics for the whole Secretariat, the comments here pertain to management level only. Naturally, one must start with the historic appointment of Dr Ngozi Okonjo-Iweala as the first woman Director-General. She then proceeded to make history by appointing two women as Deputy Director-Generals (or 50 per cent) which is a clear break with the past. The improvements with respect to women's share in the management positions within the Secretariat do not stop here. At present, six out of seventeen divisional directors are women (35.3 per cent).[37] That is almost double the share Mikic and Sharma reported (18 per cent).[38]

When it comes to the gender composition of the members' representatives in the WTO, these numbers also show an improvement, although small.[39] At present, no woman chairs the Council or the Committees. However, 33.3 per cent of chairs of the bodies reporting to the General Council are women; similarly, 33.3 per cent of chairs in the Trade Negotiating Committee are women, 35.7 per cent in the council on Goods, and 50 per cent in the Council on Plurilaterals. Only the Council on Services has no woman engaged as a chair. These chairs come from the forty women ambassadors (24.4 per cent) from the members' group and four from the WTO observers (16 per cent), which is still a significant underrepresentation of women in the most important global trade governance body.

With the ceiling seemingly being removed, the sky should be the limit. A plethora of initiatives bringing together women working in the area of trade and trade policy-making shows that there is both demand and supply for such self-organized and -driven communities aiming to strengthen women's role as influencers in the public and private sectors. Women hold an enormous amount of knowledge and skills relevant for making trade contribute to

[36] Maria V. Sokolova, Alisa DiCaprio, Nicole Bivens Collinson, 'Is It Time for Women Leaders in International Organizations?' (Trade Experettes n.d.) <www.tradeexperettes.org/blog/articles/is-it-time-for-women-leaders-in-international-organizations> accessed 8 May 2022. There is also a matter of whether the WTO should be increasing the total number of staff to properly oversee Trade and Gender work. *See* Trade Experettes, 'Time for Women Leaders in International Organizations' <www.tradeexperettes.org/podcasts/episodes/women-leaders-in-international-organizations> accessed 8 May 2022.

[37] Based on author's calculation, late 2021. On file with author.

[38] Mikic and Sharma, 'Feminizing WTO 2.0' (n 6).

[39] Based on author's calculation, late 2021. On file with author.

sustainable development and thus women should be actively encouraged to play their role in the trade community.

3.7 CONCLUSION

We have come a long way since it was acceptable to claim that trade as an economic activity and trade policy as part of economic coordination is gender neutral. It is indisputable that trade policies can (and should) be used to advance the economic and social well-being of women. Women have been, and increasingly will be, directly involved in making critical and path-changing decisions at national, regional, and global levels on how trade could be used to promote sustainable development.

Based on the performance of women in decision-making and leadership positions during the last two years of the pandemic, we should be actively placing women into jobs and roles with responsibilities for tackling current and emerging crises. Not only that, but we should also look more decisively to removing obstacles that prevent women from employing their full potential and contributing to generate prosperity and more just, responsible societies.

In this chapter, we attempted to find out about the progress of the feminization of the WTO, which is our shorthand for the implementation of the Buenos Aires Joint Declaration on Trade and Women's Economic Empowerment. While 127 WTO members and observers had joined in this Declaration, apparently showing an overwhelming interest in supporting women's economic empowerment, it still did not convert into a more ambitious self-standing MC12 multilateral declaration. Furthermore, following our review of how much of this support was translated into changes of trade rules to promote women's economic empowerment and engagement of women in trade, we were not impressed. Among all of the members' work on new rules or directions for the WTO's reform, only one (joint initiative on Services Domestic Regulation) includes a reference to gender-responsible trade policy. Despite evidence of the great importance of fisheries, agriculture, and MSMEs for women, the members missed the opportunity to build in adequate promoting provisions. While one must appreciate the existence of some progress ('WTO is not gender blind anymore'[40]), there is no time for

[40] According to the comment made by Anoush der Boghossian (WTO Trade and Gender focal point) at the recent ARTNeT and WTO webinar. *See* UN ESCAP, 'ARTNeT & WTO Webinar – Forward-Looking Conversation on "Trade for Peace"' (10 December 2021) <www.unescap.org/events/2021/artnet-wto-webinar-forward-looking-conversation-trade-peace#> accessed 8 May 2022.

complacency. If there is any chance for the disproportionate burden that women have been carrying throughout the pandemic (as in so many other crises) to be shifted and rebalanced, trade policy must become more gender responsible. The time has come to accept that work on women's equality in trade is the core of the trade agenda.

4

Global Economic Governance and Women

Why Is the WTO a Difficult Case for Women's Representation?

JUDIT FABIAN[*]

ABSTRACT

This chapter describes why the World Trade Organization (WTO) has proven such a great challenge for the representation of women and women's interests. Some progress has been made since the Aid-for-Trade programme, which cooperates with the WTO, incorporated gender mainstreaming in 2011. This includes the adoption of the 2017 Joint Declaration on Trade and Women's Economic Empowerment and the inauguration of the WTO Gender Research Hub in 2021. Nevertheless, to date the WTO has lagged behind other international organizations, including organizations of global economic governance, in representing women and their interests. The chapter posits the following reasons in historical context: (i) Women did not 'get in on the ground floor' at the WTO; (ii) The locus of power at the WTO rests with the members (exemplified by the requirement for consensus and the 'single undertaking', the importance of member proposals, and the institutional weakness of the Secretariat); (iii) The relative lateness and weakness of WTO involvement with civil society, compared to other institutions of global economic governance; (iv) The formative clashes during the 1980s and 1990s between gender and trade activism and trade liberalization; (v) The *lex specialis* nature of the WTO dispute settlement system; (vi) The WTO is primarily a 'hard-law' institution.

[*] This chapter draws on the author's PhD dissertation: Judit Fabian, 'Towards a Theory of Democratic Global Economic Governance: Hybridization of Soft and Hard Law in the Case of Gender within the World Trade Organization' (PhD Thesis, Carleton University 2015). Specifically, it draws on chapter 5 of the dissertation, entitled 'A Proxy for GEG II: Why the WTO Is the 'Hardest Case' amongst the Institutions of GEG', 258–365. The chapter has undergone significant revision.

4.1 INTRODUCTION

In June 2016, for the first time, a 'gender perspective on trade' was discussed as part of the Annual Session of the Parliamentary Conference on the WTO, entitled 'What Future for the WTO?'[1] The event was organized by the Inter-Parliamentary Union and the European Parliament on the premises of the World Trade Organization (WTO) in Geneva. This is important. Why? Because by 2016, most institutions of global governance had begun to incorporate gender perspectives, while for the most part trade governance, whether national, regional, or international, had been resistant to gender considerations despite ongoing efforts for change. This is true both for the European Union's Directorate-General for Trade (DG TRADE)[2] and the WTO (although less so for EU DG TRADE), which makes it especially remarkable that the above initiative was led by EU Members of Parliament,[3] and the discussion hosted on WTO premises. The press release for the session stated that 'parliamentarians from 57 countries and the World Trade Organization's leadership, civil society organizations, all in all around 400 participants' would be present. Thus, clearly, there was interest and, for the first time, the Outcome Document of the Annual Session made a clear statement about gender mainstreaming: 'We note that gender mainstreaming and women's empowerment are instrumental to development strategies for achieving gender equality and are key to the eradication of poverty. Therefore, we encourage policymakers to mainstreaming [*sic*] gender in macro-economic policies, especially in trade policy.'[4]

Thus, the responsibility to mainstream gender in trade policies remained to be shouldered by WTO member governments as they wished, without

1 IPU, '2016 Annual Session of the Parliamentary Conference on the WTO: What Future for the WTO?, WTO Headquarters, Geneva, 13–14 June 2016, organized jointly by the Inter-Parliamentary Union and the European Parliament' <www.ipu.org/splz-e/trade16.htm> accessed 8 May 2022.

2 Elina Viilup, 'The EU's Trade Policy: From Gender-Blind to Gender Sensitive?' (2015) In-Depth Analysis for the European Parliament, DG External Policies <www.europarl.europa.eu/RegData/etudes/IDAN/2015/549058/EXPO_IDA(2015)549058_EN.pdf> accessed 8 May 2022.

3 European Parliament, 'MEPS to Lead WTO Parliamentary Conference in Geneva' (10 June 2016).

4 IPU, '2016 Annual Session of the Parliamentary Conference on the WTO – What Future for the WTO?, Geneva, 13–14 June 2016: Outcome Document – Adopted by consensus on 14 June 2016' <www.ipu.org/splz-e/trade16/outcome.pdf> accessed 8 May 2022.

oversight, and without any formal role for the WTO. This remains true despite significant and promising developments at the WTO since 2017, including the Joint Declaration on Trade and Women's Economic Empowerment,[5] the Introduction of the Gender Focal Point, the Informal Working Group on Trade and Gender, the International Trade and Gender Research Hub, and the proposed Joint Ministerial Declaration on the Advancement of Gender Equality and Women's Economic Empowerment within Trade.[6] Indeed, the difficulty of mainstreaming gender into global trade governance was reinforced by the WTO's MC12 Outcome Document, paragraph 13 of which contained a profoundly anodyne statement 'recognizing' women's economic empowerment and 'taking note' of the work of the WTO, the United Nations Conference on Trade and Development (UNCTAD), and the International Trade Centre (ITC) on the subject.[7] The paragraph stood as proxy for the Joint Ministerial Declaration mentioned above, which, rather than being approved at MC12 as expected, was placed on hold.

The purpose of this chapter is to paint a picture of why the WTO has proved such a difficult case for the representation of women and women's interests. While other international organizations, including organizations of global economic governance, have incorporated some form of representation of women and their interests, mostly through gender mainstreaming, the WTO has long been resistant. A small exception is through its cooperation with the Aid-for-Trade Programme,[8] which incorporated gender mainstreaming in 2011. While this represented a significant milestone, many undoubtedly remain disappointed.

So why is it that the WTO remains resistant to adopting gender mainstreaming openly? The chapter answers this question by giving six reasons in the following six sections:

5 WTO, 'Buenos Aires Declaration on Women and Trade Outlines Actions to Empower Women – 12 December 2017' (2017) <www.wto.org/english/news_e/news17_e/mc11_12dec17_e.htm> accessed 8 May 2022.

6 WTO, 'Joint Ministerial Declaration on the Advancement of Gender Equality and Women's Economic Empowerment within Trade', WT/MIN(21)/4 (Draft, 10 November 2021).

7 WTO, 'MC12 Outcome Document,' WT/MIN(22)/24 (22 June 2022).

8 Aid-for-Trade is a WTO-led programme whose purpose is to provide financial assistance to developing countries, and particularly to Least-Developed Countries (LDCs), in order that they may more effectively access global trading markets and benefit from trade liberalization. *See* WTO, 'Aid for Trade Fact Sheet' <www.wto.org/english/tratop_e/devel_e/a4t_e/a4t_factsheet_e.htm> accessed 8 May 2022. It takes its ultimate origins from the Integrated Framework, which came into being in 1997 as the collaborative effort of six agencies and organizations: IMF, ITC, UNCTAD, UNDP, WTO, and the World Bank. *See* WTO, 'Enhanced Integrated Framework' <www.wto.org/english/tratop_e/devel_e/teccop_e/if_e.htm> accessed 8 May 2022.

1. Women did not 'get in on the ground floor' at the WTO;
2. The locus of power at the WTO rests with the members, as exemplified by:
   a. the requirement for consensus and the 'single undertaking';
   b. the importance of member proposals; and
   c. the institutional weakness of the Secretariat;
3. The relative lateness and weakness of WTO involvement with civil society compared to other institutions of global economic governance;
4. The formative clashes during the 1980s and the 1990s between gender and trade activism and trade liberalization;
5. The *lex specialis* nature of the WTO dispute settlement system; and
6. That the WTO is primarily a 'hard law' institution.

4.2 PATH-DEPENDENT HISTORY

4.2.1 *Reason 1: A Simple Fact – Women Did Not 'Get in on the Ground Floor'*

To begin, there was no possibility for women to 'get in on the ground floor'[9] at the founding of the WTO in 1994 because the WTO was, so to speak, built on the 'mezzanine' while the General Agreement on Tariffs and Trade (GATT) occupied the 'ground floor'. The 'ground floor' was created during the ratification of the GATT in 1947,[10] and adopted in full as part of the founding agreements of the WTO in 1994.[11] This means that the WTO was not a 'new' organization created from whole cloth. Rather, it was incorporated in full and built upon the GATT regime, the history of which spanned almost five decades.

As Vickers describes, following North,[12] 'getting in on the ground floor' is important because institutions are path-dependent; they are self-reinforcing feedback loops in which each loop makes the next loop more predictable and

[9] The phrase 'getting in on the ground floor' is borrowed from Vickers. *See* Jill Vickers, 'Is Nationalism Always "Bad for Women"? In Search of "Women-Friendly" Democracy: Gender/Nation Relations in Modern Nation-States' 2005/2006 Davidson Dunton Research Lecture, Carleton University (27 March 2006) 15.

[10] General Agreement on Tariffs and Trade 1994, 1867 UNTS 187 33 ILM 1153 (1994) (GATT 1994).

[11] Marrakesh Agreement Establishing the World Trade Organization, 15 April 1994, 1867 UNTS 154 33 ILM 1144 (1994) (Marrakesh Agreement or WTO Agreement).

[12] Douglass C. North, *Institutions, Institutional Change and Economic Performance* (Cambridge University Press 2011).

makes changing the nature of the loop more difficult. More specifically, the cost of establishing and restructuring institutions is high and most institutions are complex. This creates disincentives against restructuring and changes of direction and reinforces over time any policy direction initially taken by the institution. This means that opportunities for inclusion within institutions usually arise only at the time of establishment and times of restructuring. For example, as Underhill writes, 'those market constituencies which successfully exert influence on the process of institutionalization, particularly at its early stages, are likely to find their interests better represented than others'.[13] Walby adds that restructuring occurs almost exclusively at critical junctures, building upon the ideas of 'rounds of struggle' developed by Edwards, and 'rounds of accumulation' developed by Massey.[14] Thus, one could argue that the creation of the WTO could have been an opportunity for the representation of women and their interests provided by restructuring.

The difficulty posed by the WTO is that, as stated, the 'ground floor' was the establishment of the GATT in 1947, because it was incorporated in full as part of the founding agreements of the WTO in 1994. The GATT 1947 was entirely blind to gender and made no provision for representation of women and women's interests as such. Thus, when the WTO was established in 1994, it incorporated all the negative effects of this path-dependency that made the representation of women and women's interests especially difficult. The foundation of the WTO in 1994 was not, therefore, an opportunity to 'get in on the ground floor'. It was not an opportunity created by restructuring, since the restructuring was partial and conditioned by the GATT, by subsequent rounds of multilateral trade negotiations, and by almost five decades of global trade governance under the GATT regime. All of these factors excluded gender analysis and the representation of women and women's interests.

This failure to address the representation of women and women's interests when the WTO was founded in 1994, a failure embedded in the practices and ideas of a half-century-old path-dependent institution, kept the GATT/WTO regime on a path that did not address the representation of women and women's interests. With no opportunity to 'get in on the ground floor' in

[13] Geoffrey Underhill, 'Markets, Institutions, and Transaction Costs: The Endogeneity of Governance' (2007) World Economy & Finance Research Programme Working Paper 25, 34 <https://ideas.repec.org/p/wef/wpaper/0025.html> accessed 8 May 2022.

[14] Sylvia Walby, *Gender Transformations* (Routledge 1997) 76–78, 99. *See* also Richard Edwards, *Contested Terrain: The Transformation of the Workplace in the Twentieth Century* (Basic Books 1979); and Doreen Massey, *Spatial Divisions of Labour: Social Structures and the Geography of Production* (Macmillan 1984).

1947 or 1994, there was little likelihood that it would be considered necessary to address the lack of representation of women and women's interests during subsequent rounds of negotiations or potential restructurings.

Indeed, there was little success in raising the subject within the WTO until at least 2017. For example, the 2004 Sutherland Report[15] simply did not mention gender or women despite its mission to recommend reforms ensuring the WTO's continued viability. The 2007 Report of the First Warwick Commission, in its turn, made only fleeting mention of women and gender, and did not address either substantively in any way.[16] This is despite a relatively widespread understanding in 2007 of the gendered effects of trade, even within the WTO Secretariat.[17] As one member of the Secretariat put it in 2007:

> By now I think it's an accepted fact that in certain areas, I think more in developing countries than in developed countries, trade liberalization, or sometimes ... protectionism has a specific effect upon a sector where there [are] a lot of women working, so there is a gender aspect to it. [...] I think by now, there has been enough done by different people, academics, NGOs, [that] have proven that you can establish a link between [gender] and trade, and I would say particularly trade policies and gender, and particularly the effects on the gender balance within a sector, whether it's agriculture,

15 WTO, 'The Future of the WTO: Addressing Institutional Challenges in the New Millennium, Report by the Consultative Board to the Director-General Supachai Penitchpakdi' (2004) <www.wto.org/english/thewto_e/10anniv_e/future_wto_e.pdf> accessed 8 May 2022 (Sutherland Report). The Board's objective was 'to look at the state of the World Trade Organization as an institution, to study and clarify the institutional challenges that the system faced and to consider how the WTO could be reinforced and equipped to meet them' (ibid 2). The Report made thirty-seven recommendations that its authors considered practical and realizable (ibid 4). Chaired by Peter Sutherland, the other members were Jagdish Bhagwati, Kwesi Botchwey, Niall FitzGerald, Koichi Hamada, John H. Jackson, Celso Lafer, and Thierry de Montbrial. The Board had no woman member.

16 The Warwick Commission, 'The Multilateral Trade Regime: Which Way Forward? – The Report of the First Warwick Commission' (University of Warwick December 2007). The Report examined 'how the multilateral trade regime [could] better serve the global community' (ibid 1) and asked whether 'the sustained and uneven transformation of the global economy, with the associated rise of new powers, heightened aspirations, and considerable pockets of societal discontent, require a reconsideration of the principles and practices that currently guide the multilateral trade regime, the core of which is the World Trade Organization' (ibid 1). The First Warwick Commission was chaired by Pierre Pettigrew, Canadian Minister for International Trade under Prime Ministers Jean Chretien and Paul Martin. It included nineteen members (fourteen were men and five women).

17 Confidential interviews conducted at the WTO Secretariat (Geneva, September–October 2007) and EU DG TRADE (Brussels, September–October 2007). On file with author.

whether it's industrial, whether it's services, particularly in developing countries. [. . .] By now, as I said before, I think there is enough research or evidence on the table.[18]

Silence such as that of the Sutherland Report supports Hawkesworth's contention that feminist knowledge is erased by evidence blindness, which in turn insulates vested interests that are themselves gendered (and racialized).[19] In this way, it made sense that the traditional silence of the GATT/WTO regime concerning women and gender would be preserved and extended. Young, who was a member of the Warwick Commission, expressed this dynamic when she stated that 'structural power derives its power from the control over ideas and knowledge, and from the ability to deny access to others who hold different views'.[20] In this context, the placement of the WTO 'outside' the United Nations (UN) system as a related organization[21] becomes even more important, since the WTO falls 'outside' the mandate of UN Women to promote and advance gender mainstreaming throughout the UN system.[22]

18 Interview with senior member of WTO Secretariat (Geneva, Switzerland, October 2007). On file with author.

19 Mary Hawkesworth, 'Policy Discourse as Sanctioned Ignorance: Theorizing the Erasure of Feminist Knowledge' (2009) 3(3–4) *Critical Policy Studies* 268–289, 283–285.

20 Brigitte Young, 'Structural Power and the Gender Biases of Technocratic Network Governance in Finance' in Gülay Caglar, Elisabeth Prügl, and Susanne Zwingel (eds) *Feminist Strategies in International Governance* (Routledge 2013) 270.

21 The WTO is a related organization, technically outside of the UN system, while the World Bank and IMF are specialized organizations within the UN system. It is now widely recognized that 'the WTO system is only one part of a much broader set of international rights and obligations that bind WTO Members'. To this end, the WTO maintains 'institutional relations with . . . some 140 international organisations that have observer status in WTO bodies. The WTO also participates as an observer in the work of several international organizations. In all, the WTO Secretariat maintains working relations with almost 200 international organisations in activities ranging from statistics, research, standard-setting, and technical assistance and training. Although the extent of such cooperation varies, coordination and coherence between the work of the WTO and that of other international organizations continues to evolve'. *See* WTO, 'The WTO and Other Organizations' <www.wto.org/english/thewto_e/coher_e/coher_e.htm> accessed 8 May 2022. However, UN Women does not appear to be included in the 200 international organizations mentioned above. *See* WTO, 'International Intergovernmental Organizations Granted Observer Status to WTO Bodies' <www.wto.org/english/thewto_e/igo_obs_e.htm> accessed 8 May 2022.

22 UN Office of the Special Adviser on Gender Issues and Advancement of Women, 'Supporting Gender Mainstreaming: The Work of the Office of the Special Adviser on Gender Issues and Advancement of Women' (March 2001) <www.un.org/womenwatch/osagi/pdf/report.pdf> accessed 8 May 2022. Also *see* UN Women, 'Gender Mainstreaming' <www.un.org/womenwatch/osagi/gendermainstreaming.htm> accessed 8 May 2022.

4.3 ‘HIGH’ POLITICS

4.3.1 *Reason 2: The Locus of Power Rests with the Members*

4.3.1.1 The Requirement for Consensus and the ‘Single Undertaking’

Decisions at the WTO are made by consensus, barring certain exceptions.[23] This means that formal changes to accomplish the representation of women and women’s interests can be blocked by any single WTO member for any reason. This includes, of course, members that have shown themselves unsympathetic to gender equality.[24] Moreover, the ‘single undertaking’ requirement[25] – that nothing be agreed until everything is agreed – strengthens this

[23] *See* Art. IX of the Marrakesh Agreement. The first principle of the WTO is that it is a forum for discussion and negotiation run by its member governments. With only four exceptions, decisions are made, agreements reached, and the organization governed on the basis of consensus. The exceptions are the following: three-quarters of WTO members are sufficient to adopt an interpretation of any multilateral trade agreement; three-quarters of the Ministerial Conference is sufficient to waive a particular obligation imposed upon a member under a multilateral agreement; particular amendments to particular multilateral agreements can be approved by two-thirds of all members, with the proviso that such amendments are binding only for the members that voted to accept them; and the admission of a new member is approved by a two-thirds majority of the Ministerial Conference or the General Council. *See* WTO, ‘Whose WTO Is It Anyway?’ <www.wto.org/english/thewto_e/whatis_e/tif_e/org1_e.htm> accessed 8 May 2022. Aside from these exceptions, the WTO is governed by consensus. Having said that, it must be stressed that consensus-based decision-making in WTO proceedings entails the absence of a dissenting vote, rather than express and universal positive consensus. Politically, this alters somewhat the calculus of costs and benefits, principles and preferences that informs the vote of each WTO member. A member’s decision to absent itself from a vote can be accomplished with a lower profile than a vote upon a given question, regardless of whether the vote is visible to the public or not. This could conceivably make the process of legitimizing and advancing the representation of women and women’s interests within the WTO easier. Nevertheless, absence from a vote is a decision not to vote against a given initiative and thereby tacitly to maintain consensus. It is certainly likely to be so interpreted by parties desirous of the failure of an initiative. As such, it is entirely correct to state that adoption of a given initiative by the WTO requires the consensus of all WTO members not to vote against the initiative. This must in turn reduce the potential benefit to a WTO member of abstention or absence.

[24] For example, the countries Goetz describes as having done much to cause an impasse at the 2012 Commission on the Status of Women (CSW), scuttle the 2015 Fifth World Conference on Women, and reduce or eliminate feminist civil society participants from their CSW delegations, are by and large also WTO members. This includes Russia, Turkey, the Holy See (a WTO observer), and several North African and Middle Eastern countries. Other examples are legion. Anne Marie Goetz, ‘The New Competition in Multilateral Norm-Setting: Transnational Feminists and the Illiberal Backlash’ (2020) 149(1) *Daedalus* 165–166.

[25] WTO, ‘Ministerial Declaration – Ministerial Conference, Fourth Session, Doha, 9–14 November 2001’, WT/MIN(01)/DEC/W/1 (20 November 2001) para. 47.

veto to cover the entirety of WTO negotiations at any given time. This greatly increases the difficulty of representing women and women's interests at the WTO.

Amongst institutions of global economic governance, only in the WTO can the vote of a single member block a change in rules. By contrast, the International Monetary Fund (IMF) decides policy by majority vote of its Board of Governors, with votes allocated amongst its 187 members according to the size of their respective quotas, which are themselves based roughly upon the relative size of each member's economy.[26] Voting power at the World Bank and its component parts – International Bank for Reconstruction and Development (IBRD), International Development Association (IDA), International Finance Corporation (IFC), Multilateral Investment Guarantee Agency (MIGA) and International Centre for Settlement of Investment Disputes (ICSID) – is distributed according to each member's contribution to the capital stock of the Bank, which is roughly in accordance with the size of a given member's economy.[27]

Neither the voting system of the IMF nor that of the World Bank is democratic, but both are structurally more open to the possibility of reforms to advance the representation of women and women's interests than the consensus-based voting system of the WTO, which gives any individual member the power to veto any initiative. The same is true for the UN General Assembly and for any other organization in which decisions are taken by majority vote of all members.[28] It follows that any organization with a voting system that is not consensus-based will be more open to movement towards the representation of women and women's interests, and to the introduction of 'new issues' in general, as compared to the WTO.

Yet the hindrance to the representation of women and women's interests posed by the requirement for consensus is still greater. This is illustrated by Elsig and Cottier's 'incompatible triangle', in which they highlight that consensus combines with the 'single undertaking' and the member-driven nature of the WTO to render the decision-making process still more

[26] IMF, 'Factsheet – IMF Quotas' (25 March 2014) <www.imf.org/external/np/exr/facts/quotas.htm> accessed 8 May 2022; IMF, 'IMF Executive Directors and Voting Power' (19 August 2014) <www.imf.org/external/np/sec/memdir/eds.aspx> accessed 8 May 2022.

[27] World Bank, 'International Bank of Reconstruction and Development: Voting Power of Executive Directors' <http://siteresources.worldbank.org/BODINT/Resources/278027-1215524804501/IBRDEDsVotingTable.pdf> accessed 8 May 2022.

[28] UNGA, 'Methods and Procedures of the General Assembly', A/RES/362 (22 October 1949) Rule 82 et seq.

difficult.[29] Mentioned as one of the reasons for the difficulties of the 2001 Doha Round, the 'single undertaking' has a legal and a political aspect. The former requires that all WTO agreements be interpreted as a single treaty, but the latter is of greater concern here: it requires that nothing be agreed in WTO negotiations until everything is agreed by all members.

As such, the political aspect of the 'single undertaking' is an extension of the consensus principle, but one that strengthens the hand of a member objecting to a given initiative. It does so by giving such a member leverage over a wide scope of negotiations, rather than a single issue area or subset. In effect, this increases the power of the de facto veto that the consensus principle by implication grants to every member. By extension, this increases the power held by a hypothetical member or group of members opposed to advancing the representation of women and women's interests within the WTO.

Indeed, even without active opposition, the 'single undertaking' would reduce the likelihood of advancing the representation of women and women's interests in WTO negotiations. This is because of what Elsig and Cottier call 'a type of inherent negotiation logic among contracting parties that being a first mover in terms of making a meaningful concession is seen as a disadvantage as subsequent pressures on the other parties to follow cannot be maintained'.[30] In short, then, the 'single undertaking', as a particular extension of the consensus principle and as conditioned by the member-driven nature of the WTO, both increases the relative power of the veto of any member opposing the representation of women and women's interests, and makes a negotiated advance less likely even absent active opposition.

4.3.1.2 The Importance of Member Proposals

The importance of member proposals constitutes another obstacle to the representation of women and their interests in the WTO, as illustrated by the following quote from a senior member of the Secretariat: 'The Americans and the Canadians have come, and I said, "Ask your members to propose it." [They] never proposed [anything concerning gender or women] . . . And the DG will not do it if members are not willing. How come, you know, Norway, EC, US, how come they don't? Just a proposal.'[31]

[29] Manfred Elsig and Thomas Cottier, 'Reforming the WTO: the Decision-making Triangle Revisited' in Thomas Cottier and Manfred Elsig (eds) *Governing the World Trade Organization: Past, Present and Beyond Doha* (Cambridge University Press 2011) 291.

[30] Ibid 300.

[31] Interview with senior member of WTO Secretariat (Geneva, Switzerland, October 2007). On file with author.

It might be thought that the location of power within the WTO membership constitutes an opportunity to represent women and women's interests, since it removes the potential obstacle of an intransigent bureaucracy. However, closer examination shows it to be on balance a significant hindrance, since it resists orderly agenda creation and makes veto use institutionally simple and painless.[32] It is fundamental to the structure and identity of the WTO that it be primarily a forum for negotiation among members concerning the governance of international trade. In practice, this largely takes the form of negotiations concerning the administration of trade agreements and further liberalization of global trade. This places the burden of initiating change upon the members themselves and creates a de facto requirement that issue areas be discussed predominantly in terms of their quantified effects on trade or economic well-being, not their ethical merits or their accordance with international administrative or human rights law.

Conversely, the WTO's primary function as a forum for negotiation can create a disordered atmosphere for discussion in which any member delegation can place any issue area on the agenda, essentially without reference to other members' or external prioritization. In short, the structure that makes it easy in theory to introduce a topic is the same structure that allows any member to block any initiative for any reason, and that resists orderly construction of agendas for negotiation and the introduction of new issue areas.

Within this structure, there are four basic ways a proposal by a member could advance the representation of women and women's interests. First, a member could propose that the issue area be brought within the purview of the WTO in a manner that all members could accept. Given the difficulties of reaching consensus in general during the Doha Round, given the necessary expansion of the WTO's scope and that one member's vote can block any prospective WTO agreement, and given members' differences in gender regimes, this approach is probably impossible.

Second, a proposal could treat the representation of women and women's interests as part of 'non-trade' initiatives already within the WTO's purview, or already being considered. For example, Director-General Lamy stressed in his speeches the importance of human rights, and research was done in collaboration with the International Labour Organization (ILO) as early as 2007.[33]

[32] This does not preclude political costs of veto use, which could be painful; nevertheless, the location of power within the WTO membership means that there is no mandatory structural cost to veto use deriving from WTO law or procedural rules.

[33] Marion Jensen and Eddy Lee, 'Trade and Employment: Challenges for Policy Research' (2007) ILO and WTO Joint Study <www.ilo.org/wcmsp5/groups/public/—dgreports/—dcomm/—publ/documents/publication/wcms_091038.pdf> accessed 8 May 2022.

Although the latter did not concern gender, the ILO is explicitly concerned with redistribution. In theory, sustainable development could also provide an opening for the representation of women and women's interests, as occurred in the EU's DG TRADE.[34]

Third, many have argued for a 'social clause' in WTO agreements, which would allow 'trade-distorting' policies to be justified as a social good.[35] Such a clause was included in the 1947 Havana Charter and discussed during negotiations leading to the WTO's founding. Certainly, the representation of women and women's interests could in theory constitute a social good. However, a social clause is unlikely to be adopted, having been rejected at the December 1996 WTO Ministerial Conference because it was understood to threaten the comparative advantage of low-wage developing countries.[36] This is important because it impedes the ability of WTO members to cite labour practices that are exploitative of women to justify trade-distorting policies.

Fourth, a Generalized System of Preferences (GSP)[37] could incentivize policies in developing countries that promote the representation of women and women's interests by granting extra market access to developing countries that adopted the preferred policies.[38] This approach concerning labour standards has been implemented with success by European countries towards developing countries since 1971.[39] Moreover, the GSP was upheld by the WTO Appellate Body in 2004 as long as GSP standards were tied to 'objective' factors and the implementing WTO member did not discriminate between countries meeting the standards.[40]

---

34 Interview with member of EU DG TRADE (Brussels, Belgium, October 2007). On file with author.

35 Julien Burda, 'Chinese Women after the Accession to the World Trade Organization: A Legal Perspective on Women's Labor Rights' in Günseli Berik, Xiao-Yuan Dong, and Gale Summerfield (eds) *Gender, China and the World Trade Organization: Essays from Feminist Economics* (Routledge 2010) 263–265.

36 Ibid 264.

37 WTO, 'Differential and More Favourable Treatment, Reciprocity and Fuller Participation of Developing Countries, Decision of 28 November 1979', L/4903 (29 November 1979).

38 Burda, 'Chinese Women after the Accession to the World Trade Organization' (n 35) 268–271.

39 Ibid 269.

40 Ibid 269–270. *See also* Appellate Body Report, *European Communities – Conditions for the Granting of Tariff Preferences to Developing Countries*, WT/DS246/AB/R (31 August 2004). Although both panel report and Appellate Body report in this case determined that India's complaint was justified, the Appellate Body report also found that GSP could be made to accord with the MFN principle as long as the selection of developing countries was based on objective criteria, and all developing countries that met the criteria received the same preferences.

While GSP might create minor advances, it is unlikely to improve the representation of women and women's interests significantly because it is not properly a WTO initiative, but a member-initiated and member-specific set of preferences. Further, pursuant to the WTO Agreements, GSP can be applied only to developing countries, reducing considerably its potential to accomplish the representation of women and women's interests globally. Moreover, it is specifically designed to allow developed countries to tie trade preferences to policy preferences vis-à-vis developing countries. The connection of GSP with developing countries could also lead to its association with discourses of colonialism, creating resentment and possibly associating the representation of women and women's interests with 'the West' or 'the North' and concerns about undermining developing countries' sovereignty, culture, and traditions.[41]

4.3.1.3 The Institutional Weakness of the Secretariat

Another possible avenue for the representation of women and their interests would be for the WTO bureaucracy to lead by example, including by the gender composition of its staff and the potential to initiate research. The problem here is the institutional weakness of the Secretariat, which follows directly from the WTO's primary function as a forum for negotiation among members. This makes it very difficult for the Secretariat, the largest bureaucratic body within the WTO and the one with the most equitable gender composition, to introduce items for negotiation. It also severely restricts the Secretariat as an access point for introducing the representation of women and women's interests into the WTO. As Elsig writes, 'the role of the Secretariat in multilateral trade negotiations has to be read in conjunction with the "member-driven" nature of the WTO'.[42] The Sutherland Report similarly notes that the Secretariat cannot take a more active, agenda-setting role, and expresses regret that this should be so.[43]

41 Oona A. Hathaway, 'The Cost of Commitment' (2003) 55(5) *Stanford Law Review* 1821–1862; Elizabeth Whitsitt, 'A Comment on the Public Morals Exception in International Trade and the EC – Seal Products Case: Moral Imperialism and Other Concerns' (2014) 3(4) *Cambridge Journal of International and Comparative Law* 1376–1391.

42 Manfred Elsig, 'WTO Decision-Making: Can We Get a Little Help from the Secretariat and the Critical Mass?' in Debra P. Steger (ed) *WTO: Redesigning the World Trade Organization for the Twenty-First Century* (CIGI & Wilfrid Laurier University Press 2010) 71.

43 Sutherland Report (n 14).

What one finds upon closer inspection is that while the Secretariat became fairly successful in achieving equal representation of women and men,[44] the real loci of power within the WTO continued for a long time to be dominated by men; it remains uncertain how the Secretariat could effectively address this if the members did not want to. Indeed, while the WTO does not publish the gendered composition of its members' delegations,[45] the gendered composition of the Appellate Body and of the various Councils of Chairpersons under the General Council for two decades after the WTO's founding is very telling. Among Appellate Body members in 2013, six were men and only one a woman.[46] From 1994 until 2013, former members included fourteen men and only three women.[47] Among chairpersons of the General Council in 2013, thirteen were men and only one a woman.[48] Among chairpersons of the Trade Negotiations Committee Council, nine were men and only one a woman.[49] Of chairpersons of the Council for Trade in Goods, the 2013 division was ten men and three women.[50] For Trade in Services, remarkably enough, the division was two men and two women.[51] For chairpersons of the Committees of Plurilateral Agreements, the division in 2013 was two men and no women.[52]

This represents a significant disparity and suggests that even descriptive gender equality in the Secretariat[53] has had little effect upon the gender

44 WTO, 'Overview of the WTO Secretariat' <www.wto.org/english/thewto_e/secre_e/intro_e.htm> accessed 8 May 2022. As of 31 December 2012, the WTO Secretariat employed 349 women and 290 men. In terms of seniority, on a scale of grades where 2 is the lowest and 12 the highest, the breakdown is as follows: grade 2 – 0 women and 3 men; grade 3 – 14 women and 19 men; grade 4 – 33 women and 22 men; grade 5 – 70 women and 20 men; grade 6 – 61 women and 31 men; grade 7 – 44 women and 24 men; grade 8 – 28 women and 34 men; grade 9 – 53 women and 49 men; grade 10 – 38 women and 68 men; grade 11 – 6 women and 11 men; grade 12 – 0 women and 5 men; Deputy Director-General level – 2 women and 3 men; Director-General – 0 women and 1 man. Clearly, there remained an imbalance in the most senior grades and executive levels in favour of the descriptive representation of men.

45 *See also* Maria Sokolova and Matthew Wilson, 'Setting Up the Table Right: Women's Representation Meets Women's Inclusion in Trade Negotiations' (Chapter 7 in this book).

46 WTO, 'Appellate Body Members' <www.wto.org/english/tratop_e/dispu_e/ab_members_descrp_e.htm> accessed 8 May 2022.

47 Ibid.

48 WTO, 'Current WTO Chairpersons' <www.wto.org/english/thewto_e/secre_e/current_chairs_e.htm> accessed 8 May 2022.

49 Ibid.

50 Ibid.

51 Ibid.

52 Ibid.

53 WTO, 'Overview of the WTO Secretariat' (n 44).

composition of those bodies and councils where it was dictated by the members. Indeed, the member-centric structure of the WTO inhibited for many years any initiative to balance the gender composition of delegations to the WTO, and of course the balanced descriptive representation of women is no guarantee of the substantive representation of women's interests.

By the early 2020s, the situation had improved but only to a limited extent. It must be noted that the ongoing Appellate Body crisis has affected these figures; nevertheless, by the expiration of the term of the last sitting Appellate Body member on 30 November 2020, of twenty-seven former Appellate Body members only five were women.[54] Among chairpersons of the General Council in November 2021, nine were men and six women.[55] Among chairpersons under the Trade Negotiations Committee Council, five were men and four women (though this includes the Committee on Agriculture, Special Session, and the Sub-Committee on Cotton).[56] Of chairpersons under the Council for Trade in Goods, nine were men and five women.[57] For Trade in Services, four were men and none women.[58] Finally, the only chairperson of a Committee of Plurilateral Agreements was a woman.[59] Again, this is an improvement from the very low bar of 2013, but it is a long way from parity.

How then might the representation of women and women's interests be achieved more fully and effectively? A senior member of the Secretariat described succinctly both the technical possibility of success and the most significant impediment: 'A priori, I would *not* say that the structure of the Organization would prevent gender and trade or any other new issue . . . [from being] looked at, at least from the Secretariat's perspective. The membership, then you may have problems . . . Just say, if we can expand our research, if we can be . . . a little more of an independent Secretariat.'[60]

One possibility, initially appealing, would have the Secretariat becoming more independent and investigating the representation of women and women's interests on its own initiative. The Secretariat is the only part of the WTO with a quasi-executive capacity to which greater independence could be delegated by WTO members. However, to be made formally, any

54 WTO, 'Appellate Body Members' (n 46).
55 WTO, 'Current WTO Chairpersons' (n 48).
56 Ibid.
57 Ibid.
58 Ibid.
59 Ibid.
60 Interview with senior member of WTO Secretariat (Geneva, Switzerland, October 2007). On file with author.

such reform would require the consensus of WTO members, as would any determination to follow the Secretariat's findings. This might require expanding the scope of the WTO and would certainly require expanding the Secretariat's mandate and size. Thirteen years into the WTO's existence, it was considered highly unlikely to come to pass – 'never, never, never', as one interviewee put it.[61] Elsig echoed this sentiment three years later when he noted that 'the reluctance of Members to delegate powers to the Secretariat has not changed [since 1994]'.[62] The prospect has not become significantly more likely during the ensuing years.

The possibility that the Secretariat could develop openly, proactively, and independently its research activity to where it could investigate of its own accord the representation of women and women's interests may be dismissed quickly. To initiate research and make suggestions without the formal approval of the members, it would be necessary for the Secretariat to assume powers it currently lacks. There is currently no reason to believe that the members would allow the Secretariat to arrogate to itself any such power.

Further, interviews with its senior members show that the political culture within the Secretariat before 2010 was not amenable to proactive reform: 'There is still a lot of conservative thinking in this house. That may actually lead to, you know, opposition to trying out new things, and I've seen this in practice. … That's one thing I've experienced very much – you have a conservative school and a progressive school.'[63] Another interviewee stated plainly that 'the Secretariat in the WTO has zero initiative power. It can never propose something'.[64]

In sum, the locus of WTO power in its membership has created a number of hindrances and disincentives that have militated against the representation of women and women's interests. These are functions of the ease with which a single member can both block any initiative and introduce any topic for discussion. Further, the structure of the WTO has constrained the Secretariat's ability to promote the representation of women and women's interests. Nevertheless, acting within these constraints, the WTO and the Secretariat have since 2017 taken important steps toward addressing gender. The 2017 WTO Declaration on Trade and Women's Economic

61 Ibid.
62 Elsig, 'WTO Decision-Making' (n 42).
63 Interview with senior member of WTO Secretariat (Geneva, Switzerland, October 2007). On file with author.
64 Ibid.

Empowerment,[65] currently signed by 127 WTO members and observers,[66] is exactly the sort of initiative from which institution-level WTO engagement with gender can begin to emerge. It is member-driven but firmly within the realm of soft law and soft power, it sidesteps the weakness of the Secretariat and the requirement for consensus, but it nonetheless speaks for the WTO as an institution and constitutes a significant statement of intent. It has also given cover to the Informal Working Group on Trade and Gender, the Gender Focal Point, and the Secretariat's Gender Research Hub, which have provided fora for discussing and coordinating research on trade and gender taking place outside the WTO. It may be that in years to come, these initiatives are looked upon as the beginning of a critical mass of support for formal, institutional, member-driven engagement with gender at the WTO.

4.4 'LOW' POLITICS

4.4.1 *Reason 3: The Relative Lateness and Weakness of WTO Involvement with Civil Society*

The WTO took significantly longer to include civil society contributions than the World Bank, IMF, Asia-Pacific Economic Cooperation (APEC), and other institutions of global economic governance. This isolated the WTO to a significant degree from what True and Mintrom have called 'transnational networks of policy diffusion' which helped to promote gender mainstreaming policies in many states and international organizations (IOs).[67] This is important because, in general, it appears that IOs that engaged more extensively and earlier with civil society than the WTO also did a great deal more than the WTO between 1994 and 2014 to advance the representation of women and their interests. This is true even if 'gender mainstreaming' during this period was relatively less successful at the IMF than at the World Bank, and less

65 WTO, 'Joint Declaration on Trade and Women's Economic Empowerment on the Occasion of the WTO Ministerial Conference in Buenos Aires in December 2017' (2017) <www.wto.org/english/thewto_e/minist_e/mc11_e/genderdeclarationmc11_e.pdf> accessed 8 May 2022.

66 WTO, 'Eleventh WTO Ministerial Conference: Buenos Aires Declaration on Women and Trade Outlines Actions to Empower Women' (12 December 2017) <www.wto.org/english/news_e/news17_e/mc11_12dec17_e.htm> accessed 8 May 2022. Also WTO, 'Interim Report Following the Buenos Aires Joint Declaration on Trade and Women's Economic Empowerment' (25 September 2020) <https://docs.wto.org/dol2fe/Pages/SS/directdoc.aspx?filename=q:/WT/L/1095R1.pdf&Open=True> accessed 8 May 2022.

67 Jacqui True and Michael Mintrom, 'Transnational Networks and Policy Diffusion: The Case of Gender Mainstreaming' (2001) 45(1) *International Studies Quarterly* 27–57.

successful at the World Bank than, for example, in development projects operating under the aegis of German or European agricultural policy.[68] It is also true even if the adoption of mainstreaming at organizations such as the World Bank was more successful as policy than practice.[69] Indeed, the WTO did significantly less than other IOs to represent women and their interests during the first two decades of its existence.

True and Mintrom argue that transnational networks amongst non-state actors, particularly international non-governmental organizations (INGOs), offer the 'most compelling explanation' for the diffusion of 'gender mainstreaming' across 110 countries and numerous international organizations by 2001.[70] They show a strong correlation between openness to policy networks supportive of gender mainstreaming, adoption of gender mainstreaming policies by national governments, and adoption of high-level mechanisms to implement gender mainstreaming, such as independent central government ministerial portfolios. Even though their analysis focuses upon states, it nonetheless constitutes a strong argument that openness to such networks is an important contributory factor to institutional adoption of 'gender mainstreaming' policies in general, including within global economic governance.

The WTO's position outside the gender mainstreaming mandate of UN Women makes it crucial that it be open to transnational networks of policy diffusion. That it was more open in 2014 than in 1994 is well-established; for example, NGO attendance at WTO Ministerial Conferences increased from 108 in 1996 to 812 in 2005. Nevertheless, many experts argued that WTO engagement with NGOs and other civil society organizations (CSOs) was more superficial and slower in development than in other IOs during the same period. For example, Clark describes how the World Bank improved its relationship with CSOs during the late 1980s and 1990s.[71] The Bank expanded operational collaborations with CSOs, engaged them in 'country-level strategy and policy formation', expanded its public disclosure of information, established international structured dialogue with CSOs, including consultative forums on major topics and policies, and sought to convince member governments to pursue greater engagement with CSOs.

68 Jacqui True, 'Feminist Problems with International Norms: Gender Mainstreaming in Global Governance' in J. Ann Tickner and Laura Sjoberg (eds) *Feminism and International Relations: Conversations about the Past, Present and Future* (Routledge 2011) 81–83.

69 Ibid 81.

70 True and Mintrom, 'Transnational Networks' (n 67) 37.

71 John D. Clark, 'The World Bank and Civil Society: An Evolving Experience' in Jan Aart Scholte and Albrecht Schnabel (eds) *Civil Society and Global Finance* (Routledge 2002) 112–114.

By contrast, for most of its first two decades, the WTO did not engage or support the involvement of CSOs in a way that approached what the World Bank introduced. Thus, in 2010 Bonzon labelled 'rudimentary' three of the most important policy documents governing WTO engagement with civil society: the Decision of the General Council on the Procedures for the Circulation and De-Restriction of WTO Documents (1996; revised 2002); the Guidelines for Arrangements in Relations with Non-Governmental Organizations (1996); and the submission by civil society interests of *amicus curiae* briefs.[72] He emphasized that the Guidelines stated that NGOs could not be directly involved in WTO work,[73] and that closer cooperation with NGOs could be achieved 'through appropriate processes at the national level'.[74] This testifies to the absence of will within member governments at the time for the WTO itself to engage closely or very actively with civil society.

Conversely, as van den Bossche notes, during the same period, the UN Economic and Social Council (ECOSOC) provided for three levels of NGO engagement, granting 'general consultative status', 'special consultative status', or 'roster status'. The first of these granted rights well beyond the level of access or engagement granted by the WTO to any NGO or CSO.[75] Even the IMF may be said to have engaged civil society at least as extensively as the WTO, if not more so. In the 1990s and early 2000s IMF management began to seek closer relationships with Jubilee 2000, Caritas International, and Oxfam, amongst others, while also implementing Poverty Reduction Strategy Papers (PRSPs), the Poverty Reduction and Growth Facility (PRGF), the Heavily Indebted Poor Countries (HIPC) initiative,[76] and the Independent Evaluation Office (IEO).[77] Moreover, IMF and CSO meetings

72 Yves Bonzon, 'Options for Public Participation in the WTO: Experience from Regional Trade Agreements' in Debra P. Steger (ed) *WTO: Redesigning the World Trade Organization for the Twenty-First Century* (CIGI & Wilfrid Laurier University Press 2010) 288.

73 WTO, 'Guidelines for Arrangements on Relations with Non-Governmental Organizations', WT/L/162 (23 July 1996), para VI.

74 Ibid.

75 Peter Van Den Bossche, 'Non-governmental Organizations and the WTO: Limits to Involvement?' in Debra P. Steger (ed) *WTO: Redesigning the World Trade Organization for the Twenty-first Century* (CIGI & Wilfrid Laurier University Press 2010) 315–316.

76 IMF, 'Factsheet – Debt Relief under the Heavily Indebted Poor Countries (HIPC) Initiative' (24 March 2014) <www.imf.org/external/np/exr/facts/hipc.htm> accessed 8 May 2022.

77 Thomas C. Dawson and Gita Bhatt, 'The IMF and Civil Society: Striking a Balance' in Jan Aart Scholte and Albrecht Schnabel (eds) *Civil Society and Global Finance* (Routledge 2002) 149–154, 155; IMF, 'Standard Rules for Review and Publication of Evaluation Reports and other IEO Documents' (19 August 2002), <www.ieo-imf.org/ieo/files/origins/081902.pdf> accessed 8 May 2022; IMF, 'Completed Evaluations' <www.ieo-imf.org/ieo/pages/Completed .aspx> accessed 8 May 2022.

ranged between forty-five and seventy-five per year from 2001 through 2005, comprising interaction with 330 different CSOs annually.[78]

Finally, in 1995, APEC founded the APEC Business Advisory Council (ABAC), which contributed to the 2013 APEC Policy Partnership for Food Security (PPfFS),[79] and to the 2011 APEC Business Travel Card Programme.[80] In addition, from 1993, the APEC Study Centers Consortium (ASCC) has met annually to evaluate APEC progress and policy. It comprises fifty APEC study centres in twenty APEC member economies[81] and was established to 'foster regional cooperation among tertiary and research institutes to promote greater academic collaboration on key regional and economic challenges'.[82] Amongst the WTO's Public Forum, Institute for Training and Technical Cooperation (ITTC), and Advisory Centre on WTO Law, only the first entailed comparable engagement with civil society before 2014, and none integrated itself equally within member countries.

What one finds as a result of the WTO's much later engagement of civil society is exactly what one would expect to find if True and Mintrom's argument concerning transnational networks of policy diffusion were to hold with IOs, and if the effects of their argument were amplified by path-dependency. It appears that IOs that engaged more extensively and earlier with civil society also did a great deal more by 2014 than the WTO to advance the representation of women and their interests. For example, APEC committed to gender mainstreaming after the Women Leaders Network (WLN) began in 1996 to lobby APEC to include gender issues in its economic forum. It was promoted in 1997 by Canada, which was APEC chair at the time.[83] The support of the Canadian International Development Agency (CIDA) for WLN led to APEC's Framework for the Integration of Women in APEC,[84] which determined that all proposals related to general or sectoral policies and

78 Van Den Bossche, 'Non-Governmental Organizations and the WTO' (n 75) 320.

79 APEC, 'APEC Business Advisory Council – Achievements' <www.apec.org/Groups/Other-Groups/APEC-Business-Advisory-Council.aspx> accessed 8 May 2022.

80 APEC, 'APEC Business Travel Card' <www.apec.org/about-us/about-apec/business-resources/apec-business-travel-card.aspx> accessed 8 May 2022.

81 APEC, 'APEC Study Centers Consortium' <www.apec.org/Groups/Other-Groups/APEC-Study-Centres-Consortium.aspx> accessed 8 May 2022.

82 Ibid.

83 Christina Gabriel and Laura Macdonald, 'Managing Trade Engagements? Mapping the Contours of State Feminism and Women's Political Activism' (2005) 12(1) *Canadian Foreign Policy* 71–88, 82. The APEC chair, held by Canada at the time (1997), was shared by Lloyd Axworthy, then Minister of Foreign Affairs, and Sergio Marchi, then Minister of International Trade.

84 APEC, 'Framework for Integration of Women in APEC' (1999) <www.apec.org/~/media/Files/Groups/GFPN/02_aggi_framewk.pdf> accessed 8 May 2022.

programmes would be analysed from a gender-equality perspective to ensure positive, equitable impacts.[85] APEC thus became the only multilateral economic organization to incorporate 'gender mainstreaming' throughout its policy initiatives.

Still other international organizations engaged more closely and extensively than the WTO with civil society and made greater progress towards the representation of women and women's interests between 1994 and 2014. At the 1999 UN Conference on Financing for Development (UN-FfD), the 'Monterrey Consensus' established gender budgeting. By 2000, the UN System comprised 1,300 gender focal points.[86] Moreover, UN Security Council Resolution 1325 called for 'the integration of gender across UN security policy and operations'.[87] Even if delayed in implementation and of questionable effectiveness,[88] there remained in 2022 no WTO parallel to gender budgeting, Resolution 1325 or the 1,300 gender focal points. The World Bank and UNDP have introduced gender budgeting. This is true even if UNDP 'emphasises women's reproductive role in the care economy',[89] and even if gender budgeting at the World Bank is intended to improve the economic efficiency of women in the care economy, reducing itself to an 'investment strategy in mothers for growth'.[90] Thus, again, where an institution has engaged more extensively than the WTO with civil society, it has generally been able to represent women and women's interests earlier and at a level unmatched by the WTO.

4.4.2 *Reason 4: The Clash of Non-compromising Positions – A Brief History of Early Gender and Trade Activism versus Trade Liberalization*

Beginning in the 1980s and extending to the present, a significant proportion of gender/feminist scholars has taken an antagonistic approach to neoliberal economics and to institutions and networks perceived as neoliberal. The development of this perspective took place during the same era that saw the

85 Heather Gibb, *Gender Mainstreaming: Good Practices from the Asia Pacific Region* (Renouf Publishing 2001) 7.

86 Jacqui True, 'Gender Specialists and Global Governance: New Forms of Women's Movement Mobilisation' in Sandra Grey and Marian Sawer (eds) *Women's Movements: Flourishing or in Abeyance?* (Routledge 2008) 97.

87 Ibid.

88 Ibid 98.

89 Gülay Caglar, 'Feminist Strategies and Social Learning in International Economic Governance' in Gülay Caglar, Elisabeth Prügl and Susanne Zwingel (eds) *Feminist Strategies in International Governance* (Routledge 2013) 261.

90 Ibid.

ascendancy of the institutions and economic and political philosophies later known as neoliberal. This antagonism has extended to globalization, free trade, and international organizations involved in trade issues, such as the WTO. As a member of the WTO Secretariat noted: '[During the late 1990s] … the debate … was … very sharp. It was basically anything done in trade or WTO is bad for gender (i.e., women).'[91] This meant that very little dialogue was possible at all for some time between women's interest groups and the WTO, since women's interest groups tended generally to oppose liberalized trade, while the mandate of the WTO was to promote it.

This clash produced important results: first, the resistance of a significant proportion of women's interest groups to engaging positively with the WTO in order to build an organization more amenable to the representation of women and women's interests; and second, the expectation of WTO personnel, trade negotiators, etc. for a period of time that anyone doing work on gender and trade must be in principle against free trade and therefore the existence of the WTO. Regardless of the merits and the relatively extreme positions of either side, this conflict hindered dialogue and increased the difficulty of representing women and women's interests within the WTO.

Where did it all start? Many point to the Canadian context, where the National Action Committee on the Status of Women (NAC), argued that the 1988 Canada–US Free Trade Agreement (FTA) would impose the greatest costs upon those 'most disadvantaged in the labour force'.[92] Given the structure of the Canadian economy in the mid-1980s, these would predominantly have been women. In the event, the Conservatives were re-elected in Canada, the FTA was ratified, and the NAC's government funding was cut by more than 50 per cent.[93] Even so, as Bashevkin states, the NAC 'identified linkages between free trade … and the lives of Canadian women' that 'might have been ignored without NAC's intervention'[94] and that 'worked to articulate a feminist perspective on free trade'.[95] Moreover, the NAC's experience with the Canadian government became a very important influence in persuading

[91] Interview with senior member of WTO Secretariat (Geneva, Switzerland, October 2007). On file with author.

[92] Marjorie Cohen, 'The Macdonald Report and Its Implications for Women' (Feminist Action December 1985) cited in Sylvia B. Bashevkin, *True Patriot Love: The Politics of Canadian Nationalism* (Oxford University Press 1991) 140.

[93] Ibid 142–144. Also Jill Vickers, Pauline Rankin, and Christine Appelle, *Politics as if Women Mattered: A Political Analysis of the National Action Committee on the Status of Women* (University of Toronto Press 1993) 293–295.

[94] Bashevkin, *True Patriot Love* (n 92) 147.

[95] Ibid 145.

the Mexican women's group Mujer a Mujer to join the NAC in opposing the North American Free Trade Agreement (NAFTA).[96]

In the American context, from 1990 to 1994, the Women's Alternative Economic Network (WAEN) opposed NAFTA and the nascent WTO, and by 1997 Women's EDGE had arisen in opposition to the WTO and trade liberalization.[97] Their opposition was framed in terms that recalled those used by the NAC in opposition to the Canada–US FTA.[98] Further, gender and trade advocates participated in the Mexican Action Network on Free Trade (RMALC) coalition against NAFTA.[99] Women's NGOs were also involved in the successful broad-based civil society efforts against the Multilateral Agreement on Investment (MAI) in 1998,[100] against 'fast-track' authorization in 1997 for the Clinton Administration to extend NAFTA membership,[101] for a 'social-labour declaration' at the December 1998 Mercusor summit,[102] and against the proposed Free Trade Area of the Americas (FTAA).[103] In the context of opposition to the FTAA, 200 women's rights activists from 35 countries met in April 1998 in Santiago, Chile, for the Alternative Women's Forum at the People's Summit of the Americas.[104] Finally, gender and trade advocates were involved in opposition to the 1999 WTO Ministerial in Seattle. The 'People's Assembly' held on 29 November 1999 included a session titled 'Women Say No to WTO!'[105]

Steinkopf Rice's analysis identifies key themes advocated by gender and trade organizations that support this contention: gender equality in market structures, alternatives to free-market capitalism, bottom-up trade policies, networks, accountability through gender-specific measures, greater global/local cohesion in policies, and the democratization of decision-making processes.[106] Each of these themes is critical of neoliberalism *or* assertive of the need for gendered trade and economic analysis. More than this, Steinkopf

96 Debra Jacqueline Liebowitz, *Gender and Identity in an Era of Globalization: Transnational Political Organizing in North America* (Rutgers 2000) 74–75.
97 Ibid 97–99.
98 Ibid 93–97, 229–230.
99 Ibid 228.
100 Ibid 225–226.
101 Ibid 225.
102 Ibid.
103 Ibid 229.
104 Ibid.
105 LeeRay Costa, 'Women Say No to WTO' (2000) 4(2) *Gender, Technology and Development* 315–322.
106 Julie Steinkopf Rice, 'Viewing Trade Liberalization through a Feminist Lens: A Content Analysis of the Counterhegemonic Discourse of Gender and Trade Advocacy Groups' (2010) 30(3) *Sociological Spectrum* 289–316.

Rice shows that the nascent gender and trade movement of the late 1980s and 1990s had developed to become a 'global movement' by the mid-2000s. Her research records twenty-one distinct 'gender and trade advocacy groups'[107] worldwide, of which thirteen were in the global north, but seven were in the global south, and one was entirely internet-based.[108]

The challenge, however, is that this movement, developing for over twenty years, had taken shape during the same years in which the WTO had first sought to broaden its engagement with civil society. Thus, effectively, two contrary institutions, path-dependent not only in their institutional composition but in their knowledge production, met in the late 1990s and 2000s. One was largely committed to the neoliberal programme by means of trade liberalization, the other deeply antagonistic towards neoliberalism. Regardless of the merits of the arguments, the development and meeting of these oppositional forces made progress towards the representation of women and women's interests particularly difficult to achieve within the WTO. Paradoxically, because the WTO was the single multilateral governing institution for world trade, the same antagonism towards neoliberalism that had produced foundational insights of gender and trade analysis also produced an environment for interaction with the WTO that militated against the adoption of the insights within global trade governance. This was mostly because in many cases those who advanced the insights of gender and trade analysis were opposed to the very existence of the WTO and its body of principles and rules. In such a case, where to begin a dialogue, let alone a negotiation? It was impossible.

Thus, although the antagonism that contributed to this disjuncture was legitimate, essential, and valuable, it came with costs. As Nager and others warned in 2002, 'constructing women as universally exploited by global capital and neoliberal policies obscures the ways in which gendered subjects, in particular historically and geographically specific places, engage in complex and contradictory experiences of, and in response to, global processes'.[109]

[107] 'Gender and trade advocacy group' is Steinkopf Rice's term; the discussion uses her terminology. Ibid.

[108] Ibid 314. These figures are from a review of the contact details on the websites of the groups Steinkopf Rice lists. Her own figures give only four groups in the global south and seventeen in the north; however, her figures are contradicted in this regard by the information on the websites she gives (or, in a few cases, updated versions of the websites).

[109] Richa Nagar, Victoria Lawson, Linda McDowell and Susan Hanson, 'Locating Globalization: Feminist (Re)readings of the Subjects and Spaces of Globalization' (2002) 78(3) *Economic Geography* 257–284, 269.

4.5 INTERNATIONAL LAW

4.5.1 *Reason 5: The WTO Dispute Settlement System as* Lex Specialis – *Implications for Women's Rights as Human Rights*

WTO dispute settlement operates as *lex specialis*, a specialized sub-system of law occupying a distinct place in the interrelationships of international law. This appellation is the subject of an extended controversy in international law literature known as the Marceau–Pauwelyn debate. To simplify, Marceau argued that the dispute settlement mechanism of the WTO is *lex specialis*, whereas Pauwelyn argued that it constitutes treaty law operating normally under the rules of public international law.[110] However, the stronger arguments lie with Marceau's understanding that WTO dispute settlement is *lex specialis*. This is of significance to the representation of women and women's interests because it negates, within the context of the WTO, much of the effectiveness of the strategy of identifying women's rights with human rights, which has been prominent since the advent of the Convention on the Elimination of All Forms of Discrimination against Women (CEDAW)[111] in 1980.

The question of *lex specialis* is crucial because, in international law, '*lex specialis derogat generalis*' – 'specialized law derogates from general law'.[112] This means that in cases of conflict, the provisions of the specialized system take precedence over general treaties. Moreover, '*lex posterior generalis non derogat priori specialis*' – 'later general law does not derogate from prior special

[110] The following comprise the basics of the debate: Gabrielle Marceau, 'WTO Dispute Settlement and Human Rights' (2002) 13(4) *European Journal of International Law* 753–814; Joel Trachtman, 'The Domain of WTO Dispute Resolution' (1999) 40(2) *Harvard International Law Journal* 333–378; Pieter Jan Kuijper, 'The Law of GATT as a Special Field of International Law – Ignorance, Further Refinement or Self-Contained System of International Law' (1994) 25 *Netherlands Yearbook of International Law* 227–257; Joost Pauwelyn, 'The Role of Public International Law in the WTO: How Far Can We Go?' (2001) 95(3) *American Journal of International Law* 535–578; Mariano Garcia Rubio, 'Unilateral Measures as a Means of Forcible Execution of WTO Recommendations and Decisions' in Laura Picchio Forlati and Linos-Alexandre Sicilianos (eds), *Les sanctions economiques en droit international / Economic Sanctions in International Law* (Martinus Nijhoff Publishers 2004); Petros C. Mavroidis, 'Remedies in the WTO Legal System: Between a Rock and a Hard Place' (2000) 11(4) *European Journal of International Law* 763–813; David Palmeter and Petros C. Mavroidis, 'The WTO Legal System: Sources of Law' (1998) 92 *American Journal of International Law* 398–413.

[111] Convention on the Elimination of All Forms of Discrimination against Women, 3 September 1981, 1249 UNTS 13 (not reproduced in ILM).

[112] Marceau, 'WTO Dispute Settlement and Human Rights' (n 110) 794.

law'.[113] This is an exception from the norm under general international law that, in cases of conflict, law created later takes precedence over law created earlier.

For Marceau, the WTO treaty defines both the applicable law and the jurisdiction and competence of panels with reference to the WTO agreements. As she states, 'specific rights and obligations, specific remedies and a specific dispute settlement mechanism are mandatory and countermeasures have been regulated, [hence the] WTO can be seen as having set up a system that contains a specific applicable law, a *lex specialis* system'.[114] Since the WTO Dispute Settlement Understanding (DSU) is a *lex specialis* system, international human rights treaties cannot be invoked in a WTO or Appellate Body panel to justify the violation of a WTO obligation, although the contradiction can be highlighted. That is to say, the WTO and Appellate Body panels are not empowered to find that a human rights violation, as such, justifies the violation of a WTO obligation.[115] This means that the identification of women's rights with human rights cannot be a directly effective legal strategy for achieving the representation of women and women's interests at the WTO.

This is significant because the definition of women's rights as human rights has long been a strategy of women's organizations and accepted as fact by many. As Dorsey notes, it can be traced at least to the advent of CEDAW in 1979, and has been a developed, coherent, and successful strategy for the advancement of women's rights since the 1993 World Conference on Human Rights at Vienna, the 1994 International Conference on Population and Development at Cairo, the 1995 World Summit on Social Development at Copenhagen, and the 1995 Fourth World Conference on Women at Beijing.[116]

At a basic level, the structures exist in international law to facilitate and motivate the incorporation of gender concerns within the WTO. As Table 4.1 shows, a number of international agreements and conventions prohibit discrimination based on gender and are supported by the requirement of the 1969 Vienna Convention on the Law of Treaties (VCLT) to 'interpret in good

[113] Ibid.

[114] Ibid 764.

[115] Ibid 767.

[116] These four conferences together constituted a crucial milestone in the development of the strategy of identifying women's rights as human rights. For a fuller discussion, *see* Ellen Dorsey, 'The Global Women's Movement: Articulating a New Vision of Global Governance' in Paul F. Diehl (ed) *The Politics of Global Governance: International Organizations in an Interdependent World* (Reinner 2005) 418–430.

TABLE 4.1 *Fundamental international agreements and conventions that prohibit all forms of discrimination on the basis of gender*

The Charter of the UN
The Universal Declaration of Human Rights
The International Covenant on Economic, Social and Cultural Rights
The International Covenant on Civil and Political Rights
The Convention for the Elimination of all forms of Discrimination Against Women
The European Convention for the Protection of Human Rights & Fundamental Freedoms
The American Convention on Human Rights
The African Charter on Human & People's Rights
The Protocol on the Rights of Women in Africa

faith'.[117] As former Director-General Lamy noted, 'There is a clear consensus: all WTO member governments are committed to a narrower set of internationally recognized "core" standards – freedom of association, no forced labour, no child labour, and no discrimination at work (including gender discrimination)'.[118] The problem is that the agreements in Table 4.1 do no more than prohibit discrimination based on sex/gender; they impose no positive requirement for action. Further, they do not sway the argument concerning *lex specialis* from Marceau's position to that of Pauwelyn. WTO panellists and Appellate Body members remain barred from altering WTO agreements and from determining anything more than that an insoluble conflict exists between the obligations of a given state as a WTO member under WTO law, and the same state's obligations under international law that is not *jus cogens*.[119]

[117] Vienna Convention on the Law of Treaties, 23 May 1969, 1155 UNTS 331, Art. 31.

[118] WTO, 'Understanding the WTO: Cross-Cutting and New Issues – Labour Standards: Consensus, Coherence and Controversy; Consensus on Core Standards, Work Deferred to the ILO' <www.wto.org/english/thewto_e/whatis_e/tif_e/bey5_e.htm> accessed 8 May 2022.

[119] *Jus cogens* is Latin for 'compelling law' and is generally translated into English as 'peremptory norm'. According to Cornell University Law School's Legal Information Institute (LII), *jus cogens* 'refers to certain fundamental, overriding principles of international law, from which no derogation is ever permitted'. *See* Cornell University Law School's Legal Information Institute, 'Jus Cogens' <www.law.cornell.edu/wex/jus_cogens> accessed 8 May 2022. *See also* Ian Brownlie, *Principles of Public International Law* (Oxford University Press 5th ed. 1998); James Crawford (ed) *Brownlie's Principles of Public International Law* (Oxford University Press 8th ed. 2012) 594–597. For an excellent overview, *see also* Rafael Nieto-Navia, 'International Peremptory Norms (*Jus Cogens*) and International Humanitarian Law' in Lal Chand Vohrah et al. (eds) *Man's Inhumanity to Man* (Brill Nijhoff 2003) 595.

There is no parallel amongst other institutions of global economic governance to the *lex specialis* DSU of the WTO. Even the UN Convention on the Law of the Sea (UNCLOS) does not comprehend a mechanism for dispute settlement as robust, strong in compliance, or wide in its reach as the WTO Dispute Settlement Mechanism (DSM) (when operating as intended – i.e., prior to its present crisis). For their parts, neither the IMF nor the World Bank incorporates a robust, legalistic mechanism for dispute settlement; nor do they meet Marceau's criteria to be considered *lex specialis*, as described above. Indeed, there is no other institution of global economic governance that can be considered *lex specialis* and that combines a mechanism for dispute settlement as robust and extensive as the DSM of the WTO. This makes the WTO institutionally and structurally resistant to human rights discourse to a greater degree than its peer institutions of global economic governance, and therefore to the representation of women and women's interests (particularly as women's rights) in a way that is stronger and more severe than any other such institution.

4.5.2 *Reason 6: WTO Law Is Primarily Hard Law*

WTO law is primarily hard law, which necessarily increases the difficulty and perceived risk of introducing any reform beyond that of any organization comprised to a greater degree of soft law. Following Abbott et al., Davidson argues that law, whether hard or soft, consists of rules that regulate behaviour in society, a mechanism for compliance, and a mechanism for the settlement of disputes.[120] According to Davidson, the distinction between soft and hard law lies within these criteria and is a gradation between the binding and non-binding nature of rules, their precision or imprecision, and the settlement of disputes by a more judicial or more diplomatic model.[121] Similarly, Abbott, Keohane, and others define a gradation between soft and hard law in terms of the binding nature of the obligation, the precise nature of the rule, and the diplomatic or judicial nature of the parties to which the authority to implement, interpret, and enforce the rules is delegated.[122] The WTO agreements are considered primarily hard law because they detail their terms and obligations very precisely, they are binding upon WTO members with relatively

120 Kenneth W. Abbott, Robert O. Keohane, Andrew Moravcsik, Anne-Marie Slaughter, and Duncan Snidal, 'The Concept of Legalization' (2000) 54(3) *International Organization* 401–419, 401–404; Paul J. Davidson, 'The Role of Law in Governing Regionalism in Asia' in Nicholas Thomas (ed) *Governance and Regionalism in Asia* (Routledge 2008) 224–233.

121 Davidson, 'The Role of Law in Governing Regionalism in Asia' (n 120) 233.

122 Abbott et al., 'The Concept of Legalization' (n 120) 401.

little flexibility of application or interpretation, and they are enforced by a robust, judicial, dispute settlement process with clear sanctions for contravention. In terms of Davidson's gradation, WTO law is far closer to 'binding', 'precise', and 'judicial'. It is difficult to experiment with reform in a hard-law structure, since all members know that any hard-law reform must entail a clear and enforceable commitment. This means hard-law reform is inherently risky and makes it far more difficult to convince WTO members to introduce initiatives such as gender mainstreaming.

By contrast, APEC was able to incorporate gender mainstreaming throughout its policy initiatives fundamentally because its soft-law structure made it possible to do so. The recommendations from the 1998 APEC Ministerial Meeting on Women are illustrative of the soft-law nature of APEC gender mainstreaming commitments. For example, APEC is 'strongly urged' and 'recommendations are submitted to Leaders' toward 'integrating women into the mainstream of APEC processes and activities'. The recommendations were the following: to 'recognize' gender as a cross-cutting theme in APEC; to 'place a high priority' on the collection of sex-disaggregated data; to 'implement gender impact analysis of policy, program and project proposals as an integral component of APEC decisions, processes and activities';[123] to 'place a high priority' on the development of further studies concerning the impact of financial and economic crises upon women; to 'accelerate the process' of integrating women in the mainstream of gender processes and activities; to 'promote and encourage' the involvement of women in all APEC fora; and to 'ensure' that the recommendations be implemented and that APEC members be accountable for results.[124]

These were important initiatives of significant potential that nevertheless were soft law; framed in the language of commitments, they actually committed APEC members to very little. Only the recommendation to implement gender impact analysis mandates action, and the action in that case is further study. Moreover, each recommendation requires only that each APEC member adjust policy in the required direction to their own satisfaction. This is, however, no disparagement. Exactly where they do not require a policy result, even when it is within the power of APEC members to do so, is where they make it easier for members to agree to the recommendations. In this way, the representation of women and women's interests was made legitimate as a topic of discussion and negotiation within APEC. This

[123] APEC, 'Joint Ministerial Statement' APEC Ministerial Meeting on Women (15–16 October 1998) para. 27 c.

[124] Ibid para. 27.

constituted a meaningful advance for women within APEC and was achieved precisely because the soft-law nature of the recommendations allowed each APEC member flexibility concerning the extent and scope of its commitment. In the case of the WTO, similar progress towards 'gender mainstreaming' has proven much more difficult to attain. To a significant degree, this is because WTO agreements tend towards hard law, are made harder to attain by the requirement for consensus, and carry a greater risk for the members/ contracting parties.

4.6 CONCLUSION

In summary, the six reasons describe how the institutional structure of the WTO, as well as the nature of its interactions with civil society and the wider framework of international law, have made it such a difficult case for the representation of women and women's interests. Taken as a whole, they provide an understanding of why the WTO is resistant to the representation of women and their interests during an era in which gender mainstreaming has come to be widespread within institutions of global governance.

However, as developed by Fabian,[125] within these reasons lie clues to how the WTO can overcome its institutional resistance. Specifically, the hybridization of soft law and hard law can provide the openness, flexibility, and risk reduction necessary to introduce policies, declarations, and agreements that advance the representation of women and women's interests.[126] Equally, Aid for Trade can provide a locus for policy innovation and research towards the same end,[127] and WTO declarations and initiatives since 2017 give hope that the WTO Secretariat can take a more active role in researching measures to represent women and their interests through trade governance.[128]

[125] Fabian, 'Towards a Theory of Democratic Global Economic Governance' (n *).
[126] Ibid 429–484.
[127] Ibid 460–484.
[128] WTO, 'Joint Ministerial Declaration' (n 6). Again, these are the Joint Declaration on Trade and Women's Economic Empowerment, the Gender Focal Point, the Informal Working Group on Trade and Gender, and the International Trade and Gender Research Hub.

PART II

Current Issues in Gender Equality and Trade Policies

5

Women in the LDCs

How to Build Forward Differently for Them

SIMONETTA ZARRILLI*

ABSTRACT

Women across countries and regions face many obstacles that hamper their capacity to fully benefit from international trade and, more generally, from their participation in the economy. Those shortcomings are also found in the least-developed countries (LDCs), but they are magnified by persistent and acute development challenges that include high levels of poverty, deficient infrastructure, limited productive capacities, and a mostly low-skilled labour force. Trade has been singled out as an effective tool for a fruitful integration of the LDCs into the global economy, and preferential trade regimes have been set up to facilitate the process. However, have LDCs benefited from such regimes and, above all, has trade provided meaningful opportunities for women's economic empowerment? This chapter will try to provide an answer to these questions. First, it will look at underlying factors that play a role in determining women's likelihood to participate in trade and benefit from it, including women's level of education, time availability, agency, and participation in the labour market. Second, it will explore the role women play and the gendered obstacles they face in the female-intensive sectors of agriculture, artisanal and small-scale mining, Export Processing Zones (EPZs), and tourism. The chapter will then suggest measures that would help women benefit more from their participation in these sectors and highlight the overall economic and societal benefits that this would imply. The measures identified as being potentially beneficial to women will be checked against measures that have been put in place by the LDCs through rescue packages. This will allow a preliminary assessment of the matching between what women would need, especially in a post-pandemic environment, and what so far has been provided to them.

* The author wishes to thank Rolf Traeger for valuable comments and suggestions.

5.1 INTRODUCTION

Women across countries and regions face many obstacles that hamper their capacity to benefit fully from international trade and more generally from their participation in the economy. Hurdles include time poverty; discriminatory legal rules and social norms; limited access to productive resources and technology; and inadequate opportunities for education, training, and skill development. These shortcomings are also found in LDCs[1] and are magnified by persistent and acute development challenges that include high levels of poverty, deficient infrastructure, limited productive capacities, and a mostly low-skilled labour force.

This challenging situation has become even more dramatic as a result of the COVID-19 pandemic that has increased women's already heavy burden of domestic and care work,[2] and has escalated the instances of male violence against them.[3] Moreover, the pandemic has had a devastating economic impact on women by severely hitting sectors and occupations in which they are mainly involved.[4]

This chapter unfolds as follows: Section 5.2 provides a brief overview of the LDCs, their position in the global economy and the role of women in the economy of LDCs. Section 5.3 then explores the measures implemented by the LDCs to help people and companies to shoulder the pandemic-induced economic shock. Among the many measures put in place, it singles out those

1 As of 2022, forty-six countries were designated by the United Nations as least-developed countries (LDCs). They are grouped as the African LDCs and Haiti (Angola, Benin, Burkina Faso, Burundi, Central African Republic, Chad, Democratic Republic of the Congo, Djibouti, Eritrea, Ethiopia, the Gambia, Guinea, Guinea-Bissau, Haiti, Lesotho, Liberia, Madagascar, Malawi, Mali, Mauritania, Mozambique, Niger, Rwanda, Senegal, Sierra Leone, Somalia, South Sudan, Sudan, Togo, Uganda, United Republic of Tanzania, and Zambia); the Asian LDCs (Afghanistan, Bangladesh, Bhutan, Cambodia, Lao People's Democratic Republic, Myanmar, Nepal, and Yemen); and the Island LDCs (Comoros, Kiribati, Sao Tome and Principe, Solomon Islands, Timor-Leste, and Tuvalu).

2 UN Women, 'Whose Time to Care: Unpaid Care and Domestic Work during COVID-19' (25 November 2020) <https://data.unwomen.org/sites/default/files/inline-files/Whose-time-to-care-brief_0.pdf> accessed 8 May 2022.

3 UN Women, 'Impact of COVID-19 on Violence against Women and Girls and Service Provision: UN Women Rapid Assessment and Findings' (UN Women Brief 2020) <www.unwomen.org/-/media/headquarters/attachments/sections/library/publications/2020/impact-of-covid-19-on-violence-against-women-and-girls-and-service-provision-en.pdf?la=en&vs=0> accessed 8 May 2022, link no longer active.

4 UN, 'The Impact of COVID-19 on Women: UN Secretary-General's Policy Brief' (9 April 2020) <www.unwomen.org/sites/default/files/Headquarters/Attachments/Sections/Library/Publications/2020/Policy-brief-The-impact-of-COVID-19-on-women-en.pdf> accessed 8 May 2022.

that, directly or indirectly, by design or by coincidence, have the potential to especially benefit women. Section 5.4 then tries to answer the following questions: Is there a good match between women's needs and what so far has been provided to them through the rescue packages? What measures would be necessary to allow women to play a more active role in the economy, including in international trade, beyond the emergency measures? What are the preconditions to avoid going back to 'business as usual'? Section 5.5 concludes.

5.2 THE LDCS IN THE GLOBAL ECONOMY AND THE ROLE OF WOMEN

5.2.1 *The LDCs in the Global Economy*

LDCs face common development challenges such as persistent poverty, deficient infrastructure, limited productive capacities, low investments, high debt burden, and mostly low-skilled labour force. Structural transformation and fruitful integration into the global economy have not materialized for most LDCs.

LDCs have very high trade-to-Gross Domestic Product (GDP) ratios, since they heavily rely on trade, both imports and exports, and all have trade deficits at present. Many LDCs are dependent on the exports of primary commodities and economic diversification remains a challenge for them.

Most LDCs have been through trade reforms during recent decades, including by acceding to the World Trade Organization (WTO). They benefit from full or nearly full duty-free and quota-free market access in most developed country markets and in an increasing number of developing country markets. Their exports also benefit from less stringent rules of origin in some markets. However, most LDCs have not been able to benefit from these concessions, mainly due to their low productive capacities and the limited role played by trade policy in their development strategies.[5] Moreover, delays at borders, costly and opaque border procedures and high transport costs have contributed to the very limited integration of the LDCs into the global economy. In 2020, LDCs as a group produced only 1.4 per cent of the world's

5 UNCTAD, 'Making Trade Work for Least Developed Countries: A Handbook on Mainstreaming Trade' (2016) Trade and Poverty Paper Series No. 5 <https://unctad.org/webflyer/making-trade-work-least-developed-countries-handbook-mainstreaming-trade> accessed 8 May 2022.

GDP.[6] They accounted for 1 per cent of world exports of goods and services, and their share in world trade in goods and services was 1.2 per cent.[7]

The main shortcomings that women face in other developing countries to become more involved in economic and trade activities and benefit from them are similarly found in the LDCs. However, for LDCs, such instances are amplified by shortcomings in most development dimensions.

Women play vital roles in the key economic sectors in LDCs, including in agricultural, industry, and services sectors. The following sub-sections provide discussions on their roles in these economic sectors.

5.2.2 *The Agricultural Sector*

The agricultural sector corresponds to 24 per cent of total economic activity in the African LDCs, 17 per cent in the Asian LDCs and 22 per cent in the Island LDCs (2019 data). In 2019, it contributed to 13 per cent of all LDCs exports, 15 per cent for the African LDCs, 10 per cent for the Asian LDCs, and 43 per cent for the Island LDCs (see Table 5.1). It remains the main employer for all LDC groups, with 55 per cent of the workforce employed in agriculture in 2019.[8]

Women make up between 41 and 45 per cent of total employment in agriculture in the LDCs.[9] There is, however, a high degree of gender segregation in the crops being grown and in the production roles and responsibilities. Women are typically responsible for subsistence farming due to their traditional role to provide food security for the household. The transition from subsistence farming to commercialization and agricultural exports that has happened in several LDCs has attracted men's interest and in many cases crowded out women. Gender segregation by crop is also due to traditional expectations for women to remain close to the household. From a legal point of view, men and women have equal ownership rights to property in thirty-seven LDCs; however, customary law prevails in most societies, preventing women from owning land and other property.[10] This has a negative impact on access to credit that would enable women to expand production and participate in international trade.

6 UNCTAD, 'The Least Developed Countries in the Post-COVID World: Learning from 50 Years of Experience', UNCTAD/LDC/2021 (2021).

7 Calculations by the author based on data from the UNCTAD Stat, accessed 8 July 2022.

8 UNCTAD, 'Trade and Gender Linkages: An analysis of Least Developed Countries, Teaching Material on Trade and Gender: Module 4E', UNCTAD/DITC/2021/1 (2021).

9 Ibid.

10 Ibid.

TABLE 5.1 *Sectoral contribution to LDC GDP and exports (2019)*

Sectoral Contribution to LDC GDP, 2019 (%)				
	LDCs (all)	African LDCs	Asian LDCs	Island LDCs
Agriculture	21	24	17	22
Non-manufacturing industry (incl. mining)	16	20	12	14
Manufacturing	14	10	18	5
Services	49	46	53	59
Sectoral Contribution to LDC exports, 2019 (%)				
	LDCs (all)	African LDCs	Asian LDCs	Island LDCs
Agriculture	13	15	10	43
Non-manufacturing industry (incl. mining)	39	59	12	8
Manufacturing	28	8	55	12
Services	20	18	23	37

Source: Calculation by the author based on United Nations Conference on Trade and Development (UNCTAD) statistics.

There are gender gaps in productivity and earnings, mainly driven by the fact that women typically produce staple crops whereas men are more often involved in the production of cash crops.[11] Due to the difference in earning potential between staple and cash crops, women generate substantially less income. Household responsibilities and related time poverty contribute to making women less productive than men.

The difficulties that female farmers face is also the result of long-term problems affecting the agricultural sector in the LDCs, including import competition, especially when imported products benefit from massive subsidies; the shift of Official Development Assistance (ODA) away from agriculture; and governments' underinvestment in agricultural research and development (R&D) and extension services, with a consequent loss in knowledge and capacity. Moreover, because of the lack of dynamism of the sector, men are increasingly migrating to urban areas, leaving women with growing responsibilities for farm activities and for the well-being of the household.[12]

[11] Ibid.
[12] Ibid.

5.2.3 *The Industrial Sector*

Between 2011 and 2019, the contribution of manufacturing to GDP remained constant in the LDCs at around 10–14 per cent. In 2019, non-manufacturing industries, including mining, contributed 16 per cent to GDP, with the highest value of 20 per cent in African LDCs (see Table 5.1).

Primary commodities dominate LDC exports, with an overall 39 per cent share of total exports (59 per cent for the African LDCs) (see Table 5.1), though the share of commodities in exports is shrinking. Conversely, exports of manufactures have steadily increased, reaching 28 per cent of total exports in 2019. Manufacturing exports represent 55 per cent of Asian LDC exports, but only 8 per cent of African LDCs (see Table 5.1). Hit by the pandemic, exports of manufactures, however, significantly declined in 2020. Mirroring the low level of technology diffusion and the low skill level of the workforce, most LDC exports are concentrated in low-technology and low-skill goods.[13]

As with other developing countries, in LDCs there is a feminization of labour in low-skilled manufacturing production, especially export-oriented, and a high degree of occupational gender segregation with the concentration of women in low-skilled jobs. EPZs have played an important role in providing wage employment to women. In Cambodia, virtually all production workers are young (aged eighteen to thirty) women.[14] Women constitute around 70 per cent of employees in EPZs in Tanzania.[15]

5.2.4 *The Services Sector*

Services dominated the economy in all LDCs in 2019, representing almost 50 per cent of economic activities. Services play a particularly important role in island LDCs, where their contribution to GDP is around 60 per cent (see Table 5.1). Services exports have gained importance during the last two decades, reaching 20 per cent of total exports in 2019. In particular for island LDCs, services represent 37 per cent of their exports (see Table 5.1). Despite

[13] Ibid.

[14] Peter Warr and Jayant Menon, 'Cambodia's Special Economic Zones' (2015) ADB Economics Working Paper Series No. 459 <www.adb.org/sites/default/files/publication/175236/ewp-459.pdf> accessed 8 May 2022.

[15] Richard Adu-Gyamfi, Simplice A. Asongu, Tinaye Sonto Mmusi, Herbert Wamalwa, and Madei Mangori, 'A Comparative Study of Export Processing Zones in the Wake of the Sustainable Development Goals: The Cases of Botswana, Kenya, Tanzania, and Zimbabwe' (2020) WIDER Working Paper Series wp-2020-64 <www.wider.unu.edu/sites/default/files/Publications/Working-paper/PDF/wp2020-64.pdf> accessed 8 May 2022.

substantially growing, services exports remain concentrated in traditional transport and travel sectors.

Services' employment share rose from 21 per cent in 1995 to 32 per cent in 2019. Wholesale and retail trade make up 15–18 per cent of economic activity within services as the largest sub-sector in all the LDC groups. The wholesale and retail trade sector corresponds to high levels of female employment, reaching between 30 and 40 per cent of female share of total employment in Haiti, Liberia, Benin, Sierra Leone, Zambia, Burkina Faso, Mauritania, and Togo (in decreasing order).[16]

Tourism provides women with opportunities for employment, formal and informal, direct and indirect, and for entrepreneurship. In many LDCs, the tourism sector is marked by intense occupational segregation: men are concentrated in high-skill and managerial positions, while women primarily participate in low-skilled tasks such as room cleaning, kitchen work, and waitressing.[17] Employment in the tourism sector is mostly informal and temporary, for both men and women.

5.3 THE COVID-19 PANDEMIC, LDCS, AND WOMEN

5.3.1 *The Impact of the Pandemic on the LDCs and on Women*

The COVID-19 pandemic has spared no country; however, it has proved particularly detrimental to some countries and to specific segments of the population. It has magnified existing inequalities across and within countries.[18]

The health effects of the pandemic in the LDCs are still unclear because of the difficulty of detecting and reporting pandemic-related illness and deaths accurately. However, what is clear is that LDCs have had limited access to vaccines and the world is witnessing a global failure of collaboration in making vaccines available to all. Only 2 per cent of the population in the LDCs was vaccinated against an average of over 40 per cent in developed countries as of mid-2021.[19] The fundamental right to health is being denied.

[16] UNCTAD, 'Trade and Gender Linkages' (n 8).

[17] Ibid.

[18] UNCTAD, 'Trade and Development Report 2020 – From Global Pandemic to Prosperity for All: Avoiding Another Lost Decade', UNCTAD/TDR/2020 (2020); Nishant Yonzan, Christoph Lakner, and Daniel Gerszon Mahler, 'Is COVID-19 Increasing Global Inequality?' (World Bank 7 October 2021) <https://blogs.worldbank.org/opendata/covid-19-increasing-global-inequality> accessed 8 May 2022.

[19] UNCTAD, 'The Least Developed Countries in the Post-COVID World' (n 6).

Moreover, considering that access to vaccines is a precondition for recovery, the situation is particularly worrisome.

The global economic downturn has had disproportionately adverse economic and social effects on the LDCs. Income losses, low investments, and reduced remittances have worsened extreme poverty in the LDCs, making 2020 the worst year from a growth perspective in about three decades.[20] UNCTAD estimates an increase in the poverty headcount ratio against the USD 1.90 per day poverty line of 3.3 percentage points – from 32.2 to 35.2 per cent in the LDCs overall.[21] This means that compared to the pre-COVID-19 era, 35 million more people will live in extreme poverty in the LDCs in the post-COVID-19 era.[22] Extreme poverty, beyond being a dramatic problem in itself, has negative repercussions for human capital accumulation, knowledge development, and labour productivity, and negatively affects the environment. The COVID-19 crisis is negatively impacting other fundamental rights, such as access to education, security, and protection against violence.

Meagre domestic financial resources and high debt levels are greatly affecting LDCs' capacity to cope with pandemic-related shocks. The lesson learned from other health-related crises is that the health emergency will eventually be overcome, but if countries do not put in place the right policies, the negative economic and social repercussions will affect their development trajectory in the long run. The recovery path for the LDCs is projected to be slow and to constrain their process of structural transformation, which in turn will impact on their ability to meet the United Nations Sustainable Development Goals (SDG) Agenda 2030.

Turning to the specific impact of COVID-19 on women, the pandemic is estimated to result in millions of additional women and girls falling into extreme poverty. This means that the total number of women and girls living in extreme poverty may reach 388 million in 2022, compared to 372 million men and boys, or even increase all the way to 446 million in a 'high-damage' scenario.[23] It is also estimated that 83.7 per cent of the world's extremely poor women and girls would live in Sub-Saharan Africa (62.8 per cent) and Central and Southern Asia (20.9 per cent), where most LDCs are located.[24]

[20] Ibid.

[21] Ibid.

[22] Ibid.

[23] This scenario is based on an overall deterioration of economic and social indicators and assumes that the pandemic will leave long-lasting scars on countries.

[24] UN Women, 'Poverty Deepens for Women and Girls, According to Latest Projections' (UN Women 1 February 2022) <https://data.unwomen.org/features/poverty-deepens-women-and-girls-according-latest-projections> accessed 7 September 2022.

Economic downturns such as the present one is typically not gender-neutral. Several critical factors contribute to explain why. First, women are more at risk of losing their jobs than men because they often hold temporary, part-time, and precarious jobs that are the first ones to be cut. Second, women tend to work in the informal sector and rescue packages mainly target workers in the formal sector. Third, female-dominated sectors, such as hospitality and personal services, have been severely disrupted by the effects of the pandemic because of lockdown and social distancing measures, and travel restrictions. Fourth, access to credit is a critical factor for business survival during crises. However, particularly in developing countries, women entrepreneurs are often discriminated against when attempting to access formal lending schemes. Fifth, women have seen their burden of care work increase because of closure of schools and childcare facilities, and the provision of basic health care at home. Finally, lockdown and social isolation policies, coupled with the financial stress that families and individuals are experiencing, have dramatically exacerbated domestic violence.[25]

5.3.2 *The Rescue Measures in LDCs*

By and large, all countries have made efforts to provide support to their populations and economies to shoulder the social and economic impacts of the pandemic. According to the COVID-19 Global Gender Response Tracker,[26] a total of 4,968 measures have been put in place so far; 1,605 measures, less than a third of the total, can be regarded as gender-sensitive

[25] UN Women, 'Impact of COVID-19 on Violence against Women and Girls and Service Provision: UN Women Rapid Assessment and Findings' (2020) <www.unwomen.org/sites/default/files/Headquarters/Attachments/Sections/Library/Publications/2020/Impact-of-COVID-19-on-violence-against-women-and-girls-and-service-provision-en.pdf> accessed 8 May 2022; Isabelle Durant and Pamela Coke-Hamilton, 'COVID-19 Requires Gender-Equal Responses to Save Economies' (UNCTAD 1 April 2020) <https://unctad.org/news/covid-19-requires-gender-equal-responses-save-economies> accessed 8 May 2022.

[26] The Tracker is a joint effort by UNDP and UN Women. Information on countries' measures is collected based on publicly available information, media reports, official documents, and information provided by UNDP and UN Women country offices. Because measures change over time, some reported measures may have expired while new measures may have been introduced since the latest updated of the Tracker carried out in November 2021. Moreover, considering that at times measures included in the Tracker are based on announcements made by government officers or reported by the press, the actual implementation of such measures is not fully certain. *See* UNDP, 'Gender Tracker' <https://data.undp.org/gendertracker/> accessed 8 May 2022.

since they address unpaid care (226 measures),[27] violence against women (853),[28] and women's economic security (526).[29] Most measures are meant to support women who have been victims of violence, or the establishment of prevention and reporting mechanisms, in line with the view that women's needs are in particular found in the private sphere.

The following section provides an overview of the rescue measures put in place by LDCs as available on the COVID-19 Global Gender Response Tracker. The purpose is to assess whether and to what extent those measures are directly targeting women, are targeting economic sectors and functions where women are particularly active, or are supporting women as heads of households or as those mainly responsible for the well-being of the household. In other words, the objective is to investigate whether the rescue packages deployed by the LDCs are providing, directly or indirectly, by purpose or by coincidence, significant support to women as far as their economic security is concerned.[30]

5.3.2.1 Cash Transfers and Emergency Food Distribution

To alleviate pandemic-driven extreme poverty, almost all LDCs have resorted to cash transfers and/or emergency food distribution in favour of the most vulnerable and food-insecure households, on a monthly basis, for a determined period of time, or as a one-off intervention. Since female poverty has become particularly acute during the pandemic and is expected to last for several years to come, it can be assumed that women are benefiting from these measures, especially when, within the household, they are those directly receiving cash or food, as is the case in Sierra Leone and Togo, according to the Tracker.

27 They include: (a) social protection measures that support women and men with care responsibilities or improve services for populations with care needs and (b) labour market measures that help female and male workers with care responsibilities to cope with the rising demand for unpaid care.

28 Measures to tackle violence against women are by default gender-sensitive. They are not analysed in this chapter.

29 They include: (a) social protection measures that target women or prioritize them as the main recipients of benefits, (b) labour market measures aimed at improving women's access to paid work and training, and (c) fiscal and economic measures that channel support to female-dominated sectors of the economy.

30 This implies that this chapter considers as 'gender-sensitive' measures those that, without specifically targeting women, may benefit them. Therefore, some measures that according to the Tracker are not 'gender-sensitive' are so in our analysis.

In addition to targeting vulnerable and food-insecure households, some LDCs have identified specific categories of workers and sectors as eligible for cash transfers. They include agricultural and day labourers and domestic workers (Bangladesh), workers in the informal sector (Lesotho, Liberia, Nepal, Niger, Rwanda, Sierra Leone, Togo, and Zambia), including informal street vendors (Bangladesh, Burkina Faso, Liberia), and small businesses (Burundi, Malawi, and Mauritania).

Informal employment dominates to a large extent employment for both men and women, and especially for women, in most LDCs. More than 80 per cent of women in the non-agriculture sector work informally in Madagascar, Mali, Myanmar, Uganda, United Republic of Tanzania, and Zambia.

Street vendors, small-scale and informal cross-border traders, daily wagers, and domestic workers, occupations that include a large share of women, have been badly hit by the pandemic since lockdowns, social distancing measures, and border closures have made these activities unfeasible. It is estimated that women represent around 70 per cent of small-scale and informal cross-border traders in sub-Saharan Africa.[31] Domestic workers are among the most vulnerable groups of workers, and they mostly work informally. According to the International Labour Organization (ILO), around 80 per cent of all domestic workers are women.[32] The workers and occupations targeted for cash transfers seem, therefore, to include many women.

5.3.2.2 Micro, Small, and Medium-Sized Enterprises

The analysis now turns to measures targeting micro, small, and medium-sized enterprises (MSMEs), including both fiscal measures and cash transfers.

The health crisis has made firms face several challenges at the same time, namely, the suspension, at least during the first phase of the pandemic, of most face-to-face operations due to the need to observe social distancing and mobile restrictions, supply chain disruptions, and falling consumer demand.[33]

Globally, there are around 9.3 million formal small and medium-sized enterprises (SMEs) that are fully or partially owned by women, which

[31] UN Women, 'Unleashing the Potential of Women Informal Cross Border Traders to Transform Intra-African Trade' (2010) <www.unwomen.org/sites/default/files/Headquarters/Media/Publications/en/factsheetafricanwomentradersen.pdf> accessed 8 May 2022.

[32] International Labour Organization, 'Who Are Domestic Workers' <www.ilo.org/global/topics/domestic-workers/who/lang–en/index.htm> accessed 8 May 2022.

[33] Jesica Torres, Franklin Maduko, Isis Gaddis, Leonardo Iacovone, and Kathleen Beegle, 'The Impact of the COVID-19 Pandemic on Women-Led Businesses' (2021) World Bank Policy Research Working Paper 9817 <https://openknowledge.worldbank.org/handle/10986/36435> accessed 8 May 2022.

corresponds to approximately one-third of all formal SMEs.[34] These firms play a crucial role in the economy worldwide, including in the LDCs, as a source of employment and income generation, and as such they have been targeted in many rescue packages.

According to the LDC MSME Impact Survey, conducted in July–August 2020 across 2,245 firms in all LDCs, firms mainly operate in the sectors of tourism and catering (20 per cent), textiles and crafts (18 per cent), and industrial goods (15.3 per cent).[35] MSMEs have suffered a significant reduction in business capacity and anticipate a notable reduction in their annual revenue due to COVID-19. As much as 88 per cent of respondents indicated that they were operating on less than 75 per cent of business capacity; over 52 per cent anticipated a reduction in revenues; 34 per cent stated that they risked shutting down in the coming three months; and 35 per cent reported having laid off staff. Findings from the same survey show that the pandemic hit female-intensive sectors such as textiles and crafts, and personal and care services more severely than male-intensive sectors, such as finance, professional, and technology services. Moreover, female-led SMEs have reported higher rates of lay-offs and fewer resources to sustain their businesses in the short and medium term compared to male-owned SMEs.[36]

Cash shortages have in particular affected women-led firms. This reflects the barriers women's businesses face in securing adequate finance, a worrying situation experienced already in the pre-pandemic era. Moreover, in the pandemic era, alternative sources of finance, be they personal savings or borrowing from friends and family, have dried up.[37] Without easy and reasonable (in terms of ceilings) repayment and interest conditions, and access to credit, most companies, especially micro and small ones, are unable to shoulder the economic burden.

Angola has provided financial support to maintain minimum levels of activity of MSMEs in the manufacturing sector through funds for the payment

[34] IFC, 'Women-Owned SMEs: A Business Opportunity for Financial Institutions' (2014) <www.ifc.org/wps/wcm/connect/44b004b2-ed46-48fc-8ade-aaof485069a1/WomenOwnedSMes+Report-Final.pdf?MOD=AJPERES&CVID=kiiZZDZ> accessed 8 May 2022.

[35] IFC, 'Women-Owned SMEs: A business Opportunity for Financial Institutions: A Market and Credit Gap Assessment and IFC's Portfolio Gender Baseline' (2014) <www.ifc.org/wps/wcm/connect/44b004b2-ed46-48fc-8ade-aaof485069a1/WomenOwnedSMes+Report-Final.pdf?MOD=AJPERES&CVID=kiiZZDZ> accessed 8 May 2022; UNCDF, 'The State of Small Businesses in the LDCs Taking the Pulse of SMEs in the LDC Markets during COVID-19: LDC SME Impact Survey Technical Presentation of Preliminary Findings' (9 September 2020) <https://infogram.com/1prm101ryl2nqlagqoew595e59im5vrgzv5?live> accessed 8 May 2022.

[36] IFC, 'Women-Owned SMEs' (n 35).

[37] Torres et al., 'The Impact of the COVID-19 Pandemic on Women-Led Businesses' (n 33).

of social security contributions and the removal of some administrative procedures. It has provided special credit lines to finance family agri-business and supported the capitalization of cooperatives in the agriculture, livestock, and fisheries sector, a sector that employs 56 per cent of women. Bangladesh has enacted a rescue package for SMEs at a concessionary interest rate. More than half of the interest is borne by the government to save firms and safeguard employment. Businesses are also allowed lower interest rates for imported raw materials. Burkina Faso, Chad, and Lao PDR have implemented tax relief measures for formal and informal MSMEs, and in the case of Mauritania for the artisanal fisheries sector. The Gambia enacted deferred tax returns for the wholesale and retail trade activities, which account for 45 per cent of women's employment. Guinea has allowed banks to provide facilitated credit to MSMEs. In Liberia, the government has borne the loans owned by small and informal women traders and helped banks to increase lending to new borrowers. Senegal provides interest-free loans and subsidies to women entrepreneurs in the informal sector who have experienced significant operating losses due to the pandemic. The measures target a total of 1,000 beneficiaries working in areas such as fisheries, hairdressing, sewing, crafts, processing of agricultural products, and petty trade. In Uganda, the government has allocated funds to microfinance institutions to improve access to finance for MSMEs. The Uganda Development Bank offers low-interest financing to manufacturing, agribusiness, and other private sector firms. Malawi has put in place two measures in support of MSMEs. The first – an emergency cash transfer programme – involves small businesses which receive the equivalent of a USD 40 monthly payment, matching the country's minimum wage, through mobile cash transfer. The second measure – increasing loans under the Malawi Enterprise Development Fund – is meant to support MSMEs that have been seriously affected by the pandemic. Mauritania provided financial support for three months to small individual businesses. In consideration of women's role as micro and small entrepreneurs, it can be assumed that they could benefit from the rescue measures targeting MSMEs.

5.3.2.3 Tourism

The tourism sector was among the hardest hit by the pandemic. Social distancing measures and travel restrictions have driven the sector to an almost complete halt in 2020.[38] The situation is improving at present with the

[38] The UNWTO reports a fall in arrival of 84 per cent during January to May 2020, as compared to the same period in 2019. In an earlier assessment, the UNWTO estimates that the loss in direct tourism gross domestic product is USD 2 trillion.

relaxation of most measures; as of May 2022, the sector has recovered to almost half of the 2019 pre-pandemic levels, though geopolitical tensions, rising fuel prices, and disruptions at major airports may reverse the recovery trend.[39] Globally, tourism earnings diminished by 40 per cent during the first half of 2020 as compared to the same period in 2019, badly hitting LDCs dependent on tourism revenues, as it is the case for Sao Tome and Principe, Timor-Leste, Samoa, Vanuatu, Comoros, and the Gambia (in decreasing order) for which, in 2018, tourism contributed to more than 40 per cent of export revenues.

Employment in the tourism sector tends to be informal and temporary, for both men and women. In Tanzania, for example, 38 per cent of men and 39 per cent of women in the tourism sector do not have formal written contracts. In Mozambique, 50 per cent of men and 46 per cent of women work in the tourism sector under unclear contractual arrangements.[40]

Beyond wage employment, tourism provides women with opportunities for entrepreneurship, for example as owners of small tourism outlets, producers and sellers of handicrafts, tour guides, and providers of food services.[41] Several LDC governments have therefore put in place measures meant to support the tourism sector. Bangladesh and the Gambia have provided emergency cash transfer to hotel workers. Bhutan supports workers in the sector through cash for work and cash for reskilling. Cambodia provides wage subsidies and training for tourism workers. Guinea allows banks to provide facilitated credit to businesses operating in the hotel, restaurant, and transport sectors. Lesotho has provided a grant covering the tourism and food sectors. Burkina Faso, Cambodia, Cameroon, Madagascar, Mali, Lesotho, and Niger have implemented favourable tax measures to support the tourism sector or specific subsectors. Also in this case, we can assume that women have benefited from the rescue measures targeting the tourism sector.

5.3.2.4 Textile and Garments

Another sector badly hit by the pandemic is the textiles and garment sector, which is one of the most female-intensive sectors worldwide, including in the LDCs, and a key economic sector for some LDCs.

[39] World Tourism Organization, 'International Tourism Consolidates Strong Recovery Amidst Growing Challenges' (1 August 2022) <www.unwto.org/news/international-tourism-consolidates-strong-recovery-admidst-growing-challenges> accessed on 7 September 2022.

[40] World Tourism Organization, 'Global Report on Women in Tourism – Second Edition' (2019) <www.e-unwto.org/doi/book/10.18111/9789284420384> accessed 8 May 2022.

[41] World Tourism Organization and ILO, 'Measuring Employment in the Tourism Industries – Guide with Best Practices' (2014) <www.e-unwto.org/doi/book/10.18111/9789284416158> accessed 8 May 2022.

In 2017, 85 per cent of workers in the apparel sector were women in Cambodia,[42] and 90 per cent in Myanmar.[43] In Bangladesh, the number of women employed in the ready-made garment sector is estimated at 3.3 million, corresponding to 80 per cent of all workers in the sector.[44]

The pandemic has led to a collapse in the global demand for clothing. During the first phase of the health crisis, a number of international brands and retailers cancelled orders, including for products already fully or partially manufactured, delayed payments, or demanded discounts. In Myanmar, during 2020, garment factories saw orders fall by 75 per cent due to the pandemic, which prompted many factories to cut their workforce or permanently close.[45] In Bangladesh, half of suppliers that participated in a survey administered in March 2020 had the bulk of their production cancelled, while 80 per cent declared that they were unable to provide severance pay when order cancellation resulted in worker dismissals. By the end of March 2020, at least 1.2 million workers had already been affected by order cancellations.[46]

Bangladesh has set up a special scheme to support export-oriented garment companies. Owners are allowed an interest-free loan from the scheme to keep their factories running. Cambodia provides wage subsidies and training for workers of the garment sector and tax holidays for firms operating in the sector. Cambodia, Haiti, and Lesotho provide subsidies for workers in the textiles industry. Here again it can be concluded that women in principle can benefit from rescue measures targeting the textiles and garment sector.

5.3.3 *The Magnitude of the Problem and the Resources Available*

Once it is assessed that some rescue measures have directly targeted women, especially as heads of vulnerable households, and other measures deliberately

[42] ILO and IFC, 'Towards Gender Equality: Better Factories Cambodia' (2018) <https://betterwork.org/wp-content/uploads/2018/04/Toward-Gender-Equality-2017-18.pdf> accessed 8 May 2022.

[43] ILO, 'Weaving Gender: Challenges and Opportunities for the Myanmar Garment Industry' (2018) <www.ilo.org/wcmsp5/groups/public/—asia/—ro-bangkok/—ilo-yangon/documents/publication/wcms_672751.pdf> accessed 8 May 2022.

[44] ILO, 'Understanding the Gender Composition and Experience of Ready-Made Garment (RMG) Workers in Bangladesh', BGD/16/03/MUL (3 September 2020).

[45] Hannah Abdulla, 'Myanmar Garment Factory Orders Fall by 75 Per Cent' (Just-style 3 September 2020) <www.just-style.com/news/myanmar-garment-factory-orders-fall-by-75_id139507.aspx> accessed 8 May 2022.

[46] Mark Anner, 'Abandoned? The Impact of Covid-19 on Workers and Businesses at the Bottom of Global Garment Supply Chains' (2020) Pennsylvania State University Center for Global Workers' Rights Research Report <www.workersrights.org/wp-content/uploads/2020/03/Abandoned-Penn-State-WRC-Report-March-27-2020.pdf> accessed 8 May 2022.

or by coincidence have covered sectors and functions that include a large share of women, the next question is how effective these measures can be. Indeed, one-off interventions, transfer of very limited amounts of cash, and support provided during one or two months may be able to alleviate immediate and acute emergencies, but not to provide sufficient 'breathing space' for workers and firms to survive and plan for the future.

LDCs have been able to devote a median USD 18 per inhabitant in terms of additional spending or forgone revenues, which is a tiny fraction of the median USD 1,365 that developed countries were able to dedicate to their inhabitants.[47] Substantially higher amounts are necessary for the rescue packages to be effective and make a difference, especially for those particularly hit by the pandemic, such as women. Moreover, it is necessary to include in the rescue packages not only provisions meant to face the most acute phase of the crisis, but also measures that will allow LDCs to be back on track to meet the SDGs. Indeed, the seventeen SDGs are interlinked. Gender equality and women's and girls' empowerment will be the result not only of fully implementing SDG 5, but also other relevant SDGs. They include SDG 1 on poverty eradication, SDG 2 on ending hunger, SDG 8 on inclusive and sustainable economic growth, SDG 10 on reducing inequality within and among countries, and SDG 17 on strengthening the means of implementation and revitalizing the global partnership for sustainable development.

Domestically, LDCs need to strengthen their fiscal capacity, increase domestic resource mobilization, and improve the effectiveness of public expenditure. From the outside, they need a mix of financial resources, debt alleviation, transfer of technology, capacity-building, and inclusive and equitable trade at the global and regional level. In its 2020 LDCs Report, UNCTAD estimates that the total average expenditure needed to meet selected SDGs varies from USD 875.9 to USD 1,464.9 billion per year for the group of LDCs, once combining the forecast total social and environmental spending with estimated investments.[48]

5.4 THE WAY FORWARD

Going back to 'business as usual' is not a suitable alternative for the LDCs, especially for women living there. This chapter has provided an overview of

[47] UNCTAD, 'The Least Developed Countries Report 2020 – Productive Capacities for the New Decade', UNCTAD/LDC/2020 (2020).

[48] Ibid.

the main shortcomings that the LDC were already facing before the pandemic hit them. The situation has dramatically worsened since. If not addressed, these shortcomings will curtail LDCs' prospects for development and for a more beneficial participation in the global economy, which will reverberate for women's prospects.

LDCs have put in place a host of policy measures that aim at attenuating the adverse impact of the pandemic on their populations and economies. As this chapter has shown, several of these measures address concerns and problems faced by women in LDCs, though the funds available undoubtedly fall short of the needs.

Looking forward, LDCs need to design and implement policies and strategies aimed at their mid- to long-term development prospects in such a way that women's concerns are properly tackled. Addressing and overcoming the longstanding barriers women face in all spheres should be at the top of the new agenda of all countries, including the LDCs.

What would building forward differently mean for the LDCs and especially for women in the LDCs? A number of measures are suggested in the following. While some of them refer to deepening and broadening policy measures adopted in response to the pandemic shock, others are targeted at the long-standing development challenges of LDCs.

5.4.1 *Building Forward Differently*

- Human capital should be upgraded. Improved education for women would facilitate the shift from precarious and low-skill jobs to more stable and formal employment. In particular, enhanced access to education would increase women's openings in sectors that attract better pay and provide opportunity for skills and career development. Shortage of qualified workers is often mentioned as one of the main obstacles for firms to expand in the LDCs.[49] The emergence of advanced technology is making this constraint even more damaging. Improving the quality of education and encouraging women to enrol in STEM disciplines would provide a win–win solution.
- The business environment needs to improve. Three regional groupings in Africa – Common Market for Eastern and Southern Africa (COMESA), East African Community (EAC), and Southern African

[49] The 2007 UNCTAD LDC Report documents the issue of brain drain and brain gain. *See* UNCTAD, Least Developed Countries Report 2007 (2007).

Development Community (SADC),[50] each of them including several LDCs – have some of the longest processing times and highest costs for imports and exports compared to other regions of the world. To overcome this, a growing number of LDCs are putting in place measures to cut red tape, lower barriers to entry, foster competitiveness, and facilitate trade. Such measures may benefit actual or potential entrepreneurs, including female MSMEs and small-scale cross-border traders. Trade facilitation reforms and human capital improvements should be coordinated to ensure a switch to more productive and technology-intensive sectors, and make entrepreneurship, especially female entrepreneurship, a sustainable and growth-oriented endeavour instead of a survival economic activity. A precondition to boosting female entrepreneurship is to facilitate women's access to credit, not only as an emergency measure, but as a way to overcome a long-standing form of gender discrimination that impedes female-headed enterprises from growing and playing a more positive role in the economy.[51]

- A renewed focus is needed in agriculture and rural development. The sector should be a priority for inclusive and sustainable growth in the LDCs in consideration of its role as the main employer of men and women and its contribution to poverty alleviation and food security. Improved access to inputs and extension services, crop diversification, and agro-processing are all developments that would benefit the LDCs and women in the LDCs, provided that women's specific needs and the gender challenges that these developments can imply are addressed.
- Services are increasingly important in the economy of the LDCs, and their role in manufacturing is growing through 'servicification'.[52] The linkages between the two sectors – manufacturing and services – may contribute to them reinforcing each other and could lead to more sophisticated, technology-intensive, and value-added outcomes. Again, in this case, the distributional effects of these developments should be

[50] Agreement Establishing a Common Market for Eastern and Southern Africa, Kampala, 5 November 1993; Treaty for the Establishment of the East African Community, Tanzania, 30 November 1999; Treaty of the Southern African Development Community, Windhoek, 17 August 1992.

[51] *See* UNCTAD, Entrepreneurship Policy Framework and Implementation Guidance (2012) para. 107 et seq.

[52] *See*, for instance, UNCTAD, 'The Role of the Services Economy and Trade in Structural Transformation and Inclusive Development, Note by the Secretariat', TD/B/C.I/MEM.4/14 (14 June 2017) para. 14 et seq.

carefully assessed to avoid leaving some segments of the population, including women, behind.

- Now that the emergency is over, most safety nets have been removed'. The ongoing response to the COVID-19 pandemic has provided good examples of measures that may be beneficial in the medium run and not only to face emergencies. Several LDCs have extended their safety nets to informal workers. Such measures should continue once the health emergency is over since they are essential both for social cohesion and to accelerate inclusive economic recovery. Moreover, measures should be put in place to facilitate business formalization.
- Women's participation in decision-making needs to be enhanced. Women are playing a minor role in the task forces set up to design and implement COVID-19 rescue packages. According to the COVID-19 Global Gender Response Tracker, of the 262 task forces for which membership data is available, women make up less than a quarter of members and are not represented at all on 10 per cent of all task forces. The inclusion of explicit gender considerations in the medium- to long-term recovery plans would be greatly facilitated by the participation of women in the discussion and decision-making processes. For this to happen, ministries of gender equality and women's groups should be given adequate resources and an influential role in policymaking.

5.4.2 *Building Forward Differently through Trade*

Trade policy is one of the important tools that can be used to increase LDC inclusion in the world economy and offer new economic opportunities to women. Devising measures that promote women's participation in trade and ensuring that the benefits from trade reach women and men equally can be an effective way for LDCs to step up their efforts towards a more inclusive and gender-equal order after the pandemic.

- It is important to keep markets open. Ensuring a free, fair, non-discriminatory, transparent, predictable, and stable trade environment remains essential to ensure the availability of essential goods and promote a strong economic recovery from which all should benefit.[53]

[53] Echoing the call by the G20, *see* EU, 'G20 Ministerial Statement on Trade and Digital Economy' <https://g20-digital.go.jp/asset/pdf/g20_2019_japan_digital_statement.pdf> accessed 8 May 2022.

- Make the trade debate gender-responsive. The WTO Joint Declaration on Trade and Women's Economic Empowerment launched at the margins of the 11th Ministerial Conference of the WTO in 2017 signalled the departure of the trade community from its longstanding position that trade is 'gender-neutral'.[54] Discussions, exchange of experiences, and reviews of research work on trade and gender were held at the WTO following the adoption of the declaration and culminated in the setting up of the informal Working Group on Trade and Gender in September 2020. The Working Group took on board the ambitious task to launch a new declaration at the following Ministerial Conference, MC12. Negotiations resulted in the Draft Joint Ministerial Declaration on the Advancement of Gender Equality and Women's Economic Empowerment within Trade. One of the objectives of the declaration was to explore and analyse a gender perspective and women's economic empowerment issues in the work of the WTO. Though the declaration ultimately was not tabled at MC12, member countries may still be willing to include a gender perspective in WTO work. Such a development could lead to transformative results since the analysis on the nexus between trade and gender will permeate WTO work rather than be clustered in a specific working group or specific meetings where gender issues are on the agenda.[55] The shortcomings that women in LDCs face could then be addressed and solutions discussed in several WTO bodies, those where the link between the issues under discussion and women's economic empowerment is rather straightforward, for example trade facilitation, MSMEs, Technical Barriers to Trade (TBT), and Sanitary and Phytosanitary measures (SPS), or public procurement, but also when discussing agriculture, services, or intellectual property rights, to mention a few. While it may be less evident, there is a close link between discussions and negotiations on these issues and women's enhanced or diminished opportunities in these areas.
- Conduct *ex ante* evaluations of the gender-differentiated impacts of trade. The approach to trade negotiations has long been that the impact of a new trade agreement should be assessed for a country as a whole. Such an approach, however, fails to identify how a trade agreement or a trade

[54] WTO, 'Joint Declaration on Trade and Women's Economic Empowerment on the Occasion of the WTO Ministerial Conference in Buenos Aires in December 2017' (2017) <www.wto.org/english/thewto_e/minist_e/mc11_e/genderdeclarationmc11_e.pdf> accessed 8 May 2022.

[55] For more information and analysis on this, *see* Mia Mikic, 'Advances in Feminizing the WTO' (Chapter 3 in this book).

reform may impact different segments of the population. Identifying those who will benefit from the new measure and conversely those who may be negatively impacted by it may be the first step to put in place buffer measures, at least in an initial phase of implementing the new measure, or to reconsider the terms of the negotiations to mitigate the foreseen negative effects. Indeed, while a trade reform may overall be beneficial for a country, it may not be so, for example, for the rural population, or for the elderly, or for women and girls. The call to conduct gender assessments prior to negotiating a trade agreement was included in the 1995 Beijing Platform for Action.[56] Governments were advised to seek to ensure that trade agreements do not negatively impact women's new and traditional economic activities, and, more broadly, that macro- and microeconomic policies are assessed through an *ex ante* gender analysis and reformulated if harmful impacts are expected to occur. At present, Canada and the European Union provide the most advanced examples of conducting *ex ante* gender assessments of trade agreements. The Canadian Gender-Based Analysis Plus (GBA+) mandates the integration of GBA+ in all policies, plans, programmes, and initiatives, including trade agreements, to assess their impacts on different groups of people.[57] The GBA+ has been used for the first time with reference to a trade agreement during the Canada–Mercosur Free Trade Agreement (FTA) negotiations. In the case of the EU, Sustainability Impact Assessments (SIAs) analyse the potential economic, social, and environmental impacts of a proposed trade agreement while the negotiations are ongoing. Gender considerations are introduced to SIAs among the social themes under 'equality'. The use of *ex ante* gender assessments will hopefully expand and become a regular feature of trade negotiations. Some outstanding issues related to the scope and feasibility of the assessments remain, including data availability to conduct impact assessments that are not limited to analysing the potential impact of an agreement on women's employment in the formal sector. Moreover, a key point is to ensure that the findings of the impact assessments are duly considered during the negotiations and reflected in the outcomes. An *ex*

[56] Beijing Declaration and Platform for Action, *Beijing +5 Political Declaration and Outcome* (UN 1995, reprinted by UN Women 2015). *See also* UN Women, 'The Beijing Platform for Action: Inspiration Then and Now' <https://beijing20.unwomen.org/en/about> accessed 8 May 2022.

[57] For more information on Canada's impact assessment approach, *see* Marie-France Paquet and Georgina Wainwright-Kemdirim, 'Crafting Canada's Gender-Responsive Trade Policy' (Chapter 14 in this book).

ante gender assessment of the African Continental Free Trade Area (AfCFTA) would be especially useful to support the development of national strategies that countries are currently called upon to develop.[58] While the continental agreement is expected to provide numerous new opportunities, it is crucial to assess whether these opportunities will equally reach men and women. If they do not, measures should be introduced to rectify any foreseen negative effect.

- It is also pertinent to enhance and strengthen the collection of data. A full appreciation of the distributive effects of trade, including on women and men, requires the availability of a wide range of sex-disaggregated statistics. While data on education and health, labour force participation, and political participation are usually available in LDCs, statistics on working conditions, consumption, time use, entrepreneurship, and on policies and laws that influence gender equality, among others, are still difficult to find. This is an area where international organizations could provide support to the statistical offices of the LDCs.
- Ensuring policy coherence is quintessential. Building forward differently implies coordination between policies, both at the domestic level and between domestic policies and regional/multilateral ones. If policy coherence was necessary in the pre-pandemic era, it is even more so at present, when countries face multifaceted challenges from COVID-19.

5.5 CONCLUSION

This chapter has briefly presented the position of the LDC in the world economy and in international trade and has focused on women in the LDCs, looking at the role women play in the economy and in trade. It has highlighted the many problems that women face in the LDCs, exacerbated by unresolved development challenges and currently magnified by the pandemic.

The LDCs, as all other countries, implemented rescue measures to shelter their people and economies from the impact of the pandemic. A considerable number of measures appear to have the potential to directly or indirectly, by purpose or by coincidence, benefit women. They include those supporting MSMEs, highly female-intensive sectors such as agriculture, tourism, and the textiles and garment sectors, or informal workers. However, the amount that the LDCs have been able to devote to their inhabitants is extremely low –

[58] Agreement Establishing the African Continental Free Trade Area, Kigali, 21 March 2018.

USD 18 per inhabitant as compared to USD 1,365 in rich countries, with a consequent limited and short-term effect. To make their interventions more impactful and long-term, at the domestic level LDCs need to strengthen their fiscal capacity, increase domestic resource mobilization, and improve the effectiveness of public expenditure, while from the outside they need a mix of financial resources, debt alleviation, transfer of technology, and capacity-building.

The chapter concludes by highlighting some measures that would help the LDCs build forward differently for the benefit of their populations, and especially women. The upgrading of human capital, the overall improvement of the business environment, a renewed interest in the agricultural sector and rural development, special attention to the development and gender implications of further linking the manufacturing and the services sectors, and support for women's participation in decision-making processes, including those related to the rescue packages, were singled out. Moving more specifically to how trade could contribute to improve the prospects for women in the LDCs, the chapter emphasizes that some developments look particularly promising, including conducting on a regular basis *ex ante* gender assessments of trade agreements, strengthening the collection of data that would allow the distributive effects of trade to be grasped fully, making gender considerations a feature of all WTO work and deliberations, and ensuring that the trade environment remains free, fair, non-discriminatory, transparent, predictable, and stable. The chapter calls for policy coherence between domestic, regional, and international policies and initiatives. Coherence is identified as a precondition for countries, including the LDCs, to be able to face the unprecedented human, social, and economic challenges deriving from the pandemic and avoid women bearing a disproportionate brunt of it.

6

Gender-Inclusive Governance for e-Commerce, Digital Trade, and Trade in Services

A Look at Domestic Regulation

AMALIE GIØDESEN THYSTRUP*

ABSTRACT

The chapter builds on the author's article titled 'Gender-Inclusive Governance for E-Commerce', which broke new ground by examining electronic commerce (e-commerce) from a gender perspective, and the proposal for a provision on gender equality in services domestic regulation (services DR). Since then, both the provision and the policy landscape have developed. The provision was included in the negotiations on services DR that concluded on 2 December 2021 among the sixty-seven World Trade Organization (WTO) members participating in the Joint Statement Initiative (JSI) on Services Domestic Regulation. The chapter aims to meet the moment with a restatement of the framework that the article proposed, using original and new analysis by including the concluded text. The chapter generates new knowledge that is actionable for policymakers and stakeholders by responding to three questions: What is gender-inclusive governance? What is the relationship between gender divides, e-commerce, digital trade, and trade in services? What policy interventions are necessary, and why, to meet the moment? The goal is to discuss ways to attain gender-inclusive governance for trade policy at this unique time for implementing changes that are fit for the digital age. The

* The main body of the book chapter is a version of the author's article. *See* Amalie Giødesen Thystrup, 'Gender-Inclusive Governance for E-Commerce' (2020) 21(4) *Journal of World Trade and Investment* 595–629. The goal of this chapter is to direct the proposed framework to not solely e-commerce but also to digital trade and services trade. Thereby, the chapter adds another layer – that of the four modes of services supply and the relationship between gender, e-commerce, digital trade, and services trade. Furthermore, it unpacks and updates the article's analysis of the provision on gender equality proposed as part of the WPDR and later the JSI's disciplines on services domestic regulation. The chapter leaves out RTA experiences and other agendas included in the article to save space and to support the focus on the WTO agenda. Needless to say, all errors are entirely my own. Contact <amaliethystrup@gmail.com>

chapter argues that multi-level dedicated gender-inclusive governance can contribute to closing the gender gap.

6.1 INTRODUCTION: POLICYMAKING FOR TRADE AND GENDER

Following the 11th Ministerial Conference (MC11), World Trade Organization (WTO) debates among members have concentrated around four substantive agendas: investment facilitation; micro, small, and medium-sized enterprises (MSMEs); services DR pursuant to Article VI:4 of the General Agreement on Trade in Services; and e-commerce. The four agendas produced joint initiatives announced on 13 December 2017 during the final day of the MC11.[1] Among the four JSIs, negotiations between ultimately sixty-seven WTO members on services DR successfully concluded on 2 December 2021.[2]

The WTO discussions on the interplay between the cross-cutting agenda for gender equality anchored in the Joint Declaration on Trade and Women's Economic Empowerment on the Occasion of the WTO Ministerial Conference in Buenos Aires in December 2017 (the Buenos Aires Declaration on Women and Trade) and the four Ministerial Statements picked up steam post-MC11.[3] These efforts see the WTO hosting a series of

[1] The joint initiatives for E-Commerce, MSMEs, and investment facilitation were launched at MC11, on 13 December 2017. *See* WTO, 'Joint Statement on Electronic Commerce, Ministerial Conference Eleventh Session Buenos Aires, 10–13 December 2017', WT/MIN (17)/60 (13 December 2017); WTO, 'Joint Ministerial Statement on Investment Facilitation for Development, Ministerial Conference Eleventh Session Buenos Aires, 10–13 December 2017', WT/MIN(17)/59 (13 December 2017); and WTO, 'Joint Ministerial Statement – Declaration on the Establishment of a WTO Informal Work Programme for MSMEs', WT/MIN(17)/58 (13 December 2017). *See also* WTO, 'New Initiatives on Electronic Commerce, Investment Facilitation and MSMEs' (13 December 2017) <www.wto.org/english/news_e/news17_e/minis_13dec17_e.htm> accessed 8 May 2022. Proponents of DR had hoped for a DR outcome at the MC11, based on a consolidated text that included a provision on gender equality, but *in lieu* a Joint Ministerial Statement on services DR with more signatories was signed. *See* WTO, 'Joint Ministerial Statement on Services Domestic Regulation, Ministerial Conference Eleventh Session Buenos Aires, 10–13 December 2017', WT/MIN(17)/61 (13 December 2017).

[2] WTO, 'Negotiations on Services Domestic Regulation Conclude Successfully in Geneva' (2 December 2017) <www.wto.org/english/news_e/news21_e/jssdr_02dec21_e.htm> accessed 8 May 2022. *See also* WTO, Declaration on the Conclusion of Negotiations on Services Domestic Regulation, WT/L/1129 (2 December 2021).

[3] WTO, 'Joint Declaration on Trade and Women's Economic Empowerment on the Occasion of the WTO Ministerial Conference in Buenos Aires in December 2017' (2017) <www.wto.org/english/thewto_e/minist_e/mc11_e/genderdeclarationmc11_e.pdf> accessed 8 May

discussions sparked by the declaration on a range of specific topics to share best practices and national experiences with a view to unlocking trade benefits for women.[4] Open to all members, the Informal Working Group on Trade and Gender meets at the WTO to further the discussion.[5]

New and enhanced disciplines on services DR, including a provision on gender equality, were projected to deliver outcomes at the MC12 in June 2022, initially scheduled to be held in Geneva from 30 November until 3 December 2021. Participants in the negotiations on DR concluded text-based discussions at their meeting on 27 September 2021. Signatories to the initiative proceeded to circulate national schedules of specific commitment pursuant to the General Agreement on Trade in Services (GATS).[6]

These efforts were to pave the way for the conclusion of the negotiations by MC12 in 2021.[7] Despite the postponement of MC12,[8] negotiators persisted and reached an agreement on services DR among the JSI's sixty-seven WTO members on 2 December 2021 (JSI 2021).[9] As a plurilateral agreement within the WTO, the JSI's disciplines will be applied on a most-favoured nation (MFN) basis, and the members that are signatories will inscribe any commitments into their schedules under GATS as additional commitments.[10] This means that it will benefit the full WTO membership, and not solely the sixty-seven signatories.[11] The JSI 2021 includes a provision on gender equality

2022. *See also* Rohini Acharya, Olga Falgueras Alamo, Salma Mohamed Thabit Al-Battashi, Anoush der Boghossian, Naghm Ghei, Tania Parcero Herrera, Lee Ann Jackson, Ulla Kask, Claudia Locatelli, Gabrielle Marceau, Ioana-Virginia Motoc, Anna Caroline Müller, Nora Neufeld, Simon Padilla, Josefita Pardo de Léon, Stella Perantakou, Nadezhda Sporysheva, and Christiane Wolff, 'Trade and Women – Opportunities for Women in the Framework of the World Trade Organization'(2019) 22(3) *Journal of International Economic Law* 323–354.

4 WTO, 'DG Azevêdo: Global Cooperation on Digital Economy Vital to Unlock Trade Benefits for Women (*WTO Speeches* 1 July 2019) <www.wto.org/english/news_e/spra_e/spra268_e.htm> accessed 8 May 2022.

5 WTO, 'Informal Working Group on Trade and Gender' (2017) <www.wto.org/english/tratop_e/womenandtrade_e/iwg_trade_gender_e.htm> accessed 15 September 2022.

6 WTO, 'Joint Initiative on Services Domestic Regulation – Schedules of specific commitments', INF/SDR/3/Rev.1 (2 December 2021).

7 WTO, 'Participants in Domestic Regulation Talks Conclude Text Negotiations, on Track for MC12 Deal' (27 September 2021) <www.wto.org/english/news_e/news21_e/serv_27sep21_e.htm#.YVN1fj23jHo.linkedin> accessed 8 May 2022.

8 WTO, 'General Council Decides to Postpone MC12 Indefinitely' (26 November 2021) <www.wto.org/english/news_e/news21_e/mc12_26nov21_e.htm> accessed 8 May 2022.

9 WTO, 'Negotiations on Services Domestic Regulation Conclude Successfully in Geneva' (n 2).

10 Ibid.

11 A full account of different types of plurilateral agreements, and their implications, are given in Amalie Giødesen Thystrup, *Governing Trade in Services – Transforming Rulemaking and Trade Integration* (2017) PhD thesis, University of Copenhagen.

where a member adopts or maintains measures relating to the authorization for the supply of a service.

As a plurilateral agreement, the conclusion of JSI 2021 does not form part of the 'Geneva Package' of negotiated multilateral outcomes that MC12 secured when it was successfully concluded on 17 June 2022.[12] However, the three co-chairs of the Informal Working Group on Trade and Gender issued a statement at MC12 highlighting the achievements of WTO members' joint work and reaffirming their commitment to advancing gender equality in trade.[13]

The chapter will organize discussions of the effects of trade on gender gaps around the four modes of supply of services in GATS Article I:2 (a–d), to reflect the crucial avenues for economic participation in the economy that are at stake. After this short introduction of the trade and gender agenda, Section 6.2 outlines the economic structures driving the gender gap and specifically the gender digital divide. The chapter then turns to examining the relationship between gender, e-commerce, digital trade, and services trade in Section 6.3. Next, Section 6.4 restates a framework for gender-inclusive governance for trade and examines policy prescriptions for bridging the gender digital divide. Section 6.5 examines policy interventions in digital trade. Section 6.6 looks at policy interventions in services trade based on a close reading of the provision on gender equality introduced in DR to unlock its legal-political implications. Section 6.7 concludes.

6.2 THE GENDER GAP IN TRADE

According to the World Economic Forum's (WEF) definition, the gender gap is the difference between women and men as reflected in social, political, intellectual, cultural, or economic attainments or attitudes.[14] The chapter subscribes to the understanding that the gender gap encompasses the structural differences women face in terms of (i) the gendered composition of the labour force, (ii) women's primary responsibility for reproductive work, and

[12] *See* WTO, 'Twelfth WTO Ministerial Conference, including the MC12 outcome document', WT/MIN(22)/24 (22 June 2022).

[13] WTO, 'Trade and Gender Co-chairs Affirm Commitment to Gender Equality in Trade at MC12' (12 June 2022) <www.wto.org/english/news_e/news22_e/iwgtg_13jun22_e.htm> accessed 15 September 2022.

[14] Briony Harris, 'What Is the Gender Gap (and Why Is It Getting Wider)?' (World Economic Forum 1 November 2017) <www.weforum.org/agenda/2017/11/the-gender-gap-actually-got-worse-in-2017> accessed 8 May 2022.

(iii) women's differential access to and control over resources relative to men.[15]

Research in the last decade has begun to produce evidence that the assumption that trade reforms will benefit men and women equally does not always hold. Because of the different roles that women and men have in society, trade policy does not automatically generate gender-neutral results.[16] Simply put, trade rules are not gender-neutral.[17] Gender-based inequality in turn impacts trade patterns and trade outcomes because it influences the patterns of resource allocation and competitive advantages of countries.[18] The impact of trade on women and men differs because they tend to operate in different sectors and have differentiated access to resources.[19]

Women are impacted in various and overlapping roles as producers, employees, business owners, managers, and consumers. In turn, these factors shape different supply responses, vulnerabilities to economic change, and, more broadly, abilities to seize export opportunities and absorb adjustment costs.[20] With women as workers, but also as entrepreneurs and business owners, concentrating in less export-oriented sectors such as services, trade liberalization does not extend the same benefits of competition and broader supply that drive down prices.[21]

The International Trade Centre (ITC) finds that the gender gap in trade is largely due to the concentration of women's employment in less export-oriented sectors, notably in services sectors.[22] The Organisation for

[15] Penny Bamber and Cornelia Staritz, 'The Gender Dimensions of Global Value Chains' (2016) ICTSD Policy Paper 3 <www.tralac.org/images/docs/10585/the-gender-dimensions-of-global-value-chains-ictsd-september-2016.pdf> accessed 8 May 2022.

[16] Nadia Rocha, 'Linkages between Trade and Gender' (7 December 2018) <www.wto.org/english/tratop_e/womenandtrade_e/session_1_a_nadia_trade_and_gender_geneva_dec_2018_nr_short_version.pdf> accessed 20 September 2022. *See also* the key report World Bank and WTO, 'Women and Trade: The Role of Trade in Promoting Gender Equality' (2020) <www.wto.org/english/res_e/booksp_e/women_trade_pub2807_e.pdf> accessed 20 September 2022.

[17] The finding is supported by ITC, 'From Europe to the World: Understanding Challenges for European Businesswomen' (2019) 3; Alicia Frohmann, 'Gender Equality and Trade Policy' (2017) WTI Working Paper No. 24/2017 <www.wti.org/media/filer_public/8b/a8/8ba88d03-1a2b-4311-af6a-629d9997c54c/working_paper_no_24_2017_frohmann.pdf> accessed 8 May 2022.

[18] Bamber and Staritz, 'The Gender Dimensions of Global Value Chains' (n 15) 7.

[19] ITC, 'From Europe to the World' (n 17) 3.

[20] Ibid.

[21] Ibid 17–18.

[22] Ibid.

Economic Co-operation and Development (OECD) arrives at the same conclusion.[23]

It is not that services are less 'tradeable' than goods, though services sectors are associated with being less export-oriented than those for goods. In fact, whenever a good is exported and crosses borders, the supply of a service is involved, whether it is at the early stages of design, transportation, or delivery. Thus, GATS Article I:2 (a–d) defines trade in services as the supply of a service from the territory of one member into the territory of any other member (cross-border), in the territory of one member to the service consumer of any other member (consumption abroad), by a service supplier of one member, through commercial presence in the territory of any other member (commercial presence), or by a service supplier of one member through the presence of natural persons of a member in the territory of any other member (mode 4). Moreover, services are integral to global value chains (GVCs), to the effect that services generate trade in value added.

Contemporary research reflects that services are not as often or as easily supplied along the four modes of supply, and instead such services may be supplied domestically and without the service, the worker, or the business crossing any borders to new markets. Thereby, the supply of services would also avoid the regulatory barriers to trade that, generally speaking, are pronounced in services trade.[24] This is why GATS Article VI on DR imposes disciplines on domestic regulations in committed services sectors to discipline domestic regulations that are neither discriminatory nor quantitative in nature, where domestic regulations could nonetheless have trade-restricting effects on services.

A main reason why women tend to concentrate in services is that several of the sectors are gendered. The mining, oil, and gas sectors are examples of sectors with a low ratio of women among its labour force,[25] while high concentrations of women workers are observed in sectors such as education and healthcare.[26] Generally speaking, traditional healthcare cannot be

[23] Jane Korinek, Evdokia Moïsé, and Jakob Tange, 'Trade and Gender: A Framework of Analysis' (2021) OECD Trade Policy Papers No. 246, 3–4, 11–16, 27ff. <https://doi.org/10.1787/6db59d80-en> accessed 8 May 2022.

[24] *See* Marc Bacchetta, Valerie Cerra, Roberta Piermartini, and Maarten Smeets, 'Trade and Inclusive Growth' (2021) IMF Working Papers WP/21/74, 35.

[25] *See* Nick Johnstone and Marta Silva, 'Gender Diversity in Energy: What We Know and What We Don't Know' (*IEA* 6 March 2020) <www.iea.org/commentaries/gender-diversity-in-energy-what-we-know-and-what-we-dont-know> accessed 8 May 2022. It includes a breakdown of data in energy sectors across sub-sectors.

[26] Bacchetta et al., 'Trade and Inclusive Growth' (n 24) 13–14.

supplied at a distance cross-border, and supplying healthcare to consumers abroad requires authorization, while travelling to a different country as a healthcare provider would often require a permit or a visa. Thus, the benefits of trade liberalization would not extend to those sectors and consequently double down on the concentrations of women supplying such services. Data shows that firms that export pay higher wages.[27] More so, arguably it is to the detriment of women workers specifically if the benefits associated with trade do not extend to them.

However, trade does create jobs for women in export-oriented sectors, and those jobs also serve to bring more household resources under women's control, which in turn leads to greater investments in the health and education of future generations. However, differences in wages earned by men and women persist in all countries.[28]

Women's primary responsibility for reproductive work implies a time constraint on participating in trade as women carry most of the burden of child rearing and domestic work, which decreases flexibility.[29] The third structural difference women face pertains to access to and control over resources.[30] A woman may, for example, run the household but not control any capital, or work in agriculture but not hold property rights. Other examples would include lack of recognition before the law preventing a woman from opening a bank account in her own name, or impaired access to education, knowledge, finance, or other means of value that are prerequisites to economic participation.[31]

Against this backdrop, it is submitted that the existing patterns of trade to a large extent perpetuate structural challenges facing women in the economy at large: (i) Women face greater disadvantages in responding to new economic incentives because of gender differences in access to productive resources, including land, credit, education, skills, infrastructure, utilities, and services. (ii) Women tend to concentrate in fewer sectors, and face gendered job segregation. (iii) Time constraints dampen women's response to potential

[27] Ibid 18.

[28] Jane Korinek, 'Trade and Gender: Issues and Interactions' (2005) OECD Trade Policy Working Paper No. 24 <https://doi.org/10.1787/826133710302> accessed 8 May 2022. The OECD defines the gender wage gap as the difference between median earnings of men and women relative to median earnings of men and finds that women earn 13 per cent less than men on average across the OECD. *See* OECD, 'Gender Wage Gap (Indicator)' <https://data.oecd.org/earnwage/gender-wage-gap.htm> accessed 5 April 2022.

[29] Bamber and Staritz, 'The Gender Dimensions of Global Value Chains' (n 15).

[30] Ibid.

[31] *See* World Bank, 'Women, Business and the Law' (2018) <https://openknowledge.worldbank.org/handle/10986/29498> accessed 8 May 2022.

opportunities in new economic activities, and poor infrastructure and poor services heighten these challenges for women in developing countries.[32]

Gender-based differential access to or constraints on labour, time, and resources create a gap. We speak of a 'gender gap' to reflect how the structural differences produce *de jure* and *de facto* discrimination, and because the conditions for the gender gap are based on sex, but on gender more broadly. These structural differences can produce discrimination against more groups of individuals, reflected in a wider concept of gender equality that is sensitive to sex, status, and socio-economic norms. Thus, the gender gap is a multidimensional concept.

Structural challenges produce gender inequality in the economy that interacts in complex ways with socio-economic components such as origins and status, and with the divides in trade and the economy at large that are broadly accepted as determinants of export capabilities, in particular firm size, level of development, and level of digitalization. The gender gap, conceptually centred around labour, time, and resource constraints, interacts with such divides to the effect that the divide can deepen and the gender gap can widen by implication. Cross-cutting divides to that effect would include the trade finance gap, the divide between MSMEs and larger entities, divides between levels of development among countries, and the digital divide. The implication may be understood as the multiplicity of the gender gap.[33]

6.2.1 *The Gender Digital Divide*

Remy defines the gender digital gap as 'the gender differences in resources and capabilities to access and effectively utilise information and communications technology (ICT) within and between countries, regions, sectors and socio-economic groups'.[34] Based on the literature, Remy identifies the following root causes for the gender digital divide: (i) women's limited access to the internet and digital technologies; (ii) low technological literacy rates among women; and (iii) limited visibility of women in decision-making roles within the tech industry.[35] Women are fairly well represented across industries but, as with other gendered sectors, that is not the case in technical jobs, or in technological courses, and the issue here is one of gender stereotyping and

[32] Bamber and Staritz, 'The Gender Dimensions of Global Value Chains' (n 15) 6, cf. 9, table 1.
[33] Thystrup, 'Gender-Inclusive Governance for E-Commerce' (n *) 597 ff, including figure 1.
[34] Jan Yves Remy, 'Closing the Digital Gender Divide through Trade Rules' (CIGI 9 October 2019) <www.cigionline.org/articles/closing-digital-gender-divide-through-trade-rules/> accessed 8 May 2022.
[35] Ibid.

also its impact on education selection.[36] This structural problem produces the conditions for a gender digital divide.

The gender digital divide reflects the multidimensional nature of the gender gap and its multiplicity – indeed, the gender digital divide is a prime example of how the gender gap interacts with other divides, and to what effect. It is submitted that impaired access to information technology (IT) infrastructure and IT skills compounds or exacerbates the gender gap into a gender digital gap. Consequently, the gender digital divide produces disadvantages in seizing technology-driven opportunities because of gender discrimination combined with low access to infrastructure, finance, and IT skills. Indeed, access to these resources are imperative for seizing export opportunities in e-commerce, and arguably in digital trade too, as access to IT skills and IT infrastructure are prerequisites for participation.

6.3 THE RELATIONSHIP BETWEEN GENDER, E-COMMERCE, DIGITAL TRADE, AND TRADE IN SERVICES

One avenue for increasing gender-inclusive participation in the trading system is through e-commerce. The sector performs extremely well and has a number of advantages over traditional commerce, which was rocked by lockdowns prompted by the global pandemic that adversely affected women's economic fortunes in particular.[37] During this time, e-commerce saw the reverse trend, with demand soaring and supply following suit to the extent that the sector generated massive revenues for online shopping giants in particular, despite supply chains experiencing delays in delivery.[38]

A joint paper between the United Nations Conference on Trade and Development (UNCTAD), the WTO, and the World Bank draws on empirical analyses to provide greater clarity to the interplay between women, trade, and ICT in the face of increasing digitalization. The study analyses how

[36] Penny Bamber, 'Gender and Global Value Chains' (WTO 7 December 2018) <www.wto.org/english/tratop_e/womenandtrade_e/session_2_a_paper_4_penny_bamber.pdf> accessed 8 May 2022.

[37] UN Women, 'COVID-19 and Its Economic Toll on Women: The Story behind the Numbers' (16 September 2020) <www.unwomen.org/en/news/stories/2020/9/feature-covid-19-economic-impacts-on-women> accessed 8 May 2022.

[38] OECD, 'E-Commerce in the Time of COVID-19' (7 October 2020) <www.oecd.org/coronavirus/policy-responses/e-commerce-in-the-time-of-covid-19-3a2b78e8/> accessed 8 May 2022.

technological developments such as e-commerce platforms and other digital solutions enable and can enhance women's participation in trade.[39]

Research has also produced recommendations on policy prescriptions for how e-commerce can incorporate gender equality to meet SDG 5 by acting on the goal's explicit reference to using technology to deliver gender equality. This research presents a framework for understanding the multiplicity of gender gaps in e-commerce and provides an analysis of key regulatory and policy challenges women face in e-commerce, before advancing a multi-level approach to incorporating gender-inclusive e-commerce regulation into trade policy.[40]

Services play an increasingly important role in job creation, economic output, and in trade in countries at all development levels.[41] Moreover, the supply of services is ubiquitous to e-commerce. Trade in services is also at the heart of digital trade, which has emerged as a reference point for policy practice dedicated to online trade, almost by definition involving the supply of a service under one of the modes of supply. In the European Commission's taxonomy, and as reflected in the EU's trade policy communication, 'An Open, Sustainable and Assertive Trade Policy' from 2021, digital trade refers to commerce enabled by electronic means, including by telecommunications and/or ICT services. Digital trade covers trade in both goods and services, and it affects all sectors of the economy.[42]

Yet regardless of the policy practices devoted to the subject, trade in services remains severely understudied from a gender perspective. While a body of mainly empirical research on gender and trade in services linkages in a development context is emerging,[43] more research is needed.

39 Marie Sicat, Ankai Xu, Ermira Mehetaj, Michael Ferrantino, and Vicky Chemutai, 'Leveraging New Technologies in Closing the Gender Gaps' (2020) World Bank Working Paper No. 8 <https://openknowledge.worldbank.org/handle/10986/33165> accessed 8 May 2022.

40 Thystrup, 'Gender-Inclusive Governance for E-Commerce' (n *).

41 World Bank and WTO, 'Women and Trade' (n 16) 7.

42 European Commission, 'Digital Trade' <https://ec.europa.eu/trade/policy/accessing-markets/goods-and-services/digital-trade/> accessed 8 May 2022.

43 Enrico Nano, Gaurav Nayyar, Stela Rubínová, and Victor Stolzenburg, 'The Impact of Services Liberalization on Education: Evidence From India' (2021) WTO Staff Working Paper ERSD-2021-10 <www.wto.org/english/res_e/reser_e/ersd202110_e.pdf> accessed 20 September 2022; Gavin van der Nest, 'Women in Services Trade: An Update of Participation and Ownership Data for Sub-Saharan Africa' (2021) tralac Trade Brief No. US21TB01/2021 <www.tralac.org/publications/article/15143-women-in-services-trade-an-update-of-participation-and-ownership-data-for-sub-saharan-africa.html> accessed 20 September 2022

Moreover, e-commerce, digital trade, and trade in services might separately or in combination feed into GVCs. Bamber and Staritz reassess the idea of feminization of GVCs of trade by focusing on the implications of countries moving into higher GVC sectors, namely in technology. Here, a need for much more evidence-based research is identified but a picture emerges of a reality that is not benefiting women, with lower female participation in high-tech sectors. The picture even suggests defeminization of GVCs. When examining the cases of the Dominican Republic and Costa Rica, Bamber and Staritz find that the female intensity in the medical devices sector was higher from the outset and held steady as firms in the sector upgraded into more sophisticated products where women found quality jobs, permanent contracts, benefits, and relatively high wages. In contrast, a study on mining-related GVCs finds that the growing recourse to digital technologies has yet to translate into increased levels of female participation.[44]

This backdrop suggests that making the connection between gender, e-commerce, digital trade, and trade in services, and applying lessons learned, can advance the research agenda and provide value to policy-making.

6.3.1 *The Key Policy Challenges of Market Access, Resources, and Regulatory Aspects for Gender-Inclusive Trade*

The following section will show how key policy challenges for gender equality across the multiplicity of the gender gap in trade at large and in e-commerce, digital trade, and services trade specifically include market access, access to resources, and a regulatory aspect.

6.3.1.1 Market Access

Suominen's study of current patterns for e-commerce controls for firm size, and finds, for one, that the gender gap is not unique to e-commerce as it is a structural feature of the economy. By implication, there are no significant

[44] Bamber and Staritz, 'The Gender Dimensions of Global Value Chains' (n 15) 3; data-driven evidence from firm-level data in Danny Hamrick and Penny Bamber, 'Pakistan in the Medical Device Global Value Chain' (Duke Global Value Chains Center 2019) <https://gvcc.duke.edu/wp-content/uploads/PakistanMedicalDeviceGVC.pdf> accessed 8 May 2022; Karina Fernandez-Stark, Vivian Couto, and Penny Bamber, 'Industry 4.0 in Developing Countries: The Mine of the Future and the Role of Women?' (2019) World Bank Group Background Paper for the WBG-WTO Global Report on Trade and Gender 2019 <https://documents1.worldbank.org/curated/pt/824061568089601224/Industry-4-0-in-Developing-Countries-The-Mine-of-the-Future-and-the-Role-of-Women.pdf> accessed 8 May 2022.

differences between male and female participation rates in e-commerce relative to the wider economy. The study also finds that regardless of whether firms were run by men or women, smaller firms are uniformly less likely to export and are more hampered in e-commerce than large firms, as is the case with cross-border trade at large.[45] The impact is in the correlation – as per the findings highlighted earlier, women as workers and as suppliers tend to concentrate where the gender gap as a structural feature of the economy is felt and in those smaller firms that are uniformly less likely to export.

E-commerce offers MSMEs and small and medium-sized enterprises (SMEs) several advantages in regard to export and market access. Such advantages include lower transaction costs, access to larger or new markets, secure payment options, and, arguably, faster productivity and output growth. Thus, women in particular could stand to benefit from e-commerce because it allows them to connect directly with buyers, thereby circumventing *de jure* or *de facto* discriminatory local business or legal practices. Furthermore, evidence suggests that women increase sales volume and profits when selling to destinations further from their home country rather than over a single border.[46]

Online work and ICT-enabled services exports can be particularly empowering for women expected to stay at home, and where women lack the professional networks and resources relative to men.[47] However, getting to the stage of export, and tapping into the cross-border trade that improves conditions, is more difficult for women. First, because they may receive a lower price in product markets, as shown in a study about eBay.[48] Secondly, women exporters face more trade obstacles than men do, with 74 per cent of women-owned firms reporting challenging non-tariff measures (NTMs) compared to 54 per cent of businesses owned by men.[49]

Digitalization can help make it possible for women to trade cross-border to reap the benefits suggested earlier, and with the benefit of anonymizing the exporter's gender online. Anonymizing gender online improves the conditions

45 Kati Suominen, 'Women-Led Firms on the Web: What Are Their Regulatory Challenges – and What Are Solutions?' (2018) ICTSD Working Paper, 3, 16 <www.nextradegroupllc.com/_files/ugd/478c1a_ed3fb14c1a9b465eadd6076404d6da01.pdf> accessed 8 May 2022.

46 Sicat et al., 'Leveraging New Technologies in Closing the Gender Gap' (n 39).

47 Suominen, 'Women-Led Firms on the Web' (n 45) 8, citing World Bank, 'World Development Report 2016: Digital Dividends' (2016) <www.worldbank.org/en/publication/wdr2016> accessed 8 May 2022.

48 Tamar Kricheli-Katz and Tali Regev, 'How Many Cents on the Dollar? Women and Men in Product Markets' (2016) 2(2) *ScienceAdvances* 2.

49 ITC, 'SME Competitiveness Outlook 2016: Meeting the Standard for Trade' (2016).

for gender equality because it removes immediate bias in exporting, which carries real economic value in terms of market access and could carry the full price.[50]

However, this is not a given, and the picture of improved market access granted by anonymization of gender is more complex. Online suppliers may lose some of the benefit of gender being anonymized online since a licence is required to access the market. Even when the seller's gender is anonymous, women may receive a lower price than men would collect for the same good or service because of limited business networks, for example.

Moreover, in policy terms, anonymization is insufficient for market access when the goal is more profound change that reflects the structural aspect of gender-inclusive trade policy-making.[51] This is because anonymization does not remedy underlying issues such as limited access to financing or the persistent structural differences women face. Thus, it is submitted that the approach may not serve to consolidate a gender-inclusive trade policy.

6.3.1.2 Access to Resources

In line with the thinking underpinning anonymizing gender online,[52] a joint paper by UNCTAD, WTO, and the World Bank on the interplay between women, trade, and ICT in the face of increasing digitalization finds, inter alia, that digital solutions may reduce face-to-face interactions, which in turn improves the participation of women entrepreneurs in trade networks traditionally dominated by men. The analysis highlights payment technologies as means to ease provision of financial services for women in e-commerce.[53]

Evidence shows that it is more difficult for women to access financing than it is for men because of gender biases among investors and lenders.[54] ITC research shows that the trade finance gap that women entrepreneurs in

[50] Kricheli-Katz and Regev, 'How Many Cents on the Dollar?' (n 48). The authors found that on average, women sellers received about 80 cents for every dollar a man received when selling the identical new product and 97 cents when selling the same used product.

[51] *See* Thystrup, 'Gender-Inclusive Governance for E-Commerce' (n *).

[52] *See* ibid.

[53] Sicat et al., 'Leveraging New Technologies in Closing the Gender Gap' (n 39).

[54] Suominen, 'Women-Led Firms on the Web' (n 45) cites the following examples: Alberto F. Alesina, Fransesca Lotti, and Paulo Emilio Mistrulli, 'Do Women Pay More for Credit? Evidence from Italy' (2013) 11 *Journal of the European Economic Association* 45; Giorgio Calcagnini, Germana Giombini, and Elisa Lenti, 'Gender Differences in Bank Loan Access: An Empirical Analysis' (2014) 1 *Italian Economic Journal* 193; Sarah K. Harkness, 'Discrimination in Lending Markets: Status and the Intersections of Gender and Race' (2016) 79 *Social Psychology Quarterly* 81.

emerging markets face is around USD 260–320 billion per year.[55] Here, e-commerce is instrumental for women because digital trade would, in theory, be less costly, and therefore require less financing because participation takes place without the physical attributes of a store. Yet participation in e-commerce and digital trade alike would still require some financial infrastructure, such as e-payment systems and access to a bank account.[56] This could be lost where women suffer under a finance gap and a digital gender divide because IT infrastructure, such as broadband, and IT skills are a prerequisite for engaging in online exports.

To reflect the reality that an estimated 1 billion people in the developing world have broadband but not a debit or credit card, Sicat and others argue that an enabling environment for e-commerce should include access to broadband but also to payment mechanisms.[57]

Limited access to business networks is a key factor in women-owned or women-led SMEs facing specific challenges to grow or access market opportunities, and another key factor is that larger firms lack knowledge of women-owned or women-led SMEs in the market.[58] Access to resources such as business networks and to larger firms is another pathway to helping these SMEs tap into larger firms' supply chains, which in turn can help overcome how scale is a determinant of a firm's ability to export and unlock the benefits of participating in trade, and trade in value-added. For trade in services, such supply of services could take the form of any of the modes of supply, and it would be imperative to extend the benefits of trade in services to more sectors,

55 ITC, 'SME Competitiveness Outlook 2016' (n 49); For a recent report, *see* OECD, 'Trade Finance for SMEs in the Digital Era' (2021) OECD SME and Entrepreneurship Papers No. 24 <www.oecd.org/cfe/smes/Trade%20finance%20for%20SMEs%20in%20the%20digital%20era.pdf> accessed 8 May 2022. The report quotes Kijin Kim, Steven Beck, Mara Claire Tayag, and M. Concepcion Latoja, 'Trade Finance Gaps, Growth, and Jobs Survey' (2019) ADB Briefs <www.adb.org/publications/2019-trade-finance-gaps-jobs-survey> accessed 8 May 2022. It finds that the global trade finance gap was estimated to be USD 1.5 trillion in 2018, difficulties in measuring this gap notwithstanding.

56 For exploration of blockchain's potential for bypassing discriminatory practices or overcoming other constraints such as a lack of ID to enable women to engage in the financial and business transaction needed to participate in trade, *see* Amrita Bahri, 'Blockchaining International Trade: A Way Forward for Women's Economic Empowerment?' in Maarten Smeets et al. (eds) *Adapting to the Digital Trade Era: Challenges and Opportunities* (2020) WTO Chairs Programme <www.wto.org/english/res_e/booksp_e/adtera_e.pdf> accessed 20 September 2022.

57 Sicat et al., 'Leveraging New Technologies in Closing the Gender Gap' (n 43).

58 *See* Sheng Fang, Heba Shamseldin, and L. Colin Xu, 'Foreign Direct Investment and Female Entrepreneurship' (2019) World Bank Policy Research Working Paper No. WPS 9083 <http://documents.worldbank.org/curated/en/404861576511949229/Foreign-Direct-Investment-and-Female-Entrepreneurship> accessed 20 September 2022.

including those where women tend to concentrate, and to improving female participation in GVCs.[59]

The flexibility of online work can bridge the structural differences women face in terms of primary responsibility for reproductive work. Assuming online work requires fewer resources than opening a physical shop, e-commerce and digital trade can bridge women's differential access to resources, from networks to finance. Furthermore, servicification has a potential to diversify economies, and ICT is a major component to this end. However, it presupposes education and ICT skills.

Indeed, the International Telecommunications Union reports that the proportion of women using the internet is 12 per cent lower than the proportion of men, and this gender gap widens to around 33 per cent in least-developed countries. Research also shows that in Africa, over 40 per cent of women are not able to effectively engage with digital tools for personal and professional activities.[60] Thus, women affected by a lack of access to education or the existence of a digital divide would not readily be able to take full advantage of the opportunities associated with e-commerce and digital trade. Yet, globally, reports estimate that enabling internet access for 150 million women would contribute an estimated USD 13–18 billion to the annual Gross Domestic Product (GDP) of 144 developing countries.[61]

6.3.1.3 Regulatory Challenges

In trade in services, barriers to trade are mostly of a regulatory nature that can be time and resource consuming to overcome, for example obtaining a licence or complying with domestic regulations, such as licensing requirements, qualifications, and technical standards.[62] Thus, on the regulatory side, gender needs to be recognized before the law to ensure access to resources, anchored in enforceable rights. For example, without legal protection, women could risk being denied access to the financial infrastructure needed for

59 *See* Bamber and Staritz, 'The Gender Dimensions of Global Value Chains' (n 15).

60 WTO, 'DG Azevêdo: Global Cooperation on Digital Economy Vital to Unlock Trade Benefits for Women, Speeches – DG Azevêdo (1 July 2019), <www.wto.org/english/news_e/spra_e/spra268_e.htm> accessed 8 May 2022.

61 Ibid.

62 For recent evidence, *see* Sebastian Benz, Janos Ferencz, and Hildegunn K. Nordås, 'Regulatory Barriers to Trade In Services: A New Database and Composite Indices' (2020) 43 *World Economy* 2860–2879. It is well established, *see* for example Thystrup, *Governing Trade in Services* (n 11).

participating in trade, such as opening a bank account or cashing cheques, or they could be denied authorization to supply a given service.

This is where disciplines on DR come into the picture. The goal of developing new enhanced disciplines pursuant to GATS Article VI:4 is to address difficulties which may be faced by services suppliers in complying with measures relating to licensing requirements and procedures, qualification requirements and procedures, and technical standards of other members. In a regime that tolerates discrimination or fails to intervene in gender inequality, women could, for example, experience not being able to obtain licences such as a permit to operate as a professional service supplier. Furthermore, women would not be able to avail themselves of regulatory frameworks that support trade.

The policies and regulations that shape the digital economy also critically shape the economic prospects of women who use it or seek to partake in it, and can have an outsized impact on women. An enabling environment with internet connection and IT systems, e-commerce logistics, online payments, skilled workforces, and an accommodating regulatory environment, are required for firms to engage in cross-border e-commerce.[63]

In sum, it is proposed that the three key policy challenges of market access, resources, and regulatory aspects for gender-inclusive trade are interconnected, which may in effect reinforce their effect on differential access and gendered constraints to participation in e-commerce, digital trade, and services trade. The following framework for gender-inclusive governance can be devised to shape the necessary policy interventions.

6.4 MULTI-LEVEL FRAMEWORK FOR SECURING INCREMENTAL CHANGE FOR A COMPREHENSIVE SHIFT TOWARDS GENDER-INCLUSIVE E-COMMERCE AND TRADE POLICY

It is the central proposition of this chapter that policy intervention can counter the gender-based constraints that impede participation of women in trade. The vehicle proposed for securing incremental change for a comprehensive shift towards gender-inclusive trade policy is a multi-level framework.

Efforts to promote gender equality for economic growth from participation in trade suggest that engaging the domestic policy level is imperative for implementation. This means focusing on implementing domestic reforms, such as those identified by the World Bank.[64] In line with this thinking, a

63 Suominen, 'Women-Led Firms on the Web' (n 45).
64 World Bank, 'Women, Business and the Law' (n 32).

'bottom-up approach' consists of engaging the domestic policy level. Domestic reform then feeds into Regional Trade Agreements (RTAs), and in turn is informed by advancements in RTAs.

Research has mapped gender-related provisions across RTAs, showing a diversity in approaches that suggests much experience to draw from.[65] Regional trade policy instruments that have embraced provisions on gender equality include, inter alia, the FTA between Chile and Canada, the Comprehensive and Progressive Agreement for Trans-Pacific Partnership (CPTPP), and the African Comprehensive Free Trade Agreement (AfCFTA).[66] Regional experiences with drafting, scoping, and implementing gender-related provisions and chapters, and their interplay with other disciplines, could improve gender-inclusive governance at large, and inform WTO negotiating modalities. Namely, the experience of including chapters and provisions on gender equality in RTAs would inform policy interventions in the multilateral rules-based system, on a multilateral level, or in a plurilateral setting. The plurilateral setting encompasses the JSIs, and the JSI on services DR specifically includes a provision on gender equality.

The second component to the bottom-up approach involves policy interventions in specific issues. For e-commerce and digital trade, the bottom-up approach would direct policy intervention towards the regulatory space of an enabling environment for e-commerce as the key regulatory and policy challenges facing women can be addressed in this regulatory space to overcome

[65] *See* Amrita Bahri, 'Gender Mainstreaming in Free Trade Agreements: A Regional Analysis and Good Practice Examples' (2022) Gender, Social Inclusion and Trade Knowledge Product Series <www.genderandtrade.com/_files/ugd/86d8f7_ea7e603922c54ff7a9e1f81e594a5d9f.pdf> accessed 20 September 2022; Anoush der Boghossian, 'Trade Policies Supporting Women's Economic Empowerment: Trends in WTO Members' (2019) WTO Staff Working Paper ERSD-2019-07 <www.wto.org/english/res_e/reser_e/ersd201907_e.pdf> accessed 8 May 2022; José-Antonio Monteiro, 'Gender-related provisions in Regional Trade Agreements' (2018) WTO Staff Working Paper ERSD-2018-15 <www.wto.org/english/res_e/reser_e/ersd201815_e.pdf> accessed 8 May 2022.

[66] Canada–Chile Free Trade Agreement (enforced since July 1997); Comprehensive and Progressive Agreement for Trans-Pacific Partnership (enforced since 30 December 2018); Agreement Establishing the African Continental Free Trade Area (enforced since 30 May 2019). For research on African RTAs specifically, *see* Lolita Laperle-Forget, 'Gender Provisions in African Trade Agreements: What Commitments Are There For Reconciling Gender Equality and Trade?' (2022) Tralac Working Paper No. G21WP11/2021 <www.tralac.org/publications/article/15567-gender-provisions-in-african-trade-agreements-what-commitments-are-there-for-reconciling-gender-equality-and-trade.html> accessed 20 September 2022; Nadira Bayat, 'Advancing Gender-Equitable Outcomes in African Continental Free Trade Area (AfCFTA) Implementation' (2021), UNCTAD White Paper <www.uneca.org/sites/default/files/keymessageanddocuments/22May_Final_WhitePaper_Advancing_gender_equitable_outcomes.pdf> accessed 20 September 2022.

key challenges. The JSI on services DR encompasses policy intervention in the form of a specific provision targeting any gender-based discrimination in the authorizations for the supply of services. Specific issues and specific provisions would then lend themselves to implementing gender-inclusivity and improvement of women's participation in other issue areas and other disciplines by way of example and of policy practice. Furthermore, the modalities would be shaped to capture the multiplicity of the gender gap.

Supporting gender mainstreaming is key to a 'top-down approach' to gender-inclusive trade policy. Gender mainstreaming can engage all WTO initiatives, including the JSIs, to bring about gender-inclusive economic growth in the spirit of the SDGs and in fulfilment of the aspirations of the Buenos Aires Declaration. Such an incremental approach could help ensure implementation of gender-inclusive governance across the WTO *acquis* and anchor gender equality in the rules-based system. Building on the JSI on services DR and its landmark provision on gender equality, and the traction the trade and gender agenda had at MC12, would contribute to consolidating the agenda and exercise policy pressure on the multilateral trading system top-down as well as on the domestic level and upwards. These efforts could build on experience from RTAs incorporating gender equality in different ways.

On an institutional level, continuous strengthening of the coordination between the WTO, RTAs, UNCTAD, the World Bank, the ITC, and the OECD on modalities for supporting the necessary multi-level coordination holds promises for advancing gender-inclusive trade policy-making. Continuous efforts to mainstream gender in trade policy are crucial for sustaining the momentum for gender equality in the WTO.

Furthermore, reading gender equality into the rules-based system could help deliver an incrementally more gender-inclusive trading system across the WTO *acquis*. It would also require dedicating time, resources, and political will to continuing discussions on trade and gender in the WTO. The prospect of an outcome at the MC12 seems particularly promising to this end.

Bringing the market access component of the key policy challenges for gender-inclusivity in trade to the forefront when designing and implementing gender-inclusive programmes can support accessing markets, expand and strengthen market participation, while ensuring sustained gender-inclusion. This is operationalized by employing the multi-level framework of combining a bottom-up approach centred around domestic regulations and reform, and a top-down approach revolving around commitments and policy support.

Expanding in services and digital trade requires improving conditions for participating in all modes of supply. The reverse scenario could produce the unfortunate side effect that existing patterns of limited employment and the gendered composition of labour and education are reproduced at the expense of support for women branching into digital products and services via e-commerce and digital trade.

The multiplicity of the gender gap is not fully captured across trade policy instruments – for an on point example, see the JSI outcome on DR. If committing to such a framing, it is important not to lose sight of the broader gender equality issue and its multiplicity, and to safeguard against any gender-preclusive effects.[67] Furthermore, policymakers could prepare the ground for expanding the platform to address how gender is one part of a larger socio-economic issue of *de jure* and *de facto* discrimination based on gender, sex, sexual orientation, class, race, and origins.[68]

Finally, to support a comprehensive shift towards gender equality, it is strongly recommended to continue the effort to collect more data on all aspects of e-commerce, digital trade, trade in services, and trade at large to support policy-making and implementation of gender-inclusive governance.[69] Collecting data on implementation and the effect of the concluded disciplines on DR, including the provision on gender equality, would lend itself to an uptake in data and support policy-making.

6.5 POLICY INTERVENTION TO BRIDGE THE GENDER DIGITAL DIVIDE

The WTO does not yet offer a comprehensive multilateral response to the digitalization that drives digital trade and e-commerce. However, MC11 saw much more policy attention directed to e-commerce as seventy-one members launched the Joint Statement Initiative on Electronic Commerce (JSI on e-commerce)[70] to initiate exploratory work towards future WTO negotiations on trade-related aspects of e-commerce.[71]

If coupled with the trade and gender agenda, the JSI on e-commerce would be in line with the thinking behind the multi-level framework's bottom-up

67 *See* Thystrup, 'Gender-Inclusive Governance for E-Commerce' (n *) 623.

68 *See* ibid.

69 For a turning point on the collection of data, *see* the WTO's Database on gender provisions in RTAs, launched on 28 July 2022 during the Aid for Trade Global review, <www.wto.org/english/tratop_e/womenandtrade_e/gender_responsive_trade_agreement_db_e.htm> accessed 20 September 2022.

70 WTO, 'Joint Statement on Electronic Commerce', WT/MIN(17)/60 (13 December 2017).

71 ICTSD, 'Updating the Multilateral Rule Book on E-Commerce. WTO: Paths Forward' (2018) International Centre for Trade and Sustainable Development Policy Brief – March 2018 <www.tralac.org/component/cck/?task=download&file=app_att_01&id=13518> accessed 8 May 2022.

policy intervention in specific issues, and its top-down approach to securing incremental change towards gender-inclusive e-commerce and trade policy. Furthermore, it is the central argument that applying the framework to the modalities shaping e-commerce rules could help secure gender-inclusive e-commerce governance. Recalling the structural differences women face in terms of labour, time, and resources,[72] e-commerce provides flexibility in structuring participation in trade, new markets for employment, and pathways to control over online resources that may be cheaper than traditional business. This suggests a tangible potential for incorporating gender equality into e-commerce rules to form gender-inclusive e-commerce governance. However, it will take effort and policy commitment to overcome the gender digital divide and other aspects of the gender gap given gender-based constraints and differential access to prerequisite resources. In the absence of policy intervention, an acceleration of digitalization could deepen the gender digital divide, which in turn could reverse the status quo for participation in e-commerce and digital trade and lead to backsliding.

Factoring in the domestic aspect is important for participation in e-commerce because 90 per cent of e-commerce is in fact domestic commerce.[73] Moreover, it is necessary to overcome the divides to upscale a firm to an operation with the resources to export cross-border. Compatibility between domestic, regional, and multilateral frameworks to advance comprehensive gender-inclusive governance would be instrumental to that end.

Achieving a predictable regulatory environment for e-commerce and digital trade could link with incorporating gender equality into DR because service suppliers engaged in cross-border e-commerce might rely on obtaining licences and authorizations when meeting the requirements, regardless of gender, and the predictability of the regulatory environment would improve in consequence.

Embedding these issues within a framework for e-commerce and digital trade that connects with other trade policy agendas would drive more comprehensive implementation of gender equality into trade policy. The JSI points out that a link exists between MSMEs and e-commerce and that furthering gender equality in this nexus could be particularly beneficial for women's participation and for development. This platform could be used for providing the key access to finance, which also hinges on domestic regulation and reform.

Seeking to embed gender equality even more firmly within the MSME agenda as a development issue and connecting it to e-commerce could be

[72] *See* Thystrup, 'Gender-Inclusive Governance for E-Commerce' (n *), 598.

[73] Sicat et al., 'Leveraging New Technologies in Closing the Gender Gaps' (n 39).

anchored within Aid for Trade, where gender-inclusive initiatives can target the obstacles that women face when trading. The rapid development of technology enabling e-commerce and digital trade, while ensuring that it is gender-inclusive, promises more opportunities for women beyond the sectors where most women currently find employment or work, and could be anchored in enabling environments for e-commerce and digital trade at large.

6.5.1 *Gender-Inclusive e-Commerce Governance*

Gender-inclusive e-commerce governance aims to narrow the gender gap by overcoming the digital divide, the finance gap, and how they intersect with scale.[74] Gender-inclusive e-commerce governance addresses the key regulatory challenges of market access, access to resources, and regulatory aspects to participating in e-commerce.

Domestic policy commitments to gender equality in both the exporting country and the importing country could help leverage and upscale domestic e-commerce into cross-border e-commerce. This would improve market access with positive benefits. First, it could offset some of the vulnerabilities in the economy associated with women being concentrated in fewer sectors, and facing gendered job segregation.[75] Secondly, evidence suggests that women increase sales volume and profits when selling to destinations further from their home country rather than over a single border.[76] Access to new markets through exports could help abate some of that vulnerability and overcome the norms or structural features that produce gender discrimination and differential access.

As for access to resources, even where participation in e-commerce on a small scale is less costly or requires less financing, it would still require a backbone of IT infrastructure and financial infrastructure, such as internet access and skills, e-payment systems, and access to a bank account. IT infrastructure and financial infrastructure, including payment mechanisms, are components for an enabling environment that could have a real impact in helping women to overcome the disadvantages they face in responding to new economic incentives because of gender differences in access to resources, such as those needed for participating in e-commerce.

Thus, once again the prospect of economic empowerment from participating in e-commerce is defined by access to the prerequisites for e-commerce,

[74] *See* Thystrup, 'Gender-Inclusive Governance for E-Commerce' (n *) 625 ff.

[75] *See* ibid.

[76] *See* ibid.

such as holding a bank account, and to designing rules that establish an enabling environment that helps women respond to new economic incentives, namely access to finance and IT skills. Securing access to IT skills and finance, in particular, could improve gender equality in the digital market, and the chances that e-commerce and digital trade deliver on the promise of inclusive economic growth.

Women's opportunities in new economic activities are dampened by time constraints,[77] and thus easing regulatory barriers and improving the regulatory environment, which can be time and resource consuming, could have a positive effect on participation at large and, by implication, also on gender-inclusive e-commerce governance. The ongoing JSI on e-commerce encompasses disciplines and provisions on transparency, non-discrimination, ensuring a predictable regulatory environment, and shaping an enabling environment for e-commerce.

It is the central argument that incorporating gender equality into the e-commerce rulebook could result in positive change towards gender-inclusive governance. Transparency improves accountability, and by extension lends itself to gender-inclusive governance,[78] while non-discrimination is key to levelling the playing field. Achieving a predictable regulatory environment for e-commerce also lends itself to gender-inclusive e-commerce governance. If it were to link with incorporating gender equality into DR, service suppliers engaged in cross-border e-commerce and digital trade would then rely on obtaining licences, regardless of gender, and the predictability of the regulatory environment would improve in consequence. Finally, there are rules to establish an enabling environment, and they could have an outsized effect on operationalizing gender-inclusive e-commerce governance. The multi-level framework's bottom-up approach to specific disciplines advises exploring the potential for gender-inclusive e-commerce to shape the regulatory space for an enabling environment.

6.5.2 *An Enabling Environment for e-Commerce*

Elements of an enabling environment to facilitate online transactions were introduced into discussions at the WTO.[79] The 2019 European Union proposal for WTO disciplines and commitments relating to electronic

77 Ibid.

78 *See*, for instance, OECD, 'Policy Framework for Gender-Sensitive Public Governance', C/MIN(2021)21 (21 September 2021).

79 At the Council for Trade in Services – Special session in TN/S/W/64, May 2017 communication from the European Union. For the April 2018 policy proposal from EU, *see* European Commission, 'EU Releases Proposal on New WTO Rules for Electronic

commerce, stipulates in Article 1, 'The EU supports the open, transparent and inclusive character of these negotiations'.[80]

Gender equality could be injected into the proposal's provisions on an enabling environment in Article 2. A provision obliging members to ensure that there is no discrimination based on gender when issuing licences and authorizations could be incorporated into Article 3.6,[81] drawing on lessons learnt from the changing language in DR.[82]

Injecting gender equality into the modalities for an enabling environment in e-commerce discussions could be approached by outlining how enjoying rights, having effective redress, protection from discriminatory practices, and transparency form part of such an environment, and by emphasizing international cooperation and coordination with other national and regional bodies to this end. Thereby an enabling environment for e-commerce would be created, with regulatory space conducive to gender equality. Prescriptive measures for adopting and maintaining measures that contribute to closing the gender gaps would be coupled with a gender-inclusive prohibition against discrimination based on gender and embedded within the modalities for e-commerce.

6.6 POLICY INTERVENTION TO BRIDGE THE GENDER GAP IN SERVICES TRADE

With most barriers to trade in services being of a regulatory nature and non-tariff-related, the role of domestic regulation and measures over the border in the country receiving the supply of services by any of the means becomes even more important to services trade. Research by the WTO and OECD suggests that the reduction in trade costs from implementing the new disciplines included in the sixty-seven members' landmark conclusion of an agreement on services DR of 2 December 2021 could amount to USD 150 billion per annum globally, with particularly important gains for financial, business, communications, and transport services.[83]

Commerce' (3 May 2019) <https://trade.ec.europa.eu/doclib/press/index.cfm?id=2016> accessed 8 May 2022.

80 EU, 'EU Proposal for WTO Disciplines and Commitments Relating to Electronic Commerce', INF/ECOM/22 (26 April 2019).

81 Ibid.

82 *See* Thystrup, 'Gender-Inclusive Governance for E-Commerce' (n *) for evidence and discussion.

83 WTO and OECD, 'Services Domestic Regulation in the WTO: Cutting Red Tape, Slashing Trade Costs, and Facilitating Services Trade' (November 2021) <www.wto.org/english/news_e/news21_e/jssdr_26nov21_e.pdf> accessed 8 May 2022.

Further to the disciplines in GATS Article VI, the GATS also establishes the mandate for negotiating additional disciplines in GATS Article VI:4.[84] The provision stipulates that, with a view to ensuring that measures relating to qualification requirements and procedures, technical standards and licensing requirements do not constitute unnecessary barriers to trade in services, the Council for Trade in Services shall, through appropriate bodies it may establish, develop any necessary disciplines. Such disciplines shall aim to ensure that such requirements are, inter alia: (a) based on objective and transparent criteria, such as competence and the ability to supply the service; (b) not more burdensome than necessary to ensure the quality of the service; and (c) in the case of licensing procedures, not in themselves a restriction on the supply of the service. Thus, pursuant to GATS Article VI:4, members agree to further develop rules to ensure that domestic regulations support rather than impede the opening of services markets to trade and investment as a central task for services negotiations.[85]

As the reference paper on services regulation explains,[86] members would agree to the disciplines on DR with the objective of elaborating upon the provisions of GATS pursuant to Article VI:4. In doing so, members recognize the difficulties which may be faced by service suppliers, particularly those of developing country members, in complying with measures relating to licensing requirements and procedures, qualification requirements and procedures, and technical standards of other members, and, in particular, the specific difficulties which may be faced by service suppliers from LDCs.

The JSI on services DR is more advanced than the JSI on e-commerce in two ways: first, the JSI on services DR has concluded an agreement, and second, it includes a specific provision on gender equality. These advancements reflect the multi-level framework's bottom-up approach to policy intervention on specific issues, and its top-down approach to securing incremental change towards gender-inclusive e-commerce and trade policy, and indicate a pathway to gender-inclusive governance for services trade.

DR disciplines are for trade in services sectors positioned to address the regulatory component to the key policy challenges of market access and differential access to resources that women face, as DR disciplines regulatory

[84] Aik Hoe Lim, *WTO Domestic Regulation and Services Trade, Putting Principles into Practice* (Cambridge University Press 2014) 2.

[85] Aaditya Mattoo and Pierre Sauvé, *Domestic Regulation and Service Trade Liberalization* (World Bank 2003) 1.

[86] 'Note by the Chairperson, Joint Initiative on Services Domestic Regulation', INF/SDR/W/1/Rev.2 (18 December 2020) Section I, paragraphs 1 and 2.

measures in order to level the playing field.[87] The need for recognition before the law, evidence of gender bias adversely affecting women, and many new opportunities for employment outside the existing gendered composition of the labour force make DR all the more important for women's economic participation in the supply of services. Such supply often requires a licence or authorization. Thus, DR disciplines are key to economic participation in services trade, and are well positioned to shape the modalities for gender-inclusive trade in services, also spanning the services components to e-commerce and digital trade, where commitments have been made.[88]

6.6.1 *Negotiating Modalities for Development of Measures on Domestic Regulation pursuant to GATS Article VI:4*

In pursuit of an outcome on DR at MC11, the Friends of DR circulated a communication, dated 7 November 2017, to the members of the Working Party on Domestic Regulation (WPDR).[89] Among other provisions, under the DR GATS Article VI:4 mandate, the text includes provisions on measures relating to licensing requirements and procedures, qualification requirements and procedures, and technical standards. This section also includes a provision on gender equality originally tabled by Canada. In 2016, Canada had previously included the exact provision in the DR text during negotiations on the Trade in Services Agreement (TiSA).[90]

At the time of MC11, the DR proposal on gender equality for the WPDR read (the 2017 WPDR text):

> Gender Equality
>
> 6.2 Where a Member adopts or maintains measures relating to authorisation for the supply of a service, the Member shall ensure that such measures do not discriminate against individuals on the basis of gender.
>
> [Footnote: For greater certainty, legitimate differentiation, which means differential treatment that is reasonable and objective, and aims to achieve a legitimate purpose, and adoption by Members of temporary special measures aimed at accelerating de facto gender equality, shall not be considered discrimination for the purposes of this provision.]

[87] *See* Thystrup, 'Gender-Inclusive Governance for E-Commerce' (n *).

[88] *See* ibid on scheduling modalities.

[89] WTO, 'Working Party on Domestic Regulation', JOB/SERV/272/Rev.1 (7 November 2017).

[90] Thystrup, *Governing Trade in Services* (n 11). Annex 4 traces the changes to DR disciplines from 2016 to 2017. The exercise includes the provision on gender equality on pp. 15–16 of Annex 4.

At MC11, the Friends of DR were not successful in securing an outcome in the shape of multilateral agreement under the built-in mandate. Instead they secured support for the JSI on services DR.[91] The initiative (JSI) operates on a plurilateral basis, and has continued discussions outside the WPDR since MC11.

The JSI's text on gender equality was adjusted to the following stipulation (the 2018 JSI text):[92]

> Development of Measures
>
> If a Member adopts or maintains measures relating to authorisation for the supply of a service, the Member shall ensure that: …
>
> [(e) such measures do not discriminate between men and women.
>
> [Footnote: Differential treatment that is reasonable and objective, and aims to achieve a legitimate purpose, and adoption by Members of temporary special measures aimed at accelerating de facto equality between men and women, shall not be considered discrimination for the purposes of this provision.]].

When comparing the 2017 WPDR text with the 2018 JSI text, a change in the structure of the provision is evident, but it also embodies an evident change in wording.

The JSI proceeded to stabilize a text on DR in preparation for a plurilateral outcome coinciding with MC12 with the support of sixty-five members (the 2020 JSI text).[93] The provision on gender equality carries on the changes introduced with the JSI 2018 text, when it stipulates:

> SECTION II – DISCIPLINES ON SERVICES DOMESTIC REGULATION …
>
> Development of Measures
>
> 22. If a Member adopts or maintains measures relating to the authorization for the supply of a service, the Member shall ensure that: …
>
> [; and
>
> (d) such measures do not discriminate between men and women.
>
> [Footnote: Differential treatment that is reasonable and objective, and aims to achieve a legitimate purpose, and adoption by Members of temporary special

91 WTO, 'Joint Ministerial Statement on Services Domestic Regulation' (n 1).

92 WTO, 'Working Room Document by the Chair', DR4-D/Rev.1 (14 September 2018).

93 WTO, 'Note by the Chairperson, Joint Initiative on Services Domestic Regulation', INF/SDR/W/1/Rev.2 (18 December 2020).

measures aimed at accelerating de facto equality between men and women, shall not be considered discrimination for the purposes of this provision.]]

Compared to the 2018 JSI text, what is new to the JSI 2020 text is the inclusion of alternative disciplines on DR for Financial Services. These disciplines include a twin-provision on non-discrimination between men and women:

> [SECTION III – ALTERNATIVE DISCIPLINES ON SERVICES DOMESTIC REGULATION FOR FINANCIAL SERVICES ...
>
> Development of Measures
>
> 19. If a Member adopts or maintains measures relating to the authorization for the supply of a service, the Member shall ensure that: ...
>
> [; and
>
> (d) such measures do not discriminate between men and women.
>
> [Footnote: Differential treatment that is reasonable and objective, and aims to achieve a legitimate purpose, and adoption by Members of temporary special measures aimed at accelerating de facto equality between men and women, shall not be considered discrimination for the purposes of this provision.]]

The change in language from the 2017 WPDR text to the 2018 JSI text encompasses non-discrimination 'between men and women', rather than 'against individuals on the basis of gender'. The change in language carries legal consequences as it effectively changes the scope of the obligation. Both proposals turn on the notion of non-discrimination, likely with the intention in mind to discipline *de jure* discrimination based on gender when applying for authorization, and perhaps with less regard for *de facto* discrimination. The definitions vary, however, and, by implication, so does the scope of those protected individuals under the imperative of 'shall ensure'. In essence, the 2018 and 2020 JSI texts have been watered down to a binary categorization, compared with the broader term 'gender', used in the 2017 WPDR text, which did not make such a pronouncement.

On 27 September 2021, participants in the JSI on Domestic Regulations concluded text negotiations, on track for MC12, and proceeded to circulate national schedules of commitment pursuant to GATS.[94] Despite the postponement of MC12, on 2 December 2021 negotiators reached an agreement

[94] WTO, 'Participants in Domestic Regulation Talks Conclude Text Negotiations, on Track for MC12 Deal' (n 7).

among the JSI's now sixty-seven WTO members.[95] Except for the removal of brackets, the final text[96] is identical to the JSI 2020 text, and so it locks in the binary wording of 'between men and women' that first appeared with the 2018 JSI text, at the expense of the 2017 WPDR text's gender-inclusive language, 'on the basis of gender'.

6.6.2 *Legal–Political Implications of the Domestic Regulation Discipline on Gender Equality*

As a wider concept that reflects the multiplicity of the gender gap, the use of 'gender' does not preclude any gender from the scope of protection against discriminatory domestic measures.[97] The scope of a provision on gender equality that obliges members to ensure that domestic measures do not discriminate based on gender, should ideally capture the multiplicity of the gender gap and be gender-inclusive to economic participation. Whether a provision such as the one included in the 2017 WPDR text would yield results to that effect would depend on interpretation and implementation. Yet it is a given that such wording of a provision on gender equality lends itself to that end and comes much closer to fulfilling the aspirations of gender-inclusivity as it can also reflect the multidimensional nature of the gender gap and the multiplicity of the gender gap.

Though several policy tools, such as the Buenos Aires Declaration on Women and Trade, turn on the notion of uplifting women's participation in trade, they form part of a larger trade and gender agenda that top-down promotes gender mainstreaming in trade policy. However, the JSI 2021 text employs a binary, biological identification of sex as a man or a woman and locks in a binary wording that contrasts women and men.

Viewed through the lens of the framework for gender-inclusive governance, the concern is, for one, that the binary wording can be employed to exclude or legitimize excluding those that do not identify with it. Secondly, the binary wording does not immediately lend itself to reflect the multiplicity of the gender gap or its multidimensional occurrence.

The revised proposal fails to protect from discrimination those that are deemed outside the scope of 'women', in the sense of the sex. It is problematic

95 WTO, 'Negotiations on Services Domestic Regulation Conclude Successfully in Geneva' (n 2).

96 WTO, 'Declaration on the Conclusion of Negotiations on Services Domestic Regulation' (n 2). The attached Annex 1, INF/SDR/2, dated 26 November 2021, is the JSI on Services Domestic Regulation's reference paper which includes the disciplines.

97 *See* Thystrup, 'Gender-Inclusive Governance for E-Commerce' (n *).

to not include every gender in an improvement based on non-discrimination because, while it uplifts women, it leaves those that are not captured by the improvement at the status quo. While it may be a function of the trading landscape that policymakers had to navigate in order to conclude complicated negotiations, such an approach falls short of the aspiration of gender-inclusivity. A deeper concern would be that language effectively precluding some could produce gender-precluding results, even resulting in backsliding for those excluded. The binary wording could even be (mis)used to legitimize or promote an interpretation that excludes LGBTQ+ from protection against discriminatory measures relating to authorization for the supply of services.

Furthermore, the wording seems to rest on the flawed assumption that all men have better access to resources and fewer constraints to participating in the supply of services than women do. Employing 'men' as the comparator for non-discrimination is problematic for operationalizing the provision because individuals who are biologically of the male sex may also be socially vulnerable and face differential access to opportunities in trade because of socio-economic stratification, for example based on origins. In practice, this could undermine the implementation of the provision as stipulated in the 2021 JSI texts, which would also be a disservice to those immediately within its scope.

The footnotes included in both proposals seek to clarify 'discrimination' to ensure the legality of differential treatment that is reasonable and objective, and aims to achieve a legitimate purpose, and adoption by members of temporary special measures aimed at accelerating *de facto* equality between men and women. It is reasonable to assume that the footnote is intended to, for example, safeguard domestic measures involving services authorization that encompass affirmative action. The footnote then establishes criteria that such domestic measures are to meet for the differential treatment not to be considered the kind of discrimination that the provision obliges members to protect against. The criteria of reasonability, objectivity, and legitimacy apply to differential treatment, but not to temporary special measures aimed at accelerating de facto equality between men and women.

As for the footnote's first part on differential treatment, an issue may arise if a member who has made commitments under the provision enacts affirmative action directed at men and socio-economic attributes specific to them. If, for example, such a member enacted domestic measures relating to authorization to intervene in the disadvantage of precarious or dangerous employment in the mining sector, which, for the purpose of this experiment, is assumed to be exclusively male, it would be problematic if such a measure could be struck down as incompatible. However, interpretation that looks to the aim of the provision would supposedly ensure the compatibility of such a measure.

As for the footnote's second part, an issue would arise if a special measure aimed at accelerating *de facto* equality between men and women is not of a temporary duration. This issue could be harder to reconcile, firstly, because 'temporary' is left to interpretation and, secondly, because some domestic measures may be designed to correct engrained inequalities, which takes time. Viewed through the lens of the framework for gender-inclusive governance, which specifically emphasizes the importance of domestic reforms and of compatibility, in this sense, and because it reproduces the binary wording, the footnote leaves room for improvement.

Still, by implication of the exclusion from the definition of 'discrimination', the footnote can protect policy tools such as positive discrimination and affirmative action aimed at accelerating *de facto* gender equality from being struck down as incompatible with the DR discipline. In effect, the clarification reads like a policy space reservation that ensures the legality of domestic affirmative programmes that meet the criteria.

This is crucial for two reasons. First, the disciplines of DR are aimed at domestic law and regulations, behind the border, so the legality of domestic measures of this kind need to be secured. Second, the World Bank has collected and analysed data on the effect of domestic laws and regulations on limiting women's economic participation, citing research that calls into question the notion that economic growth alone increases gender equality when rather continuous policy commitments to gender equality are required to achieve the goal.[98] The report establishes how domestic reform is key to improving conditions for women's participation in economic activities, including cross-border.[99] Arguably, incompatibility with WTO law of domestic reforms to narrow the gender gap would undermine such efforts. Third, more broadly speaking, ensuring compatibility between domestic, regional, and multilateral frameworks is key to advancing comprehensive gender-inclusive governance.

The same criticisms apply to the reproduction of the binary wording in Section III's alternative disciplines on domestic regulation for financial services. This is where it is advised to counter any adverse effect on women of trade reform and to include safeguard provisions.[100]

98 World Bank, 'Women, Business and the Law' (n 32). It cites Esther Duflo, 'Women Empowerment and Economic Development' (2012) 50 *Journal of Economic Literature* 1051–1079.

99 Ibid.

100 As advised by, inter alia, Mariama Williams, *Gender and Trade: Impacts and Implications for Financial Resources for Gender Equality* (Commonwealth Secretariat 2007).

That being said, the value of the policy intervention that the provision embodies is two-fold. First, the provision on non-discrimination goes to the very heart of access to finance and banking which is a main driver among the key challenges identified with regard to women's differential access to resources.[101] Second, the sectoral focus shines an important light on the importance of financial services as they are a prerequisite to any form of trade, across all four modes of supply of services, to e-commerce and to digital trade.[102] Thus, the addition is quite promising for narrowing the gender finance gap.

In sum, the multi-level framework helps show how the provision on gender equality included in the WPDR 2017 text with its gender-inclusive language is preferable over the provision included in the JSI 2021 text that was agreed upon because the WPDR 2017 policy intervention is directed at a deeper level. This would have a positive effect on a wider array of implications of differential access and constraints in services trade, and as it better reflects the multiplicity of gender inequalities. Furthermore, the framework shines a light on how the agreed provision leaves room for improvement in terms of addressing the multidimensional nature of the gender gap, and to what effect *de facto*. While it seems to aim squarely at *de jure* discrimination when applying for an authorization, while de facto discrimination is wrapped up in a less-than-ideal footnote.

However, the 2018, 2020, and now the concluded 2021 JSI texts' provision is positioned to build on the significant traction for women's participation in trade at this moment of renewed commitments to the trade and gender agenda at MC12. The platform provided by the JSI 2021 outcome can help application incrementally reflect the many dimensions of and multiplicity of gender gaps and ensure its rooting in gender-inclusivity. Provided that gender-preclusivity does not lead to backsliding, eventually the approach locked in with the 2021 JSI text would yield results incrementally, specifically for women. However, building on this traction and the anchoring in trade regimes, under the multilevel framework the measures could incrementally expand to produce positive effects from participation in trade in line with the aspirations of gender-inclusivity.

The promise of the provision depends on implementation though, and for services DR implementation involves bottom-up implementation

[101] *See* Thystrup, 'Gender-Inclusive Governance for E-Commerce' (n *).

[102] *See* ibid. Also see Sicat et al., 'Leveraging New Technologies in Closing the Gender Gaps' (n 39).

domestically, as well as technical implementation in the GATS schedules of specific commitments given the modalities of the JSIs in general and given the specifics of the JSI on services DR.

6.6.3 *Scheduling Modalities*

What is new in the 2020 JSI text, compared to previous iterations, is the following paragraph 9 on sectoral coverage and scheduling:

> SECTION I
>
> Sectoral Coverage and Scheduling Modalities
>
> 7. Members shall inscribe the disciplines in Section II in their Schedules as additional commitments under Article XVIII of the Agreement. Members may choose to inscribe the alternative disciplines in Section III for their commitments in financial services.
>
> 8. The disciplines inscribed pursuant to paragraph 7 of this Section apply where specific commitments are undertaken. In addition, Members are encouraged to inscribe in their Schedules additional sectors to which the disciplines apply.
>
> 9. [Members may exclude the discipline set out in paragraph 22 (d) of Section II and paragraph 19 (d) of Section III from the additional commitments scheduled under paragraph 7 of this Section].

Sectoral coverage and scheduling follow particular modalities. As Section I, paragraph 7 outlines, WTO members shall inscribe the disciplines in Section II in their schedules of commitment as additional commitments under GATS Article XVIII. Members may choose to inscribe the alternative disciplines in Section III for their commitments in financial services.

Except for the removal of brackets, the final text in JSI 2021 is identical to the JSI 2020 text, and so it also locks in paragraph 9's opt-out, which first appeared with the JSI 2020 text.

Paragraph 8 stipulates how the disciplines inscribed pursuant to paragraph 7 apply where specific commitments are undertaken. In addition, members are encouraged to note in their schedules additional sectors to which the disciplines apply. However, in effect paragraph 9 introduces an opt-out by allowing a member to avoid the two provisions on non-discrimination between men and women when scheduling additional commitments pursuant to paragraph 7. This is a very unfortunate development in the text because of several legal-political implications. First, it creates a back door which undermines the standard-setting effect of the discipline. Second, allowing for an opt-out could be construed as almost legitimizing any discrimination or gender-exclusive effects causing backsliding. Third, it could be an unfortunate precedent that runs counter to the aspirations for incremental change set out in Section 6.6.2. Therefore, the opt-out included in the agreed JSI 2021 text is a hard pill to swallow.

The silver lining is, first, that it can also be used by members implementing domestic reforms who are concerned that affirmative action and special measures to accelerate gender equality that are not outright temporary in nature are protected from being struck down as incompatible. It seems counter-intuitive but perhaps it is to the benefit of such advancements. Second, it also lends itself to those that find the binary wording irreconcilable with domestic policy, or whose gender-inclusive domestic reforms in other ways cannot be reconciled with the binary provision and its implications.

The specific schedules of commitments are integral to scheduling market access, and to operationalizing new rules, such as the provision on gender equality. Time and policy practice will show how members inscribe their additional commitments in accordance with the agreement in their GATS commitments. Hereafter, they will apply on an MFN basis. Time and policy practice will also shed light on how commitments to ensuring non-discrimination between men and women in relation to authorizations for supply of services are implemented in domestic regimes. Once implemented in domestic regimes, generally speaking, such rules would apply to all within their jurisdiction and scope.

Thus, despite its flaws and the opt-out, the provision is set to discipline and generate value for the services sectors covered by it. Furthermore, where commitments are made, it is set to affect the reduction of barriers in services that may have a spill-over effect as those services form part of e-commerce or digital trade. Policy-wise, beyond MC12, it might strengthen the agenda and energize further advancements on gender equality. The developments so far allow for extrapolating important lessons – positive as well as negative ones – that can serve as fuel across the multi-level framework for the advancement of gender-inclusive e-commerce governance.

Indeed, factoring in existing and accelerating gender gaps, including the gender digital divide implicating e-commerce and digital trade, and the risk of producing gender-exclusion is imperative to improving policy practice. Therefore, it is the central argument that it takes multi-level dedicated gender-inclusive governance to make advances in closing the gender gap.

6.7 CONCLUSIONS

Gender-inclusive governance responds to the multiplicity of the gender gap, and how it is a multidimensional concept in the nature of its occurrence, the dynamics of its development, and the manifold ways it interrelates with other divides.

The relationship between gender divides, e-commerce, digital trade, and trade in services can be observed through the lenses of the different modes of supply and in trade patterns. The relationship reflects key policy challenges to participation in that trade – market access, resources, and a regulatory component. Moving towards gender-inclusive governance for e-commerce, digital trade, and trade in services is imperative for sustainable trade policy as digitalization can serve to fuel women's participation in trade, but in the absence of policy interventions, a deepening of the gender digital divide could have negative effects on gender inequalities.

The proposed multi-level framework shows the regulatory space for gender equality in creating an enabling environment for e-commerce and digital trade, and for incorporating gender equality into the new and enhanced regulatory layer of DR disciplines for trade in services.

What policy interventions are necessary, and why, to meet the moment? This chapter proposes a multi-level gender-inclusive framework for comprehensive narrowing of the gender gap in trade. Addressing the global, structural issue of gender inequality with multi-level approaches to the negotiating modalities, coupled with gender-inclusive governance for e-commerce, digital trade, and services trade, can contribute to closing the gender gap. E-commerce and digital trade alone, despite the promise of digitalization, cannot close the gender gap in trade. Services trade is ubiquitous and an extremely important area of trade that gender-inclusive governance could unlock to the benefit of gender equality. Examining trade in services also point squarely to the role of regulatory barriers and their interconnectedness with market access and access to resources. Disciplining DR pursuant to GATS Article VI and new disciplines pursuant to Article VI:4 may address this head-on. The provision on gender equality has been reduced to its detriment but it still shows a way forward and allows for important lessons that can inform gender-inclusive governance for trade when seizing this moment.

Leveraging the multi-level framework, and extrapolating lessons from policy practice, namely the concluded provision on gender equality in the JSI on services DR, could foster gender-inclusive governance. In that regard, the WTO and its JSIs could help deliver on the imperative of SDG 5 to achieve gender equality and turn high stakes into high reward for its members.

7

Setting Up the Table Right

Women's Representation Meets Women's Inclusion in Trade Negotiations

MARIA V. SOKOLOVA AND MATTHEW WILSON*

ABSTRACT

This chapter looks at women's representation in multilateral trade negotiations within the context of the overall goal of achieving more gender-sensitive outcomes in trade policy. Although trade negotiations have increased in scope and scale, this has not resulted in a concomitant increase in the representation of women as experts, negotiators and diplomats. The expansion and more complex nature of trade negotiations puts greater pressure on developing nations, especially on smaller delegations, as illustrated by data from the diplomatic missions to the United Nations and the World Trade Organization in Geneva. The chapter discusses the current structure and challenges of trade negotiations, highlighting both the challenges of the career and the changing character of persons engaged in trade negotiations. Lastly, the chapter draws attention to the distinction between women participating in trade negotiations and having the interests of women reflected in trade negotiation outcomes. This distinction is particularly important if one wants to place trade policy in the context of the overall societal movement towards gender equality. In its conclusion, this chapter sets out a list of actionable advice to improve the current situation to facilitate greater contribution of trade negotiations to global gender equality.

7.1 INTRODUCTION

Over the course of the last two decades in particular, trade negotiations have increased in scope, scale and complexity, involving more experts, negotiators

* The authors are very grateful for the research assistance of Imane Cherifi, and to all the interviewees – both active and retired negotiators – that contributed their knowledge and experience.

and diplomats. This has resulted in additional pressure on smaller developing countries that often have either a limited complement of staff in missions or have only non-resident representation in Geneva, which is the seat of multilateral trade negotiations at the WTO. Furthermore, the increasingly technical nature of trade negotiations can also place a strain on national expertise which is necessary to inform, backstop and support the negotiating process. The evidence confirms that trade missions from small island developing states (SIDS) and least-developed countries (LDCs) have a much lower staff complement, and in turn fewer women, than the average in the UN or the WTO missions in Geneva.[1] This can impact the ability of these economies to represent their interests in all relevant aspects of the negotiating agenda. This chapter looks at the representation of women in multilateral trade negotiations, specifically in the context of the WTO, and places it in the context of the overall goal of achieving more gender-sensitive outcomes from trade policy.

An important question is whether the gender make-up of representation has an impact on gender-sensitive outcomes emanating from trade negotiations. Recently it was recognized by the WTO members that trade has an important gender element. But the actual question is whether it has been a result of changing global norms around gender mainstreaming and gender inclusion or is a reflection of more gender-equal representation across the trade landscape – nationally and at the level of the missions in Geneva.

References to gender are present in some of the existing trade agreements,[2] and at the 11th Ministerial Conference held in Argentina in 2017, some WTO members, supported by the work of the International Trade Centre (ITC) and other actors, agreed to the Buenos Aires Declaration on Trade and Women's Economic Empowerment.[3] Ahead of Ministerial Conference 12 (MC12), gender seemed to be one of the key topics to see significant advancement.[4] At MC12, held in June 2022, we saw the highest number of women present at the negotiations – negotiating for food security, health and other

[1] Based on empirical research the authors have carried out. On file with authors.

[2] José-Antonio Monteiro, 'The Evolution of Gender-Related Provisions in Regional Trade Agreements' (2018) WTO Staff Working Paper ERSD-2018-15 <www.wto.org/english/res_e/reser_e/ersd201815_e.pdf> accessed 8 May 2022.

[3] WTO, 'Joint Declaration on Trade and Women's Economic Empowerment on the Occasion of the WTO Ministerial Conference in Buenos Aires in December 2017' (2017) <www.wto.org/english/thewto_e/minist_e/mc11_e/genderdeclarationmc11_e.pdf> accessed 8 May 2022 (Buenos Aires Declaration).

[4] The Joint Ministerial Declaration on the Advancement of Gender Equality and Women's Economic Empowerment within Trade signed by eighty-nine countries in November 2021 can be seen as a step forward.

themes of trade policy. Yet the term 'gender' was absent from the key negotiated outcomes. There was some progress made on the outskirts, and a side event, 'Unlocking Trade for Women's Empowerment and Sustainable Development', discussed the operational issues of trade and gender, such as the need to ensure trade and trade agreements contribute to greater gender equality through enhancing gender-sensitive data, better gender-based reporting and greater attention to women owned micro, small and medium-sized enterprises (MSMEs). But the 'side-ness' of the event indicates that we have still a long way to go.

While some of the trade agreements do include gender provisions and chapters, and there is momentum to take this further, it is worth looking at the process involved in concluding a trade agreement and ask how women are represented in those trade negotiations and whether greater representation translates into more gender-sensitive outcomes. The existing research on causality is limited but we provide a framework to analyse how, and at what stages, women are part of the negotiating value chain and survey the current representation of women in trade negotiations in Geneva. We argue that, while women's representation has a positive impact on trade negotiations, it should not be seen as a substitute for active inclusion of gender considerations in negotiated trade policy. There is a lack of literature and data on representation of women in the trade negotiation cycle, which we have sought to partly address by collecting data on the gender composition of the UN and the WTO missions and conducting confidential interviews with women and men involved throughout their careers in trade negotiations. While the names of interviewees will remain confidential, the authors have ensured geographic, gender and thematic diversity of persons interviewed.[5]

This chapter is organized as follows: Section 7.2 covers the changes in the nature of trade negotiations and how this has affected the demands on negotiators; Section 7.3 provides collected gendered data on the staff composition of the UN and WTO missions, showing diverging representation among member states; Section 7.4 highlights the importance of networks in supporting the job of a trade negotiator and how gendered socio-economic systems have historically placed women at a disadvantage for such positions; Section 7.5 binds together the altered nature of what trade negotiations are and which challenges women face in trade negotiations as a career choice. Section 7.6 highlights the importance of making a distinction between women participating in trade negotiations and the interests of women being included in trade

[5] Details are on file with the authors.

negotiations. In Section 7.7, we analyse women's representation as a tool for gender equality. We conclude the chapter, in Section 7.8, with a set of actionable suggestions that can improve the inclusion of issues around women in trade negotiations.

7.2 TRADE NEGOTIATIONS HAVE EXPANDED IN SCALE AND SCOPE

Trade negotiations have expanded in scale, scope and depth.[6] Trade negotiators are increasingly expected to contribute technical and multidisciplinary input and expertise and/or to be able to galvanize these technical inputs from their capital-based experts. New trade agreements tend to build on the already complex scope of agreements under the WTO or in existing bilateral agreements, hence sometimes forcing newcomers to the trade negotiation game to follow the lead that has already been set.

This is particularly the case for smaller countries which may naturally be party to less complex trade negotiations at the bilateral or regional levels. However, it is worth noting that since 2016, every WTO member has been a member of at least one regional trade agreement.[7] This certainly signifies an explosion in the number of negotiations that would naturally have to precede completed trade agreements – both non-WTO and WTO – even though there are different levels of complexities to consider.

The vast majority of the agreements concluded outside of the WTO have been 'WTO-plus' – meaning that they go deeper than already existing trade agreements at the WTO. Quite often the 'plus' relating to discussions that also happen inside the WTO with a more limited set of countries involved in plurilaterals such as investment, elements of environment, services, gender and others.[8] The reasons for this are rather obvious: fewer partners to negotiate

6 For information on size and originality of the agreements, *see* Wolfgang Alschner, Julia Seiermann and Dmitriy Skougarevskiy, 'Text of Trade Agreements (ToTA) – A Structured Corpus for the Text-as-Data Analysis of Preferential Trade Agreements' (2018) 15(3) *Journal of Empirical Legal Studies* 648–666. For the type of provisions and trends in enforceability, *see* Claudia Homann, Alberto Osnago and Michele Ruta, 'Horizontal Depth: A New Database on the Content of Preferential Trade Agreements' (2017) World Bank Policy Research Working Paper 7981 <https://openknowledge.worldbank.org/handle/10986/26148> accessed 8 May 2022.

7 WTO, 'Regional Trade Agreements Database' <https://rtais.wto.org/UI/PublicMaintainRTAHome.aspx> accessed 8 May 2022.

8 For example, Canada, the EU, New Zealand, Chile and the United States started including environment chapters in their trade agreements, but as they are driven by national policy these chapters differ in their design. It is safe to assume that should there be a WTO agreement on the environment, these chapters would have been of a more similar structure.

with; a more like-minded approach between partners; and the ability to develop agreement-specific implementation, monitoring and dispute systems. The expectation is that every WTO member will notify its trade agreements to the WTO to ensure that it does not violate the existing multilateral commitments.[9]

However, the reality can be a bit more complex given the tension between the notions of 'globalization' (through the WTO) and 'regionalization' (through regional trade agreements – RTAs) of trade liberalization.[10] For the past decade – accelerated by limited success at concluding multilateral agreements (with the Trade Facilitation Agreement and recent Fisheries Subsidies Agreements being exceptions) and emergence of more plurilateral negotiations at the WTO – the balance has shifted from 'ideological competitors' to 'complementary allies.' Views on regionalization have matured from being seen as undermining trade globalization, to now being viewed as an extension of trade globalization moving the needle forward and complementing the WTO rules.[11] RTAs are now accepted as avenues for deepening trade liberalization and informing the scope and ambition of multilateral agreements. We are seeing this happen in the area of gender and trade, e-commerce and investment facilitation.[12]

Trade is widely seen as one of the main vessels for inclusive and sustainable growth. It permeates the United Nations Sustainable Development Goals (UN SDGs)[13] and during the COVID-19 pandemic it was key to vaccine distribution.[14] Ideological differences still persist on what 'kind' of trade is best

[9] Notification of RTAs that cover goods are in paragraphs 4 to 10 of Article XXIV of GATT, trade in services is under Article V of GATS. The only exception from 'deeper' trade agreements than WTO is the Enabling Clause (the 1979 Decision on Differential and More Favourable Treatment, Reciprocity and Fuller Participation of Developing Countries) that gave more favourable arrangements for trade in goods between developed and developing countries.

[10] For example, Sangmoon Kim and Eui-Hang Shin, 'A Longitudinal Analysis of Globalization and Regionalization in International Trade: A Social Network Approach' (2002) 81(1) *Social Forces* 445–471.

[11] For time trend analysis of key regional indicators, *see* WEF, 'Regionalization vs Globalization: What Is the Future Direction of Trade?' (15 July 2021) <www.weforum.org/agenda/2021/07/regionalization-globalization-future-direction-trade/> accessed 8 May 2022. Regionalism has been fuelling globalization and is projected to be the key force in future global trade.

[12] For example, in the case of gender there were a number of various provisions in trade agreements addressing gender inequality, some of them predating the Buenos Aires Declaration, and most going beyond the declarations. *See* ITC, 'Mainstreaming Gender in Free Trade Agreements' (2020) <https://intracen.org/media/file/2411> accessed 8 May 2022.

[13] WTO, 'The WTO and the Sustainable Development Goals' <www.wto.org/english/thewto_e/coher_e/sdgs_e/sdgs_e.htm> accessed 8 May 2022.

[14] *See* Reinhilde Veugelers, Niclas Poitiers and Lionel Guetta-Jeanrenaud, 'A World Divided: Global Vaccine Trade and Production' (Bruegel 20 July 2021) <www.bruegel.org/blog-post/

for the environment, equality and sustainability, but there is growing recognition that it does have divergent effects on men and women.[15] A growing number of RTAs now include gender chapters.[16] However, these chapters are primarily persuasive in intention as in general they do not have enforcement mechanisms attached to them.[17] At the same time, if one takes a deeper look at the 2017 Buenos Aires Declaration, it has pushed the needle forward by leading to the formation of an Informal Working Group (IWG) on Trade and Gender in the WTO.[18] This group addresses trade and gender issues by encouraging members to exchange practices on mainstreaming gender considerations into programmes and strategies and increase gendered data collection, amongst others.[19]

Given this increased attention to gender in trade, one can expect that modern trade policy would become more gender-equal not only in its effects, but also in its creation.

Based on the interviews conducted for this chapter, we can conclude that in trade negotiations, women's representation has often been a proxy for 'having women's voices heard', and therefore more gender-inclusive policy proposals being created throughout the negotiations. We argue, however, that women's representation in trade negotiations, while having a positive effect, should not be confused with inclusion of issues of importance to women in the context of trade negotiations and agreements – that is, a result that leads to a more gender-equalizing effect of negotiated trade policy.

Women's representation is a necessary, but not a sufficient condition for a more gender-inclusive trade policy. Gender inclusion is a responsibility of all

world-divided-global-vaccine-trade-and-production> accessed 8 May 2022; Margaret Labban, 'Vaccine Trade Becomes a Key Factor in Global Diplomacy' (27 July 2021) <www.pharmaceutical-technology.com/pricing-and-market-access/vaccine-trade-becomes-a-key-factor-in-global-diplomacy-html/> accessed 8 May 2022.

15 For the purpose of this chapter we rely on a simplistic split of genders as 'men' and 'women' but acknowledge that the gender spectrum can be seen as far more complex. *See*, for example, the World Bank and WTO, 'Women and Trade: The Role of Trade in Promoting Gender Equality' (23 July 2020) <www.worldbank.org/en/topic/trade/publication/women-and-trade-the-role-of-trade-in-promoting-womens-equality> accessed 8 May 2022.

16 The most prominent first case was the Canada–Chile FTA, which included commitments on women's access to education, digital know-how and skills development.

17 For more details, *see* Javiera Cáceres Bustamante and Felipe Muñoz Navia, 'South America's Leadership in Gender Mainstreaming in Trade Agreements' (Chapter 12 in this book).

18 WTO, 'Informal Working Group on Trade and Gender' <www.wto.org/english/tratop_e/womenandtrade_e/iwg_trade_gender_e.htm> accessed 8 May 2022.

19 WTO, 'Trade and Gender Informal Working Group Co-chairs Present Draft Outcome Document for MC12' (23 September 2021) <www.wto.org/english/news_e/news21_e/women_23sep21_e.htm> accessed 8 May 2022.

genders, and although it is ideal to have all of these genders involved in the crafting of gender-sensitive trade policies, as a second-best option it can be assumed that men would be able to sufficiently represent the interests of women with the right tools at hand. However, in the twenty-first century, this scenario is far from ideal.

7.3 ABILITY TO PARTICIPATE IN NEGOTIATIONS VARIES

It is difficult to obtain information on women's representation in the process of trade negotiations, as quite often this information is confidential, or it is hard to estimate who is engaged in trade negotiations, and at what point. As most of the multilateral trade discussions are led by Geneva missions, we use Geneva for our data collection exercise to survey the overall picture on women's involvement in trade negotiations.

According to data we collected,[20] there are 182 missions to the UN in Geneva, and 175 missions to the WTO. The average size of professional staff in a UN mission is ten people, but with a wide range of one person to seventy people. Of the total staff in UN missions, 37 per cent identify as women. Remarkably, the average WTO mission – sometimes a subset of the larger UN mission – is six people, ranging from one to thirty people, and with 40 per cent identifying as women. This signals that there is similar attention, on average, given to trade representation in Geneva as there is to humanitarian affairs, human rights, health, labour and so on combined. It is worth recalling that discussions at the WTO also now cover the environment, gender, health and other topics. This is supported by the fact that in the case of 105 countries,[21] the mission carries out a double function – meaning that the head of the delegation leads both the mission to the UN and to the WTO.

Amongst others, the following conclusions can be drawn from the data presented in Table 7.1:

- On average, the size of the WTO mission of a country is almost half the size of the UN mission. This illustrates the fact that Geneva, while being a regional UN headquarters and centre for many other discussions, is also seen as a global centre of multilateral trade negotiations;

[20] Data is collected from the UN blue book, official websites and sources of the WTO and WTO missions. The data was collected in September 2021, and the most recent available data is accounted as current. On file with authors.

[21] The EU and its member states are counted as separate entities.

TABLE 7.1 *Breakdown of the staff (incl. gendered) of the UN and WTO missions in Geneva, by region and country groups*

	Separate function of UN & WTO missions	Double function of UN & WTO missions	Average size UN mission	Average share of women, UN mission	Average size WTO mission	Average share of women, WTO mission	Share of women heads of WTO delegation
Overall	58	105	10	0.4	5.7	0.37	0.3
Regional breakdown							
Asia	16	25	11.8	0.33	6.9	0.3	0.24
Europe & Northern America	14	28	14.3	0.47	6.1	0.43	0.36
Latin America & Caribbean	17	12	6.6	0.54	5.2	0.41	0.24
Oceania (including Pacific countries)	4	1	4.6	0.52	4.3	0.45	0.5
Africa	7	39	8	0.3	5	0.35	0.33
Country groupings							
OECD	12	19	17	0.49	7.7	0.44	0.29
SIDS	8	8	3.3	0.5	3.1	0.4	0.5
LDC	7	31	6.5	0.27	4.6	0.33	0.27
Developed	18	31	15	0.47	6.5	0.42	0.34
Developing	40	74	8	0.37	5.4	0.35	0.28
Industrialized	14	24	18	0.47	7.8	0.44	0.25
Emerging industrialized	13	15	11	0.44	6.4	0.38	0.04
Country income groups							
High-income	22	31	13.8	0.46	6.8	0.41	0.23
Upper-middle-income	16	26	9.8	0.43	5.8	0.38	0.43
Lower-middle-income	15	22	8.7	0.41	4.7	0.36	0.32
Low-income	5	26	6.9	0.24	5.3	0.32	0.21

Source: authors' collection of data (based on interviews and discussions with relevant stakeholders; details withheld. On file with authors).
Averages are simple arithmetic averages.

- Every two out of three missions in Geneva double as both mission to the UN and mission to the WTO, which implies that they do not concentrate solely on trade issues;
- It is no surprise that the countries of the Organisation for Economic Development and Co-operation (OECD), developed countries, industrialized countries and high-income countries have larger UN and WTO missions than other subgroups of countries;
- Women are present at a rate of under 50 per cent in both UN and WTO mission staff, but score over 30 per cent for almost all subgroups;
- Women are present less frequently than men as heads of WTO delegations in the missions of industrialized countries, with low- and high-income countries having the lowest share;
- Europe and North America have 50 per cent larger UN missions than the rest of the world, but the difference is much smaller for the WTO missions; Asia also has larger UN missions than average (18 per cent), and the largest trade missions (20 per cent larger).
- Regarding women's representation, Asia and Africa have on average fewer women present in the missions, but Latin America and the Caribbean and Asia have the lowest share (24 per cent) of women heads of WTO missions.
- Irrespective of groupings, women are on average less present in WTO missions than men.

While we are only able to collect information on the Geneva diplomatic sphere and hence may not capture the gender make-up of the capital and regional counterparts of trade diplomacy, it is still telling that women from all regions are underrepresented in Geneva, which is the epicentre of the multilateral trading system. Altogether, these facts paint a very complex picture of Geneva diplomacy. There are currently 516 active RTAs,[22] with 17 RTAs notified to the WTO in the first half of 2021.[23] At the same time, the WTO itself has a complex structure with at least thirty-three active committees, councils or working groups (aside from the dispute settlement processes). As Geneva is considered a capital of trade policy, it is useful to look at the sheer number of meetings facilitated by the WTO and the UN Conference on Trade and Development (UNCTAD), which on average can reach more than 1,000 per year, with a common occurrence of 4–5 meetings a day. In addition,

[22] Based on data from ITC, WTO and WCO, 'Rules of Origin Facilitator' <https://findrulesoforigin.org/> accessed 8 May 2022.

[23] WTO, 'Regional Trade Agreements Database' (n 7).

there are bilateral meetings, lobbying and some cross-issue meetings in other organizations such as the ITC, the World Intellectual Property Organization (WIPO) and the International Telecommunications Union (ITU), and various other discussion fora on human rights, labour rights, some aspects of disarmament, intellectual property, health and others. As a mission is assumed to generally cover all topics in Geneva, or at least have an understanding of the ecosystem, mission staff are often faced with making hard choices on which issues and meetings to follow. Many smaller missions are not able to have dedicated personnel solely focused on trade issues.

The 37 per cent representation of women in WTO missions is a score that can seem relatively close to parity. However, one should be careful in interpreting this number as an indicator for gender inclusion in resulting trade policy. The gendered effects of trade are multifaceted and require not only a multitude of experts to account for, but also a vast network during the process of negotiation to get certain concessions or commitments through. However, the presence of women in trade negotiations is an improvement to the overall 'masculinity' of trade and negotiations and is a first step to creating a more gender-inclusive trade policy.

7.4 TRADE NEGOTIATIONS NEED NETWORKS

Trade negotiations are a complex process that rely on the ability of chief negotiators and their whole team to influence the other party and ensure win–win outcomes. A fundamental component of an effective negotiating strategy is the ability to connect to institutions and expertise in their own capitals.[24]

Quite often, negotiations are pictured as two or more parties sitting at different sides of the table having different interests. We see people sitting at the table signing papers next to each other on front pages of newspapers as a symbol of concluded trade negotiations. This image is misleading not only because people on these front pages are usually not the ones doing the negotiations, but it can also give an inaccurate message about the process of negotiation, and the diverging goals of the negotiating parties. The common goal of negotiating parties is to reach an agreement – this was confirmed by the Brexit process, where despite the diverging interests and various

24 Role of negotiation scripts and national culture discussed using the example of negotiations with China: Rajesh Kumar and Verner Worm, 'Social Capital and the Dynamics of Business Negotiations between the Northern Europeans and the Chinese' (2003) 20(3) *International Marketing Review* 262–285.

difficulties, the 'no-deal' scenario was avoided as it was apparent that no agreement was the least preferred scenario on either side of the table.[25]

Processes and people matter for successful negotiations. There are certainly some personal traits that can contribute to a more successful outcome at the negotiating table, such as persuasion, charisma, assertiveness and communication skills. Successful negotiators are quite often branded with such images as 'punching above their weight', 'heavy hitters' and 'aggressive players'.[26] These are viewed 'traditionally' as male skills and characteristics,[27] as gendered power systems tend to assign such skills to 'men's jobs', which require a generally higher level of power and fewer women tend to apply for them.[28] One can argue that such a traditional, and frankly inaccurate, perception of negotiation as a 'man's job' could be one reason for fewer women choosing such a career. After all, if one looks at gender stereotypes, one can also say that women tend to be more collaborative in their decision making.[29] In addition, our interviews also show the anecdotal evidence that a higher presence of women at the negotiating table may lead to faster compromises and conclusion of the trade agreement.[30]

However, the biggest success factor of negotiations may lie outside of the negotiating room: the connection with the capital. As described above, the negotiation process has a double location – at the negotiating table and in the capital. Achieving the ultimate goal of negotiations (conclusion of a trade agreement where both sides gain more than they lose) requires receiving guidance and expertise from the capital, approving of texts and positions and requiring quick feedback and decisions. One can assume, in most of the cases, that this will require a number of inter-agency and inter-ministry

[25] Jim Brunsden and George Parker, 'UK and EU to Resume Talks in Final Push for Post-Brexit Trade Deal' (*Financial Times* 22 October 2020) <www.ft.com/content/27d46f3b-a718-421e-b5d6-b007c08a441d> accessed 8 May 2022.

[26] These quotes are unattributable to the interviews, but Malhotra and Bazerman give a good overview of the key skills of a successful negotiator – and they resemble the ones we list from the interviews. *See* Deepak Malhotra and Max Bazerman, *Negotiation Genius: How to Overcome Obstacles and Achieve Brilliant Results at the Bargaining Table and Beyond* (Bantam 2008).

[27] Gill Whitty-Collins, *Why Men Win at Work… and How We Can Make Inequality History* (Luath Press 2020).

[28] Roxana Barbulescu and Matthew Bidwell, 'Do Women Choose Different Jobs from Men? Mechanisms of Application Segregation in the Market for Managerial Workers' (2012) 24(3) *Organization Science* 737–756.

[29] Renee Cullinan, 'In Collaborative Work Cultures, Women Disproportionately Carry More of the Weight' (*Harvard Business Review* 24 July 2018) <https://hbr.org/2018/07/in-collaborative-work-cultures-women-carry-more-of-the-weight> accessed 8 May 2022.

[30] The authors would welcome further research on this.

consultations, verifications and active lobbying with the business community and civil society for certain concessions. Additionally, every step involves not only political consensus, but also certain administrative steps – be it sending a memo between different ministries or associations, or just registering incoming documents. To speed up the response from the capital and overcome or make more efficient these 'red tape' processes, personal connections and political aptness are key for negotiators.

Historically, diplomatic and political connections in any country were in the hands of men, and this can explain the relatively lower presence of women in trade (and the UN) missions today. Changing the gender make-up of a profession can take generations. Based on the collected data on missions in Geneva, it is not a surprise that the presence of women trade experts, diplomats and negotiators is higher in countries that score better on gender equality domestically. Active encouragement of women to pursue government-related careers could help bring more women to positions where they are engaged in the negotiation process. There is evidence that even when quotas for women were introduced, women have tended to fall out of government careers[31] – a phenomenon that is yet to be studied further. What could be the reasons for women not staying in the government positions, and can these reasons be curtailed in order to enhance women's participation?

A first relevant factor is that trade negotiations take years. The greater the number of participating countries, the longer will be the negotiations. Overall, the trade negotiation process can be described in several steps:[32]

(1) Consultative process of negotiations;
(2) Development of country position and possible scenarios for the concessions;
(3) Negotiation of the process of negotiation: determination of the number of rounds, chapters to be negotiated, when and where;
(4) Actual process of negotiation: party-to-party interaction; and
(5) Formal conclusion: the official 'signature' moment, ratification in the executive body, official notification to the WTO and other trading partners.

While the beginning and end of the negotiations are set points in time, the intermediate steps can be repeated many times and span many years. These

[31] UN Women, 'Women in Politics: 2021' <www.unwomen.org/sites/default/files/Headquarters/Attachments/Sections/Library/Publications/2021/Women-in-politics-2021-en.pdf> accessed 8 May 2022.

[32] Based on data collected by the authors and their experience.

intermediary steps may never come to fruition – for example, in the case of the Transatlantic Trade and Investment Partnership (TTIP) – but if they do, the signature process is a huge political success.

Quite often during the process of multilateral and regional negotiations, the process is split into stages of active face-to-face negotiations in a predetermined location and time to lobby/gather feedback in the capital – requiring much travelling in between.[33]

Negotiations at the WTO are premised on consensus-building with the hitherto unused option of majority voting available.[34] Finding a common position among 164 countries requires building alliances that are ever more nuanced and therefore require even larger networks. In the world where there are so many trade topics in many trade fora, countries are naturally drawn to build strategic alliances and partnerships, pooling resources and accessing information.

Just having women present in trade negotiations does not control for women as a population group having similar access to the benefits of trade agreements as men. Research shows that gains from trade liberalization are distributed unequally between men and women due to the systemic issues across different areas of human activity, including access to finance, skills, prohibitive laws and social norms.[35] Expecting a woman negotiator to be an expert not only in her field of expertise, but also in all other fields that interact with gender, or being able to forecast the gendered impact of trade policy taking into account all these dimensions, is an unrealistic assumption. Of course, every woman negotiator brings her own experience and perspective as a woman to the table, but it does not substitute for gender inclusion in the process of negotiation.

A separate remark has to be made about the effect of the COVID-19 pandemic on trade negotiations. The overall move of negotiations to virtual/hybrid format and higher reliance of government officials on computer-enabled processes had the potential to improve the general speed of interaction and reaction of the capital. At the same time, it had an ambiguous effect on the ability of negotiators to build connection and trust during the

[33] The back-and-forth between the capital and negotiation seat is quite often combined with actual physical travel. As women are traditionally left in charge of unpaid care work for children and the elderly more often than men, such a work routine could be a greater burden.

[34] Art. XI, WTO Agreement: Marrakesh Agreement Establishing the World Trade Organization, 15 April 1994, 1867 UNTS 154 33 ILM 1144 (1994) (Marrakesh Agreement or WTO Agreement).

[35] World Bank and WTO, 'Women and Trade' (n 15).

negotiations.[36] The pandemic definitely has opened the door to creating a more inclusive structure of trade negotiations, but it is yet to be understood how this can be successfully utilized to achieve the common goal of any trade negotiation – conclusion of trade agreements that benefit its addressees.

7.5 TO BE A NEGOTIATOR IS A CAREER CHOICE, TRADE NEGOTIATIONS ARE NOT

While it is safe to assume that having sufficient women representatives in trade negotiations is a positive development for the negotiations themselves due to women's higher propensity to achieve more collaborative interactions,[37] tasking women negotiators to represent the whole multitude of 'women's interests' in trade negotiations is misplaced. The larger question is how do we systemically ensure that 'women's interests' can be reflected in trade negotiations?

Trade negotiations increasingly cover more and more topics, both in the WTO and at the regional level. Independent from the type of negotiation, the interviews have indicated that expertise in the negotiating party can be split into two fields – 'generalist' and 'expert' negotiators. The generalist negotiators are often responsible for the overall process of negotiation – exchange of positions, ensuring fulfilment of the procedural code, getting a response from the opposite party. Their key skills are institutional memory and diplomatic connections that they can use to try to get a better offer from the opposing party. The more experienced the generalists in trade negotiations, the more a country can 'punch above its weight' in trade negotiations.[38] Where women are present in these roles, this mostly happens in countries where gender equality has been targeted internally for decades.

The 'expert' negotiator deals with the more technical side – the aspect that has been gaining in prominence – such as covering Technical Barriers to Trade (TBT), Sanitary and Phytosanitary Measures (SPS), climate change, rules of origin, environmental issues or other related issues. The complexity of these issues varies with the agreement and the countries, but it requires specialist knowledge given that the impact goes beyond the scope of diplomacy and to the heart of domestic policy development. One can think of the

36 Connection and trust are key in successful negotiations. *See* Malhotra and Bazerman, *Negotiation Genius* (n 26).

37 Eduardo Araújo, Nuno AM Araújo, André A Moreira, Hans J Herrmann and José S Andrade Jr, 'Gender Differences in Scientific Collaborations: Women Are More Egalitarian than Men' (2017) 12(5) *PLoS ONE*.

38 Based on the authors' experience and empirical research.

example of the trade facilitation negotiations where many of the experts were from customs and other border agencies and not necessarily from the foreign affairs or foreign trade office. The same can be seen in the fisheries subsidies negotiations where many large countries are able to be represented by officials and experts from the agriculture, fisheries or environmental ministries. Their involvement is dynamic, and often issue-specific.

This vast scope of specialists that are involved in trade negotiations serve as a bridge to the issues to which women are 'traditionally' assigned, as in many countries women's segregation by profession is still present.[39] So when women are present in trade negotiations, are they mostly assigned to 'expert' fields, or do they occupy more 'generalist' positions? Based on the authors' experience, there is no clear-cut answer on that. Moreover, while women heading negotiations does indeed have the potential to lead to greater inclusion of some women's interests in the absence of overall gender inclusion, having women specialized in certain topics can bring more tailored and specialized gender inclusion and is overall a stronger indicator of a more gender-equal society.

With the increasing complexity of issues covered by trade agreements – gender, environment, technology, IP, investment, human rights – one can be certain that there will be an increase of negotiating teams to include experts from those fields.[40] The increasing technical charge of trade agreements and growing political tensions around trade will also increase the need to bridge between expert jargon and generalists' political messaging.

Based on the information collected in the preparation of this chapter, it became obvious that there is no common structure in the order of engaging different types of negotiators. In some cases, both 'generalists' and 'experts' are present in the negotiating room; sometimes they take turns negotiating by chapters; sometimes generalists are well-prepared and can negotiate just checking in with experts; sometimes experts are placed in the capital, with generalists consulting with them constantly.

The expansion of trade negotiation teams is not universal – as with the size of trade missions in Geneva, some countries have limited diplomatic resources for trade policy and even less financial resources.[41] In many smaller countries,

[39] Some anecdotal evidence gathered for this chapter suggests that women play a bigger role in topics that are 'unpopular' or 'marginal', but as these topics gain attention men start being more engaged with them. This could be the case for gender, the climate and labour issues in trade agreements.

[40] For some of the conducted interviews, the negotiating party was already reaching 100 people.

[41] For example: Benin removed its mission. *See* Simon Petit, 'Une ambassade à Genève, un luxe? Oui, a repondu le Benin' (*Le Temps* 28 August 2020) <www.letemps.ch/monde/une-ambassade-geneve-un-luxe-oui-repondu-benin> accessed 8 May 2022; Fiji reinstated its

or 'latecomers' to trade negotiations, the 'expert' and 'generalist' is often the same person, and there is sometimes a need to rely on international experts for support, paradoxically often funded by their negotiating opponents. Organizations such as the South Centre, the Commonwealth Secretariat and the Advisory Center on WTO Law (ACWL) also provide legal, technical and analytical support to developing countries as part of their mandate.[42]

Some of these small countries and 'latecomers' may have a harder time catching up, facing the tension between being locked out from the integration processes and not having enough trade policy expertise at home to protect national interests. Interviews with small delegations have confirmed that such latecomers have greater difficulties crafting their own position and may quite often outsource the underlying trade analysis to experts in other countries or international institutions.

A separate remark has to be made about the importance of training of officials provided by international organizations. Training provided by the WTO, the UNCTAD, the ITC and other organizations[43] tend to be built on a best-practices approach, and therefore can provide a timely source of knowledge on the latest topics in trade, sometimes being the sole source of affordable expertise on such issues as gender and trade, trade and environment, or financing for trade for government officials.

7.6 WOMEN'S REPRESENTATION VERSUS WOMEN'S INCLUSION IN TRADE NEGOTIATIONS

The purpose of this chapter is not simply to discuss whether women are represented at trade negotiations – but also to highlight that women

mission in 2014 after a decade of absence. *See* ABC News, 'Fiji Reinstated to the Commonwealth Following "Credible Elections"' (26 September 2014) <www.abc.net.au/news/2014-09-27/fiji-reinstated-to-the-commonwealth-following-elections/5773330> accessed 8 May 2022; Mexico has decreased the overall size of negotiating teams as a part of austerity politics. *See* Mary Beth Sheridan, 'López Obrador's Cost-Cutting Spree Is Transforming Mexico – and Drawing Blowback from Bureaucrats' (*Washington Post* 14 July 2019) <www.washingtonpost.com/world/the_americas/lopez-obradors-cost-cutting-spree-is-transforming-mexico–and-drawing-blowback-from-bureaucrats/2019/07/14/5e187b5e-66c2-11e9-a698-2a8f808c9cfb_story.html> accessed 8 May 2022.

42 For further information, *see* ACWL, 'Home' <www.acwl.ch> accessed 8 May 2022; South Centre <www.southcentre.int> accessed 8 May 2022; Commonwealth <https://climate.thecommonwealth.org> accessed 8 May 2022.

43 For example, *see* courses available for registration at ITC, 'SME Trade Academy' <https://learning.intracen.org> accessed 8 May 2022; UNCTAD, 'Virtual Institute' <https://vi.unctad.org> accessed 8 May 2022; WTO, 'e-Learning Institute' <www.learning.wto.org/> accessed 8 May 2022.

representation in trade negotiations does not guarantee that 'women's interests' are included in the resulting negotiated text of a trade agreement. This puts trade negotiations into a wider context of achieving global gender equality.

Women's representation is quite often a misleading proxy for including women's interests. Therefore, when women's representation is discussed, it is often intended to serve not as a role model of a particular career, but also as the channel to include women's interests at large – to create gender inclusion in a trade agreement. It is important to recognize the difference between the two. While there are positive benefits of women's representation on gender equality (see next section) in the negotiated trade agreement, it is not a sufficient element to ensure the gender inclusion of the negotiated outcome and that the interests of women are fully reflected. This can be ensured only when negotiation is gender-sensitive and/or gender is a part of the analysis in the process of negotiation.[44]

As we discussed, the negotiation itself is a highly technical process that involves many different types of expertise, including both professional negotiators and specialists in a particular field. Women's representation in the trade negotiations therefore depends on encouraging women to take on these kinds of jobs and to ensure the environment is supportive of growing responsibility for these women. Access to skills and training, family-friendly policies for diplomats and negotiators and mentorship are all important elements to attract and maintain women's representation in this career.

Can we assume that the inclusion of women in trade negotiations implies that gender equality is improving as a result of what is negotiated? Trade negotiations are a success when they result with the conclusion of a trade agreement. Trade agreements in turn contain not only preferential trade terms between countries, but also better regulatory frameworks, means to liberalize

44 Historically, gender was introduced as a part of sustainability concepts, and was first bundled into sustainability analysis of trade agreements. Right now, there are multiple frameworks available on how to incorporate gender into trade policy proposals. *See* ITC, 'Mainstreaming Gender in Free Trade Agreements' (n 12); Jane Korinek, Evdokia Moïsé and Jakob Tange, 'Trade and Gender: A Framework of Analysis' (2021) OECD Policy Paper 246 <https://doi.org/10.1787/6db59d80-en> accessed 8 May 2022. There are also country-specific initiatives, for example, Canada's gender-based analysis used for all development cooperation programmes. *See* Government of Canada, 'Gender Analysis' <www.international.gc.ca/world-monde/funding-financement/gender_analysis-analyse_comparative.aspx?lang=eng> accessed 8 May 2022, and EIGE, 'Gender Mainstreaming' <https://eige.europa.eu/gender-mainstreaming> accessed 8 May 2022.

trade and improve development outcomes. Recent data[45] shows that trade agreements are hard to implement, and developing countries are lagging behind even on implementing existing agreements and using certain preferential rates. When we take into account the social complexity of addressing gender, regional trade agreements have the potential to both improve and worsen the situation of women if the unequal distribution of trade effects domestically are not controlled for.

There is evidence that trade agreements improve gender equality – but this is dependent on agreement-specific factors.[46] This, along with the generally unequally distributed gains from trade liberalization, brings us to the conclusion that the biggest possible positive effect of a trade agreement on gender equality can be only achieved in its gender-inclusive implementation at home.

While the existing gender chapters do not have specific commitments or enforcement mechanisms,[47] they signify a huge step forward in recognizing that to control for diverging impacts on men and women, trade agreements should not be assumed to be gender-neutral, but should be actively gender-inclusive.[48] There is yet an unproven effect on gender equality of trade and gender chapters, and the high cultural sensitivity of gender issues makes it unlikely that such gender chapters can be included in all upcoming trade negotiations. Inability to have gender provisions or chapters does not automatically undermine the inclusion of issues of importance to women in trade agreements as there are other ways of incorporating them – such as adding

45 For example, *see* Rohini Acharya, 'Regional Trade Agreements: Challenges and Opportunities. Proliferation of Trade Accords Has Potential to Increase Trade – and Make Trade Relations More Complex' (ITC News 20 December 2018) <https://intracen.org/news-and-events/news/regional-trade-agreements-challenges-and-opportunities> accessed 8 May 2022.

46 Amelia U. Santos-Paulino, Alisa DiCaprio and Maria V. Sokolova, 'The Development Trinity: How Regional Integration Impacts Growth, Inequality and Poverty' (2019) 42(7) *World Economy* 1961–1993.

47 For example, Articles 121–122 of the East African Community treaty endorses women roles in economic, social and political development of the region – with no specific commitments or enforcement. However, using the more general Article 6(d) that includes commitment to equal opportunities and gender equality among others, they have launched the Gender Policy that introduces gender strategies into different institutional policies that are aimed at integration. On the other hand, the Canada–Israel FTA that includes a gender chapter (Chapter 13) with provisions on cooperation in various areas that can improve gender equality (e.g. access to finance, female entrepreneurship, GBA implementation) also permits parties to have recourse on consent to the dispute settlement mechanism established under the FTA – making it, legally speaking, clearer on how to monitor and enforce advances in gender equality in FTAs.

48 For more discussion on this, *see* Marie-France Paquet and Georgina Wainwright-Kemdirim, 'Crafting Canada's Gender-Responsive Trade Policy' (Chapter 14 in this book).

gender as a dimension to be considered during the analysis of the potential effects of trade agreements at the negotiation stage.[49]

The existence of SDG 5 creates the sentiment and a set of indicators,[50] but there is no recipe on how it should or can be implemented in each country. There is a lingering lack of gendered data – both in trade and globally. Collection and transparency about such data can be more problematic in some societies due to cultural sensitivity but it is often as a result of the appropriate systems not being in place to capture this important disaggregated data. This disaggregated data is not only essential to ensuring that trade agreements are gender-sensitive but gives governments the means to monitor and measure the consequent impact of the agreements on women.

There is a misleading sentiment that only women should be in charge of gender-inclusion issues. While it is undeniable that there is a positive effect of having greater women's representation and women role models it is inaccurate to assume that a woman put into the lead negotiator position will automatically have the understanding of how to propose policies that are gender-inclusive on a large scale. This is why it is crucial that systemic changes are made at all stages of the trade negotiating cycle to infuse gender-sensitivity, gender-disaggregated data and gender training irrespective of which gender is leading the negotiations.

Given the uneven representation of women in negotiations and the general lack of gender mainstreaming, having women negotiators is better than having no women at all, but it does not automatically ensure greater inclusion of gender issues in trade policy.

7.7 WOMEN'S REPRESENTATION AS A TOOL FOR GENDER EQUALITY

Women have been notoriously absent in history[51] and despite greater awareness and anxiety around issues of gender equality today, there is still a clear divide, with women not only earning less than men for the same job, but also

49 One such approach is the gender-based Analysis Plus (GBA+) that allows for assessing how diverse groups of women and men experience various policy proposals. At the moment, the Canadian government is the first to implement a comprehensive GBA+ analysis of the full scope of trade agreements and its effects. For more details, *see* ibid.

50 SDG 5: Achieve gender equality and empower all women and girls. *See* UNECOSOC, 'Achieve Gender Equality and Empower All Women and Girls' <https://sdgs.un.org/goals/goal5> accessed 8 May 2022.

51 Christine Fauré, 'Absent from History' (Lillian S. Robinson trans) (1981) 7(1) *Journal of Women in Culture and Society* 71–80.

having more limited access to basic human rights and suffering greater effects from economic and climate shocks.[52] Much of this disparity is not only dependent on socio-economic factors, but also connected to cultural and religious factors. This makes the global advancement of gender equality not only institutionally complex, but also highly charged politically. Although it is beyond the remit of this chapter, the situation is even more dire when elements such as race, ethnicity and socio-economic status are brought into the picture.

In such a globally unequal situation, women's representation has not always been seen as an overall improvement, but rather as a 'patch' to the situation. There has even been a backlash, and scepticism regarding the competency of women placed in positions of power.[53] Nevertheless, the overarching positive impact of greater representation of women, specifically in trade-related activities, cannot be ignored.

First of all, role models matter, especially for roles where there is a gender bias, and more so in developing countries.[54] Having women negotiators sends a powerful signal of career possibilities (as discussed earlier, networks and influence are key components of a negotiator's job).

Secondly, women overall have different sets of skills and perspectives – partially invigorated by systemic limitations and disadvantages – and can bring different dynamics and views to the process of negotiation. While this requires further research, the anecdotal evidence that the authors collected during the interviews proves that having a sufficient number of women negotiators changes the dynamics of the process – potentially making it less charged and more efficient.[55]

[52] UN Women, 'Explainer: How Gender Inequality and Climate Change Are Interconnected' <www.unwomen.org/en/news-stories/explainer/2022/02/explainer-how-gender-inequality-and-climate-change-are-interconnected> accessed 8 May 2022; Elisabeth Reichert, 'Women's Rights Are Human Rights: Platform for Action' (1998) 41(3) *International Social Work* 371–384; Eric Neumayer and Thomas Plümper, 'The Gendered Nature of Natural Disasters: The Impact of Catastrophic Events on the Gender Gap in Life Expectancy, 1981–2002' (2007) 97(3) *Annals of the Association of American Geographers* 551–566.

[53] From the recent cases of biased attention on women in power one can look at the election of Ngozi Okonjo-Iweala as the head of the WTO and coverage in the media. *See* Euronews, 'Swiss Newspaper Apologises for "Inappropriate" Headline about New WTO Director-General' (1 March 2021) <www.euronews.com/2021/03/01/swiss-newspaper-apologises-for-inappropriate-headline-about-new-wto-director-general> accessed 8 May 2022.

[54] Maria V. Sokolova, 'On the Role of Women Trade Trainers' (Trade Experettes n.d.) <www.tradeexperettes.org/blog/articles/on-the-role-of-women-trade-trainers> accessed 8 May 2022.

[55] Remarkably, based on the interviews, different tones of the negotiations seem to appear when a number of women – close to one-third – were engaged in the negotiations. On file with authors.

Thirdly, in the absence of the overall common understanding of the nexus of trade and gender, having women at the negotiation table – and involved in the negotiation process at large – provides a source of knowledge on these issues and their experiences. Women engaged as experts in the negotiations inevitably bring their gender-specific experience into policy analysis, assessing the impact of different negotiated concessions not only from the economic standpoint, but also through the gender lens. Women negotiators can also channel their knowledge into the negotiations, improving the gendered effect of negotiated policies.

All in all, while women's representation may not be the perfect tool to address gender inequality, the key benefits outlined can turn trade negotiations into a tool for better gender equality. The more gender-informed and inclusive the process of trade negotiations, the higher are the chances of more gender-inclusive outcomes.

7.8 THE WAY FORWARD

While there may have been progress, there is no doubt that improvements are needed to enhance the presence and impact of women in current trade negotiations, However, the system can also be systematically inclusive if, along with gender awareness, the appropriate incentives are provided for women to pursue diplomatic careers in trade and government positions overall.

Women's representation has a positive effect on trade negotiations in terms of both the negotiation process and the substance of negotiations. The complexity of modern trade negotiations requires experts from a variety of fields, and to secure women's representation overall it needs to be improved throughout various fields. Women can be encouraged to pursue diplomatic careers, and gender disparities (both vertical and horizontal) in other areas of government careers should be addressed – for example, through gender strategies.

But while women's representation at trade negotiations should not be a goal in itself, the inclusion of women's interests should be. A woman negotiator brings her soft and hard skills and her experiences, including her gender-specific experiences, into the negotiation process – this can improve both the process and outcome of the negotiation. However, it is a flawed logic that a woman placed at the negotiation table should be in charge of representing the interests of all women in the country. Trade touches a variety of fields of expertise and therefore has a multidimensional intersection with gender issues that are specific to each field. Representing the interests of all women in the country is only possible when these interests are included in the analysis of how the negotiated outcomes impact women who are active in these fields.

This can only be done when using appropriate tools and when gender equality is mainstreamed throughout the overall priorities and policies of the country.

Therefore, gender aspects should be included in the analysis of policy proposals during the stage of trade negotiations. This analysis can result in subsequent creation of specific chapters or provisions, or just serve as the background papers that inform the more traditional trade concessions that will have a more positive (or rather, less negative) impact on women.

Geneva remains a centre of international trade law and policy making, but there is an uneven capacity in diplomatic missions to serve all the ongoing negotiations, with much higher pressure on staff from developing and small countries. In such circumstances, countries have to prioritize among different topics that are being negotiated, and gender often is not given top priority, overshadowed by such issues as climate change, carbon offsetting, health, security and others – all issues which have a very clear gender dimension as well.

The persistent lack of data about the gendered effects of trade policy can be addressed at the multilateral level through the Trade Policy Review mechanism of the WTO[56] and through data collection initiatives such as ITC's SheTrades Outlook.[57] Including on a systematic basis a gender component in the WTO's trade policy reviews of countries will not only provide more information about the current state of play and practices, but will also educate the countries to pay attention to these issues.

We need to realize that gender inclusion is not the sole responsibility of women, but of all genders. There is no doubt that the presence of women trade negotiators improves the speed and overall structure of how trade negotiations are conducted. But charging women trade negotiators to represent women's interests for the whole economy is as much a retrograde step as having no women involved in trade negotiations. Prioritizing women's interests in trade negotiations is important. Bringing more women to the negotiating table is important. We have to be able to do both at the same time, but it has to be the responsibility of everyone.

[56] WTO, 'Amendment to the Trade Policy Review Mechanism', WT/L/1014 (27 July 2017) 1.

[57] ITC, 'SheTrades Outlook' <www.shetrades.com/outlook/home> accessed 8 May 2022.

8

The Importance of Gender-Responsive Standards for Trade Policy

GABRIELLE WHITE AND MICHELLE PARKOUDA

ABSTRACT

For decades, standards were perceived to be gender-neutral. However, recent research by the Standards Council of Canada has challenged that assumption. The research found that standardization was associated with a reduction in unintentional fatalities for men, but not for women. The research aligns with sector-specific research and anecdotal evidence that standards are more effective at protecting men compared to women. This is significant because standards form the building blocks of how products, processes, and services are designed and made to be interoperable. Therefore, standards, and the products and services that are standardized according to them, are largely designed by men, for men. This chapter aims to explore the interconnected nature of gender, standards, and trade to argue that the lack of gender-responsiveness of standards has a negative impact on the safety and well-being of women. Furthermore, the link between standardization and trade will highlight the importance of improving the gender-responsiveness of standards given their role in the proliferation of goods, and the different initiatives that are currently underway.

8.1 INTRODUCTION

Because I am a woman, I am at a greater risk of being seriously injured or killed if I am involved in a car accident.[1] Because I am a woman, my personal

[1] Jason Forman, Gerald S. Poplin, C. Greg Shaw, Timothy L. McMurry, Kristin Schmidt, Joseph Ash, and Cecilia Sunnevang, 'Automobile Injury Trends in the Contemporary Fleet: Belted Occupants in Frontal Collisions' (2019) 20(6) *Traffic Injury Prevention* 607–612.

protective equipment (PPE) does not protect me as well as it protects my husband, brother, father, or son.[2] Because I am a woman, voice-recognition software has difficulty understanding me.[3]

These are just a few of the consequences women face because they live in a world built for men. Women are consistently and persistently underrepresented in the data that is used to design and engineer our world,[4] and this includes the development of standards for crash test dummies, personal protective equipment, and artificial intelligence, among other things. This results in inequitable outcomes for women relative to men.

The persistence of gender gaps in all aspects of society indicates that the following does bear repeating:

> Women and girls account for half the world's population and therefore *represent half of its potential*. Gender equality is central to all areas of a healthy society, from reducing poverty to promoting health, education, welfare, and well-being of girls and boys. Reducing the gender gap promotes economic development. Societies are unable to unlock their potential and meet the challenges of rapid economic and technological change without harnessing the skills and ideas of their *entire population*.[5]

Consequently, closing all forms of gender gaps, including the gender gap in standardization, needs to be a priority. The United Nations Economic Commission for Europe (UNECE) Working Party on Regulatory Cooperation and Standardization Policies (WP.6) has been a leader in bringing attention to the gender gap in standardization and taking action to address it. In 2016, members approved the development of a 'roadmap and

[2] *See* for example Centers for Disease Control and Prevention, *Characteristics of Health Care Personnel with COVID-19 – United States*, 12 February to 9 April 2020 (2020) 69(15) Morbidity and Mortality Weekly Report 477–481; Olga Algayerova and Alia El-Yassir, 'Personal Protective Equipment Standards Must Respond to Women's Needs to Ensure the Safety of All Frontline Workers during the COVID-19 Pandemic' (UN Women 2 May 2020) <https://unece.org/general-unece/news/personal-protective-equipment-standards-must-respond-womens-needs-ensure-safety> accessed 8 May 2022.

[3] Rachel Tatman, 'Gender and Dialect Bias in YouTube's Automatic Captions' (2017) Proceedings of the First ACL Workshop on Ethics in Natural Language Processing, Valencia, Spain. Association for Computational Linguistics <https://aclanthology.org/W17-1606.pdf> accessed 25 May 2023.

[4] Kirsten M. A. Madeira-Revell, Katie J. Parnell, Joy Richardson, Kiome A. Pope, Daniel T. Fay Siobhan E. Merriman, and Katherine L. Plant, 'How Can We Close the Gender Data Gap in Transportation Research?' (2021) 32(1) *Ergonomics SA: Journal of the Ergonomics Society of South Africa* 19–26.

[5] World Bank and WTO, 'Women and Trade: The Role of Trade in Promoting Gender Equality' (2020) <www.wto.org/english/res_e/booksp_e/women_trade_pub2807_e.pdf> accessed 8 May 2022 (emphasis added).

recommendation on mainstreaming gender into standards and regulatory policies at national and international levels'.[6] Subsequently, the Gender Responsive Standards Initiative began with the acknowledgement that:

(a) Prevailing gender norms present barriers to women's participation in the development of standards;
(b) [The d]ominance of male representation in standard-setting affects the way that standards are produced, with insufficient consideration of women specificities in the deliverables; and
(c) Standards are generally presumed to be gender-neutral and are developed without recognizing the differences between male and female standard users.[7]

In 2018, the UNECE Declaration for Gender Responsive Standards and Standards Development was approved.[8] The Declaration is significant because it was the first initiative that targeted standards development organizations and national standards bodies, providing them with tangible and concrete actions that they can undertake to address the gender gap. The Declaration has been an effective catalyst for getting gender on the agenda of national standards bodies and raising awareness amongst standards organizations of the importance of considering gender in standardization. The Declaration was open for signature in May 2019 during an international signing event and as of February 2023, there were eighty-one signatories who committed to take action to address the gender gap in standards development.

The gender gap in standardization has widespread consequences, as it can introduce biases wherever those standards are applied. As such, the usage of standards in Free Trade Agreements (FTAs) and trade policies can exacerbate inequitable outcomes for men and women. In effect, the absence of gender-responsive standards has resulted in the proliferation of goods that are not designed to keep women as safe as men. Trade policy can be leveraged as an effective tool to improve gender-responsiveness in standardization and advance women's economic empowerment.

To understand the relationship between gender, standardization, and trade policy, Section 8.2 will begin by providing an overview of the role of

[6] Steering Committee on Trade Capacity and Standards, 'Working Party on Regulatory Cooperation and Standardization Policies, Gender Mainstreaming in Standards', ECE/SCTCS/WP.6/2016/3 (2016) 2.

[7] Ibid 2–3.

[8] *See* UNECE, 'Gender Responsive Standards Initiative' <https://unece.org/gender-responsive-standards-initiative> accessed 8 May 2022.

standardization in trade agreements. Next, Section 8.3 will elaborate on the gender gap in standardization and why it is dangerous. Finally, Section 8.4 will discuss how addressing the gender gap in standardization can lead to more inclusive trade. Section 8.5 concludes.

8.2 STANDARDS IN TRADE AGREEMENTS

While FTAs help to foster the movement of goods and services across borders, the chapters on standards, technical regulations, and conformity assessment procedures are a vital, though perhaps less well-understood, part of trade agreements. In FTAs, obligations on standards and conformity assessment are found in Technical Barriers to Trade (TBT) chapters. To varying degrees, these chapters incorporate or reference portions of the World Trade Organization (WTO) TBT Agreement.[9] According to the Government of New Zealand, TBT chapters 'aim to reduce the impact of TBTs on global trade and create a fair, facilitative and sustainable trading environment'.[10] These chapters focus on the structures and practices that reinforce the transparency and openness of the systems that underpin the development, adoption, and use of standards, technical regulations, and conformity assessment, to ultimately improve the predictability of global markets and reduce the occurrence of technical requirements causing unnecessary barriers to trade.

FTAs have been a powerful tool to reduce tariffs to support the flow of goods and services between countries. However, as tariffs have reduced, there has been an increased focus on non-tariff measures (NTMs) and their impact on free trade. The Economic and Social Commission for Asia and the Pacific and the UN Conference on Trade and Development (UNCTAD) have estimated that NTMs cost twice as much as ordinary customs tariffs.[11] Research from the US government has shown that up to 93 per cent of global trade is impacted by technical regulations, which can include

[9] Agreement on Subsidies and Countervailing Measures, 15 April 1994, LT/UR/A-1A/10. *See* for example the TBT chapter of the United States–Mexico–Canada Agreement (USMCA) (enforced on 1 July 2020), TBT chapter in the Comprehensive and Progressive Agreement for Trans-Pacific Partnership, and the TBT chapter in the EU–Mercosur Trade Agreement, Agreement in Principle, 1 July 2019.

[10] Government of New Zealand, 'Technical Barriers to Trade (TBT) Strategy' (2018) 4. *See* also Caroline Lesser, 'Do Bilateral and Regional Approaches for Reducing Technical Barriers to Trade Converge towards the Multilateral Trading System?' (2007) OECD Trade Policy Paper No. 58 <https://doi.org/10.1787/051058723767> accessed 8 May 2022.

[11] UN ESCAP, 'The Rise of Non-Tariff Measures' (2019) <www.unescap.org/sites/default/d8files/aptir2019_introduction.pdf> accessed 8 May 2022.

standards.[12] Given the impact that NTMs can have on trade, it is not surprising that increasingly progressive trade agreements are bolstering their technical barriers to trade chapters. For example, the Canada–European Union Comprehensive and Economic Trade Agreement[13] (CETA) includes a unique Protocol on the mutual acceptance of the results of conformity assessment,[14] which is far more ambitious in reducing NTMs than any other FTA Canada currently has in place. The Protocol attempts to deal with the long-standing issue of in-country conformity assessment requirements by allowing Canadian manufacturers to have their products certified to the EU requirements in Canada, and vice versa.

8.2.1 *What Are Standards?*

Standards are an important regulatory tool that have significant trade implications. Generally speaking, standards are voluntary documents that outline specifications, characteristics, or production methods for products, processes, or services. They are written by a group of people, typically volunteers, representing relevant stakeholder categories, who arrive at the content of the standard through consensus.[15] Standards are often described as invisible infrastructure.[16] They permeate everyday life, and their role is influential in shaping the design of social life and public infrastructure. And yet they often go unnoticed. Everything from your car to your mobile phone, to your

[12] Jeff Okun-Kozlowicki, 'Standards and Regulations: Measuring the Link to Goods Trade' (2016) US Department of Commerce, Office of Standards and Investment Policy Paper <https://legacy.trade.gov/td/osip/documents/osip_standards_trade_full_paper.pdf> accessed 8 May 2022.

[13] EU–Canada Comprehensive Economic and Trade Agreement (CETA) (enforced since 21 September 2017).

[14] *See* Text of the Comprehensive Economic and Trade Agreement – Protocol on the mutual acceptance of the results of conformity assessment (2017) <www.international.gc.ca/trade-commerce/trade-agreements-accords-commerciaux/agr-acc/ceta-aecg/text-texte/P2.aspx?lang=eng> accessed 8 May 2022.

[15] The process for developing standards varies from country to country, but for more information on how standards are developed in Canada, *see* Standards Council of Canada, 'Requirements & Guidance – Accreditation of Standards Development Organizations' (2019) <www.scc.ca/en/about-scc/publications/requirements-and-procedures-accreditation/requirements-guidance-accreditation-standards-development-organizations> accessed 8 May 2022. This document provides the detailed requirements for standards development organizations to develop voluntary standards in Canada under the Standards Council of Canada's accreditation.

[16] *See* for example Government of Canada, 'International Standards: Targeted Regulatory Review – Regulatory Roadmap' (2021), <https://tc.canada.ca/en/corporate-services/acts-regulations/international-standards-targeted-regulatory-review-regulatory-roadmap> accessed 22 September 2022.

toothbrush is based on standards. Because of their ubiquity, it is essential to understand the myriad ways in which they can alleviate or exacerbate the gender gap in the products, processes, and services that we use as well as those we import and export.

Standards play an important role in international trade for a number of reasons. For the purposes of this chapter, three areas are noteworthy:

- The first, and perhaps the most basic one, is that standards allow goods and services to be produced and reproduced in a consistent and repeatable manner. For producers, this can improve efficiency while also ensuring the quality of products. For consumers, this predictability increases user confidence and expectations.
- Second, standards are important for interoperability. Interoperability is the ability for two or more products or systems to interpret and exchange information. Interoperability allows trains to travel across national borders where tracks have been standardized. Geographic differences in standard requirements can result in a lack of interoperability; for example, travellers are often reliant on adapters because voltage requirements tend to be regionally standardized. A lack of interoperability is also seen with the need for unique cords to charge different electronic devices because their ports are different. Indeed, this has come to be such a problematic issue that the European Commission is proposing to revise the Radio Equipment Directive to require all handheld devices to standardize to one common charging port.[17]
- The third reason is the health and safety of humans, animals, and the environment. A key component of standards is ensuring that products are safe for use. Standards can specify exposure limits for chemicals, safety requirements for machinery, the requirements for personal protective equipment, and so forth. The protection of health and safety, and the environment, are considered legitimate objectives for regulations by the TBT Agreement, so long as the measures are not more trade-restrictive than necessary.[18] For example, construction standards will differ due to climate; building on permafrost will require different specifications than building in a desert.

[17] European Commission, 'Pulling the Plug on Consumer Frustration and e-Waste: Commission Proposes a Common Charger for Electronic Devices' (23 September 2021) <https://ec.europa.eu/commission/presscorner/detail/en/IP_21_4613> accessed 8 May 2022.

[18] Agreement on Technical Barriers to Trade, 15 April 1994, Marrakesh Agreement Establishing the World Trade Organization, Annex 1A, 1868 UNTS 120, Art. 2.2 (TBT Agreement).

For these reasons, among others, governments have recognized that standards are effective regulatory tools that can be a cost-effective way of leveraging prevailing knowledge and expertise.

In the context of the WTO TBT Agreement, standards and technical regulations are distinguished between voluntary and mandatory. Specifically, a technical regulation is a '[d]ocument which lays down product characteristics or their related processes and production methods, including the applicable administrative provisions, with which *compliance is mandatory*. It may also include or deal exclusively with terminology, symbols, packaging, marking or labelling requirements as they apply to a product, process or production method'.[19]

In Canada, as in many other jurisdictions, standards are voluntary when they are developed. However, voluntary standards may become part of a technical regulation when incorporated into regulations and therefore take on the force of law. For example, in Canada alone, there are over 1,500 references to standards in Federal regulations and almost 5,000 references in Provincial and Territorial regulations.[20] Therefore, for the purposes of this chapter, both standards and technical regulations are relevant for the discussion at hand since standards may come to form the basis, or part of, technical regulations.

Within the TBT Agreement, there is preference for the use of international rather than domestic standards in technical regulations. Specifically, Article 2.4 states:

> [w]here technical regulations are required and *relevant international standards exist* or their completion is imminent, *Members shall use them,* or the relevant parts of them, as a basis for their technical regulations except when such international standards or relevant parts would be an ineffective or inappropriate means for the fulfilment of the legitimate objectives pursued.[21]

Moreover, members are encouraged to participate in the development of international standards so that they reflect the needs and realities of their domestic economies and will therefore be more easily integrated into domestic technical regulations or standards. The reason for this is that broad use of international standards allows for more efficient trade. According to research conducted by the US National Research Council, '[w]hen different countries

[19] TBT Agreement, Annex 1 (emphasis added).

[20] Internal data of the Standards Council of Canada: Diane Liao, 'Annual Facts & Figures' (Standards Council of Canada 2022).

[21] TBT Agreement, Art. 2.4 (emphasis added).

or regions have different technical standards for essentially the same product, manufacturers selling into multiple markets are forced to produce multiple versions of the same product. For example, automobile production lines must be switched between right-hand and left-hand drive cars for the United Kingdom and continental Europe'.[22] In this regard, it is important to note the influential role of international standards for trade.

Finally, because standards are so influential in international trade, and ubiquitous in our daily lives, the content of standards really matters. According to the WTO TBT Agreement, standards should contain requirements that are performance based. Specifically, Article 2.8 states, '[w]herever appropriate, Members *shall specify technical regulations based on product requirements in terms of performance* rather than design or descriptive characteristics'.[23] The focus on performance is meant to help address the trade dimension of standards while attempting to counteract potential bias in terms of provenance. This element is particularly relevant for the topic at hand because it fails to explicitly address one key question: performance for whom? As this chapter will explore further in Section 8.3, the male perspective has long been held as universal. In fact, according to Criado-Perez, 'we rely on data from studies done on men as if they apply to women. Specifically, Caucasian men aged 25–30, who weigh 70kg. This is "Reference Man"'.[24] Developing standards for reference man has implications for women, as well as for those men who are outside the norm for 'reference man'.

8.2.2 *What Is Conformity Assessment?*

Any discussion of standards is not complete without addressing the role of conformity assessment. As noted, voluntary standards can be useful in situations where risks to health and safety, the environment, and national security are lower. However, typically, if a product, process, or service requires a standard by law,[25] then conformity assessment will be used to demonstrate

22 National Research Council, *Standards, Conformity Assessment and Trade: Into the 21st Century* (National Academies Press 1995) 106.

23 TBT Agreement, Art. 2.8 (emphasis added).

24 Caroline Criado-Perez, *Invisible Women: Exposing Data Bias in a World Designed for Men* (Vintage Publishing 2020) 116.

25 According to the United Nations Conference on Trade and Development (UNCTAD), '[t]he principle [*sic*] difference between a technical regulation and a standard is that compliance with a technical regulation is mandatory, while compliance with a standard is voluntary'. *See* UNCTAD, 'Dispute Settlement, World Trade Organization, Technical Barriers to Trade' (2003) 9 <https://unctad.org/system/files/official-document/edmmisc232add22_en.pdf> accessed 8 May 2022.

compliance with the standard. According to the International Electrotechnical Commission (IEC), conformity assessment is:

> [a]ny activity that determines whether a product, system, service and sometimes people fulfil the requirements and characteristics described in a standard or specification. Such requirements can include performance, safety, efficiency, effectiveness, reliability, durability, or environmental impacts such as pollution or noise, for example. Verification is generally done through testing or/and inspection. This may or may not include on-going verification.[26]

In other words, conformity assessment allows for an independent verification that a product or process meets the requirements established by a specific standard. While not all products or services require third-party conformity assessment, as the IEC definition notes, there are times when an independent verification is necessary to ensure they can be safely used. For example, conformity assessment is used to ensure that your vacuum cleaner operates the way it should and that it does not catch fire or electrocute you while you are using it. Conformity assessment is an essential element of the TBT Agreement as it plays an important, and somewhat distinct, role in the movement of goods across borders. Indeed, conformity assessment procedures are directly linked to the efficient functioning of international markets: 'Even when standards in different countries have been harmonized, the free flow of trade is inhibited if products are subjected to redundant testing and certification requirements in multiple export markets.'[27] Depending on the conformity assessment requirements in different markets, exporters may need to ship their goods to the destination market for costly and duplicate testing, or to pay for foreign inspectors to visit domestic production sites in order to obtain the necessary conformity assessment mark.

Conformity assessment requirements can also have implications for economic opportunities. International trade is an important source of economic growth. However, globally, small and medium-sized enterprises (SMEs) are less likely to be involved in international trade.[28] SMEs are less likely to have the resources needed to navigate complex regulatory requirements, which can include conformity assessment requirements. Women-owned businesses are more likely to be SMEs, and in Canada, women-owned SMEs are even less

[26] IEC, 'What Is Conformity Assessment' (2021) <www.iec.ch/conformity-assessment/what-conformity-assessment> access on 8 May 2022.

[27] National Research Council, Standards, Conformity Assessment and Trade.

[28] *See* OECD, 'Small and Medium-Sized Enterprises and Trade' <www.oecd.org/trade/topics/small-and-medium-enterprises-and-trade> accessed 8 May 2022.

likely to export than those owned by men.[29] While conformity assessment is an essential part of the quality infrastructure to safeguard citizens, it can also inadvertently limit the economic advancement of some businesses, including women-owned businesses which often have less capital.[30]

8.2.3 *How Can Trade Policy Leverage Standards and Conformity Assessment to Advance More Inclusive Trade?*

Understanding the linkages between gender, standards, conformity assessment, and trade is important because it helps illustrate the significant impact this invisible infrastructure has on our day-to-day lives. Goods are required to meet technical regulations of the market they are entering. Consequently, standards and conformity assessment play an integral role in the movement of goods across borders. Standards dictate the minimum requirements for those goods coming into a country, and conformity assessment procedures explain the process the goods must undergo to demonstrate compliance with those standards. As noted, the characteristics of standards and the necessity of meeting conformity assessment requirements have gender implications. Their usage in FTAs serves to amplify those effects, for good and for bad. Thus, it is essential that the gender impacts of standards, conformity assessment, and trade policy are explicitly considered and addressed.

To that end, in 2017, the Government of Canada signed Canada's first FTA with Chile that included a chapter on trade and gender, which was also the first such agreement for any G20 country.[31] Later that year, Canada joined 117 other WTO members to endorse the Buenos Aires Declaration on Women and Trade.[32] The Declaration seeks to remove barriers to, and foster, women's economic empowerment. Since then, the Canadian government has affirmed that moving forward with including gender and trade chapters in FTAs is a priority.

[29] Government of Canada, 'Majority-Female Owned Exporting SMEs in Canada' (2020) <www.tradecommissioner.gc.ca/businesswomen-femmesdaffaires/2016-MFO_SMES-PME_EDMF.aspx?lang=eng> accessed 8 May 2022.

[30] Claire Leitch, Friederike Welter, and Colette Henry, 'Women Entrepreneurs' Financing Revisited: Taking Stock and Looking Forward: New Perspectives on Women Entrepreneurs and Finance' (2018) 20(2) *Venture Capital* 103–114.

[31] Government of Canada, 'Trade and Gender in Free Trade Agreements: The Canadian Approach' (2021) <www.international.gc.ca/trade-commerce/gender_equality-egalite_genres/trade_gender_fta-ale-commerce_genre.aspx?lang=eng> accessed 8 May 2022.

[32] WTO, 'Buenos Aires Declaration on Women and Trade Outlines Actions to Empower Women' (2017) <www.wto.org/english/news_e/news17_e/mc11_12dec17_e.htm> accessed 8 May 2022.

Although this chapter focuses on the impact of standards on trade and how the lack of gender-responsive standards results in uneven benefits for women and men, it is important to note that trade impacts women disproportionately in other ways. A report from the WTO found that women face higher tariff burdens. The report explains the 'higher burden is the result of higher applied tariffs and greater spending on imported goods by women consumers. In the textile sector, for instance, the tariff burden on women's apparel was USD 2.77 billion higher than on men's clothing, and this gender gap grew about 11 percent in real terms between 2006 and 2016'.[33] In addition to the uneven impact of tariffs is the consideration of the impact of NTMs on women.

As previously discussed, the costs associated with complying with technical regulations, such as the cost of obtaining conformity assessment for goods, are often prohibitive for SMEs. Particularly if the market you are exporting to requires conformity assessment to a different standard or a technical regulation, this might require testing the product more than once. It may even require a complete redesign of the product to meet new or different requirements. The impact of this is significant when considering how they can be compounded: 'Combined with the fact that women are more likely to own and run SMEs than large firms and that they often export and import a smaller amount of goods, this pattern also suggests that NTMs affect women entrepreneurs more severely than men.'[34]

FTAs and trade policy have the potential to improve gender equality by removing some of the trade barriers that make women more economically vulnerable than men. Moreover, their reach can be even further when the gender impacts of technical regulations are considered. Specifically, if we can ensure standards are gender-responsive through their performance requirements, then those products and services are proliferated through trade in a way that keeps everyone safe. However, as we will explain in the next section, the vast majority of standards are not currently gender-responsive, which means that products and services are *not* proliferated through trade in a way that keeps everyone safe.

8.3 THE GENDER GAP IN STANDARDIZATION

Standards are powerful tools because they dictate the design, performance, and functionality of a good or a service. Therefore, the expertise of those who develop standards matters, as standards are shaped by the knowledge and

33 World Bank and WTO, 'Women and Trade' (n 5) 5.

34 Ibid 88.

experience of those who develop them. While there are often requirements for committees to ensure balanced representation of stakeholder categories, little consideration has historically been given to the personal attributes (e.g., gender) of those who develop standards. The result is that women are significantly underrepresented in standards development. At the International Organization for Standardization (ISO), only about one-third of technical committee members were women in 2020.[35] While you do not need to be a woman to develop a gender-responsive standard, it can be difficult to come up with solutions to problems you have not faced.

The preponderance of men, both historically and currently, participating in the development of standards does not help with androcentrism in standardization. Androcentrism is the tendency to view men as 'representative' or 'default' and women as 'niche'.[36] Androcentrism privileges men's experiences. It also results in research based solely on men being overgeneralized and applied to both men and women.[37] This has had unfortunate consequences. In medical research, medications have been withdrawn from the market because they were not adequately tested on women and, in fact, had serious side effects for women.[38]

The low representation of women in standardization compounds the lack of awareness of the importance of considering gender in standardization. When ISO and IEC surveyed the leadership of their technical committees in 2020 to identify what actions were taken by the committees to consider gender, only 25 per cent of committees said they considered gender in the work of their technical committee.[39] While a quarter of responding technical committees had considered gender, only 13 per cent indicated that sex-specific

[35] Remarks made by Sergio Mujica, ISO Secretary-General at the Standards Accelerator Online Event (14 October 2021) <www.worldstandardsday.org/contents/posts/events/the-standards-accelerator.html> accessed 8 May 2022.

[36] April H. Bailey, Marianne LaFrance, and John F. Dovidio, 'Is Man the Measure of All Things? A Social Cognitive Account of Androcentrism' (2019) 23(4) *Personality and Social Psychology Review* 307–331.

[37] Theresa A. Beery, 'Gender Bias in the Diagnosis and Treatment of Coronary Artery Disease' (1995) 24(6) *Heart & Lung* 427–435.

[38] Janet Heinrich, 'Drug Safety: Most Drugs Withdrawn in Recent Years Had Greater Health Risks for Women. A Letter to the Honorable Tom Harkin, the Honorable Olympia J. Snowe, The Honorable Barbara A. Mikulski, United States Senate, the Honorable Henry Waxman, House of Representatives' (*United States General Accounting Office* 19 January 2001) <www.gao.gov/assets/gao-01-286r.pdf> accessed 8 May 2022.

[39] IEC, 'Disappointing Results of Gender Survey in Technical Committees' (21 June 2021) <www.iec.ch/blog/disappointing-results-gender-survey-technical-committees> accessed 8 May 2022.

requirements were included in their standards.[40] In other words, the vast majority of ISO and IEC technical committees do not consider gender when developing standards. Among technical committees that did not consider gender, almost 80 per cent said that gender is not relevant to their sector.[41] The perception that standards are gender-neutral, or gender-blind, is both pervasive and insidious – and can have real consequences.

The fact that standards are often applied to inanimate objects, such as technologies, feeds the narrative that they are (gender) neutral in application. However, when inanimate objects are created and shaped by people, they can perpetuate biases. Artificial intelligence (AI) is a prime example of how technologies can be imbued with bias. It is now widely recognized that AI has perpetuated existing biases in hiring, credit limits, and health-care prioritization, to name a few areas.[42] Gender bias can also be seen with physical products. For products that require a specific fit (e.g., PPE and dimensions for operator space envelopes), or require physical manipulation, do they take into account the differing size and strength of men and women? As evidenced by the survey of ISO and IEC technical committee members, there is still a significant gender gap in standardization.

8.3.1 *What Are Gender-Responsive Standards?*

If standards are not gender-neutral, then what would make them gender-responsive? As outlined in the UNECE guidelines for developing gender-responsive standards, a gender-responsive standard is developed with consideration for how gender impacts the content, requirements, and application of standards.[43] They ensure that both women's and men's needs, experiences, and concerns are an integral dimension in the design and performance of the product, process, or service undergoing standardization.

Gender-responsive standards should take into account both sex and gender. Biological and socio-cultural differences in men and women can impact the way men and women experience a standard. The COVID-19 pandemic provides an example of how sex and gender can differentially impact

[40] Ibid.

[41] Ibid.

[42] Genevieve Smith and Ishita Rustagi, 'When Good Algorithms Go Sexist: Why and How to Advance AI Gender Equity' (Stanford Social Innovation Review 31 March 2021) <https://ssir.org/articles/entry/when_good_algorithms_go_sexist_why_and_how_to_advance_ai_gender_equity> accessed 8 May 2022.

[43] Under development: UNECE expects to publish the final guidelines in 2023.

prevalence and mortality. COVID-19 has killed more men than women.[44] At the same time, in part due to prevailing gender norms, women are more likely to work in health care and there have been concerns that women health-care practitioners are at a greater risk of contracting COVID-19 because PPE has been designed for the average European or American man.[45] While researchers are still trying to understand why men are at a greater risk from contracting the coronavirus, it is clear that sex and gender can play a role in risk factors for contracting the virus and the prognosis. It is hoped that greater clarity around what constitutes a gender-responsive standard will prompt standards developers to collect the necessary data to determine whether there are gender considerations and what action needs to be taken to address them.

8.3.2 *Why Does Gender-Responsiveness Matter in Standardization?*

The current lack of gender-responsiveness in standards has consequences. These consequences can at times be minor inconveniences. For example, ventilation standards are based on men's metabolism.[46] As a result, women are more likely to be cold in the workplace. Being cold at work is not merely a matter of comfort. It is associated with reduced typing speed and decreased cognitive performance.[47] In other words, the lack of gender-responsiveness in ventilation standards can be detrimental to an organization's overall productivity and performance.

A failure to consider gender in standardization can also be fatal. Research in multiple countries has shown that women are more likely to be seriously injured or killed when they are involved in a car accident because crash test dummies are based on male anthropometry. Research on gender considerations in car accidents dates back to at least the 1960s, and yet action has been slow.[48] However, it does appear that efforts to address this gap are finally

44 Richard B. Reeves and Beyond Deng, 'At Least 65,000 More Men than Women Have Died from COVID-19 in the US' (Brookings 19 October 2021) <www.brookings.edu/blog/up-front/2021/10/19/at-least-65000-more-men-than-women-have-died-from-covid-19-in-the-us/> accessed 8 May 2022.

45 *See* for example D. J. Janson, B. C. Clift, and V. Dhokia, 'PPE Fit of Healthcare Workers during the COVID-19 Pandemic' (2022) 99/103610 *Applied Ergonomics* 1–8.

46 Boris Kingma and Wouter van Marken Lichtenbelt, 'Energy Consumption in Buildings and Female Thermal Demand' (2015) 5(12) *Nature Climate Change* 1054–1056.

47 T. Y. Chang and A. Kajackaite, 'Battle for the Thermostat: Gender and the Effect of Temperature on Cognitive Performance' (2019) 14(5) *PLoS ONE*.

48 Anna Carlsson, *Addressing Female Whiplash Injury Protection – A Step towards 50th Percentile Female Rear Impact Occupant Models* (PhD Thesis, Chalmers University of Technology 2012).

gaining more traction. In 2021, the UNECE Working Party on Passive Safety released a proposal supported by Canada, France, Germany, Japan, Netherlands, Spain, and Sweden for an informal working group to examine sex- and size-neutral crash safety. The informal working group will analyse UNECE regulations and determine if changes are needed to ensure equal safety for men and women as well as individuals of differing sizes.[49]

Sector-specific research such as on crash test dummies and anecdotal evidence have pointed to the impacts of standards that are not gender-responsive. Research in the health sector also illustrates the consequences of not accounting for gender (e.g., the increased mortality of women from heart attacks).[50] However, more recently a study using data from almost 100 countries examined the relationship between standardization activity and the number of men and women who die as a result of unintentional injuries. The premise of the research is that if standards can help to ensure the safety of products, processes, and services, then countries that are more involved in standardization should have fewer people dying as a result of unintentional injuries. Indeed, research has shown that greater standardization is associated with a reduction in the number of unintentional injuries even after controlling for the wealth and education levels of the country.[51]

Given the lack of gender-responsiveness in standardization, it was important to consider the unintentional fatalities separately for men and women. Globally, men are more likely to die as a result of an unintentional injury.[52] And yet, when examining the impact of standardization on unintentional fatalities for men and women, we found that there was a significant negative relationship between standardization and unintentional fatalities for men, even after controlling for wealth and education.[53] In other words, the more a country was involved in standardization, the less likely it was that men died

49 UNECE, 'Terms of Reference for Informal Working Group on Sex and Size Neutral Crash Safety' GRSP-70-01 (7 September 2021).

50 *See* for example P. J. Kudenchuk, C. Maynard, J. S. Martin, M. Wirkus, and W. D. Weaver, 'Comparison of Presentation, Treatment, and Outcome of Acute Myocardial Infarction in Men versus Women (the Myocardial Infarction Triage and Intervention Registry)' (1996) 78 (1) *American Journal of Cardiology* 9–14.

51 Michelle Parkouda, 'An Ounce of Prevention: Standards as a Tool to Prevent Accidental Fatalities' (Standards Council of Canada 2019) <www.scc.ca/en/system/files/publications/SCC_Gender_Safety_Report_EN.pdf> accessed 8 May 2022.

52 WHO, 'Global Health Estimates 2015: Deaths by Cause, Age, Sex, by Country and by Region, 2000–2015' (2016). Note that unintentional injuries include road injury, poisonings, falls, fire, heat and host substances, drowning, exposure to mechanical forces, natural disasters and other unintentional injuries.

53 Parkouda, 'An Ounce of Prevention' (n 51).

as a result of unintentional injuries. When the analysis was repeated to see the impact on women, there was no significant effect. Standardization was not actively associated with reducing deaths due to unintentional injuries for women. This report was the first of its kind to demonstrate the devastating consequences of not considering gender in standardization across a sample of almost 100 countries. It highlights the need to address the gender gap in standardization because unintentional injuries are preventable. Clearly standards can, and must, do more to protect women.

8.3.3 *What Is Being Done about It?*

The UNECE Gender Declaration has spurred action in this area. The declaration is explicit in asking signatories to take action to develop gender action plans for their organization and track progress towards improving participation rates and gender-responsiveness in standards.[54] The authors of this chapter developed the Standards Council of Canada's (SCC) action plan. In SCC's action plan, the authors prioritized three areas:

1. Increasing participation of women in standards development;
2. Developing guidance on how to develop gender-responsive standards; and
3. Contributing sound research to better understand the implications of gender on standards.[55]

Many other national standards bodies have developed their own gender strategies.[56] These national strategies have been complemented by international work. The UNECE is currently finalizing guidance on how to develop gender-responsive standards. This guidance is meant to be broadly applicable to standards developers to give them the practical tools needed to help them increase representation of women in standards development and to ensure standards are gender-responsive, regardless of who is developing them.

ISO and IEC have also formed a Joint Strategic Advisory Group (JSAG) on gender-responsive standards. The JSAG has gathered data from technical committee experts to understand the degree to which gender is a consideration for technical committees. It is also developing guidance specific to ISO and IEC for how committees can ensure their standards are gender-responsive. These

54 UNECE, 'Declaration for Gender Responsive Standards and Standards Development' (2019).

55 Standards Council of Canada, 'Gender and Standardization Strategy' (2019) <www.scc.ca/en/system/files/publications/SCC_Gender-and-Standardization-Strategy-2019-2025_FINAL_EN.pdf> accessed 8 May 2022.

56 UNECE, 'Gender-Responsive Standards Initiative' <https://unece.org/gender-responsive-standards-initiative> accessed 8 May 2022.

initiatives have received a high level of support from the leaders of the respective organizations, which will be important for implementation.[57]

8.4 ADDRESSING THE GENDER GAP IN STANDARDIZATION FOR MORE INCLUSIVE TRADE

Gender-responsive standards are essential for inclusive trade. As we have noted, currently, standards are not doing enough to protect and support women. This means that when goods and services that rely on standards are traded, they are perpetuating inequality. By ensuring that standards, including those referenced in regulation, have addressed their gender gap, we can advance equality and improve outcomes for women.

While all standards would benefit from a gender lens to ensure that products that are not as safe for women are not inadvertently proliferated, targeted standards can also be a useful tool to promote gender equality in trade. In March 2021, ISO published an International Workshop Agreement (IWA) on Women's Entrepreneurship – Key Definitions and General Criteria.[58] By developing an accepted definition of women-owned and -led businesses, the IWA has enabled governments, businesses, statistical agencies, and non-government organizations to clearly track progress and have targeted initiatives to advance economic opportunities for women.[59]

In Canada, a publicly available specification was developed in support of the Government of Canada's 50–30 Challenge. The 50–30 Challenge aims to increase representation of women and underrepresented groups in senior management and on Canadian boards.[60] As the name states, the government is challenging companies to achieve gender parity in senior management and on Canadian boards and to ensure that underrepresented individuals comprise 30 per cent of senior management and members of Canadian boards. The publicly available specification defines how to determine whether the

[57] Remarks made by Sergio Mujica, ISO Secretary-General and Philippe Metzger IEC General Secretary & CEO, at the Standards Accelerator Online Event (14 October 2021) <www.worldstandardsday.org/contents/posts/events/the-standards-accelerator.html> accessed 8 May 2022.

[58] ISO, 'Women's Entrepreneurship – Key Definitions and General Criteria' (IWA 34:2021) <https://www.iso.org/standard/79585.html> accessed 8 May 2022.

[59] Swedish Institute for Standards, 'ISO/IWA 34 – Definition of a "Woman-Owned Business" and Guidance on Its Use' (2021) <www.sis.se/en/about_sis/isoiwa-34-definition-of-a-womanowned-business-and-guidance-on-its-use/> accessed 8May 2022.

[60] Government of Canada, 'The 50–30 Challenge: Your Diversity Advantage' (Innovation, Science and Economic Development Canada 2021) <www.ic.gc.ca/eic/site/icgc.nsf/eng/07706.html> accessed 8 May 2022.

targets have been met.[61] Measurement is imperative to track progress and target initiatives to meet the objectives of the challenge.

The WTO can also play an important role in addressing the gender gap in standardization. The WTO is one of the only places where standards and technical regulations are disciplined. As such, it has an opportunity and obligation to ensure that standards and technical regulations are used to promote equity and advance economic opportunities for women. In fact, a report from the WTO delineated the ways in which trade can promote gender equality, stating:

> Trade policy itself is a critical determinant in lowering the trade costs faced by women and improving women's access to international markets. Discriminatory trade policies that make women-dominated industries less competitive and productive than their male counterparts are widespread. Women's market access can be increased by addressing tariff and nontariff measures that hurt women traders and consumers, improving trade facilitation that enables women to trade as safely and easily as men, and expanding access to trade finance that empowers women to connect with international markets.[62]

The Government of Canada has explicitly stated that it participates in trade negotiations and agreements because 'it is in the Canadian interest to do so'.[63] Undoubtedly, Canada is not unique in this. International trade accrues many benefits for countries and their citizens. And yet, as we have highlighted, more needs to be done so that everyone is benefited equally.

8.5 CONCLUSION

This chapter argues that by addressing the gender gap in standardization and ensuring that the standards included in technical regulations are gender-responsive, we will increase the safety of products for women and contribute to women's economic empowerment. By requiring gender-responsiveness in standards and trade agreements, countries can make meaningful progress towards addressing discriminatory social institutions and improving gender equality, which will benefit everyone.

61 Diversity Institute, 'The 50–30 Challenge, Publicly Available Specification (PAS)' (2021) <https://secureservercdn.net/192.169.220.85/bom.396.myftpupload.com/wp-content/uploads/2021/08/Publicly-Available-Specification-PAS.pdf> accessed 8 May 2022.

62 World Bank and WTO, 'Women and Trade' (n 5) 11.

63 Government of Canada, 'International Trade Agreements and Local Government: A Guide for Canadian Municipalities' (Global Affairs Canada 2021) <www.international.gc.ca/trade-agreements-accords-commerciaux/ressources/fcm/complete-guide-complet.aspx?lang=en> accessed 8 May 2022.

9

Mainstreaming Gender in Investment Treaties and Its Prevailing Trends

The Actions of MNEs in the Americas

RENATA VARGAS AMARAL AND LILLYANA SOPHIA DAZA JALLER

ABSTRACT

Foreign direct investment (FDI) inflows can lead to more opportunities for women in the job market but may also exacerbate gender disparities. While gender mainstreaming in trade agreements has been extensively discussed over the past few years, demonstrating the need for reform, the discussion on gender mainstreaming in investment treaties is incipient, although extremely interesting. The inclusion of gender provisions in investment treaties is one of the pillars for a successful strategy to overcome gender inequality. It needs to be addressed along with gender policies by multinational enterprises (MNEs) leading the foreign investment process. This chapter aims to address the role of women as levers of change and the opportunity for MNEs to be the drivers of this change. To this end, it reviews the recent evolution of gender provisions in investment agreements and demonstrates how FDI can foment much-needed change by providing examples of actions and policies by MNEs in the Americas towards promoting more opportunities for women.

9.1 INTRODUCTION

The impacts that foreign direct investment (FDI) can have on gender issues are increasingly drawing the attention of policymakers and are gradually occupying more space in the decision-making processes of companies. As we are going to demonstrate in this chapter, particularly when investing in developing countries – such as the ones in Latin America and the Caribbean (LAC) – the lack of meaningful gender policies by multinational enterprises that guarantee participation by women may lead the MNEs to miss out on the tremendous impact they could have on gender equality.[1]

Gender mainstreaming is defined as 'the process of assessing the implications for women and men of any planned action, including legislation, policies or programmes, in all areas and at all levels'.[2] Gender provisions can be found in regional trade agreements as far back as 1957, and their inclusion has steadily increased over the years.[3] Governments seeking to foster equality between men and women can also include gender considerations and concerns in the drafting and implementation of investment agreements. Similarly, corporations can include gender perspectives in the design, implementation, and assessment of their policies and programmes to ensure that they benefit men and women equally.

The World Economic Forum's (WEF) Global Gender Gap Report 2021 predicts that it will take another 136 years to achieve gender equality based on the current rate of progress.[4] The estimate is more pessimistic than the one cited in the 2019 report,[5] mainly due to the disproportionate effect the COVID-19 pandemic crisis has had on women. However, the timeline is substantially smaller for the Americas, where it is estimated that gender gaps could be closed in 60–70 years. North America comes in second to Europe with regard to progress towards gender parity, followed by Latin America and the Caribbean coming in at third place. This gives multinational enterprises in the region an opportunity to contribute to the local economy and society in general, by implementing policies that advance gender equality.

This chapter unfolds as follows. In Section 9.2, we demonstrate why women are levers of change and the opportunities MNEs have in promoting women's empowerment within their organizations and the communities where they operate. Then, in Section 9.3, we discuss the urgency of gender provisions in investment agreements in light of the evolution observed in recent years, particularly in bilateral investment treaties (BITs). Finally, in Section 9.4, we address forms in which FDI can be the driver of necessary

1 UNCTAD, 'Multinational Enterprises and the International Transmission of Gender Policies and Practices', UNCTAD/DIAE/INF/2021/1 (8 March 2021).

2 UN, 'Report of the Fourth World Conference on Women, Beijing, 4–15 September 1995', A/CONF.177/20/REV.1 (1996) Chap. I, Resolution 1, Annex II.

3 José-Antonio Monteiro, 'Gender-Related Provisions in Regional Trade Agreements' (2018) WTO Economic Research and Statistics Division Staff Working Paper ERSD-2018-15 <www.wto.org/english/res_e/reser_e/ersd201815_e.pdf> accessed 8 May 2022.

4 World Economic Forum, 'Global Gender Gap Report' (March 2021) <www3.weforum.org/docs/WEF_GGGR_2021.pdf> accessed 8 May 2022.

5 Ibid.

changes, and how public, private, domestic, and international investment policies are of fundamental importance to further women's economic empowerment. Section 9.5 concludes.

9.2 WOMEN AS LEVERS OF CHANGE: THE OPPORTUNITY FOR MNES

Gender equality is a crucial factor for economic development.[6] It can contribute to poverty reduction and higher levels of human capital for future generations.[7] Companies with gender diversity in emerging markets had a 13 per cent rise in their internal rate of return.[8]

9.2.1 *Current State*

Many reasons support the need to address gender inequality issues in the workforce. Although participation of women in the labour market has been on the rise, it remains a challenge along with the vast gender pay gaps across all occupations.[9] A study carried out among 278 Canadian firms found that international firms are less likely to have women in management roles.[10] The authors believe that this may be based on gender bias at the time of hiring for international positions, as women may be considered less capable of entering business networks due to their restrictive schedules or to negative stereotypes in the countries where they would work.[11]

Social stereotypes deem women less capable than men of holding positions of leadership or working in certain fields, such as those requiring degrees in science, technology, engineering, and mathematics (STEM). Additionally, women are more likely to face microaggressions that undermine them professionally, such as being interrupted or spoken over, having their judgement questioned in their area of expertise, or having others comment on their

6 IADB, 'Una olimpíada desigual: La equidad de género en las empresas latinoamericanas y del Caribe' (August 2021) BID Nota Técnica No. IDB-TN-2255 <https://publications.iadb.org/publications/spanish/document/Una-olimpiada-desigual-la-equidad-de-genero-en-las-empresas-latinoamericanas-y-del-Caribe.pdf> accessed 8 May 2022.

7 Ibid.

8 Onu Mujeres, 'Catalizando la Igualdad' (2021) <https://lac.unwomen.org/es/digiteca/publicaciones/2021/07/catalizando-la-igualdad> accessed 8 May 2022.

9 Magdalena Barafani and Angeles Barral Verna, 'Género y comercio: Una relación a distintas velocidades' (2020) IBD Note Técnica No. IDB-NT-2006 <https://publications.iadb.org/es/genero-y-comercio-una-relacion-distintas-velocidades> accessed 8 May 2022.

10 Eddy S. Ng and Greg J. Sears, 'The Glass Ceiling in Context: The Influence of CEO Gender, Recruitment Practices and Firm Internationalisation on the Representation of Women in Management' (2017) 27(1) *Human Resource Management Journal* 133–151.

11 Ibid.

emotional state.[12] Notably, the percentage of women reporting microaggressions in the United States is higher for women in leadership as well as women of colour.[13]

Women tend to be considered responsible for unpaid labour such as homemaking and childcare, leaving them with little time to dedicate to professional development. In the United States, women are responsible for almost twice as much unpaid care and domestic work as men.[14] While 54 per cent of women report shouldering all or most of the household responsibilities, only 22 per cent of the men have this additional work.[15] On a daily basis, almost half of the Latina workforce in the United States spend five or more hours on housework and caregiving.[16] In many cases, these women are responsible for the care of children as well as adults in the family, such as an elderly family member.[17] This unequal share was exacerbated during the COVID-19 pandemic, which resulted in an average increase of over five hours on the time women around the world spend just on childcare in one week.[18] In 2021, 42 per cent of female employees in the United States said they were consistently burned out and 33 per cent reported having considered leaving the workforce or downshifting their careers due to them being overburdened with household work.[19]

In recent years, there has been a rise in the number of female board members worldwide. However, Latin America stands out as lagging in the number of women in boardrooms.[20] In fact, different from the global trend,[21] there are no known quotas to increase the number of women on corporate

[12] McKinsey & Company & LeanIn.Org, 'Women in the Workplace' (2021) <www.mckinsey.com/featured-insights/diversity-and-inclusion/women-in-the-workplace> accessed 8 May 2022.

[13] Ibid.

[14] McKinsey & Company, 'The Power of Parity: Advancing Women's Equality in the United States' (2016) <www.mckinsey.com/featured-insights/employment-and-growth/the-power-of-parity-advancing-womens-equality-in-the-united-states> accessed 8 May 2022.

[15] Ibid.

[16] McKinsey & Company & LeanIn.Org, 'Women in the Workplace' (n 12).

[17] Ibid.

[18] Gary Barker, Aapta Garg, Brian Heilman, Nikki van der Gaag, and Rachel Mehaffey, 'State of the World's Fathers: Structural Solutions to Achieve Equality in Care Work' (MenCare 2021) <https://men-care.org/wp-content/uploads/2021/06/210610_BLS21042_PRO_SOWF.v08.pdf> accessed 8 May 2022.

[19] McKinsey & Company & LeanIn.Org, 'Women in the Workplace' (n 12).

[20] Marie Froehlicher, Lotte Knuckles Griek, Azadeh Nematzadeh, Lindsey Hall, and Nathan Stoval, 'Gender Equality in the Workplace: Going beyond Women on the Board' (S&P Global 5 February 2021) <www.spglobal.com/esg/csa/yearbook/articles/gender-equality-workplace-going-beyond-women-on-the-board> accessed 8 May 2022.

[21] Ibid. Countries that have legislated boardroom quotas – whether the quotas are binding or non-binding – perform better in terms of board gender composition. Following a European

boards in Latin America and the Caribbean. In the United States, the representation of women in the workforce drops at every level of the corporate ladder.[22] While 48 per cent of employees at entry-level positions are female, women account for only 24 per cent of C-suite leaders.[23] The figure is even more staggering when it comes to women of colour, who only represent 4 per cent of the C-suite.[24] The state of California has taken the lead in this regard, seeking to reap the benefits of gender diversity. In 2018, it introduced Women on Boards, a law that requires all publicly held domestic or foreign corporations headquartered in the state of California to have at least one woman on the board.[25] Depending on the size of the company, the law may require two or more female board members. The enactment of the law has resulted in a 10 per cent increase in the number of women on boards over a four-year period.[26]

Gender inequality in Latin America and the Caribbean can be due to a variety of factors. Stereotypes hold women responsible for most unpaid work at home and makes it difficult for them to access new labour opportunities.[27] Labour segregation also places women in low-quality jobs that limit their professional development.[28] This results in a large number of women working in the informal sector of the economy.[29] Additionally, women are faced with regulatory and cultural biases and limited access to capital and information that hinder their development as entrepreneurs.[30]

Union directive proposal to improve gender balance on corporate boards, six member states adopted binding quotas for gender board diversity, and nine others introduced non-binding quotas. Norway's gender quota, adopted in 2003, was the first in the world to require that at least 40 per cent of the board be female; France and Iceland later took a similar approach. Belgium, Italy, Portugal, Germany, Austria, and France have binding quotas; Denmark, Ireland, Spain, Luxemburg, the Netherlands, Poland, Finland, Slovenia, and Sweden have non-binding quotas. India, Pakistan, and Israel require that boards have at least one female director, while Malaysia has a 30 per cent binding quota.

22 McKinsey & Company & LeanIn.Org, 'Women in the Workplace' (n 12).

23 Ibid.

24 Ibid.

25 An act to add Sections 301.3 and 2115.5 to the Corporations Code, relating to corporations, Cal. Sen. B. 826, Chapter 954 (State of California, USA 2018) <https://leginfo.legislature.ca.gov/faces/billTextClient.xhtml?bill_id=201720180SB826> accessed 8 May 2022.

26 Marina Gertsberg, Johanna Mollerstrom, and Michaela Pagel, 'Gender Quotas and Support for Women in Board Elections' (2021) National Bureau of Economic Research Working Paper 28463 <www.nber.org/papers/w28463> accessed 8 May 2022.

27 IADB, 'Una olimpíada desigual' (n 6) 25.

28 Ibid 3.

29 Ibid 25.

30 Ibid 3.

The region of Latin America and the Caribbean provides a unique opportunity for investors to finance the recovery of the region through women.[31] Women hold only 15 per cent of management positions, own only 14 per cent of companies in the region,[32] and hold the top manager position in only 11 per cent of the companies.[33] At the same time, a higher proportion of women are in lower positions (36 per cent) while only 25 per cent are in higher positions.[34]

Participation by women predominates in areas that are usually lower-paid – or 'soft' (those that do not require STEM skills), according to the report.[35] For example, women make up 64 per cent of the workforce in human resources, and 63 per cent in communications and public relations.[36] In other areas, such as foreign trade, women represent less than 35 per cent of the employees.[37] Studies have found that throughout the Americas, women make up less than half of the workforce with STEM degrees.[38] However, women with the same qualifications as men find it hard to get hired, likely due to social stereotypes and discrimination.[39] In the United States, women with STEM degrees are more likely to work in health and education while men tend to hold positions in technology, engineering, business, and management.[40]

More data on the LAC region indicates that women represent only 35 per cent of the workforce that uses advanced technologies.[41] This could be due to a lack of demand, discrimination, or the erroneous idea that women are less capable of handling technology.[42] Another reason could be the lack of women with the required skills in the labour market.[43] Interestingly, women-led businesses were found to be more likely to employ women in positions that use technology.[44]

Finally, six out of ten companies do not provide any type of maternity leave beyond what is determined by law and only 15 per cent of companies analyse

31 Ibid 4.
32 Ibid 8.
33 Ibid 34.
34 Ibid 5.
35 Ibid 5.
36 Ibid 26.
37 Ibid 61.
38 Ibid 22.
39 Ibid 15.
40 Shulamit Kahn and Donna Ginther, 'Women and STEM' (2017) NBER Working Paper No. w23525 <https://ssrn.com/abstract=2988746> accessed 8 May 2022.
41 IADB, 'Una olimpíada desigual' (n 6) 27.
42 Ibid.
43 Ibid.
44 Ibid.

the existence of salary gaps within their organization;[45] 28 per cent of firms reported giving lower salaries to women compared to men with the same qualifications. In this regard, women-led companies stand out again, being more equitable when it comes to employee salaries.[46] However, only a third of companies surveyed in LAC have boards with at least 30 per cent of women.[47]

9.2.2 *What Women Offer: The Business Case for Gender Equality*

Companies that integrate gender equality into their business model can expect benefits in terms of profitability and success as well as social impact.[48] According to an International Labour Organization (ILO) analysis of data from 186 countries over a twenty-six-year period, there is a positive correlation between an increase in female employment and Gross Domestic Product (GDP) growth.[49] McKinsey & Company estimates that the global annual GDP could increase by USD 12 trillion by 2025 if gender inequality is addressed around the world.[50] The report goes further and imagines a best-case scenario, where women attain full gender parity around the world, resulting in a USD 28 trillion addition to the global GDP within the same timeframe.

Women generally have characteristics that are considered 'soft skills', such as effective communication, empathy, and self-awareness. In a survey carried out among Fortune's 100 Best Companies to Work for, Chief Executive Officers (CEOs) cited these skills as the most desirable attributes in employees.[51] Additionally, women tend to perform better than men in emotional intelligence competencies correlated with effective leadership, such as con-

45 Ibid 5–6.

46 ILO and UN Women, 'Win–Win: Gender Equality Means Good Business' (August 2017) <https://ganarganar.lim.ilo.org/en/> accessed 8 May 2022.

47 Ibid.

48 Acumen, 'Women and Social Enterprises: How Gender Integration can Boost Entrepreneurial Solutions to Poverty' (2015) <https://acumen.org/wp-content/uploads/2017/09/Women_And_Social_Enterprises_Report_Acumen_ICRW_2015.pdf> accessed 8 May 2022.

49 ILO, 'Women in Business and Management: The Business Case for Change' (2019) <www.ilo.org/global/publications/books/WCMS_700953/lang–en/index.htm> accessed 8 May 2022.

50 McKinsey & Company, 'How Advancing Women's Equality Can Add $12 Trillion to Global Growth' (2015) <www.mckinsey.com/featured-insights/employment-and-growth/how-advancing-womens-equality-can-add-12-trillion-to-global-growth> accessed 8 May 2022.

51 Laura Entis, 'This Is the No. 1 Thing These CEOs Look For in Job Candidates' (Fortune 26 March 2017) <https://fortune.com/2017/03/26/ceos-ideal-job-candidates/> accessed 8 May 2022.

flict management, adaptability, and teamwork.[52] These traits place women at a competitive advantage in the workforce and should incentivize companies to promote a gender-diverse workplace, to take advantage of the best qualities of both genders.

PROFITABILITY Companies with higher levels of gender diversity are more profitable, particularly companies with women in leadership roles.[53] In a survey conducted among 13,000 companies around the world, almost 60 per cent of the respondents reported that gender-diversity initiatives improved business outcomes.[54] In LAC, almost 75 per cent of companies surveyed saw profit increases between 5 and 20 per cent as a result of improving gender diversity in the workplace.[55] Research has shown that companies with women in leadership roles have better sales figures and equity value.[56] A 2016 study carried out by Credit Suisse Research Institute analysed the impact of diversity in the boardroom and the executive suite at over 3,000 companies around the world.[57] The study showed that having more women on both levels results in higher returns without taking more risks.[58] Additionally, among the sample of companies, share price performance was higher for companies with at least one woman on the board as well as for companies with more women in senior management – particularly for companies with more than 50 per cent women in senior management.[59]

Women in leadership roles provide an important perspective, leading to significant returns on investment. The evidence shows that companies with more women on boards and in leadership positions have significantly better

[52] Korn Ferry, 'Women Outperform Men in 11 of 12 Key Emotional Intelligence Competencies' (2016) <www.kornferry.com/about-us//press/new-research-shows-women-are-better-at-using-soft-skills-crucial-for-effective-leadership> accessed 8 May 2022.

[53] McKinsey & Company, 'Diversity Wins: How Inclusion Matters' (2020) <www.mckinsey.com/featured-insights/diversity-and-inclusion/diversity-wins-how-inclusion-matters> accessed 8 May 2022.

[54] ILO, 'Women in Business and Management' (n 49).

[55] ILO and UN Women, 'Win–Win' (n 46).

[56] Yasmina Zaidan, 'Five Reasons Social Enterprises Are Applying a Gender Lens to their Businesses' (*Acumen* 24 May 2016) <https://acumen.org/blog/five-reasons-social-enterprises-are-applying-a-gender-lens-to-their-businesses/> accessed 8 May 2022.

[57] Credit Suisse Research Institute, 'The CS Gender 3000: Reward for Change' (2016) <https://evolveetfs.com/wp-content/uploads/2017/08/Credit-Suisse-Reward-for-Change_1495660293279_2.pdf> accessed 8 May 2022.

[58] Ibid.

[59] Ibid.

financial performance.[60] A 2020 McKinsey report highlighted that the most gender-diverse companies are 28 per cent more likely to perform better financially.[61] A rise in female board members is correlated with less excessive risk-taking and a reduction in aggressive tax strategies.[62] Importantly, a balance between the number of men and women in leadership and board positions also has a positive effect on financial performance.[63] The goal should not be all-women boards or only women leaders but diversity across all hierarchical levels of the company. Research has shown that there need to be at least three women on corporate boards for gender diversity to contribute to the financial performance of the company.[64] Gender balance in boardrooms could also motivate women to aspire to positions of power and diminish negative stereotypes around women's capabilities in the workplace.

Gender diversity in the boardroom also has been shown to result in better decision-making, likely due to the greater diversity in background, experience, and perspective.[65] Diverse teams are less prone to groupthink, allowing them to evaluate different options more carefully. In a study of 108 technology companies, Morgan Stanley also found that those that have gender-inclusive policies had better returns on equity and lower volatility.[66] Gender-diverse companies also have less regulatory and operational risks.[67] Finally, a more diverse workforce has been positively associated with higher-quality work, greater team satisfaction, and more equality.[68]

60 Calvert Impact Capital, 'Just Good Investing: Why Gender Matters to Your Portfolio and What You Can Do about It' (2018) <https://assets.ctfassets.net/40aw9man1yeu/2X1gLdNUrUPFhRAJbAXp1q/205876bdd2d7e076fce05d5771183dfe/calvert-impact-capital-gender-report.pdf> accessed 8 May 2022.

61 McKinsey & Company, 'Diversity Wins' (n 53) .

62 Froehlicher et al., 'Gender Equality in the Workplace' (n 20).

63 Calvert Impact Capital, 'Just Good Investing' (n 60).

64 Cynthia Soledad, Karoline Vinsrygg, Ashley Summerfield, and Jennifer Reingold, *2018 Global Board Diversity Tracker: Who's Really on Board?* (Egon Zehnder 2018) 11.

65 Bob Zukis, 'How Women Will Save the Future, One Corporate Board at a Time' (*Forbes* 30 June 2020) <www.forbes.com/sites/bobzukis/2020/06/30/how-women-will-save-the-future-one-corporate-board-at-a-time/?sh=44915c207bc9> accessed 8 May 2022.

66 Morgan Stanley, 'Gender Diversity Is a Competitive Advantage' (2016) <www.morganstanley.com/pub/content/dam/msdotcom/ideas/gender-diversity-toolkit/Gender-Diversity-Investing-Primer.pdf> accessed 8 May 2022.

67 Froehlicher et al., 'Gender Equality in the Workplace' (n 20).

68 Robin J. Ely and David A. Thomas, 'Getting Serious about Diversity: Enough Already with the Business Case' (Harvard Business Review November–December 2010) <https://hbr.org/2020/11/getting-serious-about-diversity-enough-already-with-the-business-case> accessed 8 May 2022.

9.2.2.1 Market Expansion and Productivity

A focus on female consumers leads to significant market expansion. Women are usually responsible for household purchases[69] and they account for 85 per cent of consumer purchases,[70] making them an important consumer base. Companies need to understand how to market their goods and services to female consumers, including convenient times and locations according to their lifestyles.[71] Alignment with female customers' challenges and preferences can lead to a rise in their loyalty and an increase in sales.[72] Women involved in the design and production process of goods and services take the female perspective into account, providing insights that amplify profitability for the company.[73] Finally, gender integration in companies' business models can lead to increased perception of value by consumers, and therefore increased use and adoption of the goods and services offered.[74]

A rise in female employment increases productivity throughout value chains.[75] Giving women access to jobs usually reserved for men can increase the companies' productivity.[76] Companies with male and female employees can take full advantage of the different capabilities of both genders.[77] Employment of women in sales and distribution teams can lead to increased trust by female consumers, resulting in an expansion in customer base and increased customer retention and brand reputation.[78] According to a report by the ILO, gender-diverse companies report improvements in creativity, innovation, openness, and enhanced reputation.[79] Finally, research has shown that gender-diverse teams are more likely to produce radical innovation.[80]

69 Millennium Challenge Corporation, 'Gender Equality: A Smart Proposition for Business' (2015) <www.mcc.gov/resources/story/story-kin-apr-2015-gender-equality-a-smart-business-proposition#ref-4-a> accessed 8 May 2022.

70 She-conomy, 'Marketing to Women Quick Facts' <http://she-conomy.com/report/marketing-to-women-quick-facts> accessed 8 May 2022.

71 Acumen, 'Women and Social Enterprises' (n 48) 11.

72 Ibid 12.

73 Ibid 46.

74 Ibid 11.

75 Ibid 46.

76 Ibid 39.

77 Ibid.

78 Ibid 12.

79 ILO, 'Women in Business and Management' (n 49).

80 Cristina Díaz-García, Angela González-Moreno, and Francisco Jose Sáez-Martínez, 'Gender Diversity within R&D Teams: Its Impact on Radicalness of Innovation' (2012) 15(2) *Innovation* 149–160.

Companies should strive to have gender balance in the research and development teams, to take advantage of what both men and women have to offer.

9.2.2.2 Social Impact

Women in higher positions foster greater gender equality within their companies, promoting the implementation of diversity policies for the well-being of women within the firm.[81] Firms with a female general manager employ more women than those led by a man, and are committed to help them grow professionally through mentoring, offering equal opportunities to those given to men, and eliminating bias in employment and pay.[82] Additionally, women managers have been shown to provide more support to their teams, in terms of well-being and workload, than their male counterparts.[83] Women in leadership positions may be more committed to gender equality than men, having been exposed to inequality throughout their professional careers and personal lives.[84] Furthermore, they are more in tune with the difficulties faced by women and therefore can allow more flexibility in the workplace. Companies with women board members tend to have more remote work options and flexible working arrangements.[85] An increase in the number of women in leadership positions results in a broader candidate pool, leading to more qualified women available for board nominations. Finally, companies with a female CEO tend to have a higher percentage of women in managerial positions.[86]

9.3 EMERGENCE OF GENDER PROVISIONS IN INVESTMENT AGREEMENTS

FDI is a main feature of economic globalization, and it indicates long-term commitment and economic ties, with different levels of impact on the social, economic, cultural, and gender structures of the region receiving the investment. FDI is, for the most part, regulated by international investment treaties (IIAs) signed between governments – the government of the country receiving the investment and the government of the home of the investor.

[81] IADB, 'Una olimpíada desigual' (n 6).
[82] Ibid.
[83] ILO and UN Women, 'Win–Win' (n 46).
[84] Ibid.
[85] Froehlicher et al., 'Gender Equality in the Workplace' (n 20).
[86] Ng and Sears, 'The Glass Ceiling in Context' (n 10).

IIAs are categorized in two types: (i) bilateral investment treaties and (ii) treaties with investment provisions. A BIT is an agreement between two countries regarding the promotion and protection of investments made by parties from the respective countries in each other's territory. They are international agreements establishing the terms and conditions for private investment by natural and legal persons of one state in another state. The great majority of IIAs are BITs,[87] and this section will focus on those, and in particular on model BITs proposed by governments, as those are the types of international investment agreements where relevant gender provisions are currently being developed.

There are clear linkages through which trade and investment policies and agreements can affect gender dynamics. Negotiators of international trade agreements have progressively included the discussions on gender provisions or gender chapters in free trade agreements (FTAs). Both individual provisions and chapters mostly cover issues ranging from cooperation activities to institutional arrangements, including the establishment of a trade and gender committee and consultation procedures. Other gender-related provisions can be found spread throughout the text of an FTA – in the preamble, in chapters on labour, on investment, on cooperation, on sustainable development, or on small and medium-sized enterprises (SMEs).[88] Although mostly welcome and in continuous development, so far the commitments that address gender through those instruments are mostly aspirational. It is worth noting that a few FTAs contain binding and enforceable gender-related provisions, with the US–Mexico–Canada agreement (USMCA) being the most recent one, notably in Chapter 23 – Labor.[89]

On the other hand, in the realm of international investment agreements, very few model BITs currently include gender provisions. Even when they do, these provisions do not impose binding obligations on corporations. Out of eighty-four model agreements published online by the United Nations Conference on Trade and Development's (UNCTAD) Investment Policy

87 UNCTAD, 'Investment Policy Hub' <https://investmentpolicy.unctad.org/international-investment-agreements/model-agreements> accessed 8 May 2022.

88 *See* for example the United States–Mexico–Canada (USMCA), that includes gender provisions in the Labor Chapter and the Comprehensive and Progressive Agreement for Trans-Pacific Partnership (CPTPP) that addresses gender concerns in the Development Chapter.

89 United States–Mexico–Canada Agreement Implementation Act, H.R. 5430, Public Law 116–113, Chapter 23, <https://ustr.gov/sites/default/files/files/agreements/FTA/USMCA/Text/23%20Labor.pdf> accessed 8 May 2022.

Hub,[90] only seven explicitly address gender, albeit through broad provisions that refer to 'fair and equitable treatment' between men and women.[91]

Among the few examples of countries that have submitted model BITs containing gender provisions are the Netherlands (model revised in 2019)[92] and Canada (model revised in 2021).[93] Amid the interesting changes introduced by the Netherlands, the 2019 model agreement includes a commitment to promote equal opportunities and participation for women and men in the economy. The preamble recognizes the importance of gender equality in international trade and investment policies, and Article 6, paragraph 3 of the model agreement underscores 'the importance of incorporating a gender perspective into the promotion of inclusive economic growth' and that 'Contracting Parties commit to promote equal opportunities and participation for women and men in the economy'.

More recently, in May 2021, the Government of Canada introduced its model BIT with several provisions addressing gender issues. Among the main changes included in this model, Canada highlights provisions on gender equality, including 'a number of new provisions that aim to help women and other groups benefit more from the agreements, and to ensure that investment protections do not impede policies promoting gender equality'.[94] Special attention in that regard should be paid to Article 3 (Right to Regulate), Article 8 (Minimum Standard of Treatment), and Article 16 (Responsible Business Conduct).

The Dutch and the Canadian model BITs are relevant because they set the scene for a new generation of IIAs, as they highlight the importance of incorporating a gender perspective in the promotion of inclusive growth and equal opportunities between men and women. Previously, when investment agreements mentioned gender, they mostly focused on gender equality in arbitral dispute resolution and the gender division among arbitrators. This

[90] UNCTAD, 'Investment Policy Hub' (n 87).

[91] The Model BITs that mention gender were signed by Morocco, Belgium-Luxemburg, Netherlands, Slovakia, India, and Serbia.

[92] Kingdom of the Netherlands, 'Model Investment Agreement' (2019) <https://investmentpolicy.unctad.org/international-investment-agreements/treaty-files/5832/download> accessed 8 May 2022.

[93] Government of Canada, '2021 Model FIPA' <www.international.gc.ca/trade-commerce/trade-agreements-accords-commerciaux/agr-acc/fipa-apie/2021_model_fipa-2021_modele_apie.aspx?lang=eng> accessed 8 May 2022.

[94] Government of Canada, '2021 FIPA Model – Summary of Main Changes' <www.international.gc.ca/trade-commerce/trade-agreements-accords-commerciaux/agr-acc/fipa-apie/2021_model_fipa_summary-2021_modele_apie_resume.aspx?lang=eng> accessed 8 May 2022.

seems to be changing in light of the recent model BITs, but the impact of investment treaties and foreign direct investment on gender equality are notions that need to have more concrete ground in international investment treaties.

It is worth noting that having gender provisions in government model BITs is not a precondition for signatories to include gender provisions in the BITs they negotiate and sign. In fact, a quick overview in the most recently signed BITs in force[95] shows that there is little correlation between countries that addressed gender in their model BITs and countries that signed BITs addressing gender. For example, whereas Brazil stood out as one of the few countries whose recent model investment agreement did not address gender, the government addresses the issue in most of its recently signed investment cooperation and facilitation treaties.[96] Conversely, whereas Morocco's 2019 model BIT[97] addressed gender, its most recent BIT – signed with Japan in August 2020[98] – does not.

9.4 FDI CAN BE THE DRIVER OF NECESSARY CHANGES

The private sector can have a very active role in promoting gender equality, and investment policies by MNEs can be conducive to creating more employment opportunities for women.[99] FDI inflows can lead to more opportunities for women in the job market but may also exacerbate disparities. In fact, according to Blanton and Blanton, 'traditional arguments about the linkages between socio-political factors and FDI – particularly in developing

[95] According to the UNCTAD Investment Policy Hub, currently there are 2,270 BITs in force <https://investmentpolicy.unctad.org/international-investment-agreements>.

[96] *See* for example the Cooperation and Facilitation Investment Agreement between Brazil and the United Arab Emirates <https://investmentpolicy.unctad.org/international-investment-agreements/treaty-files/5855/download> accessed 8 May 2022; For more information, *see* Ana Sarmento, 'The Scope of New Brazilian Investment Protections: Intellectual Property and the Limits of an Alternate Approach', (2021) 52(2) *University of Miami Inter-American Law Review* n.p.

[97] Kingdom of Morocco, 'Model Investment Treaty' (June 2019) <https://investmentpolicy.unctad.org/international-investment-agreements/treaty-files/5895/download> accessed 8 May 2022.

[98] UNCTAD, 'Agreement between the Kingdom of Morocco and Japan for the Promotion and Protection of Investment' <https://investmentpolicy.unctad.org/international-investment-agreements/treaty-files/5908/download> accessed 8 May 2022.

[99] Renata Vargas Amaral and Lillyana Daza Jaller, 'The Role of Regulations and MNEs in Ensuring Equal Opportunities for Women' (2020) 27(3) *UNCTAD Transnational Corporations Journal* 183–202.

countries – anticipate an inverse relationship between the rights and welfare of women and foreign investment'.[100]

FDI can be the driver of necessary changes and although it would be natural to believe that a rise of trade and investment in the economy would lead to more opportunities for women, studies consistently show that trade and investment policies are not gender-neutral. While the current trade and investment paradigms are supposed to increase growth, decrease inequalities and promote employment, evidence shows (especially in developing countries such as those in Latin America and the Caribbean) that a more globalized economy and a boost of foreign direct investment by MNEs may increase inequalities, 'especially across sectors, income, gender and social groups'.[101]

When planning and implementing investments in a foreign country, MNEs can set the tone and go beyond the gender provisions where they exist in domestic legislation and IIAs. In fact, corporations' gender policies have in many ways led the efforts to raise awareness around the inequality with which women are treated in the workforce in all regions of the world.

9.4.1 *What Women Need*

Implementing employment policies that create an enabling environment for men and women can improve companies' access to talent as well as employee retention.[102] Offering flexible work arrangements and using governmental programmes to promote gender equality within the organization are strong contributing factors to improve the working environment for women and to create more opportunities for them.[103]

Access to training, mentorship, and professional development can help women rise, enhancing their leadership and decision-making skills.[104] Increased purchasing power for women leads to more women purchasing from and investing in companies that take their social impact into account.[105] Furthermore, companies whose workforce uses advanced technologies tend to

[100] Robert Blanton and Shannon Lindsey Blanton, 'Is Foreign Direct Investment Gender Blind? Women's Rights as a Determination of US FDI' (2015) 21(4) *Feminist Economics* 61–88.
[101] Ranja Sengupta, 'The Gender Dynamics of Trade and Investment and the Post-2015 Development Agenda: A Developing-Country Perspective' (2013) Third World Network Briefing Paper 68 <www.twn.my/title2/briefing_papers/No68.pdf> accessed 8 May 2022.
[102] Acumen, 'Women and Social Enterprises' (n 48).
[103] IADB, 'Una olimpíada desigual' (n 6).
[104] Acumen, 'Women and Social Enterprises' (n 48).
[105] Ibid.

be more equitable in terms of gender.[106] In a study carried out in Mexico, the introduction of computer technology helped ease the physical effort required by women in blue-collar jobs.[107] This led to a higher female participation rate and higher relative salaries.

9.4.2 Initiatives by Corporations in the Americas

MNEs can go beyond the requirements imposed on them by domestic legislation and IIAs. For example, by imposing their own quotas for women's representation at senior managerial levels, their investment practices will be aligned with UN Sustainable Development Goal 5 on gender equality.[108] As a result of the COVID-19 pandemic, several corporations have implemented measures to address the struggle employees were facing due to the increase in their domestic responsibilities. As an example, Microsoft introduced different parental leave programmes for parents with children at home due to school closures and online learning.[109]

Some may claim that corporations are opportunistic, using human rights rhetoric, including that of gender equality, as part of their marketing strategy.[110] However, regardless of the intentions behind the actions of corporations, these initiatives have positive business outcomes for the company as well as social outcomes, including raising awareness about these issues. By prioritizing a diverse and inclusive work environment, MNEs can have a positive impact on the lives of women employees as well as women in the communities where the MNEs operate. Finally, these transformative actions can benefit society as a whole by driving the development of local communities and national economies.[111]

An example of an MNE that is implementing interesting projects in Latin America and the Caribbean is United Parcel Service (UPS). In 2021, UPS launched its Women Exporter programme in fifteen countries in Latin America, including Mexico, Chile, and Barbados .[112] The corporation has

[106] IADB, 'Una olimpíada desigual' (n 6).
[107] Ibid.
[108] Froehlicher et al., 'Gender Equality in the Workplace' (n 20).
[109] Holly Corbett, 'How Companies Are Supporting Working Parents in the COVID Economy' (Forbes 30 July 2020) <www.forbes.com/sites/hollycorbett/2020/07/30/how-companies-are-supporting-working-parents-in-the-covid-economy/?sh=52bbb64e328f> accessed 8 May 2022.
[110] Marianna Leite, 'Pluralizing Discourses: Multinationals and Gender Equality' (2019) 20(3) *Journal of International Women's Studies* 116–138.
[111] ILO and UN Women, 'Win–Win' (n 46).
[112] UPS, 'Women Exporters Program' <www.ups.com/ba/en/services/small-business/women-exporters-program.page> accessed 8 May 2022.

committed its resources and industry know-how to empower women through the programme, assisting small or medium-sized enterprises with international trade and e-commerce. Another example is ExxonMobil, which works with Vital Voices, to support advanced training for women business owners in LAC and other regions. Since 2005, the corporation has had global gender policies to help women around the world invest in themselves and their communities.[113]

Unilever has had a strong presence in the region and beyond, adopting internal gender policies – it supports and works with United Nations (UN) Women in Latin America. In 2021, the corporation celebrated the fact that Unilever Colombia achieved gender balance on its board of directors, with 50 per cent of the positions held by women. Unilever also closed the gender gap in managerial roles, with 53 per cent of managerial positions covered by female talent. This is the largest representation of women in leadership positions in the history of the company in Colombia.[114] Moreover, the corporation intends to generate better living conditions for women in its extended chain in Colombia through programmes such as Shakti – an inclusive micro-distribution project through which the company offers training and additional income opportunities. This initiative has already benefited more than 10,000 Colombian women – most of them heads of household – in 463 rural localities around the country.[115]

9.5 CONCLUDING REMARKS

The future of the international economic order is contingent on the ability of governments and the private sector to distribute the benefits of economic growth equally to all.[116] Maximizing the benefits for women in terms of FDI by MNEs requires action from both the public and private sectors, at the national and the international levels. The mere existence of gender provisions (and maybe chapters) in IIAs does not guarantee that gender concerns will be

[113] ExxonMobil, 'Community Engagement: Women's Economic Opportunity' <https://corporate.exxonmobil.com/Sustainability/Community-engagement/Womens-economic-opportunity> accessed 8 May 2022.

[114] Unilever, 'Promoting Gender Equality throughout our Value Chain in Colombia' <www.unilever-southlatam.com/news/comunicados-de-prensa/2021/promoting-gender-equality-throughout-our-value-chain-in-colombia.html> accessed 8 May 2022.

[115] Ibid.

[116] Padideh Alai and Renata Amaral, 'The Importance (and Complexity) of Mainstreaming Gender in Trade Agreements' (CIGI October 2019) <www.cigionline.org/articles/importance-and-complexity-mainstreaming-gender-trade-agreements/> accessed 8 May 2022.

implemented and enforced at the firm level, the policy level or through domestic legislation.

Public, private, domestic, and international investment policies are of fundamental importance to further women's economic empowerment, creating opportunities for employment, entrepreneurship, and inclusive growth. Domestically, legal reform and enforcement of gender policies by local governments in the countries where an MNE operates is crucial. As discussed previously in scholarship,[117] legal frameworks around the world have vastly improved in terms of the rights granted to women, but there is still much room for growth. Research shows that focused domestic legal reform leads to smaller gender gaps and higher investments, together with societal and economic benefits.

MNEs in the private sector have been leading this change around the globe in many respects. With gender policies focused on the composition of boards, for example, corporations have been changing the decision-making landscape for the past years. However, especially when talking about foreign investments in different countries, many initiatives are still needed in the private sector to create an enabling environment for women as well as opportunities to attract, train, retain, and promote women.

[117] Amaral and Daza Jaller, 'The Role of Regulations and MNEs' (n 99).

PART III

Regional Approaches

10

Gender Approaches in Regional Trade Agreements and a Possible Gender Protocol under the African Continental Free Trade Area

A Comparative Assessment

KATRIN KUHLMANN*

ABSTRACT

With gender and trade now linked on the international agenda, gender approaches in regional trade agreements (RTAs) could have significant implications for women entrepreneurs and traders around the world. Building on the foundation of African Regional Economic Communities (RECs), the African Continental Free Trade Area (AfCFTA) includes gender as an express priority alongside sustainable and inclusive socio-economic development. Yet this is only a starting point. A gender-focused AfCFTA protocol is under negotiation, representing a significant opportunity to reassess RTA provisions on gender and consider more tailored, contextual approaches that could benefit women on the African continent and around the world. This chapter will present a comparative assessment of approaches for evaluating and categorizing gender and trade approaches in RTAs. These include a focus on gender responsiveness and incorporation of international and domestic legal design options for 'inclusive law and regulation' in order to use RTAs to address more holistically the concrete challenges facing women. The chapter also includes a contextual analysis of how trade rules could more actively support women's work, reduce procedural hurdles in the market, enhance access to finance and digital inclusion, and promote food security under the AfCFTA and future RTAs.

* The author would like to thank Ruth Gitau, who received a Masters of Law degree from Georgetown University Law Center, for her invaluable research support. Special thanks also to the Georgetown Law International Economic Law Colloquium and to Cristen Bauer and Aline Bertolin for comments on earlier versions of this work.

10.1 INTRODUCTION

The legal basis exists for a deeper focus on gender through the African Continental Free Trade Area (AfCFTA).[1] The 2017 Joint Declaration on Trade and Women's Economic Empowerment on the Occasion of the WTO Ministerial Conference in Buenos Aires (Declaration)[2] was heralded as a landmark initiative for putting gender on the trade agenda,[3] and gender is also a strong focus of the African Union (AU) Agenda 2063.[4] Although in legal terms these are soft law instruments without binding obligations, they set the stage for deeper work globally and under regional trade agreements (RTAs) such as the AfCFTA. These instruments also align with important human rights instruments, including the UN Convention on the Elimination of All Forms of Discrimination Against Women (CEDAW),[5] UN Sustainable Development Goals (UN SDGs), in particular, Goal 5 on Gender Equality,[6] and the African Charter on Human and Peoples' Rights Protocol on the Rights of Women in Africa (Maputo Protocol; also referred to as the AU Protocol on Women's Rights).[7]

RTAs are increasingly incorporating gender priorities,[8] sometimes in the form of more tangible commitments through gender-focused provisions and

[1] Agreement Establishing the African Continental Free Trade Area, Art. 3, 21 March 2018, 58 ILM 1028 (AfCFTA) <https://au.int/en/treaties/agreement-establishing-african-continental-free-trade-area> accessed 2 May 2023.

[2] WTO, 'Joint Declaration on Trade and Women's Economic Empowerment on the Occasion of the WTO Ministerial Conference in Buenos Aires in December 2017' (2017) <www.wto.org/english/thewto_e/minist_e/mc11_e/genderdeclarationmc11_e.pdf> accessed 4 May 2023.

[3] *See* José-Antonio Monteiro, 'The Evolution of Gender-Related Provisions in Regional Trade Agreements' (2018) World Trade Organization Staff Working Paper ERSD-2021-8 <www.wto.org/english/res_e/reser_e/ersd201815_e.pdf> accessed 8 May 2022.

[4] AU Commission, 'African Union (AU) Agenda 2063: The Africa We Want' (2015) <https://au.int/sites/default/files/documents/36204-doc-agenda2063_popular_version_en.pdf> accessed 8 May 2022.

[5] UN, 'Convention on the Elimination of All Forms of Discrimination Against Women', UNGA Res. 34/180 (18 December 1979) (CEDAW).

[6] Amrita Bahri, 'Measuring the Gender-Responsiveness of Free Trade Agreements: Using a Self-Evaluation Maturity Framework' (2019) 14(2) *Global Trade & Customs Journal* 517–527. She refers to CEDAW and the UN, 'Transforming Our World: The 2030 Agenda for Sustainable Development', UNGA Res. A/RES/70/1 (25–27 September 2015).

[7] AU, 'Protocol to the African Charter on Human and Peoples' Rights on the Rights of Women in Africa' (2005) <https://au.int/en/treaties/protocol-african-charter-human-and-peoples-rights-rights-women-africa> accessed 8 May 2022.

[8] Ideally, gender should be interpreted broadly to include sex, gender identity, and gender expression. Further, as noted in Clair Gammage and Mariam Momodu, 'The Economic Empowerment of Women in Africa: Regional Approaches to Gender-Sensitive Trade Policies' (2020) 1 *African Journal of International Economic Law* 5: 'African women and their

chapters.[9] Not only is this a global trend, but it has strong roots in the African continent, where substantive gender commitments are included in obligations through Regional Economic Communities (RECs) and 'gender-sensitive trade policy has ... been a distinct feature' for years.[10] As of September 2022, the World Trade Organization (WTO) reported that out of 353 RTAs in force and notified to the WTO, 101 contain provisions on gender and women's issues.[11] Among the recent RTAs that include gender provisions, several incorporate a separate gender chapter, such as the Chile–Uruguay, Canada–Chile, Argentina–Chile, Chile–Brazil, and Canada–Israel Free Trade Agreements (FTAs),[12] as well as the 2020 United Kingdom–Japan

experiences are not homogenous and their historical and present experiences differ from one community to another.' An understanding of these experiences should be both 'intersectional' and 'multidimensional'. As referenced in Gammage and Momodu, 'The Economic Empowerment of Women in Africa' (fn 11 and 12), intersectionality was developed by Kimberlé Crenshaw Williams, 'Demarginalizing the Intersection of Race and Sex: A Black Feminist Critique of Antidiscrimination Doctrine, Feminist Theory and Antiracist Politics' (1989) University of Chicago Legal Forum; on multidimensionality, *see* James Gathii, 'Writing Race and Identity in a Global Context: What CRT and TWAIL Can Learn from Each Other' (2020) 67 *UCLA Law Review* 1610–1650.

9 *See* Monteiro, 'The Evolution of Gender-Related Provisions' (n 3); Bahri, 'Measuring the Gender-Responsiveness of Free Trade Agreements' (n 6); and Sama Al Mutair, Dora Konomi, and Lisa Page, 'Trade & Gender: Exploring International Practices That Promote Women's Economic Empowerment' (TradeLab 17 May 2018) <www.tradelab.org/single-post/2018/05/17/Trade-and-Gender-1> accessed 8 May 2022.

10 Gender and trade approaches in Africa date back to the 1980s. *See* Gammage and Momodu, 'The Economic Empowerment of Women in Africa' (n 8) 4. *See also* Lolita Laperle-Forget, 'Gender Responsiveness in Trade Agreements – How Does the AfCFTA Fare' (Tralac 17 March 2021) <www.tralac.org/blog/article/15141-gender-responsiveness-in-trade-agreements-how-does-the-afcfta-fare.html> accessed 8 May 2022; and Amrita Bahri, 'Gender Mainstreaming in Free Trade Agreements: A Regional Analysis and Good Practice Examples' (Gender, Social Inclusion and Trade Knowledge Product Series 2021), <https://wtochairs.org/sites/default/files/7.%20Gender%20mainstreaming%20in%20FTAs_final%20%286%29.pdf> accessed 8 May 2022.

11 WTO, 'Informal Working Group on Trade and Gender: Trade and Gender-related Provisions in Regional Trade Agreements' INF/TGE/COM/4 (WTO 2022) <https://docs.wto.org/dol2fe/Pages/SS/directdoc.aspx?filename=q:/INF/TGE/COM_4.pdf&Open=True> accessed 2 May 2023.

12 Chile–Uruguay Free Trade Agreement (Chile–Uruguay FTA) (2016); Chile–Canada Free Trade Agreement (CCFTA) (2019); Chile–Argentina Free Trade Agreement (Chile–Argentina FTA) (2019); Canada–Israel Free Trade Agreement (CIFTA) (2018); *see also* Katrin Kuhlmann, Tara Francis, Indulekha Thomas, Malou Le Graet, Mushfiqur Rahman, Fabiola Madrigal, Maya Cohen, and Ata Nalbantoglu, 'Reconceptualizing Free Trade Agreements through a Sustainable Development Lens' (27 July 2020) <https://cb4fec8a-9641-471c-9042-2712ac32ce3e.filesusr.com/ugd/095963_8b66c44bd19b4683b974eaa267fd4070.pdf> accessed 8 May 2022.

Comprehensive Economic Partnership Agreement.[13] Some African RECs, such as the Common Market for Eastern and Southern Africa (COMESA) and Southern African Development Community (SADD), as well as the Canada–Israel FTA, notably subject gender provisions to dispute settlement, which must often follow an attempt to pursue amicable avenues for resolving disputes.[14] While subjecting gender provisions to dispute settlement is a rather unusual feature among RTAs, it is likely that it is more cosmetic than compulsory.

Despite the proliferation of gender provisions and chapters, current approaches merely scratch the surface of what is possible. Most provisions on gender contain softer obligations and do not establish binding legal standards, which can be important for small enterprises and vulnerable communities. Further, gender provisions often fall short of enhancing equity and inclusion by not directly addressing the concrete challenges women face and the sectors in which they work. As gender chapters continue to evolve, they will likely be under increasing scrutiny regarding the depth of provisions, the degree to which they are gender responsive, and the extent to which they foster equitable and inclusive opportunities for women. This chapter will examine both current approaches and options for the future, with a particular focus on how trade rules could be designed to respond to the challenges that women traders, especially micro, small, and medium-sized enterprises (MSMEs) and small and medium-sized enterprises (SMEs), face in their day-to-day work.[15]

This assessment is critical in light of the announcement of a gender-related protocol under the AfCFTA,[16] which is the world's largest RTA in terms of

[13] Treaty Establishing the Common Market for Eastern and Southern Africa (5 November 1993) (COMESA Treaty) <www.comesa.int/wp-content/uploads/2019/02/comesa-treaty-revised-20092012_with-zaire_final.pdf> accessed 8 May 2022; SADC Protocol on Gender and Development, Arts. 20, 22 (17 August 2008) <www.sadc.int/sites/default/files/2021-08/Protocol_on_Gender_and_Development_2008.pdf> accessed 2 May 2023; SADC; and Agreement between the United Kingdom of Great Britain and Northern Ireland and Japan for a Comprehensive Economic Partnership, 23 October 2020.

[14] *See* Kuhlmann et al., 'Reconceptualizing Free Trade Agreements' (n 12).

[15] This is a significant gap in trade agreements, both regionally and multilaterally. *See*, for instance, Gammage and Momodu, 'The Economic Empowerment of Women in Africa' (n 8); and Kuhlmann et al., 'Reconceptualizing Free Trade Agreements' (n 12).

[16] Xinhua, 'AfCFTA Secretariat Mulls Protocol to Promote Gender, Youth Interests' (The Standard 27 April 2021) <www.standardmedia.co.ke/business-news/article/2001411063/afcfta-secretariat-mulls-protocol-to-promote-gender-youth-interests> accessed 8 May 2022; *see also* Eleni Giokos, 'Now for the Hard Part, Says Secretary-General of African Continental Free Trade Area' (CNN Business 16 June 2021) <https://edition.cnn.com/2021/06/16/business/wamkele-mene-afcfta-spc-intl/index.html?utm_source=fbCNNi&utm_campaign=africa&

member states and is an agreement that has the potential to reset the rules well beyond the African continent.[17] Although the Protocol on Women and Youth in Trade under the AfCFTA is still taking shape, several provisions in the current AfCFTA provide a high-level glimpse into what may follow,[18] and some of these are quite innovative in their design. Treaties establishing other African RECs contain gender provisions as well, including the East African Community (EAC),[19] COMESA,[20] SADC,[21] Economic Community of West African States (ECOWAS),[22] and Economic Community of Central African States (ECCAS),[23] establishing a foundation on which to build.[24] Given some of the particular challenges facing women traders and entrepreneurs on the African continent,[25] including complex and inconsistent market rules and gaps in digital inclusion and access to finance, the AfCFTA provides a fresh opportunity to go beyond this start and address gender and trade in a meaningful way.

The sections below will examine RTA approaches on gender and trade to date, including the structure of RTA provisions on gender, the gender responsiveness of RTA provisions, and inclusive legal design approaches.[26] Together, these provide a comparative assessment of approaches, provisions, and legal design innovations (drawn from RTAs, WTO rules, hard and soft

utm_medium=social&fbclid=IwARox7fg7mRaFL_O5P61fKhR30jBM6bfow9_MQRtX6fvgKKQ6fB5h337uYyA> accessed 8 May 2022.

17 Katrin Kuhlmann and Akinyi Lisa Agutu, 'The African Continental Free Trade Area: Toward a New Model for Trade and Development Law' (2020) 51(4) *Georgetown Journal of International Law* 853–808.

18 Laperle-Forget, 'Gender Responsiveness in Trade Agreements' (n 10).

19 Treaty for the Establishment of the East African Community, Art. 1 (1999) (EAC Treaty).

20 COMESA Treaty (n 13).

21 SADC Protocol on Gender and Development (n 13).

22 Treaty of the Economic Community of West African States Treaty (28 May 1975) (ECOWAS Treaty (Original)); Revised Treaty of the Economic Community of West African States Treaty (24 July 1993) (ECOWAS Treaty (Revised)).

23 Treaty for the Establishment of the Economic Community of Central African States, Art. 60(2)(b) (1983) (ECCAS Treaty).

24 Laperle-Forget, 'Gender Responsiveness in Trade Agreements' (n 10) 2. For a comprehensive assessment of gender provisions in African RECs, *see* Gammage and Momodu, 'The Economic Empowerment of Women in Africa' (n 8).

25 *See*, for instance, UN Women, 'Opportunities for Women Entrepreneurs in the African Continental Free Trade Area' (2019) <https://africa.unwomen.org/en/digital-library/publications/2019/07/opportunities-for-women-in-the-acfta> accessed 8 May 2022.

26 Katrin Kuhlmann, 'Mapping Inclusive Law and Regulation: A Comparative Agenda for Trade and Development' (2021) 2 *African Journal of International Economic Law* 48–87.

law, and domestic law) that could be used to address gender considerations in the context of inclusive development under the AfCFTA going forward.[27]

The chapter unfolds as follows. Section 10.2 compares the approaches to assess trade and gender rules. Section 10.3 provides a contextual analysis of the options and innovations with respect to trade measures affecting women, access to finance, digital inclusion, and food security, under the AfCFTA and for future RTAs.

10.2 A BRIEF COMPARISON OF APPROACHES TO ASSESS TRADE AND GENDER RULES

Although the practice and literature are still evolving on gender and trade, several approaches on how to assess gender and trade rules are relevant to the AfCFTA and other future RTAs. These include analysis of the structural nature of RTA provisions on gender, evaluation of the degree to which RTA provisions are gender responsive, and assessment of the equity and inclusivity dimension of gender and trade provisions. These different approaches intersect and are presented briefly below, and they all inform the contextual analysis in Section 10.3 focused on women's needs in the market.

10.2.1 *Structure of RTA Provisions on Gender*

Structurally, the word 'gender' appears in RTAs in various forms (Table 10.1), including in agreements' preambles and objectives (including, e.g., the Preamble to the AfCFTA); annexes; non-specific articles on related issues such as labour, agriculture, and intellectual property;[28] specific articles on gender; side agreements, which are often focused on related issues such as labour (e.g., Canada–Colombia and Canada–Costa Rica FTAs); and even stand-alone gender chapters (e.g., Chile–Uruguay FTA) in RTAs and

[27] To this end, *see* additional work on inclusive regulation, including, for example, Kuhlmann (ibid); Katrin Kuhlmann and Bhramar Dey, 'Using Regulatory Flexibility to Address Market Informality in Seed Systems: A Global Study' (2021) 11(2) 377 *Agronomy* 1–27, 16; Katrin Kuhlmann, 'Flexibility and Innovation in International Economic Law: Enhancing Rule of Law, Inclusivity, and Resilience in the Time of COVID-19' (Afronomicslaw 27 February 2020) <www.afronomicslaw.org/2020/08/27/flexibility-and-innovation-in-international-economic-law-enhancing-rule-of-law-inclusivity-and-resilience-in-the-time-of-covid-19/> accessed 8 May 2022.

[28] These include the Chile-Uruguay FTA (Chapter 11.9/6 on labour) and USMCA (Article 14.17 on corporate social responsibility, Article 23.9 on sex-based discrimination in the workplace, Article 25.2 on investment and SMEs), as referenced in Bahri, 'Measuring the Gender-Responsiveness of Free Trade Agreements' (n 6) 5.

TABLE 10.1 *Main structures of gender-related provisions*

Structure of gender-related provisions	Number of RTAs
Main text of the RTA:	**76**
Preamble	12
Non-specific article(s) on gender	64
Specific article on gender	10
Specific chapter on gender	9
Annex(es)	17
Side document(s) to the RTA:	**12**
Side Letters	1
Joint statement(s)	1
Protocol(s)	2
Labour cooperation agreement	8
Post-RTA agreements/decisions on gender:	**13**
Declaration(s)	4
Decision(s)/resolution(s)/directive(s)	6
Agreement(s)	3

Source: José-Antonio Monteiro, 'The Evolution of Gender-Related Provisions in Regional Trade Agreements', (2021) World Trade Organization Staff Working Paper ERSD-2021-8, 14.

protocols, such as the SADC Protocol on Gender and Development.[29] These structural aspects of gender and trade have been comprehensively assessed;[30] they inform how gender is incorporated into trade agreements, and they impact the degree and depth of commitments.

Within these structures, gender commitments tend to include common elements: '(i) affirmations of the importance of eliminating discrimination against women; (ii) recognition and adherence to other international agreements on gender; (iii) cooperation on gender issues (iv) institutional provisions including the establishment of committees for cooperation and exchange of information; and (v) soft committee-based dispute resolution mechanisms to amicably resolve differences'.[31]

[29] SADC Protocol on Gender and Development (n 13) Arts. 20, 22; *see generally*, Monteiro, 'The Evolution of Gender-Related Provisions' (n 3) 15; *see also* Bahri, 'Measuring the Gender-Responsiveness of Free Trade Agreements' (n 6) 4.

[30] *See* Monteiro, 'The Evolution of Gender-Related Provisions' (n 3).

[31] Kuhlmann et al., 'Reconceptualizing Free Trade Agreements' (n 12). *See also* ITC, 'Mainstreaming Gender in Free Trade Agreements' (2020) <https://intracen.org/resources/publications/mainstreaming-gender-in-free-trade-agreements> accessed 2 May 2023.

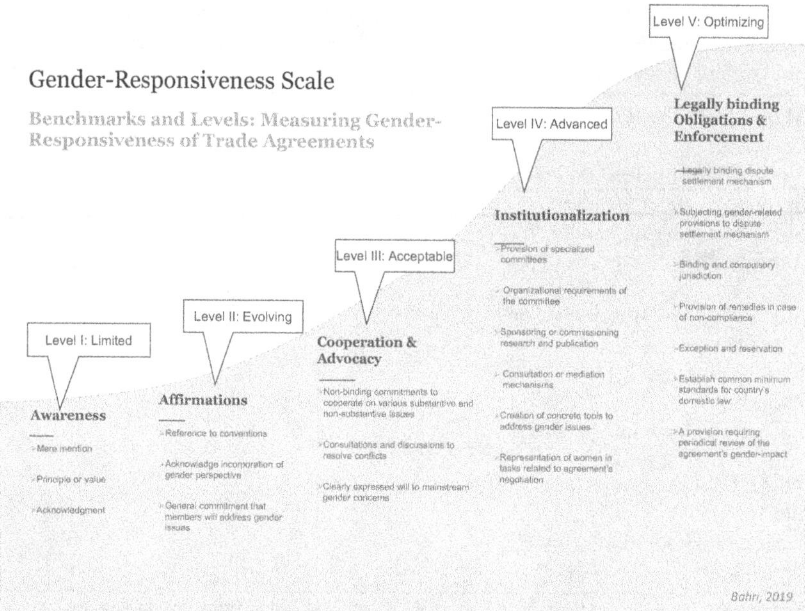

FIGURE 10.1 **Gender-responsiveness maturity framework.**
Source: Amrita Bahri, 'Measuring the Gender-Responsiveness of Free Trade Agreements: Using a Self-Evaluation Maturity Framework' (2019) 14(2) *Global Trade & Customs Journal* 517–527.

10.2.2 *Gender Responsiveness of RTA Provisions*

Going beyond structure, gender responsiveness is an important consideration in assessing RTA approaches. Bahri has advanced an instrumental Gender-Responsiveness Scale based on a maturity framework (Figure 10.1) which categorizes RTA provisions based on their gender responsiveness into five groups: limited, evolving, acceptable, advanced, and optimizing.[32] These benchmarks and levels allow for comparison across RTA provisions that go beyond their structure and begin to evaluate their impact.

[32] Bahri's study focuses on explicit gender-related provisions (those that 'use the terms relating to gender, women, female or a similar expression in the provision in an explicit manner') and implicit gender-related provisions ('those which, without making any explicit reference to gender, address the issues of gender in an indirect manner through human rights, vulnerable groups focus, labour discrimination, corporate social responsibility, intellectual property rights and small and medium enterprises'). Bahri, 'Measuring the Gender-Responsiveness of Free Trade Agreements' (n 6) 9, fn 31. *See also* Monteiro, 'The Evolution of Gender-Related Provisions' (n 3).

Applying this framework to the AfCFTA, the AfCFTA contains Level I commitments in the Preamble ('Recognising the importance of international security, democracy, human rights, gender equality, and the rule of law, for the development of international trade and economic cooperation') and General Objectives (Article 3 (e) under the General Objectives contains the objective to 'promote and attain sustainable and inclusive socio-economic development, gender equality and structural transformation of the State Parties').[33] Even though the AfCFTA's General Objectives contain a non-binding mention of gender equality, the inclusion of the language 'promote and attain' suggests a higher level of commitment than other general gender references.[34] Further, the language in the AfCFTA Preamble draws an explicit link between gender and 'the development of international trade and economic cooperation', implying that the AfCFTA as a whole should be interpreted in this context.[35]

Notably, two of the AfCFTA's protocols also contain gender-related provisions.[36] The AfCFTA Protocol on Trade in Services includes a reference to women in Article 27(2)(d) on Technical Assistance, Capacity Building, and Cooperation that could be considered a Level III commitment under Bahri's scale ('State Parties agree, where possible, to mobilise resources, in collaboration with development partners, and implement measures, in support of the domestic efforts of State Parties, with a view to, *inter alia*, ... improving the export capacity of both formal and informal service suppliers, with particular attention to micro, small and medium size; women and youth service suppliers').[37] The AfCFTA Protocol on the Free Movement of Persons contains a binding commitment with the use of mandatory language 'shall', stating that 'States Parties *shall* not discriminate against nationals of another Member State entering, residing or established in their territory, on the basis of their ... sex'.[38] This provision is particularly innovative, as it links non-discrimination with the free movement of persons and explicitly prohibits discrimination based on sex in this context.[39] The AfCFTA also includes a number of other provisions, including on special and differential treatment (S&DT), that could impact women as well (*see* Table 10.2).

33 AfCFTA (n 1) Preamble and General Objectives (Article 3 (e)).

34 Laperle-Forget, 'Gender Responsiveness in Trade Agreements' (n 10).

35 Ibid.

36 Ibid.

37 AfCFTA, Protocol on Trade in Services, Art. 27(2)(d), 21 March 2018, 58 ILM 1028, 1053 (AfCFTA Protocol on Trade in Services).

38 AfCFTA, Protocol on the Free Movement of Persons, 21 March 2018, 58 ILM 1028, 1053.

39 Laperle-Forget, 'Gender Responsiveness in Trade Agreements' (n 10).

TABLE 10.2 *Inclusive legal and regulatory approach*

Inclusive legal/regulatory dimension	Example RTA options
(1) Differentiation for vulnerable parties [special & differential treatment (S&DT)][a]	• RTA provisions on S&DT related to goods and services (e.g., AfCFTA S&DT provisions) could incorporate a gender context. • Globally, the LDC Services Waiver could be used to provide preferential market access for services in 'sectors employing predominantly women'.[b] • AfCFTA Protocol on Trade in Services references 'formal and *informal* service suppliers, with particular attention to . . . women'.
(2) Flexibility in design and application of rules	• 'Review and revise' provisions in RTAs, such as the AfCFTA 'rendezvous clause',[c] which allow for agreements to be adapted as circumstances change. • Consultation provisions focused on vulnerable groups and women could inform use of flexibility to reassess and build out commitments subject to circumstances and needs.
(3) Sustainable development	• Sustainable development provisions could be tailored to gender priorities. • Green Box domestic support measures could be assessed, consistent with the WTO Agreement on Agriculture (AoA), based on how to address women's needs,[d] particularly in the context of climate and food security, which could be part of a more comprehensive approach on food security and gender through RTAs.
(4) Equity[e]	• Minimum legal standards on women's access to land, non-discrimination, equal pay for equal work, inheritance, and other areas of law related to women's role in the economy[f] could enhance equity through RTAs and domestic law. • In addition to non-discrimination, building on the WTO Joint Initiative on Services Domestic Regulation, provisions could be incorporated into services schedules to guarantee gender-responsive financial services. • Permissible subsidies could be considered to provide treatment for 'assistance to disadvantaged groups, such as women and ethnic minorities'.[g] • Provisions could be added on migration and anti-trafficking. • Digital inclusion provisions could be integrated that include gender, and gender could be noted in the

Inclusive legal/regulatory dimension	Example RTA options
	context of data privacy (along with human rights, sexual orientation, transgender status, etc.). • AfCFTA and other RTAs could incorporate provisions on gender-responsive standards in line with the United Nations Economic Commission for Europe Declaration for Gender Responsive Standards and Standards Development.[h]
(5) Engagement and transparency	• Engagement provisions could be incorporated (Bahri Level 3) and linked with 'review and revise' RTA provisions to provide an avenue for addressing women's needs on an ongoing basis, coupling engagement with 'responsiveness'. • Transparency provisions could be tailored to women's needs, drawing upon good practices and lessons learned. • Engagement should be broadly designed to include civil society and the private sector, including enterprises of all sizes and women entrepreneurs across sectors.
(6) Reduction of legal and regulatory gateways	• Measures to address regulatory hurdles facing women could be more systematically assessed and prioritized, with a focus on regulatory design and implementation to enhance women's engagement in the market (e.g., focus on processes and procedures in trade facilitation, standards, sanitary and phytosanitary measures, streamlined business registration processes, etc.). • Mapping of specific processes that affect women could be done, with a focus on regulatory design and implementation to enhance women's engagement in the market. • AfCFTA Simplified Trade Regime and Non-Tariff Barrier Reporting, Monitoring, and Eliminating Mechanism could be gender responsive.
(7) Implementation and impact	• Provisions could be integrated requiring gender assessment and gender impact review, along with focused engagement on implementation that actively involves women affected by trade rules.

Source: Katrin Kuhlmann, 'Mapping Inclusive Law and Regulation: A Comparative Agenda for Trade and Development' (2021) 2 *African Journal of International Economic Law* 48–87.

[a] This most often takes the form of special and differential treatment, or special rights, for developing countries at the international law level. Kuhlmann, 'Mapping Inclusive Law and Regulation'.

[b] Acharya et al., 'Trade and Women', 346.
[c] AfCFTA, Part. II Art. 7. *See also* Kuhlmann, 'Mapping Inclusive Law and Regulation', and Gammage and Momodu, 'The Economic Empowerment of Women in Africa'.
[d] Acharya et al., 'Trade and Women', 337.
[e] Equity encompasses impartiality in law, with an emphasis on ensuring inclusivity for vulnerable groups addressing past injustices through law.
[f] *See* ITC, 'What Role for Women in International Trade?' (2019) <https://intracen.org/news-and-events/news/what-role-for-women-in-international-trade> accessed 2 May 2023; Kuhlmann et al., 'Reconceptualizing Free Trade Agreements'. At the WTO level, this could take the form of a plurilateral agreement on women in trade, which could 'codify the elimination of discrimination against women in trade [by eliminating] domestic laws that perpetuate such discrimination and ensur[ing] compliance with the principles of equal access and opportunity for trade'. Laura Lane and Penny Nass, 'Women in Trade Can Reinvigorate the WTO and Global Economy' (CIGI 27 April 2020) 6 <www.cigionline.org/articles/women-trade-can-reinvigorate-wto-and-global-economy/> accessed 8 May 2022.
[g] Acharya et al., 'Trade and Women', 342. They note that the WTO Agreement on Subsidies and Countervailing Measures (SCM Agreement) provides for significant policy space that could be used to empower women and disadvantaged groups.
[h] *See* Lane and Nass, 'Women in Trade Can Reinvigorate the WTO and Global Economy'.

Yet, despite these innovations, the AfCFTA's provisions on gender merely scratch the surface,[40] and movement towards an AfCFTA Protocol on Women and Youth in Trade could propel the AfCFTA in the direction of more comprehensive gender commitments, perhaps even reaching Level V on Bahri's scale. As the following section will argue, an AfCFTA protocol could innovate beyond existing Level V commitments and be tailored to address particular challenges facing women traders and entrepreneurs in the market.

10.2.3 *Inclusive Legal Design Approach*

In addition to the approaches discussed above, another important aspect of assessing RTA approaches revolves around equity and inclusion in legal design.[41] To date, RTA provisions on gender, whether explicit or implicit, have focused primarily on cooperation and consultation and have not fully addressed more direct equity considerations.[42]

40 As Laperle-Forget (ibid) highlights, of the thirty-six states that have ratified the AfCFTA, thirty-four (excluding only Mauritania and the Republic Democratic of Sahwari Arab) have undertaken stronger gender commitments in other RTAs, including in RTAs with the European Union.

41 Kuhlmann, 'Mapping Inclusive Law and Regulation' (n 26).

42 Ibid 82.

Cooperation and consultations provisions are common in RTAs and are not limited to gender. They also appear in other RTA chapters, such as those on labour, the environment, SMEs/MSMEs, government procurement, agriculture, services, and intellectual property rights (IPRs).[43] These provisions fall within Level III in Bahri's Gender-Responsiveness Scale and can be a useful tool when combined with other RTA commitments.

Assessing RTA design options through a lens of inclusion and equity requires a deeper dive into relevant legal design (encompassing a range of instruments, including treaties, soft law, domestic law and regulation, customary law, etc.), diverse legal and regulatory innovations, and the needs of vulnerable and marginalized stakeholders.[44] This is presented here based on an approach to 'Inclusive Law and Regulation' (Kuhlmann), applied to trade rules in a gender context (Table 10.2),[45] following an analytical framework that provides a basis to evaluate economic law and regulation (including RTAs) in the context of inclusive trade and development.[46] Additional options that fall within this analytical framework are presented in Section 10.3.

As Table 10.2 highlights, trade provisions and measures could be designed and applied based on a framework that fosters inclusion and equity. Additional examples that track these dimensions of inclusive law and regulation are presented in section 10.3.

Finally, and critically, there is also a political dimension to gender and trade. Despite the proliferation of gender provisions in trade instruments, gender and trade commitments are sometimes viewed with scepticism from the perspective of preserving policy flexibility (or 'policy space') and avoiding disguised protectionism.[47] These are important considerations and are

43 Bahri, 'Measuring the Gender-Responsiveness of Free Trade Agreements' (n 6) 11.

44 Kuhlmann, 'Mapping Inclusive Law and Regulation' (n 26).

45 Ibid. Legal instruments also include aspects of WTO law comprehensively assessed through a gender lens in Rohini Acharya, Olga Falgueras Alamo, Salma Mohamed Thabit Al-Battashi, Anoush der Boghossian, Naghm Ghei, Tania Parcero Herrera, Lee Ann Jackson, Ulla Kask, Claudia Locatelli, Gabrielle Marceau, Ioana-Virginia Motoc, Anna Caroline Müller, Nora Neufeld, Simon Padilla, Josefita Pardo de Léon, Stella Perantakou, Nadezhda Sporysheva, and Christiane Wolff, 'Trade and Women – Opportunities for Women in the Framework of the World Trade Organization' (2019) 22(3) *Journal of International Economic Law* 323–354.

46 Kuhlmann, 'Mapping Inclusive Law and Regulation' (n 26).

47 Similar concerns have been raised regarding human rights, labour, environment, and sustainable development provisions. India, in particular, has voiced concerns with linking gender and trade at the multilateral level. *See* Ananya Singh, 'Explained: India's Refusal to Back WTO Declaration on Gender Equality in Trade' (QRIUS 15 December 2017) <https://qrius.com/explained-india-refusal-gender-equality-trade/> accessed 8 May 2022; *see also* Suresh Prabhu, 'Indian Minister of Industry and Commerce' (Indian Press Conference, WTO Ministerial Conference, Buenos Aires, 11 December 2017).

approached here in three interconnected ways, recognizing that these issues are complex and multidimensional. First, states and regions need to consider the most appropriate way to use the legal instruments of international trade to meet particular gender and development needs. For this reason, the following section presents options for consideration and not prescriptive solutions. Second, as far as possible, any options for RTAs should be tracked with innovations in regional and domestic law, which can act as a proxy for supported principles and approaches. In this case, innovations in the design of African law at the international/regional and domestic levels are highlighted, bearing in mind that a more substantial review would be beneficial in the AfCFTA context. Finally, options presented in the following section are linked with actual challenges women face in sub-Saharan Africa, suggesting a balance between policy space and women's needs and drawing a connection between RTA provisions and those they are meant to serve, ultimately linking macro-level trade agreements with micro-level challenges and opportunities. This final dimension is also worthy of greater study, as it is an important gap in trade law and trade agreements that should be more systematically addressed.[48]

10.3 CONTEXTUAL ANALYSIS OF OPTIONS AND INNOVATIONS FOR THE AFCFTA AND FUTURE RTAS

The preceding section presented a brief summary of three interconnected approaches to assess possible RTA provisions on gender and trade: a structural approach, a gender-responsive approach, and a design-focused approach based on inclusive law and regulation. This section draws from these approaches and frames RTA options for the AfCFTA in the context of challenges women face in the market. These challenges include issues related to the sectors in which women are engaged, including challenges related to work in both goods and services (and the high degree of work in the informal sector), non-tariff measures and regulatory hurdles, gaps in access to finance, lack of digital inclusion, and issues related to women's role in the agricultural sector and food security.[49] Although current African RTAs (including the AfCFTA) do contain legal innovations, they do not fully recognize women's particular

[48] *See* Kuhlmann, 'Mapping Inclusive Law and Regulation' (n 26).

[49] *See*, for instance: UN Women, 'Opportunities for Women Entrepreneurs' (n 25); and UNECA, 'Advancing Gender-Equitable Outcomes in African Continental Free Trade Area (AfCFTA) Implementation' (2021) <www.uneca.org/sites/default/files/keymessageanddocuments/22May_Final_WhitePaper_Advancing_gender_equitable_outcomes.pdf> accessed 8 May 2022.

needs or the roles that women hold in an economy, highlighting an important gap.[50] The AfCFTA could, however, innovate further through the new protocol and through a comprehensive, whole-agreement approach to address women's needs.[51]

Important lessons and options can be drawn from the design of both gender-specific and broader provisions in existing RTAs, WTO rules, and African law. The legal dimension of gender and trade should be comprehensively assessed across legal instruments (Table 10.3), although a full legal assessment is beyond the scope of this chapter. Assessing the legal dimension of RTAs must, however, go beyond RTA text, structure, and enforcement and extend to other international legal instruments and national law as well, encompassing the 'various laws and norms that influence gender roles and women's opportunities and constraints within a particular country' (or region) (*see* Table 10.3).[52]

Domestic law is one of the most important sources of information on how RTA parties approach gender. Although states have innovative rules addressing gender, there are still critical gaps. According to the International Trade Centre, over 90 per cent of states have laws that limit women's ability to engage in the market. These can take the form, for example, of rules and regulations that restrict women's ownership of land, differentiated processes for business registration, and limitations on women's participation in global trade.[53]

In lieu of a comprehensive legal review, the WTO Trade Policy Review Mechanism (TPRM) provides important insight into how women's empowerment is incorporated into the trade policies of WTO members.[54]

50 These agreements fail to recognize 'the diverse roles of women as traders, workers, and consumers in African economies [which] has sustained inequalities through the guise of the development discourse'. *See* Gammage and Momodu, 'The Economic Empowerment of Women in Africa' (n 8) 1.

51 *See* Nadirya Bayat, 'A Whole Agreement Approach to Gender Mainstreaming in the AfCFTA' (Friedrich Ebert Stiftung March 2022).

52 Eugenia McGill, 'Trade and Gender' in Arthur Appleton, Patrick Macrory, and Michael Plummer (eds), *The World Trade Organization – Legal, Economic, and Political Analysis* (Springer Science and Business Media 2005) 36, referencing Rekha Mehra and Sarah Gammage, 'Trends, Countertrends, and Gaps in Women's Employment' (1999) 27(3) *World Development* 533–550. *See also* Marceline White, Carols Salas, and Sarah Gammage, 'Trade Impact Review: Mexico Case Study; NAFTA and the FTAA: A Gender Analysis of Employment and Poverty Impacts in Agriculture' (Women's Edge Coalition 2003) <www.iatp.org/sites/default/files/NAFTA_and_the_FTAA_A_Gender_Analysis_of_Employ.pdf> accessed 8 May 2022.

53 ITC, 'What Role for Women in International Trade?' (2019) <https://intracen.org/news-and-events/news/what-role-for-women-in-international-trade> accessed 2 May 2023, referenced in Acharya et al., 'Trade and Women' (n 45) 324.

54 Acharya et al., 'Trade and Women' (n 45) 327–328.

TABLE 10.3 *Legal instruments related to gender and trade*

Legal Instrument	Example
International instruments 'relevant to gender equality and human rights'[a]	International treaties such as CEDAW, International Labour Organization (ILO) conventions, and the Maputo Protocol/AU Protocol on Women's Rights; soft law, such as the UN SDGs (incorporated by reference in RTAs)
National constitutions	Constitution of Kenya (2010), for example[b]
National and subnational laws, regulations, policies, and other instruments 'that benefit women and other disadvantaged groups'	(a) Non-discrimination/equal treatment laws; (b) Affirmative action and laws to address gender disparity and promote equality;[c] (c) Laws related to fair wages, food labelling, and health and safety, as well as non-tariff measures in other areas, for example trade facilitation provisions; (d) Procurement rules related to women; and (e) Laws and regulations facilitating development of sectors in which women work (including agriculture, manufacturing, and services), as well as digital regulation and provisions on digital inclusion.
'Gaps or biases in the application or enforcement of laws that benefit women'	Labour laws, land titling, banking regulation[d]
'Religious, traditional, or customary laws and practices' (including 'living law')	Land tenure rules, inheritance rules

Source: Adapted from McGill, 'Trade and Gender', 37–38, with author's additions, also referencing Christine Chinkin and Florance Butegwa, *Gender Mainstreaming in Legal and Constitutional Affairs: A Reference Manual for Governments and Other Stakeholders* (Commonwealth Secretariat 2001) and Mehra and Gammage, 'Trends, Countertrends and Gaps', R 26.

[a] McGill, 'Trade and Gender', 37.

[b] Constitution of Kenya, 2010 (Laws of Kenya), Arts. 27(8), 59(2), 60(1)(f), 81(b), 91(f), 172(2)(b), 175(c), 197(1), and 250(11). With respect to government procurement, *see also* Constitution of Kenya, 2010 (Laws of Kenya) Art. 227(1) and Public Procurement and Asset Disposal Act (Kenya), 2015, Section 53(6).

[c] According to McGill, 'Trade and Gender', fn 93, such 'special measures aimed at accelerating de facto equality between men and women' are expressly authorized under CEDAW.' See CEDAW, Art. 4.1.

[d] Based on McGill, 'Trade and Gender', 38. McGill notes that '[f]acially neutral laws can … be applied in a discriminatory manner … [and] can also disadvantage women because of their more limited access to assets and employment opportunities'.

Based on a sampling of TPR submissions, the majority (70 per cent) of members' policies contain gender-responsive provisions.[55] These include (1) financial and non-financial incentives to the private sector and women-owned/led MSMEs and SMEs (30 per cent reported 'trade policies that support women-owned/led companies', including economic empowerment in the export sector; (2) 'agriculture and fisheries policies that support women's empowerment' (15.5 per cent); and (3) 'government procurement policies that support women's empowerment' (9 per cent).[56]

Possible RTA options should further 'be informed by an understanding of the social, economic and political context in which the relevant trade or investment activity is taking place, including the opportunities and constraints facing women and other disadvantaged groups'.[57] This aligns with an important aspect of gender mainstreaming, which calls for incorporating the 'experience, knowledge, and interests of women … on the development agenda',[58] as well as increasing focus on sectors that provide opportunities for women and ways in which to assist women-owned businesses to benefit from international trade and investment.[59]

The sub-sections that follow discuss four priority areas: (a) women's work in the goods and services sectors (including informal work) and trade measures affecting women (including impact of market rules on women); (b) access to finance; (c) digital inclusion; and (d) women's responsibilities related to agriculture and food security, with relevant RTA options summarized. The options below track closely with the 'inclusive law and regulation' approach summarized in Table 10.2 and also integrate aspects of the gender-responsive approach in Figure 10.1. Although they relate mainly to the AfCFTA, they are

[55] Anoush der Boghossian, 'Trade Policies Supporting Women's Economic Empowerment: Trends in WTO Members' (2019) WTO Staff Working Paper ERSD-2019-07 <www.wto.org/english/res_e/reser_e/ersd201907_e.htm> accessed 8 May 2022.

[56] Acharya et al., 'Trade and Women' (n 45) 327–328. Categorization based on the TPR submissions of 111 (out of 164) WTO members.

[57] McGill, 'Trade and Gender' (n 52) 36.

[58] According to the UNECOSOC, building upon the Platform for Action adopted at the 1995 United Nations Fourth World Conference on Women, in Beijing, China, gender mainstreaming involves: 'the process of assessing the implications for women and men of any planned action, including legislation, policies, or programmes, in any area and at all levels' (1997). See ILO, 'Definition of Gender Mainstreaming' <www.ilo.org/public/english/bureau/gender/newsite2002/about/defin.htm> accessed 8 May 2022.

[59] Commission on the Status of Women, 'Report on the Forty-Sixth Session' Ch. I.A., Draft Resolution III.A, para. 5, in *Economic and Social Council Official Records 2002, Supp.* No. 7, U.N. Doc. E/2002/27-E/CN.6/2002/13 (2002).

applicable to other RTAs as well and also draw upon WTO disciplines as noted.[60]

10.3.1 *Women's Work and Trade Measures Affecting Women*

One of the most fundamental aspects of trade and gender centres around the nature of women's work and engagement in the market. Women's employment encompasses the goods and services sectors,[61] and women have faced considerable disruptions in respect of both goods and services work due to the COVID-19 pandemic.[62] A number of these challenges are due to the more precarious nature of women's work, the lack of social safety nets, and women's role in unpaid and informal work.[63] Tourism services, which are dominated by women, were also hit particularly hard during the pandemic.[64]

Overall, women are increasingly involved in services, ranging from retail and financial services to tourism and hospitality, to health care,[65] including cross-border delivery of medical care that has been so critical during the COVID-19 pandemic. Women continue to play a strong role in manufacturing sectors as well, particularly export-driven manufacturing such as garments.[66]

Women are disproportionately involved in the informal sector, and the United Nations (UN) estimates that 89 per cent of women in Africa work

[60] For a comprehensive discussion of the relationship between gender and WTO rules, *see* McGill, 'Trade and Gender' (n 52) and Acharya et al., 'Trade and Women' (n 45).

[61] *See*, for instance, Katrin Kuhlmann, 'U.S. Preference Programs: How Well Do They Work?' (*US Senate Finance Committee* 16 May 2007) <www.finance.senate.gov/hearings/us-preference-programs-how-well-do-they-workd> accessed 8 May 2022.

[62] A number of gender-differentiated impacts have resulted from the COVID-19 pandemic, including disproportionate effects on women's work, lack of social safety nets, and gender-based violence. *See* UNCTAD, 'Impact of the COVID-19 Pandemic on Trade and Development: Transitioning to a New Normal' (2020) <https://unctad.org/system/files/official-document/osg2020d1_en.pdf> accessed 8 May 2022. Lessons can also be drawn from the gender-differentiated impact resulting from the financial crisis. *See*, for instance, Maria Floro and Gary Dymski, 'Financial Crisis, Gender, and Power: An Analytical Framework' (2000) 28 *World Development* 1269–1283; Joseph Y. Lim, 'The Effects of the East Asian Crisis on the Employment of Women and Men: the Philippine Case' (2000) 28 *World Development* 1285–1306; Ajit Singh and Ann Zammit, 'International Capital Flows: Identifying the Gender Dimension' (2000) 28 *World Development* 1249–1268.

[63] UNCTAD, 'Impact of the COVID-19 Pandemic on Trade and Development' (n 62) 31–32.

[64] Ibid 33.

[65] Acharya et al., 'Trade and Women' (n 45) 344.

[66] Export-driven manufacturing is often labour-intensive and subject to poor working conditions, frequent turnover, and unpredictability due to changes in capital and skills requirements (particularly in export processing zones). McGill, 'Trade and Gender' (n 52) 12.

informally (as a percentage of full employment).[67] While informal work can sometimes be more flexible, it can also offer little security and room for advancement.[68] Within the informal sector, migrant women face some of the most significant challenges, as the pandemic has underscored.[69] The immense challenge of addressing trafficking of women and girls remains as well,[70] which is linked with trade and transport corridors and global value chains.

Women traders struggle with a number of regulatory roadblocks, or 'regulatory gateways',[71] that limit their participation in the markets. These include domestic rules and regulations that relate to non-tariff measures (NTMs) in the form of standards, sanitary and phytosanitary (SPS) measures, and border measures, many of which are not gender responsive.[72] In terms of border measures, although the WTO Trade Facilitation Agreement[73] (and African governments) have pressed for simplification of measures and encouraged digitalization of border procedures in order to reduce waiting times, women traders still face procedural challenges and safety issues at the border.[74] Women traders also often lack information on cross-border regulations and procedures,[75] putting them at a disadvantage vis-à-vis larger businesses and

67 UN Women, 'Women in Informal Economy' (2021) <www.unwomen.org/en/news/in-focus/csw61/women-in-informal-economy> accessed 8 May 2022.

68 Informal work includes part-time work, home-based work, and other informal sector activity. McGill, 'Trade and Gender' (n 52) 13.

69 UNCTAD, 'Impact of the COVID-19 Pandemic on Trade and Development' (n 62) 36. *See also* Joan Fitzpatrick and Katrina R. Kelly, 'Gendered Aspects of Migration: Law and the Female Migrant' (1998) 22(1) *Hastings International and Comparative Law Review* 47–112.

70 McGill, 'Trade and Gender' (n 52) 34.

71 'Legal and Regulatory Gateways' are the decision points and hurdles contained within a legal or regulatory process (licence, registration, or permit, for example) that 'correspond with practical steps that enterprises and other stakeholders encounter in navigating a particular aspect of the legal and regulatory system'. They also 'signify intervention points to make the rules more equitable, inclusive, and efficient'. Kuhlmann, 'Mapping Inclusive Law and Regulation' (n 26) 70.

72 These measures are all linked to WTO disciplines as well. *See* Acharya et al., 'Trade and Women' (n 45).

73 WTO, 'Protocol Amending the Marrakesh Agreement Establishing the World Trade Organization', WT/L/940 (22 February 2017).

74 *See* Philomena Apiko, Sean Woolfrey, and Bruce Byiers, 'The Promise of the Africa Continental Free Trade Area (AfCFTA)' (ECDPM 2020) <https://ecdpm.org/publications/promise-african-continental-free-trade-area-afcfta/> accessed 8 May 2022.

75 *See* Taku Fundira, 'Informal Cross-Border Trading – Review of the Simplified Trade Regimes in East and Southern Africa' (TRALAC 2018) <www.tralac.org/publications/article/12825-informal-cross-border-trading-review-of-the-simplified-trade-regimes-in-east-and-southern-africa.html> accessed 8 May 2022.

subjecting them to delays at border crossings.[76] In addition, women tend to lack access to transport, which impacts opportunities for small-scale women traders, particularly those dealing in perishable goods (this was exacerbated during the pandemic due to border closures).[77]

A number of RTA options could be considered to address women's work and trade, as elaborated upon below.

- For example, current RTAs tend to address women's work more indirectly through provisions on labour, often including reference to the ILO Convention on Employment Discrimination.[78] While integrating ILO Conventions is important, this is just a start, and the AfCFTA and other future RTAs could incorporate both hard legal obligations and soft law instruments relevant to women's work, such as UN SDG targets and indicators and business and human rights principles, enhancing the equity dimension of RTAs. Services commitments could be shaped in a gender context through horizontal commitments (spanning all services sectors) on non-discrimination,[79] strengthening the equity dimension of the AfCFTA. This would put the AfCFTA in a position to lead globally as well (aligning, for example, with the 2021 WTO Joint Initiative on Domestic Services Regulation that includes a provision to ensure that services measures 'do not discriminate between men and women').[80]
- The AfCFTA already incorporates differentiated treatment with respect to both goods and services, which is a notable innovation that could be built upon in a gender context.[81] In particular, the language in the AfCFTA Protocol on Trade in Services that mentions 'formal and

[76] EASSI, 'Annual Report' (2020) 12, 14 <https://eassi.org/annual-reports/> accessed 8 May 2022.

[77] Ibid.

[78] ILO C111, 'Discrimination (Employment and Occupation) Convention' (1958) (in force, 7 May 2001). *See also* Bahri, 'Measuring the Gender-Responsiveness of Free Trade Agreements' (n 6).

[79] Laura Lane and Penny Nass, 'Women in Trade Can Reinvigorate the WTO and Global Economy' (CIGI 27 April 2020) 6 <www.cigionline.org/articles/women-trade-can-reinvigorate-wto-and-global-economy/> accessed 8 May 2022, 2. A number of the multilateral recommendations made by Lane and Nass are relevant in an RTA context, as noted and referenced herein.

[80] WTO Joint Initiative on Services Domestic Regulation, 'Declaration on the Conclusion of Negotiations on Services Domestic Regulation' WT/L/1129, Section III 19 (d) (WTO 2021) <https://docs.wto.org/dol2fe/Pages/SS/directdoc.aspx?filename=q:/WT/L/1129.pdf&Open=True> accessed 4 May 2023; *See also* Lane and Nass, 'Women in Trade Can Reinvigorate the WTO and Global Economy' (n 79) 345.

[81] Kuhlmann and Agutu, 'The African Continental Free Trade Area' (n 17).

informal service suppliers, with particular attention to … women',[82] is unique among RTAs and could inspire more binding commitments under the new protocol.

- The AfCFTA could place special emphasis on women's migration and trafficking in women and girls, innovating in these areas beyond current approaches. For example, the AfCFTA could include commitments in these important areas and incorporate other relevant instruments, such as the Ten Year Action Plan to Eradicate Child Labour, Forced Labour, Human Trafficking and Modern Slavery (2020–2030), adopted in February 2020 by African Heads of States and Government,[83] which aligns with AU Agenda 2063, and UN SDG Target 8.7. With respect to migration, the AfCFTA could include provisions on free movement of persons and give effect to aspects of the UN Global Compact for Safe, Orderly and Regular Migration, including provisions on mutual recognition of qualifications for migrant workers (Global Compact Objective 18) and other aspects related to human rights, trafficking, and decent work.[84]
- Drawing upon lessons from the pandemic, the AfCFTA could also include provisions on essential services, such as procedural liberalizations, mutual recognition of professional qualifications, and use of green lanes for essential travellers, including service providers.[85]
- The AfCFTA could incorporate gender-specific non-discrimination provisions related to NTMs, such as gender-specific commitments on licensing requirements and licensing procedures for goods and services, along with qualification requirements and procedures in services.[86]

82 AfCFTA Protocol on Trade in Services (n 37) (emphasis added).

83 AU, 'Ten Year Action Plan to Eradicate Child Labour, Forced Labour, Human Trafficking and Modern Slavery (2020–2030)' (2019) <https://au.int/sites/default/files/newsevents/workingdocuments/40112-wd-child_labour_action_plan-final-english.pdf> accessed 8 May 2022. *See also* AU, 'African Union Is Committed to Ending Child Labour and Other Forms of Human Exploitation' (29 May 2021) <https://au.int/en/articles/african-union-committed-ending-child-labour-and-other-forms-human-exploitation> accessed 8 May 2022.

84 UN, 'Global Compact for Safe, Orderly and Regular Migration' (13 July 2018) <https://refugeesmigrants.un.org/migration-compact> accessed 8 May 2022.

85 Katrin Kuhlmann, 'Handbook on Provisions and Options for Trade in Times of Crisis and Pandemic' (UNESCAP 2021) 36–40 <www.unescap.org/kp/2021/handbook-provisions-and-options-trade-times-crisis-and-pandemic> accessed 8 May 2022.

86 *See* Lane and Nass, 'Women in Trade Can Reinvigorate the WTO and Global Economy' (n 79); in the context of the General Agreement on Trade and Services, *see* WTO, 'Communication from Argentina, Canada, Colombia, Iceland, and Uruguay: Domestic Regulation – Development of Measures, Gender Equality', JOB/SERV/258 (2017).

- The AfCFTA and other RTAs could incorporate provisions on gender-responsive standards, building upon the UNECE Declaration for Gender Responsive Standards and Standards Development.[87]
- Provisions on addressing NTMs could be strengthened and made more gender responsive, building upon existing innovations to reduce regulatory gateways including the AfCFTA Simplified Trade Regime and Non-Tariff Barrier Reporting, Monitoring, and Eliminating Mechanism, with parallels to the NTM mechanisms in African RECs such as the EAC, ECOWAS, and the Tripartite Free Trade Area, as well as the Simplified Trade Regimes (STRs) in COMESA and the EAC, and the EAC 'Simplified Guide for Micro and Small-Scale Cross-Border Traders and Service Providers within the EAC'.[88] Going forward, these mechanisms could increasingly be approached from a gender perspective,[89] with implementation focused, in particular, on reducing barriers for women traders and linked to ongoing consultations to ensure that they are widely known and used in practice.
- Transparency provisions could be tailored to increase information available to women traders and promote engagement and inclusiveness, expanding upon those included in Article X of the General Agreement on Tariffs and Trade (GATT),[90] as well as a number of RTAs.[91] Some areas of focus could include using designated contact points or enquiry points and formal and informal dialogue structures,[92] approached in a gender context.
- The AfCFTA could also build upon trade facilitation provisions and the STRs to address women's needs,[93] focusing on important regulatory gateways. Customs fast track lanes and green lanes, the latter of which appear in some of Africa's trade corridors and have proven to be helpful

[87] UNECE, 'Gender Responsive Standards Initiative' <https://unece.org/gender-responsive-standards-initiative> accessed 8 May 2022. *See also* Lane and Nass, 'Women in Trade Can Reinvigorate the WTO and Global Economy' (n 79). For more details on gender-responsive standards, *see* Gabrielle White and Michelle Parkouda, 'The Importance of Gender-Responsive Standards for Trade Policy' (Chapter 8 in this book).

[88] *See* Gammage and Momodu, 'The Economic Empowerment of Women in Africa' (n 8) 36.

[89] This could be combined with mapping of the regulatory processes and procedures from a gender perspective, using the Regulatory Systems Map approach developed by the New Markets Lab to pinpoint precise areas in which law and regulation could be made more gender responsive. Kuhlmann, 'Mapping Inclusive Law and Regulation' (n 26).

[90] Acharya et al., 'Trade and Women' (n 45) 329.

[91] Kuhlmann, 'Handbook on Provisions and Options for Trade in Times of Crisis and Pandemic' (n 85) 135.

[92] Ibid 145, 147–148.

[93] *See also* Apiko et al., 'The Promise of the Africa Continental Free Trade Area' (n 74).

during the COVID-19 pandemic,[94] could help facilitate trade for women, including small-scale traders, as could *de minimis* provisions to exempt trade below a certain monetary threshold from duties and other requirements. Further, RTA provisions could address the challenges women face in accessing services, such as transport.

- The AfCFTA could include gender-specific references in the context of procurement in order to increase women's participation in the market, consistent with the WTO Agreement on Government Procurement and AU proposal for a 40 per cent government procurement share for women,[95] as well as trends in African domestic law.[96] For example, Section 53 of Kenya's recent Public Procurement and Asset Disposal Act (2015) requires that 30 per cent of government procurement be reserved for women.[97] Because implementation of such commitments has already been flagged as a challenge, the AfCFTA could include provisions on implementation, actively engaging women in tracking whether these commitments are applied in practice.
- Across all areas, the AfCFTA could also require collection of sex-disaggregated data and gender impact assessments of trade rules, consistent with articulated continental priorities and the WTO Declaration.[98] The degree to which AfCFTA provisions are binding and subject to dispute settlement will also be an overarching area for further consideration.

10.3.2 *Access to Finance*

Across the African continent, women face challenges in accessing affordable finance and credit,[99] which often acts as a factor limiting women's work and trade (for example, lack of finance could keep women involved in the production of low value-added, unprocessed agriculture instead of processed

94 Kuhlmann, 'Handbook on Provisions and Options for Trade in Times of Crisis and Pandemic' (n 85) 57.

95 *See* APO Group, 'Piecing the Puzzle of African Integration: The Successes and Exponential Potential' (2020) <www.africanews.com/2021/07/16/piecing-the-puzzle-of-african-integration-the-successes-and-exponential-potential/> accessed 8 May 2022.

96 Lane and Nass, 'Women in Trade Can Reinvigorate the WTO and Global Economy' (n 79) 2.

97 ICRW, 'Gender Mainstreaming in Kenya' (2020) <www.icrw.org/wp-content/uploads/2020/09/Women-in-Manufacturing-Policy-Brief_9.20_ICRW.pdf> accessed 8 May 2022.

98 Nadira Bayat, 'A "Business Unusual" Approach for Gender Equality under the AfCFTA' (2020) 9(1) ECDPM Great Insights Magazine.

99 *See* UNECA, 'Advancing Gender-Equitable Outcomes' (n 49); *see also* Afrieximbank, 'African Trade Report: Informal Cross-Border Trade in Africa in the Context of the AfCFTA' (2020) <https://afr-corp-media-prod.s3-eu-west-1.amazonaws.com/afrexim/African-Trade-Report-2020.pdf> accessed 8 May 2022.

products with a higher premium in regional and international markets) and opportunities for specialization, growth, and entrepreneurship.

Further, limitations on women's ownership of land limits women's access to credit and economic opportunities. Collateral requirements tend to favour land-based collateral, and in doing so disadvantage women due to restrictions on women's landownership.[100] When combined with strict financial sector loan conditions, high interest rates,[101] and lack of tailored financial services products for women, these restrictions can limit women to informal cross-border trade without sufficient opportunities to engage in the market.

A number of RTA options could be considered to address access to finance for women.

- For example, RTA parties could agree to horizontal commitments to reduce gender-based discrimination and improve women's access to services (equity-enhancing provisions), as noted in Table 10.2 and Section 10.3.1.
- RTAs, including the AfCFTA, could enhance equity by introducing binding rules related to gender, as noted in Table 10.2, which are consistent with REC provisions in a number of contexts.[102] These could include access to land, inheritance, and even expanded rules on collateral, including perhaps lease financing, acceptance of moveable property and contracts as collateral, and creation of an electronic collateral securities registry,[103] which could be done in a gender-responsive way. Binding rules could address other areas as well, such as non-discrimination and equal pay for equal work, which would reinforce the other options in this section and help ensure that RTAs are designed to support equity and inclusion. While these rules would address significant aspects of access to finance, they would be important all across women's work and livelihood.

[100] Louis N. Ndumbe, 'Unshackling Women Traders: Cross-Border Trade of Eru from Cameroon to Nigeria' (2013) Africa Trade Policy Note 38 <https://documents1.worldbank.org/curated/en/262591468292477021/pdf/797110BRI0PN380B0x0377384B00PUBLIC0.pdf> accessed 8 May 2022.

[101] Emma Marie Bugingo, 'Empowering Women by Supporting Small-Scale Cross-Border Trade' (2018) 7(4) *Tralac: Bridges Africa – Supporting Small-Scale Cross-Border Traders across Africa* 11–13.

[102] *See* Lane and Nass, 'Women in Trade Can Reinvigorate the WTO and Global Economy' (n 79); Kuhlmann et al., 'Reconceptualizing Free Trade Agreements' (n 12); and ITC, 'Mainstreaming Gender in Free Trade Agreements' (n 31).

[103] *See* Edward Katende and Katrin Kuhlmann, 'Building a Regulatory Environment for Agricultural Finance' (*Uganda Banker's Association* June 2019) <https://cb4fec8a-9641-471c-9042-2712ac32ce3e.filesusr.com/ugd/095963_a0e1d52d6040405c86334e2bfd8084dc.pdf> accessed 8 May 2022.

- RTA parties could agree to financial services commitments to encourage gender-responsive financial services products. These could include services sector commitments, both horizontal and sector specific. They could also emphasize important aspects such as mobile money, which has significant implications for women traders.[104]
- Some African states, including Burundi, Egypt, Nigeria, and Zambia, have put in place policies that promote financial inclusion and gender-inclusive finance,[105] highlighting national-level support in this area and areas in which the AfCFTA could build out pan-African commitments. Training and building awareness on access to finance could be linked with the AfCFTA, including through ongoing initiatives, such as the African Development Bank's Affirmative Finance Action for Women in Africa (AFAWA) programme and 50 Million African Women Speak Platform (50MAWS). Over time, the AfCFTA could become a platform for financial education and regulatory alignment.[106]

10.3.3 *Digital Inclusion*

Addressing digital inclusion and inequality in digital trade will be significant across all aspects of women's economic engagement.[107] Although women stand to gain significantly from digital trade, they are also particularly affected by the digital divide.[108] Information and Communication Technology (ICT) and financial services, including online payments services, could be better leveraged by women entrepreneurs and traders.[109] However, this also depends upon physical infrastructure and access to the internet.

[104] Simonetta Zarelli and Mariana Lopez, 'Leveraging Digital Solutions to Seize the Potential of Informal Cross-Border Trade' (*UNCTAD* 29 April 2020) <unctad.org/es/node/2394> accessed 8 May 2022.

[105] Alliance for Financial Inclusion, 'Policy and Regulatory Reforms in the AFI Network 2019' (2019) 15–26 <www.afi-global.org/sites/default/files/publications/2020-07/AFI_P%26amp%3BRR__G_2019_AW.pdf> accessed 8 May 2022.

[106] *See* Sone Osakwe, 'Extending MSMEs' Access to Trade Finance under the AFCFTA' (2021) Centre for the Study of Economies of Africa 5 <https://papers.ssrn.com/sol3/papers.cfm?abstract_id=3780767> accessed 8 May 2022.

[107] AU and UNDP, 'The Futures Report, Making the AfCFTA Work for Women and Youth' (2020) 22 <https://www.oecd.org/digital/au.int/en/documents/20201202/making-afcta-work-women-and-youth> accessed 8 May 2022.

[108] *See* OECD, 'Bridging the Gender Digital Divide' (2018) <bridging-the-digital-gender-divide.pdf> accessed 8 May 2022.

[109] UNCTAD, 'Harnessing E-commerce for Sustainable Development' (WTO 2017) <www.wto.org\\english\\res_e\\booksp_e\\aid4trade17_chap7_e.pdf> accessed 8 May 2022.

Digital inclusion and opportunities in digital trade go hand in hand, and digital opportunities could be better harnessed to the benefit of women entrepreneurs and in furtherance of the UN SDGs,[110] namely UN SDG 5 and Target 5.b: 'Enhance the use of enabling technology, in particular ICT, to promote empowerment of women.'[111] Digital trade has already been highlighted as a priority issue for the next phase of the AfCFTA, with a digital trade protocol under negotiation,[112] which, in tandem with the gender and youth protocol, provides an opportunity to address digital inclusion and consider ways in which to tailor provisions to address women's needs.

RTAs could address digital inclusion in a number of ways.

- Although few RTAs deal with digital inclusion, the Digital Economy Partnership Agreement (DEPA) among Chile, New Zealand, and Singapore (China and South Korea have also initiated the process of joining)[113] includes specific language that emphasizes digital inclusion for indigenous communities, women, rural populations, and low socio-economic groups.[114] The DEPA explicitly references gender in the context of digital inclusion: 'To this end, the Parties shall cooperate on matters relating to digital inclusion, including participation of women, rural populations, low socio-economic groups and Indigenous Peoples.'[115] The DEPA goes on to state that 'cooperation may include' a number of things, such as sharing experiences and good practices, 'promoting inclusive and sustainable growth', 'addressing barriers in accessing digital economy opportunities', and others.[116] The cooperation aspect of the DEPA bears similarity to the cooperation provisions in existing gender and trade provisions and chapters, and this language provides a baseline upon which to build more performative obligations in the AfCFTA and future RTAs. The draft negotiated text for the Partnership Agreement between the European Union and the members

[110] Kuhlmann, 'Handbook on Provisions and Options for Trade in Times of Crisis and Pandemic' (n 85) 102.

[111] UN Women, 'SDG 5: Achieve gender equality and empower all women and girls' <www.unwomen.org\\en\\news\\in-focus\\women-and-the-sdgs\\sdg-5-gender-equality> accessed 8 May 2022.

[112] AU, 'Decision of the African Continental Free Trade Area (2020), Assembly/AU/4/(XXXIII).

[113] Government of Singapore, 'Digital Economy Partnership Agreement' (2020) <www.mti.gov.sg/Trade/Digital-Economy-Agreements/The-Digital-Economy-Partnership-Agreement> accessed 8 May 2022.

[114] Ibid Art. 11.1. *See also* Kuhlmann, 'Flexibility and Innovation in International Economic Law' (n 27).

[115] Government of Singapore, 'Digital Economy Partnership Agreement' (n 113).

[116] Ibid.

of the Organisation of African, Caribbean and Pacific States (OACPS) also contains important provisions on reducing the digital divide and supporting digital entrepreneurship, particularly by women and youth.[117]

- African national policies and rules on financial digital inclusion, such as those in Mozambique, Madagascar, Tanzania, and Zambia,[118] show national support for digital inclusion that could pave the way for broader strategies under the AfCFTA.
- Gender needs could also be explicitly taken into account in the context of data protection, and the UN Human Rights Council and the UN General Assembly have called upon UN members to 'develop or maintain ... measures ... regarding the right to privacy in the digital age that may affect all individuals, including ... women ... and persons in vulnerable situations or marginalized groups'.[119] Within African regional law, the ECOWAS data protection rules reference human rights and 'fundamental liberties' of the data holders,[120] which is also notable and could be even further tailored to gender. Some countries' laws contain innovations in this area, including India's Personal Data Protection Bill (2019), which, if passed into law, would treat data on health, caste or tribe, sexual orientation, and transgender status with heightened privacy protection.[121]

10.3.4 *Agriculture and Food Security*

African women play many roles in the agricultural sector – as primary producers of food and providers for their households, and also as traders and processors of agricultural products – creating strong links between agricultural trade and human rights, food security, health, livelihoods,[122] and, of course,

[117] Draft Negotiated Text of the Partnership Agreement between the European Union/Member States of the European Union and Organisation of African, Caribbean and Pacific States, Article 48(1) and (3); negotiated agreement text initialled by EU and OACPS negotiators 11 April 2021.

[118] *See* Better than Cash Alliance, Women's World Banking and World Bank, 'Advancing Women's Digital Financial Inclusion' (2020) <www.mfw4a.org/sites/default/files/resources/saudig20_women_compressed.pdf> accessed 8 May 2022.

[119] UNHRC, 'Right to Privacy in the Digital Age', A/HRC/RES/34/7 (7 April 2017); UNGA, 'Right to Privacy in the Digital Age', A/RES/71/199 (25 January 2017).

[120] ECOWAS, 'Supplementary Act A/SA.1/01/10 on Personal Data Protection within ECOWAS' (16 February 2015) <www.tit.comm.ecowas.int/wp-content/uploads/2015/11/SIGNED-Data-Protection-Act.pdf> accessed 8 May 2022.

[121] Government of India, Personal Data Protection Bill, 2019.

[122] *See* McGill, 'Trade and Gender' (n 52); and Katrin Kuhlmann, 'The Human Face of Trade and Food Security: Lessons on the Enabling Environment from Kenya and India' (CSIS 2017) <www.csis.org/analysis/human-face-trade-and-food-security> accessed 8 May 2022.

the SDGs.[123] In sub-Saharan Africa, women tend to be primarily responsible for household food security, in addition to their involvement in the production of both cash and subsistence crops.[124] Non-traditional agricultural exports, such as cut flowers and fruit and vegetables, present enhanced trade and work opportunities for women, and, in the case of non-traditional food crops, they can provide important benefits in terms of food security as well.[125] However, trade's differential impact on women needs to be carefully considered, particularly in the agricultural sector where export-oriented agriculture can displace women-dominated subsistence farming.[126]

Despite their prominent role in the agricultural sector, women continue to struggle with limited landownership and access rights and challenges with access to credit.[127]. Women's limited access to agricultural inputs, including seeds, technology, and extension services, impacts the ability to transition into higher value-added production and ultimately benefit from trade opportunities.[128]

Women also tend to face particularly challenging regulatory hurdles in the agricultural sector, including compliance with standards and SPS measures, which can require significant investment, economies of scale, and technical capacity.[129] The WTO SPS Agreement, with which most RTAs largely align,

[123] Nadira Bayat and David Luke, 'Gender Mainstreaming in AfCFTA National Strategies: Why It Matters for the SDGs' (IISD 20 February 2020) <http://sdg.iisd.org/commentary/guest-articles/gender-mainstreaming-in-afcfta-national-strategies-why-it-matters-for-the-sdgs/> accessed 8 May 2022.

[124] McGill, 'Trade and Gender' (n 52) 55–56; *see also* Lynn R. Brown, Hilary Feldstein, Lawrence Haddad, Christine Pena, and Agnes Quisumbing, 'Generating Food Security in the Year 2020: Women as Producers, Gatekeepers, and Shock Absorbers' (1995) International Food Policy Research Institute 2020 Vision Brief 17 <www.semanticscholar.org/paper/GENERATING-FOOD-SECURITY-IN-THE-YEAR-2020%3A-WOMEN-AS-Brown-Feldstein/01f19be2a78245ec09e5ccde6c7c36d96187a929> accessed 8 May 2022.

[125] *See* Kuhlmann, 'The Human Face of Trade and Food Security' (n 122).

[126] *See* Bayat, 'A Whole Agreement Approach to Gender Mainstreaming in the AfCFTA' (n 51) 4.

[127] *See*, for instance, Acharya et al., 'Trade and Women' (n 45); Kuhlmann, 'The Human Face of Trade and Food Security' (n 122); McGill, 'Trade and Gender' (n 52); Mehra and Gammage, 'Trends, Countertrends, and Gaps in Women's Employment' (n 52) 539.

[128] *See* FAO, 'The State of Food and Agriculture' (2015) <www.fao.org/publications/sofa/2015/en/> accessed 8 May 2022; *see also* UNCTAD, 'Borderline: Women in Informal Cross-Border Trade in Malawi, The United Republic of Tanzania and Zambia' (2019) 42 <https://unctad.org/system/files/official-document/ditc2018d3_en.pdf> accessed 8 May 2022; STDF, 'STDF Briefing Note, Inclusive Trade Solutions: Women in SPS Capacity Building' (2015) <www.standardsfacility.org/sites/default/files/STDF_Briefing_note_13.pdf> accessed 8 May 2022.

[129] *See* Acharya et al., 'Trade and Women' (n 45) 338; Spencer Henson, 'Gender and Sanitary and Phytosanitary Measures in the Context of Trade: A Review of Issues and Policy Recommendations' (ICSTD 2018) <https://standardsfacility.org/sites/default/files/Gender_

including African RECs and the AfCFTA, contains important disciplines and an emphasis on capacity building and S&DT.[130]

There are a number of RTA options for integrating agriculture and food security.

- For example, the AfCFTA could include provisions reaffirming the space for governments to put in place gender-responsive domestic support measures related to agriculture that are consistent with AoA 'Green Box' measures, such as training, research, extension, and advisory services.[131] A gender lens could also be applied to agricultural input subsidies for resource-poor farmers in line with Article 6.2 of the AoA.[132]
- The AfCFTA, building upon the precedent created through the RECs, is scheduled to address agricultural inputs in a more comprehensive way, creating another avenue for gender-responsive domestic support commitments and other provisions, including enhanced gender representation on inputs committees, that would complement the new protocol on gender.
- While RTAs have not comprehensively addressed food security, this is an area that could be pioneered under the AfCFTA in line with broader sustainable development considerations and the SDGs.[133] Food security could be addressed more comprehensively through detailed provisions on export restrictions, safeguards, tailored domestic support, climate adaptation, and links with agricultural inputs and other areas of regulation,[134] all

SPS_measures_in_the_context_of_trade_Henson_ICTSD_Nov_18.pdf> accessed 8 May 2022.

[130] *See*, in particular, Agreement on the Application of Sanitary and Phytosanitary Measures, 15 April 1994, Marrakesh Agreement Establishing the World Trade Organization, Annex 1C, 1869 UNTS 299, 33 ILM 1197 Arts. 9–10. The WTO Standards and Trade Development Facility (STDF) has played a central role in mainstreaming gender into SPS capacity-building activities Acharya et al., 'Trade and Women' (n 45) 339.

[131] These can also include measures related to land reform and rural livelihood security, such as rural employment programmes and issuance of property titles, which could be important to women's livelihood and work. Acharya et al., 'Trade and Women' (n 45) 337. *See also* McGill, 'Trade and Gender' (n 52).

[132] Acharya et al., 'Trade and Women' (n 45) 338.

[133] Annex 2 of the Agreement on Agriculture covers government stockpiling programmes for food security, and Article XI of the General Agreement on Tariffs and Trade allows for limited and temporary application of export restrictions to 'prevent or relieve critical shortages of foodstuffs'; while they tend to be incorporated into RTAs, there are limitations to these disciplines. Agreement on Agriculture, 15 April 1994, Marrakesh Agreement Establishing the World Trade Organization, Annex 1A, 1867 UNTS 410.

[134] Katrin Kuhlmann, 'Why the United States and Africa Should Lead a Collaborative, Rules-Based Approach to Food Security' (CSIS 2020) <www.csis.org/analysis/why-united-states-and-africa-should-lead-collaborative-rules-based-approach-food-securit> accessed 8 May 2022.

of which could be aligned with WTO disciplines and other areas of international law and approached through a gender and equity lens.

- RTA measures to improve transparency and enhance capacity building could be strengthened, enhancing engagement and inclusion, with a particular focus on women's role in the agricultural sector. This could work in tandem with tools for notifying and responding to SPS issues, such as the AfCFTA Simplified Trade Regime and Non-Tariff Barrier Reporting, Monitoring, and Eliminating Mechanism, and other programmes noted, in addition to the ePing Alert System of the UN Department of Economic and Social Affairs and ITC that improves access to SPS and TBT regulations, including through SMS alerts for small traders.[135] These programmes could all be tailored to women's needs.

10.3.5 *Overarching RTA Options*

Finally, several RTA design options could address challenges across the four areas that are the focus of sections 10.3.1, 10.3.2, 10.3.3, and 10.3.4. These include cooperation and consultation provisions, which are already present in current RTAs (these align with Bahri's Gender Responsiveness Levels III and IV and Kuhlmann's Engagement Dimension of Inclusive Law and Regulation), and can be important across priority areas to promote enhanced skills, entrepreneurship, access to finance, and bridging the digital divide, among others.[136] Capacity-building provisions, while common in RTAs, could be enhanced to include the creation of gender committees and application of good practices and standards, as well as the collection and use of sex-disaggregated data.[137] However, while consultation, cooperation, and capacity-building provisions are important,[138] these mechanisms alone are insufficient to directly address women's needs. These RTA options should

[135] Acharya et al., 'Trade and Women' (n 45) 339; *see* 'E-Ping' <www.epingalert.org/en> accessed 8 May 2022.

[136] Bahri, 'Measuring the Gender-Responsiveness of Free Trade Agreements' (n 6) 11.

[137] *See* World Bank and WTO, 'Women and Trade: The Role of Trade in Promoting Gender Equality' (WTO 2020) <www.wto.org/english/res_e/booksp_e/women_trade_pub2807_e.pdf> accessed 8 May 2022; and Kuhlmann, 'Handbook on Provisions and Options for Trade in Times of Crisis and Pandemic' (n 85).

[138] Mia Mikic and Vanika Sharma, 'Feminising WTO 2.0' in Simon J. Evenett and Richard Baldwin (eds), *Revitalizing Multilateral Trade Cooperation: Pragmatic Ideas for the New WTO Director-General* (VoxEU 2020) 171–185.

be considered in combination with binding commitments (and softer commitments where appropriate) discussed in particular in Section 10.3.2 that would establish more performative obligations likely to lead to concrete action and provide a clearer channel for women to exercise rights.

RTAs could also address gender on a more systemic level, drawing from pan-African priorities and proposals at the global level, the latter of which includes a possible plurilateral agreement on trade and gender. Both multilateral and regional rules could incorporate expansion of general exceptions clauses modelled on GATT Article XX, which many RTAs, including the AfCFTA, contain.[139] While this could be helpful for incorporating gender and leveraging policy space, exceptions should not take the place of affirmative commitments on gender and trade. Finally, comprehensive gender strategies at the national and regional levels and use of gender-disaggregated data should be widespread practices. On the African continent, the UN has emphasized that gender mainstreaming needs to be integrated into the operationalization of the AfCFTA through countries' national implementation strategies,[140] a proposal that would support many of the options discussed in this chapter.

10.4 CONCLUSION

As this chapter illustrates, gender-responsive rules can promote inclusive trade and development and generate significant benefits for women; however, the design and implementation of these rules will be critical. The AfCFTA already has a solid foundation on which a new gender-focused protocol could build, drawing from inclusive legal design options and innovations and broader lessons learned within and outside of the African continent to address real challenges in women's work and trade, access to finance, digital inclusion, and agriculture and food security. The options highlighted in this chapter attempt to balance between policy discretion and establishment of binding commitments that would give greater certainty to women-led MSMEs and SMEs. The AfCFTA holds great promise, both in enhancing

[139] Some experts have argued for expanded use of the 'public morals' exception in a gender context as well. *See* James Harrison, *The Human Rights Impact of the World Trade Organization* (Hart Publishing 1st ed. 2007) 207–209; Liane M. Jarvis, 'Women's Rights and the Public Morals Exception of GATT Article 20' (2000) 22 *Michigan Journal of International Law* 219–238, 237.

[140] Bayat, 'A "Business Unusual" Approach' (n 98).

existing innovations in legal design and in ensuring that women's voices are heard as new trade rules are developed and existing rules are applied. The options for inclusive law and regulation presented in this chapter, which could be incorporated into new RTA chapters and protocols or combined into an inclusive whole-of-agreement approach, provide an entry point for gender-responsive trade provisions and an opportunity for resetting the rules on gender and trade.

11

Leave No Woman Behind

Gender and Trade Policy in CARICOM SIDS

TONNI BRODBER AND JAN YVES REMY*

ABSTRACT

The Caribbean women's rights agenda has been framed by the broader agenda of international platforms for action 'adapted to national and regional priorities'. Yet the Caribbean feminist agenda is hardly present in international trade discussions and negotiations. The chapter will examine the development of gender equality/ feminism in the Caribbean and its intersections with trade; highlight and examine the current feminist agenda in the Caribbean; and ultimately consider whether and if so how that agenda manifests itself in domestic and regional policy and practice in the Caribbean. It will do so against the backdrop of broader efforts internationally to mainstream gender and will make recommendations about how the Caribbean should approach trade and gender in the future.

11.1 INTRODUCTION

Trade policy remains a critical development strategy and is increasingly used to promote gender equality. However, within feminist economist circles, many efforts to engage in gender-responsive trade policies are considered merely decorative. This is because, while trade has increased opportunities for some women, many others find it difficult to participate in trade because of structural gender-based inequalities. Moreover, trade policies and strategies are too often gender-neutral, assuming that if the tide rises and trade opportunities increase, men and women will benefit equally.

As countries which are among the most open, trade-dependent, and vulnerable (both economically and geographically) in the world, the Caribbean region

* The authors wish to thank Selisha Gilchrist, Shineco Sutherland and Tara Padmore for research assistance provided in drafting this chapter.

presents a fascinating case to explore the history of women in trade, the gender considerations within the existing trade framework, and the implications of these for sustainable development broadly, and gender equality specifically. Among the Americas, the Caribbean sub-region is unique because, unlike other case studies in North and South America featured in this book, this sub-region has not embraced gender mainstreaming in its trade negotiations and agreements. This is the case even though the region still encounters stubborn obstacles to gender equality which negatively impact women's economic empowerment.

Using the Caribbean Community (CARICOM) – a sub-grouping of fifteen Caribbean countries that aim towards economic and social cooperation and integration – as a case study, this chapter assesses the impact of CARICOM's current trade policies on women, considers whether and how gender is mainstreamed in CARICOM trade and development policy, and briefly concludes with recommendations on how gender can be better integrated into CARICOM trade policy.

The chapter is organized as follows: Section 11.2 begins by framing the gender and trade issue by providing a snapshot of CARICOM's trade environment and women's participation in trade and the economy. In Section 11.3, we assess CARICOM's approach to gender equality and women's economic empowerment, including the extent to which gender has been mainstreamed in CARICOM's trade policy and negotiations. We argue that CARICOM Member States must begin to use trade policy to deliver on the promises enshrined under instruments such as the UN Sustainable Development Goals (SDGs). Finally, Section 11.4 concludes with some recommendations for achieving gender-responsive and gender-transformative trade policy to spur gender equality and sustainable development in the region.

11.2 BACKGROUND TO WOMEN'S PARTICIPATION IN CARICOM TRADE

11.2.1 *CARICOM Trade Profile*

The group of countries of the CARICOM[1] comprises small island developing states (SIDS)[2] which geographically surround the Caribbean Sea. As they are

1 The members of CARICOM are Antigua and Barbuda, Bahamas, Barbados, Belize, Dominica, Grenada, Guyana, Haiti, Jamaica, Montserrat, St. Kitts and Nevis, St. Lucia, St. Vincent and the Grenadines, Suriname, and Trinidad and Tobago. *See* CARICOM – Caribbean Community, 'Member States and Associate Members' <https://caricom.org/member-states-and-associate-members/> accessed 29 September 2022.

2 This is so even though some CARICOM countries, such as Guyana and Belize, are not islands.

among the most trade-dependent, vulnerable, and open economies of the world, trade constitutes a major cornerstone of their economies, critical to their economic growth and development. For the CARICOM region, two sets of international obligations dominate the trade agenda: those arising under their membership of CARICOM, established in 1973 and revised in 2001, whose aim is to integrate their economies towards a single market and economy through a policy of open regionalism, and those arising from membership of the World Trade Organization (WTO),[3] which binds them to a neo-liberal agenda that seeks to liberalize multilateral trade through the gradual dismantling of barriers in the trade of goods and services. Beyond these obligations, CARICOM has also concluded formal trading arrangements with other countries, ranging from partial scope agreements to free trade agreements (FTAs).[4]

Extra-regional trade is dominated by relations with traditional trade partners such as the United States, the United Kingdom, the European Union (EU), Canada, and, increasingly, China.[5] The region is also a net foreign direct investment (FDI) importer, recording an estimated USD 2,794 million in FDI inflows in 2019 compared to USD 763 million in FDI outflows.[6] Intra-regional trade is poor compared to other regional groupings and accounted for 12.5 per cent of CARICOM's total exports in 2016.[7]

Although most countries in the region have evolved out of agriculture-based economies,[8] today, most CARICOM economies rely on the services sector. Services account for about 60 per cent of gross domestic product (GDP), with tradable services focused predominantly on the tourism and financial services

[3] Currently, except Montserrat and the Bahamas, all other CARICOM Member States are members of the WTO. The Bahamas is currently under process to accede to the WTO.

[4] The FTAs include: the CARIFORUM–EU EPA (2008) and the CARIFORUM–UK EPA (2019); and the partial scope agreements include: CARICOM–Venezuela Trade, Economic, and Technical Cooperation Agreement (1992), CARICOM–Colombia Trade, Economic and Technical Cooperation Agreement (1994), CARICOM–Dominican Republic FTA (1998), CARICOM–Cuba Trade and Economic Cooperation Agreement (2000), CARICOM–Costa Rica FTA (2004).

[5] See generally, Daniel Rune, 'Reimagining the U.S. Strategy in the Caribbean' (Center for Strategic and International Studies 2021) <www.csis.org/analysis/reimagining-us-strategy-caribbean> accessed 13 September 2022.

[6] Chelcee Brathwaite, Alicia Nicholls, and Jan Yves Remy, 'Trading Our Way to Recovery during COVID-19: Recommendations for CARICOM Countries' (SRC 2020) 15 <https://shridathramphalcentre.com/wp-content/uploads/2020/10/SRC-COVID-19-Policy-Document-October-2020_FINAL.pdf> accessed 16 December 2021 (SRC Policy Document).

[7] CARICOM Secretariat, 'Snapshot of CARICOM's Trade Series 1: CARICOM's Intra-Regional Trade 2011–2016' (CARICOM 2018) <https://statistics.caricom.org/Files/Publications/Snapshot/Series_1_2011–2016.pdf> accessed 16 December 2021.

[8] SRC Policy Document (n 6) 14.

sectors. According to some estimates, CARICOM service exports in 2018 amounted to USD 14.36 billion, of which 80 per cent or USD 11.55 billion was from travel services.[9] However, countries such as Belize, Guyana, Suriname, and Trinidad and Tobago also depend on the oil and gas and mining sectors. Also due to their larger land masses, such countries depend on agriculture. For the majority of CARICOM countries where agricultural export trade remains stagnant, imports account for 80 per cent of food in the region, and the food import bill was valued in excess of USD 5 billion in 2019.[10] Manufacturing for export remains a small proportion of the traded sectors, although energy-rich Trinidad and Tobago is something of an outlier for the region, with manufacturing accounting for 19 per cent of GDP.[11]

CARICOM's trade performance over the past four decades has declined or stagnated, and it is generally considered one of the least competitive regions in the world. Intra-regional CARICOM trade, predominantly in merchandise, amounted to 2 per cent of GDP in the mid-1980s, 4 per cent of GDP in the 1990s, and then plateaued in the 2000s. Additionally, the region's most prominent service industry, tourism, records a mere 5 to 10 per cent receipts from intra-regional tourism. This trade performance compares poorly with that of regions such as the EU, with trade amounting to 13 to 20 per cent of GDP.[12] The region's susceptibility to natural disasters as well as its chronic indebtedness means that governments are constantly struggling to meet public expenditure on basic social systems like health and education, which impacts marginalized and low-income groups. Most recently, the economic shutdowns and global supply disruptions occasioned by the COVID-19 pandemic have also wreaked havoc on fragile economies, and according to the UN World Travel Organization (UN WTO), the impact of the COVID-19 pandemic resulted in a 71 per cent decline in international arrivals globally by the end of 2020.[13] In comparison, the Caribbean recorded a 60 per cent decline in tourist arrivals and 60 per cent reduction in receipts from tourism.[14]

9 CARICOM Secretariat, 'CARICOM's Statistics on International Trade in Services 2012–2018' (CARICOM 2021) <http://statistics.caricom.org/Files/Publications/Trade%20in%20Services/TIS_2012–2018.pdf > accessed 16 December 2021.

10 SRC Policy Document (n 6) 38.

11 Ibid 14.

12 See OECD, 'Special Feature: The Caribbean Small States' <www.oecd.org/dev/americas/LEO-2019-Chapter-6.pdf> accessed 13 September 2022.

13 UN WTO, 'Global and Regional Tourism Performance' <www.unwto.org/tourism-data/international-tourism-and-covid-19>.

14 Ibid.

CARICOM's economic and climatic vulnerabilities have serious repercussions for vulnerable groups, especially women. To paraphrase the UN Women COVID-19 Impact Summary Report, these intersecting vulnerabilities mean women are more exposed than men to negative shocks like COVID-19.[15]

11.2.2 *A Snapshot of CARICOM Women's Participation in Trade*

The Caribbean trade liberalization policy has not been sensitive to the differentiated impact on men and women and has failed to take into account the historical and current profile of women as producers, traders, and consumers. Although statistics are hard to come by, women in the region were traditionally involved in agricultural production, especially during and after the colonial period.[16] For instance, in many islands of the Eastern Caribbean, when banana production shifted from plantations to smaller scale farms, it was women who managed these smaller holdings while caring for families. The loss of preferential trading arrangements therefore resulted in a significant decline in the women's livelihoods, with a 1999 study by Caribbean Association Feminist Research and Action (CAFRA) confirming that the living conditions of rural women in the Eastern Caribbean had worsened over the previous five years because of the decline in banana prices.[17] Since the 1990s, most women in smallholdings participate in intra-regional trade, focusing on products such as onions and other cash crops. Anecdotal evidence indicates that this has impacted food security and nutrition on many islands, where women's subsistence farming has declined, and women often rely on cheaper processed imports to feed their families.

Another feature of women's participation in trade-related sectors across CARICOM has been their employment in Special Economic Zones (SEZs) and Exclusive Economic Zones (EEZs), especially in Jamaica in the 1980s and 1990s, as well as in Trinidad and Tobago and Haiti.[18] Overall, these sectors did not result in sustainable economic growth or empowerment for

[15] Tara Padmore, 'Summary Status of Women and Men Report – The Impacts of COVID-19' (UN Women 2021) <https://caribbean.unwomen.org/en/materials/publications/2021/3/summary-report—status-of-women-and-men-in-covid-19> accessed 16 December 2021.

[16] Tessa Barry, Levi Gahman, Adaeze Greenidge, and Atiyah Mohamed, 'Wrestling with Race and Colonialism in Caribbean Agriculture: Toward a (Food) Sovereign and (Gender) Just Future' (2020) 109 *Geoforum* 106–110.

[17] CAFRA, *Gender and Trade in the Caribbean*, 15 November 2002 <www.cafra.org/article391.html> accessed 30 May 2023.

[18] See IDB-CARICOM Report, 'Progress and Challenges of the Integration Agenda' (IDB/CARICOM 2020) 57 <https://publications.iadb.org/en/caricom-report-progress-and-challenges-integration-agenda> accessed 16 December 2021.

women, as companies exploited low wages without improving skill sets. In Jamaica, for example, with the closing of the EEZs, 40,000 people, mostly women, were left without employment. The tourism sector effectively absorbed many of these women and tourism has therefore served as a social safety net of a sort for employment and Caribbean exports, generally benefiting women in the lower socio-economic classes.[19]

A consequence of the demise of agriculture was an expansion in exportable services from the region since the beginning in the 1990s, a sector which is predominantly run by women today. Service exports of CARICOM Member States totalled USD 14.36 billion in 2018,[20] and an estimated 87 per cent of employed women in Caribbean small states are involved in the services industry.[21] While difficult to measure in Caribbean SIDS, as noted in Section 11.2.1, the main sources of services exported in the Caribbean are from tourism and related sectors, more specifically travel.[22] Travel comprised 80 per cent of CARICOM's total service exports in 2018,[23] with the largest regional service exporters being the Dominican Republic, Trinidad and Tobago, the Bahamas, Jamaica, and Barbados.[24] Women continue to occupy lower paid positions in that sector[25] and are particularly susceptible to external shocks. For instance, according to one study by the Economic Commission for Latin America and the Caribbean,[26] on account of COVID-19, the first

[19] ILO, 'ILO: Tourism Recovery Is Key to Overcoming COVID-19 Labour Crisis in Latin America and the Caribbean' (ILO Press Release 30 June 2021) <www.ilo.org/caribbean/newsroom/WCMS_809331/lang–en/index.htm> accessed 16 December 2021; George Gmelch, *Behind the Smile: The Working Lives of Caribbean Tourism* (Indiana University Press 2nd ed. 2012).

[20] CARICOM Secretariat, 'CARICOM's Statistics on International Trade in Services 2012–2018' (n 9).

[21] See ILOSTAT Database <https://ilostat.ilo.org/> accessed 16 December 2021. Figures represent 2018 average across thirteen Caribbean small states.

[22] CEDA, 'Caribbean Export Outlook 2016' (CEDA 2017) <https://issuu.com/caribbeanexport/docs/caribbean_export_outlook_2016> accessed 16 December 2021.

[23] CARICOM Secretariat, 'CARICOM's Statistics on International Trade in Services 2012–2018' (n 9).

[24] CEDA, 'Caribbean Export Outlook 2016' (n 22); CARICOM Secretariat, 'CARICOM's Statistics on International Trade in Services 2012–2018' (n 9).

[25] Annelle Bellony, Alejandro Hoyos, and Hugo Ñopo, 'Gender Earnings Gaps in the Caribbean: Evidence from Barbados and Jamaica' (IADB 2010) <https://publications.iadb.org/publications/english/document/Gender-Earnings-Gaps-in-the-Caribbean-Evidence-from-Barbados-and-Jamaica.pdf> accessed 16 December 2021.

[26] See UN ECLAC Gender Equality Observatory for Latin America and the Caribbean, 'International Trade: A Means to a Recovery with Gender Equality?' (ECLAC Notes No. 31, 24 February 2021), <https://oig.cepal.org/sites/default/files/note_for_equality_gender_and_trade_n31.pdf> accessed 16 December 2021.

half of 2020 saw regional exports of services fall in value terms by 30 per cent, explained mainly by the halt in tourism from April 2020 onward, which resulted in a 53 per cent decrease in income on the region's travel account. The situation is particularly serious for Caribbean women, 17 per cent of who were employed in the tourism sector pre-pandemic, compared to 9.7 per cent of men.[27]

Other sectors with export potential in the region, including agri-business, continue to be dominated by men. While there is some data that women-owned micro, small and medium enterprises (MSMEs) are increasingly creating a niche for themselves as entrepreneurs in small community-based or national markets, there are some worrying trends. As of 2015, only 8 per cent of women in the Caribbean were considered entrepreneurs, in comparison to 19 per cent of men. Most women entrepreneurs are managers of themselves only and are located within low growth sectors because they are predominantly in the hospitality sectors of restaurants, hotels, and retail. This can limit their ability to engage effectively in exports as they are outcompeted by larger and more agile firms producing cheaper products. Additionally, very few female entrepreneurs have been able to engage effectively in exports.[28] Some studies note that women do not have as much access to financing as men entrepreneurs do, one of the factors which is responsible for the slow growth of female entrepreneurs' enterprises.[29] For instance, it is estimated that angel investors, seed capital, and venture capital funds are available to 1 per cent of female entrepreneurs in comparison to 7 per cent of their male counterparts.[30] Recent anecdotal and empirical data has also demonstrated that many women entrepreneurs do not necessarily enter entrepreneurship because of their love for entrepreneurial endeavours, but rather out of necessity – when they no longer have steady employment and create a business to

[27] Authors' own calculations of average employment in the accommodation and food industry (used as a proxy for the tourism industry) across Anguilla, Antigua and Barbuda, The Bahamas, Dominica, Grenada, Guyana, Jamaica, Saint Lucia, Saint Kitts and Nevis, Saint Vincent and the Grenadines, and Trinidad and Tobago. Data sourced from latest available year national Labour Force Surveys.

[28] InfoDev, 'Profiling Caribbean Women Entrepreneurs: Business Environment, Sectoral Constraints and Programming Lessons' (World Bank and Inter-American Development Bank 2017); Sylvia Dohnert, Gustavo Crespi, and Alessandro Maffioli (eds.), *Exploring Firm-Level Innovation and Productivity In Developing Countries: The Perspective of Caribbean Small States* (IADB 2017).

[29] InfoDev, 'Profiling Caribbean Women Entrepreneurs' (n 28); Dohnert et al., *Exploring Firm-Level Innovation and Productivity In Developing Countries* (n 28).

[30] Irene Arias Hofman, 'More Female Entrepreneurs Please' (Caribbean DEVTrends+ 5 December 2019) <https://blogs.iadb.org/caribbean-dev-trends/en/more-female-entrepreneurs-please/> accessed 16 December 2021.

secure a livelihood for themselves and their families. Enterprise Surveys showed that 32 per cent of women started businesses due to a lack of employment opportunities.[31] Other women enter entrepreneurship for the flexibility it affords them to manage their care responsibilities, not because of market signals or because of a desire to grow their businesses and take on additional risk.[32]

A final feature of women's participation in the labour market is its informality. Most women-owned businesses are not registered and such businesses constitute approximately 58.7 per cent of women's total employment in the region.[33] Informal employment refers to income-generating activities occurring outside of the formal and normative regulatory framework of the state (i.e., not formally registered, operating outside labour laws and regulations, often not paying income taxes, and often not contributing to, or covered by, the state's formal social protection framework). Common informal jobs include domestic workers, vendors, 'casual' labourers, construction workers, and hospitality staff. Operating outside of the state's social safety net, including labour regulations (such as protection from unfair dismissal) and social protection, informal workers are more vulnerable to economic precarity and instability.

For many women managing households on their own, informal care work has not only been integral to them and their families' livelihoods, but to Caribbean economies as a whole. Efforts to support the transition from women entrepreneurs in the informal sector to the formal sector have not been successful. Some reports indicate that women entrepreneurs in the formal economy prefer the autonomy of the informal space – for example, they can set their own working hours. Also, research from some countries demonstrates that there can be low trust in the taxes and regulatory burden of formalization[34] translating into the benefits of a well-resourced contributory social protection system for them individually.[35]

[31] Ibid.

[32] Carol Ferdinand (ed.), 'Jobs, Gender and Small Enterprises in the Caribbean: Lessons from Barbados, Suriname and Trinidad and Tobago' (2001) SEED Working Paper No. 19 <www.ilo.org/wcmsp5/groups/public/—ed_emp/—emp_ent/documents/publication/wcms_113771.pdf> accessed 16 December 2021.

[33] ILO, *Women and Men in the Informal Economy: A Statistical Picture* (ILO 3rd ed. 2018).

[34] IDB, 'Estimating the Size of the Informal Economy in Caribbean States' (IDB 2017) <https://publications.iadb.org/publications/english/document/Estimating-the-Size-of-the-Informal-Economy-in-Caribbean-States.pdf> accessed 16 December 2021.

[35] Carla Marques, Carmem Leal, João Ferreira, and Vanessa Ratten, 'The Formal–Informal Dilemma for Women Micro-Entrepreneurs: Evidence from Brazil' (2018) 14 *Journal of Enterprising Communities: People and Places in the Global Economy* 5.

Finally, women in the Caribbean experience trade policy as consumers and heads of single-parent households. In Jamaica, 37 per cent of children were reported as having no father figure in the home; and in 2018, 45.6 per cent of households were women-led.[36] In Barbados, 56 per cent of households with a young person are headed by a woman, compared to 44 per cent headed by a man.[37] In Trinidad and Tobago, 32 per cent of households are headed by women.[38] Women's roles as primary caregivers means they are often responsible for food, security, and nutrition.[39] With declining economic fortunes in many of the islands, cheaper imported food – often less nutritious than local produce – has provided the means for many women to feed their families. This has contributed to the region's high import food bill and translates into limited expenditure and fiscal space for governments to support robust social programmes such as subsidized care, health, and education that impact women and their families.

It is therefore evident that women in the labour force are not effectively participating in CARICOM's trade, or benefiting from the enhanced economic opportunities that access to external markets provide. Incentivizing and supporting women to participate in trade presents an opportunity to enhance women's economic empowerment, and leverage women's productive capabilities for regional development.

11.3 THE GENDER AND TRADE AGENDAS IN CARICOM

11.3.1 *Gender Equality and Economic Empowerment in CARICOM*

CARICOM countries have made significant gains in achieving some of the indicators of gender equality. For example, most gender-based discriminatory

[36] PIOJ and STATIN, 'Jamaica Survey of Living Conditions 2018' (PIOJ/STATIN 2018).

[37] UNICEF Office for the Eastern Caribbean and Barbados Ministry of Youth and Community Empowerment, 'Generation Unlimited: The Wellbeing of Young People in Barbados Summary Findings' (UNICEF 2020) <www.unicef.org/easterncaribbean/media/2171/file/Generation%20Unlimited%20Barbados%20factsheet.pdf> accessed 16 December 2021.

[38] Ministry of Social Development and Family Services, Central Statistical Office and UNICEF, 'Trinidad and Tobago Multiple Indicator Cluster Survey 2011, Key Findings & Tables' (Port of Spain, Trinidad and Tobago: Ministry of Social Development and Family Services, Central Statistical Office and UNICEF).

[39] Lotsmart Fonjong, 'The Role of Women's Nutrition Literacy in Food Security: The Case of Africa' (August 2022) Observer Research Foundation Issue Brief No. 572; Preety Gadhoke, '"We're Changing Our Ways": Women as Primary Caregivers and Adaptations of Food and Physical Activity Related Health Behaviors in Semi-Rural and Rural American Indian/Alaska Native Households', Conference: 141st APHA Annual Meeting and Exposition 2013, November 2013, November 2013, Project: OPREVENT Project.

legislation has been removed;[40] there are equal numbers of girls and boys in education; and women tend to be more likely to pursue tertiary education than men. Nonetheless, stubborn obstacles to gender equality remain which impact women's economic empowerment. These include high levels of gender-based violence,[41] poor integration of women's leadership in organizations, unemployment[42] and inadequate access to resources, lack of formal recognition of unpaid care work burdens,[43] lack of state-supported measures to address the burden of unpaid care such as robust parental leave policies or subsidized child-care,[44] and low numbers of women entrepreneurs.[45]

The women's rights agenda in CARICOM has gone through a number of movements. Indeed, the early feminist agenda in the region was framed within the broader agenda of international platforms for voting rights and women's rights to public spheres within the context of independence and anti-racist movements for action 'adapted to national and regional priorities'.[46] The international community, including independent Caribbean states, recognized the need for a convention focused on the need to address women's substantive right to equality and, in 1979, the Convention on the Elimination of all Forms of Discrimination Against Women (CEDAW)[47] was signed into force. All CARICOM SIDS have ratified the CEDAW, which is a legally binding treaty.

Between the 1960s and 1990s, women's inequalities were addressed through efforts to integrate women into national economies and create equal opportunities for women. This was done successively under the 'Women in Development' approach, followed by a 'Women and Development' approach, and thereafter a 'Gender and Development' approach.[48] The Women in

[40] Notable exceptions include the countries where marital rape remains legal.

[41] UN Women, CARICOM and CDB, 'Caribbean Women Count: Ending Violence against Women and Girls Data Hub' (UN Women, CARICOM, CDB n.d.) <https://caribbeanwomencount.unwomen.org/> accessed 16 December 2021.

[42] Padmore, 'Summary Status of Women and Men Report' (n 15).

[43] No country in CARICOM currently has data to measure SDG indicator 5.4.1 on unpaid domestic and care work.

[44] Deborah Budlender and Isiuwa Iyahen, 'Status of Women and Men Report: Productive Employment and Decent Work for All' (UN Women 2019) <https://caribbean.unwomen.org/en/materials/publications/2019/10/status-of-women-and-men-report-productive-employment-and-decent-work-for-all#view> accessed 13 September 2022.

[45] InfoDev, 'Profiling Caribbean Women Entrepreneurs' (n 28).

[46] Ibid.

[47] Convention on the Elimination of All Forms of Discrimination Against Women, 18 December 1979, 1249 UNTS 13 (Not reproduced in ILM).

[48] Gabriel Hosein, Tricia Basdeo-Gobin, and Lydia Gény, 'Gender Mainstreaming in National Sustainable Development Planning in the Caribbean' (ECLAC Subregional Headquarters for

Development approach prominent in the 1970s represents the groundbreaking recognition that women should be economically empowered through small-scale projects as their productive contributions support economic growth and development. While pivotal, this approach ignored the structural barriers that contributed to gender inequalities and therefore ushered in the Women and Development approach in the 1980s which better addressed these structural inequalities. Women and Development emphasized women's role in the development process more broadly, along with the intersectionality of vulnerabilities along the lines of class, ethnicity, gender, etc. The Gender and Development approach that followed in the 1990s shifted this thinking from being a women's issue to a gender issue, deconstructing gender-neutral development discourse and supporting a 'gender lens' and gender mainstreaming across all social, economic, and political work.

The Caribbean region participated in these movements, through the CAFRA – a non-governmental feminist umbrella organization advocating for gender equality and women's rights across the region. CAFRA, the Women and Development Unit (WAND), established in August 1978 in the context of the UN Decade for Women and Development Alternatives with Women for a New Era (DAWN), and a network of feminist scholars, researchers, and activists from the Global South working for economic and gender justice and sustainable and democratic development established in 1984, were significant in galvanizing CARICOM's participation in the Fourth World Conference on Women in Beijing in 1995, where countries agreed to twelve critical areas of concern under the Beijing Platform for Action (BPfA), one of which involved Women and the Economy.[49]

CAFRA's influence has waned somewhat since the 1980s and 1990s, and today the women's movement in CARICOM is not as cohesive as it once was. Many feminist activists now operate as individual activists or within informal groups, most focusing on gender-based violence prevention and response. The lack of funding to feminist and women's organizations has often been cited for

the Caribbean 2020), 14 <www.cepal.org/sites/default/files/publication/files/45086/S1901209_en.pdf> accessed 16 December 2021.

49 Strategic Objective F2 speaks specifically to trade, noting that governments should take action 'to facilitate women's equal access to resources, employment, markets and trade', and offering a clear roadmap to governments and private sector organizations to take the necessary steps to ensure equal access to trade, to 'create non-discriminatory support services, including investment funds for women's businesses, and to target women, particularly low-income women, in trade promotion programmes'.

the decline.[50] However, since 2018 there has been a significant increase in funding for feminist and women-led organizations, through the Government of Canada-supported Women's Voice and Leadership Program[51] and the European Union and United Nations Spotlight Initiative.[52] However, despite the increased funding to feminist and women's organizations generally, the civil society space has tended to focus more on issues such as gender-based violence, women's leadership, and political participation, while women's economic empowerment has been less prioritized by these organisations.

Today, beyond a general rejection of trade liberalization, the specifics regarding the gender and trade agenda amongst the network of Caribbean women's and gender equality organizations are focused on creating an enabling environment for women to equitably engage in trade. This includes the promotion of gender-responsive social protection measures such as subsidized childcare, paid parental leave, and equal pay for equal work. The private sector and international community have engaged in supporting women-owned businesses through skills strengthening and increased access to financing, as well as networking opportunities. The Compete Caribbean project by the Inter-American Development Bank (IADB) and the WeEmpower project by the Caribbean Export Development Agency are examples of this approach aimed at strengthening women-owned businesses' capacities for trade. Similarly, the SheTrades Outlook policy tool developed by the International Trade Centre (ITC) captures new trade and gender data to better inform policy and programme formulation to support women in business. Through this platform, countries can identify data gaps and areas for potential reform and discover good practices.[53] Coverage for SheTrades Outlook includes

[50] Alicia Wallace, 'Challenges in Activism to End Gender-Based Violence in the Caribbean' (FAR 6 December 2020), <https://feministallianceforrights.org/blog/2020/12/16/challenges-in-activism-to-end-gender-based-violence-in-the-caribbean/> accessed 16 December 2021.

[51] Announced in July 2017 under Canada's Feminist International Assistance Policy, it is designed to meet the needs of local women's organizations in developing countries. The Caribbean programme has a maximum contribution of CAD 4,800,000. See <www.international.gc.ca/world-monde/issues_development-enjeux_developpement/gender_equality-egalite_des_genres/wvl_projects-projets_vlf.aspx?lang=eng> accessed 16 December 2021.

[52] The €500 million EU and UN global Spotlight Initiative is being implemented through six Caribbean country programmes and one regional programme. Support to women's organizations is one of the six guiding pillars of the Spotlight Initiative. See Spotlight Initiative, 'Where We Work' <www.spotlightinitiative.org/where-we-work?region=153> accessed 16 December 2021.

[53] Story-editor, 'Trinidad Launches National SheTrades Hub' (*St. Kitts Observer* 21 September 2020) <www.thestkittsnevisobserver.com/trinidad-launches-national-shetrades-hub/> accessed 16 December 2021.

several Caribbean countries, such as Barbados, Guyana, Jamaica, St. Lucia, St. Vincent and the Grenadines, and Trinidad and Tobago. Trinidad and Tobago was the first country in the Caribbean to officially launch an ITC SheTrades Hub in October 2020.[54] The platform offers opportunities for Trinidad and Tobago's women-owned MSMEs to access global supply chains and trade which is in line with Trinidad's trade policy's commitment to remove obstacles to the full participation of women in the development of trade.

11.4 GENDER MAINSTREAMING IN CARICOM TRADE POLICY AND NEGOTIATIONS

Although feminist economists have for a long time advocated for more gender-responsive approaches to trade,[55] gender has not traditionally been part of the official trade agenda at the WTO or in other trade-related fora. But the situation is changing. Since the Beijing Declaration and Platform for Action in 1995, the 2015 Addis Ababa Action Agenda – an integral part of the 2030 Sustainable Development Agenda – has explicitly made the connection between gender and international trade. In 2016, at the XIV United Nations Conference on Trade and Development (UNCTAD) Conference held in Nairobi, Kenya, UNCTAD members called for a continuation of work on the link between gender equality and trade, and most recently at the XV UNCTAD Conference in Barbados, an inaugural Gender and Development Conference was hosted.[56] Although there is no formal committee on gender and trade at the WTO, some progress has been made in getting WTO members to begin discussion on the topic. At the 2017 WTO Ministerial Conference in Buenos Aires, 118 WTO members signed a Joint Declaration on Trade and Women's Economic Empowerment,[57] which promotes the collection and analysis of gender-disaggregated data,[58] sharing

[54] MTI_WebAdmin, 'The SheTrades T&T Movement Is Here' (Ministry of Trade and Industry 29 October 2020) <https://tradeind.gov.tt/shetrades-tt-launch-mr/> accessed 16 December 2021.

[55] Drucilla Barker, 'Beyond Women and Economics: Rereading "Women's Work"' (2005) 30(4) *Journal of Women in Culture and Society* 2189–2209.

[56] UNCTAD, 'The Inaugural Gender and Development Forum at the Fifteenth Session of the United Nations Conference on Trade and Development, Bridgetown Declaration', TD/INF.71 (7 October 2021).

[57] WTO, 'Buenos Aires Declaration on Women and Trade Outlines Actions to Empower Women' <www.wto.org/english/news_e/news17_e/mc11_12dec17_e.htm> accessed 13 September 2022.

[58] Ibid para. 3.

of country experiences and good practices,[59] and promotion of collaboration to raise the profile of the link between trade and gender. In anticipation of the 12th Ministerial Conference in Geneva, WTO members prepared a Joint Ministerial Declaration on the Advancement of Gender Equality and Women's Economic Empowerment within Trade,[60] in which they agreed to continue improving the collection of gender-segregated data,[61] use research to inform trade policies,[62] explore women's empowerment issues,[63] promote collaboration between gender and trade,[64] and discuss the impact of COVID-19 on women. However, this declaration was never adopted.

The global recognition that gender equality is an indispensable component of the achievement of the UN SDGs – Goal 5 is to 'achieve gender equality and empower all women and girls' – has no doubt also contributed to the mainstreaming of gender in international economic policy, including trade policy. While there is no specific reference to trade within SDG 5, a closer look at the targets and indicators associated with it illustrate how progressive gender-related policies can lead to economic empowerment, increase their outcomes as workers and owners, and increase access to technology, all of which are linked to topics of international trade. This particularly stands for the most vulnerable, including those who are subjects of economic exploitation, unpaid care workers, and beneficiaries of public service expenditure.[65]

59 Ibid para. 1.

60 WTO, 'Joint Ministerial Declaration on the Advancement of Gender Equality and Women's Economic Empowerment within Trade', WT/MIN(21)/4 (10 November 2021) <https://docs.wto.org/dol2fe/Pages/FE_Search/FE_S_S009-DP.aspx?language=E&CatalogueIdList=278631,278632,278621&CurrentCatalogueIdIndex=1&FullTextHash=371857150&HasEnglishRecord=True&HasFrenchRecord=True&HasSpanishRecord=False> accessed 16 December 2021.

61 Ibid para. 1.

62 Ibid para. 2.

63 Ibid para. 3.

64 Ibid para. 4.

65 See for instance, Target 5.1: 'End all forms of discrimination against all women and girls everywhere'; Target 5.2: 'Eliminate all forms of violence against all women and girls in the public and private spheres, including trafficking and sexual and other types of exploitation'; Target 5.4: 'Recognize and value unpaid care and domestic work through the provision of public services, infrastructure and social protection'; Target 5.5: 'Ensure women's full and effective participation and equal opportunities for leadership at all levels of decision-making in political, economic and public life'; Target 5.a: 'Undertake reforms to give women equal rights to economic resources, as well as access to ownership and control over land and other forms of property, financial services, inheritance and natural resources, in accordance with national laws'; Target 5.b:' Enhance the use of enabling technology, in particular information and communications technology, to promote the empowerment of women'; Target 5.c: 'Adopt and strengthen sound policies and enforceable legislation for the promotion of gender equality and the empowerment of all women and girls at all levels'.

Despite the changes at the international levels, not all countries have adapted and streamlined gender policy into the development and trade agendas. Some countries, such as Sweden and Canada, explicitly acknowledge the role trade policy has in contributing to gender equality and have led the way through far-reaching agreements. For example, Canada's FTAs with Israel and Chile reaffirm its gender-related obligations under international agreements such as those recommended the CEDAW.[66] Additionally, Canada has committed to adopt policies, regulations, and best practices for gender equality nationally.[67] Sweden has created a national policy space which prioritizes gender mainstreaming and allows better articulation of the country's negotiating position on gender-related matters. For instance, Sweden has since 1994 required that all national statistics be disaggregated by sex, budgeting processes are informed by gender equality agendas, public sector agencies and officials are trained in gender equality, and various anti-discriminatory legislations are enacted.[68] Within CARICOM, by comparison, much work remains to be done in better streamlining gender into trade agreements and sustainable development policies, and in particular addressing some of the gender inequalities that persist in the region.

According to a 2020 study conducted by the UN ECLAC on the status of gender mainstreaming in the sustainable development policy frameworks of twenty-nine Caribbean States, as of 2019 the most frequent themes addressed in the national development plans have been: quality education (SDG 4), decent work and economic growth (SDG 8), sustainable cities and communities (SDG 11), climate action and peace (SDG 13), and peace, justice, and strong institutions (SDG 19). One of the weakest linkages to the SDG goals, however, includes gender equality (SDG 5).[69] Out of the twenty-nine Caribbean Member States reviewed, eight have national development plans that mainstream gender. These states include Antigua and Barbuda, Bahamas, Belize, Dominica, Dominican Republic, Jamaica, St. Vincent and the

[66] Canada–Israel Free Trade Agreement (CIFTA) was modernized in 2014 to include provisions on gender in chapter 13. *See* Government of Canada, 'Canada–Israel Free Trade Agreement' <www.international.gc.ca/trade-commerce/trade-agreements-accords-commerciaux/agr-acc/israel/fta-ale/text-texte/toc-tdm.aspx?lang=eng&_ga=2.4276787.1009792136.1642363194-531467218.1642363194> accessed 13 September 2022.

[67] Jose-Antonio Monteiro, 'Gender Related Provisions in Regional Trade Agreements' (2018) WTO Staff Working Paper ERSD-2018-15, 20–22 <www.wto.org/english/res_e/reser_e/ersd201815_e.pdf> accessed 13 September 2022.

[68] EIGE, 'Sweden – Gender Mainstreaming' <https://eige.europa.eu/gender-mainstreaming/countries/sweden> accessed 29 September 2022.

[69] Hosein et al., 'Gender Mainstreaming in National Sustainable Development Planning in the Caribbean' (n 48) 14.

Grenadines, and Trinidad and Tobago. However, as the UN ECLAC study demonstrates, the measures in the country's national development plans are limited to the areas of gender-based violence, education, and employment, and are not integrated in 'transformational ways', especially when addressing cross-cutting issues.[70] As highlighted by UN ECLAC, the trade sector especially continues to remain virtually gender-neutral despite its widely accepted gender dimensions. The study also highlighted the fact that eleven Caribbean states have existing gender equality policies or related action plans. Upon further analysis, out of these eleven states, gender equality policies or related action plans in Jamaica, Trinidad and Tobago, and especially Grenada have addressed trade in different ways. However, oftentimes these policies do not reference each other; nor are there robust monitoring and evaluation frameworks to assess the success of policy implementation.

CARICOM's incorporation of gender provisions into its trade agreements has also been underwhelming. Although some CARICOM Member States – Barbados, Dominica, Grenada, Guyana, Haiti, Jamaica, St. Kitts and Nevis, and St. Vincent and the Grenadines – have signed up to the 2017 Buenos Aires Declaration, as a region it is among the lowest performing in terms of the incorporation of gender provisions.

A 2021 Study by UN Women considered CARICOM's incorporation of gender in its trade agreements by reviewing all six free trade and partial scope agreements which are currently in force.[71] The 'gender-inclusive lens' was applied to the agreements, using the ITC's gender-responsive trade agreement survey tool[72] to determine the extent to which the agreements' texts were sensitive to informed or committed to gender equality. CARICOM's FTAs were analysed and found to be 'completely or close to gender-blind or gender-neutral' because they failed to mainstream gender concerns.[73] The reasons given by the authors of the UN Women study for the poor gender mainstreaming in trade agreements included that: trade officials were unsure of the protocols they needed to follow to allow their negotiations to advocate for gender-responsive trade agreements; there are limited meaningful

70 Ibid.

71 Lebrechtta N. O. Hesse Bayne and Robin Haarr (eds.), *Role of Gender in CARICOM and CARIFORUM Regional Trade Agreements* (UN Women 2021) <https://caribbean.eclac.org/publications/role-gender-caricom-and-cariforum-regional-trade-agreements> accessed 16 December 2021.

72 See ITC, 'Mainstreaming Gender in Free Trade Agreements' (2020) <https://intracen.org/media/file/2411> accessed 13 September 2022.

73 Hesse Bayne and Haarr, *Role of Gender in CARICOM and CARIFORUM Regional Trade Agreements* (n 71).

consultations with national or regional offices responsible for gender-related matters, which denies the opportunity to adequately understand as well as subsequently prioritize gender concerns in trade negotiations; and insufficient allocation of resources to properly monitor and evaluate the implementation of trade agreements and their provisions which may have gender implications.[74]

The most expansive reference in existing agreements, the EU–CARIFORUM Economic Partnership Agreement[75] (also UK–CEPA), includes two gender equality considerations in the agreement's text. One such commitment is in Article 191, under which the parties reaffirm their commitment to the internationally recognized core labour standards, as defined by the relevant International Labour Organization (ILO) Conventions, in particular under the ILO Declaration on Fundamental Principles and Rights at Work and its Follow-Up (1998). The parties have also committed to promote the development of international trade in a way that is conducive to full and productive employment and decent work for all, including men, women, and young people. Another commitment is found in Article 5, wherein parties have undertaken to review the operation of the Agreement to ensure that it is implemented for the benefit of men as well as women. While the commitment for impact assessment might be considered a best practice provision, its utility is undervalued by the fact that the parties do not commit to any affirmative action in this respect, in the form of either cooperation or a binding commitment. They also do not identify how this review or impact assessment may be carried out and whether it would be an *ex ante* or *ex post* assessment.[76]

A promising prospect for a more gender-responsive trade agreement has been provided in the recently concluded post-Cotonou EU/African–Caribbean–Pacific Partnership Agreement.[77] While not formally a trade agreement, it does provide the basis for future economic relations and a partnership between the EU and Caribbean. The pact does include more specific gender provisions than any of the existing agreements to which CARICOM states are party. The preamble, for instance, reaffirms that gender

74 Ibid.

75 Economic Partnership Agreement between the CARIFORUM States, of the one part, and the European Community and its Member States, of the other part (28 October 2008).

76 Countries can use the UNCTAD's toolbox on trade and gender for conducting these assessments. More details at UNCTAD, 'UNCTAD Trade and Gender Tool Box' (UNCTAD 2017) <https://unctad.org/webflyer/unctad-trade-and-gender-tool-box> accessed 16 December 2021.

77 EU African–Caribbean–Pacific Partnership Agreement, 2021.

equality and empowerment of women and girls are essential to achieving inclusive and sustainable development. Moreover, a specific provision (Article 10) addresses gender equality and in the Caribbean Protocol, Article 48 specifically 'reinforces women's economic rights, including by facilitating their access to economic opportunities, financial services, enabling technology, employment and the control and use of land and other productive assets'.

Beyond CARICOM, other Caribbean states have demonstrated more expansive approaches to trade and gender. For instance, in the EU-Overseas Countries and Territories (OCT),[78] the parties have committed to non-discrimination based on sex as one of the main objectives of the agreement. In United States–Dominican Republic–Central America FTA (CAFTA-DR),[79] Parties have reserved a right to craft government procurement schemes that may be favourable for certain groups, including women.[80] Given that public procurement accounts for around one-fifth of global GDP[81] and the relative underrepresentation of women entrepreneurs,[82] it is a positive development that CARICOM states could well embrace.

At the institutional level, some work has been done by CARICOM to advance gender concerns, but this has focused on social and health-related themes and addressing sexual violence against women and girls. In particular, the 2005 CARICOM Plan of Action[83] for gender equity and equality has provided a regional framework to guide the process of gender mainstreaming in priority areas such as education with a focus on building human capital, and health with a focus on HIV/AIDS and poverty. The economy including trade was included as the third priority area, but it is unclear what has emerged from that effort.

78 European Commission, 'The Overseas Countries and Territories (OCT)' (European Commission) <https://ec.europa.eu/taxation_customs/customs-4/international-affairs/origin-goods/general-aspects-preferential-origin/overseas-countries-and-territories-oct_en> accessed 16 December 2021.

79 CAFTA-DR (Dominican Republic-Central America FTA).

80 Annex 9.1.2(b)(i) of Chapter 9 'Government Procurement' of the CAFTA–DR (Dominican Republic–Central America FTA).

81 ITC, 'Empowering Women through Public Procurement' (2014) <www.intracen.org/uploadedFiles/intracenorg/Content/Publications/Women%20procurement%20guide-final-web.pdf> accessed 16 December 2021.

82 Ibid; Erin Kepler and Shane Scott, 'Are Male and Female Entrepreneurs Really That Different?' (2007) Office of Advocacy Small Business Working Papers 07ekss, US Small Business Administration, Office of Advocacy.

83 CARICOM Secretariat, 'Plan of Action to 2005: Framework for Mainstreaming Gender into Key CARICOM Programmes' (CARICOM 2005) <https://caricom.org/documents/11303-plan_of_action_to_2005.pdf> accessed 16 December 2021.

More recently, as of February 2019, consultations have been underway on a draft CARICOM Regional Gender Equality Strategy with priority areas identified including equality and social inclusion, freedom from violence, access to health services, access to education, good governance, and economic empowerment.[84] At face value, it is unclear whether the link between trade and gender has been considered or will be addressed in this strategy. The draft strategy is being refined and should be finalized in 2023. This presents an opportunity to incorporate trade and gender considerations for the region. CARICOM markets especially should be explored for opportunities that would enable businesses owned by women to expand their operations.

11.5 FINAL THOUGHTS

In spite of the multiple vulnerabilities they face as SIDS, CARICOM states are among the most open and trade dependent in the world. Trade is therefore an indispensable tool for economic growth and development, which must be inclusive, sustainable, and leave no group behind, including women and girls. Despite increasing recognition globally of the interlinkages between trade and gender, and the role that trade can play in advancing women's empowerment, CARICOM Member States have not demonstrated a clear understanding of the differentiated impact on women who encounter the trade space as producers, traders, and consumers; nor have they sufficiently mainstreamed gender provisions into their trade agreements to date.

Trade represents a fertile, albeit unrealized, opportunity for CARICOM Member States to reduce and overcome these structural inequalities that stifle the economic, social, and cultural advancement of women and gender equality. If negotiated with a gender lens, trade can translate into more job opportunities, better business connections, enhanced market access, and fewer barriers to access finances and other productive resources for women, all of which present obstacles to women's advancement in CARICOM states.

The authors recommend a few simple but essential policies for the attention of gender and trade officials in CARICOM. First, reliable sex-disaggregated data must be collected so that a better understanding can be gained of how trade policies impact women and more targeted interventions can be made. Efforts by UN Women and CARICOM to create CARICOM

84 CANA, 'CARICOM Hosting National Consultations on Draft Regional Gender Policy' (Caribbean Communications Network 8 February 2019), <www.tv6tnt.com/news/regional/caricom-hosting-national-consultations-on-draft-regional-gender-policy/article_e4df18a8-2baf-11e9-bdb7-b705294ad47a.html> accessed 16 December 2021.

Gender Equality Indicators, which are aligned to the SDGs, has been a good start. Caribbean SIDS should ensure the effective collection of this data, especially as it is related to women's economic engagement. A better understanding of time use, as measured by SDG 5.4.1 (Proportion of time spent on unpaid domestic and care work), will allow governments to reflect on the contribution of the unpaid care economy to GDP and inform equitable policies for women to engage more fully in the formal economy and trade sectors.

Another key recommendation is to break the silos between trade policy and gender, and mainstream gender into all significant national development strategies. In spite of the enormous impact of trade policy on women – whether as importers, producers, entrepreneurs, or consumers – consultations with gender departments, women's organizations and community groups have not been prioritized in the development of trade policy. Gender indicators should be developed for all trade policies, and trade negotiation teams should include gender and socio-economic specialists. Moreover, SIDS should ensure all that trade policy is inclusive of tourism policies, and that both are fully gender responsive. Gender policies should not be siloed from national development strategies.

Finally, CARICOM should utilize existing mechanisms in trade agreements to revisit and renegotiate provisions so that they focus on gender inequalities that persist in CARICOM, including women's lack of participation in commercial and entrepreneurial sectors, and lack of access to capital and finance. Trade agreements should explicitly reference provisions such as capacity development for women-owned businesses, as well as temporary special measures for export by women-owned businesses. Priority in the region should be on negotiating outcomes that focus on enhancing the participation of women in newer areas that hold promise, such as in the ecommerce and renewable energy sectors.

12

South America's Leadership in Gender Mainstreaming in Trade Agreements

JAVIERA CÁCERES BUSTAMANTE AND FELIPE MUÑOZ NAVIA

ABSTRACT

There is a growing awareness that trade affects women and men differently based on their position in the economy, and that it also affects women's empowerment and well-being. Although countries in South America have traditionally imported provisions of trade agreements from developed countries, they have also demonstrated their ability to innovate and design gender-sensible trade regulations. Mainstreaming gender elements into economic and trade policies is crucial for women's empowerment and will have a positive effect on both women's and the region's social and economic development. While some trade agreements have incorporated gender references in their preambles and in provisions relating to cooperation, the very first standalone trade and gender chapter was incorporated in the Chile–Uruguay Free Trade Agreement (FTA). This was followed by other South American countries such as Argentina, Brazil, and Ecuador, that have also incorporated this kind of chapter in their FTAs. Through a review of gender provisions in South American bilateral trade agreements and in the region's main integration processes (Pacific Alliance and Mercosur), this chapter will demonstrate how South America has advanced gender-sensitive trade policymaking which has expanded to other regions.

12.1 INTRODUCTION

There is a growing awareness amongst academics, government officials, and experts from international and non-governmental organizations (NGOs) that economic policies impact men and women differently. The difference is probably the result of social systems where different kinds of inequalities exist.

In these systems, social relational contexts are fundamental as they shape a gender regime which conditions sex segregation in jobs, division of labour, and gender differences in social positions in authority, among others.[1] Therefore, it has been recognized that mainstreaming gender perspectives into policymaking is crucial to ensure women's economic autonomy and has a positive effect on development.[2] In this context, gender issues have been included in international trade policy agendas, acknowledging that countries with higher levels of political and economic participation by women are closer to achieving gender equality as well as a higher level of global competitiveness.[3]

New preferential trade agreements (PTAs) include gender considerations because: more women are part of policymaking than before; an increasing number of women own or manage export firms and trade in international markets; advocacy campaigns are raising awareness of the relevance of gender equality issues; research is being conducted on the gender dimension of trade policy; and there is a widespread belief that trade can be instrumental for long-lasting development only if it is more inclusive and its benefits are more equally shared.[4]

South American countries have adopted a proactive attitude towards the inclusion of a gender perspective within their trade policymaking. For example, at the regional level, the Pacific Alliance can be highlighted due to the implementation of a roadmap to address women's economic autonomy and empowerment[5] and, at the bilateral level, the Chile–Uruguay FTA became the first to include a gender and trade chapter.[6] This chapter became a template for trade negotiations worldwide, as well as a stepping stone for the evolution of such chapters in other agreements.

1 Cecilia Ridgeway and Shelley Correll, 'Unpacking the Gender System: A Theoretical Perspective on Gender Beliefs and Social Relations' (2004) 18 *Gender Society* 510; Javiera Cáceres and Felipe Muñoz, 'The Gendered Impact of COVID-19 Crisis in Latin America' in Pablo Baisotti and Pierfrancesco Moscuzza (eds.), *Reframing Globalization after COVID-19: Pandemic Diplomacy amid the Failure of Multilateral Cooperation* (Sussex Academic Press 2022) 66–96.

2 Simonetta Zarrilli, 'The New Way of Addressing Gender Inequality Issues in Trade Agreements: Is It a True Revolution?' (UNCTAD 2017) <https://unctad.org/system/files/official-document/presspb2017d2_en.pdf> accessed 8 May 2022.

3 Alejandra Mora, 'COVID-19 in Women's Lives: Reasons to Recognize the Differential Impacts' (Reliefweb 2020) <https://reliefweb.int/report/world/covid-19-women-s-lives-reasons-recognize-differential-impacts> accessed 8 May 2022.

4 Zarrilli, 'The New Way of Addressing Gender Inequality Issues in Trade Agreements' (n 2).

5 Pacific Alliance/Alianza del Pacífico <https://alianzapacifico.net/en/> accessed 8 May 2022.

6 UNCTAD, 'Chile–Uruguay FTA' (4 October 2016) <https://investmentpolicy.unctad.org/international-investment-agreements/treaty-files/5408/download> accessed 8 May 2022.

The main objective of this chapter is to analyse how South American economies have mainstreamed gender issues in their trade agreements, and to identify common elements in such agreements and their evolution. For this purpose, the chapter reviews the incorporation of gender provisions in bilateral trade agreements and the region's integration processes (Pacific Alliance and Mercosur). With respect to the methodology used, this chapter analyses and compares primary and secondary sources, and, in particular, presidential declarations from integration processes and the contents of the text of various FTAs, their enforcement and governance. Moreover, in-depth semi-structured interviews with key stakeholders from the public sector were conducted to complement previous analysis, looking into the motivations and reasons behind the different legal clauses.[7] The results of the interviews are woven into the text of the chapter, which also includes analysis in specific sections. The field research – which includes face-to-face and virtual interviews prior to the pandemic, and online zoom interviews after lockdown and during social distancing measures – was conducted between December 2018 and October 2021 and entailed interviews with stakeholders from Argentina, Chile, Colombia, Peru, and Mexico, as well as representatives from international organizations. In total, thirty-four interviews were carried out with a variety of stakeholders, including former trade ministers, vice ministers, negotiators, experts from international organizations, and academics. Due to the positions interviewees hold, the results have been anonymized. Moreover, although there is consensus regarding the incorporation of gender provisions in international trade agreements, a divergence in opinions is found between members who hold public office and members from international organizations and academia. This chapter demonstrates how South American countries have advanced their trade policymaking regarding gender-sensible regulations, which has been influential for trade and gender negotiations in other regions.

This chapter is divided into the following sections. Section 12.2 reviews the relevant literature regarding the inclusion of gender issues in trade policy. Section 12.3 revises gender mainstreaming in the Pacific Alliance and Mercosur. Then, Section 12.4 presents an overview of gender inclusion in South American PTAs. Section 12.5 presents analysis of the inclusion of gender provisions in South America's FTAs. To conclude, Section 12.6 contains final remarks and policy recommendations.

7 Interviewees were informed that participation was voluntary and that results would be published anonymously.

12.2 GENDER MAINSTREAMING IN TRADE POLICY INSTRUMENTS

It is crucial to analyse FTAs through a gender perspective. This would contribute to determining whether the decisions of a society favour the search for social and economic justice and the scope and limitations of macroeconomic policies. The literature has established that trade strategies which are focused on lowering labour costs and maintaining gender disparities can cement a path of underdevelopment and obstruct the transition to sustainable development.[8] Through the incorporation of a gender perspective into FTAs, governments can push their trade partners to develop laws and processes that decrease obstacles to women's access to trade.[9]

The first multilateral step towards including gender in international trade policy goes back to the World Trade Organization's (WTO) claim that trade liberalization is linked to greater accumulation of education, skills, and increased gender equality.[10] This claim has led international organizations and governments to incorporate a gender-based perspective within their trade agenda, making it a worldwide priority.[11] Nevertheless, there is no consensus to include gender within multilateral negotiations amongst WTO members. Many WTO members have argued that the WTO should deal only with trade-related issues that imply trade distortions, but not social issues such as gender inequality.[12] Some NGOs have argued the opposite, as gender equality contributes to economic growth and poverty reduction, and women make up 70 per cent of the world's poorest share of the population.[13] Although it

[8] Diane Elson, Caren Grown, and Nilüfer Çaæatay, 'Mainstream, Heterodox, and Feminist Trade Theory' in Irene van Staveren, Diane Elson, Caren Grown, and Nilufer Cagatay (eds), *The Feminist Economics of Trade* (Routledge 2012); Alicia Frohmann, 'Género y emprendimiento exportador: iniciativas de cooperación regional' (ECLAC 2018) <www.cepal.org/es/publicaciones/43287-genero-emprendimiento-exportador-iniciativas-cooperacion-regional> accessed 8 May 2022.

[9] Amrita Bahri, 'Measuring the Gender-Responsiveness of Free Trade Agreements: Using a Self-Evaluation Maturity Framework' (2019) 14(11/12) *Global Trade Customs Journal* 517–527.

[10] Paul Schultz, *Does the Liberalization of Trade Advance Gender Equality in Schooling and Health?* (Routledge 2014).

[11] Dorotea López, Felipe Muñoz, and Javiera Cáceres, *Gender Inclusion in Chilean Free Trade Agreements* (Institute of International Studies University of Chile 2019).

[12] Baogang He and Hannah Murphy, 'Global Social Justice at the WTO? The Role of NGOs in Constructing Global Social Contracts' (2007) 83(4) *International Affairs* 707–727; Robyn Eckersley, 'The Big Chill: The WTO and Multilateral Environmental Agreements' (2004) 4 (2) *Global Environmental Politics* 24–50; Montserrat González-Garibay, 'The Trade-Labour and Trade-Environment Linkages: Together or Apart?' (2011) 10(2) *Journal of International Trade Law and Policy* 165–184.

[13] Elina Viilup, 'The EU's Trade Policy: From Gender-Blind to Gender Sensitive?' (2015) In-Depth Analysis for the European Parliament, DG External Policies <www.europarl.europa

was not included in the trade negotiation agenda, the 2017 Buenos Aires Declaration on Women and Trade,[14] which aims to promote and remove impediments to women's economic empowerment, was endorsed by 118 WTO members and observers.[15] Moreover, in the WTO's 12th Ministerial Conference, held in Geneva in June 2022, members recognized the relevance of women's economic empowerment and the work that international organizations such as the WTO, the United Nations Conference on Trade and Development (UNCTAD), and the International Trade Centre (ITC) are doing in this respect.[16]

Gender considerations must be a part of the integral design of the different trade policies.[17] The literature has identified the following trade policy tools that could contribute to gender equality:

- First, gathering specific trade and gender information can mitigate the lack of data about women in economic roles.[18] Since December 2017, following the Buenos Aires Declaration, countries have sought to exchange methodologies and processes for collecting gender-disaggregated data and analysing gender-focused trade statistics.[19]
- Second, the participation of civil society and private stakeholders, including business chambers and women's organizations, can be instrumental in identifying gender objectives within trade policy and advocating for this change in the future.
- Third, *ex ante* and *ex post* evaluation of the impact of an agreement on women, and the necessary adaptation and compensation for the impact of trade on women, are important to produce evidence on how trade

.eu/RegData/etudes/IDAN/2015/549058/EXPO_IDA(2015)549058_EN.pdf> accessed 8 May 2022.

14 WTO, 'Joint Declaration on Trade and Women's Economic Empowerment on the Occasion of the WTO Ministerial Conference in Buenos Aires in December 2017' (2017) <www.wto.org/english/thewto_e/minist_e/mc11_e/genderdeclarationmc11_e.pdf> accessed 8 May 2022.

15 As of September 2022, 127 members had endorsed this Declaration.

16 WTO, 'MC12 Outcome Document – Adopted on 17 June 2022', WT/MIN(22)/24 (22 June 2022) <https://docs.wto.org/dol2fe/Pages/SS/directdoc.aspx?filename=q:/WT/MIN22/24.pdf&Open=True> accessed 12 September 2022.

17 Frohmann, 'Género y emprendimiento exportador' (n 8).

18 World Bank and WTO, 'Women and Trade. The Role of Trade in Promoting Gender Equality' (WTO 2020) <www.wto.org/english/res_e/booksp_e/women_trade_pub2807_e.pdf> accessed 8 May 2022.

19 UNCTAD, 'Gender and Trade: Assessing the impact of Trade Agreements on Gender Equality: Canada-EU Comprehensive Economic and Trade Agreement' (2020) <https://unctad.org/system/files/official-document/UNWomen_2020d1_en.pdf> accessed 8 May 2022.

impacts gender concerns.[20] Trade policies that will favour women's well-being and empowerment and mitigate gender disparities can use an *ex ante* assessment to analyse the potential impacts on specific segments of the population.[21]

- Fourth, the increasing participation of women in the policymaking process, international markets, and the awareness brought by different campaigns for gender equality in the last few years have allowed the incorporation of gender chapters in trade agreements.[22]
- Fifth, mainstreaming gender in all trade disciplines can be achieved through the prohibition of gender discrimination, the inclusion of affirmative actions, and reservations in areas where the state's regulatory power over gender equality must be protected.
- Sixth, the implementation of trade facilitation measures including borders and customs, commerce and transportation infrastructure, and logistics which may benefit women by ensuring a more predictable and inclusive workplace.[23]
- Seventh, the promotion of women's export entrepreneurship, and the elimination of restrictions and legal barriers to access financing can also help in addressing gender concerns within the trade policy context. The inclusion of women entrepreneurs and workers in higher-level sectors such as knowledge-intensive activities may promote a more gender-equal society. This can be reinforced by enhancing women's participation in leadership positions within productive structures, including regional and global value chains. Moreover, the latest developments due to the COVID-19 pandemic have raised the awareness of the care economy and women's participation in the digital economy.[24] Against that background, the following section provides a discussion on how the existing

20 Different approaches towards ex-ante and ex-post evaluations have been developed by international organisations and governments. Amongst them, it can be highlighted UNCTAD's trade and gender toolbox, the OECD's framework of analysis, and Canada's Gender Based Approach (GBA+).

21 Zarrilli, 'The New Way of Addressing Gender Inequality Issues in Trade Agreements' (n 2).

22 Javiera Cáceres, Felipe Muñoz, Brayan Alarcón, Martín Fierro, Constanza Montenegro, Antonia Pérez, María Jesús Ramírez, Tomas Rogaler, Lida Chávez, Libertad Guzmán, Valentina Hidalgo, and Andrea Martínez, *Propuestas para la incorporación de disposiciones de género en el Protocolo Adicional de la Alianza del Pacífico* (Integración y Comercio 2021) 76–103.

23 Frohmann, 'Género y emprendimiento exportador' (n 8).

24 ECLAC, 'La autonomía económica de las mujeres en la recuperación sostenible y con igualdad' (2021) Informe Especial COVID-19 No. 9 <www.cepal.org/es/publicaciones/46633-la-autonomia-economica-mujeres-la-recuperacion-sostenible-igualdad> accessed 8 May 2022.

trade agreements in South America have embraced these gender-mainstreaming tools.

12.3 GENDER MAINSTREAMING IN SOUTH AMERICA'S MAIN INTEGRATION PROCESSES

The most important processes of economic integration in South America include Mercosur and the Pacific Alliance. Mercosur was established in 1991 by Argentina, Brazil, Paraguay, and Uruguay, with the objective of creating a deep integration process in the region to foster economic and investment opportunities. The Pacific Alliance is a more recent initiative established in 2011 by Chile, Colombia, Mexico, and Peru to promote members' higher economic growth and competitiveness through a mechanism of economic, political, and social articulation.

12.3.1 *Gender-Specific Policies under Mercosur*

The incorporation of women and gender has been a longstanding topic of discussion in Mercosur's working agenda. Members have incorporated different actions in their integration process work, including the Specialized Meeting of Women, a body that was created in 1997. This body was established in response to the increasing demand of civil society and women's movements for a forum to foster the analysis of women's situations and contribute to the social, economic, and cultural development of various communities. Amongst other issues, the meeting recommended male–female parity in the composition of the Mercosur Parliament.[25] Moreover, in 2008, a project to strengthen gender institutions and policies was implemented in cooperation with the Spanish Agency of International Cooperation.

Mercosur members have also worked towards the collection of gender-disaggregated data, for which a diagnosis on indicators on domestic violence was released in 2010. In 2011, on the occasion of the 100th Summit of the International Labour Organization (ILO), a Joint Statement was issued to support ILO Convention 189 on decent work for domestic workers. In the same year, the gender perspective was incorporated into the Strategic Social Action Plan, following which the Women's Ministers and High Official Meeting of Mercosur (RMAAM) was established. This led to the Mercosur

[25] Alma Espino, *Impacting MERCOSUR's Gender Policies: Experiences, Lessons Learned, and the Ongoing Work of Civil Society in Latin America* (Montreal International Forum 2008).

Gender Equity Policy, built in collaboration with various regional forums and women's organizations.

Another important topic analysed by Mercosur members relates to trafficking of women, and in particular the identification of domestic and international routes used for such trafficking. This led to the establishment of a Mercosur Guide on awareness of women victims of trafficking with the purpose of sexual exploitation.[26] In 2014, the Mercosur Guidelines on Gender Policy were approved, setting the ground for equality and non-discrimination of women in the region from a feminist and human rights perspective.

As stated, while Mercosur has acknowledged the relevance of incorporating a gender perspective in its social and governance agenda, it has not yet addressed this topic in relation to trade or trade agreements. In this context, Mercosur's trade liberalization has been argued to have mixed and potentially detrimental effects.[27] Further, analyses show that current Mercosur international trade patterns tend to benefit male-oriented sectors, and do not contribute to women's employment.[28] Hence, the mainstreaming of gender into trade policymaking becomes an opportunity for the next steps in this regional integration process in order to foster inclusive and sustainable development.

12.3.2 *Gender-Specific Policies under the Pacific Alliance*

The Pacific Alliance's Additional Protocol has not yet incorporated specific gender-related provisions.[29] In 2015, members agreed on a gender approach at the Tenth Summit of the Pacific Alliance. The Gender Technical Working

[26] Florencia Cadario, Florencia Fantin, and Mariana Jacques, 'La trata de personas con fines de explotación sexual en el contexto de pandemia: un análisis institucional desde el Mercosur y la Argentina' (2021) 26 *Nueva Serie Documentos de Trabajo* 53–60; Nueva Serie Documentos de Trabajo MERCOSUR, 'Guía MERCOSUR de atención a mujeres en situación de trata con fines de explotación sexual', MERCOSUR/CMC/REC No. 09/12 (2012).

[27] Leonith Hinojosa, 'EU–Mercosur Trade Agreement: Potential Impacts on Rural Livelihoods and Gender (with Focus on Bio-Fuels Feedstock Expansion)' (2009) 1(4) *Sustainability* 1120–1143; Andrea Ribeiro Hoffmann, 'Gender Mainstreaming in Mercosur and Mercosur–EU Trade Relations' in Anna van der Vleuten, Anouka van Eerdewijk, and Conny Roggeband (eds.), *Gender Equality Norms in Regional Governance: Transnational Dynamics in Europe, South America and Southern Africa* (Springer 2014).

[28] Paola Azar, Alma Espino, and Soledad Salvador, *Los vínculos entre comercio, género y equidad. Un análisis para seis países de América Latina* (Red Internacional de Género y Comercio 2007).

[29] Pacific Alliance Additional Protocol <https://alianzapacifico.net/?wpdmdl=1118> accessed 8 May 2022.

Group (GTG) was created to promote the gender perspective throughout the Alliance, to incorporate women leaders in exports, and to establish virtual platforms to address trade and gender, mainstreaming a gender perspective into cooperation, SMEs, export promotion agencies, the digital agenda, and innovation groups. In the Eleventh Summit, the Presidential Mandate[30] proposed the incorporation of female entrepreneurs into the export process, and the establishment of virtual platforms to promote gender and trade dialogues. Following this, the Alliance commissioned the Organisation for Economic Co-operation and Development (OECD) to assess gender equality in the member economies.

The 2017 Presidential Declaration[31] referred to the contribution of the gender perspective for the fulfilment of the 2030 United Nations' Agenda for Sustainable Development Goals (UN SDGs).[32] This led to the creation of the Virtual Community of Female Entrepreneurs and the III Forum of female entrepreneurs of Colombia, Chile, Mexico, and Peru.

In 2018, the Women Entrepreneurs Community platform, which is linked to ConnectAmericas, was established. The work under this initiative is complemented by *Mujeres del Pacífico* (Women of the Pacific), a private initiative that works with the Chilean Economic Development Agency (CORFO), the Inter-American Development Bank (IADB), and the Association of Entrepreneurs of Latin America (ASELA) through its Multilateral Investment Fund. In the same year, the Pacific Alliance Observatory issued a report identifying women-oriented programmes.[33] This report displayed the differences in the number of women-favouring programmes offered by each country, Colombia (twenty-three), Chile (fourteen), Mexico (eleven), and Peru (three), and highlighted that only 18 per cent of them referred to the need to mitigate sexist stereotypes.

In 2019, to clarify the understanding of concepts such as discrimination and gender equality, amongst others, the GTG created the Gender Glossary.[34] The GTG with IADB conducted a survey of 1933 women-owned businesses in Chile, Colombia, Mexico, and Peru. Preliminary results, presented at the

30 Pacific Alliance, 'Mandatos Grupo Técnico de Género' [Gender Technical Group Mandate] (2019) <https://alianzapacifico.net/?wpdmdl=17500> accessed 8 May 2022.

31 Pacific Alliance, 'Declaración de Cali: XII Cumbre de la Alianza del Pacífico' (2017) <https://alianzapacifico.net/?wpdmdl=1167> accessed 8 May 2022.

32 Pacific Alliance Presidential Declaration (2017) <https://alianzapacifico.net/?wpdmdl=1167> accessed 8 May 2022.

33 Observatorio Estratégico de la Alianza del Pacífico, Programas de Apoyo al Emprendimiento Femenino en la Alianza del Pacífico (2018).

34 Pacific Alliance, 'Gender Glossary' (2019).

Pacific Alliance Webinar on Women and International Trade in 2020, show that 78 per cent of surveyed businesswomen were sole/majority shareholders of companies, out of which 73 per cent were micro companies, 20 per cent small, 5 per cent medium, and 2 per cent were big enterprises.[35] Services, food, and beverage industries constitute the majority of sectors in which they work, except in Peru, where textiles and clothing are key industries where women engage as entrepreneurs and business-owners.

In 2020, the GTG launched the Guidelines for the Use of Inclusive Language in Technical Groups of the Pacific Alliance.[36] The study, with IADB, was expanded to include the effects of the COVID-19 crisis. The Pacific Alliance countries conducted a series of webinars to support the digitalization of women's businesses and issued a Presidential Declaration on Gender Equality with a Roadmap for Women's Autonomy and Economic Empowerment.[37] This roadmap reiterated the role of international agreements regarding women's rights and commits to centring women in reactivation strategies and economic recovery. Additionally, the roadmap identifies priority actions to promote women's entrepreneurship, labour participation, access to leadership positions, and decision-making in the political, economic, and social spheres; eliminate barriers to women's autonomy; reduce the gender digital gap; and generate gender-disaggregated data.

Therefore, the Pacific Alliance has recognized the relevance of mainstreaming gender for sustainable development in its presidential declarations, technical groups, and the Roadmap for Women's Autonomy and Economic Empowerment. However, current programmes should move into solid commitments included within the Pacific Alliance Additional Protocol (trade protocol), giving stability and permanence to the objective of gender equity.[38]

[35] Marisa Bircher, Dana Chahín, Carolina López, Isabel Mejía, and Alejandra Villota, 'Estudio de Diagnóstico, Radiografía de la participación de las mujeres empresarias de la Alianza del Pacífico en el comercio exterior' (November 2020) <https://alianzapacifico.net/wp-content/uploads/Estudio-de-Diagnostico-Participacion-de-las-mujeres-empresarias-de-la-AP-en-el-comercio-exterior-NOV2020.pdf> accessed 8 May 2022.

[36] Pacific Alliance, 'Guidelines for the Use of Inclusive Language' (2020) <https://alianzapacifico.net/wp-content/uploads/Guia_LenguajeInclusivo_vf.pdf> accessed 8 May 2022.

[37] Pacific Alliance, 'Declaración Presidencial sobre Igualdad de Género' [Presidential Declaration on Gender Equality] (2020) <https://alianzapacifico.net/?wpdmdl=21208> accessed 8 May 2022.

[38] Cáceres and Muñoz, 'The Gendered Impact of COVID-19' (n 1).

12.4 GENDER MAINSTREAMING IN SOUTH AMERICAN TRADE AGREEMENTS

The inclusion of a gender perspective has been a latecomer in bilateral trade agreements. Whereas the word 'women' has been used to address gender issues in the past, the expression 'gender' has only appeared recently.[39] Nevertheless, the evolution of the language from 'women' to 'gender' is correlated with the progressive development of the gender mainstreaming paradigm, which flourished after the 1995 Beijing Platform for Action.[40]

Although some WTO members have included provisions on gender in their FTAs, the scope, the form, and the enforceability of these provisions have been diverse. As of December 2020, from the 577 PTAs notified to the WTO, 83 (14 per cent) of them include at least one provision related to gender, and 257 (44 per cent) refer implicitly to gender impacts.[41] Regarding commitments, some agreements have a single clause on substantial duties for the contracting parties, while others have a dedicated chapter on gender. However, such provisions and chapters are not legally binding. While most of these clauses are included in the main text of the agreements, some clauses are tucked away in subsidiary agreements, appendices, or protocols. Reaffirmation provisions, for example, require members to repeat legal obligations made under other international treaties such as the Convention on the Elimination of All Forms of Discrimination Against Women (CEDAW), ILO conventions, or the UN SDGs.[42] Within South America, countries such as Chile and Uruguay have suggested a new paradigm in which free trade agreements are viewed as tools for attaining women's economic empowerment.[43]

Within this context, the opportunities of negotiations with like-minded countries have led to the creation and inclusion of gender chapters within free trade agreements. This has represented a shift in the way gender equality

[39] The first mention was in the Chile–Canada FTA (1997).

[40] Haifa Bensalem, 'Gender as Included in Bilateral and Multi-Party Trade and Integration Agreements' (CUTS 2017) <www.cuts-geneva.org/pdf/study%20-%20gender%20and%20trade.pdf> accessed 8 May 2022.

[41] José-Antonio Monteiro, 'The Evolution of Gender-Related Provisions in Regional Trade Agreements' (2021) WTO Staff Working Paper ERSD-2021-8 <www.wto.org/english/res_e/reser_e/ersd202108_e.pdf> accessed 8 May 2022.

[42] UNGA, 'Convention on the Elimination of All Forms of Discrimination Against Women', 1249 UNTS 13 (18 December 1979) ILO Equal Remuneration Convention, 1951 (No. 100); UNGA, 'Transforming Our World: The 2030 Agenda for Sustainable Development', A/RES/70/1 (21 October 2015).

[43] Bahri, 'Measuring the Gender-Responsiveness of Free Trade Agreements' (n 9).

issues were treated within trade agreements, as in previous trade agreements parties usually made a reference to gender issues in the preambles of the agreements or only addressed them as a general issue.[44] For instance, the Chile–Vietnam FTA (2014) proposes gender as one of the spheres of cooperation within its cooperation chapter,[45] and the Peru–Australia FTA (2020) refers to women and economic growth within its development chapter.[46] In the provision titled 'Women and Economic Growth', the contracting parties in this agreement have recognized the necessity to enhance opportunities for women so as to contribute to economic development, for which it promotes cooperation activities that will improve the ability of women to fully access and benefit from the opportunities created by the agreement.

The Chile–Uruguay FTA (2016)[47] marked the first inclusion of a dedicated chapter on gender and trade in the framework of a bilateral FTA. In the case of Chile, gender became an explicit component of trade policy during Michelle Bachelet's second government (2014–2018). The relevance of this topic during her administration was based on two main elements: (i) women's role as supporters of the economy; and (ii) the lack of information, discussion, proposals, and institutional participation. In addition to the Ministry of Women and Gender Equity created in 2016,[48] in terms of trade policy formulation and implementation, the General Directorate of International Economic Relations (DIRECON) included a gender-perspective approach in its work agenda,[49] to identify relevant spaces where gender-sensitive measures could be addressed.[50] In the case of Uruguay, under the second mandate of President Tabaré Vasquez (2015–2020), a process of bilateral free trade agreements negotiated outside Mercosur was initiated.[51] Both governments' coalitions had a progressive agenda in place, which gave gender issues a

44 Zarrilli, 'The New Way of Addressing Gender Inequality Issues in Trade Agreements' (n 2).

45 Art. 9.3, Chile–Vietnam FTA (2014).

46 Art. 22.4, Peru–Australia FTA (2020).

47 Chile–Uruguay FTA (2016).

48 This Ministry is in charge of developing policies and programmes that will benefit women, trying to eliminate all kinds of gender discrimination. Before this Ministry, since 1991, the National Service for Women (Sernam because of its name in Spanish) oversaw these affairs.

49 In 2016, a Gender Department was established responsible for follow-up on gender topics, enhancing internal gender policies, and managing the programmes to promote and support women's participation in international trade.

50 Dorotea López and Felipe Muñoz, 'Trade Policy and Women in the Pacific Alliance' (2018) 25 *Agenda Internacional* 133–150.

51 Camilo López and María Cecilia Míguez, 'Uruguay como Estado pequeño en el MERCOSUR (1991–2020): Una lectura desde la autonomía regional' (2021) *Lua Nova: Revista de Cultura e Política* 181–216.

prominent position within their public policies. This created suitable conditions for the inclusion of a gender chapter in their bilateral FTAs.

Following the Chile–Uruguay agreement, Chile incorporated gender issues in its negotiation processes. The agreements between Canada and Chile (June 2017), Argentina and Chile (November 2017), Brazil and Chile (December 2018), and Chile and Ecuador (August 2020) each included a trade and gender chapter.[52] The Chile–Canada FTA is a modernized version of the 1997 agreement, which corresponds to a progressive trade agenda as a response to the worldwide rise of anti-globalization populism and the concentration of trade gains at the top of the income scale that have left women, among others, behind.[53] The Chile–Uruguay FTA, Argentina–Chile FTA, and Brazil–Chile FTA are established in the context of the Economic Complementation Agreement 35 among Chile and Mercosur parties.[54] In particular, the Chile–Brazil FTA includes a framework of good regulatory practices in order to promote an open, fair, and predictable environment for companies in Chile and Brazil,[55] in order to respect, amongst others, issues relating to the environment and gender issues. Regarding the Chile–Ecuador FTA, the objective of modernizing the existing agreement was to include new issues related to trade in services and to achieve a deeper level of integration, comprising an inclusive approach under which gender provisions were incorporated.

In a multilateral arena, in 2018, Canada, Chile, and New Zealand established the Inclusive Action Group (ITAG) to create progressive and inclusive trade policies to guarantee that benefits from trade and investment are equally distributed. In 2020, they signed the Global Trade and Gender Arrangement (GTAGA) to stimulate women's participation in international trade, recognizing the relevance of having a gender perspective in the promotion of an inclusive economic growth.[56] This agreement acknowledges parties' equality

52 Canada–Chile FTA (2017); Argentina–Chile FTA (2017); Brazil–Chile FTA (2018); Chile–Ecuador FTA (2020); Brazil–Chile FTA (2022); and Chile–Ecuador FTA (2022). All official texts available at <www.subrei.gob.cl/acuerdos-comerciales/acuerdos-comerciales-vigentes> accessed 8 May 2022.

53 Dan Ciuriak, 'Canada's Progressive Trade Agenda and the NAFTA Renegotiation' (2018) CD Howe Institute Commentary No. 516 <www.cdhowe.org/sites/default/files/attachments/research_papers/mixed/Final%20June%2011%20Commentary_516.pdf> accessed 8 May 2022.

54 Economic Complementation Agreement 35 among Chile and Mercosur parties, ACE No. 35.

55 Patricia Schüller, 'Senado aprobó acuerdo de libre comercio entre Chile y Brasil' (*La Nación* 12 August 2020) <www.lanacion.cl/senado-aprobo-acuerdo-de-libre-comercio-entre-chile-y-brasil/> accessed 8 May 2022.

56 Government of Canada, 'GTAGA' <www.international.gc.ca/trade-commerce/inclusive_trade-commerce_inclusif/itag-gaci/arrangement.aspx?lang=eng> accessed 8 May 2022.

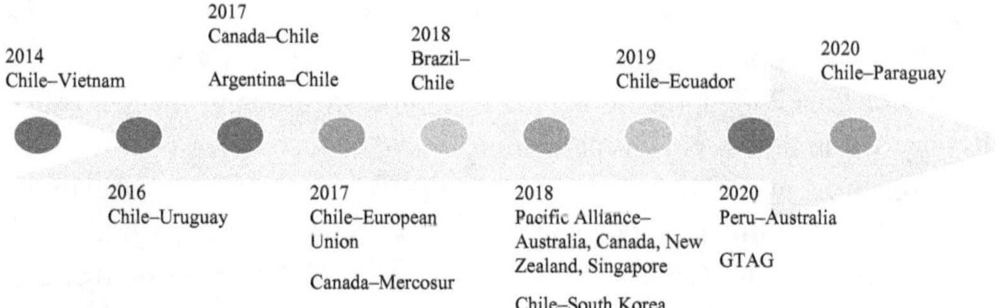

FIGURE 12.1 Timeline of South America's gender references in trade agreements.
Source: Authors' elaboration.

laws and regulations, calling on members not to weaken or reduce their protection in order to increase their trade and investment benefits. The three countries, by signing this agreement, have sought to ensure that trade policies are inclusive and that they become more inclusive with time, which is relevant for the post-pandemic economic recovery. The agreement's coverage has expanded as Mexico (6 October 2021), Colombia (13 June 2022), and Peru (13 June 2022) have acceded to it.

Moreover, the ongoing trade negotiation mandates on several FTAs including Canada–Mercosur, Chile–European Union, Chile–South Korea, Chile–Paraguay, and the associate members of the Pacific Alliance include trade and gender issues (Figure 12.1). As these negotiations are still in process, it is not clear which instrument or approach will be used to establish commitments on gender issues. Nevertheless, during the field research, interviewees expressed that it was most likely that trade and gender chapters would be used, following the templates of previous FTAs.[57] The consideration of gender chapters in the ongoing negotiations highlights the instrumental role that gender policies may play towards a sustainable socioeconomic development and reinforce the parties' commitment to effectively implement their normative policies and good practices towards gender equality and equity.[58]

12.5 ASSESSMENT OF GENDER ISSUES IN SOUTH AMERICAN FTAS

In order to understand how South American economies have mainstreamed gender issues, the trade and gender chapters in FTAs, as well as those in the GTAGA, are reviewed. This section provides an assessment of their content,

57 Informal communication with key stakeholders during fieldwork held by researchers. On file with author.

58 Carlos D'Elia, 'Análisis del TLC Chile-Uruguay' (Conexión INTAL 2017) <https://conexionintal.iadb.org/2017/09/01/analisis-del-tlc-chile-uruguay/> accessed 8 May 2022.

their enforcement, and their governance.[59] Table 12.1 presents a detailed comparison of the agreements' texts in the following dispositions: general provisions, international commitments, cooperation activities, and the establishment of trade and gender committees.[60]

12.5.1 *Content*

As the GTAGA is the most recent agreement and is solely focused on trade and gender, it is not surprising that it contains more gender-related sections. This agreement includes new sections focused on deepening commitments. For instance, Section 5 titled 'Gender and Responsible Business Conduct' aims for the parties to incorporate the principles of internationally recognized standards that address gender equality in their jurisdictions. Section 6 titled 'Discrimination in the Workplace' focuses on the participants that support the goal of promoting gender equality in the workplace. Section 7 titled 'Transparency' and Section 10 titled 'Trade and Gender Working Group" have been created to define the actions of the working group in gender cooperation. Finally, Section 13 refers to parties' options to invite other economies interested in pursuing inclusive trade and investment approaches to join them. Following this provision, in the context of the 2021 OECD Trade Ministers' meeting, Mexico was formally accepted into the GTAGA.[61]

It must be stated that the five agreements[62] analysed in this section were accomplished in a short period of time, and that they have a very similar structure. Moreover, they went through an important imitation process, being the first agreements and providing a template for those that followed. In this regard, they share the same structure. In general, the sections contained in all

[59] The classification of provisions used is from Lore Van den Putte and Jan Orbie, 'EU Bilateral Trade Agreements and the Surprising Rise of Labour Provisions' (2015) 31(3) *International Journal of Comparative Labour Law Industrial Relations* 263–283.

[60] Even though the chapter has referred to twelve agreements, on the one hand, Chile–Vietnam and Peru–Australia do not contain a trade and gender chapter and, on the other hand, as only the negotiation mandates are available for the negotiations between Canada and Mercosur, the Pacific Alliance and its associate members, and Chile with the European Union, South Korea, and Paraguay, these agreements are not thoroughly analysed.

[61] SUBREI, 'México ingresa al Arreglo Global de Comercio y Género integrado por Canadá, Chile y Nueva Zelandia' (2021) <www.subrei.gob.cl/sala-de-prensa/noticias/detalle-noticias/2021/10/06/m%C3%A9xico-ingresa-al-arreglo-global-de-comercio-y-g%C3%A9nero-integrado-por-canad%C3%A1-chile-y-nueva-zelandia> accessed 8 May 2022.

[62] The FTAs analysed were Chile–Uruguay, Chile–Canada, Chile–Argentina, Chile–Brazil, and Chile–Ecuador.

TABLE 12.1 *Gender and trade provisions in South American FTAs*

Agreement	Specific Chapter	Dispositions			
		General provisions	International commitments	Cooperation activities	Trade and gender committee
Chile–Uruguay FTA[a] Additional Protocol (ACE 35) Chile–Mercosur	Chapter 14	– Common objective – No reference to Goal 5 of SDG	– Overall commitment towards the effective implementation of international agreements	Skills enhancement; financial inclusion; agency and leadership; access to science, technology, and innovation; entrepreneurship	It should discuss potential cooperation activities, exchange information, discuss joint proposals, and manage administrate future topics
Chile–Canada FTA[b] (Modernisation)	Appendix II, Chapter N bis	– Common objective – SDG 5 – Agreement on Labour Cooperation and the OECD Guidelines for Multinational Enterprises	CEDAW Convention	Skills enhancement; financial inclusion; agency and leadership; access to science and engineering, technology, and innovation; entrepreneurship	It should discuss potential cooperation activities, exchange information, discuss joint proposals, and manage administrate future topics
Chile–Argentina FTA[c] Additional Protocol (ACE 35) Chile–Mercosur	Chapter 15	– Common objective – SDG 5	– CEDAW Convention – ILO Conventions (No. 100, 111, 156)	Skills enhancement; financial inclusion; agency and leadership; access to science, technology, and innovation; entrepreneurship	It should discuss potential cooperation activities, exchange information, discuss joint proposals, and manage administrate future topics

Chile–Brazil FTA[d] Additional Protocol (ACE 35) Chile–Mercosur	Chapter 18	– Common objective – SDG 5	– CEDAW Convention – Belem do Para	Skills enhancement; financial inclusion; agency and leadership; access to science, technology, and innovation; entrepreneurship	It should discuss potential cooperation activities, exchange information, discuss joint proposals, and manage administrate future topics
Chile–Ecuador[e]	Chapter 18	– Common objective – SDG 5	– CEDAW Convention – Belem do Para – Beijing Action Plan	Skills enhancement; financial inclusion; agency and leadership; access to science, technology, and innovation; entrepreneurship – Reference to funding sources	It should discuss potential cooperation activities, exchange information, discuss joint proposals, and manage future topics
Global Trade and Gender Arrangement, ITAG[f] (Chile, Canada, Colombia,	N/A	– Common objective – SDG 5	– CEDAW Convention – WTO Buenos Aires Declaration	Seventeen areas of cooperation aimed at enhancing the ability of women, including workers, entrepreneurs, businesswomen and business owners, to fully	It should discuss potential cooperation activities and its funding, exchange information, discuss joint proposals, and manage future topics

(*continued*)

TABLE 12.1 (*continued*)

Agreement	Specific Chapter	Dispositions			
		General provisions	International commitments	Cooperation activities	Trade and gender committee
Mexico, New Zealand, Peru)				access and benefit from the opportunities created by this Arrangement. – Reference to external funding sources	

Source: Authors' elaboration based on Cáceres *et al* (2021).

[a] Government of Chile, 'Chile–Uruguay FTA' <www.subrei.gob.cl/docs/default-source/acuerdos/uruguay/capitulos-uruguay/14-capitulo-14-g%C3%A9nero-y-comercio.pdf?sfvrsn=962199b6_2> accessed 19 April 2022.

[b] Government of Chile, 'Chile–Canada FTA' <www.subrei.gob.cl/docs/default-source/acuerdos/canad%C3%A1/modernizaci%C3%B3n-del-acuerdo/acuerdo-modificatorio-inversiones-genero-y-comercio.pdf?sfvrsn=2c5ae24d_2> accessed 8 May 2022.

[c] Government of Chile, 'Chile–Argentina FTA' <www.subrei.gob.cl/docs/default-source/acuerdos/argentina/capitulos-argentina/15-capitulo-15-g%C3%A9nero.pdf?sfvrsn=8326c19d_2> accessed 8 May 2022.

[d] SICE - OAS, 'Chile–Brazil FTA' <www.sice.oas.org/TPD/BRA_CHL/FTA_CHL_BRA_s.pdf> accessed 8 May 2022.

[e] SICE – OAS, 'Chile–Ecuador FTA' <www.sice.oas.org/Trade/CHL_ECU/Cap_18_s.pdf> accessed 8 May 2022.

[f] Government of Canada, 'GTGA' <www.international.gc.ca/trade-commerce/inclusive_trade-commerce_inclusif/itag-gaci/arrangement.aspx?lang=eng> accessed 8 May 2022.

agreements, except for the GTAGA, are: 'General Provisions', 'International Commitments', 'Cooperation Activities', 'Trade and Gender Committee', 'Consultations', and 'Non-application of Dispute Resolution'. In fact, these agreements not only share a similar structure, but the content of the legal texts is almost identical. This is not a new phenomenon in the negotiation of trade agreements, which are usually settled using common templates.[63]

Even though the chapters contain some mandatory elements, none of them requires a change in domestic regulations, as they mainly refer to cooperation activities. The chapters, within their general provisions, acknowledge the importance of incorporating a gender perspective into the promotion of inclusive economic growth. Moreover, they reaffirm parties' commitments towards multilateral conventions, such as equal pay for equal work, maternity protection, and the balance of family and professional life.

In the Canada–Chile FTA, the Argentina–Chile FTA, the Brazil–Chile FTA, the Chile–Ecuador FTA, and the GTAGA, as stated by a high-level government official,[64] agreements were reached to carry out Goal 5 of the SDGs. A mention of the SDGs was omitted in the Chile–Uruguay FTA, as the SDGs were just being implemented at the time the agreement was negotiated. In this vein, scholastic research argues that mainstreaming gender in trade policy is deemed a vehicle and an accelerator for achieving the SDGs,[65] since trade policy has a vital role in promoting many other SDGs in addition to SDG 5 on gender equality, such as alleviation of poverty (SDG 1), improvement of education (SDG 4), promotion of decent working conditions for economic growth (SDG 8), and reduction of inequalities (SDG 10).

Within the 'General Provisions', the recognition that increasing labour participation, decent jobs, and economic autonomy of women contribute to sustainable economic development is part of all agreements. Nevertheless, they differ in how the provision is incorporated according to the parties' international commitments. For instance, the Chile–Canada FTA and the GTAGA reaffirm the work done in OECD, which is not included in the other

63 Leonardo Baccini, Andrea Dür, Manfred Elsig, and Karolina Milewicz, 'The Design of Preferential Trade Agreements: A New Dataset in the Making' (2011) WTO Staff Working Paper No. ERSD-2011-10 <www.wto.org/english/res_e/reser_e/ersd201110_e.pdf> accessed 8 May 2022.

64 Personal communications with negotiators during fieldwork conducted by researchers. On file with authors.

65 Bensalem, 'Gender as Included in Bilateral and Multi-Party Trade and Integration Agreements' (n 40); Jeni Klugman, 'The 2030 Agenda and the Potential Contribution of Trade to Gender Equality' (ICSTD 2016) <www.tralac.org/images/docs/10610/the-2030-agenda-and-the-potential-contribution-of-trade-to-gender-equality-ictsd-september-2016.pdf> accessed 8 May 2022.

FTAs because Argentina, Brazil, Ecuador, and Uruguay are not members of the OECD.

An interesting difference within the agreements can be found in their second section, titled 'International Agreements'. The Chile–Uruguay FTA only refers to an overall commitment towards the effective implementation of international agreements. The agreements between Chile and Canada, Argentina and Chile, Chile and Ecuador, Brazil and Chile, and the GTAGA explicitly include the CEDAW; and Argentina also includes references to ILO Conventions on remuneration equity (No. 100), on work and occupation discrimination (No. 111), and on workers' family responsibilities (No. 156). As the GTAGA was signed after the 2017 WTO Ministerial Conference, it recalls the objectives of the WTO Joint Declaration on Trade and Women's Economic Empowerment and refers to the implementation of 'obligations under any other international agreements addressing women's rights or gender equality to which they are party' (Article 3.b). As explained by a high-level government official, this shows the quick evolution of gender-related chapters, and that countries have managed to include specific references to relevant international gender-related agreements in a short time. For instance, the Chile–Brazil FTA and the Chile–Ecuador FTA recall the Belem do Para Convention.[66] Chile and Ecuador have also made a commitment in their bilateral FTA to implement the 1995 Beijing Declaration and Platform for Action on the rights of women and girls and their empowerment. In this way, FTAs may signal the importance of various international treaties towards the accomplishment of a general well-being objective.

In terms of 'Cooperation Activities', all the above-mentioned FTAs as well as the GTAGA include almost identical provisions. This is the core of the trade and gender chapters, with activities that can be beneficial for women, considering areas such as skills enhancement; financial inclusion, agency, and leadership; access to science, technology, and innovation; entrepreneurship; and with respect to how trade and gender provisions are to be treated in the relevant chapters of the agreement. In addition, the Chile–Vietnam FTA and the Peru–Australia FTA also included 'gender' directly in their cooperation activities.

Nevertheless, it must be highlighted that the trade and gender chapters do not include a specific programme on cooperation, and do not define budgets,

[66] OAS, 'Inter-American Convention on the Prevention, Punishment and Eradication of Violence against Women' <www.oas.org/juridico/english/treaties/a-61.html> accessed 8 May 2022.

baselines, targets, objectives, measurements, or other relevant characteristics to enforce the cooperation. In this sense, cooperation activities are subject to the will of in-office administrations. Nevertheless, it can be argued that the most recent agreements (GTAGA and the Chile–Ecuador FTA) explicitly refer to parties' commitments to find international donors, private sector entities, and NGOs to assist in the development and implementation of cooperation activities.

The chapter on trade and gender in the Chile–Canada FTA is the only FTA which contains sections on 'Relation to the Agreement on Labour Cooperation' and 'Definitions'. With respect to labour cooperation, the section states that if there is any inconsistency between the chapter and the Agreement on Labour Cooperation or its successor, the latter will prevail to the extent of the inconsistency. Regarding 'Definitions', the Agreement on Labour Cooperation and the Agreement on Environmental Cooperation are defined and contextualized. Hence, there is a clear priority given to labour provisions over gender issues in this agreement.

12.5.2 *Enforcement*

One of the most important articles examined is the final provision within these chapters on the 'Non-application of Dispute Resolution'. Amongst international treaties, a crucial characteristic of trade agreements has been their lack of enforceability. This has been possible due to the exclusion of these provisions and chapters from the jurisdiction of the agreements' dispute resolution mechanisms that could use the annulment of trade preferences as a leverage mechanism to ensure parties' compliance. As stated in Article 14.6 of the Chile–Uruguay FTA, Article N bis-06 of the Chile–Canada FTA, Article 15.6 of the Chile–Argentina FTA, Article 18.9 of the Chile–Ecuador FTA, and Article 18.7 of the Chile–Brazil FTA, no party may initiate a dispute for a breach of gender-related provisions.

It can be argued that such an exclusion makes the commitments on gender hortatory in nature. Therefore, the effective implementation of 'International Agreements' or 'Cooperation activities' are left to the willingness of the parties (and incumbent administrations), as the breach of gender-related provisions is not subject to any kind of retaliation. In this context, two lines of thought were encountered during the interviews.[67] On the one hand, some interviewees, especially from the public sector, argue that as the main impact of the

[67] Personal communication with key stakeholders during research fieldwork. On file with authors.

inclusion of gender chapters in FTAs may not be on trade relations, the mere inclusion of a chapter reflects government's willingness to incorporate and visualize this topic, which validates a gender perspective within trade policy agendas. On the other hand, interviewees from academia and international organizations have pointed out that including current chapters to the dispute settlement mechanism is not useful as they do not contain strong provisions to be enforced and they are built on cooperation activities without concrete legal commitments.

This situation is very similar to the evolution of environmental and labour clauses within trade agreements, which, at the beginning, were included as side agreements. However, they are now becoming a substantial part of trade negotiation agendas. The same can be argued for regulations relating to trade in services, which have been included at the multilateral level since the Uruguay Round negotiations that established the WTO (1986–1994). However, during the 1990s, not every economy wanted to include them in their bilateral treaties. Nowadays, almost every trade agreement includes not only a trade-in-services chapter, but also specific services-related chapters such as financial services, telecommunication services, movement of businesspersons, digital trade, amongst others. Therefore, it is not unlikely that new agreements may include gender-related chapters, with enforceable provisions.

12.5.3 *Governance*

In each of the above-mentioned FTAs, a Trade and Gender Committee is established to manage the possible outcomes of the agreement in areas such as potential cooperation activities, exchange information, discuss joint proposals, and manage any other related topic that may arise in the future.[68] This committee is supposed to meet at least once a year and it should review the implementation of the chapter after two years. Regarding the 'Consultations' section, the five chapters state that the contracting parties will make all necessary efforts to solve any issues that may arise regarding the chapter's application and interpretation, through consultations and dialogue.[69] The GTAGA states that each participant will designate a contact point for trade

[68] Trade and Gender Committees are referred to in: Art. 14.4, Chile–Uruguay FTA; Art. N bis-04, Chile–Canada FTA; Art. 15.4, Chile–Argentina FTA; Art. 18.4, Chile–Brazil FTA; Art. 18.5, Chile–Ecuador FTA; Art. 10, GTAGA.

[69] Consultations are referred to in: Art. 14.5, Chile–Uruguay FTA; Art. N bis-05, Chile–Canada FTA; Art. 15.5, Chile–Argentina FTA; Art. 18.6, Chile–Brazil FTA; Art. 18.8, Chile–Ecuador FTA.

and gender to coordinate the implementation of this arrangement.[70] Even though it contains the section on 'Differences in interpretation and implementation', it only states that participants should resolve any differences on the interpretation or application of this arrangement amicably and in good faith. However, there are no proper mechanisms set up for the consultation processes. The most advanced provisions in this respect can be found in the Chile–Ecuador FTA, which entered into force in May 2022. This agreement not only defines contact points and functions but also provides for a consultation procedure.[71] This process is based on a mutually satisfactory resolution establishing timelines for each step. First, the affected party will present a request through contact points to solve the matter; if it is not solved, the request is transferred to the committee; and in case there is no resolution, it may be raised to the related ministers. At any step, good offices and conciliation can be used, and if an agreement is reached, the final report will be publicly available.

As the discussions show, these chapters have made various strides in mainstreaming gender in trade agreements, but they have various deficiencies. First, instead of including specific gender-related standards that could affect trade under the agreements, reference is made to the implementation of gender equality commitments included in global conventions. Second, milestones or specific goals are not included. Third, dispute-settlement mechanisms do not apply to such provisions. Fourth, the harmonization of gender-related legislation between the parties is not mandated. Fifth, potential impacts of trade liberalization pursued under the agreements on women's well-being and economic empowerment are not addressed or mentioned in these agreements.[72]

12.6 CONCLUSION

In South America, a gender perspective has been included in foreign affairs as well as in trade policies. The region has pioneered the incorporation of gender in trade policies, including in both trade negotiations and trade promotion. This is particularly true in the case of Chile. This chapter has analysed how South American economies have mainstreamed gender issues in their trade agreements, identifying their common elements and evolution. For this

[70] Art. 11, GTAGA.
[71] *See* Art. 18.7, Chile–Ecuador FTA.
[72] Zarrilli, 'The New Way of Addressing Gender Inequality Issues in Trade Agreements' (n 2).

purpose, the chapter has reviewed the incorporation of gender provisions in bilateral trade agreements, Mercosur, and the Pacific Alliance.

At a regional level, both Mercosur and the Pacific Alliance have incorporated gender issues into their working agendas. Nevertheless, most of the work related to gender has been on social or institutional policymaking and not with respect to trade instruments. In other words, trade instruments lack a gender perspective or gender-related provisions, especially in regional economic integration instruments. It has been recognized that incorporating a gender perspective into trade policymaking can aid in achieving inclusive and sustainable development. Moreover, as both Mercosur and the Pacific Alliance have referred to their interest in gender topics, this may become a stepping stone towards regional convergence.[73]

Regarding bilateral agreements, the inclusion of a gender-related chapter has become a common element in the latest agreements that are in operation, such as in the Chile–Uruguay FTA, the Chile–Canada FTA, the Argentina–Chile FTA, the Brazil–Chile FTA, and the Chile–Ecuador FTA. These trade and gender chapters consider trade as an engine for economic growth, thereby improving women's access to opportunities and removing barriers to enhance their participation in national and international economies, and contributing to sustainable and inclusive economic development, competitiveness, prosperity and society's well-being. These objectives have been reaffirmed by the GTAGA.

Although legally there is no mechanism to enforce the parties' commitments on trade and gender, the mere inclusion of gender-related chapters is not only an important step towards guaranteeing that trade may benefit women and men equally, but a representation of an important milestone towards gender equity. First, the inclusion of such chapters is a recognition of the relevance of incorporating a gender perspective within trade negotiations. These chapters take into consideration the relevance of the nexus between trade and gender, and the importance for countries to take actions towards allowing women to benefit from trade liberalization. They identify ways to enhance women's participation in international trade, as well as the relevance of sound public policies that may be directed to use trade as a tool for achieving gender equity.

Second, the evolution of the chapters' negotiations allows the relevant elements in the trade and gender relationship to be identified and assessed. As reviewed in this chapter, the Chile–Uruguay FTA does not deepen the

[73] Cáceres and Muñoz, 'The Gendered Impact of COVID-19' (n 1).

legality of commitments in certain provisions. For example, the recent FTAs signed between Brazil and Chile, Chile and Ecuador, and the GTAGA, have shown detailed specifications in certain elements and references to international agreements (such as the UN SDGs, CEDAW, or the ILO conventions). However, the Chile–Uruguay FTA does not refer to any agreement in particular. In this way, as new chapters are negotiated, more specific issues are encompassed within the agreement, allowing the best policies to be formulated.

Third, the evolution of agreements must be taken into consideration. Although at this point gender-related chapters are not subject to dispute-resolution mechanisms, agreements do evolve. For instance, the FTAs between Chile and Canada, and Chile and Ecuador have been outcomes of a renegotiation process of their predecessors. This evolution must be considered for each agreement, and for trade negotiations in general. As new topics arise, they are initially included as side agreements or non-enforceable chapters (which is the case for gender chapters). However, once the topic is more widely accepted by the international community as relevant and important, new agreements are more likely to include these topics as binding and enforceable commitments.

Nevertheless, for trade policy instruments to be drivers for women's economic empowerment, it is necessary to strengthen commitments, elaborate concrete programmes for the development of cooperation activities, and conduct periodical *ex ante* and *ex post* assessments. Trade and gender chapters should not only contain declarative provisions, but also obligations to undertake regulatory changes at the domestic level and guarantee their compliance. Moreover, cooperation activities, which are the core of these agreements, need to be planned accordingly, for which timelines, specific activities, areas to cover, and budgets are required. Besides, for countries to improve women's participation in trade, women's presence in each economic sector should be studied and acknowledged through sex-disaggregated data. This will become the first step towards conducting quantitative and qualitative assessments to see the expected impacts of trade policies on women, as well as the actual changes in the economy after their implementation.

13

Gender Mainstreaming in Trade Agreements

Best Practice Examples and Challenges in the Asia-Pacific

AMRITA BAHRI

ABSTRACT

In recent years, more and more countries have included different kinds of gender considerations in their trade agreements. Yet many countries have still not signed their very first agreement with a gender equality-related provision. Though most of the agreements negotiated by countries in the Asia-Pacific region have not explicitly accommodated gender concerns, a limited number of trade agreements signed by countries in the region have presented a distinct approach: the nature of provisions, drafting style, location in the agreements, and topic coverage of such provisions contrast with the gender-mainstreaming approach employed by the Americas or other regions. This chapter provides a comprehensive account and assessment of gender-related provisions included in the existing trade agreements negotiated by countries in the Asia-Pacific, explains the extent to which gender concerns are mainstreamed in these agreements, and summarizes the factors that impede such mainstreaming efforts in the region.

13.1 INTRODUCTION

Without exception, women across the globe have suffered from the economic and social consequences of the COVID-19 pandemic.[1] In particular, women

[1] WTO, 'The Economic Impact of COVID-19 on Women in Vulnerable Sectors and Economies' (2020) <https://doi.org/10.30875/74a82a3d-en> accessed 8 May 2022. The study outlines the economic impact of the pandemic on vulnerable sectors including women; Amrita Bahri, 'Women at the Frontline of COVID-19: Can Gender Mainstreaming in Free Trade Agreements Help?' (2020) 23(3) *Journal of International Economic Law* 563–582. The

entrepreneurs and employees have been disproportionately impacted due to the pre-pandemic disadvantages they have faced in the economic, social, financial, and regulatory ecosystems in which they operate.[2] These disadvantages may include, but are not limited to, lack of access to educational opportunities; the digital divide between men and women caused by lack of affordability and digital know-how; lack of access to productive resources such as land, finances, and other assets; disproportionately high tariff and non-tariff barriers faced by women-owned businesses engaged in agriculture and textiles; lack of access to trade-related information and business networks; and disproportionately high burdens in discharging household responsibilities.[3] The COVID-19 pandemic is magnifying the impact of the pre-existing barriers that women face, bringing about massive loss of jobs and business opportunities, declining access to education as it goes online, spiralling increases in household responsibilities, and domestic violence against women.[4] Recent studies have shown how limited gains made in respect of gender equality are now at serious risk of being rolled back.[5]

Countries can employ two different approaches to counter these challenges: a bottom-up and a top-down approach. Using a bottom-up approach, countries can directly try to change national laws, culture, and social norms at the domestic level, which then permeates to the higher levels of policy making. Alternatively (or complementarily), in the top-down approach, they can use international law to create incentives to bring about a change at the domestic level.

In the realm of women's empowerment, international trade law and policies can form part of this 'top-down' approach. The WTO's Joint Declaration

author presents multiple reasons for how COVID-19 has put women in the frontline and explores how trade agreements can help.

2 These barriers are discussed in World Bank, 'Women, Business and the Law' (World Bank Reports 2010, 2012, 2014, 2016, 2018, 2019 and 2020); World Bank and WTO 'Women and Trade: The Role of Trade in Promoting Gender Equality' (2020) <https://wbl.worldbank.org/en/wbl> accessed 8 May 2022.

3 ITC, 'Unlocking Markets for Women to Trade' (2015) <https://intracen.org/resources/publications/unlocking-markets-for-women-to-trade> accessed 8 May 2022.

4 Simonetta Zarrilli and Henri Luomaranta, 'Gender and Unemployment: Lessons from the COVID-19 Pandemic' (UNCTAD 8 April 2021) <https://unctad.org/news/gender-and-unemployment-lessons-covid-19-pandemic> accessed 8 May 2022; Gabriela Ramos, 'Women at the Core of the Fight against COVID-19 Crisis' (OECD 1 April 2020) <www.oecd.org/coronavirus/policy-responses/women-at-the-core-of-the-fight-against-covid-19-crisis-553a8269/> accessed 8 May 2022.

5 WTO, 'The Economic Impact of COVID-19 on Women' (n 1); Bahri, 'Women at the Frontline of COVID-19' (n 1); World Bank, 'Women, Business and the Law' (n 2).

on Trade and Women's Economic Empowerment[6] is an important step in this direction. The Declaration, signed in December 2017 at Buenos Aires by almost 70 per cent of the WTO membership, reaffirms that 'international trade and investment are engines of economic growth for both developing and developed countries, and that improving women's access to opportunities and removing barriers to their participation in national and international economies contributes to sustainable economic development'.[7] The Declaration is aligned with and complements the United Nations (UN) Convention on the Elimination of all Forms of Discrimination Against Women (CEDAW) 1979[8] and Goal 5 of the Sustainable Development Goals (UN SDGs) in the UN 2030 Agenda for Sustainable Development.[9]

Moreover, recent trends show a promise in terms of the role that Free Trade Agreements (FTAs) can play in this respect.[10] Since 2016, there has been an upsurge of FTAs that are carving out space for gender-equality concerns through the incorporation of provisions and chapters on trade and gender. These trends show that FTAs can act as laboratories in which to experiment with the complex amalgamation of trade and gender concerns. In this race towards making trade more inclusive, have FTAs proven to be trend-setters? This chapter shows that they have pushed for an inclusive trade agenda aiming to distribute trade benefits in a gender-just manner.

This chapter provides a comprehensive account and assessment of gender-related provisions included in the existing trade agreements negotiated by countries in the Asia-Pacific, considers the extent to which gender concerns are mainstreamed in these agreements, and examines the reasons that impede such mainstreaming efforts in the region. Section 13.2 provides an overview of different gender-mainstreaming trends in trade agreements. Section 13.3 clarifies what gender mainstreaming entails in the trade policy context. Section 13.4 provides an overview of those trade agreements signed by Asia-Pacific countries that have accommodated gender-equality concerns. Section

6 WTO, 'Joint Declaration on Trade and Women's Economic Empowerment on the Occasion of the WTO Ministerial Conference in Buenos Aires in December 2017' (2017) <www.wto.org/english/thewto_e/minist_e/mc11_e/genderdeclarationmc11_e.pdf> accessed 8 May 2022 (Declaration 2017).

7 Ibid.

8 UN, 'Convention on the Elimination of All Forms of Discrimination against Women', UNGA Res. 34/180 (18 December 1979).

9 UNDP, 'The Sustainable Development Goals' (2015) Goal 5.

10 The expression 'free trade agreement' or 'FTA' in this chapter is used to refer to all international trade agreements (except the WTO multilateral agreements) and may include regional trade agreements, plurilateral agreements, bilateral agreements, economic partnership agreements, association agreements, strategic partnership agreements, and others.

13.5 concludes and provides a discussion on potential barriers and hesitations that impede gender-mainstreaming efforts in this region.

13.2 AN OVERVIEW OF FTAS MAINSTREAMING GENDER CONCERNS

In recent years, more and more countries have included gender considerations in their trade agreements, albeit in different ways, formats, and drafting styles. Some FTAs have a whole chapter with a number of provisions on trade and gender, but no compulsory and enforceable obligations.[11] Some FTAs have a single gender-explicit provision, but that single provision creates a legally binding obligation.[12] Some countries have sought to work on these concerns via cooperative actions, including exchange of best practices and organization of capacity-building workshops;[13] while others have reserved the right to regulate particular services that directly impact women or services related to nutrition or childcare for instance.[14] In some agreements, all we find are general statements wherein parties acknowledge the importance of the role of women in trade and commerce.[15] In other agreements, we find affirming and reaffirming provisions, wherein parties commit to engaging in concrete actions or reaffirm their commitments made under other international instruments.[16] Moreover, several agreements are completely silent or merely make a single mention of expressions relating to gender equality,

[11] Modernized Canada–Chile Free Trade Agreement (CCFTA) (enforced on 5 February 2019) and Modernized Canada–Israel Free Trade Agreement (CIFTA) (enforced on 1 September 2019). Both include standalone chapters on gender; Canada–Chile FTA (chapter N bis) and Canada–Israel FTA (chapter 13).

[12] Stabilisation and Association Agreement between the European Communities and their Member States, of the one part, and the Republic of Montenegro, of the other part (1 May 2010) Art. 101. It obliges Montenegro to adjust its domestic legislation to provide for working conditions and equal opportunities for women and men.

[13] Modernized Canada–Chile Free Trade Agreement (CCFTA) (5 February 2019). It includes multiple cooperation activities focused on enhancing women's access to trade as employees, employers and consumers.

[14] Free Trade Agreement between New Zealand and the Republic of Korea (20 December 2015).

[15] The Canada–Honduras Free Trade Agreement (1 October 2014). It only contains a general statement on the importance of gender equality within Annex 1; it is a cooperation activity mentioned in best endeavour language.

[16] The Free Trade Agreement between the United States of America and the Republic of Korea (15 March 2012) (Parties reaffirm their commitments to ILO Conventions); Modernized Canada–Chile Free Trade Agreement (CCFTA) (enforced on 5 February 2019) (Parties reaffirm their commitments to CEDAW).

and others mention gender-explicit expressions more than forty times in their main text.[17]

In most agreements, gender-related provisions are non-binding, and are drafted with non-mandatory expressions and 'soft' permissive grammatical constructions.[18] However, a handful of countries have drafted such provisions with legally binding obligations.[19] Gender-related provisions are considered legally binding when they are drafted with mandatory verbs (such as 'shall' or 'must') and their implementation is compulsory in nature, and enforceable under dispute settlement mechanisms.[20] Most of the gender-related provisions are found in chapters on cooperation, which mostly are excluded from the agreement's dispute settlement mechanism's scope.

The topics addressed in gender provisions also vary from one region to the other, as some regions have included provisions on social and healthcare concerns of women (such as Asia-Pacific),[21] and others have covered purely economic and market-oriented interests (such as North or South America).[22] The location of gender provisions in different agreements is also diverse, as they are included in agreements' preambles, objectives and principles clauses, stand-alone chapters, side agreements, specific provisions, cross-cutting provisions or chapters, protocols, arrangements, and even annexes.[23]

Variations are also found in the level of readiness countries have developed over the years to discuss and negotiate gender concerns in the context of trade policy. On one hand, various countries in North and South America, Africa, and the European Union are leading gender-mainstreaming efforts.[24] On the other hand, many countries are yet to take their very first step in this regard.[25]

[17] For instance, Modernized Canada–Chile Free Trade Agreement (CCFTA) (5 February 2019).

[18] Modernized Canada–Chile Free Trade Agreement (CCFTA) (5 February 2019); Modernized Canada–Israel Free Trade Agreement (CIFTA) (1 September 2019).

[19] For instance, Agreement establishing an Association between the European Union and its Member States, on the one hand, and Central America on the other, OJL 346 (15 December 2012) and the United States–Mexico–Canada Agreement (USMCA) (1 July 2020).

[20] Graham Cook, *A Digest of WTO Jurisprudence on Public International Law Concepts and Principles* (Cambridge University Press 2015) chapters 15 and 16, 225–360.

[21] Amrita Bahri, 'Gender Mainstreaming in Free Trade Agreements: A Regional Analysis and Good Practice Examples' (Gender, Social Inclusion and Trade Knowledge Product Series 2021), <https://wtochairs.org/sites/default/files/7.%20Gender%20mainstreaming%20in%20FTAs_final%20%286%29.pdf> accessed 8 May 2022.

[22] Ibid.

[23] José-Antonio Monteiro, 'Gender-Related Provisions in Regional Trade Agreements' (2021) WTO Staff Working Papers ERSD-2018-15 <www.wto.org/english/res_e/reser_e/ersd201815_e.pdf> accessed 8 May 2022.

[24] Bahri, 'Gender Mainstreaming in Free Trade Agreements' (n 21).

[25] Ibid.

For example, several countries in Asia-Pacific have either opposed the inclusion of gender concerns in trade policy instruments or are reluctant to engage in such negotiations without fully comprehending the impact such provisions can have on their trade, economy, sovereignty, and social concerns.[26]

Most of the agreements negotiated by countries in Asia-Pacific are gender-blind, as they do not contain any gender-related or gender-considerate provision.[27] As compared to other regions, the Asia-Pacific countries have negotiated the lowest number of agreements with provisions relating to gender-equality concerns. For example, 38 per cent of trade agreements signed by North American countries have included at least one gender-explicit provision.[28] For South American countries, this number is just over 20 per cent, and it is 32 per cent in the case of African countries.[29] As many as 78 per cent of the EU's agreements contain at least one gender-explicit provision, even though most of these agreements are not merely trade agreements in a strict sense, and are drafted as association or integration agreements that include gender commitments in social or cooperation pillars of such agreements.[30] Out of all trade agreements signed by the Asia-Pacific countries, only 14 per cent have incorporated one or more gender-related or gender-explicit provision.[31]

26 Ibid.

27 For instance, Korea–India FTA (1 January 2010) and Korea–Viet Nam FTA (20 December 2015).

28 Author's calculations. For the purpose of this study, the author has assessed all trade agreements that are currently in force and notified to the WTO (as of 15 June 2021), independent of the relative importance of trade flows between parties. Agreements or economic integration mechanisms not yet notified to the WTO or not yet in force are excluded from this study. However, selected trade agreements that are not yet notified or not yet in force are considered to a limited extent if they contain gender-related best practice provisions that can add new or support existing findings presented in this study. Those provisions which use terms directly related to 'gender', 'women', 'female', 'maternity', or a similar expression in the provision in an explicit manner are considered 'gender-explicit provisions' in this study. 'Gender-implicit provisions' are those provisions which address the issues of gender in an indirect and implicit manner through areas such as, but not limited to, human rights, vulnerable groups focus, labour discrimination, corporate social responsibility, intellectual property rights, and SMEs. These findings are initially published in Bahri, 'Gender Mainstreaming in Free Trade Agreements' (n 21).

29 Author's calculations.

30 Author's calculations.

31 The focus of this section is on bilateral trade agreements notified to the WTO and does not address gender issues in regional or transregional integration mechanisms such as the Asia-Pacific Economic Cooperation (APEC) forum, nor within the Association of Southeast Asian Nations (ASEAN) or the Comprehensive and Progressive Trans-Pacific Partnership (CPTPP).

These numbers show that the Asia-Pacific is behind other regions in respect of using trade agreements to further gender equality concerns. Moreover, unlike gender provisions on market, employment, or resource access negotiated by countries in the Americas or East Africa, the focus of gender-related provisions in Asia-Pacific has been on women's personal welfare concerns.[32] A handful of agreements that have included such commitments have mainly envisaged women as mothers as they have focused on enhancing women's access to affordable childcare facilities, and other maternity benefits, and protection of healthcare interests.[33] In addition, the style of these provisions is in stark contrast to how such provisions have been drafted by countries in other regions.

13.3 WHAT IS GENDER MAINSTREAMING IN A TRADE POLICY CONTEXT?

Gender mainstreaming can be defined as 'the (re)organization, improvement, development, and evaluation of policy processes so that gender equality perspective is incorporated in all policies at all levels at all stages, by the actors normally involved in policymaking'.[34] It is a means to achieve gender equality. Gender mainstreaming in FTAs means the inclusion of gender concerns in the drafting and implementation of FTAs. This is a process by which parties seek to include the gender perspective in trade liberalization efforts and policies. The process of mainstreaming affirms a country's commitment, understanding, and political will to reduce gender inequalities through trade policies and agreements. The process also aims to maximize the positive impact and minimize the negative impact of trade agreements on women's empowerment goals. The term 'gender responsiveness' is also used extensively in this chapter, and refers to an assessment of how sensitive, informed, or committed the provisions of a trade agreement are to gender equality.[35] In

[32] Bahri, 'Gender Mainstreaming in Free Trade Agreements' (n 21).

[33] Australia–New Zealand Closer Economic Relations Trade Agreement (1 January 1983 (G), 1 January 1989 (G)); Hong Kong, China–New Zealand Closer Economic Partnership Agreement (1 January 2011).

[34] This is the definition proposed by an expert group convened by the Council of Europe (1998).

[35] As defined within the UN Gender Equality Glossary, 'gender' refers to 'the roles, behaviors, activities, and attributes that a given society at a given time considers appropriate for men and women. In addition to the social attributes and opportunities associated with being male and female and the relationships between women and men and girls and boys, gender also refers to the relations between women and those between men. These attributes, opportunities and relationships are socially constructed and are learned through socialization processes. They are context/time-specific and changeable. Gender determines what is expected, allowed and

other words, the way and extent to which an agreement mainstreams gender equality considerations defines how responsive that agreement is to gender equality concerns.

Gender mainstreaming in trade agreements can be employed to strengthen women's empowerment. FTAs can play an important role in reducing gender inequality because countries can encourage their trade partners to create laws and procedures that can reduce barriers and create encouraging conditions for women's participation in trade and commerce.[36] In this manner, countries can use these negotiating instruments to incentivize change at the domestic level in other countries in exchange for enhanced or unfettered market access. In short, the lure of market access to important markets can be used to enhance gender equality through FTAs.

13.4 TRADE AGREEMENTS SIGNED BY ASIA-PACIFIC COUNTRIES: BEST PRACTICE EXAMPLES

The Asia-Pacific region is home to almost half of the world's population, and hence any action to reduce gender inequality by countries in this region can impact the lives of many women in the world. Moreover, the region accounts for almost 37 per cent of world GDP at purchasing power parity and major economic powers such as the United States, China, Australia, India, Singapore, Japan, and Taiwan are also situated here.[37] These states in Asia-Pacific play an important economic role as they contribute significantly to the world economy.[38]

valued in a woman or a man in a given context'. Gender equality 'refers to the equal rights, responsibilities and opportunities of women and men and girls and boys. Equality does not mean that women and men will become the same but that women's and men's rights, responsibilities and opportunities will not depend on whether they are born male or female. Gender equality implies that the interests, needs and priorities of both women and men are taken into consideration, recognizing the diversity of different groups of women and men. Gender equality is not a women's issue but should concern and fully engage men as well as women. Equality between women and men is seen both as a human rights issue and as a precondition for, and indicator of, sustainable people-centered development'. See UN Women, 'Gender Equality Glossary' <www.un.org/womenwatch/osagi/conceptsandefinitions.htm> accessed 8 May 2022.

36 Amrita Bahri, 'Measuring the Gender-Responsiveness of Free Trade Agreements: Using a Self-Evaluation Maturity Framework' (2019) 14(11) *Global Trade & Customs Journal* 517–527.

37 World Population Review, 'Asia-Pacific Countries 2022' <https://worldpopulationreview.com/country-rankings/apac-countries> accessed 8 May 2022.

38 IMF, 'Regional Economic Outlook for Asia and Pacific' (October 2021) <www.imf.org/en/Publications/REO/APAC/Issues/2021/10/15/regional-economic-outlook-for-asia-and-pacific-october-2021> accessed 8 May 2022; FAO, 'Economic and Demographic Developments' <www.fao.org/3/w7705e/w7705e07.htm> accessed 8 May 2022.

In total, the 66 countries in the Asia-Pacific region have notified a total of 152 trade agreements to the WTO that are currently in force.[39] Amongst these, 22 agreements have gender-explicit provisions; that is, only about 14 per cent of its agreements have some sort of gender consideration.[40] The countries that lead the gender mainstreaming trend in this region are Australia, New Zealand, Singapore, South Korea, and Vietnam, and most recently Japan. The most commonly found provisions are drafted in the form of 'right to regulate' reservations. These reservations help countries to strike a balance between protection of investment or trade liberalization and the signatory's policy space to regulate on issues such as national security, public health, environment, and gender equality, among others.[41]

13.4.1 *Best Practice Examples*

The FTAs' gender provisions negotiated by countries in this region mostly relate to women's personal welfare concerns. Access to affordable childcare, and other maternity benefits, protection of healthcare interests, and physical safety are considered some of the effective enablers for empowering women in this region. The Australia–New Zealand Closer Economic Agreement (ANZCERTA),[42] for example, contains a reservation wherein New Zealand reserves the right to regulate in the area of social services, including childcare.[43] Childcare challenges pose a significant barrier to work, especially for mothers, who disproportionately take on unpaid responsibilities when they cannot find affordable childcare.[44] Provision of affordable childcare facilities is therefore vital, as their absence limits women's employment opportunities and educational aspirations.

39 WTO, 'Regional Trade Agreements Database' <https://rtais.wto.org/UI/PublicMaintainRTAHome.aspx> accessed 8 September 2022

40 The focus of this section is on bilateral trade agreements notified to the WTO and does not address gender issues in regional or transregional integration mechanisms such as the APEC forum, or within the ASEAN or CPTPP. Findings initially presented in: Bahri, 'Gender Mainstreaming in Free Trade Agreements' (n 21).

41 David Gaukrodger, 'The Balance between Investor Protection and the Right to Regulate in Investment Treaties: A Scoping Paper' (2017) OECD Working Papers on International Investment No. 2017/02 <https://doi.org/10.1787/82786801-en> accessed 8 May 2022.

42 Australia–New Zealand Closer Economic Relations Trade Agreement (1 January 1989).

43 Ibid Annex II.

44 ILO, 'The Gender Gap in Employment: What's Holding Women Back?' (ILO Infostories 2017) <www.ilo.org/infostories/en-GB/Stories/Employment/barriers-women#footer> accessed 8 May 2022.

Similar provisions regarding the right to regulate in respect of childcare services are also found in the Peru–South Korea FTA[45] and the South Korea–Central America FTA.[46] In addition, in Annex I to the South Korea–Central America FTA, Costa Rica reserves the right to prevent the issuance of licences to sell alcoholic beverages in certain zones and areas (such as near child nutrition centres). This is not a gender-explicit provision per se, but it is relevant in the sense that it prohibits the selling of alcohol around child nutrition centres, and it is mostly women that are responsible for child nutrition and other caregiving responsibilities, which include accompanying children to such centres.[47] Therefore, such a restriction may enhance the physical safety of mothers regarding people who may, under the influence of alcohol, engage in socially undesirable behaviour and hence may become a cause of concern for their safety.

The signatories to the FTA between Hong Kong, China, and New Zealand[48] reserve the right to regulate certain services that relate to female professionals and women's health interests. In Annex II and III to Chapter 13 on Services, the signatories reserve the right to regulate services provided by nurses, a profession which is significantly dominated by female professionals.[49] The reservation also extends to services relating to childcare, maternity care, services provided by midwives, services relating to supervision during pregnancy, childbirth, and the supervision of the mother after birth.

In the agreement between Association of Southeast Asian Nations and South Korea,[50] Singapore reserves the right to regulate certain types of social services including statutory supervision services related to the provision of accommodation for women and girls detained in a place of safety under

45 Free Trade Agreement between the Republic of Korea and the Republic of Peru (1 August 2011).

46 Republic of Korea–Central America Free Trade Agreement (1 November 2019).

47 Lisa C. Smith, Usha Ramakrishnan, Aida Ndiaye, Lawrence Haddad, and Reynaldo Martorell, 'The Importance of Women's Status for Child Nutrition in Developing Countries' (2003) International Food Policy Research Institute Research Report No. 131 <https://ebrary.ifpri.org/utils/getfile/collection/p15738coll2/id/48032/filename/43490.pdf> accessed 8 May 2022.

48 Free Trade Agreement between the Government of the People's Republic of China and the Government of New Zealand (1 October 2008).

49 Nuriye Buyukkayaci Duman, 'Reflections of Female Domination in the Profession over the Nursing Strength: Turkey Sample' (2012) 3(24) *International Journal of Business and Social Science* 182–187.

50 Agreement on trade in goods under the framework agreement on Comprehensive Economic Cooperation among the Governments of the Member Countries of the Association of Southeast Asian Nations and the Republic of Korea (1 January 2010).

Section 160 of the Singapore's Women's Charter (CPC 93312).[51] Section 160 stipulates four cases in which the Director-General (DG)[52] may order the detention or commitment of a woman or girl: (a) where a lawful guardian has requested the DG to detain her in a place of safety or to commit her to the care of a fit individual; or (b) if the DG feels that she is in need of protection and whose lawful guardian cannot be found; or (c) if the DG believes that she has been ill-treated and is in need of protection; (d) for whom the DG considers to be in moral danger. In these cases, Singapore reserves the right to regulate its supervision services for women and girls. This provision can be construed as both favourable and unfavourable for women and girls. It can be seen as a favourable provision as it seeks to ensure the physical safety of women and girls. However, the fourth instance mentioned above, where the DG can order detention or 'commitment' if a woman or a girl is considered to be in moral danger, gives unfettered discretion to the DG. This is because the concept of 'morality' is highly subjective and may change or evolve from place to place and with the passage of time. Another problem with this provision is the use of the word 'commitment'. It is not defined in the statute itself, but the scope of this expression could extend to decisions relating to adoption, allocation to foster care homes or welfare centres, or even decisions related to matrimony. If that is the case, and if the statute is interpreted to allow the DG to interfere with a woman's or a girl's life in all these aspects owing to the DG's moral judgement, it could be seen as an undue interference with, and a violation of, women's right to freedom. Hence, in this sense, such a legal provision could be a double-edged sword and its impact would depend on how it is applied by the country.

The above-mentioned examples show that, unlike in other regions, several countries in the Asia-Pacific region have signed FTAs with legally binding reservations. South Korea and New Zealand seem to have currently led this approach, as they have negotiated several agreements with a binding 'right to regulate' provision. In the New Zealand–South Korea FTA,[53] parties have reserved the right to regulate certain health and social services that relate to female professionals and women's health interests. In Annex II, which relates to Services and Investment, parties have reserved the right to adopt or

51 Singapore's Women's Charter (CPC 93312) §120 <https://sso.agc.gov.sg/Act/WC1961?ProvIds=P1I-#pr2-> accessed 8 May 2022.

52 'Director-General' means the Director-General of Social Welfare and includes any person who is authorized by him to perform any of the duties or exercise any of the powers of the Director-General under this Act (Part I, Act).

53 Free Trade Agreement between New Zealand and the Republic of Korea (20 December 2015).

maintain any measure with respect to maternity and related services, including services provided by midwives, and with respect to childcare. In the South Korea–Singapore FTA,[54] Chapter 9 on cross-border trade in services does not apply to subsidies or grants (including government-supported loans, guarantees, and insurance) or social services provided in conjunction with childcare (Article 9.2). Also, in Chapter 10 on investment, parties have reserved the right to regulate foreign investment in respect of childcare services (Article 10.2).

Though countries in the Asia-Pacific region have not engaged previously in negotiating a standalone chapter on trade and gender in their trade agreements, a recent development is worth mentioning. Japan and the United Kingdom have signed a Comprehensive Economic Partnership Agreement with a standalone chapter titled 'Trade and Women's Economic Empowerment'.[55] This includes declarative statements on the importance of enhancing opportunities for women in the domestic and global economy. It also contains parties' affirmations on cooperation activities aimed at improving the access of women to markets, technology and financing, and developing women's leadership and business networks. Parties have also committed to work on activities related to the WTO's Joint Declaration on Trade and Women's Economic Empowerment. Japan and the United Kingdom have also agreed to establish a Working Group to oversee and implement the cooperation activities mentioned in the chapter. The agreement's preamble is gender-explicit, and states that the parties seek to 'increase women's access to and ability to benefit from the opportunities created by this Agreement and to support the conditions for women to participate equitably in the domestic and global economy'.[56] Such provisions in a trade agreement are unique in this region.

As can be seen from these examples, several agreements in this region seek to protect maternity and safety concerns of women. Hence, signatories to these agreements have envisaged the role of women as mothers and caretakers and not as employees, entrepreneurs, or decision-makers. This discussion shows why there is merely a slightly opened door in FTAs that countries in this region need to push further by recognizing women's economic interests and including commitments on enhancing women's participation in their markets and economies. Moreover, as noted before, only about 14 per cent of bilateral

[54] Free Trade Agreement between the Government of the Republic of Korea and the Government of the Republic of Singapore (2 March 2006).

[55] UK–Japan Agreement for a Comprehensive Economic Partnership (31 December 2020). This agreement is not considered in the calculation of gender-explicit words found in agreements in this region, as the agreement was not notified to the WTO at the date of this writing).

[56] Ibid Preamble.

trade agreements in this region contain provisions with gender-explicit expressions.[57] This can be attributed to various hesitations that may impede such efforts in this region. The following section provides a discussion on three such factors.

13.4.2 *Potential Factors Impeding Gender Mainstreaming Efforts*

There are various factors that could have hindered the negotiation of bilateral trade agreements with gender provisions in this region. These factors may include, among others, lack of understanding and expertise, paucity of gender-disaggregated data, lack of political willingness, fear of protectionism, high cost and low probability of compliance, and fears of cultural imperialism.[58] The discussions in this section focus on the latter three factors – i.e., the high cost and low probability of compliance; fears of cultural imperialism; and lack of understanding and relevant expertise.

A first deterrent for countries in the Asia-Pacific region could be the high cost and low probability of compliance. Countries' willingness and appetite for such inducements rely on their domestic conditions as countries may not be willing to be a part of agreements that contain obligations they cannot comply with.[59] Hence, countries may not usually engage in cooperation efforts that require departure from their domestic policies and practices or the ones that require countries to act differently than they would otherwise. The cost of compliance is therefore fundamental to a country's decision to join an agreement which may require that country to change the status quo in respect of its laws, policies, and practices.

The further a country's practices and policies discourage gender inequality and adhere to universally accepted gender equality norms, the more likely it is that the country will accept such a commitment in its trade policy

[57] However, the large and comprehensive regional and trans-regional economic integration mechanisms to which countries in the region are party, such as APEC, ASEAN, and the CPTPP, include gender issues to a certain extent. APEC is pioneering in this respect.

[58] Based on findings gathered during interviews with trade negotiators and policymakers (details withheld).

[59] George W. Downs, David Rocke, and Peter Barsoom, 'Is the Good News About Compliance Good News about Cooperation?' (1996) 50(3) *International Organization* 379–406; *see also* James C. Murdoch and Todd Sandler, 'The Voluntary Provision of a Pure Public Good: The Case of Reduced CFC Emissions and the Montreal Protocol' (1997) 63(3) *Journal of Public Economics* 331–349; Contrary view in Beth A. Simmons, 'International Law and State Behavior: Commitment and Compliance in International Monetary Affairs' (2000) 94(4) *American Political Science Review* 819–835 (authors observe that 'international legal rules do alter governments' interests in compliant behavior').

instruments. Countries with practices and policies that do not adhere to commonly accepted norms (such as the elimination of discrimination based on sex) and hence are ranked poorly in gender-related indexes, might be less likely to accept such a provision.[60] Together with this cost of compliance, another deterrent could be the uncertainty as to the inconvenience countries might face with such gender commitments, as countries can invoke these provisions to justify a value that may either be related only remotely to gender equality or be a value that is not shared or observed by other countries.

The cost of compliance associated with gender-responsive trade agreements for several countries in this region could be discouragingly high, as most are found to have the widest inequality between women and men across health, education, economy, laws, and politics (with few exception of countries that score a high rating such as Japan, Australia, and New Zealand) as per Global Gender Gap Reports[61] or World Bank's Women, Business and the Law Reports.[62] Hence, negotiating gender-responsive trade agreements may often require a departure from domestic policies for some of these countries and countries may also face difficulties in the ratification and implementation of such agreements, especially if they require changes in domestic laws, policies, and practices.

A second deterrent may be the fear of cultural imperialism. Trade agreements with commitments on gender equality or interpretation of gender-explicit provisions can allow another country (i.e., a trade partner) to effectively define the moral or cultural values of foreign jurisdictions without regard for their moral norms. If country A justifies a measure that bans or restricts trade with country B because country B ranks poorly on WEF Gender Gap Reports or because it does not adhere to its commitments under International Labour Organization (ILO) conventions, country B could perceive this as country A's attempt to impose its own cultural standards on country B. An actual WTO case demonstrates this problem. The WTO Appellate Body's (AB) ruling in *EC – Seals*[63] may be seen as legitimizing the moral imperialism that was inherent in the EU Seal Regime, since it could be seen as an attempt by the EU to impose its moral values on foreign jurisdictions without any

60 Oona A. Hathaway, 'The Cost of Commitment' (2003) 55(5) *Stanford Law Review* 1821–1862. The author has referred to this as the 'sovereignty view', wherein countries take into account the cost of such a commitment to their national sovereignty.

61 WEF, 'Closing the Gender Gap Accelerators' <www.weforum.org/projects/closing-the-gender-gap-accelerators> accessed 8 May 2022.

62 World Bank, 'Women, Business and the Law' (n 2).

63 WTO Appellate Body Reports, *European Communities – Measures Prohibiting the Importation and Marketing of Seal Products*, WT/DS400/AB/R and WT/DS401/AB/R (18 June 2014) 7.

consideration for their moral interests.[64] This imposition in a sense also contradicted the traditions and cultural practices related to seal hunting in Canada and Norway. In other words, by giving legitimacy to animal welfare concerns as a public moral concern, both the WTO panel and the AB subordinated the moral concerns of the indigenous sealing communities in other countries to those of the EU's animal welfare concerns. This is a classic example that reflects how justifying a trade measure under a vaguely defined value (such as morality or gender equality) may allow the responding country to effectively define the moral concerns of foreign jurisdictions without any regard for their morals or even sometimes at the cost of destroying their comparative advantage in a particular product or industry.[65]

Another associated consideration may be the risk of eliminating a country's competitive advantage, given the low cost of women's labour in a particular labour-intensive industry in several countries of this region.[66] 'Cultural imperialism' could therefore be perceived as a protectionist weapon to take advantage of unequal market power, as countries may use gender provisions to enhance their own competitive advantage by imposing their social or cultural model on countries that have a different set of values and concerns. At the European Parliament, some members have openly voiced opposition to the incorporation of gender equality in trade agreements owing to their fears that it might be seen as 'colonialist behaviour'. Joachim Starbatty of the European Conservatives and Reformists Group said the following: 'If we start putting forward clauses such as the one you are proposing, then we will be laughed at … We cannot impose our vision of gender on the world. It's colonialist behaviour.'[67] The fears of cultural imperialism and the use of gender standards for protection of domestic industries are in fact the main concerns several countries have voiced when they have resisted or opposed any development in respect of trade and gender, such as the signing of the WTO 2017 Declaration, or even for joining the recently formed WTO informal group to discuss these matters.[68]

64 Elizabeth Whitsitt, 'A Comment on the Public Morals Exception in International Trade and the EC – Seal Products Case: Moral Imperialism and Other Concerns' (2014) 3(4) *Cambridge Journal of International and Comparative Law* 1376, 1390.

65 Ibid.

66 Ibid.

67 Claire Guyot, 'EP Wants to Include Gender Equality in Free-Trade Agreements' (EURACTIV 14 March 2018) <www.euractiv.com/section/politics/news/ep-wants-to-include-gender-equality-in-free-trade-agreements/> accessed 8 May 2022.

68 Ananya Singh, 'Explained: India's Refusal to Back WTO Declaration on Gender Equality in Trade' (QRIUS 15 December 2017) <https://qrius.com/explained-india-refusal-gender-equality-trade/> accessed 8 May 2022; APWLD, 'Statement: Women's Rights Groups Call on

In this connection, one might question how some countries, including Japan, have signed trade accords with gender-related commitments; 'cultural imperialism', and the risk of 'reduced competitive advantage' could act as limiting factors for these countries as well. The explanation seems to be particularly apt in the case of the UK–Japan Agreement, where both parties share similar levels of human development (i.e., they are both highly developed free market economies).[69] This finding is in line with a recent study that has shown that parties are more willing to accept gender-related commitments when they are negotiating these provisions with countries that are similarly situated in terms of gender development levels (as measured by the gender development index).[70] Having trade partners with similar domestic conditions minimizes fears of cultural imperialism. In the Asia-Pacific region, Japan is the only country that has signed a trade agreement (the UK–Japan CEPA) with a stand-alone chapter on trade and gender and a set of best practice provisions that seek to empower women economically within the trade policy context. Japan and the United Kingdom were both willing to negotiate gender-related legal provisions.[71] Hence, another important factor is whether both trading partners in a particular agreement are willing and able to assume gender commitments within their trade policy context.

A third factor may be a lack of understanding and relevant expertise. The nexus between trade and gender is far from straightforward, and globalization and trade liberalization have contradictory effects on women's employment and livelihoods.[72] In some cases, they generate employment and business

Governments to Reject the WTO Declaration on Women's Economic Empowerment' (12 December 2017) <https://apwld.org/statement-womens-rights-groups-call-on-governments-to-reject-the-wto-declaration-on-womens-economic-empowerment/> accessed 8 May 2022.

69 UN, 'World Economic Situation and Prospects 2014: Country Classification' (2014) <www.un.org/en/development/desa/policy/wesp/wesp_current/2014wesp_country_classification.pdf> accessed 8 May 2022.

70 Monteiro, 'Gender-Related Provisions in Regional Trade Agreements' (n 23).

71 The UK government has committed to formulating a post-Brexit trade policy that will uphold gender equality. More information in 'Gender Sensitive Trade Policy' (UK Policy Briefings, September 2019) <https://wbg.org.uk/wp-content/uploads/2019/09/FINAL-.pdf> accessed 8 May 2022. For more information on the UK government's commitments to 'gender-responsive trade', *see* Government of the United Kingdom, 'Export Strategy: Supporting and Connecting Businesses to Grow on the World Stage' (2018) GOV.UK Policy Paper <www.gov.uk/government/publications/export-strategy-supporting-and-connecting-businesses-to-grow-on-the-world-stage/export-strategy-supporting-and-connecting-businesses-to-grow-on-the-world-stage> accessed 8 May 2022.

72 Markéta von Hagen, 'Trade and Gender – Exploring a Reciprocal Relationship: Approaches to Mitigate and Measure Gender-Related Trade Impacts' (OECD 2014) <www.oecd.org/dac/gender-development/GIZ_Trade%20and%20Gender_Exploring%20a%20reciprocal%20relationship.pdf> accessed 8 May 2022.

opportunities for women; in others, they create burdens by disrupting industries that employ women or are prevalent with small businesses run by women.[73] Lack of understanding and awareness on how international trade and gender equality are related impede gender mainstreaming efforts. Lack of understanding may also manifest itself in disbelief in and indifference to this approach.

Even though increased international visibility is being given to the gender equality dimension of trade, multiple countries fail to understand how these two different issues are interrelated. Several countries believe that FTAs are trade instruments concerned with market access issues, and hence they are not appropriate forums to discuss gender issues.[74] To overcome this impediment, countries need to ensure that their policymakers and negotiators gain an understanding of how trade can have gendered implications and how inclusion of women in economies is not merely the morally right thing to do but also has a compelling business case.[75] The government officials at the negotiating table must understand the gender equality implications of all substantive issues they are negotiating as part of the package. Enhancing this understanding within relevant government ministries responsible for trade negotiations is vital.

Even though multiple advances are made in research on enhancing understanding of this nexus, it has to some extent been held back by limited sex-disaggregated data. Multiple studies have shown a clear correlation between international trade and women as employees, business actors, and customers. However, what remains to be done is the gathering of concrete numbers that can attest to this correlation. Hence, the paucity of country-wise and industry-wise gender-disaggregated data on how trade disciplines impact women is perhaps slowing down the gender-mainstreaming efforts in trade negotiations.

Lack of understanding, data, and political willingness can translate to a complete absence of expertise within government offices in this respect. One trade negotiator has for instance noted that some trading partners just do not

[73] UN Women, 'Gender Equality & Trade Policy' (2011) UN Women Watch Resource Paper <www.un.org/womenwatch/feature/trade/gender_equality_and_trade_policy.pdf> accessed 8 May 2022.

[74] Suresh Prabhu, 'Indian Minister of Industry and Commerce' (Indian Press Conference, WTO Ministerial Conference, Buenos Aires, 11 December 2017).

[75] Jonathan Woetzel, Anu Madgavkar, Kweilin Elingrud, Eric Labaye, Sandrine Devillard, Eric Kutcher, James Manyika, Richard Dobbs, and Mekala Krishnan, 'The Power of Parity: How Advancing Women's Equality Can Add $12 Trillion' (Mckinsey Global Institute September 2015) <www.mckinsey.com/featured-insights/employment-and-growth/how-advancing-womens-equality-can-add-12-trillion-to-global-growth> accessed 8 May 2022.

want to talk about gender while they are engaged in trade negotiations on the grounds that trade is gender-neutral, that FTA negotiations are no place for gender considerations, or that a FTA is not a tool to advance social issues.[76] Countries holding these views have no incentive or motivation to create capacity and expertise in negotiating agreements with a gender lens. The absence of expertise on gender issues within government departments responsible for carrying out trade negotiations is therefore another impediment that needs to be overcome in this respect.

Negotiators need to possess expertise on how to add a gender lens to the process of negotiations, drafting, and implementation of trade agreements. To build this expertise, negotiators and policymakers should be provided with up-to-date knowledge and developments on these issues through inclusion of debate on them in parliamentary discussions and high-level conferences, requiring negotiators to read relevant studies, and carrying out exchange visits to discuss and share experiences with negotiators from other countries in this respect. In addition, negotiators and policymakers can receive hands-on training on the following: (i) How are gender considerations mainstreamed by other countries? (ii) What are some best-practice provisions in this respect? (iii) What benefits have other countries realized from gender mainstreaming in the past few years? (iv) What are the main arguments behind mainstreaming gender in trade instruments? (v) What are the different ways of including gender considerations in trade agreements? (vi) How can the negotiators measure the gender-responsiveness of the trade agreements they are either negotiating or renegotiating, and if needed increase this responsiveness content? Answers to such questions would increase the understanding of negotiators and policymakers to reorient trade negotiations by mainstreaming gender equality concerns.

13.5 CONCLUSION

As discussed in this chapter, most of the agreements negotiated by countries in Asia-Pacific are gender-blind, as they do not contain any gender-related or gender-considerate provisions. The ones that contain gender-related provisions do not include commitments relating to women's economic interests or economic empowerment as they mainly relate to their personal welfare concerns. However, recent developments show that the trade community in this region is slowly recognizing that trade policy can be used as a tool to

[76] Interview with a trade negotiator (details withheld).

empower women, which represents a positive change in the trade policy-making mindset. Yet, to ensure that the gender commitments that are included in trade agreements can become a 'game-changer' for women in the future, it is crucial to think about overcoming limitations and challenges that continue to impede gender-mainstreaming efforts in several countries including those of the Asia-Pacific region.

14

Crafting Canada's Gender-Responsive Trade Policy

MARIE-FRANCE PAQUET AND GEORGINA WAINWRIGHT-KEMDIRIM*

ABSTRACT

Public concerns about the impacts of globalization and in particular the perception that benefits of trade have not been shared widely make it harder to continue to advocate for more and open trade at the multilateral level or in some cases at the bilateral level. The Government of Canada, therefore, has committed to making trade work for all, including women. Understanding the effects of trade on people in Canada is important. Global Affairs Canada (GAC) is undertaking a new analytical approach based on four complementary elements to help craft a coherent gender responsive and inclusive trade policy for Canada: (1) Research and analysis of the participation in trade of women-owned businesses in Canada; (2) *Ex ante* economic impact analysis using a computable general equilibrium (CGE) model and adding a labour market module; (3) *Ex post* quantitative assessment of free trade agreements (FTAs); and (4) Comprehensive dynamic gender-based analysis plus (GBA Plus) of a trade negotiation. The purpose of this chapter is to examine what Canada has been doing on these four elements and show how they are helping Canada craft a gender-responsive and inclusive trade policy so that others can determine whether this approach might be useful for application in their own countries.

* The views expressed in this chapter are those of the authors only and should not be attributed to the Government of Canada.

14.1 INTRODUCTION

The public concerns of the impacts of globalization,[1] and in particular the perception that benefits of trade have not been shared widely,[2] make it harder to continue to advocate for more and open trade at the multilateral level or in some cases at the bilateral level. At the same time, it is important to recognize that some of the benefits of trade are very tangible: consumers may enjoy a wide variety of products and at lower prices, businesses can benefit from economies of scale, and workers may benefit from increased wages.[3]

Canada is a trading nation: the value of exports and imports of goods and services amounted to 63 per cent of gross domestic product (GDP) in 2020.[4] Canada depends on international trade to sustain high living standards. Improving access to international markets and participation in international trade and ensuring that everyone benefits from it is of paramount importance. Access to international markets is achieved through multilateral and bilateral trade agreements. Canada now benefits from a wide network of trade agreements providing preferential access through fifteen FTAs covering fifty-one countries, which represents 1.5 billion consumers and about 60 per cent of world GDP.[5] Increasing participation in international trade means understanding the challenges that firms might face in trying to access international markets. Ensuring widespread benefits means understanding how trade in general, and how a specific FTA in particular, can affect workers. To determine if different groups are affected equally or not, it is important to analyse disaggregated data on dimensions such as gender.

The starting point is to recognize from the outset that the effects of trade might not be gender-neutral, including in Canada. The impacts of a trade agreement might affect workers differently since the distribution of men and women as workers or as business owners is not balanced between tradeable

[1] Dani Rodrik, *The Globalization Paradox: Democracy and the Future of the World Economy* (Norton 2011); Nicolas Lamp, 'How Should We Think about the Winners and Losers from Globalization?' (2019) 30(4) *European Journal of International Law* 1359–1397.

[2] OECD, 'Making Trade Work for All' (2017) OECD Trade Policy Papers No. 202 <http://dx.doi.org/10.1787/6e27effd-en> accessed 8 May 2022.

[3] For a full review of the benefits of trade on Canada, *see* Government of Canada, 'International Trade and Its Benefits to Canada' (2012) <www.international.gc.ca/trade-commerce/economist-economiste/state_of_trade-commerce_international/special_feature-2012-article_special.aspx?lang=eng> accessed 8 May 2022.

[4] Government of Canada, 'Canada's State of Trade 2020 – The Early Impacts of COVID-19 on Trade' (2020) 54.

[5] Ibid Minister's Message.

and non-tradeable sectors.[6] Understanding the barriers that owners, in particular underrepresented groups, of small and medium-sized enterprises (SMEs) face in trying to participate in international trade is key. It allows for the development of better policies and programmes, and overall better outcomes.

Section 14.2 will present an overview of the evolution of trade policy in Canada and the nexus between trade and gender, including how the transition from general policy on inclusion and equality transitioned to inform Canada's current practice. Section 14.3 will present and explain the four elements that constitute the analysis and research behind Canada's gender-responsive and inclusive trade policies. Section 14.4 concludes.

14.2 BACKGROUND

14.2.1 *The Evolution of Canada's Trade Policy*

Canada's trade policy is based on three mutually reinforcing priorities: supporting the rules-based international system which is the foundation of its trade policy; diversifying its trade and investment to new exporters and new markets; and championing inclusive trade which seeks to ensure that the benefits of trade are more widely shared.

Canada is highly dependent on the rules-based international trading system and has played a role in helping to build a global order based on the rule of law and an aspiration to free and more open trade. Canada is committed to upholding and actively participating in the rules-based multilateral trading system with the World Trade Organization (WTO) at its core. This system is necessary for creating a predictable and fair economic environment in which businesses can thrive, which is essential to increasing the economic well-being of all WTO members, contributing to a more prosperous and stable world. Canada believes that more trade and investment is essential for global economic growth to build prosperity and create jobs, and now more than ever given the effects of the COVID-19 pandemic and the need to ensure a resilient and sustainable economic recovery.

Canada also has a long history of negotiating comprehensive and ambitious free trade agreements (FTAs), starting with the Canada–US Free Trade Agreement (CUSFTA) in 1989[7] and then the North American Free Trade

6 Felipe Benguria, 'The Matching and Sorting of Exporting and Importing Firms: Theory and Evidence' (2021) 131/103430 *Journal of International Economics* 1–49.

7 US–Canada Free Trade Agreement, 1 January 1989, 27 ILM 281.

Agreement (NAFTA) in 1994.[8] Since these historic agreements, Canada continues to make significant efforts to diversify its trade, with the aim of allowing exporters to take advantage of opportunities in large and emerging markets. Bilateral and regional FTAs have represented a key tool for Canada in pursuit of trade diversification. As of September 2021, Canada had fifteen FTAs in force with fifty-one countries, representing about two-thirds of the global economy.[9] Following the entry into force of the Comprehensive and Progressive Agreement for Trans-Pacific Partnership (CPTPP) on 30 December 2018,[10] Canada became the only Group of Seven (G7) country to have FTAs with every other member of the G7, connecting Canadian businesses to over 1.5 billion consumers. Canada is currently engaged in FTA negotiations with other countries and trading blocs (e.g., Mercosur, Association of Southeast Asian Nations – ASEAN, Indonesia, the United Kingdom, and India) which reflects the importance that it places on free trade and the goal of establishing high-quality, ambitious, and comprehensive FTAs through improved market access benefiting companies of all sizes in a diverse range of markets.

Canada's recent approach to negotiating FTAs has been informed by the public and political debates on trade and globalization in Canada. There are public perceptions that trade agreements lack transparency in the negotiating process; provide special rights and privileges to corporations; have negative effects on certain population groups (particularly the middle class and workers in traditional industries); and threaten the environment, health, safety, consumer standards, and governments' right to regulate.[11] These concerns affect support for free trade, and hence the Government of Canada recognizes that trade policies need to respond and contribute more meaningfully to domestic economic, social, and environmental policy priorities, including its Feminist International Assistance Policy.[12]

[8] North American Free Trade Agreement (NAFTA), 1 January 1994, 32 ILM 289.

[9] Chile (1997, 2019); Colombia (2011); Costa Rica (2002); European Free Trade Association (2009); European Union (2017); Honduras (2014); Israel (1997, 2019); Jordan (2012); Panama (2013); Peru (2009); South Korea (2015); Ukraine (2017); the United States and Mexico (NAFTA 1994, CUSMA 2020); Comprehensive and Progressive Agreement for Trans-Pacific Partnership (CPTPP) (2018); Canada–UK Trade Continuity Agreement (2021).

[10] CPTPP (2018).

[11] *See* Government of Canada, 'Canada's Inclusive Approach to Trade' <www.international.gc.ca/trade-commerce/gender_equality-egalite_genres/approach-can-approche.aspx?lang=eng> accessed 8 May 2022.

[12] Government of Canada, 'Canada's Feminist International Assistance Policy' <www.international.gc.ca/world-monde/issues_development-enjeux_developpement/priorities-priorites/policy-politique.aspx?lang=eng> accessed 8 May 2022.

Informed by these developments, Canada is pursuing an inclusive approach to trade as part of its overall export diversification strategy.[13] Canada's approach aims to ensure that the benefits and opportunities that flow from trade are more widely shared, including with underrepresented groups such as women, SMEs, and Indigenous Peoples. This trade policy approach is based on three pillars: informed and inclusive trade policy-making; provisions in trade agreements that are responsible, sustainable, transparent, and inclusive; and international engagement to advance support for responsible, transparent, and inclusive trade initiatives.

Canada has a long history of integrating gender-related clauses into the preamble of its agreements and also gender provisions in labour chapters and side agreements starting with NAFTA in 1994. Recently, Canada has been advancing comprehensive, binding, and enforceable commitments in its labour chapters related to gender, such as in CPTPP[14] and in the Canada–United States–Mexico Agreement (CUSMA or USMCA).[15] In these agreements, the parties are required to promote employment equity and address gender-based discrimination in the workplace and adopt programmes and policies that address the gender wage gap and barriers to the full participation of women in the workforce.[16]

Building on these successes, Canada has successfully advanced inclusive trade provisions in its modernized FTAs with Chile (2019)[17] and Israel (2019),[18] with the inclusion of dedicated trade and gender chapters in both agreements. In addition, at their first Joint Committee meeting in September 2018, Canada and the European Union (EU) agreed to three recommendations under the Canada–EU Comprehensive Economic and Trade Agreement (CETA) on Trade and Gender,[19] Trade and SMEs,[20] and Trade

[13] Government of Canada, 'Diversifying Canada's Trade and Investment Opportunities' <www.international.gc.ca/gac-amc/campaign-campagne/trade-diversification-commerce/index.aspx?lang=eng> accessed 8 May 2022.

[14] Consolidated TPP Text, Chapter 19, Art. 19.

[15] CUSMA (2020).

[16] CUSMA, Art. 23.9.

[17] Canada–Chile FTA, Appendix II – Chapter N bis.

[18] Canada–Israel FTA, Art. 13.

[19] CETA Joint Committee on Trade and Gender, 'Recommendation 002/2018 of 26 September 2018 of the CETA Joint Committee on Trade and Gender' (2018) <www.international.gc.ca/trade-commerce/trade-agreements-accords-commerciaux/agr-acc/ceta-aecg/rec-002.aspx?lang=eng> accessed 8 May 2022.

[20] CETA Joint Committee on Small and Medium-Sized Enterprises, 'Recommendation 003/2018 of 26 September 2018 of the CETA Joint Committee on Small- and Medium-sized Enterprises (SMEs)' (2018) <www.international.gc.ca/trade-commerce/trade-agreements-accords-commerciaux/agr-acc/ceta-aecg/rec-003.aspx?lang=eng> accessed 8 May 2022.

and Climate Change.[21] The CPTPP contains Canada's first chapter on SMEs, a chapter also included in the modernized Canada–Israel FTA and the CUSMA.

Canada has also concluded the Global Trade and Gender Arrangement (GTAGA)[22] with Chile and New Zealand in August 2020. The GTAGA is modelled on the trade and gender chapters Canada has negotiated in its trade agreements and aims to remove barriers to women's participation in trade as business owners and workers. The GTAGA is an innovative non-binding plurilateral trade instrument, which is open for other countries to join. Mexico signed on to GTAGA and joined the Inclusive Trade Action Group (ITAG) in October 2021.[23] Peru and Colombia signed onto GTAGA in June 2022, and Ecuador and Costa Rica will join both GTAGA and ITAG soon.

14.2.2 *Trade and Gender Nexus*

Trade affects people differently, based on a wide range of factors, including gender.[24] Therefore, it is important to incorporate gender perspectives into trade policy in order to pursue inclusive and sustainable economic development and to achieve outcomes that are more beneficial for all, including workers, business owners, and entrepreneurs.

In Canada, women are overrepresented in lower-growth and lower-wage industries, such as the retail trade, and in less export-intensive services such as accommodation and food services.[25] In comparison, men dominate sectors where trade plays a significant role, such as manufacturing, agriculture, and

[21] CETA Joint Committee on Trade, Climate Action and the Paris, 'Recommendation 001/2018 of 26 September 2018 of the CETA Joint Committee on Trade, Climate Action and the Paris Agreement' (2018) <www.international.gc.ca/trade-commerce/trade-agreements-accords-commerciaux/agr-acc/ceta-aecg/rec-001.aspx?lang=eng> accessed 8 May 2022.

[22] Government of Canada, 'Global Trade and Gender Arrangement' <www.international.gc.ca/trade-commerce/inclusive_trade-commerce_inclusif/itag-gaci/arrangement.aspx?lang=eng> accessed 8 May 2022.

[23] Government of Canada, 'Inclusive Trade Action Group' <www.international.gc.ca/trade-commerce/inclusive_trade-commerce_inclusif/itag-gaci/index.aspx?lang=eng> accessed 8 May 2022.

[24] This has, for instance, been assessed in the framework of CETA. *See* UNCTAD, 'Trade and Gender – Assessing the Impact of Trade Agreements on Gender Equality: Canada–EU Comprehensive Economic and Trade Agreement' <https://unctad.org/system/files/official-document/UNWomen_2020d1_en.pdf> accessed 8 May 2022.

[25] Audrey Ann Bélanger Baur, 'Women-Owned Exporting Small and Medium Enterprises – Descriptive and Comparative Analysis' (2019) <www.international.gc.ca/trade-commerce/economist-economiste/analysis-analyse/women_owned-export-entreprises_femmes.aspx?lang=eng> accessed 8 May 2022.

resource extraction. Women account for a larger share of the workforce in service sectors, such as health services, where 81 per cent of workers are women, and in education services. Therefore, trade policies can have different effects on women and men as workers, depending on the sector in which they are employed and whether that sector is likely to expand or contract because of a trade agreement. Accordingly, trade policies need to consider gender-related factors during FTA negotiations so there is a better understanding of the risks and opportunities for particular population groups in the economy.

14.3 ADVANCING INCLUSIVITY AND GENDER EQUALITY THROUGH TRADE POLICY: FROM POLICY TO PRACTICE

Canada launched FTA negotiations with Mercosur in March 2018[26] with a vision to pursue a comprehensive, ambitious, inclusive, and gender-responsive FTA in order to ensure that the benefits and opportunities flowing from international trade are more widely shared, including among traditionally underrepresented groups in international trade. Mercosur Member States and Canada were committed to ensuring that this FTA would realize benefits for all population groups and achieve lasting economic growth and development for all people, including women-owned businesses.[27]

In these trade negotiations, Canada pursued a two-pronged approach: incorporation of dedicated cooperation-based inclusive trade chapters (such as trade and gender) and mainstreaming gender-responsive and inclusive provisions across the full agreement. This two-pronged approach is considered important because both strategies contribute to achieving a final agreement that supports women's economic empowerment and gender equality.

A dedicated trade and gender chapter is important because it has value in terms of establishing as a priority identifying and removing barriers to women's participation in trade and advancing women's economic empowerment and gender equality. The trade and gender chapter recognizes the importance of

[26] Global Affairs Canada, 'Minister Champagne Welcomes Agreement to Launch Trade Negotiations with Mercosur' (GAC 9 March 2018) <www.canada.ca/en/global-affairs/news/2018/03/minister-champagne-welcomes-agreement-to-launch-trade-negotiations-with-mercosur.html> accessed 8 May 2022.

[27] Global Affairs Canada, 'Joint Statement on the Launch of Negotiations toward a Comprehensive Free Trade Agreement between Canada and the Mercosur Member States' (9 March 2018) <www.international.gc.ca/trade-commerce/trade-agreements-accords-commerciaux/agr-acc/mercosur/joint_statement-declaration_commune.aspx?lang=eng> accessed 8 May 2022.

mutually supportive trade and gender policies and incorporating a gender perspective into trade. It also recognizes the importance of not weakening gender equality laws in order to attract trade or investment, and recognizes the importance of implementing international instruments that advance gender equality and women's economic empowerment (such as the UN Convention on the Elimination of Discrimination Against Women (CEDAW) and the Joint Declaration on Trade and Women's Economic Empowerment).[28] It also establishes a framework to undertake cooperation activities and a bilateral committee to oversee the activities and report publicly on progress. These chapters are an important communication tool, giving recognition to the trade and gender nexus, helping build knowledge and understanding of the parties on the issues, and the barriers and challenges faced by women. Because they are cooperation based, they are a no-risk/high-reward opportunity, pragmatic, open to innovation, and customizable based on the needs of FTA partners. The long list of potential cooperation activities demonstrates the challenges faced by women workers or business owners that need to be addressed. These chapters can inspire domestic action as flanking policies and programmes may be developed in response to barriers identified. They also help deliver on SDG 5 and support a march to the top rather than a race to the bottom.

Canada recognizes that there are many misperceptions around the value of trade and gender chapters in trade agreements. Based on the gathering of empirical insights from stakeholders and trade negotiating partners, some of the criticisms include: the chapter is not valuable because it is not enforceable and parties will not take it seriously; the chapter is primarily best-efforts language and allows for a reduced commitment on the part of signatories and thus no real progress on gender equality is achieved; the chapter meddles in social policy or seeks to use a trade agreement to transform societies; the chapter is a hidden pathway to creating non-tariff barriers if parties do not support gender equality or women's economic empowerment domestically; and if there is a trade and gender chapter in an agreement, there is no need to mainstream gender into other chapters of a FTA.[29] Canada disagrees with all of these critiques and firmly believes that pursuing only a trade and gender chapter in a trade agreement will not leverage an important opportunity to

[28] *See* Convention on the Elimination of All Forms of Discrimination against Women, A/RES/34/180 (18 December 1979); WTO Joint Declaration on Trade and Women's Economic Empowerment on the Occasion of the WTO Ministerial Conference in Buenos Aires in December 2017 (2017) <www.wto.org/english/thewto_e/minist_e/mc11_e/genderdeclarationmc11_e.pdf> accessed 8 May 2022.

[29] Insights based on empirical research (details withheld).

utilize a trade agreement to advance women's economic empowerment and gender equality.

While Canada believes that trade and gender chapters are very important, mainstreaming gender across a trade agreement is equally important. Mainstreaming gender will not only help deliver on inclusive trade and support delivery of the SDGs, but it will also have many other benefits. For example, mainstreaming gender in other chapters will ensure that those provisions are enforceable under the agreement's dispute settlement mechanism as typically to date trade and gender chapters have not been binding (except for the unique circumstance of the modernized Canada–Israel FTA,[30] which has a modified dispute settlement approach). Mainstreaming demonstrates that trade is not gender-neutral and that gender is relevant in all chapters of an FTA, and also in committee work following entry into force. It also helps move beyond narrowly defined sectoral rules and policies; inspires domestic policy development and implementation in women's economic empowerment and gender equality areas; helps achieve overall domestic and trade policy coherence; and supports a holistic and whole-of-government approach to trade and gender policies. In addition, it serves to get governments to lead by example in addressing trade and gender issues and thus potentially inspire action by the business sector.

To that end, Canada is conducting comprehensive analysis and research to inform these negotiations. The overall findings are based on four elements:

- Element 1: Understanding the characteristics of women-owned SMEs, their propensity to export, and the obstacles they face;
- Element 2: *Ex ante* economic impact assessment;
- Element 3: *Ex post* analysis; and,
- Element 4: Comprehensive and dynamic GBA Plus.

Part of this analysis is conducted in parallel with the negotiations to ensure that findings are taken into account during the negotiations whenever possible. For example, the *ex ante* economic assessment and the initial GBA Plus are conducted before launching free trade negotiations. Therefore, the results of the economic impact assessment can inform the initial GBA Plus from the outset and during the negotiations.

[30] *See* Government of Canada, 'Canada–Israel Free Trade Agreement (CIFTA) – Building on 20 Years of Growth' <www.international.gc.ca/trade-commerce/trade-agreements-accords-commerciaux/agr-acc/israel/fta-ale/index.aspx?lang=eng&_ga=2.172535846.441821398.1638973123-2080543025.1611591818> accessed 8 May 2022.

14.3.1 *Element 1: Understanding the Characteristics of Women-Owned SMEs, Their Propensity to Export and the Obstacles They Face*

Studies have shown that women-owned businesses contribute $150 billion to the Canadian economy[31] and employ over 1.5 million people.[32] Furthermore, women start businesses at a greater rate than men in Canada, but women-owned businesses account for less than 16 per cent of SMEs[33] in Canada, and only 11 per cent of them export.[34]

Using data from Statistics Canada's Survey on Financing and Growth of Small and Medium Enterprises (2011, 2014, 2017), a study by Bélanger Baur[35] looked at the trends and business characteristics of Canadian exporting SMEs by gender of ownership. Women-owned SMEs are those where women's representation is greater than 50 per cent, which can mean 100 per cent women ownership or a majority of it. One of the main findings of the study is that women-owned SMEs, in contrast to men-owned SMEs and equally owned SMEs, saw their export propensity (share of firms that export) more than double, growing from 5.0 per cent to 11.1 per cent, from 2011 to 2017.

The use of online tools to conclude sales could contribute to explaining this shift. Some preliminary research using firm-level data and controlling for firms' size, labour productivity, sector, education, management experience, and age of firm,[36] shows that innovation and e-commerce allow women-owned SMEs to succeed internationally. Having an online payment feature is actually increasing the probability to export by 40 per cent compared to 20 per cent for men-owned and equally owned SMEs. Marketing innovation, or new ways to sell, leads to an increase in probability to export of 25 per cent for women-owned SMEs compared to 18 per cent for men-owned and equally

[31] Laura Cooper, 'Canadian Women Grabbing the Baton' (RBC Economics Research October 2013) <www.rbc.com/economics/economic-reports/pdf/other-reports/canadianwomengrabbingthebaton.pdf> accessed 8 May 2022.

[32] BMO Financial Group, 'BMO Women's Day Study: Majority of Canadian Women Would Start Their Own Business' (2 March 2012) <https://newsroom.bmo.com/2012-03-02-BMO-Womens-Day-Study-Majority-of-Canadian-Women-Would-Start-Their-Own-Business> accessed 8 May 2022.

[33] Ibid 25; Bélanger Baur, 'Women-Owned Exporting Small and Medium Enterprises' (n 25).

[34] Bélanger Baur, 'Women-Owned Exporting Small and Medium Enterprises' (n 25).

[35] Ibid.

[36] *See* Julia V. Sekkel and Weimin Wang, 'Closing the Gender Gap in Exporting: Identifying Women's Exporting Successes Using Firm-Level Data in Canada' (in press WTO publication, September 2023). For a short version of the paper<www.international.gc.ca/trade-commerce/economist-economiste/index.aspx?lang=eng> accessed 29 September 2022.

TABLE 14.1 *Exporting SMEs that considered these obstacles as moderate or major when exporting (%)*

	Women-owned	Equally owned	Men-owned	All SMEs
Logistical	23.9	19.1	18.6	19.5
Border	21.7	16.8	17.2	17.8
Foreign administration	19.2	20.7	14.3	16.3
Financial risk	10.7	15.5	15.8	14.9
Marketing knowledge	10.8	15.8	13.5	13.5
Lack of financing or cash-flow	9.3	9.6	14.3	12.7
Domestic administration	11.5	7.6	10.0	9.7
IP issues	3.3	2.3	6.6	5.3
Other	5.5	12.8	9.1	9.3

Data: Statistics Canada, Survey on Financing and Growth of Small and Medium Enterprises, 2017.
Source: Office of the Chief Economist, Global Affairs Canada; and see Julia V. Sekkel, 'Women-Owned SMEs and Trade Barriers' (2020) <www.international.gc.ca/trade-commerce/economist-economiste/analysis-analyse/women_owned_smes_trade-pme_commerce_appartenant_femmes.aspx?lang=eng>

owned SMEs.[37] This emphasizes the importance of e-commerce for SMEs in general, but even more so for women-owned SMEs.

Using the data from Statistics Canada's Survey on Financing and Growth of Small and Medium Enterprises (2017),[38] Sekkel shows the percentage of exporting SMEs that considered obstacles while exporting as moderate or major, disaggregated by gender of ownership (Table 14.1).[39] Women-owned SMEs are more likely to cite logistical, border, and foreign administrative obstacles as an impediment to exporting. Logistical obstacles relate to distance to customers, transportation costs, and brokerage fees. Border obstacles include tariffs, non-tariff barriers, and import quotas, while foreign administrative obstacles refer to foreign customer requirements, product standards,

[37] Ibid.

[38] For a summary, *see* Government of Canada, 'Summary of the Survey on Financing and Growth of Small and Medium Enterprises, 2017' (2018) <www.ic.gc.ca/eic/site/061.nsf/vwapj/SFGSME_Summary-EFCPME_Sommaire_2017_eng-V2.pdf/$file/SFGSME_Summary-EFCPME_Sommaire_2017_eng-V2.pdf> accessed 8 May 2022.

[39] Julia V. Sekkel, 'Women-Owned SMEs and Trade Barriers' (2020) <www.international.gc.ca/trade-commerce/economist-economiste/analysis-analyse/women_owned_smes_trade-pme_commerce_appartenant_femmes.aspx?lang=eng> accessed 8 May 2022.

and technology requirements. Since women-owned SMEs represent a larger proportion of exporters to non-US markets (e.g., Europe, India, others) relative to men-owned SMEs, this could explain their perception about logistical obstacles. The lack of financing or cash flow is perceived as an obstacle but to a lesser degree and is less of an impediment than for men-owned SMEs. According to Huang and Rivard (2020), women are more likely than men to be approved for credit but also to be discouraged from borrowing.[40]

Other research has shown that women-owned businesses around the world also face other challenges, such as lack of financing or violence and harassment at border crossings, which can affect their ability and willingness to participate in trade.[41]

14.3.2 Element 2: *Ex ante* Economic Impact Assessment

In order to produce an Economic Impact Assessment (EIA) of potential FTAs, the Office of the Chief Economist at Global Affairs Canada has employed a Computable General-Equilibrium (CGE) model for many years. A CGE model is a mathematical representation of the structure of the economy and the behavioural response of firms, households, and the government. The model includes different countries and regions of the world with which Canada trades. Such a model provides for a simulation as opposed to a forecast. It allows for a comparison between a base case scenario (i.e., the current economy and trade) and a scenario based on what the economy would

[40] Lyming Huang and Patrice Rivard, 'Financing of Women-Owned Small and Medium-Sized Enterprises in Canada' (2021) <www-ic.fjgc-gccf.gc.ca/eic/site/061.nsf/vwapj/2021_Fin_women-owned-SMEs_Canada_EN4.pdf/$file/2021_Fin_women-owned-SMEs_Canada_EN4.pdf> accessed 8 May 2022.

[41] A. Atkinson and F. Messy, 'Measuring Financial Literacy – Results of the OECD / International Network on Financial Education (INFE) Pilot Study' (2012) OECD Working Papers on Finance, Insurance and Private Pensions No. 15, 43 <https://doi.org/10.1787/5k9csfs90fr4-en> accessed 8 May 2022; Government of Canada, 'Majority-Female Owned Exporting SMEs in Canada' (2016) <https://tradecommissioner.gc.ca/businesswomen-femmesdaffaires/assets/pdfs/majority-female_owned_exporting_smes_canada_eng.pdf?_ga=2.159767997.1696028190.1649271305-1421400920.1649056212> accessed 8 May 2022; Marco Marchese, 'Policy Brief on Access to Business Start-Up Finance for Inclusive Entrepreneurship – Entrepreneurial Activities in Europe' (2014) 19 <www.oecd.org/cfe/leed/Finacing%20inclusive%20entrepreneurship%20policy%20brief%20EN.pdf> accessed 8 May 2022; Government of Canada, 'Survey on Financing and Growth of Small and Medium Enterprises' (2014) Table 25 <www.ic.gc.ca/eic/site/061.nsf/vwapj/SummarySFGSMEs-ResumeEFCPME_2014_eng.pdf/$file/SummarySFGSMEs-ResumeEFCPME_2014_eng.pdf> accessed 8 May 2022; World Bank, 'Women, Business and the Law' (2019) <http://pubdocs.worldbank.org/en/702301554216687135/WBL-DECADE-OF-REFORM-2019-WEB-04-01.pdf> accessed 8 May 2022.

look like once the policy shock has been implemented and time has allowed the economy to adjust. Here, the policy shock is a new trade agreement which can be incorporated in phases in the model to account for immediate and gradual tariff reduction. The difference between these two states is the impact of the shock.

The impact of a new FTA comes from changes in factor prices and allows a country to reallocate its resources from sectors where there is a comparative advantage. An improved allocation of resources in the economy provides for a more efficient outcome, hence a better economic outcome globally.

However, a more efficient allocation of resources does not automatically mean more employment. An increase in production in a specific sector might be achieved through an increase in capital, not labour. It is also possible that an increase in production in another sector is achieved through an increase in labour. In an economy where labour markets operate freely, changes in output in expanding sectors would result in more employment in that sector, to the detriment of sectors that are contracting. Hence, the overall impact on employment could seem to be small.

In light of the desire to assess if and how a free trade agreement would impact men and women differently, the Office of the Chief Economist at Global Affairs Canada expanded its existing modelling capacity to include a newly developed labour market module. The model follows the structure of the Global Trade Analysis Project (GTAP) model developed and supported by Purdue University,[42] but has been expanded to include a labour market with some friction. This expanded model takes into account the potential impacts on gender, age, and the distribution of Canadian workers across eight different occupational groups and sixty-five sectors of the economy.

The labour module allows for substitution between workers of different age groups, substitution between men and women, and between occupations. The friction in the labour market means that, at any point in time, there is no longer full employment. Rather, changes occur in unemployment and movements in and out of the labour market for men and women separately. Trade liberalization can generate both smooth job transitions and involuntary unemployment as some firms expand, while others are forced to cut back output and reduce their workforce in response to a loss of market share due to imports. Further, trade liberalization could also have an impact on labour

[42] Martina Brockmeier, 'A Graphical Exposition of the GTAP Model' (1996, as revised in 2001) GTAP Technical Paper No. 8 <www.gtap.agecon.purdue.edu/resources/download/181.pdf> accessed 8 May 2022.

force participation: higher real wages and associated job creation may encourage those who are not in the labour force to seek work.

Canada used its CGE model to assess the potential impacts of trade liberalization under the proposed Canada–Mercosur FTA. This model allowed Canada to look at new dimensions such as the potential impacts on overall employment, employment by gender, employment by age groups, or employment by occupation. For the purpose of this analysis, complete elimination of tariffs is assumed between Canada and the four Mercosur countries, with no exception made for 'sensitive products'.

Based on full implementation of the agreement, the results on the Canadian economy by 2040 suggest that the benefits could be widely shared from an inclusive trade perspective.[43]

Under the potential Canada–Mercosur FTA, the sectors projected to add the most jobs would be in services and domestic trade. Given that there is a higher proportion of women workers in these sectors, the Agreement would generate a disproportionately larger demand for female workers. Accordingly, the overall demand for female workers would increase by 4,489, compared to a net increase of male employment of 4,086.

The potential FTA could lead to an expansion in participation of the Canadian labour force by attracting workers from the non-participating working-age population and distributing the income gains more widely. Further, the increase would be moderately weighted in favour of women, which shows that this FTA would benefit women and improve gender equity.

The findings from the EIA suggest that enhancing economic cooperation in the form of an FTA between Canada and Mercosur countries is desirable, and would generate economic benefits for both economies, including positive effects for underrepresented groups in Canada's economy.[44] The expansion of trade between Canada and Mercosur countries would drive economic gains, generate jobs and promote gender balance in the Canadian economy, and encourage youth employment and greater labour participation. All these effects would support a broader sharing of the benefits of the Agreement, including amongst traditionally underrepresented groups in the economy and trade.[45] Unfortunately, it is not possible to evaluate the similar impacts on the other negotiating parties. The CGE model used only has the extension for

[43] Global Affairs Canada, 'Summary of Initial GBA+ for Canada Mercosur FTA Negotiations' (2019) Online Stakeholder Consultations Paper <www.international.gc.ca/trade-commerce/assets/pdfs/gba_plus_summary-acs_plus_resume_eng.pdf> accessed 8 May 2022.

[44] Ibid.

[45] Ibid.

the Canadian labour market due the availability of extensive gender-disaggregated data.

Canada has also used this methodology in its EIA of the CUSMA.[46] The implementation of the CUSMA outcome secures GDP gains of $6.8 billion (USD 5.1 billion), or 0.25 per cent, which would have been lost if the United States had withdrawn from NAFTA.[47] From a labour perspective, CUSMA can secure nearly 38,000 jobs that would otherwise be lost while preserving real wage gains for Canadian workers, particularly machinery operators, manual labourers, and sales workers. From a gender perspective, the jobs secured are expected to be almost evenly split between men and women (18,708 jobs held by men that were preserved and 18,853 jobs held by women that were preserved).[48] Overall, these outcomes could have a positive impact on middle-class jobs and improve income equality in Canada.

14.3.3 Element 3: *Ex post* Analysis

In order to study the long-term impacts of an FTA on labour market outcomes, leading researchers[49] have used longitudinal employer–employee data from Canada for the years 1984–2004. The employment of workers employed in 1988 in industries affected by tariff reductions was followed and the long-run effects of the CUSFTA[50] was examined on labour market outcomes including cumulative earnings, and whether the worker was more likely to be separated from their initial employer, leave their initial industry, or experience periods of unemployment. The longitudinal nature of the data allowed for the examination of these trajectories in detail while controlling for pre-existing conditions and trends for affected workers.

The study also provides results by gender to assess how the CUSFTA might have differentially affected labour market outcomes for women, including workforce separations and lifetime earnings. The main findings related to gender impacts of the CUSFTA are as follows: (i) among low-attachment

46 Global Affairs Canada, 'The Canada–United States–Mexico Agreement, Economic Impact Assessment' (2020) <www.international.gc.ca/trade-commerce/trade-agreements-accords-commerciaux/agr-acc/cusma-aceum/economic_assessment-analyse_economiques.aspx?lang=eng> accessed 8 May 2022.

47 Ibid 7.

48 Ibid.

49 Allison Devlin, Brian K. Kovak, and Peter Morrow, 'The Long-Run Labour Market Effects of the Canada–U.S. Free Trade Agreement' (2020) Research Report prepared for Global Affairs Canada <www.aeaweb.org/conference/2021/preliminary/paper/9ibAiHk4> accessed 8 May 2022.

50 Canada–US FTA (no longer in force).

workers,[51] men have lower lifetime earnings overall with a larger effect on earnings at the initial employer while women have experienced no discernible effects; (ii) men and women have benefited equally from US concessions, particularly with respect to strong positive effects on earnings at the initial employers; (iii) for high-attachment workers,[52] women have benefited from Canadian concessions, with much of the effect coming from earnings at the initial employer while for men there is no effect of Canadian concessions on either type of income.

These results show that workers can be affected in many different ways, depending on their attachment to the labour market, the sector in which they operate, and how the sector is affected by concessions. It also shows that indirect but positive benefits can be found in the long run. An FTA that stimulates the economy overall can also stimulate in a positive way sectors of the economy not directly affected by concessions. Prospects in sectors that are less trade-intensive such as retail trade and some services can improve and provide for better conditions overall.

14.3.4 *Element 4: Dynamic GBA Plus*

The gender impact assessment of the Canada–Mercosur FTA was conducted using gender-based analysis plus (GBA Plus).[53] GBA Plus is an analytical process used by the Government of Canada to assess how domestic and international policies, programmes, initiatives, organizations, and activities may affect diverse groups of women, men, and non-binary people.[54] The *plus* of GBA Plus aims to ensure that policymakers consider other overlapping identity factors of the Canadian population such as Indigeneity, race, ethnicity, culture, religion, immigration status, disability, age, sexual orientation, and geographic region of residence (urban, rural, remote, coastal, or northern) when they are developing policy. The aim behind this approach is to put people at the heart of decision-making and ensure that policies do not perpetuate or exacerbate existing inequalities. Applying the GBA Plus

[51] Low-attachment workers are defined as those who earned less than the equivalent of 1,600 annual hours of work at the nominal provincial minimum wage in every year between 1985 and 1988.

[52] High-attachment workers are defined as those who earned at least the equivalent of 1,600 annual hours of work at the nominal provincial minimum wage in every year between 1985 and 1988.

[53] Government of Canada, ‘Gender-Based Analysis Plus (GBA+)’ <https://women-gender-equality.canada.ca/en/gender-based-analysis-plus.html> accessed 8 May 2022.

[54] Ibid.

analytical framework to trade policy and an ongoing FTA negotiation is breaking new ground and realizing value-added benefits to the negotiations. GBA Plus is in fact changing the way Canada does trade policy.[55]

14.3.4.1 Overview of GBA Plus

Canada is conducting a GBA Plus on each of the twenty-five chapters[56] currently under negotiation as part of the potential Canada–Mercosur FTA. This requires that the lead negotiators of these chapters conduct an analysis on the potential GBA Plus effects and opportunities associated with each chapter's provisions.

Supported by a custom-designed questionnaire to guide them in their analysis, lead negotiators were tasked to consider a range of effects (positive and negative, direct and indirect, intended and unintended) associated with their chapters' provisions on various industries and sectors of the economy, as they related to men and women performing various roles – such as workers, business owners, entrepreneurs, and consumers. They were also asked to consider any different effects of the chapter on men and women based on other intersectional characteristics, with Indigeneity and SMEs as priority issues to consider, and any other relevant considerations which might arise and for which data or other evidence were available. They were asked to consider how they could mitigate a negative effect or enhance a positive opportunity through a new trade policy provision in their chapter. In addition, lead negotiators were asked to regularly update their GBA Plus before each round of negotiations with Mercosur by integrating information on progress to date, adding new data and evidence as it is identified, and analysing these

55 Government of Canada, 'Overview: Trade Policy and Gender-Based Analysis Plus' <www.international.gc.ca/trade-commerce/gender_equality-egalite_genres/gba_plus-acs_plus.aspx?lang=eng> accessed 8 May 2022.

56 The twenty-five chapters are grouped into four sets of related chapters: Goods (National Treatment and Market Access for Goods; Rules of Origin; Origin Procedures; Customs and Trade Facilitation; Sanitary and Phyto-sanitary Measures; Technical Barriers to Trade; Good Regulatory Practices; Trade Remedies); Services, investment, and government procurement (Cross-Border Trade in Services; Temporary Entry; Telecommunications; Electronic Commerce; Financial Services; Investment; State-Owned Enterprises; Competition Policy; Intellectual Property Government Procurement); Inclusive trade (Environment; Labour; Trade and Gender; Micro, Small and Medium-Sized Enterprises (MSMEs); Trade and Indigenous Peoples); Institutional and dispute settlement (Preamble and five institutional chapters [Initial Provisions and General Definitions; Institutional and Administrative Provisions; Exceptions and General Provisions; Transparency, Anti-Corruption, Corporate Social Responsibility and Responsible Business Conduct; Final Provisions]; and Dispute Settlement).

inputs to reveal findings to inform the negotiation strategy through the development of new provisions. This process is ongoing (at the time of this writing), and the GBA Plus continues to be updated as Canada tables new provisions in negotiations with Mercosur. GBA Plus is a dynamic process which is continually realizing benefits to the negotiations and allows for tabling of new provisions in real time. With the help of the findings collected through this process, to date fifteen of twenty-five chapters in its negotiations with Mercosur have presented opportunities for Canada to propose at least one new inclusive or gender-responsive trade policy provision.

Canada's analysis was also informed by the Economic Impact Assessment (see Element 3) and feedback received from a diverse range of stakeholders between September and December of 2018. A summary of the initial GBA Plus for the Canada–Mercosur FTA negotiations was published in August 2019 for public review and comment over a ninety-day period.[57] A 'What We Heard' report was published in June 2020 that summarizes the comments received from stakeholders and experts.[58] Lead negotiators were subsequently informed of these comments, so they can consider and address them wherever possible.

14.3.4.2 GBA Plus Case Studies

Among others, two chapters in particular present opportunities to integrate inclusive and gender-responsive trade policy provisions in trade agreements: Electronic Commerce and Government Procurement.

CASE STUDY 1: ELECTRONIC COMMERCE Canada's model electronic commerce chapter that it has tabled in negotiations aims to facilitate the use of electronic commerce as a means of facilitating trade in goods and services. It enhances the viability of the digital economy by ensuring that impediments to both consumers and businesses embracing this medium of trade are addressed. Canada recognizes that the successful integration of electronic commerce into the global economy is dependent upon the level of trust and confidence businesses and consumers have in the digital environment.

In doing the research to support the GBA Plus, the leads found an OECD study that suggests the use of digital platforms, mobile phones, and mobile money could lead to an overall increase in women's participation in the

57 Global Affairs Canada, 'Summary of Initial GBA+ for Canada Mercosur FTA Negotiations' (n 44).

58 Ibid.

economy.[59] The use of digital platforms may offer women many additional opportunities, including the possibility to overcome challenges related to physical immobility, gain access to new markets and knowledge, enjoy flexible working hours, and supplement their household income. The Organisation for Economic Co-operation and Development (OECD) also notes that the use of digital trade platforms may therefore result in higher female employment rates than in traditional industries or businesses.[60] The OECD also notes that greater digitalization and cheaper online access can benefit in particular women-owned businesses that tend to be smaller and more vulnerable to downturns in the economy.[61]

The GBA Plus also found that Canada's model FTA chapter on electronic commerce could affect all sectors of the economy that engage in digital trade and may have different effects on men and women operating in the sector. Within the category of 'electronic shopping', nearly an equivalent number of men and women are employed in Canada. However, there continues to be a considerable gap in salaries – the average women's salary is more than 50 per cent below the average salary for men.[62] In terms of diversity, Indigenous Peoples occupied 2 per cent of jobs within the Canadian electronic shopping sector. Furthermore, an international study of micro, small, and medium-sized enterprises (MSMEs) found that while only 25 per cent of traditional offline businesses are women-owned, women-owned online businesses represent 50 per cent of the total number.[63] A growth in electronic commerce will likely also have a positive impact on Indigenous Peoples' participation in economic activities of various sectors.

The GBA Plus found that electronic commerce has the potential to act as a tool to advance gender equality and close the gender digital divide by facilitating access to international markets for SMEs owned by women, Indigenous Peoples, and other underrepresented groups, such as persons with disabilities and those living in rural, remote, or northern regions of Canada. In this

59 OECD, 'Going Digital: The Future of Work for Women' (2017) Policy Brief on the Future of Work <www.oecd.org/employment/Going-Digital-the-Future-of-Work-for-Women.pdf> accessed 8 May 2022.

60 Ibid.

61 Jane Korinek, Evdokia Moïsé, and Jakob Tange, 'Trade and Gender: A Framework of Analysis' (2021) OECD Trade Policy Papers No. 246 <https://doi.org/10.1787/6db59d80-en> accessed 8 May 2022.

62 Statistics Canada, 'North American Industry Classification System (NAICS) Canada 2012, All Demographics' <www.statcan.gc.ca/en/subjects/standard/naics/2012/index> accessed 8 May 2022.

63 ITC, 'New Pathways to E-Commerce: A Global MSME Competitiveness Survey' (2017) <https://intracen.org/media/file/2437> accessed 8 May 2022.

regard, two new e-commerce-related commitments have been advanced to address potential negative effects/risks and leverage positive opportunities for women and other underrepresented groups in the economy and trade, namely:

- a provision in the cooperation article to promote accessibility to information and communications technologies for underrepresented groups/ people with specific needs, including women and girls, Indigenous Peoples, and persons with disabilities; and
- a provision in the Personal Information Protection article that commits the parties to ensure that they maintain a domestic legal framework that provides for the protection of personal information of electronic commerce users. (This provision may also be of particular importance to LGBTQI+ communities concerned about protecting their private lives from employer, state, or public scrutiny).

CASE STUDY 2: GOVERNMENT PROCUREMENT Canada's model government procurement (GP) chapter that has been tabled in negotiations aims to secure preferential access to trading partners' GP markets, while retaining the necessary domestic policy space to achieve socio-economic objectives. The proposed GP chapter for negotiations with Mercosur contains two sections: the procedural rules laid out in the chapter and the market access commitments listed in the Annexes. The procedural rules, which establish the manner in which GP is conducted, are governed by four core principles: national treatment, fairness, transparency, and accountability. These rules support the primary objective of providing Canadian businesses with an increased ability to access GP opportunities in foreign markets.[64]

The estimated annual value of contracts awarded by Canada's federal government departments and agencies is about $22 billion, accounting for about 1.2 per cent of GDP.[65] These procurements occur across all sectors and industries. Considering that Canada's existing procurement market is generally open to foreign suppliers, any economic effects from the GP chapter

[64] The market access commitments set out the GP opportunities to which these rules apply and identify the government entities, contract value thresholds, goods and services, and other exclusions that are used to determine whether a procurement is 'covered' by the obligations of the GP chapter.

[65] Government of Canada, 'Public Services and Procurement Canada Unveils Plan to Modernize Federal Procurement' (5 March 2019) <www.canada.ca/en/public-services-procurement/news/2019/03/public-services-and-procurement-canada-unveils-plan-to-modernize-federal-procurement.html> accessed 8 May 2022.

would be largely dependent on the value of the market access commitments provided by Mercosur. Canadian suppliers of goods and services would benefit from access to GP opportunities in the Mercosur countries in various areas such as information and communications technology, telecommunications, energy technologies, and environmental goods and services. In doing the research to support the GBA Plus, the lead negotiators found that in Canada, women-owned SMEs are active in all of these sectors and industries, but particularly in environmental goods and services.

In line with these findings, in the Canada–Mercosur FTA negotiations, Canada seeks to mainstream gender equality and inclusivity provisions in the GP chapter. In the GP chapter, the GBA Plus found that there is an opportunity to increase the participation of women- and Indigenous-owned businesses and other SMEs in the GP market in Canada in order to build their capacity and grow their businesses. Canada can seek the inclusion of a provision in its Market Access Schedule to maintain flexibility to take into account socio-economic considerations in procurements so as to increase the participation of these groups in accessing GP opportunities in Canada.

These two case studies show that there are opportunities to advance inclusive and gender-responsive provisions in various chapters. However, while some chapters do not have direct gender-responsive or inclusive trade provisions appearing in the chapter texts, this does not mean that they do not have gender-related benefits. For example, many of the chapters, especially those related to goods, aim to make trade rules transparent and predictable and to reduce costs for businesses; this is especially important for SMEs, in particular for women-owned businesses that tend to be even smaller than men-owned SMEs,[66] and tend to have a higher proportion of fixed costs as a percentage of expenditures. In addition, while cooperation activities listed in some chapters – particularly those relating to gender, MSMEs, and Indigenous Peoples – advance gender equality, women's economic empowerment and inclusivity, it will be especially important to effectively implement these activities and demonstrate value-added and positive results over time.

14.3.5 *Assessing Canada's Experience in Respect of the GBA Plus Process*

In order to promote sustainable and inclusive economic growth through evidence-based policies, Canada has conducted a quantitative and qualitative assessment of the possible effects on Canadians of the potential Canada–

[66] *See* Bélanger Baur, 'Women-Owned Exporting Small and Medium Enterprises' (n 25).

Mercosur FTA. This approach may help deliver a more gender-responsive and inclusive FTA where women realize the benefits and opportunities of trade as much as men do. GBA Plus can help make an FTA a tool to achieve women's economic empowerment and gender equality outcomes – not only in Canada but also with willing negotiating partners who realize the value of fully integrating women into the economy and trade. In fact, a GBA Plus of trade policies – bilateral, regional, plurilateral, and multilateral – can help achieve not only gender equality outcomes but also sustainable economic development and prosperity for all, consistent with the SDGs that all countries have endorsed.

There are strengths in Canada's approach of applying GBA Plus to an ongoing trade negotiation. The approach includes both a quantitative and a qualitative dimension, with the former informing the latter. The quantitative side is led by the Office of the Chief Economist at Global Affairs Canada using data from Statistics Canada, and the qualitative side is led by negotiators who know their chapters and are well supported by the Gender Focal Point for trade policy and negotiations. As GBA Plus is applied to a variety of trade policy initiatives, this approach is also proving adaptable to different scenarios – new FTAs, modernizations, and accessions; *ex ante* and *ex post* scenarios; and, bilateral, plurilateral, and multilateral contexts. This approach also provides an opportunity for stakeholder feedback and it supports transparency and accountability. When GBA Plus is applied, negotiators are able to table new innovative provisions to address findings in real time at the negotiating table and brief the trade partner on the rationale behind the new proposal, thus building buy-in for the approach and the importance of advancing women's economic empowerment and gender equality through the FTA. In addition, this approach helps Canada promote alignment with and development of domestic flanking policies as required.

There are limitations in applying GBA Plus to FTA negotiations that are important to recognize. For example, a limitation could be that a GBA Plus finding cannot be addressed through a policy provision in a trade agreement. This would mean that addressing the finding would need to be undertaken by another ministry in the government – beyond the trade negotiators. A close and integrated communication must therefore exist among ministries so that they can work together and develop a coherent domestic policy response to a GBA Plus finding in a trade agreement negotiation. In some instances, it may be necessary for the country applying this process to redesign or develop new domestic policies and programmes to mitigate risks or enhance opportunities. In addition, GBA Plus reveals and confirms what is well known: that trade outcomes that benefit one group (for example, consumers who benefit from lower-priced products) may negatively affect another population segment (for example, workers in an industry that would lose its protection once tariffs are removed). Hence, GBA Plus, while uncovering or confirming this tension, may not necessarily produce an immediate win–win solution. However, it may help identify the population group most at risk so those impacts and implications can be taken into account during negotiations and domestic implementation. Another limitation in the successful application of GBA Plus to FTA negotiations may be the lack of gender-disaggregated data across a range of important variables. This gap, however, should not impede analysis if other evidence can be collected through consultations or case studies. It is important to undertake the GBA Plus work in an iterative way, building skills and knowledge, as the challenges for women are generally/intuitively well-known and further delay for the collection and analysis of data will only make things worse for the women who need support.

While the GBA Plus process applied to an ongoing trade negotiation has some limitations, early benefits have already been realized: it is recognized by Canada's trade negotiators that conducting GBA Plus on the ongoing Mercosur FTA negotiations has been a valuable undertaking. It is providing trade negotiators with a richer sense of the impacts and effects of FTA provisions on Canadian workers, entrepreneurs, business owners, and consumers; it is helping officials develop in real time and on an ongoing basis new and innovative gender-responsive and inclusive trade policy provisions to address effects and opportunities; it is supporting the continuous strengthening and innovating of Canada's FTA chapters; and it has effectively informed the FTA negotiation strategy to date.

GBA Plus has also served to highlight data and knowledge gaps that need to be addressed in order to ensure effective GBA Plus of future FTA chapters (for example, indirect employment effects by industry, gender, and other intersectional characteristics; consumer effects). GBA Plus has also highlighted that FTAs do more than seek lower tariffs and increase market access opportunities: FTAs can positively influence a range of factors that affect participation in the economy, such as transparency, cutting red tape, and advancing global norms and standards. The overall benefit of applying GBA Plus to FTA negotiations is that it has the potential to help craft and deliver a more gender-responsive and inclusive trade agreement than ever before.

In terms of ensuring effective GBA Plus of trade agreements on an *ex ante* basis, there are some key success factors that need to be considered. These include: collection and analysis of substantial gender-disaggregated data across a number of economic and trade variables; capacity to interpret the data in a trade policy context and to develop and implement advanced economic modelling with it; a willingness to move beyond some common assumptions such as that trade is gender-neutral; well-functioning government ministries that consult each other regularly; training and guidance for negotiators on how to conduct GBA Plus of their chapters; and strong internal governance systems to ensure implementation of the GBA Plus policy.

14.4 CONCLUDING REMARKS

In the span of a few years, Canada has been able to analyse, develop, and implement changes in its approach to trade policy, in particular as it relates to gender. Canada went from few considerations on gender to specific provisions in CPTPP to dedicated chapters on trade and gender in the Canada–Chile and Canada–Israel FTAs, to a full GBA Plus assessment for the ongoing Canada–Mercosur FTA, and can undertake this approach, with any necessary modifications based on learning, in all future FTA negotiations, including with ASEAN, Indonesia,[67] United Kingdom,[68] and Ukraine.[69]

A better understanding of women-owned SMEs' participation in international trade and the barriers they face also allows the Trade Commissioner Service[70] of Global Affairs Canada to better target their programming activities through the Business Women in International Trade,[71] trade missions tailored to the needs of women entrepreneurs, or through trade promotion activities when new trade agreements come into force. The extension in the analysis to assess potential impacts of a FTA on gender through the labour markets provides a better understanding of the impacts on the labour markets in general and helps in assessing if any adaptation measures are needed in the short or medium term. In the long term, based on evidence

[67] Government of Canada, 'Summary of Initial GBA Plus for the Canada–Indonesia CEPA negotiations' <www.international.gc.ca/trade-commerce/trade-agreements-accords-commerciaux/agr-acc/indonesia-indonesie/cepa-apeg/summary-gba-acs-resume.aspx?lang=eng> accessed 11 September 2022.

[68] Government of Canada, 'Summary of Initial GBA Plus for the Canada–UK FTA negotiations' <www.international.gc.ca/trade-commerce/trade-agreements-accords-commerciaux/agr-acc/canada_uk_fta-ale_canada_ru/summary-gba-init-resume-acs.aspx?lang=eng> accessed 11 September 2022.

[69] Government of Canada, Summary of Initial GBA Plus for Negotiations to Modernize the Canada–Ukraine FTA <www.international.gc.ca/trade-commerce/trade-agreements-accords-commerciaux/agr-acc/ukraine/summary_gba-acs_sommaire.aspx?lang=eng> accessed 16 May 2023.

[70] Government of Canada, 'Trade Commissioner Service' <www.tradecommissioner.gc.ca/index.aspx?lang=eng> accessed 8 May 2022.

[71] Government of Canada, 'Business Women in International Trade' <www.tradecommissioner.gc.ca/businesswomen-femmesdaffaires/index.aspx?lang=eng> accessed 8 May 2022.

from the *ex post* analysis of the CUSFTA, some sectors can benefit directly from the concessions, others could benefit indirectly because of the overall impact of the economy leading to more activities in other sectors, but some workers in sectors affected might need time to adjust to the new realities.

The dynamic GBA Plus that Canada has piloted with the Canada–Mercosur FTA negotiations has resulted in the identification of opportunities in fifteen of twenty five chapters to present new, innovative gender responsive inclusive provisions in real time at the negotiating table to help ensure that women and other underrepresented groups in trade can share more in the benefits of this potential trade agreement. Canada is committed to applying learning from this analysis and negotiations to future trade negotiations bilaterally. There is also an opportunity for Canada to share its experience with trade partners in plurilateral and multilateral contexts. For example, Canada could support the comprehensive application of GBA Plus to the work of the WTO, including its negotiating, reporting, and monitoring functions, as well as implementation of agreements. This would help deliver on the commitments that WTO members made in December 2017 in the Buenos Aires Declaration on Trade and Women's Economic Empowerment[72] at the WTO 11th Ministerial Conference (MC11).

There is no doubt that Canada has made great progress, but it is just the start of the journey. It continues to try to understand better how trade affects other underrepresented groups such as Indigenous Peoples, new immigrants, and visible minorities. As it understands better the linkages between trade and gender, Canada is committed to refine its approach.

[72] WTO, 'Buenos Aires Declaration on Women and Trade Outlines Actions to Empower Women' (12 December 2017) <www.wto.org/english/news_e/news17_e/mc11_12dec17_e.htm> accessed 8 May 2022.

Bibliography

CHAPTER 1: INTRODUCTION (BAHRI/LOPEZ/REMY)

BOOKS

Roberts A and Lamp N, *Six Faces of Globalization: Who Wins, Who Loses, and Why It Matters* (Harvard University Press 2022).

BOOK CHAPTERS

Chen YZ and Tanaka H, 'Women's Empowerment' in Michalos AC (ed.), *Encyclopaedia of Quality of Life and Well-Being Research* (Springer 2014).

ARTICLES

Bahri M, 'Measuring the Gender-Responsiveness of Free Trade Agreements: Using a Self-Evaluation Maturity Framework' (2019) 14(11/12) *Global Trade and Customs Journal* 517–527.

Bøler EA, Javorcik B and Ulltveit-Moe KH, 'Working across Time Zones: Exporters and the Gender Wage Gap' (2018) 111(C) *Journal of International Economics* 122–133.

Broda C and Weinstein DE, 'Globalization and the Gains from Variety' (2006) 121(2) *Quarterly Journal of Economics* 541–585.

Ghosh J, 'Globalization, Export-Oriented Employment for Women and Social Policy: A Case Study of India' (2002) 30(11) *Social Scientist* 17–60.

Melanson K, 'An Examination of the Gendered Effects of Trade Liberalisation' (2005) 2(1) *Policy Perspectives* 10–17.

Oostendorp R, 'Globalization and the Gender Wage Gap' (2009) 23(1) *World Bank Economic Review* 141–161.

Sauvé P and Zoabi H, 'International Trade, the Gender Wage Gap and Female Labor Force Participation' (2014) 111(C) *Journal of Development Economics* 17–33.

Standing G, 'Global Feminization through Flexible Labour (1989) 17(7) *World Development* 1077–1095.

'Global Feminization through Flexible Labour: A Theme Revisited' (1999) 27(3) *World Development* 583–602.

Verloo M, 'Reflections on the Concept and Practice of the Council of Europe Approach to Gender Mainstreaming and Gender Equality' (2005) 12(3) *Social Politics: International Studies in Gender, State & Society* 344–365.

WORKING PAPERS

Alon T, Doepke M, Olmstead-Rumsey J and Tertilt M, 'The Impact of COVID-19 on Gender Equality' (2020) NBER Working Paper No. 26947 <www.nber.org/papers/w26947> accessed 8 May 2022.

Deardorff AV and Stern RM, 'Measurement of Non-Tariff Barriers' (1997) OECD Working Paper No. 179 <www.oecd-ilibrary.org/docserver/568705648470.pdf?expires=1655752963&id=id&accname=guest&checksum=E8E491E03C3B460002DACE6A08B4D75B> accessed 8 May 2022.

Monteiro JA, 'The Evolution of Gender-Related Provisions in Regional Trade Agreements' (2021) WTO Staff Working Paper ERSD-2021-8 <www.wto.org/english/res_e/reser_e/ersd202108_e.htm> accessed 8 May 2022.

von Hagen M, 'Trade and Gender – Exploring a Reciprocal Relationship: Approaches to Mitigate and Measure Gender-Related Trade Impacts' (2014) *Deutsche Gesellschaft für Internationale Zusammenarbeit* <www.oecd.org/dac/gender-development/GIZ_Trade%20and%20Gender_Exploring%20a%20reciprocal%20relationship.pdf> accessed 8 May 2022.

INSTITUTIONAL AND GOVERNMENTAL DOCUMENTS

ILO, 'Women and Men in the Informal Economy: A Statistical Picture' (2018) <www.ilo.org/wcmsp5/groups/public/—dgreports/—dcomm/documents/publication/wcms_626831.pdf> accessed 8 May 2022.

OECD, 'Trade and Gender: A Framework of Analysis' (March 2021) <www.oecd.org/publications/trade-and-gender-6db59d80-en.htm> accessed 8 May 2022.

UNCTAD, 'Mainstreaming Gender in Trade Policy, Note by the UNCTAD secretariat', TD/B/C.I/EM.2/2/Rev.1 (2009) <www.unctad.org/en/docs/ciem2d2_en.pdf> accessed 8 May 2022.

UNCTAD, 'Mainstreaming Gender in Trade Policy', TD/B/C.I/EM.2/2/Rev.1 (19 March 2019).

UNFPA, 'COVID-19: A Gender Lens, Technical Brief Protecting Sexual and Reproductive Health and Rights, and Promoting Gender Equality' (March 2020) <www.unfpa.org/resources/covid-19-gender-lens> accessed 8 May 2022.

UNGA, 'Addis Ababa Action Agenda of the Third International Conference on Financing for Development (Addis Ababa Action Agenda)', A/Res/69/313 (2015), para. 90.

'Transforming Our World: The 2030 Agenda for Sustainable Development', A/RES/70/1 (21 October 2015) <www.refworld.org/docid/57b6e3e44.html> accessed 8 May 2022.

World Bank and WTO, 'Women and Trade: The Role of Trade in Promoting Gender Equality' (30 July 2020) <https://openknowledge.worldbank.org/handle/10986/34140> accessed 8 May 2022.

WTO, 'Gender Aware Trade Policy: A Springboard for Women's Economic Empowerment' 4 <www.wto.org/english/news_e/news17_e/dgra_21jun17_e.pdf> accessed 8 May 2022.

REPORTS AND STUDIES

Bahri A, 'Mainstreaming Gender in Free Trade Agreements' (ITC, 2020) <https://intracen.org/resources/publications/mainstreaming-gender-in-free-trade-agreements> accessed 8 May 2022.

Fontana M and Paciello C, 'Gender Dimensions of Agricultural and Rural Employment: Differentiated Pathways out of Poverty' (FAO, IFAD and ILO, 2010) <www.ilo.org/employment/Whatwedo/Publications/WCMS_150558/lang–en/index.htm> accessed 8 May 2022.

Fontana M, 'Gender Justice in Trade Policy – The Gender Effects of Economic Partnership Agreements' (One World Action, 2009) <https://oneworldaction.org.uk/GendJustTrad.pdf> accessed 8 May 2022.

'The Gender Effects of Trade Liberalization in Developing Countries: A Review of Literature' (Institute of Development Studies, 2009) <www.ids.ac.uk/publications/the-gender-effects-of-trade-liberalization-in-developing-countries-a-review-of-the-literature/> accessed 8 May 2022.

Kutlina-Dimitrova Z, Rueda-Cantuche JM, Amores AF and Román V, 'How Important Are EU Exports for Jobs in the EU?' (EU Chief Economist Note, November 2018) <https://econpapers.repec.org/paper/risdgtcen/2018_5f004.htm> accessed 8 May 2022.

WEBSITES, BLOGS AND NEWS ARTICLES

IIRR, 'Building Back Best: Strengthening Rural Women's Resilience Amid the COVID-19 Pandemic' (March 2021) <https://iirr.org/building-back-best-strengthening-rural-womens-resilience-amid-the-covid-19-pandemic/> accessed 8 May 2022.

UN Women, 'Concepts and Definitions' <www.un.org/womenwatch/osagi/conceptsandefinitions.htm> accessed 8 May 2022.

UN Women, 'On the 25th Anniversary of Landmark Beijing Declaration on Women's Rights, UN Women Calls for Accelerating Its Unfinished Business' (4 September 2020) <www.unwomen.org/en/news/stories/2020/9/press-release-25th-anniversary-of-the-beijing-declaration-on-womens-rights> accessed 8 May 2022.

UN, 'Third International Conference on Financing for Development (FfD3)' (13–16 July 2015) <www.un.org/esa/ffd/ffd3/conference.html> accessed 8 May 2022.

WTO, 'Informal Working Group on Trade and Gender' <www.wto.org/english/tratop_e/womenandtrade_e/iwg_trade_gender_e.htm> accessed 8 May 2022.

'Women and Trade: The Role of Trade in Promoting Gender Equality' (July 2020) <www.wto.org/english/res_e/publications_e/women_trade_pub2807_e.htm> accessed 8 May 2022.

CHAPTER 2: GENDER-RESPONSIVE WTO: MAKING TRADE RULES AND POLICIES WORK FOR WOMEN (DER BOGHOSSIAN)

ARTICLES

Morrow Roberson C, 'Global Parcel Volumes Expected to Double by 2026 on e-Commerce Boom' (2020) *Journal of Commerce Online* <www.joc.com/international-logistics/global-parcel-volumes-expected-double-2026-e-commerce-boom_20201012.html> accessed 8 May 2022.

WORKING PAPERS

Bouet A, Pace K and Glauber JW, 'Informal Cross-Border Trade in Africa: How Much? Why? And What Impact?' (2018) FPRI Discussion Paper <www.ifpri.org/publication/informal-cross-border-trade-africa-how-much-why-and-what-impact> accessed 8 May 2022.

der Boghossian A, 'Trade Policies Supporting Women's Economic Empowerment: Trends in WTO Members' (2019) WTO Staff Working Paper ERSD-2019-07 <www.wto.org/english/res_e/reser_e/ersd201907_e.pdf> accessed 8 May 2022.

'Women's Economic Empowerment: An Inherent Part of Aid for Trade' (2019) WTO Staff Working Paper ERSD-2019-08 <www.wto.org/english/res_e/reser_e/ersd201908_e.htm> accessed 8 May 2022.

DiCaprio A, Yao Y and Simms R, 'Women and Trade: Gender's Impact on Trade Finance and Fintech' (2017) ADBI Working Paper Series No. 797 <www.adb.org/sites/default/files/publication/389186/adbi-wp797.pdf> accessed 8 May 2022.

Elborgh-Woytek K, Newiak M, Kochhar K, Fabrizio S, Kpodar K, Wingender P, Clements B and Schwartz G, 'Women, Work, and the Economy: Macroeconomic Gains from Gender Equity' (2013) IMF Staff Discussion Note SDN/13/10 <www.imf.org/external/pubs/ft/sdn/2013/sdn1310.pdf> accessed 8 May 2022.

Fernández R, Isakova A, Luna F and Rambousek B, 'Gender Equality and Inclusive Growth' (2021) IMF Working Paper WP/21/59 <www.imf.org/en/Publications/WP/Issues/2021/03/03/Gender-Equality-and-Inclusive-Growth-50147> accessed 8 May 2022.

Franić R and Kovačićek T, 'The Professional Status of Rural Women in the EU' (2019) Study requested by the European Parliament FEMM Committee <www.europarl.europa.eu/RegData/etudes/STUD/2019/608868/IPOL_STU(2019)608868_EN.pdf> accessed 8 May 2022.

Kyvik Nordås H, 'Is Trade Liberalization a Window of Opportunity for Women?' (2003) WTO Staff Working Paper ERSD-2003-03 <www.wto.org/english/res_e/reser_e/ersd200303_e.htm> accessed 8 May 2022.

Morsy H, 'Access to Finance – Mind the Gender Gap' (2017) EBRD Working Paper No. 202 <www.ebrd.com/publications/working-papers/access-to-finance> accessed 8 May 2022.

USAID, 'Women in Cross-Border Agricultural Trade' (2012) USAID Policy Brief No. 4 <www.agrilinks.org/sites/default/files/resource/files/EAT_PolicyBrief_WomenCrossBorderAgTrade_Oct2012_FINAL.pdf> accessed 8 May 2022.

INSTITUTIONAL AND GOVERNMENTAL DOCUMENTS

ADB, '2019 Asian Development Bank Annual Report' (ADB, 2019) <www.adb.org/sites/default/files/institutional-document/650011/adb-annual-report-2019.pdf> accessed 8 May 2022.

Aid for Trade Task Force, 'Recommendations of the Task Force on Aid for Trade', WT/AFT/1 (27 July 2006).

FAO, 'The State of Food and Agriculture 2010–2011' (2011) <www.fao.org/3/i2050e/i2050e.pdf> accessed 8 May 2022.

Government of India, 'All India Report of Sixth Economic Consensus' (2016) <https://msme.gov.in/sites/default/files/All%20India%20Report%20of%20Sixth%20Economic%20Census.pdf> accessed 8 May 2022.

IFC, 'IFC Annual Report 2010: Where Innovation Meets Impact' (IFC/World Bank, 2010) <www.ifc.org/wps/wcm/connect/16494d0c-77b8-474a-bafd-f8f8a928ff8c/AR2010_English.pdf?MOD=AJPERES&CVID=iYNAdVZ> accessed 8 May 2022.

ILO, 'World Employment Social Outlook – Trends for Women 2017' (2017) <www.ilo.org/wcmsp5/groups/public/—dgreports/—inst/documents/publication/wcms_557245.pdf> accessed 8 May 2022.

IMF, *Pursuing Women's Economic Empowerment* (2018) <www.imf.org/en/Publications/Policy-Papers/Issues/2018/05/31/pp053118pursuing-womens-economic-empowerment> accessed 8 May 2022

International Livestock Research Institute, 'Why Women Are Essential in Livestock Development – and Why Livestock Are Essential in Women's Lives' (11 February 2022) <www.ilri.org/knowledge/stories/why-women-are-essential-livestock-development-and-why-livestock-are-essential> accessed 19 May 2023.

Permanent Mission of the Kingdom of Saudi Arabia to the WTO, 'Vision 2030, an Economic Diversification Strategy and Women's Economic Empowerment' (23 June 2021) <www.wto.org/english/tratop_e/womenandtrade_e/230621_saudi_arabia.pdf> accessed 8 May 2022.

SADC, 'Food and Nutrition Security Strategy 2015–2025' (2014) <www.resakss.org/sites/default/files/SADC%202014%20Food%20and%20Nutrition%20Security%20Strategy%202015%20-%202025.pdf> accessed 8 May 2022.

UN, 'The UN Sustainable Agenda' <www.un.org/sustainabledevelopment/development-agenda/#:~:text=Sustainable%20development%20has%20been%20defined,to%20meet%20their%20own%20needs> accessed 8 May 2022.

UNDP, 'Afghanistan Socio-Economic Outlook 2021–2022: Averting a Basic Needs Crisis' (1 December 2021) <www.undp.org/publications/afghanistan-socio-economic-outlook-2021-2022-averting-basic-needs-crisis> accessed 8 May 2022.

UNECOSOC, 'Meeting Coverage of the 63rd Commission on the Status of Women', WOM/2175 (13 March 2019) <www.un.org/press/en/2019/wom2175.doc.htm> accessed 8 May 2022.

World Bank and WTO, 'Women and Trade. The Role of Trade in Promoting Gender Equality' (WB/WTO, 2020) <www.wto.org/english/res_e/booksp_e/women_trade_pub2807_e.pdf> accessed 8 May 2022.

World Commission on the Environment and Development, 'Our Common Future' (1987).

WTO, 'Agreement on Trade Facilitation' <www.wto.org/english/docs_e/legal_e/tfa-nov14_e.htm> accessed 8 May 2022.

'Biennial Technical Assistance and Training Plan, Revision 2018–19', WT/COMTD/W/227/Rev.1 (23 October 2017).

'Biennial Technical Assistance and Training Plan, Revision 2020–2021', WT/COMTD/W/248/Rev.1 (1 November 2019).

'Declaration on the Conclusion of Negotiations on Services Domestic Regulation', WT/L/1129 (2 December 2021).

'Guidelines for Arrangements on Relations with Non-Governmental Organizations', WT/L/162 (23 July 1996).

'Hong Kong Ministerial Declaration', WT/MIN(05)/DEC (22 December 2005).

'Interim Report Following the Buenos Aires Joint Declaration on Trade and Women's Economic Empowerment', WT/L/1095/Rev.1 (25 September 2020).

'Joint Declaration on Trade and Women's Economic Empowerment on the Occasion of the WTO Ministerial Conference in Buenos Aires in December 2017' <www.wto.org/english/thewto_e/minist_e/mc11_e/genderdeclarationmc11_e.pdf> accessed 8 May 2022.

'Trade Policy Review – Japan – Minutes of the Meeting, Addendum', WT/TPR/M/310/Add.1 (9 and 11 March 2015).

'Trade Policy Review – Pakistan', WT/TPR/S/311 (17 February 2015).

'Trade Policy Review – Report by Chile', WT/TPR/G/315/Rev.1 (7 October 2015).

'Trade Policy Review – Report by Egypt', WT/TPR/G/367 (16 January 2018).

'Trade Policy Review – Report by Guyana', WT/TPR/G/320 (28 July 2016).

'Trade Policy Review – Report by Iceland' WT/TPR/G/361 (30 August 2017).

'Trade Policy Review – Report by Japan', WT/TPR/G/310 (9 and 11 March 2015).

'Trade Policy Review – Report by Mozambique', WT/TPR/G/354, 7 (29 March 2017).

'Trade Policy Review – Report by Nigeria', WT/TPR/G/356 (7 May 2017).

'Trade Policy Review – Report by Paraguay', WT/TPR/G/360 (2 August 2017).

'Trade Policy Review – Report by the Secretariat – India', WT/TPR/S/313 (28 April 2015).

'Trade Policy Review – Report by the Secretariat – Southern African Customs Union', WT/TPR/S/324 (30 September 2015).

'Trade Policy Review – Report by The Gambia', WT/TPR/G/365, (21 November 2017).

'Trade Policy Review – Report by United Arab Emirates', WT/TPR/G/338 (27 April 2016).

'Trade Policy Review – Report by the United States', WT/TPR/G/350 (14 November 2016).

'Trade Policy Review – Separate Customs Territory of Taiwan, Pehghu, Kinmen and Matsu – Minutes of the Meeting', WT/TPR/M/377/Add.1 (28 January 2019).

'Trade Policy Review – The Maldives – Minutes of the Meeting', WT/TPR/M/332/Add.1 (7 June 2016).

'Trade Policy Review – The Philippines – Minutes of the Meeting, Addendum', WT/TPR/M/368/Add.1 (28 May 2018).

'Trade Policy Review – Zambia – Minutes of the Meeting', WT/TPR/M/340/Add.1 (19 September 2016).

REPORTS AND STUDIES

Etsy, 'Celebrating Creative Entrepreneurship around the Globe' (Etsy Global Seller Census Report 2019' (2019) <https://extfiles.etsy.com/advocacy/Etsy_GlobalSellerCensus_4.2019.pdf> accessed 8 May 2022.

Etsy, 'Unlocking Opportunity – Annual Report 2018' (2018) <http://s23.q4cdn.com/775204224/files/doc_downloads/2018-Annual-Report-(1).pdf> accessed 8 May 2022.

General Authority for Statistics (Saudi Arabia), 'Saudi Unemployment at 11.0%, Overall Unemployment at 6.9% in Q42021' (2021) <www.stats.gov.sa/sites/default/files/LMS%20Q042021E.pdf> accessed 8 May 2022.

Global Alliance for Trade Facilitation, 'WTO's Trade Facilitation Agreement through Gender Lens, Global Alliance for Trade Facilitation' (2020) <www.tradefacilitation.org/content/uploads/2020/05/2020-tfa-through-a-gender-lens-final.pdf> accessed 8 May 2022.

Global Entrepreneurship Monitor, 'GEM Global Report 2016/17' (GERA, 2017) <www.gemconsortium.org/report/gem-2016-2017-global-report> accessed 8 May 2022.

MasterCard, 'Mastercard Index of Women Entrepreneurs (MIWE) 2018' (2018) <www.mastercard.com/news/media/phwevxcc/the-mastercard-index-of-women-entrepreneurs.pdf> accessed 8 May 2022.

Morsy H, 'Access to Finance: Why Aren't Women Leaning In?' (*IMF – Finance & Development Magazine*, March 2020) <www.imf.org/external/pubs/ft/fandd/2020/03/pdf/africa-gender-gap-access-to-finance-morsy.pdf> accessed 8 May 2022.

Southern Africa Trust, 'The Experiences and Challenges of Women in the SADC Region: The Case of Trade and Agriculture Sectors' (January 2018) <https://media.africaportal.org/documents/Experiences_and_challenges_of_women_in_SADC.pdf> accessed 8 May 2022.

Weldegiorgis F, Lawson L, Verbrugge H, 'Women in Artisanal and Small-Scale Mining: Challenges and Opportunities for Greater Participation' (*IISD*, 12 May 2018) <www.iisd.org/publications/report/women-artisanal-and-small-scale-mining-challenges-and-opportunities-greater> accessed 8 May 2022.

WEBSITES, BLOGS AND NEWS ARTICLES

Benton D, 'Global Mining Industry Suffering a Major Skills Shortage Problem, Chamber of Mines Finds' (*Mining*, 17 May 2022) <https://miningglobal.com/supply-chain-and-operations/global-mining-industry-suffering-major-skills-shortage-problem-chamber-mines-finds> accessed 8 May 2022.

Business Standard, 'Indian Textile & Handicrafts Industry Is the Largest Employment Generator after Agri: Ajay Tamta' (*Business Standard*, 9 November 2017) <www.business-standard.com/article/news-cm/indian-textile-handicrafts-industry-is-the-largest-employment-generator-after-agri-ajay-tamta-117110900180_1.html> accessed 8 May 2022.

EIF, 'Delivering Change in Mali: Investing in Women and Beyond' (*Trade for Development News EIF*, October 2016) <https://enhancedif.org/en/publication/2016-10/delivering-change-mali-investing-women-and-beyond> accessed 8 May 2022, link no longer active.

EIGE, 'Gender Blindness' <https://eige.europa.eu/thesaurus/terms/1157> accessed 8 May 2022.

European Innovation Council, 'EU Launches Women TechEU Pilot to Put Women at the Forefront of Deep Tech' (13 July 2021) <https://eic.ec.europa.eu/news/eu-launches-women-techeu-pilot-put-women-forefront-deep-tech-2021-07-13_en> accessed 8 May 2022.

Eurostat, 'Farm Indicators by Agricultural Area, Type of Farm, Standard Output, Sex and Age of the Manager and NUTS 2 Regions' (22 February 2021) <https://ec.europa.eu/eurostat/databrowser/view/EF_M_FARMANG__custom_636393/bookmark/table?lang=en&bookmarkId=f146257b-e328–43b7-b338–48c769ab000f> accessed 8 May 2022.

Fair Trade Africa, 'I Am Back as a Woman' (4 September 2020) <https://fairtradeafrica.net/i-am-coming-back-as-a-woman/> accessed 8 May 2022.

FAO, 'Women Farmers and Resilience in the Face of Climate Change' <www.fao.org/climate-smart-agriculture/news/detail/zh/c/881891/> accessed 8 May 2022.

Fredenburgh J, 'The "Invisible" Women at the Heart of the Chocolate Industry' (BBC, n.d.) <www.bbc.com/future/bespoke/follow-the-food/the-invisible-women-farmers-of-ivory-coast.html> accessed 8 May 2022.

ILO, 'Employment in Agriculture, Female (% of Female Employment) (Modelled ILO Estimate)' (29 January 2021) <https://data.worldbank.org/indicator/SL.AGR.EMPL.FE.ZS> accessed 8 May 2022.

International Gender Champions, 'About' <https://genderchampions.com/about#:~:text=The%20International%20Gender%20Champions%20> accessed 8 May 2022.

ISO, 'IWA 34:2021, Women's Entrepreneurship – Key Definitions and General Criteria' <www.iso.org/standard/79585.html> accessed 8 May 2022.

ITU, 'Bridging the Gender Divide' (July 2021) <www.itu.int/en/mediacentre/backgrounders/Pages/bridging-the-gender-divide.aspx> accessed 8 May 2022.

Kingdom of Saudi Arabia, Vision 2030' <www.vision2030.gov.sa> accessed 8 May 2022.

Knowles M, 'Mali Mango Project Is "Bearing Fruit"', 2 June 2017 <www.fruitnet.com/eurofruit/mali-mango-project-is-bearing-fruit/172388.article> accessed 19 May 2023.

Lusaka Times, 'Mines are Battling to Attract Skilled and Experienced People – Chamber of Mines' (23 June 2017) <www.lusakatimes.com/2017/06/23/mines-battling-attract-skilled-experienced-people-chamber-mines/> accessed 8 May 2022.

Musumeci M and Miyamoto K, 'Strengthening the Gender Dimension of Aid for Trade in the Least Developed Countries' (Enhanced Integrated Framework, 25 June 2019) <https://trade4devnews.enhancedif.org/en/news/strengthening-gender-dimension-aid-trade-least-developed-countries> accessed 8 May 2022.

PwC Nigeria, 'Impact of Women on Nigeria's Economy' (PwC, 12 March 2020) <www.pwc.com/ng/en/publications/impact-of-women-on-nigerias-economy .html> accessed 8 May 2022.

SAWDF, 'International Women Entrepreneurs Summit – 2018' <https://sawdf.org/port folio-item/international-women-entrepreneurs-summit-2018/> accessed 8 May 2022.

Women at the Table, 'Home' <www.womenatthetable.net/> accessed 8 May 2022.

Women Entrepreneurship Knowledge Hub, 'The State of Women's Entrepreneurship in Canada 2021' (June 2021) <https://wekh.ca/research/the-state-of-womens-entre preneurship-in-canada-2021/> accessed 8 May 2022.

World Bank, 'Breaking the "Grass Ceiling": Empowering Women Farmers' (6 March 2018) <www.worldbank.org/en/news/feature/2018/03/06/breaking-the-grass-ceil ing-empowering-women-farmers> accessed 8 May 2022.

WTO, 'Informal Working Group on Trade and Gender' (WTO, 26 February 2021) <www.wto.org/english/tratop_e/womenandtrade_e/iwg_trade_gender_e.htm> accessed 8 May 2022.

OTHER

WTO, 'Workshop on Enhancing the Participation of Women Entrepreneurs and Traders in Government Procurement Hosted by the Republic of Moldova Organized in cooperation with the WTO, ITC and EBRD' (25 June 2018) <www.wto.org/eng lish/tratop_e/womenandtrade_e/programme_workshop_e.htm> accessed 8 May 2022.

WTO survey, Assessing Women Entrepreneurs' Knowledge Gap on Trade in East Africa, South Asia, and Latin America (2019–2020) (Unpublished. on file with author).

CHAPTER 3: ADVANCES IN FEMINIZING THE WTO (MIKIC)

BOOKS

Tran-Nguyen AN and Beviglia Zampetti A (eds), *Trade and Gender: Opportunities and Challenges for Developing Countries* (UNCTAD 2004).

BOOK CHAPTERS

Mikic M and Sharma V, 'Feminizing WTO 2.0' in Evenett SJ and Baldwin R (eds.), *Revitalising Multilateralism: Pragmatic Ideas for the New WTO Director-General* (Centre for Economic Policy Research Press 2020).

ARTICLES

Cagatay N, 'Asian and Pacific Developing Economies and the First WTO Ministerial Conference: Issues of Concern' (1996) 22 *Studies in Trade and Investment* 323–334.

Erten B and Keskin P, 'Trade-Offs? The Impact of WTO Accession on Intimate Partner Violence in Cambodia' (2021) No. 14918 *Review of Economics and Statistics* 1–40.

WORKING PAPERS

der Boghossian A, 'Women's Economic Empowerment: An Inherent Part of Aid for Trade' (2019) WTO Staff Working Paper ERSD-2019-08 <www.wto.org/english/res_e/reser_e/ersd201908_e.pdf> accessed 8 May 2022.

Fitzgerald OE, Acharya R, Aydiner-Avsar N, Babiak O, Baka S, Beliakova A, Champagne F-P, María de la Mora L, Elson D, Fontana M, Goff P, González A, Honey S, Kinnear M, Malcorra S, Panezi M, Pinchis-Paulsen M, Piovani C, Rajagopal B, Seiermann J, Steger D, Cherise Valles C and Zarrilli S, 'Reshaping Trade through Women's Economic Empowerment' (2018) CIGI Special Report <www.cigionline.org/sites/default/files/documents/Women%20and%20Trade.pdf> accessed 8 May 2022.

Korinek J, Moïsé E and Tange J, 'Trade and Gender: A Framework of Analysis' (2021) OECD Trade Policy Papers No. 246 <https://doi.org/10.1787/6db59d80-en> accessed 8 May 2022.

Rubinova S and Sebti M, 'The WTO Trade Cost Index and Its Determinants' (2021) WTO Staff Working Paper ERSD-2021-6 <www.wto.org/english/res_e/reser_e/ersd202106_e.pdf> accessed 8 May 2022.

Shepherd B and Stone S, 'Trade and Women' (2017) ADBI Working Paper Series No. 648 <www.adb.org/sites/default/files/publication/224666/adbi-wp648.pdf> accessed 8 May 2022.

Tyers-Chowdhury A and Binder G, 'What We Know about the Gender Digital Divide for Girls: A Literature Review' (UNICEF Gender and Innovation Evidence Briefs, 2021) <www.unicef.org/eap/media/8311/file/What%20we%20know%20about%20the%20gender%20digital%20divide%20for%20girls:%20A%20literature%20review.pdf> accessed 8 May 2022.

Upadhayay NB, 'Are Only Men Fighting Trade Wars? Empirical Evidence from the Temporary Trade Barriers (TTB) Data' (2020) ERUDITE Working Papers 2020 <https://erudite.univ-paris-est.fr/fileadmin/public/ERUDITE/erudwp/ERU-03-20-nu.pdf> accessed 8 May 2022.

Wolff AW, '"WTO 2025: Constructing an Executive Branch': PIIE Working Paper 22-8 (May 2022) <www.piie.com/sites/default/files/documents/wp22-8.pdf> accessed 22 April 2023.

INSTITUTIONAL AND GOVERNMENTAL DOCUMENTS

UN ESCAP, 'Asia-Pacific Trade and Investment Trends 2021–2022: Preferential Trade Agreements in Asia and the Pacific, United Nations, Bangkok' (2020) <www.unescap.org/sites/default/d8files/knowledge-products/APTIT_PTA_20212022.pdf> accessed 8 May 2022.

'Economic and Social Commission for Asia and the Pacific: Annual Report, 2 May 1995–24 April 1996', E/1996/36 E/ESCAP/1044 (Economic and Social Council Official Records, 1996).

UNCTAD, 'Trade and Gender: Opportunities and Challenges for Developing Countries', UNCTAD/EDM/2004/2 (23 May 2004).

World Bank and WTO, 'Women and Trade: The Role of Trade in Promoting Gender Equality' (2020) <www.wto.org/english/res_e/booksp_e/women_trade_pub2807_e.pdf> accessed 8 May 2022.

WTO Trade Cost Index, 'Who Faces Higher Trade Costs? Trade Costs by Gender' <http://tradecosts.wto.org/categories.html> accessed 8 May 2022.

'Committee on Agriculture in Special Session – Report by the Chairperson, HE Ms Gloria Abraham Peralta to the Trade Negotiations Committee', TN/AG/50 (23 November 2021).

'COVID-19 and World Trade' <www.wto.org/english/tratop_e/covid19_e/covid19_e.htm> accessed 8 May 2022.

'Declaration on the Conclusion of Negotiations on Services Domestic Regulation', WT/L/1129 (2 December 2021).

'Final Work Plan for Implementing Activities under the Informal Working Group on Trade and Gender', INF/TGE/W/1/Rev.2 (29 March 2021).

'Informal Working Group on MSMEs, Declaration on Micro, Small and Medium-Sized Enterprises (MSMEs)', INF/MSME/4/Rev.2 (6 October 2021).

'Joint Ministerial Declaration on the Advancement of Gender Equality and Women's Economic Empowerment within Trade 12th WTO Ministerial Conference', WT/MIN21/4 (10 November 2021).

'Report on G20 Trade Measures' (28 October 2021) <www.wto.org/english/news_e/news21_e/report_trdev_nov21_e.pdf> accessed 8 May 2022.

'Singapore Ministerial Declaration', WT/MIN(96)/DEC (18 December 1996).

'Statement on the Inclusive Trade and Gender Equality from the Co-Chairs of the Informal Working Group on Trade and Gender', WT/MIN(22)/7 (12 June 2022).

'WTO Secretariat Talking Points' (16 July 2021) <www.wto.org/english/tratop_e/womenandtrade_e/16july21/statement_from_wto_secretariat.pdf> accessed 8 May 2022.

'WTO Trade Cost Index: Evolution, Incidence and Determinants, Background Note' (March 2021) <http://tradecosts.wto.org/> accessed 8 May 2022.

REPORTS AND STUDIES

der Boghossian A, 'WTO Technical Assistance on Trade and Gender: New Strategy 2021–2026' (WTO, 2021) <www.wto.org/english/tratop_e/womenandtrade_e/16july21/item_3.4.d._wto_secretariat.pdf> accessed 8 May 2022.

ITC, 'Delivering on the Buenos Aires Declaration on Trade and Women's Economic Empowerment' (2020) <www.wto.org/english/tratop_e/womenandtrade_e/tig_rpt_dec20_e.pdf> accessed 8 May 2022.

Joekes S, 'A Primer on Gender and Trade' <www.genderandtrade.com/_files/ugd/c947e9_a7141ac8ff644bff8bcd006731b9fa7c.pdf> accessed 8 May 2022.

WEBSITES, BLOGS AND NEWS ARTICLES

Dommen C, 'WTO Advances Gender Agenda Amidst Calls for Broader Gender Lens' (IISD, 2021) <https://sdg.iisd.org/news/wto-advances-gender-agenda-amidst-calls-for-broader-gender-lens/> accessed 8 May 2022.

Fitzgerald OE, 'Modernizing the World Trade Organization' (CIGI, 2020) <www.cigionline.org/articles/modernizing-world-trade-organization/> accessed 8 May 2022.

Government of Canada, 'Minister Ng Promotes Benefits of Global Trade and Gender Arrangement at OECD' (9 June 2021) <www.canada.ca/en/global-affairs/news/2021/06/minister-ng-promotes-benefits-of-global-trade-and-gender-arrangement-at-oecd.html> accessed 8 May 2022.

Gromova K, Anderson R and Gupta G, 'Opening a Global Conversation about the Gender Digital Divide' (World Bank, 4 November 2021) <https://blogs.worldbank.org/digital-development/opening-global-conversation-about-gender-digital-divide> accessed 8 May 2022.

New Zealand Foreign Affairs and Trade, 'Inclusive Trade Action Group (ITAG)' <www.mfat.govt.nz/kr/trade/nz-trade-policy/inclusive-trade-action-group-itag/> accessed 8 May 2022.

OECD, 'How Trade Can Support Women's Economic Empowerment Global Trade and Gender Arrangement (GTAGA): An Innovative Initiative to Support Women's Economic Empowerment through Trade' (9 June 2021) <www.oecd.org/trade/events/trade-women-economic-empowerment/> accessed 8 May 2022.

OECD, 'Trade and Gender: A Framework Analysis' (2021) <www.oecd.org/trade/topics/trade-and-gender/> accessed 8 May 2022.

Sokolova MV, DiCaprio A, Bivens Collinson N, 'Is It Time for Women Leaders in International Organizations?' (Trade Experettes, n.d.) <www.tradeexperettes.org/blog/articles/is-it-time-for-women-leaders-in-international-organizations> accessed 8 May 2022.

Trade Experettes, 'Time for Women Leaders in International Organizations' <www.tradeexperettes.org/podcasts/episodes/women-leaders-in-international-organizations> accessed 8 May 2022.

Ueno A, 'Erosion of the Non-discrimination Principle through Waves of Preferential Trade Agreements: A Warning from the Sutherland Report' (REITI, n.d.) <www.rieti.go.jp/en/columns/a01_0163.html> accessed 8 May 2022.

UN ESCAP, 'ARTNeT & WTO Webinar – Forward-Looking Conversation on "Trade for Peace"' (10 December 2021) <www.unescap.org/events/2021/artnet-wto-webinar-forward-looking-conversation-trade-peace#> accessed 8 May 2022.

WTO, 'Buenos Aires Declaration on Women and Trade Outlines Actions to Empower Women' <www.wto.org/english/news_e/news17_e/mc11_12dec17_e.htm> accessed 8 May 2022.

Informal Working Group on Trade and Gender <www.wto.org/english/tratop_e/womenandtrade_e/iwg_trade_gender_e.htm> accessed 8 May 2022.

'Meetings of the Informal Working Group' <www.wto.org/english/tratop_e/womenandtrade_e/iwg_trade_gender_e.htm#meetings> accessed 8 May 2022.

'Ministerial Conferences: Twelfth WTO Ministerial Conference' <www.wto.org/english/thewto_e/minist_e/mc12_e/documents_e.htm> accessed 8 May 2022.

'Trade and Gender Informal Working Group Co-chairs Present Draft Outcome Document for MC12' (WTO News, 23 September 2021) <www.wto.org/english/news_e/news21_e/women_23sep21_e.htm> accessed 8 May 2022.

'Trade and Labour Standards' <www.wto.org/english/thewto_e/minist_e/min96_e/labstand.htm> accessed 8 May 2022.

'Twelfth WTO Ministerial Conference' <www.wto.org/english/thewto_e/minist_e/mc12_e/mc12_e.htm> accessed 8 May 2022.

WTO Conference Services, 'From Gender Research to Action for a Post COVID-19 Resilient World' (YouTube, 29 September 2021) <www.youtube.com/watch?v=hLHW27FyVdo> accessed 8 May 2022.

CHAPTER 4: GLOBAL ECONOMIC GOVERNANCE AND WOMEN: WHY IS THE WTO A DIFFICULT CASE FOR WOMEN'S REPRESENTATION? (FABIAN)

BOOKS

Bashevkin SB, *True Patriot Love: The Politics of Canadian Nationalism* (Oxford University Press 1991).

Brownlie I, *Principles of Public International Law* (Oxford University Press 5th ed. 1998).

Crawford J (ed), *Brownlie's Principles of Public International Law* (Oxford University Press 8th ed. 2012).

Edwards R, *Contested Terrain: The Transformation of the Workplace in the Twentieth Century* (Basic Books 1979).

Gibb H, *Gender Mainstreaming: Good Practices from the Asia Pacific Region* (Renouf Publishing 2001).

Liebowitz DJ, *Gender and Identity in an Era of Globalization: Transnational Political Organizing in North America* (Rutgers 2000).

Massey D, *Spatial Divisions of Labour: Social Structures and the Geography of Production* (Macmillan 1984).

North DC, *Institutions, Institutional Change and Economic Performance* (Cambridge University Press 2011).

Vickers J, Rankin P and Appelle C, *Politics as if Women Mattered: A Political Analysis of the National Action Committee on the Status of Women* (University of Toronto Press 1993).

Walby S, *Gender Transformations* (Routledge 1997).

BOOK CHAPTERS

Bonzon Y, 'Options for Public Participation in the WTO: Experience from Regional Trade Agreements' in Steger DP (ed.), *WTO: Redesigning the World Trade Organization for the Twenty-first Century* (CIGI & Wilfrid Laurier University Press 2010).

Burda J, 'Chinese Women after the Accession to the World Trade Organization: A Legal Perspective on Women's Labor Rights' in Berik G, Dong XY and Summerfield G (eds.), *Gender, China and the World Trade Organization: Essays from Feminist Economics* (Routledge 2010).

Caglar G, 'Feminist Strategies and Social Learning in International Economic Governance' in Caglar G, Prügl E and Zwingel S (eds.), *Feminist Strategies in International Governance* (Routledge 2013).

Clark JD, 'The World Bank and Civil Society: An Evolving Experience' in Scholte JA and Schnabel A (eds.), *Civil Society and Global Finance* (Routledge 2002).

Davidson PJ, 'The Role of Law in Governing Regionalism in Asia' in Thomas N (ed.), *Governance and Regionalism in Asia* (Routledge 2008).

Dawson TC and Bhatt G, 'The IMF and Civil Society: Striking a Balance' in Scholte JA and Schnabel A (eds.), *Civil Society and Global Finance* (Routledge 2002).

Dorsey E, 'The Global Women's Movement: Articulating a New Vision of Global Governance' in Diehl PF (ed.), *The Politics of Global Governance: International Organizations in an Interdependent World* (Reinner 2005).

Elsig M and Cottier T, 'Reforming the WTO: The Decision-Making Triangle Revisited' in Cottier T and Elsig M (eds.), *Governing the World Trade Organization: Past, Present and Beyond Doha* (Cambridge University Press 2011).

Elsig M, 'WTO Decision-Making: Can We Get a Little Help from the Secretariat and the Critical Mass?' in Steger DP (ed.), *WTO: Redesigning the World Trade Organization for the Twenty-first Century* (CIGI & Wilfrid Laurier University Press 2010).

Garcia Rubio M, 'Unilateral Measures as a Means of Forcible Execution of WTO Recommendations and Decisions' in Picchio Forlati L and Sicilianos LA (eds.), *Les sanctions economiques en droit international / Economic Sanctions in International Law* (Martinus Nijhoff Publishers 2004).

Nieto-Navia R, 'International Peremptory Norms (*Jus Cogens*) and International Humanitarian Law' in Lal Chand V et al. (eds.), *Man's Inhumanity to Man* (Brill Nijhoff 2003).

True J, 'Feminist Problems with International Norms: Gender Mainstreaming in Global Governance' in Tickner JA and Sjoberg L (eds.), *Feminism and International Relations: Conversations about the Past, Present and Future* (Routledge 2011).

'Gender Specialists and Global Governance: New Forms of Women's Movement Mobilisation' in Grey S and Sawer M (eds.), *Women's Movements: Flourishing or in Abeyance?* (Routledge 2008).

Van den Bossche P, 'Non-Governmental Organizations and the WTO: Limits to Involvement?' in Steger DP (ed.), *WTO: Redesigning the World Trade Organization for the Twenty-First Century* (CIGI & Wilfrid Laurier University Press 2010).

Young B, 'Structural Power and the Gender Biases of Technocratic Network Governance in Finance' in Caglar G, Prügl E and Zwingel S (eds.), *Feminist Strategies in International Governance* (Routledge 2013).

ARTICLES

Abbott KW, Keohane RO, Moravcsik A, Slaughter AM and Snidal D, 'The Concept of Legalization' (2000) 54(3) *International Organization* 401–419.

Costa L, 'Women Say No to WTO' (2000) 4(2) *Gender, Technology and Development* 315–322.

Gabriel C and Macdonald L, 'Managing Trade Engagements? Mapping the Contours of State Feminism and Women's Political Activism' (2005) 12(1) *Canadian Foreign Policy* 71-88, 82.

Goetz AM, 'The New Competition in Multilateral Norm-Setting: Transnational Feminists and the Illiberal Backlash' (2020) 149(1) *Daedalus* 165–166.

Hathaway OA, 'The Cost of Commitment' (2003) 55(5) *Stanford Law Review* 1821–1862.

Hawkesworth M, 'Policy Discourse as Sanctioned Ignorance: Theorizing the Erasure of Feminist Knowledge' (2009) 3(3–4) *Critical Policy Studies* 268–289.

Kuijper PJ, 'The Law of GATT as a Special Field of International Law – Ignorance, Further Refinement or Self-Contained System of International Law' (1994) 25 *Netherlands Yearbook of International Law*, 227–257.

Marceau G, 'WTO Dispute Settlement and Human Rights' (2002) 13(4) *European Journal of International Law* 753–814.

Mavroidis PC, 'Remedies in the WTO Legal System: Between a Rock and a Hard Place' (2000) 11(4) *European Journal of International Law* 763–813.

Nagar R, Lawson V, McDowell L and Hanson S, 'Locating Globalization: Feminist (Re)readings of the Subjects and Spaces of Globalization' (2002) 78(3) *Economic Geography* 257–284.

Palmeter D and Mavroidis PC, 'The WTO Legal System: Sources of Law' (1998) 92 *American Journal of International Law* 398–413.

Pauwelyn J, 'The Role of Public International Law in the WTO: How Far Can We Go?' (2001) 95(3) *American Journal of International Law* 535–578.

Steinkopf Rice J, 'Viewing Trade Liberalization through a Feminist Lens: A Content Analysis of the Counterhegemonic Discourse of Gender and Trade Advocacy Groups' (2010) 30(3) *Sociological Spectrum* 289–316.

Trachtman J, 'The Domain of WTO Dispute Resolution' (1999) 40(2) *Harvard International Law Journal* 333–378.

True J and Mintrom M, 'Transnational Networks and Policy Diffusion: The Case of Gender Mainstreaming' (2001) 45(1) *International Studies Quarterly* 27–57.

Whitsitt E, 'A Comment on the Public Morals Exception in International Trade and the EC – Seal Products Case: Moral Imperialism and Other Concerns' (2014) 3 (4) *Cambridge Journal of International and Comparative Law* 1376–1391.

WORKING PAPERS

Jensen M and Lee E, 'Trade and Employment: Challenges for Policy Research' (2007) ILO and WTO Joint Study <www.ilo.org/wcmsp5/groups/public/—dgreports/—dcomm/—publ/documents/publication/wcms_091038.pdf> accessed 8 May 2022.

Underhill G, 'Markets, Institutions, and Transaction Costs: The Endogeneity of Governance' (2007) World Economy & Finance Research Programme Working Paper <https://ideas.repec.org/p/wef/wpaper/0025.html> accessed 8 May 2022.

Vickers J, 'Is Nationalism Always "Bad for Women"? In Search of "Women-Friendly" Democracy: Gender/Nation Relations in Modern Nation-States' 2005/2006 Davidson Dunton Research Lecture, Carleton University (27 March 2006).

Viilup E, 'The EU's Trade Policy: From Gender-Blind to Gender Sensitive?' (2015) In-Depth Analysis for the European Parliament, DG External Policies <www.europarl.europa.eu/RegData/etudes/IDAN/2015/549058/EXPO_IDA(2015)549058_EN.pdf> accessed 8 May 2022.

INSTITUTIONAL AND GOVERNMENTAL DOCUMENTS

APEC, 'Framework for Integration of Women in APEC' (1999) <www.apec.org/~/media/Files/Groups/GFPN/02_aggi_framewk.pdf> accessed 8 May 2022.

'Joint Ministerial Statement' APEC Ministerial Meeting on Women (15–16 October 1998).

IMF, 'Standard Rules for Review and Publication of Evaluation Reports and other IEO Documents' (19 August 2002) <www.ieo-imf.org/ieo/files/origins/081902.pdf> accessed 8 May 2022.

IPU, '2016 Annual Session of the Parliamentary Conference on the WTO: What Future for the WTO?, WTO Headquarters, Geneva, 13–14 June 2016, organized jointly by the Inter-Parliamentary Union and the European Parliament' <www.ipu.org/splz-e/trade16.htm> accessed 8 May 2022.

UN Office of the Special Adviser on Gender Issues and Advancement of Women, 'Supporting Gender Mainstreaming: The Work of the Office of the Special Adviser on Gender Issues and Advancement of Women' (March 2001) <www.un.org/womenwatch/osagi/pdf/report.pdf> accessed 8 May 2022.

UNGA, 'Methods and Procedures of the General Assembly', A/RES/362 (22 October 1949) Rule 82 et seq.

World Bank, 'International Bank of Reconstruction and Development: Voting Power of Executive Directors' <http://siteresources.worldbank.org/BODINT/Resources/278027-1215524804501/IBRDEDsVotingTable.pdf> accessed 8 May 2022.

WTO, 'Buenos Aires Declaration on Women and Trade Outlines Actions to Empower Women – 12 December 2017' (2017) <www.wto.org/english/news_e/news17_e/mc11_12dec17_e.htm> accessed 8 May 2022.

'Differential and More Favourable Treatment, Reciprocity and Fuller Participation of Developing Countries, Decision of 28 November 1979', L/4903 (29 November 1979).

'Eleventh WTO Ministerial Conference: Buenos Aires Declaration on Women and Trade outlines actions to empower women' (12 December 2017) <www.wto.org/english/news_e/news17_e/mc11_12dec17_e.htm> accessed 8 May 2022.

'Guidelines for Arrangements on Relations with Non-Governmental Organizations', WT/L/162 (23 July 1996).

'Interim Report Following the Buenos Aires Joint Declaration on Trade and Women's Economic Empowerment' (25 September 2020) <https://docs.wto.org/dol2fe/Pages/SS/directdoc.aspx?filename=q:/WT/L/1095R1.pdf&Open=True> accessed 8 May 2022.

'Joint Declaration on Trade and Women's Economic Empowerment on the Occasion of the WTO Ministerial Conference in Buenos Aires in December 2017' (2017) <www.wto.org/english/thewto_e/minist_e/mc11_e/genderdeclarationmc11_e.pdf> accessed 8 May 2022.

'Joint Ministerial Declaration on the Advancement of Gender Equality and Women's Economic Empowerment within Trade', WT/MIN(21)/4 (10 November 2021).

'Ministerial Declaration – Ministerial Conference, Fourth Session, Doha, 9–14 November 2001', WT/MIN(01)/DEC/W/1 (20 November 2001) para. 47.

'The Future of the WTO: Addressing Institutional Challenges in the New Millennium, Report by the Consultative Board to the Director-General Supachai Panitchpakdi' (2004) <www.wto.org/english/thewto_e/10anniv_e/future_wto_e.pdf> accessed 8 May 2022.

REPORTS AND STUDIES

Appellate Body Report, European Communities – Conditions for the Granting of Tariff Preferences to Developing Countries, WT/DS246/AB/R (31 August 2004).

Cohen M, 'The Macdonald Report and Its Implications for Women' Feminist Action (December 1985).

The Warwick Commission, 'The Multilateral Trade Regime: Which Way Forward? – The Report of the First Warwick Commission' (University of Warwick December 2007).

WEBSITES, BLOGS AND NEWS ARTICLES

APEC, 'APEC Business Advisory Council – Achievements' <www.apec.org/Groups/Other-Groups/APEC-Business-Advisory-Council.aspx> accessed 8 May 2022.

'APEC Business Travel Card' <www.apec.org/about-us/about-apec/business-resources/apec-business-travel-card.aspx> accessed 8 May 2022.

'APEC Study Centers Consortium' <www.apec.org/Groups/Other-Groups/APEC-Study-Centres-Consortium.aspx> accessed 8 May 2022.

Cornell University Law School's Legal Information Institute, 'Jus Cogens' <www.law.cornell.edu/wex/jus_cogens> accessed 8 May 2022.

IMF, 'Completed Evaluations' <www.ieo-imf.org/ieo/pages/Completed.aspx> accessed 8 May 2022.

'Factsheet – Debt Relief under the Heavily Indebted Poor Countries (HIPC) Initiative' (24 March 2014) <www.imf.org/external/np/exr/facts/hipc.htm> accessed 8 May 2022.

'Factsheet – IMF Quotas' (25 March 2014) <www.imf.org/external/np/exr/facts/quotas.htm> accessed 8 May 2022.

'IMF Executive Directors and Voting Power' (19 August 2014) <www.imf.org/external/np/sec/memdir/eds.aspx> accessed 8 May 2022.

IPU, '2016 Annual Session of the Parliamentary Conference on the WTO – What Future for the WTO?, Geneva, 13–14 June 2016: Outcome Document – Adopted by consensus on 14 June 2016' <www.ipu.org/splz-e/trade16/outcome.pdf> accessed 8 May 2022.

UN Women, 'Gender Mainstreaming' <www.un.org/womenwatch/osagi/gendermainstreaming.htm> accessed 8 May 2022.

WTO, 'Aid for Trade Fact Sheet' <www.wto.org/english/tratop_e/devel_e/a4t_e/a4t_factsheet_e.htm> accessed 8 May 2022.

'Appellate Body Members' <www.wto.org/english/tratop_e/dispu_e/ab_members_descrp_e.htm> accessed 8 May 2022.
'Current WTO Chairpersons' <www.wto.org/english/thewto_e/secre_e/current_chairs_e.htm> accessed 8 May 2022.
'Enhanced Integrated Framework' <www.wto.org/english/tratop_e/devel_e/teccop_e/if_e.htm> accessed 8 May 2022.
'International Intergovernmental Organizations Granted Observer Status to WTO Bodies' <www.wto.org/english/thewto_e/igo_obs_e.htm> accessed 8 May 2022.
'Overview of the WTO Secretariat' <www.wto.org/english/thewto_e/secre_e/intro_e.htm> accessed 8 May 2022.
'The WTO and Other Organizations' <www.wto.org/english/thewto_e/coher_e/coher_e.htm> accessed 8 May 2022.
'Understanding the WTO: Cross-Cutting and New Issues – Labour Standards: Consensus, Coherence and Controversy; Consensus on Core Standards, Work Deferred to the ILO' <www.wto.org/english/thewto_e/whatis_e/tif_e/bey5_e.htm> accessed 8 May 2022.
'Whose WTO Is It Anyway?' <www.wto.org/english/thewto_e/whatis_e/tif_e/org1_e.htm> accessed 8 May 2022.

OTHER

European Parliament, 'MEPS to Lead WTO Parliamentary Conference in Geneva' (10 June 2016).

CHAPTER 5: WOMEN IN THE LDCS: HOW TO BUILD FORWARD DIFFERENTLY FOR THEM? (ZARILLI)

WORKING PAPERS

Adu-Gyamfi R, Asongu SA, Sonto Mmusi T, Wamalwa H and Mangori M, 'A Comparative Study of Export Processing Zones in the Wake of the Sustainable Development Goals: The Cases of Botswana, Kenya, Tanzania, and Zimbabwe' (2020) WIDER Working Paper Series wp-2020-64 <www.wider.unu.edu/sites/default/files/Publications/Working-paper/PDF/wp2020-64.pdf> accessed 8 May 2022.
Anner M, 'Abandoned? The Impact of Covid-19 on Workers and Businesses at the Bottom of Global Garment Supply Chains' (2020) Pennsylvania State University Center for Global Workers' Rights Research Report <www.workersrights.org/wp-content/uploads/2020/03/Abandoned-Penn-State-WRC-Report-March-27-2020.pdf> accessed 8 May 2022.
Torres J, Maduko F, Gaddis I, Iacovone L and Beegle K, 'The Impact of the COVID-19 Pandemic on Women-Led Businesses' (2021) World Bank Policy Research Working Paper 9817 <https://openknowledge.worldbank.org/handle/10986/36435> accessed 8 May 2022.

UNCTAD, 'Making Trade Work for Least Developed Countries: A Handbook on Mainstreaming Trade' (2016) Trade and Poverty Paper Series No. 5 <https://unctad.org/webflyer/making-trade-work-least-developed-countries-handbook-mainstreaming-trade> accessed 8 May 2022.

Warr P and Menon J, 'Cambodia's Special Economic Zones' (2015) ADB Economics Working Paper Series No. 459 <www.adb.org/sites/default/files/publication/175236/ewp-459.pdf> accessed 8 May 2022.

INSTITUTIONAL AND GOVERNMENTAL DOCUMENTS

IFC, 'Women-Owned SMEs: A Business Opportunity for Financial Institutions' (2014) <www.ifc.org/wps/wcm/connect/44b004b2-ed46-48fc-8ade-aa0f485069a1/WomenOwnedSMes+Report-Final.pdf?MOD=AJPERES&CVID=kiiZZDZ> accessed 8 May 2022.

ILO, 'Understanding the Gender Composition and Experience of Ready-Made Garment (RMG) Workers in Bangladesh', BGD/16/03/MUL (3 September 2020).

'Weaving Gender. Challenges and Opportunities for the Myanmar Garment Industry' (2018) <www.ilo.org/wcmsp5/groups/public/—asia/—ro-bangkok/—ilo-yangon/documents/publication/wcms_672751.pdf> accessed 8 May 2022.

ILO and IFC, 'Towards Gender Equality: Better Factories Cambodia' (2018) <https://betterwork.org/wp-content/uploads/2018/04/Toward-Gender-Equality-2017-18.pdf> accessed 8 May 2022.

UN, 'The Impact of COVID-19 on Women: UN Secretary-General's Policy Brief' (9 April 2020) <www.unwomen.org/sites/default/files/Headquarters/Attachments/Sections/Library/Publications/2020/Policy-brief-The-impact-of-COVID-19-on-women-en.pdf> accessed 8 May 2022.

UN Women, 'Impact of COVID-19 on Violence against Women and Girls and Service Provision: UN Women Rapid Assessment and Findings' (UN Women Brief, 2020) <www.unwomen.org/sites/default/files/Headquarters/Attachments/Sections/Library/Publications/2020/Impact-of-COVID-19-on-violence-against-women-and-girls-and-service-provision-en.pdf> accessed 8 May 2022.

'Unleashing the Potential of Women Informal Cross Border Traders to Transform Intra-African Trade' (2010) <www.unwomen.org/sites/default/files/Headquarters/Media/Publications/en/factsheetafricanwomentradersen.pdf> accessed 8 May 2022.

'Whose Time to Care: Unpaid Care and Domestic Work during COVID-19' (25 November 2020) <https://data.unwomen.org/sites/default/files/inline-files/Whose-time-to-care-brief_0.pdf> accessed 8 May 2022.

UNCTAD, Entrepreneurship Policy Framework and Implementation Guidance (2012).

'The Least Developed Countries in the Post-COVID World: Learning from 50 Years of Experience', UNCTAD/LDC/2021 (2021).

Least Developed Countries Report 2007 (2007).

'The Least Developed Countries Report 2020 – Productive Capacities for the New Decade', UNCTAD/LDC/2020 (2020).

'The Role of the Services Economy and Trade in Structural Transformation and Inclusive Development, Note by the Secretariat', TD/B/C.I/MEM.4/14 (14 June 2017).

'Trade and Development Report 2020 – From Global Pandemic to Prosperity for All: Avoiding Another Lost Decade', UNCTAD/TDR/2020 (2020).

'Trade and Gender Linkages: An Analysis of Least Developed Countries, Teaching Material on Trade and Gender: Module 4E', UNCTAD/DITC/2021/1 (2021).

World Tourism Organization, 'Global Report on Women in Tourism – Second Edition' (2019) <www.e-unwto.org/doi/book/10.18111/9789284420384> accessed 8 May 2022.

World Tourism Organization and ILO, 'Measuring Employment in the Tourism Industries – Guide with Best Practices' (2014) <www.e-unwto.org/doi/book/10.18111/9789284416158> accessed 8 May 2022.

WTO, 'Joint Declaration on Trade and Women's Economic Empowerment on the Occasion of the WTO Ministerial Conference in Buenos Aires in December 2017' (2017) <www.wto.org/english/thewto_e/minist_e/mc11_e/genderdeclarationmc11_e.pdf> accessed 8 May 2022.

WEBSITES, BLOGS AND NEWS ARTICLES

Abdulla H, 'Myanmar Garment Factory Orders Fall by 75 Per Cent' (*Just-style*, 3 September 2020) <www.just-style.com/news/myanmar-garment-factory-orders-fall-by-75/> accessed 8 May 2022.

Durant I and Coke-Hamilton P, 'COVID-19 Requires Gender-Equal Responses to Save Economies' (UNCTAD, 1 April 2020) <https://unctad.org/news/covid-19-requires-gender-equal-responses-save-economies> accessed 8 May 2022.

International Labour Organization, 'Who Are Domestic Workers' <www.ilo.org/global/topics/domestic-workers/who/lang--en/index.htm> accessed 8 May 2022.

UN Women, 'The Beijing Platform for Action: Inspiration Then and Now' <https://beijing20.unwomen.org/en/about> accessed 8 May 2022.

UNDP, 'Gender Tracker' <https://data.undp.org/gendertracker/> accessed 8 May 2022.

Yonzan N, Lakner C and Gerszon Mahler D, 'Is COVID-19 Increasing Global Inequality?' (World Bank, 7 October 2021) <https://blogs.worldbank.org/opendata/covid-19-increasing-global-inequality> accessed 8 May 2022.

CHAPTER 6: GENDER-INCLUSIVE GOVERNANCE FOR E-COMMERCE, DIGITAL TRADE, AND TRADE IN SERVICES: A LOOK AT DOMESTIC REGULATION (THYSTRUP)

BOOKS

Giødesen Thystrup A, *Governing Trade in Services – Transforming Rulemaking and Trade Integration* (PhD thesis, University of Copenhagen 2017).

Lim AH, *WTO Domestic Regulation and Services Trade, Putting Principles into Practice* (Cambridge University Press 2014).

Mattoo A and Sauvé P (eds), *Domestic Regulation and Service Trade Liberalization* (World Bank 2003).

Williams M, *Gender and Trade: Impacts and Implications for Financial Resources for Gender Equality* (Commonwealth Secretariat 2007).

BOOK CHAPTERS

Bahri A, 'Blockchaining International Trade: A Way Forward for Women's Economic Empowerment?' in M Smeets et al. (eds.), *Adapting to the Digital Trade Era: Challenges and Opportunities* (WTO 2020) <www.wto-ilibrary.org/content/books/9789287043030s008-c002#> accessed 20 September 2022.

ARTICLES

Acharya R, Alamo FO, Al-Battashi SMT, der Boghossian A, Ghei N, Herrera TP, Jackson LA, Kask U, Locatelli C, Marceau G, Motoc I-V, Müller AC, Neufeld N, Padilla S, Pardo de Léon J, Perantakou S, Sporysheva N and Wolff C, 'Trade and Women – Opportunities for Women in the Framework of the World Trade Organization' (2019) 22(3) *Journal of International Economic Law* 323–354.

Alesina AF, Lotti F and Mistrulli PE, 'Do Women Pay More for Credit? Evidence from Italy' (2013) 11 *Journal of the European Economic Association* 45–66.

Banda F and MacKinnon CA, 'Sex, Gender, and International Law' (2006) 100 *Proceedings of the Annual Meeting American Society of International Law* 243–248.

Benz S, Ferencz J and Nordås HK, 'Regulatory Barriers to Trade in Services: A New Database and Composite Indices' (2020) 43 *World Economy* 2860–2879.

Calcagnini G, Giombini G and Lenti E, 'Gender Differences in Bank Loan Access: An Empirical Analysis' (2014) 1 *Italian Economic Journal* 193.

Duflo E, 'Women Empowerment and Economic Development' (2012) 50 *Journal of Economic Literature* 1051–1079.

Harkness SK, 'Discrimination in Lending Markets: Status and the Intersections of Gender and Race' (2016) 79 *Social Psychology Quarterly*, 81–93.

Kricheli-Katz T and Regev T, 'How Many Cents on the Dollar? Women and Men in Product Markets' (2016) 2(2) *ScienceAdvances* 2.

Thystrup AG, 'Gender-Inclusive Governance for E-Commerce' (2020) 21(4) *Journal of World Trade and Investment* 595–629.

WORKING PAPERS

Bacchetta M, Cerra V, Piermartini R and Smeets M, 'Trade and Inclusive Growth' (2021) IMF Working Papers WP/21/74.

Bamber P and Staritz C, 'The Gender Dimensions of Global Value Chains' (2016) ICTSD Policy Paper <www.tralac.org/images/docs/10585/the-gender-dimensions-of-global-value-chains-ictsd-september-2016.pdf> accessed 8 May 2022.

der Boghossian A, 'Trade Policies Supporting Women's Economic Empowerment: Trends in WTO Members' (2019) WTO Staff Working Paper ERSD-2019-07 <www.wto.org/english/res_e/reser_e/ersd201907_e.pdf> accessed 8 May 2022.

Fang S, Shamseldin H and Xu LC, 'Foreign Direct Investment and Female Entrepreneurship' (2019) World Bank Policy Research Working Paper No. WPS 9083 <http://documents.worldbank.org/curated/en/404861576511949229/Foreign-Direct-Investment-and-Female-Entrepreneurship> accessed 20 September 2022.

Fernandez-Stark K, Couto V and Bamber P, 'Industry 4.0 in Developing Countries: The Mine of the Future and the Role of Women?' (2019) World Bank Group Background Paper for the WBG-WTO Global Report on Trade and Gender 2019 <https://documents1.worldbank.org/curated/pt/824061568089601224/Industry-4-0-in-Developing-Countries-The-Mine-of-the-Future-and-the-Role-of-Women.pdf> accessed 8 May 2022.

Ferrantino M, Sicat M, Xu A, Mehetaj E and Chemutai V, 'Leveraging New Technologies in Closing the Gender Gaps' (2020) World Bank Working Paper No. 8.

Fontana M, 'Gender Equality in Trade Agreements' (2016) European Parliament Study for the FEMM Committee <www.europarl.europa.eu/RegData/etudes/STUD/2016/571388/IPOL_STU(2016)571388_EN.pdf> accessed 8 May 2022.

Frohmann A, 'Gender Equality and Trade Policy' (2017) WTI Working Paper No. 24/2017 <www.wti.org/media/filer_public/8b/a8/8ba88d03-1a2b-4311-af6a-629d9997c54c/working_paper_no_24_2017_frohmann.pdf> accessed 8 May 2022.

Hamrick D and Bamber P, 'Pakistan in the Medical Device Global Value Chain' (Duke Global Value Chains Center 2019) <https://gvcc.duke.edu/wp-content/uploads/PakistanMedicalDeviceGVC.pdf> accessed 8 May 2022.

ICTSD, 'Updating the Multilateral Rule Book on E-Commerce. WTO: Paths Forward' (2018) International Centre for Trade and Sustainable Development Policy Brief – March 2018 <www.tralac.org/component/cck/?task=download&file=app_att_01&id=13518> accessed 8 May 2022.

Kim K, Beck S, Tayag MC and Latoja LM, 'Trade Finance Gaps, Growth, and Jobs Survey' (2019) ADB Briefs <www.adb.org/publications/2019-trade-finance-gaps-jobs-survey> accessed 8 May 2022.

Korinek J, 'Trade and Gender: Issues and Interactions' (2005) OECD Trade Policy Working Paper No. 24 <https://doi.org/10.1787/826133710302> accessed 8 May 2022.

Korinek J, Moïsé E and Tange J, 'Trade and Gender: A Framework of Analysis' (2021) OECD Trade Policy Papers No. 246, 3–4, 11–16, 27ff <https://doi.org/10.1787/6db59d80-en> accessed 8 May 2022.

Laperle-Forget L, 'Gender Provisions in African Trade Agreements: What Commitments Are There For Reconciling Gender Equality and Trade?' (2022) Tralac Working Paper No. G21WP11/2021 <www.tralac.org/publications/article/15567-gender-provisions-in-african-trade-agreements-what-commitments-are-there-for-reconciling-gender-equality-and-trade.html> accessed 20 September 2022.

Monteiro JA, 'Gender-Related Provisions in Regional Trade Agreements' (2018) WTO Staff Working Paper ERSD-2018-15 <www.wto.org/english/res_e/reser_e/ersd201815_e.pdf> accessed 8 May 2022.

Nano E, Nayyar G, Rubínová S and Stolzenburg V, 'The Impact of Services Liberalization on Education: Evidence From India' (2021) WTO Staff Working Paper ERSD-2021-10 <www.wto.org/english/res_e/reser_e/ersd202110_e.pdf> accessed 20 September 2022

OECD, 'Trade Finance for SMEs in the Digital Era' (2021) OECD SME and Entrepreneurship Papers No. 24 <www.oecd.org/cfe/smes/Trade%20finance%20for%20SMEs%20in%20the%20digital%20era.pdf> accessed 8 May 2022.

Sicat M, Xu A, Mehetaj E, Ferrantino M and Chemutai V, 'Leveraging New Technologies in Closing the Gender Gaps' (2020) World Bank Working Paper No. 8 <https://openknowledge.worldbank.org/handle/10986/33165> accessed 8 May 2022.

Sicat M, Xu A, Mehetaj E, Ferrantino M and Chemutai V, 'Leveraging New Technologies in Closing the Gender Gaps' (2020) World Bank Working Paper No. 8 <https://openknowledge.worldbank.org/handle/10986/33165> accessed 8 May 2022.

Sicat M, Xu A, Mehetaj E, Ferrantino M and Chemutai V, 'Leveraging New Technologies in Closing the Gender Gaps' (2020) World Bank Working Paper No. 8 <https://openknowledge.worldbank.org/handle/10986/33165> accessed 8 May 2022.

Suominen K, 'Women-Led Firms on the Web: What Are Their Regulatory Challenges – and What Are Solutions?' (2018) ICTSD Working Paper, 3, 9–10, 16 <www.nextradegroupllc.com/_files/ugd/478c1a_ed3fb14c1a9b465eadd6076404d6da01.pdf> accessed 8 May 2022.

INSTITUTIONAL AND GOVERNMENTAL DOCUMENTS

Bahri A, 'Gender Mainstreaming in Free Trade Agreements: A Regional Analysis and Good Practice Examples' (2022) Gender, Social Inclusion and Trade Knowledge Product Series <www.genderandtrade.com/_files/ugd/86d8f7_ea7e603922c54ff7a9e1f81e594a5d9f.pdf> accessed 20 September 2022.

ITC, 'From Europe to the World: Understanding Challenges for European Businesswomen' (2019).

'SME Competitiveness Outlook 2016: Meeting the Standard for Trade' (2016).

OECD, 'Policy Framework for Gender-Sensitive Public Governance', C/MIN(2021)21 (21 September 2021).

World Bank, 'Women, Business and the Law 2018' <https://openknowledge.worldbank.org/handle/10986/29498> accessed 8 May 2022.

'World Development Report 2016: Digital Dividends' (2016) <www.worldbank.org/en/publication/wdr2016> accessed 8 May 2022.

World Bank and WTO, 'Women and Trade: The Role of Trade in Promoting Gender Equality' (2020) <www.wto.org/english/res_e/booksp_e/women_trade_pub2807_e.pdf> accessed 20 September 2022.

WTO, 'Declaration on the Conclusion of Negotiations on Services Domestic Regulation', WT/L/1129 (2 December 2021).

'EU Proposal for WTO Disciplines and Commitments Relating to Electronic Commerce', INF/ECOM/22 (26 April 2019) <www.europarl.europa.eu/RegData/

etudes/ATAG/2020/659263/EPRS_ATA(2020)659263_EN.pdf> accessed 23 May 2023.

'Joint Declaration on Trade and Women's Economic Empowerment on the Occasion of the WTO Ministerial Conference in Buenos Aires in December 2017' (2017) <www.wto.org/english/thewto_e/minist_e/mc11_e/genderdeclarationmc11_e.pdf> accessed 8 May 2022.

'Joint Initiative on Services Domestic Regulation – Schedules of specific commitments', INF/SDR/3/Rev.1 (2 December 2021).

'Joint Ministerial Statement – Declaration on the Establishment of a WTO Informal Work Programme for MSMEs', WT/MIN(17)/58 (13 December 2017).

'Joint Ministerial Statement on Investment Facilitation for Development, Ministerial Conference Eleventh Session Buenos Aires, 10–13 December 2017', WT/MIN(17)/59 (13 December 2017).

'Joint Ministerial Statement on Services Domestic Regulation, Ministerial Conference Eleventh Session Buenos Aires, 10–13 December 2017', WT/MIN (17)/61 (13 December 2017).

'Joint Ministerial Statement on Services Domestic Regulation', WT/MIN(17)/61 (13 December 2017).

'Joint Statement on Electronic Commerce, Ministerial Conference Eleventh Session Buenos Aires, 10–13 December 2017', WT/MIN(17)/60 (13 December 2017).

'Joint Statement on Electronic Commerce', WT/MIN(17)/60 (13 December 2017).

'Note by the Chairperson, Joint Initiative on Services Domestic Regulation', INF/SDR/W/1/Rev.2 (18 December 2020) Section I, paragraphs 1 and 2.

'Note by the Chairperson, Joint Initiative on Services Domestic Regulation', INF/SDR/W/1/Rev.2 (18 December 2020).

'Questions on Domestic Regulation, Submissions by the African Group', JOB/SERV/269 (27 September 2017).

'Working Party on Domestic Regulation', JOB/SERV/272/Rev.1 (7 November 2017).

'Working Room Document by the Chair', DR4-D/Rev.1 (14 September 2018).

WTO and OECD, 'Services Domestic Regulation in the WTO: Cutting Red Tape, Slashing Trade Costs, and Facilitating Services Trade' (November 2021) <www.wto.org/english/news_e/news21_e/jssdr_26nov21_e.pdf> accessed 8 May 2022.

WEBSITES, BLOGS AND NEWS ARTICLES

European Commission, 'Digital Trade' <https://ec.europa.eu/trade/policy/accessing-markets/goods-and-services/digital-trade/> accessed 8 May 2022.

'EU Releases Proposal on New WTO Rules for Electronic Commerce' (3 May 2019), <https://trade.ec.europa.eu/doclib/press/index.cfm?id=2016> accessed 8 May 2022.

Harris B, 'What Is the Gender Gap (and Why Is It Getting Wider)?' (World Economic Forum, 1 November 2017) <www.weforum.org/agenda/2017/11/the-gender-gap-actually-got-worse-in-2017> accessed 8 May 2022.

Johnstone N and Silva M, 'Gender Diversity in Energy: What We Know and What We Don't Know' (IEA, 6 March 2020) <www.iea.org/commentaries/gender-diversity-in-energy-what-we-know-and-what-we-dont-know> accessed 8 May 2022.

OECD, 'E-Commerce in the Time of COVID-19' (7 October 2020) <www.oecd.org/coronavirus/policy-responses/e-commerce-in-the-time-of-covid-19-3a2b78e8/> accessed 8 May 2022.

'Gender Wage Gap (Indicator)' <https://data.oecd.org/earnwage/gender-wage-gap.htm> accessed 5 April 2022.

Remy JY, 'Closing the Digital Gender Divide through Trade Rules,' (CIGI, 9 October 2019) <www.cigionline.org/articles/closing-digital-gender-divide-through-trade-rules/> accessed 8 May 2022.

UN Women, 'COVID-19 and Its Economic Toll on Women: The Story behind the Numbers' (16 September 2020) <www.unwomen.org/en/news/stories/2020/9/feature-covid-19-economic-impacts-on-women/> accessed 8 May 2022.

WTO, 'DG Azevêdo: Global Cooperation on Digital Economy Vital to Unlock Trade Benefits for Women (WTO Speeches, 1 July 2019) <www.wto.org/english/news_e/spra_e/spra268_e.htm> accessed 8 May 2022.

'General Council Decides to Postpone MC12 Indefinitely' (WTO News, 26 November 2021) <www.wto.org/english/news_e/news21_e/mc12_26nov21_e.htm> accessed 8 May 2022.

'Informal Working Group on Trade and Gender' (2017) <www.wto.org/english/tratop_e/womenandtrade_e/iwg_trade_gender_e.htm> accessed 15 September 2022

'Negotiations on Services Domestic Regulation Conclude Successfully in Geneva' (WTO News, 2 December 2021) <www.wto.org/english/news_e/news21_e/jssdr_02dec21_e.htm> accessed 8 May 2022.

'New Initiatives on Electronic Commerce, Investment Facilitation and MSMEs' (WTO News, 13 December 2017) <www.wto.org/english/news_e/news17_e/minis_13dec17_e.htm> accessed 8 May 2022.

'Participants in Domestic Regulation Talks Conclude Text Negotiations, on Track for MC12 Deal' (WTO News, 27 September 2021) <www.wto.org/english/news_e/news21_e/serv_27sep21_e.htm#.YVN1fj23jHo.linkedin> accessed 8 May 2022.

'Trade and Gender Co-chairs Affirm Commitment to Gender Equality in Trade at MC12' (12 June 2022) <www.wto.org/english/news_e/news22_e/iwgtg_13jun22_e.htm> accessed 15 September 2022.

'Twelfth WTO Ministerial Conference, including the MC12 Outcome Document', WT/MIN(22)/24 (22 June 2022) <www.wto.org/english/thewto_e/minist_e/mc12_e/mc12_e.htm#:~:text=The%20WTO's%2012th%20Ministerial%20Conference,future%20work%20of%20the%20WTO> accessed 23 May 2023.

OTHER

Bamber P, 'Gender and Global Value Chains' (WTO, 7 December 2018) <www.wto.org/english/tratop_e/womenandtrade_e/session_2_a_paper_4_penny_bamber.pdf> accessed 8 May 2022.

Rocha N, 'Linkages between Trade and Gender' (WTO, 7 December 2018) <www.wto.org/english/tratop_e/womenandtrade_e/session_1_a_nadia_trade_and_gender_geneva_dec_2018_nr_short_version.pdf> accessed 8 May 2022.

CHAPTER 7: SETTING UP THE TABLE RIGHT: WOMEN'S REPRESENTATION MEETS WOMEN'S INCLUSION IN TRADE NEGOTIATIONS (SOKOLOVA/WILSON)

BOOKS

Malhotra D and Bazerman M, *Negotiation Genius: How to Overcome Obstacles and Achieve Brilliant Results at the Bargaining Table and Beyond* (Bantam 2008).

Whitty-Collins G, *Why Men Win at Work... and How We Can Make Inequality History* (Luath Press 2020).

ARTICLES

Alschner W, Seiermann J and Skougarevskiy D, 'Text of Trade Agreements (ToTA) – A Structured Corpus for the Text-as-Data Analysis of Preferential Trade Agreements' (2018) 15(3) *Journal of Empirical Legal Studies* 648–666.

Araújo E, Araújo NAM, Moreira AA, Herrmann HJ and Andrade Jr. JS, 'Gender Differences in Scientific Collaborations: Women Are More Egalitarian than Men' (2017) 12(5) *PLoS ONE*.

Barbulescu R and Bidwell M, 'Do Women Choose Different Jobs from Men? Mechanisms of Application Segregation in the Market for Managerial Workers' (2012) 24(3) *Organization Science* 737–756.

Fauré C, 'Absent from History' (LS Robinson trans) (1981) 7(1) *Journal of Women in Culture and Society* 71–80.

Kim S and Shin EH, 'A Longitudinal Analysis of Globalization and Regionalization in International Trade: A Social Network Approach' (2002) 81(1) *Social Forces* 445-471.

Kumar R and Worm V, 'Social Capital and the Dynamics of Business Negotiations between the Northern Europeans and the Chinese' (2003) 20(3) *International Marketing Review* 262–285.

Neumayer E and Plümper T, 'The Gendered Nature of Natural Disasters: The Impact of Catastrophic Events on the Gender Gap in Life Expectancy, 1981–2002' (2007) 97(3) *Annals of the Association of American Geographers* 551–566.

Reichert E, 'Women's Rights Are Human Rights: Platform for Action' (1998) 41(3) *International Social Work* 371–384.

Santos-Paulino AU, DiCaprio A and Sokolova MV, 'The Development Trinity: How Regional Integration Impacts Growth, Inequality and Poverty' (2019) 42(7) *World Economy* 1961–1993.

WORKING PAPERS

Homann C, Osnago A and Ruta M, 'Horizontal Depth: A New Database on the Content of Preferential Trade Agreements' (2017) World Bank Policy Research Working Paper 7981 <https://openknowledge.worldbank.org/handle/10986/26148> accessed 8 May 2022.

Korinek J, Moïsé E and Tange J, 'Trade and Gender: A Framework of Analysis' (2021) OECD Policy Paper 246 <https://doi.org/10.1787/6db59d80-en> accessed 8 May 2022;.

Monteiro JA, 'The Evolution of Gender-Related Provisions in Regional Trade Agreements' (2018) WTO Staff Working Paper ERSD-2018-15 <www.wto.org/english/res_e/reser_e/ersd201815_e.pdf> accessed 8 May 2022.

INSTITUTIONAL AND GOVERNMENTAL DOCUMENTS

ITC, 'Mainstreaming Gender in Free Trade Agreements' (2020), <https://intracen.org/resources/publications/mainstreaming-gender-in-free-trade-agreements> accessed 8 May 2022.

UN Women, 'Women in Politics: 2021' <www.unwomen.org/sites/default/files/Headquarters/Attachments/Sections/Library/Publications/2021/Women-in-politics-2021-en.pdf> accessed 8 May 2022.

World Bank and WTO, 'Women and Trade. The Role of Trade in Promoting Gender Equality' (23 July 2020) <www.worldbank.org/en/topic/trade/publication/women-and-trade-the-role-of-trade-in-promoting-womens-equality> accessed 8 May 2022.

WTO, 'Amendment to the Trade Policy Review Mechanism', WT/L/1014 (27 July 2017).

'Joint Declaration on Trade and Women's Economic Empowerment on the Occasion of the WTO Ministerial Conference in Buenos Aires in December 2017' (2017) <www.wto.org/english/thewto_e/minist_e/mc11_e/genderdeclarationmc11_e.pdf> accessed 8 May 2022.

WEBSITES, BLOGS AND NEWS ARTICLES

ABC News, 'Fiji Reinstated to the Commonwealth Following "Credible Elections"' (26 September 2014) <www.abc.net.au/news/2014-09-27/fiji-reinstated-to-the-commonwealth-following-elections/5773330> accessed 8 May 2022.

Acharya R, 'Regional Trade Agreements: Challenges and Opportunities. Proliferation of Trade Accords has Potential to Increase Trade – and Make Trade Relations More Complex' (ITC News, 20 December 2018) <www.intracen.org/news/Regional-trade-agreements-challenges-and-opportunities/> accessed 8 May 2022.

ACWL, 'Home' <www.acwl.ch> accessed 8 May 2022.

Brunsden J and Parker G, 'UK and EU to Resume Talks in Final Push for Post-Brexit Trade Deal' (*Financial Times*, 22 October 2020) <www.ft.com/content/27d46f3b-a718-421e-b5d6-b007c08a441d> accessed 8 May 2022.

Commonwealth, 'Environment and Climate Change' <https://climate.thecommonwealth.org> accessed 8 May 2022.

Cullinan R, 'In Collaborative Work Cultures, Women Disproportionately Carry More of the Weight' (*Harvard Business Review*, 24 July 2018) <https://hbr.org/2018/07/in-collaborative-work-cultures-women-carry-more-of-the-weight> accessed 8 May 2022.

EIGE, 'Gender Mainstreaming' <https://eige.europa.eu/gender-mainstreaming> accessed 8 May 2022.

Euronews, 'Swiss Newspaper Apologises for "Inappropriate" Headline about New WTO Director-General' (1 March 2021) <www.euronews.com/2021/03/01/swiss-newspaper-apologises-for-inappropriate-headline-about-new-wto-director-general> accessed 8 May 2022.

Government of Canada, 'Gender Analysis' <www.international.gc.ca/world-monde/funding-financement/gender_analysis-analyse_comparative.aspx?lang=eng> accessed 8 May 2022.

ITC, 'SheTrades Outlook' <www.shetrades.com/outlook/home> accessed 8 May 2022.

'SME Trade Academy' <https://learning.intracen.org> accessed 8 May 2022.

WTO and WCO, 'Rules of Origin Facilitator' <https://findrulesoforigin.org/> accessed 8 May 2022.

Labban M, 'Vaccine Trade Becomes a Key Factor in Global Diplomacy' <www.pharmaceutical-technology.com/pricing-and-market-access/vaccine-trade-becomes-a-key-factor-in-global-diplomacy-html/> accessed 8 May 2022.

Petit S, 'Une ambassade à Genève, un luxe? Oui, a repondu le Benin' (*Le Temps*, 28 August 2020) <www.letemps.ch/monde/une-ambassade-geneve-un-luxe-oui-repondu-benin> accessed 8 May 2022.

Sheridan MB, 'López Obrador's Cost-Cutting Spree Is Transforming Mexico — and Drawing Blowback from Bureaucrats' (*Washington Post*, 14 July 2019) <www.washingtonpost.com/world/the_americas/lopez-obradors-cost-cutting-spree-is-transforming-mexico–and-drawing-blowback-from-bureaucrats/2019/07/14/5e187b5e-66c2-11e9-a698-2a8f808c9cfb_story.html> accessed 8 May 2022.

Sokolova MV, 'On the Role of Women Trade Trainers' (Trade Experettes, n.d.) <www.tradeexperettes.org/blog/articles/on-the-role-of-women-trade-trainers> accessed 8 May 2022.

South Centre <www.southcentre.int> accessed 8 May 2022.

UN Women, 'Explainer: How Gender Inequality and Climate Change Are Interconnected' <www.unwomen.org/en/news-stories/explainer/2022/02/explainer-how-gender-inequality-and-climate-change-are-interconnected> accessed 8 May 2022.

UNCTAD 'Virtual Institute' <https://vi.unctad.org> accessed 8 May 2022.

UNECOSOC, 'Achieve Gender Equality and Empower All Women and Girls' <https://sdgs.un.org/goals/goal5> accessed 8 May 2022.

Veugelers R, Poitiers N and Guetta-Jeanrenaud L, 'A World Divided: Global Vaccine Trade and Production' (Bruegel, 20 July 2021) <www.bruegel.org/blog-post/world-divided-global-vaccine-trade-and-production> accessed 8 May 2022.

WEF, 'Regionalization vs Globalization: What Is the Future Direction of Trade?' (15 July 2021) <www.weforum.org/agenda/2021/07/regionalization-globalization-future-direction-trade/> accessed 8 May 2022.

WTO, 'e-Learning Institute' <https://wtolearning.csod.com/client/wtolearning/default.aspx> accessed 8 May 2022.

'Informal Working Group on Trade and Gender' <www.wto.org/english/tratop_e/womenandtrade_e/iwg_trade_gender_e.htm> accessed 8 May 2022.

'Regional Trade Agreements Database' <https://rtais.wto.org/UI/PublicMaintainRTAHome.aspx> accessed 8 May 2022.

'The WTO and the Sustainable Development Goals' <www.wto.org/english/thewto_e/coher_e/sdgs_e/sdgs_e.htm> accessed 8 May 2022.

'Trade and Gender Informal Working Group Co-chairs Present Draft Outcome Document for MC12' (23 September 2021) <www.wto.org/english/news_e/news21_e/women_23sep21_e.htm> accessed 8 May 2022.

CHAPTER 8: THE IMPORTANCE OF GENDER-RESPONSIVE STANDARDS FOR TRADE POLICY (WHITE/PARKOUDA)

BOOKS

Carlsson A, *Addressing Female Whiplash Injury Protection – A Step towards 50th Percentile Female Rear Impact Occupant Models* (PhD thesis, Chalmers University of Technology 2012).

Criado-Perez C, *Invisible Women: Exposing Data Bias in a World Designed for Men* (Vintage 2020).

National Research Council, *Standards, Conformity Assessment and Trade: Into the 21st Century* (National Academies Press 1995).

ARTICLES

Bailey AH, LaFrance M and Dovidio JF, 'Is Man the Measure of All Things? A Social Cognitive Account of Androcentrism' (2019) 23(4) *Personality and Social Psychology Review* 307–331.

Beery TA, 'Gender Bias in the Diagnosis and Treatment of Coronary Artery Disease' (1995) 24(6) *Heart & Lung* 427–435.

Centers for Disease Control and Prevention, 'Characteristics of Health Care Personnel with COVID-19 – United States, 12 February to 9 April 2020', (2020) 69(15) *Morbidity and Mortality Weekly Report* 477–481.

Chang TY and Kajackaite A, 'Battle for the Thermostat: Gender and the Effect of Temperature on Cognitive Performance' (2019) 14(5) *PloS ONE*.

Forman J, Poplin GS, Shaw CG, McMurry TL, Schmidt K, Ash J and Sunnevang C, 'Automobile Injury Trends in the Contemporary Fleet: Belted Occupants in Frontal Collisions' (2019) 20(6) *Traffic Injury Prevention* 607–612.

Janson DJ, Clift BC and Dhokia V, 'PPE Fit of Healthcare Workers during the COVID-19 Pandemic' (2022) 99/103610 *Applied Ergonomics* 1–8.

Kingma B and van Marken Lichtenbelt W, 'Energy Consumption in Buildings and Female Thermal Demand' (2015) 5(12) *Nature Climate Change* 1054–1056.

Kudenchuk PJ, Maynard C, Martin JS, Wirkus M and Weaver WD, 'Comparison of Presentation, Treatment, and Outcome of Acute Myocardial Infarction in Men versus Women (the Myocardial Infarction Triage and Intervention Registry)' (1996) 78(1) *American Journal of Cardiology* 9–14.

Leitch C, Welter F and Henry C, 'Women Entrepreneurs' Financing Revisited: Taking Stock and Looking Forward: New Perspectives on Women Entrepreneurs and Finance' (2018) 20(2) *Venture Capital* 103–114.

Madeira-Revell KMA, Parnell KJ, Richardson J, Pope KA, Fay DT, Merriman SE and Plant KL, 'How Can We Close the Gender Data Gap in Transportation Research?' (2021) 32(1) *Ergonomics SA: Journal of the Ergonomics Society of South Africa* 19–26.

Tatman R, 'Gender and Dialect Bias in YouTube's Automatic Captions' (2017) Proceedings of the First ACL Workshop on Ethics in Natural Language Processing, Valencia, Spain. Association for Computational Linguistics <https://aclanthology.org/W17-1606.pdf> accessed 25 May 2023.

WORKING PAPERS

Lesser C, 'Do Bilateral and Regional Approaches for Reducing Technical Barriers to Trade Converge towards the Multilateral Trading System?' (2007) OECD Trade Policy Papers No. 58 <https://doi.org/10.1787/051058723767> accessed 8 May 2022.

Okun-Kozlowicki J, 'Standards and Regulations: Measuring the Link to Goods Trade' (2016) US Department of Commerce, Office of Standards and Investment Policy Paper <https://legacy.trade.gov/td/osip/documents/osip_standards_trade_full_paper.pdf> accessed 8 May 2022.

INSTITUTIONAL AND GOVERNMENTAL DOCUMENTS

Government of Canada, International Standards: Targeted Regulatory Review – Regulatory Roadmap (2021).

Government of New Zealand, 'Technical Barriers to Trade (TBT) Strategy' (2018).

Standards Council of Canada, 'Gender and Standardization Strategy' (2019) <www.scc.ca/en/system/files/publications/SCC_Gender-and-Standardization-Strategy-2019-2025_FINAL_EN.pdf> accessed 8 May 2022.

Standards Council of Canada, 'Requirements & Guidance – Accreditation of Standards Development Organizations' (2019) <www.scc.ca/en/about-scc/publications/requirements-and-procedures-accreditation/requirements-guidance-accreditation-standards-development-organizations> accessed 8 May 2022.

Steering Committee on Trade Capacity and Standards, 'Working Party on Regulatory Cooperation and Standardization Policies, Gender Mainstreaming in Standards', ECE/SCTCS/WP.6/2016/3 (2016) 2.

UN ESCAP, 'The Rise of Non-tariff Measures' (2019) <www.unescap.org/sites/default/d8files/APTIR2019_Introduction.pdf> accessed 8 May 2022.

UNCTAD, 'Dispute Settlement, World Trade Organization, Technical Barriers to Trade' (2003) <https://unctad.org/system/files/official-document/edmmisc232add22_en.pdf> accessed 8 May 2022.

UNECE, 'Declaration for Gender Responsive Standards and Standards Development' (2019).

'Terms of Reference for Informal Working Group on Sex and Size Neutral Crash Safety' GRSP-70-01 (7 September 2021).

WHO, 'Global Health Estimates 2015: Deaths by Cause, Age, Sex, by Country and by Region, 2000–2015' (2016).

World Bank and WTO, 'Women and Trade: The Role of Trade in Promoting Gender Equality' (2020) <www.wto.org/english/res_e/booksp_e/women_trade_pub2807_e.pdf> accessed 8 May 2022.

REPORTS AND STUDIES

Diversity Institute, 'The 50–30 Challenge, Publicly Available Specification (PAS)' (2021) <https://secureservercdn.net/192.169.220.85/bom.396.myftpupload.com/wp-content/uploads/2021/08/Publicly-Available-Specification-PAS.pdf> accessed 8 May 2022.

Heinrich J, 'Drug Safety: Most Drugs Withdrawn in Recent Years Had Greater Health Risks for Women. A Letter to the Honorable Tom Harkin, the Honorable Olympia J. Snowe, The Honorable Barbara A. Mikulski, United States Senate, the Honorable Henry Waxman, House of Representatives' (United States General Accounting Office, 19 January 2001) <www.gao.gov/assets/gao-01-286r.pdf> accessed 8 May 2022.

Liao D, 'Annual Facts & Figures' (Standards Council of Canada, 2021).

Parkouda M, 'An Ounce of Prevention: Standards as a Tool to Prevent Accidental Fatalities' (Standards Council of Canada, 2019) <www.scc.ca/en/system/files/publications/SCC_Gender_Safety_Report_EN.pdf> accessed 8 May 2022.

WEBSITES, BLOGS AND NEWS ARTICLES

Algayerova O and El-Yassir A, 'Personal Protective Equipment Standards Must Respond to Women's Needs to Ensure the Safety of All Frontline Workers during the COVID-19 Pandemic' (UN Women, 2 May 2020) <https://unece.org/general-unece/news/personal-protective-equipment-standards-must-respond-womens-needs-ensure-safety> accessed 8 May 2022.

European Commission, 'Pulling the Plug on Consumer Frustration and e-Waste: Commission Proposes a Common Charger for Electronic Devices' (23 September 2021) <https://ec.europa.eu/commission/presscorner/detail/en/IP_21_4613> accessed 8 May 2022.

Government of Canada, 'International Trade Agreements and Local Government: A Guide for Canadian Municipalities' (Global Affairs Canada, 2021) <www.international.gc.ca/trade-agreements-accords-commerciaux/ressources/fcm/complete-guide-complet.aspx?lang=en> accessed 8 May 2022.

'Majority-Female Owned Exporting SMEs in Canada' (2020) <www.tradecommissioner.gc.ca/businesswomen-femmesdaffaires/2016-MFO_SMES-PME_EDMF.aspx?lang=eng> accessed 8 May 2022.

'The 50–30 Challenge: Your Diversity Advantage' (Innovation, Science and Economic Development Canada, 2021) <www.ic.gc.ca/eic/site/icgc.nsf/eng/07706.html> accessed 8 May 2022.

'Trade and Gender in Free Trade Agreements: The Canadian Approach' (2021) <www.international.gc.ca/trade-commerce/gender_equality-egalite_genres/trade_gender_fta-ale-commerce_genre.aspx?lang=eng> accessed 8 May 2022.

IEC, 'Disappointing Results of Gender Survey in Technical Committees' (21 June 2021) <www.iec.ch/blog/disappointing-results-gender-survey-technical-committees> accessed 8 May 2022.

'What Is Conformity Assessment' (2021) <www.iec.ch/conformity-assessment/what-conformity-assessment> access on 8 May 2022.

ISO, 'Women's Entrepreneurship – Key Definitions and General Criteria' (IWA 34:2021) <www.iso.org/standard/79585.html> accessed 8 May 2022.

Mujica S, ISO Secretary-General and Philippe Metzger IEC General Secretary & CEO, at the Standards Accelerator Online Event (14 October 2021) <www.worldstandardsday.org/contents/posts/events/the-standards-accelerator.html> accessed 8 May 2022.

ISO Secretary-General at the Standards Accelerator Online Event (14 October 2021) <www.worldstandardsday.org/contents/posts/events/the-standards-accelerator.html> accessed 8 May 2022.

OECD, 'Small and Medium-Sized Enterprises and Trade' <www.oecd.org/trade/topics/small-and-medium-enterprises-and-trade> accessed 8 May 2022.

Reeves RB and Deng B, 'At Least 65,000 More Men than Women Have Died from COVID-19 in the US' (Brookings, 19 October 2021) <www.brookings.edu/blog/up-front/2021/10/19/at-least-65000-more-men-than-women-have-died-from-covid-19-in-the-us/> accessed 8 May 2022.

Smith G and Rustagi I, 'When Good Algorithms Go Sexist: Why and How to Advance AI Gender Equity' (*Stanford Social Innovation Review*, 31 March 2021) <https://ssir.org/articles/entry/when_good_algorithms_go_sexist_why_and_how_to_advance_ai_gender_equity> accessed 8 May 2022.

Swedish Institute for Standards, 'ISO/IWA 34 – Definition of a "Woman-Owned Business" and Guidance on Its Use' (2021) <www.sis.se/en/about_sis/isoiwa-34-definition-of-a-womanowned-business-and-guidance-on-its-use/> accessed 8 May 2022.

UNECE, 'Gender Responsive Standards Initiative' <https://unece.org/gender-responsive-standards-initiative> accessed 8 May 2022.

WTO, 'Buenos Aires Declaration on Women and Trade Outlines Actions to Empower Women' (2017) <www.wto.org/english/news_e/news17_e/mc11_12dec17_e.htm> accessed 8 May 2022.

CHAPTER 9: MAINSTREAMING GENDER IN INVESTMENT TREATIES AND ITS PREVAILING TRENDS: THE ACTIONS OF MNES IN THE AMERICAS (AMARAL/JALLER)

BOOKS

Soledad C, Vinsrygg K, Summerfield A and Reingold J, *2018 Global Board Diversity Tracker: Who's Really on Board?* (Egon Zehnder 2018).

ARTICLES

Blanton R and Blanton SL, 'Is Foreign Direct Investment Gender Blind? Women's Rights as a Determination of US FDI' (2015) 21(4) *Feminist Economics* 61–88.

Díaz-García C, González-Moreno A and Sáez-Martínez FJ, 'Gender Diversity within R&D Teams: Its Impact on Radicalness of Innovation' (2012) 15(2) *Innovation* 149–160.

Leite M, 'Pluralizing Discourses: Multinationals and Gender Equality' (2019) 20(3) *Journal of International Women's Studies* 116–138.

Ng ES and Sears GJ, 'The Glass Ceiling in Context: The Influence of CEO Gender, Recruitment Practices and Firm Internationalisation on the Representation of Women in Management' (2017) 27(1) *Human Resource Management Journal* 133–151.

Sarmento A, 'The Scope of New Brazilian Investment Protections: Intellectual Property and the Limits of an Alternate Approach' (2021) 52(2) *University of Miami Inter-American Law Review* n.p.

Vargas AR and Daza JL, 'The Role of Regulations and MNEs in Ensuring Equal Opportunities for Women' (2020) 27(3) *UNCTAD Transnational Corporations Journal* 183–202.

WORKING PAPERS

Alai P and Amaral R, 'The Importance (and Complexity) of Mainstreaming Gender in Trade Agreements' (Centre for International Governance Innovation, October 2019) <www.cigionline.org/articles/importance-and-complexity-mainstreaming-gender-trade-agreements/> accessed 8 May 2022.

Barafani M and Barral VA, 'Género y comercio: Una relación a distintas velocidades' (2020) IBD Note Técnica No. IDB-NT-2006 <https://publications.iadb.org/es/genero-y-comercio-una-relacion-distintas-velocidades> accessed 8 May 2022.

Gertsberg M, Mollerstrom J and Pagel M, 'Gender Quotas and Support for Women in Board Elections' (2021) National Bureau of Economic Research Working Paper 28463 <www.nber.org/papers/w28463> accessed 8 May 2022.

Kahn S and Ginther D, 'Women and STEM' (2017) NBER Working Paper No. w23525 <https://ssrn.com/abstract=2988746> accessed 8 May 2022.

Monteiro JA, 'Gender-Related Provisions in Regional Trade Agreements' (2018) WTO Economic Research and Statistics Division Staff Working Paper ERSD-2018-15 <www.wto.org/english/res_e/reser_e/ersd201815_e.pdf> accessed 8 May 2022.

Sengupta R, 'The Gender Dynamics of Trade and Investment and the Post-2015 Development Agenda: A Developing-Country Perspective' (2013) Third World Network Briefing Paper 68 <www.twn.my/title2/briefing_papers/No68.pdf> accessed 8 May 2022.

INSTITUTIONAL AND GOVERNMENTAL DOCUMENTS

Government of Canada, '2021 Model FIPA' <www.international.gc.ca/trade-commerce/trade-agreements-accords-commerciaux/agr-acc/fipa-apie/2021_model_fipa-2021_modele_apie.aspx?lang=eng> accessed 8 May 2022.

IADB, 'Una olimpíada desigual: La equidad de género en las empresas latinoamericanas y del Caribe' (August 2021) BID Nota Técnica No. IDB-TN-2255 <https://publications.iadb.org/publications/spanish/document/Una-olimpiada-desigual-la-equidad-de-genero-en-las-empresas-latinoamericanas-y-del-Caribe.pdf> accessed 8 May 2022.

ILO, 'Women in Business and Management: The Business Case for Change' (2019) <www.ilo.org/wcmsp5/groups/public/—dgreports/—dcomm/—publ/documents/publication/wcms_700953.pdf> accessed 8 May 2022.

Kingdom of Morocco, 'Model Investment Treaty' (June 2019) <https://investmentpolicy.unctad.org/international-investment-agreements/treaty-files/5895/download> accessed 8 May 2022.

Kingdom of the Netherlands, 'Model Investment Agreement' (2019) <https://investmentpolicy.unctad.org/international-investment-agreements/treaty-files/5832/download> accessed 8 May 2022.

UN, 'Report of the Fourth World Conference on Women, Beijing, 4–15 September 1995', A/CONF.177/20/REV.1 (1996) Chap. I, Resolution 1, Annex II.

UNCTAD, 'Agreement between the Kingdom of Morocco and Japan for the Promotion and Protection of Investment' <https://investmentpolicy.unctad.org/international-investment-agreements/treaty-files/5908/download> accessed 8 May 2022.

'Multinational Enterprises and the International Transmission of Gender Policies and Practices', UNCTAD/DIAE/INF/2021/1 (8 March 2021).

World Economic Forum, 'Global Gender Gap Report' (March 2021) <www3.weforum.org/docs/WEF_GGGR_2021.pdf> accessed 8 May 2022.

REPORTS AND STUDIES

Acumen, 'Women and Social Enterprises: How Gender Integration Can Boost Entrepreneurial Solutions to Poverty' (2015) <https://acumen.org/wp-content/uploads/2017/09/Women_And_Social_Enterprises_Report_Acumen_ICRW_2015.pdf> accessed 8 May 2022.

Calvert Impact Capital, 'Just Good Investing: Why Gender Matters to Your Portfolio and What You Can Do about It' (2018) <https://assets.ctfassets.net/4oaw9man1yeu/2X1gLdNUrUPFhRAJbAXp1q/205876bdd2d7e076fce05d5771183dfe/calvert-impact-capital-gender-report.pdf> accessed 8 May 2022.

Credit Suisse Research Institute, 'The CS Gender 3000: Reward for Change' (2016) <https://evolveetfs.com/wp-content/uploads/2017/08/Credit-Suisse-Reward-for-Change_1495660293279_2.pdf> accessed 8 May 2022.

Morgan Stanley, 'Gender Diversity Is a Competitive Advantage' (2016) <www.morganstanley.com/pub/content/dam/msdotcom/ideas/gender-diversity-toolkit/Gender-Diversity-Investing-Primer.pdf> accessed 8 May 2022.

Mujeres O, 'Catalizando la Igualdad' (2021) <https://lac.unwomen.org/es/digiteca/publicaciones/2021/07/catalizando-la-igualdad> accessed 8 May 2022.

WEBSITES, BLOGS AND NEWS ARTICLES

Barker G, Garg A, Heilman B, van der Gaag N and Mehaffey R, 'State of the World's Fathers: Structural Solutions to Achieve Equality in Care Work' (MenCare, 2021)

<https://men-care.org/wp-content/uploads/2021/06/210610_BLS21042_PRO_SOWF.v08.pdf> accessed 8 May 2022.

Corbett H, 'How Companies Are Supporting Working Parents in the COVID Economy' (Forbes, 30 July 2020) <www.forbes.com/sites/hollycorbett/2020/07/30/how-companies-are-supporting-working-parents-in-the-covid-economy/?sh=52bbb64e328f> accessed 8 May 2022.

Ely RJ and Thomas DA, 'Getting Serious about Diversity: Enough Already with the Business Case' (*Harvard Business Review*, November–December 2020) <https://hbr.org/2020/11/getting-serious-about-diversity-enough-already-with-the-business-case> accessed 8 May 2022.

ExxonMobil, 'Community Engagement: Women's Economic Opportunity' <https://corporate.exxonmobil.com/Sustainability/Community-engagement/Womens-economic-opportunity> accessed 8 May 2022.

Entis L, 'This Is the No. 1 Thing These CEOs Look For in Job Candidates' (Fortune, 26 March 2017) <https://fortune.com/2017/03/26/ceos-ideal-job-candidates/> accessed 8 May 2022.

Froehlicher M, Knuckles Griek L, Nematzadeh A, Hall L, and Stovall N, 'Gender Equality in the Workplace: Going Beyond Women on the Board' (S&P Global, 5 February 2021) <www.spglobal.com/esg/csa/yearbook/articles/gender-equality-workplace-going-beyond-women-on-the-board> accessed 8 May 2022.

Government of Canada, '2021 FIPA Model – Summary of Main Changes' <www.international.gc.ca/trade-commerce/trade-agreements-accords-commerciaux/agr-acc/fipa-apie/2021_model_fipa_summary-2021_modele_apie_resume.aspx?lang=eng> accessed 8 May 2022.

ILO and UN Women, 'Win–Win: Gender Equality Means Good Business' (August 2017) <https://ganarganar.lim.ilo.org/en/> accessed 8 May 2022.

Korn Ferry, 'Women Outperform Men in 11 of 12 Key Emotional Intelligence Competencies' (2016) <www.kornferry.com/about-us//press/new-research-shows-women-are-better-at-using-soft-skills-crucial-for-effective-leadership> accessed 8 May 2022.

McKinsey & Company, 'Diversity Wins: How Inclusion Matters' (2020) <www.mckinsey.com/featured-insights/diversity-and-inclusion/diversity-wins-how-inclusion-matters> accessed 8 May 2022.

McKinsey & Company, 'How Advancing Women's Equality Can Add $12 Trillion to Global Growth' (2015) <www.mckinsey.com/featured-insights/employment-and-growth/how-advancing-womens-equality-can-add-12-trillion-to-global-growth> accessed 8 May 2022.

McKinsey & Company, 'The Power of Parity: Advancing Women's Equality in the United States' (2016) <www.mckinsey.com/featured-insights/employment-and-growth/the-power-of-parity-advancing-womens-equality-in-the-united-states> accessed 8 May 2022.

McKinsey & Company & LeanIn.Org, 'Women in the Workplace' (2021) <www.mckinsey.com/featured-insights/diversity-and-inclusion/women-in-the-workplace> accessed 8 May 2022.

Millennium Challenge Corporation, 'Gender Equality: A Smart Proposition for Business' (2015) <www.mcc.gov/resources/story/story-kin-apr-2015-gender-equality-a-smart-business-proposition#ref-4-a> accessed 8 May 2022.

She-conomy, 'Marketing to Women Quick Facts' <http://she-conomy.com/report/marketing-to-women-quick-facts> accessed 8 May 2022.

UNCTAD, 'Investment Policy Hub' <https://investmentpolicy.unctad.org/international-investment-agreements/model-agreements> accessed 8 May 2022.

Unilever, 'Promoting Gender Equality throughout Our Value Chain in Colombia' <www.unilever-southlatam.com/news/comunicados-de-prensa/2021/promoting-gender-equality-throughout-our-value-chain-in-colombia.html> accessed 8 May 2022.

UPS, 'Women Exporters Program' <www.ups.com/ba/en/services/small-business/women-exporters-program.page> accessed 8 May 2022.

Zaidan Y, 'Five Reasons Social Enterprises Are Applying a Gender Lens to Their Businesses' (Acumen, 24 May 2016) <https://acumen.org/blog/five-reasons-social-enterprises-are-applying-a-gender-lens-to-their-businesses/> accessed 8 May 2022.

Zukis B, 'How Women Will Save the Future, One Corporate Board at a Time' (Forbes, 30 June 2020) <www.forbes.com/sites/bobzukis/2020/06/30/how-women-will-save-the-future-one-corporate-board-at-a-time/?sh=44915c207bc9> accessed 8 May 2022.

CHAPTER 10: GENDER APPROACHES IN REGIONAL TRADE AGREEMENTS AND A POSSIBLE GENDER PROTOCOL UNDER THE AFRICAN CONTINENTAL FREE TRADE AREA: A COMPARATIVE ASSESSMENT (KUHLMANN)

BOOKS

Harrison J, *The Human Rights Impact of the World Trade Organization* (Hart Publishing 1st ed 2007).

BOOK CHAPTERS

Chinkin C and Butegwa F, *Gender Mainstreaming in Legal and Constitutional Affairs: A Reference Manual for Governments and Other Stakeholders* (Commonwealth Secretariat 2001).

McGill E, 'Trade and Gender' in Appleton A, Macrory P and Plummer M (eds.), *The World Trade Organization – Legal, Economic, and Political Analysis* (Springer Science and Business Media 2005).

Mikic M and Sharma V, 'Feminising WTO 2.0' in Evenett SJ and Baldwin R (eds.), *Revitalizing Multilateral Trade Cooperation: Pragmatic Ideas for The New WTO Director-General* (VoxEU 2020).

ARTICLES

Acharya R, Falgueras Alamo O, Thabit Al-Battashi SM, der Boghossian A, Ghei N, Parcero Herrera T, Jackson LA, Kask U, Locatelli C, Marceau G, Motoc IV,

Müller AC, Neufeld N, Padilla S, Pardo de Léon J, Perantakou S, Sporysheva N, Wolff C, 'Trade and Women – Opportunities for Women in the Framework of the World Trade Organization' (2019) 22(3) *Journal of International Economic Law* 323–354.

Bahri A, 'Measuring the Gender-Responsiveness of Free Trade Agreements: Using a Self-Evaluation Maturity Framework' (2019) 14(2) *Global Trade & Customs Journal* 517–527.

Bayat N, 'A "Business Unusual" Approach for Gender Equality under the AfCFTA' (2020) 9(1) *ECDPM Great Insights Magazine* n.p.

Bugingo EM, 'Empowering Women by Supporting Small-Scale Cross-Border Trade' (2018) 7(4) *Tralac: Bridges Africa – Supporting Small-Scale Cross-Border Traders across Africa* 11–13.

Crenshaw Williams K, 'Demarginalizing the Intersection of Race and Sex: A Black Feminist Critique of Antidiscrimination Doctrine, Feminist Theory and Antiracist Politics' (1989) 1 University of Chicago Legal Forum <https://chicagounbound.uchicago.edu/cgi/viewcontent.cgi?article=1052&context=uclf> accessed 25 May 2023.

Fitzpatrick J and Kelly KR, 'Gendered Aspects of Migration: Law and the Female Migrant' (1998) 22(1) *Hastings International and Comparative Law Review* 47–112.

Floro M and Dymski G, 'Financial Crisis, Gender, and Power: An Analytical Framework' (2000) 28 *World Development* 1269–1283.

Gammage C and Momodu M, 'The Economic Empowerment of Women in Africa: Regional Approaches to Gender-Sensitive Trade Policies' (2020) 1 *African Journal of International Economic Law* 5.

Gathii J, 'Writing Race and Identity in a Global Context: What CRT and TWAIL Can Learn from Each Other' (2020) 67 *UCLA Law Review* 1610–1650.

Jarvis LM, 'Women's Rights and the Public Morals Exception of GATT Article 20' (2000) 22 *Michigan Journal of International Law* 219–238.

Kuhlmann K and Agutu AL, 'The African Continental Free Trade Area: Toward A New Model for Trade and Development Law' (2020) 51(4) *Georgetown Journal of International Law* 853–808.

Kuhlmann K and Dey B, 'Using Regulatory Flexibility to Address Market Informality in Seed Systems: A Global Study' (2021) 11(2) 377 *Agronomy* 1–27.

Kuhlmann K, 'Mapping Inclusive Law and Regulation: A Comparative Agenda for Trade and Development' (2021) 2 *African Journal of International Economic Law* 48–87.

Lim JY, 'The Effects of the East Asian Crisis on the Employment of Women and Men: The Philippine Case' (2000) 28 *World Development* 1285–1306.

Mehra R and Gammage S, 'Trends, Countertrends, and Gaps in Women's Employment' (1999) 27(3) *World Development* 533–550.

Singh A and Zammit A, 'International Capital Flows: Identifying the Gender Dimension' (2000) 28 *World Development* 1249–1268.

WORKING PAPERS

Bayat N, 'A "Business Unusual" Approach for Gender Equality under the AfCFTA' (2020) 9(1) *ECDPM Great Insights Magazine*.

Brown LR, Feldstein H, Haddad L, Pena C and Quisumbing A, 'Generating Food Security in the Year 2020: Women as Producers, Gatekeepers, and Shock Absorbers' (1995) International Food Policy Research Institute 2020 Vision Brief 17 <www.semanticscholar.org/paper/GENERATING-FOOD-SECURITY-IN-THE-YEAR-2020%3A-WOMEN-AS-Brown-Feldstein/01f19be2a78245ec09e5ccde6c7c36d96187a929> accessed 8 May 2022.

der Boghossian A, 'Trade Policies Supporting Women's Economic Empowerment: Trends in WTO Members' (2019) WTO Staff Working Paper ERSD-2019-07 <www.wto.org/english/res_e/reser_e/ersd201907_e.htm> accessed 8 May 2022.

Monteiro JA, 'The Evolution of Gender-Related Provisions in Regional Trade Agreements', (2018) World Trade Organization Staff Working Paper ERSD-2021-8 <www.wto.org/english/res_e/reser_e/ersd201815_e.pdf> accessed 8 May 2022.

Ndumbe LN, 'Unshackling Women Traders: Cross-Border Trade of Eru from Cameroon to Nigeria' (2013) Africa Trade Policy Note 38 <https://documents1.worldbank.org/curated/en/262591468292477021/pdf/797110BRI0PN380B0x0377384B00PUBLIC0.pdf> accessed 8 May 2022.

Osakwe S, 'Extending MSMEs' Access to Trade Finance under the AFCFTA' (2021) Centre for the Study of Economies of Africa <https://papers.ssrn.com/sol3/papers.cfm?abstract_id=3780767> accessed 8 May 2022.

White M, Salas C, and Gammage S, 'Trade Impact Review: Mexico Case Study; NAFTA and the FTAA: A Gender Analysis of Employment Poverty Impacts in Agriculture' (2003) Women's Edge Coalition <www.iatp.org/sites/default/files/NAFTA_and_the_FTAA_A_Gender_Analysis_of_Employ.pdf> accessed 8 May 2022.

INSTITUTIONAL AND GOVERNMENTAL DOCUMENTS

AU, 'Decision of the African Continental Free Trade Area (2020), Assembly/AU/4/(XXXIII).

'Ten Year Action Plan to Eradicate Child Labour, Forced Labour, Human Trafficking and Modern Slavery (2020–2030)' (2019) <https://au.int/sites/default/files/newsevents/workingdocuments/40112-wd-child_labour_action_plan-final-english.pdf> accessed 8 May 2022.

AU and UNDP, 'The Futures Report, Making the AfCFTA Work for Women and Youth' (2020) 22 <https://au.int/en/documents/20201202/making-afcta-work-women-and-youth> accessed 8 May 2022.

AU Commission, 'African Union (AU) Agenda 2063: The Africa We Want' (2015) <https://au.int/sites/default/files/documents/36204-doc-agenda2063_popular_version_en.pdf> accessed 8 May 2022.

CEDAW and the UN, 'Transforming Our World: The 2030 Agenda for Sustainable Development', UNGA Res. A/RES/70/1 (25–27 September 2015).

Commission on the Status of Women, 'Report on the Forty-Sixth Session' Ch. I.A., Draft Resolution III.A, U.N. Doc. E/2002/27-E/CN.6/2002/13 (2002).

ECOWAS, 'Supplementary Act A/SA.1/01/10 on Personal Data Protection within ECOWAS' (16 February 2015) <www.tit.comm.ecowas.int/wp-content/uploads/2015/11/SIGNED-Data-Protection-Act.pdf> accessed 8 May 2022.

FAO, 'The State of Food and Agriculture' (2015) <www.fao.org/publications/sofa/2015/en/> accessed 8 May 2022.

Government of Singapore, 'Digital Economy Partnership Agreement' (2020) <www.mti.gov.sg/Trade/Digital-Economy-Agreements/The-Digital-Economy-Partnership-Agreement> accessed 8 May 2022.

ICRW, 'Gender Mainstreaming in Kenya' (2020) <www.icrw.org/wp-content/uploads/2020/09/Women-in-Manufacturing-Policy-Brief_9.20_ICRW.pdf> accessed 8 May 2022.

ITC, 'Mainstreaming Gender in Free Trade Agreements' (2020) <https://intracen.org/resources/publications/mainstreaming-gender-in-free-trade-agreements> accessed 8 May 2022.

'What Role for Women in International Trade?' (2019) <https://intracen.org/news-and-events/news/what-role-for-women-in-international-trade> accessed 8 May 2022.

Katende E and Kuhlmann K, 'Building a Regulatory Environment for Agricultural Finance' (Uganda Banker's Association, June 2019) <https://cb4fec8a-9641-471c-9042-2712ac32ce3e.filesusr.com/ugd/095963_a0e1d52d6040405c86334e2bfd8084dc.pdf> accessed 8 May 2022.

OECD, 'Bridging the Gender Digital Divide' (2018) <www.oecd.org/digital/bridging-the-digital-gender-divide.pdf> accessed 8 May 2022.

UNCTAD, 'Borderline: Women in Informal Cross-Border Trade in Malawi, the United Republic of Tanzania and Zambia' (2019) <https://unctad.org/system/files/official-document/ditc2018d3_en.pdf> accessed 8 May 2022.

'Harnessing E-Commerce for Sustainable Development' (WTO, 2017) <www.wto.org/english/res_e/booksp_e/aid4trade17_chap7_e.pdf> accessed 8 May 2022.

'Impact of the COVID-19 Pandemic on Trade and Development: Transitioning to a New Normal' (2020) <https://unctad.org/system/files/official-document/osg2020d1_en.pdf> accessed 8 May 2022.

UNECA, 'Advancing Gender-Equitable Outcomes in African Continental Free Trade Area (AfCFTA) Implementation' (2021) <www.uneca.org/sites/default/files/keymessageanddocuments/22May_Final_WhitePaper_Advancing_gender_equitable_outcomes.pdf> accessed 8 May 2022.

UNGA, 'Right to Privacy in the Digital Age', A/RES/71/199 (25 January 2017).

UNHRC, 'Right to Privacy in the Digital Age', A/HRC/RES/34/7 (7 April 2017).

World Bank and WTO, 'Women and Trade: The Role of Trade in Promoting Gender Equality' (WTO, 2020) <www.wto.org/english/res_e/booksp_e/women_trade_pub2807_e.pdf> accessed 8 May 2022.

WTO, 'Communication from Argentina, Canada, Colombia, Iceland, and Uruguay: Domestic Regulation – Development of Measures, Gender Equality', JOB/SERV/258 (2017).

'Informal Working Group on Trade and Gender: Trade and Gender-Related Provisions in Regional Trade Agreements' INF/TGE/COM/4 (WTO 2022) <https://docs.wto.org/dol2fe/Pages/SS/directdoc.aspx?filename=q:/INF/TGE/COM_4.pdf&Open=True> accessed 2 May 2023.

'Joint Declaration on Trade and Women's Economic Empowerment on the Occasion of the WTO Ministerial Conference in Buenos Aires in December 2017' (2017) <www.wto.org/english/thewto_e/minist_e/mc11_e/genderdeclarationmc11_e.pdf> accessed 8 May 2022.

REPORTS AND STUDIES

Afrieximbank, ‘African Trade Report: Informal Cross-Border Trade in Africa in the Context of the AfCFTA’ (2020) <https://afr-corp-media-prod.s3-eu-west-1.amazonaws.com/afrexim/African-Trade-Report-2020.pdf> accessed 8 May 2022.

Alliance for Financial Inclusion, ‘Policy and Regulatory Reforms in the AFI Network 2019’ (2019) <www.afi-global.org/sites/default/files/publications/2020-07/AFI_P%26amp%3BRR__G_2019_AW.pdf> accessed 8 May 2022.

Apiko P, Woolfrey S and Byiers B, ‘The Promise of the Africa Continental Free Trade Area (AfCFTA)’ (ECDPM, 2020) <https://ecdpm.org/publications/promise-african-continental-free-trade-area-afcfta/> accessed 8 May 2022.

Bahri A, ‘Gender Mainstreaming in Free Trade Agreements: A Regional Analysis and Good Practice Examples’ (Gender, Social Inclusion and Trade Knowledge Product Series, 2021) <https://wtochairs.org/sites/default/files/7.%20Gender%20mainstreaming%20in%20FTAs_final%20%286%29.pdf> accessed 8 May 2022.

Better than Cash Alliance, Women’s World Banking and World Bank, ‘Advancing Women’s Digital Financial Inclusion’ (2020) <www.mfw4a.org/sites/default/files/resources/saudig20_women_compressed.pdf> accessed 8 May 2022.

EASSI, ‘Annual Report’ (2020) <https://eassi.org/annual-reports/> accessed 8 May 2022.

Henson S, ‘Gender and Sanitary and Phytosanitary Measures in the Context of Trade: A Review of Issues and Policy Recommendations’ (2018) <https://standardsfacility.org/sites/default/files/Gender_SPS_measures_in_the_context_of_trade_Henson_ICTSD_Nov_18.pdf> accessed 8 May 2022.

Kuhlmann K, ‘Handbook on Provisions and Options for Trade in Times of Crisis and Pandemic’ (UNESCAP, 2021) <www.unescap.org/kp/2021/handbook-provisions-and-options-trade-times-crisis-and-pandemic> accessed 8 May 2022.

‘The Human Face of Trade and Food Security: Lessons on the Enabling Environment from Kenya and India’ (Centre for Strategic and International Studies, 2017) <www.csis.org/analysis/human-face-trade-and-food-security> accessed 8 May 2022.

‘U.S. Preference Programs: How Well Do They Work?’ (US Senate Finance Committee, 16 May 2007) <www.finance.senate.gov/hearings/us-preference-programs-how-well-do-they-workd> accessed 8 May 2022.

‘Why the United States and Africa Should Lead a Collaborative, Rules-Based Approach to Food Security’ (Center for Strategic and International Studies, 2020) <www.csis.org/analysis/why-united-states-and-africa-should-lead-collaborative-rules-based-approach-food-security> accessed 8 May 2022.

Kuhlmann K, Francis T, Thomas I, Le Great M, Rahman M, Madrigal F, Cohen M and Nalbantoglu A, ‘Reconceptualizing Free Trade Agreements through a Sustainable Development Lens’ (27 July 2020) <https://cb4fec8a-9641-471c-9042-2712ac32ce3e.filesusr.com/ugd/095963_8b66c44bd19b4683b974eaa267fd4070.pdf> accessed 8 May 2022.

STDF, ‘STDF Briefing Note, Inclusive Trade Solutions: Women in SPS Capacity Building’ (2015) <www.standardsfacility.org/sites/default/files/STDF_Briefing_note_13.pdf> accessed 8 May 2022.

WEBSITES, BLOGS AND NEWS ARTICLES

AU, 'Protocol to the African Charter on Human and Peoples' Rights on the Rights of Women in Africa' (2005), <https://au.int/en/treaties/protocol-african-charter-human-and-peoples-rights-rights-women-africa> accessed 8 May 2022

Al Mutair S, Konomi D and Page L, 'Trade & Gender: Exploring International Practices That Promote Women's Economic Empowerment' (TradeLab, 17 May 2018) <www.tradelab.org/single-post/2018/05/17/Trade-and-Gender-1> accessed 8 May 2022.

APO Group, 'Piecing the Puzzle of African Integration: The Successes and Exponential Potential' (2020) <www.africanews.com/2021/07/16/piecing-the-puzzle-of-african-integration-the-successes-and-exponential-potential/> accessed 8 May 2022.

AU, 'African Union Is Committed to Ending Child Labour and Other Forms of Human Exploitation' (29 May 2021) <https://au.int/en/articles/african-union-committed-ending-child-labour-and-other-forms-human-exploitation> accessed 8 May 2022.

Bayat N and Luke D, 'Gender Mainstreaming in AfCFTA National Strategies: Why It Matters for the SDGs' (IISD, 20 February 2020) <http://sdg.iisd.org/commentary/guest-articles/gender-mainstreaming-in-afcfta-national-strategies-why-it-matters-for-the-sdgs/> accessed 8 May 2022.

'E-Ping' <www.epingalert.org/en> accessed 8 May 2022.

Fundira T, 'Informal Cross-Border Trading – Review of the Simplified Trade Regimes in East and Southern Africa' (TRALAC, 2018) <www.tralac.org/publications/article/12825-informal-cross-border-trading-review-of-the-simplified-trade-regimes-in-east-and-southern-africa.html> accessed 8 May 2022.

Giokos E, 'Now for the Hard Part, Says Secretary-General of African Continental Free Trade Area' (CNN Business, 16 June 2021) <https://edition.cnn.com/2021/06/16/business/wamkele-mene-afcfta-spc-intl/index.html?utm_source=fbCNNi&utm_campaign=africa&utm_medium=social&fbclid=IwAR0x7fg7mRaFL_O5P61fKhR30jBM6bfow9_MQRtX6fvgKKQ6fB5h337uYyA> accessed 8 May 2022.

ILO, 'Definition of Gender Mainstreaming' <www.ilo.org/public/english/bureau/gender/newsite2002/about/defin.htm> accessed 8 May 2022.

Kuhlmann K, 'Flexibility and Innovation in International Economic Law: Enhancing Rule of Law, Inclusivity, and Resilience in the Time of COVID-19' (Afronomicslaw, 27 February 2020) <www.afronomicslaw.org/2020/08/27/flexibility-and-innovation-in-international-economic-law-enhancing-rule-of-law-inclusivity-and-resilience-in-the-time-of-covid-19/> accessed 8 May 2022.

Lane L and Nass P, 'Women in Trade Can Reinvigorate the WTO and Global Economy' (CIGI, 27 April 2020) <www.cigionline.org/articles/women-trade-can-reinvigorate-wto-and-global-economy/> accessed 8 May 2022.

Laperle-Forget L, 'Gender Responsiveness in Trade Agreements – How Does the AfCFTA Fare' (Tralac, 17 March 2021) <www.tralac.org/blog/article/15141-gender-responsiveness-in-trade-agreements-how-does-the-afcfta-fare.html> accessed 8 May 2022.

UN, 'Convention on the Elimination of All Forms of Discrimination Against Women', UNGA Res. 34/180 (18 December 1979) (CEDAW). <www.ohchr.org/en/instru

ments-mechanisms/instruments/convention-elimination-all-forms-discrimination-against-women> accessed 23 May 2023.

'Global Compact for Safe, Orderly and Regular Migration' (13 July 2018), <https://refugeesmigrants.un.org/migration-compact> accessed 8 May 2022.

UN Women, 'Opportunities for Women Entrepreneurs in the African Continental Free Trade Area' (2019) <https://africa.unwomen.org/en/digital-library/publications/2019/07/opportunities-for-women-in-the-acfta> accessed 8 May 2022.

'SDG 5: Achieve Gender Equality and Empower All Women and Girls' <www.unwomen.org/en/news/in-focus/women-and-the-sdgs/sdg-5-gender-equality> accessed 8 May 2022.

'Women in Informal Economy' (2021) <www.unwomen.org/en/news/in-focus/csw61/women-in-informal-economy> accessed 8 May 2022.

UNECE, 'Gender Responsive Standards Initiative' <https://unece.org/gender-responsive-standards-initiative> accessed 8 May 2022.

Xinhua, 'AfCFTA Secretariat Mulls Protocol to Promote Gender, Youth Interests' (*The Standard*, 27 April 2021) <www.standardmedia.co.ke/business-news/article/2001411063/afcfta-secretariat-mulls-protocol-to-promote-gender-youth-interests> accessed 8 May 2022.

Zarelli S and Lopez M, 'Leveraging Digital Solutions to Seize the Potential of Informal Cross-Border Trade' (UNCTAD, 29 April 2020) <https://unctad.org/es/node/2394> accessed 8 May 2022.

OTHER

Prabhu S, 'Indian Minister of Industry and Commerce' (Indian Press Conference, WTO Ministerial Conference, Buenos Aires, 11 December 2017).

CHAPTER 11: LEAVE NO WOMAN BEHIND: TOWARDS A MORE HOLISTIC GENDER AND TRADE POLICY IN CARICORUM (BRODBER/REMY)

BOOKS

Dohnert S, Crespi G and Maffioli A (eds.), *Exploring Firm-Level Innovation and Productivity in Developing Countries: The Perspective of Caribbean Small States* (IADB 2017).

Gmelch G, *Behind the Smile: The Working Lives of Caribbean Tourism* (Indiana University Press 2nd ed. 2012).

ARTICLES

Barker D, 'Beyond Women and Economics: Rereading "Women's Work"' (2005) 30 (4) *Journal of Women in Culture and Society* 2189–2209.

Barry T, Gahman L, Greenidge A and Mohamed A, 'Wrestling with Race and Colonialism in Caribbean Agriculture: Toward a (Food) Sovereign and (Gender) Just Future' (2020) 109 *Geoforum* 106–110.

Marques C, Leal C, Ferreira J and Ratten V, 'The Formal–Informal Dilemma for Women Micro-Entrepreneurs: Evidence from Brazil' (2018) 14 *Journal of Enterprising Communities: People and Places in the Global Economy* 5.

WORKING PAPERS

Ferdinand C (ed), 'Jobs, Gender and Small Enterprises in the Caribbean: Lessons from Barbados, Suriname and Trinidad and Tobago' (2001) SEED Working Paper No. 19 <www.ilo.org/wcmsp5/groups/public/—ed_emp/—emp_ent/documents/publication/wcms_113771.pdf> accessed 16 December 2021.

Fonjong L, 'The Role of Women's Nutrition Literacy in Food Security: The Case of Africa' (August 2022) Observer Research Foundation Issue Brief No. 572.

Kepler E and Scott S, 'Are Male and Female Entrepreneurs Really That Different?' (2007) Office of Advocacy Small Business Working Papers 07ekss, US Small Business Administration, Office of Advocacy.

Monteiro JA, 'Gender Related Provisions in Regional Trade Agreements' (2018) WTO Staff Working Paper ERSD-2018-15, 20–22 <www.wto.org/english/res_e/reser_e/ersd201815_e.pdf> accessed 13 September 2022.

UN ECLAC Gender Equality Observatory for Latin America and the Caribbean, 'International Trade: A Means to a Recovery with Gender Equality?', (ECLAC Notes No 31, 24 February 2021) <https://oig.cepal.org/sites/default/files/note_for_equality_gender_and_trade_n31.pdf> accessed 16 December 2021.

INSTITUTIONAL AND GOVERNMENTAL DOCUMENTS

CAFRA, *Gender and Trade in the Caribbean*, November 15, 2002.

CARICOM Secretariat, 'CARICOM's Statistics on International Trade in Services 2012–2018' (CARICOM 2021) <http://statistics.caricom.org/Files/Publications/Trade%20in%20Services/TIS_2012–2018.pdf> accessed 16 December 2021.

'Plan of Action to 2005: Framework for Mainstreaming Gender into Key CARICOM Programmes' (CARICOM 2005) <https://caricom.org/documents/11303-plan_of_action_to_2005.pdf> accessed 16 December 2021.

'Snapshot of CARICOM's Trade Series 1: CARICOM's Intra-Regional Trade 2011–2016' (CARICOM, 2018) <https://statistics.caricom.org/Files/Publications/Snapshot/Series_1_2011–2016.pdf> accessed 16 December 2021.

CEDA, 'Caribbean Export Outlook 2016' (CEDA, 2017) <http://statistics.caricom.org/snapshot.html> accessed 16 December 2021.

Hesse Bayne LNO and Haarr R (eds), 'Role of Gender in CARICOM and CARIFORUM Regional Trade Agreements' (UN Women, 2021) <https://caribbean.eclac.org/publications/role-gender-caricom-and-cariforum-regional-trade-agreements> accessed 16 December 2021.

IDB, 'Estimating the Size of the Informal Economy in Caribbean States' (IDB, 2017) <https://publications.iadb.org/publications/english/document/Estimating-the-

Size-of-the-Informal-Economy-in-Caribbean-States.pdf> accessed 16 December 2021.

IDB-CARICOM Report, 'Progress and Challenges of the Integration Agenda', (IDB/CARICOM, 2020) <https://publications.iadb.org/en/caricom-report-progress-and-challenges-integration-agenda> accessed 16 December 2021.

ITC, 'Empowering Women through Public Procurement' (2014) <www.intracen.org/uploadedFiles/intracenorg/Content/Publications/Women%20procurement%20guide-final-web.pdf> accessed 16 December 2021.

'Mainstreaming Gender in Free Trade Agreements' (2020) <https://intracen.org/resources/publications/mainstreaming-gender-in-free-trade-agreements> accessed 13 September 2022.

Ministry of Social Development and Family Services, Central Statistical Office and UNICEF, 'Trinidad and Tobago Multiple Indicator Cluster Survey 2011, Key Findings & Tables' (Port of Spain, Trinidad and Tobago: Ministry of Social Development and Family Services, Central Statistical Office and UNICEF).

OECD, 'Special Feature: The Caribbean Small States' <www.oecd.org/dev/americas/LEO-2019-Chapter-6.pdf> accessed 13 September 2022.

PIOJ and STATIN, 'Jamaica Survey of Living Conditions 2018' (PIOJ/STATIN, 2018).

UN WTO, 'Global and Regional Tourism Performance' <www.unwto.org/tourism-data/global-and-regional-tourism-performance> accessed 16 December 2021.

UNCTAD, 'The Inaugural Gender and Development Forum at the Fifteenth Session of the United Nations Conference on Trade and Development, Bridgetown Declaration', TD/INF.71 (7 October 2021).

'UNCTAD Trade and Gender Tool Box' (UNCTAD, 2017) <https://unctad.org/webflyer/unctad-trade-and-gender-tool-box> accessed 16 December 2021.

UNGA, 'Convention on the Elimination of All Forms of Discrimination Against Women', 1249 UNTS 13 (18 December 1979) ILO Equal Remuneration Convention, 1951 (No. 100);

'Transforming Our World: The 2030 Agenda for Sustainable Development', A/RES/70/1 (21 October 2015).

UNICEF Office for the Eastern Caribbean and Barbados Ministry of Youth and Community Empowerment, 'Generation Unlimited: The Wellbeing of Young People in Barbados Summary Findings' (UNICEF, 2020) <www.unicef.org/easterncaribbean/media/2171/file/generation%20unlimited%20barbados%20factsheet.pdf> accessed 16 December 2021.

WTO, 'Joint Ministerial Declaration on the Advancement of Gender Equality and Women's Economic Empowerment within Trade', WT/MIN(21)/4 (10 November 2021).

REPORTS AND STUDIES

Bellony A, Hoyos A and Ñopo H, 'Gender Earnings Gaps in the Caribbean: Evidence from Barbados and Jamaica' (IADB, 2010) <https://publications.iadb.org/publications/english/document/Gender-Earnings-Gaps-in-the-Caribbean-Evidence-from-Barbados-and-Jamaica.pdf> accessed 16 December 2021.

Brathwaite C, Nicholls A and Remy JY, 'Trading Our Way to Recovery during COVID-19: Recommendations for CARICOM Countries' (SRC, 2020) <https://shridathramphalcentre.com/wp-content/uploads/2020/10/SRC-COVID-19-Policy-Document-October-2020_FINAL.pdf> accessed 16 December 2021.

Budlender D and Iyahen I, 'Status of Women and Men Report: Productive Employment and Decent Work for All' (UN Women, 2019) <https://caribbean.unwomen.org/en/materials/publications/2019/10/status-of-women-and-men-report-productive-employment-and-decent-work-for-all#view> accessed 13 September 2022.

Hosein G, Basdeo-Gobin T and Gény L, 'Gender Mainstreaming in National Sustainable Development Planning in the Caribbean' (ECLAC Subregional Headquarters for the Caribbean, 2020) <www.cepal.org/sites/default/files/publication/files/45086/S1901209_en.pdf> accessed 16 December 2021.

ILO, *Women and Men in the Informal Economy: A Statistical Picture* (ILO, 3rd ed. 2018).

InfoDev, 'Profiling Caribbean Women Entrepreneurs: Business Environment, Sectoral Constraints and Programming Lessons' (World Bank and Inter-American Development Bank, 2017).

Padmore T, 'Summary Status of Women and Men Report – The Impacts of COVID-19' (UN Women, 2021) <https://caribbean.unwomen.org/en/materials/publications/2021/3/summary-report—status-of-women-and-men-in-covid-19> accessed 16 December 2021.

Rune D, 'Reimagining the U.S. Strategy in the Caribbean' (Center for Strategic and International Studies, 2021) <www.csis.org/analysis/reimagining-us-strategy-caribbean> accessed 13 September 2022.

WEBSITES, BLOGS AND NEWS ARTICLES

Arias Hofman I, 'More Female Entrepreneurs Please' (Caribbean DEVTrends+, 5 December 2019) <https://blogs.iadb.org/caribbean-dev-trends/en/more-female-entrepreneurs-please/> accessed 16 December 2021.

CANA, 'CARICOM Hosting National Consultations on Draft Regional Gender Policy' (Caribbean Communications Network, 8 February 2019) <www.tv6tnt.com/news/regional/caricom-hosting-national-consultations-on-draft-regional-gender-policy/article_e4df18a8-2baf-11e9-bdb7-b705294ad47a.html> accessed 16 December 2021.

CARICOM – Caribbean Community, 'Member States and Associate Members' <https://caricom.org/member-states-and-associate-members/> accessed 29 September 2022.

EIGE, 'Sweden – Gender Mainstreaming' <https://eige.europa.eu/gender-mainstreaming/countries/sweden> accessed 29 September 2022.

European Commission, 'The Overseas Countries and Territories (OCT)' (European Commission) <https://ec.europa.eu/taxation_customs/customs-4/international-affairs/origin-goods/general-aspects-preferential-origin/overseas-countries-and-territories-oct_en> accessed 16 December 2021.

ILO, 'ILO: Tourism Recovery Is Key to Overcoming COVID-19 Labour Crisis in Latin America and the Caribbean' (ILO Press Release, 30 June 2021) <www.ilo.org/caribbean/newsroom/WCMS_809331/lang–en/index.htm> accessed 16 December 2021.

ILOSTAT Database <https://ilostat.ilo.org/> accessed 16 December 2021.

MTI_WebAdmin, 'The SheTrades T&T Movement Is Here' (Ministry of Trade and Industry, 29 October 2020) <https://tradeind.gov.tt/shetrades-tt-launch-mr/> accessed 16 December 2021.

Spotlight Initiative, 'Where We Work' <www.spotlightinitiative.org/> accessed 16 December 2021.

Story-editor, 'Trinidad Launches National SheTrades Hub' (*St. Kitts Observer*, 21 September 2020) <www.thestkittsnevisobserver.com/trinidad-launches-national-shetrades-hub/> accessed 16 December 2021.

UN Women, CARICOM and CDB, 'Caribbean Women Count: Ending Violence against Women and Girls Data Hub' (UN Women, CARICOM, CDB, n.d.) <https://caribbeanwomencount.unwomen.org/> accessed 16 December 2021.

Wallace A, 'Challenges in Activism to End Gender-Based Violence in the Caribbean' (FAR, 6 December 2020), <https://feministallianceforrights.org/blog/2020/12/16/challenges-in-activism-to-end-gender-based-violence-in-the-caribbean/> accessed 16 December 2021.

WTO, 'Buenos Aires Declaration on Women and Trade Outlines Actions to Empower Women' <www.wto.org/english/news_e/news17_e/mc11_12dec17_e.htm> accessed 13 September 2022.

OTHER

Gadhoke P, '"We're Changing Our Ways": Women as Primary Caregivers and Adaptations of Food and Physical Activity Related Health Behaviors in Semi-Rural and Rural American Indian/Alaska Native Households', Conference: 141st APHA Annual Meeting and Exposition 2013, November 2013, Project: OPREVENT Project.

CHAPTER 12: SOUTH AMERICA'S LEADERSHIP IN GENDER MAINSTREAMING IN TRADE AGREEMENTS (CÁRACERES BUSTAMANTE/ MUÑOZ NAVIA)

BOOKS

Azar P, Espino A and Salvador S, *Los vínculos entre comercio, género y equidad. Un análisis para seis países de América Latina* (Red Internacional de Género y Comercio 2007).

Cáceres J, Muñoz F, Alarcón B, Fierro M, Montenegro C, Pérez A, Ramírez MJ, Rogaler T, Chávez L, Guzmán L, Hidalgo V and Martínez V, *Propuestas para la incorporación de disposiciones de género en el Protocolo Adicional de la Alianza del Pacífico* (Integración y Comercio 2021).

Espino A, *Impacting MERCOSUR's Gender Policies: Experiences, Lessons Learned, and the Ongoing Work of Civil Society in Latin America* (Montreal International Forum 2008).

López D, Muñoz F and Cáceres J, *Gender Inclusion in Chilean Free Trade Agreements* (Institute of International Studies University of Chile 2019).

Schultz P, *Does the Liberalization of Trade Advance Gender Equality in Schooling and Health?* (Routledge 2014).

BOOK CHAPTERS

Cáceres J and Muñoz F, 'The Gendered Impact of COVID-19 Crisis in Latin America' in Baisotti P and Moscuzza P (eds.), *New Paths of International Relations: Configuring Power in Times of Pandemic* (Sussex Academic Press in press).

Elson D, Grown C and Çaæatay N, 'Mainstream, Heterodox, and Feminist Trade Theory' in van Staveren I, Elson D, Grown C and Çaæatay N (eds.), *The Feminist Economics of Trade* (Routledge 2012).

Ribeiro Hoffmann A, 'Gender Mainstreaming in Mercosur and Mercosur–EU Trade Relations' in van der Vleuten A, van Eerdewijk A and Roggeband C (eds.), *Gender Equality Norms in Regional Governance: Transnational Dynamics in Europe, South America and Southern Africa* (Springer 2014).

ARTICLES

Bahri A, 'Measuring the Gender-Responsiveness of Free Trade Agreements: Using a Self-Evaluation Maturity Framework' (2019) 14(11/12) *Global Trade Customs Journal* 517–527.

Cadario F, Fantin F and Jacques M, 'La trata de personas con fines de explotación sexual en el contexto de pandemia: un análisis institucional desde el Mercosur y la Argentina' (2021) 26 *Nueva Serie Documentos de Trabajo* 53–60.

Eckersley R, 'The Big Chill: The WTO and Multilateral Environmental Agreements' (2004) 4(2) *Global Environmental Politics* 24–50.

González-Garibay M, 'The Trade–Labour and Trade–Environment Linkages: Together or Apart?' (2011) 10(2) *Journal of International Trade Law and Policy* 165–184.

He B and Murphy H, 'Global Social Justice at the WTO? The Role of NGOs in Constructing Global Social Contracts' (2007) 83(4) *International Affairs* 707–727.

Hinojosa L, 'EU-Mercosur Trade Agreement: Potential Impacts on Rural Livelihoods and Gender (with Focus on Bio-Fuels Feedstock Expansion)' (2009) 1(4) *Sustainability* 1120–1143.

López C and Míguez MC, 'Uruguay como Estado pequeño en el MERCOSUR (1991-2020): Una lectura desde la autonomía regional' (2021) 112 *Lua Nova: Revista de Cultura e Política* 181–216.

López D and Muñoz F, 'Trade Policy and Women in the Pacific Alliance' (2018) 25 *Agenda Internacional* 133–150.

Ridgeway C and Correll S, 'Unpacking the Gender System: A Theoretical Perspective on Gender Beliefs and Social Relations' (2004) 18 *Gender Society* 510.

Van den Putte L and Orbie J, 'EU Bilateral Trade Agreements and the Surprising Rise of Labour Provisions' (2015) 31(3) *International Journal of Comparative Labour Law Industrial Relations* 263–283.

WORKING PAPERS

Baccini L, Dür A, Elsig M and Milewicz K, 'The Design of Preferential Trade Agreements: A New Dataset in the Making' (2011) WTO Staff Working Paper No. ERSD-2011-10 <www.wto.org/english/res_e/reser_e/ersd201110_e.pdf> accessed 8 May 2022.

Ciuriak D, 'Canada's Progressive Trade Agenda and the NAFTA Renegotiation' (2018) CD Howe Institute Commentary No. 516 <www.cdhowe.org/sites/default/files/attachments/research_papers/mixed/Final%20June%2011%20Commentary_516.pdf> accessed 8 May 2022.

ECLAC, 'La autonomía económica de las mujeres en la recuperación sostenible y con igualdad' (2021) Informe Especial COVID-19 No. 9 <www.cepal.org/es/publicaciones/46633-la-autonomia-economica-mujeres-la-recuperacion-sostenible-igualdad> accessed 8 May 2022.

Monteiro JA, 'The Evolution of Gender-Related Provisions in Regional Trade Agreements' (2018) WTO Staff Working Paper ERSD-2018-15 <www.wto.org/english/res_e/reser_e/ersd201815_e.pdf> accessed 8 May 2022.

INSTITUTIONAL AND GOVERNMENTAL DOCUMENTS

Government of Canada, 'GTAGA' <www.international.gc.ca/trade-commerce/inclusive_trade-commerce_inclusif/itag-gaci/arrangement.aspx?lang=eng> accessed 8 May 2022.

Nueva Serie Documentos de Trabajo MERCOSUR, 'Guía MERCOSUR de atención a mujeres en situación de trata con fines de explotación sexual', MERCOSUR/CMC/REC No. 09/12 (2012).

OAS, 'Inter-American Convention on the Prevention, Punishment and Eradication of Violence against Women' <www.oas.org/juridico/english/treaties/a-61.html> accessed 8 May 2022.

Observatorio Estratégico de la Alianza del Pacífico, Programas de Apoyo al Emprendimiento Femenino en la Alianza del Pacífico (2018).

UNCTAD, 'Chile–Uruguay FTA' (4 October 2016) <https://investmentpolicy.unctad.org/international-investment-agreements/treaty-files/5408/download> accessed 8 May 2022.

'Gender and Trade: Assessing the Impact of Trade Agreements on Gender Equality: Canada–EU Comprehensive Economic and Trade Agreement' (2020) <https://unctad.org/system/files/official-document/UNWomen_2020d1_en.pdf> accessed 8 May 2022.

World Bank and WTO, 'Women and Trade. The Role of Trade in Promoting Gender Equality' (WTO, 2020) <www.wto.org/english/res_e/booksp_e/women_trade_pub2807_e.pdf> accessed 8 May 2022.

WTO, 'Joint Declaration on Trade and Women's Economic Empowerment on the Occasion of the WTO Ministerial Conference in Buenos Aires in December 2017') <www.wto.org/english/thewto_e/minist_e/mc11_e/genderdeclarationmc11_e.pdf> accessed 8 May 2022.

REPORTS AND STUDIES

Bensalem H, 'Gender as Included in Bilateral and Multi-Party Trade and Integration Agreements' (CUTS, 2017) <www.cuts-geneva.org/pdf/STUDY%20-%20Gender%20and%20Trade.pdf> accessed 8 May 2022.

Bircher M, Chahín D, López C, Mejía I and Villota A, 'Estudio de Diagnóstico, Radiografía de la participación de las mujeres empresarias de la Alianza del Pacífico en el comercio exterior (November 2020) <https://alianzapacifico.net/wp-content/uploads/Estudio-de-Diagnostico-Participacion-de-las-mujeres-empresarias-de-la-AP-en-el-comercio-exterior-NOV2020.pdf> accessed 8 May 2022.

Frohmann A, 'Género y emprendimiento exportador: iniciativas de cooperación regional' (ECLAC, 2018) <www.cepal.org/es/publicaciones/43287-genero-emprendimiento-exportador-iniciativas-cooperacion-regional> accessed 8 May 2022.

Klugman J, 'The 2030 Agenda and the Potential Contribution of Trade to Gender Equality' (ICSTD, 2016) <www.tralac.org/images/docs/10610/the-2030-agenda-and-the-potential-contribution-of-trade-to-gender-equality-ictsd-september-2016.pdf> accessed 8 May 2022.

Mora A, 'COVID-19 in Women's Lives: Reasons to Recognize the Differential Impacts' (Reliefweb, 2020) <https://reliefweb.int/report/world/covid-19-women-s-lives-reasons-recognize-differential-impacts> accessed 8 May 2022.

Pacific Alliance, Additional Protocol <https://alianzapacifico.net/?wpdmdl=1118> accessed 8 May 2022.

'Declaración de Cali: XII Cumbre de la Alianza del Pacífico' (2017) <https://alianzapacifico.net/?wpdmdl=1167> accessed 8 May 2022.

'Declaración Presidencial sobre Igualdad de Género' [Presidential Declaration on Gender Equality] (2020) <https://alianzapacifico.net/?wpdmdl=21208> accessed 8 May 2022.

'Guidelines for the Use of Inclusive Language' (2020) <https://alianzapacifico.net/wp-content/uploads/Guia_LenguajeInclusivo_vf.pdf> accessed 8 May 2022.

'Mandatos Grupo Técnico de Género [Gender Technical Group Mandate]' (2019) <https://alianzapacifico.net/?wpdmdl=17500> accessed 8 May 2022.

Presidential Declaration (2017) <https://alianzapacifico.net/?wpdmdl=1167> accessed 8 May 2022.

Viilup E, 'The EU's Trade Policy: From Gender-Blind to Gender Sensitive?' (2015) In-Depth Analysis for the European Parliament, DG External Policies <www.europarl.europa.eu/RegData/etudes/IDAN/2015/549058/EXPO_IDA(2015)549058_EN.pdf> accessed 8 May 2022.

Zarrilli S, 'The New Way of Addressing Gender Inequality Issues in Trade Agreements: Is It a True Revolution?' (UNCTAD, 2017) <https://unctad.org/system/files/official-document/presspb2017d2_en.pdf> accessed 8 May 2022.

WEBSITES, BLOGS AND NEWS ARTICLES

D'Elia C, 'Análisis del TLC Chile–Uruguay' (Conexión INTAL, 2017) <https://conexionintal.iadb.org/2017/09/01/analisis-del-tlc-chile-uruguay/> accessed 8 May 2022.

Pacific Alliance/Alianza del Pacífico <https://alianzapacifico.net/en/> accessed 8 May 2022.

Schüller P, 'Senado aprobó acuerdo de libre comercio entre Chile y Brasil' (*La Nación*, 12 August 2020) <www.lanacion.cl/senado-aprobo-acuerdo-de-libre-comercio-entre-chile-y-brasil/> accessed 8 May 2022.

SUBREI, 'México ingresa al Arreglo Global de Comercio y Género integrado por Canadá, Chile y Nueva Zelandia' (2021) <www.subrei.gob.cl/sala-de-prensa/noticias/detalle-noticias/2021/10/06/m%C3%A9xico-ingresa-al-arreglo-global-de-comercio-y-g%C3%A9nero-integrado-por-canad%C3%A1-chile-y-nueva-zelandia> accessed 8 May 2022.

OTHER

Pacific Alliance, 'Gender Glossary' (2019) <https://alianzapacifico.net/en/?s=gender+glossary> accessed 25 May 2023.

CHAPTER 13: GENDER MAINSTREAMING IN TRADE AGREEMENTS: BEST PRACTICE EXAMPLES AND CHALLENGES IN THE ASIA PACIFIC (BAHRI)

BOOKS

Cook G, *A Digest of WTO Jurisprudence on Public International Law Concepts and Principles* (Cambridge University Press 2015).

ARTICLES

Bahri A, 'Measuring the Gender-Responsiveness of Free Trade Agreements: Using a Self-Evaluation Maturity Framework' (2019) 14(11) *Global Trade & Customs Journal* 517–527.

'Women at the Frontline of COVID-19: Can Gender Mainstreaming in Free Trade Agreements Help?' (2020) 23(3) *Journal of International Economic Law* 563–582.

Buyukkayaci DN, 'Reflections of Female Domination in the Profession over the Nursing Strength: Turkey Sample' (2012) 3(24) *International Journal of Business and Social Science* 182–187.

Downs GW, Rocke D and Barsoom P, 'Is the Good News about Compliance Good News about Cooperation?' (1996) 50(3) *International Organization* 379–406.

Hathaway OA, 'The Cost of Commitment' (2003) 55(5) *Stanford Law Review* 1821–1862.

Murdoch JC and Sandler T, 'The Voluntary Provision of a Pure Public Good: The Case of Reduced CFC Emissions and the Montreal Protocol' (1997) 63(3) *Journal of Public Economics* 331–349.

Simmons BA, 'International Law and State Behavior: Commitment and Compliance in International Monetary Affairs' (2000) 94(4) *American Political Science Review* 819–835.

Whitsitt E, 'A Comment on the Public Morals Exception in International Trade and the EC – Seal Products Case: Moral Imperialism and Other Concerns' (2014) 3 (4) *Cambridge Journal of International and Comparative Law* 1376.

WORKING PAPERS

Gaukrodger D, 'The Balance between Investor Protection and the Right to Regulate in Investment Treaties: A Scoping Paper' (2017) OECD Working Papers on International Investment No. 2017/02 <https://doi.org/10.1787/82786801-en> accessed 8 May 2022.

Monteiro JA, 'Gender-Related Provisions in Regional Trade Agreements' (2021) WTO Staff Working Papers ERSD-2018-15 <www.wto.org/english/res_e/reser_e/ersd201815_e.pdf> accessed 8 May 2022.

Smith LC, Ramakrishnan U, Ndiaye A, Haddad L and Martorell R, 'The Importance of Women's Status for Child Nutrition in Developing Countries' (2003) International Food Policy Research Institute Research Report No. 131 <https://ebrary.ifpri.org/utils/getfile/collection/p15738coll2/id/48032/filename/43490.pdf> accessed 8 May 2022.

UN Women, 'Gender Equality & Trade Policy' (2011) UN Women Watch Resource Paper <www.un.org/womenwatch/feature/trade/gender_equality_and_trade_policy.pdf> accessed 8 May 2022.

INSTITUTIONAL AND GOVERNMENTAL DOCUMENTS

Government of the United Kingdom, 'Export Strategy: Supporting and Connecting Businesses to Grow on the World Stage' (2018) GOV.UK Policy Paper <www.gov.uk/government/publications/export-strategy-supporting-and-connecting-businesses-to-grow-on-the-world-stage/export-strategy-supporting-and-connecting-businesses-to-grow-on-the-world-stage> accessed 8 May 2022.

IMF, 'Regional Economic Outlook for Asia and Pacific' (October 2021) <www.imf.org/en/Publications/REO/APAC/Issues/2021/10/15/regional-economic-outlook-for-asia-and-pacific-october-2021> accessed 8 May 2022;

ITC, 'Unlocking Markets for Women to Trade' (2015) <https://intracen.org/resources/publications/unlocking-markets-for-women-to-trade> accessed 8 May 2022.

UK Policy Briefings (September 2019) <https://wbg.org.uk/wp-content/uploads/2019/09/FINAL-.pdf> accessed 8 May 2022.

UN, 'World Economic Situation and Prospects 2014: Country Classification' (2014) <www.un.org/en/development/desa/policy/wesp/wesp_current/2014wesp_country_classification.pdf> accessed 8 May 2022.

World Bank, 'Women, Business and the Law' (World Bank Reports 2010, 2012, 2014, 2016, 2018, 2019 and 2020).

World Bank and WTO, 'Women and Trade: The Role of Trade in Promoting Gender Equality' (2020) <https://wbl.worldbank.org/en/wbl> accessed 8 May 2022.

WTO, 'Joint Declaration on Trade and Women's Economic Empowerment on the Occasion of the WTO Ministerial Conference in Buenos Aires in December 2017' (2017) <www.wto.org/english/thewto_e/minist_e/mc11_e/genderdeclarationmc11_e.pdf> accessed 8 May 2022.

'The Economic Impact of COVID-19 on Women in Vulnerable Sectors and Economies' (2020) <https://doi.org/10.30875/74a82a3d-en> accessed 8 May 2022.

REPORTS AND STUDIES

Bahri A, 'Gender Mainstreaming in Free Trade Agreements: A Regional Analysis and Good Practice Examples' (Gender, Social Inclusion and Trade Knowledge Product Series, 2021), <https://wtochairs.org/sites/default/files/7.%20Gender%20mainstreaming%20in%20FTAs_final%20%286%29.pdf> accessed 8 May 2022.

Ramos G, 'Women at the Core of the Fight against COVID-19 Crisis' (OECD, 1 April 2020) <www.oecd.org/coronavirus/policy-responses/women-at-the-core-of-the-fight-against-covid-19-crisis-553a8269/> accessed 8 May 2022.

von Hagen M, 'Trade and Gender – Exploring a Reciprocal Relationship: Approaches to Mitigate and Measure Gender-Related Trade Impacts' (OECD, 2014) <www.oecd.org/dac/gender-development/GIZ_Trade%20and%20Gender_Exploring%20a%20reciprocal%20relationship.pdf> accessed 8 May 2022.

WEBSITES, BLOGS AND NEWS ARTICLES

APWLD, 'Statement: Women's Rights Groups Call on Governments to Reject the WTO Declaration on Women's Economic Empowerment' (12 December 2017) <https://apwld.org/statement-womens-rights-groups-call-on-governments-to-reject-the-wto-declaration-on-womens-economic-empowerment/> accessed 8 May 2022.

FAO, 'Economic and Demographic Developments' <www.fao.org/3/w7705e/w7705e07.htm> accessed 8 May 2022.

Guyot C, 'EP Wants to Include Gender Equality in Free-Trade Agreements' (EURACTIV, 14 March 2018) <www.euractiv.com/section/politics/news/ep-wants-to-include-gender-equality-in-free-trade-agreements/> accessed 8 May 2022.

ILO, 'The Gender Gap in Employment: What's Holding Women Back?' (ILO Infostories, 2017) <www.ilo.org/infostories/en-GB/Stories/Employment/barriers-women#footer> accessed 8 May 2022.

Singh A, 'Explained: India's Refusal to Back WTO Declaration on Gender Equality in Trade' (QRIUS, 15 December 2017) <https://qrius.com/explained-india-refusal-gender-equality-trade/> accessed 8 May 2022.

UN Women, Gender Equality Glossary, <www.un.org/womenwatch/osagi/conceptsandefinitions.htm> accessed 8 May 2022.

WEF, 'Closing the Gender Gap Accelerators' <www.weforum.org/projects/closing-the-gender-gap-accelerators> accessed 8 May 2022.

Woetzel J, Madgavkar A, Elingrud K, Labaye E, Devillard S, Kutcher E, Manyika J, Dobbs R and Krishnan M, 'The Power of Parity: How Advancing Women's Equality can Add $12 Trillion' (Mckinsey Global Institute, September 2015) <www.mckinsey.com/featured-insights/employment-and-growth/how-advancing-womens-equality-can-add-12-trillion-to-global-growth> accessed 8 May 2022.

World Population Review, 'Asia-Pacific Countries' <https://worldpopulationreview.com/country-rankings/apac-countries> accessed 8 May 2022.

Zarrilli S and Luomaranta H, 'Gender and Unemployment: Lessons from the COVID-19 Pandemic' (UNCTAD, 8 April 2021) <https://unctad.org/news/gender-and-unemployment-lessons-covid-19-pandemic> accessed 8 May 2022.

OTHER

Prabhu S, 'Indian Minister of Industry and Commerce' (Indian Press Conference, WTO Ministerial Conference, Buenos Aires, 11 December 2017).

CHAPTER 14: CRAFTING CANADA'S GENDER-RESPONSIVE TRADE POLICY (PAQUET/WAINWRIGHT-KEMDIRIM)

BOOKS

Rodrik D, *The Globalization Paradox: Democracy and the Future of the World Economy* (Norton 2011).

ARTICLES

Benguria F, 'The Matching and Sorting of Exporting and Importing Firms: Theory and Evidence' (2021) 131/103430 *Journal of International Economics* 1–49.

Lamp N, 'How Should We Think about the Winners and Losers from Globalization?' (2019) 30(4) *European Journal of International Law* 1359–1397.

WORKING PAPERS

Atkinson A and Messy F, 'Measuring Financial Literacy – Results of the OECD / International Network on Financial Education (INFE) Pilot Study' (2012) OECD Working Papers on Finance, Insurance and Private Pensions No. 15, 43 <https://doi.org/10.1787/5k9csfs90fr4-en> accessed 8 May 2022.

Brockmeier M, 'A Graphical Exposition of the GTAP Model' (1996, as revised in 2001) GTAP Technical Paper No. 8 <www.gtap.agecon.purdue.edu/resources/download/181.pdf> accessed 8 May 2022.

Devlin A, Kovak BK and Morrow P, 'The Long-Run Labour Market Effects of the Canada-U.S. Free Trade Agreement' (2020) Research Report prepared for Global Affairs Canada <www.aeaweb.org/conference/2021/preliminary/paper/9ibAiHk4> accessed 8 May 2022.

Huang L and Rivard P, 'Financing of Women-Owned Small and Medium-Sized Enterprises in Canada' (2021) <www-ic.fjgc-gccf.gc.ca/eic/site/061.nsf/vwapj/2021_Fin_women-owned-SMEs_Canada_EN4.pdf/$file/2021_Fin_women-owned-SMEs_Canada_EN4.pdf> accessed 8 May 2022.

ITC, 'New Pathways to E-Commerce: A Global MSME Competitiveness Survey' (2017) <https://intracen.org/media/file/2437> accessed 8 May 2022.

Korinek J, Moïsé E and Tange J, 'Trade and Gender: A Framework of Analysis' (2021) OECD Trade Policy Papers No. 246 <https://doi.org/10.1787/6db59d80-en> accessed 8 May 2022.

Marchese M, 'Policy Brief on Access to Business Start-Up Finance for Inclusive Entrepreneurship – Entrepreneurial Activities in Europe' (2014) <www.oecd.org/cfe/leed/Finacing%20inclusive%20entrepreneurship%20policy%20brief%20EN.pdf> accessed 8 May 2022.

Palladini J, Sekkel J and Wang W, 'Gender and SME Exporters' (in press) <www.international.gc.ca/trade-commerce/economist-economiste/index.aspx?lang=eng> accessed 8 May 2022.

INSTITUTIONAL AND GOVERNMENTAL DOCUMENTS

CETA Joint Committee on Small and Medium-sized Enterprises, 'Recommendation 003/2018 of 26 September 2018 of the CETA Joint Committee on Small- and Medium-Sized Enterprises (SMEs)' (2018) <www.international.gc.ca/trade-commerce/trade-agreements-accords-commerciaux/agr-acc/ceta-aecg/rec-003.aspx?lang=eng> accessed 8 May 2022.

CETA Joint Committee on Trade and Gender, 'Recommendation 002/2018 of 26 September 2018 of the CETA Joint Committee on Trade and Gender' (2018) <www.international.gc.ca/trade-commerce/trade-agreements-accords-commerciaux/agr-acc/ceta-aecg/rec-002.aspx?lang=eng> accessed 8 May 2022.

CETA Joint Committee on Trade, Climate Action and the Paris Agreement, 'Recommendation 001/2018 of 26 September 2018 of the CETA Joint Committee on Trade, Climate Action and the Paris Agreement' (2018) <www.international.gc.ca/trade-commerce/trade-agreements-accords-commerciaux/agr-acc/ceta-aecg/rec-001.aspx?lang=eng> accessed 8 May 2022.

Global Affairs Canada, 'Joint Statement on the Launch of Negotiations toward a Comprehensive Free Trade Agreement between Canada and the Mercosur Member States' (9 March 2018) <www.international.gc.ca/trade-commerce/trade-agreements-accords-commerciaux/agr-acc/mercosur/joint_statement-declaration_commune.aspx?lang=eng> accessed 8 May 2022.

'Minister Champagne Welcomes Agreement to Launch Trade Negotiations with Mercosur' (GAC, 9 March 2018) <www.canada.ca/en/global-affairs/news/2018/03/minister-champagne-welcomes-agreement-to-launch-trade-negotiations-with-mercosur.html> accessed 8 May 2022.

'Summary of Initial GBA+ for Canada Mercosur FTA Negotiations' (2019) Online Stakeholder Consultations Paper <www.international.gc.ca/trade-commerce/assets/pdfs/gba_plus_summary-acs_plus_resume_eng.pdf> accessed 8 May 2022.

'The Canada–United States–Mexico Agreement, Economic Impact Assessment' (2020) <www.international.gc.ca/trade-commerce/trade-agreements-accords-commerciaux/agr-acc/cusma-aceum/economic_assessment-analyse_economiques.aspx?lang=eng> accessed 8 May 2022.

'Business Women in International Trade' <www.tradecommissioner.gc.ca/businesswomen-femmesdaffaires/index.aspx?lang=eng> accessed 8 May 2022.

'Canada's Feminist International Assistance Policy' <www.international.gc.ca/world-monde/issues_development-enjeux_developpement/priorities-priorites/policy-politique.aspx?lang=eng> accessed 8 May 2022.

'Canada's Inclusive Approach to Trade' <www.international.gc.ca/trade-commerce/gender_equality-egalite_genres/approach-can-approche.aspx?lang=eng> accessed 8 May 2022.

'Canada's State of Trade 2020 – The Early Impacts of COVID-19 on Trade' (2020) <www.international.gc.ca/gac-amc/publications/economist-economiste/state-of-trade-commerce-international-2020.aspx?lang=eng#20> accessed 25 May 2023.

'Canada–Israel Free Trade Agreement (CIFTA) – Building on 20 Years of Growth' <www.international.gc.ca/trade-commerce/trade-agreements-accords-commerciaux/agr-acc/israel/fta-ale/index.aspx?lang=eng&_ga=2.172535846.441821398.1638973123-2080543025.1611591818> accessed 8 May 2022.

'Diversifying Canada's Trade and Investment Opportunities' <www.international.gc.ca/gac-amc/campaign-campagne/trade-diversification-commerce/index.aspx?lang=eng> accessed 8 May 2022.

'Gender-Based Analysis Plus (GBA+)' <https://women-gender-equality.canada.ca/en/gender-based-analysis-plus.html> accessed 8 May 2022.

'Global Trade and Gender Arrangement' <www.international.gc.ca/trade-commerce/inclusive_trade-commerce_inclusif/itag-gaci/arrangement.aspx?lang=eng> accessed 8 May 2022.

'Inclusive Trade Action Group' <www.international.gc.ca/trade-commerce/inclusive_trade-commerce_inclusif/itag-gaci/index.aspx?lang=eng> accessed 8 May 2022.

'International Trade and Its Benefits to Canada' (2012) <www.international.gc.ca/trade-commerce/economist-economiste/state_of_trade-commerce_international/special_feature-2012-article_special.aspx?lang=eng> accessed 8 May 2022.

'Majority-Female Owned Exporting SMEs in Canada' (2016) <https://tradecommissioner.gc.ca/businesswomen-femmesdaffaires/assets/pdfs/majority-female_owned_exporting_smes_canada_eng.pdf?_ga=2.159767997.1696028190.1649271305-1421400920.1649056212> accessed 8 May 2022.

'Overview: Trade Policy and Gender-Based Analysis Plus' <www.international.gc.ca/trade-commerce/gender_equality-egalite_genres/gba_plus-acs_plus.aspx?lang=eng> accessed 8 May 2022.

'Public Services and Procurement Canada Unveils Plan to Modernize Federal Procurement' (5 March 2019) <www.canada.ca/en/public-services-procurement/news/2019/03/public-services-and-procurement-canada-unveils-plan-to-modernize-federal-procurement.html> accessed 8 May 2022.

'Summary of Initial GBA Plus for the Canada–Indonesia CEPA negotiations' <www.international.gc.ca/trade-commerce/trade-agreements-accords-commerciaux/agr-acc/indonesia-indonesie/cepa-apeg/summary-gba-acs-resume.aspx?lang=eng> accessed 11 September 2022.

'Summary of Initial GBA Plus for the Canada–UK FTA negotiations' <www.international.gc.ca/trade-commerce/trade-agreements-accords-commerciaux/agr-acc/canada_uk_fta-ale_canada_ru/summary-gba-init-resume-acs.aspx?lang=eng> accessed 11 September 2022.

'Summary of Initial GBA Plus for Negotiations to Modernize the Canada–Ukraine FTA' <www.international.gc.ca/trade-commerce/trade-agreements-accords-commerciaux/agr-acc/ukraine/summary_gba-acs_sommaire.aspx?lang=eng> accessed 16 May 2023.

'Summary of the Survey on Financing and Growth of Small and Medium Enterprises, 2017' (2018) <www.ic.gc.ca/eic/site/061.nsf/vwapj/SFGSME_Summary-EFCPME_Sommaire_2017_eng-V2.pdf/$file/SFGSME_Summary-EFCPME_Sommaire_2017_eng-V2.pdf> accessed 8 May 2022.

'Survey on Financing and Growth of Small and Medium Enterprises' (2014) Table 25, <www.ic.gc.ca/eic/site/061.nsf/vwapj/SummarySFGSMEs-ResumeEFCPME_2014_eng.pdf/$file/SummarySFGSMEs-ResumeEFCPME_2014_eng.pdf> accessed 8 May 2022.

'Trade Commissioner Service' <www.tradecommissioner.gc.ca/index.aspx?lang=eng> accessed 8 May 2022.

OECD, 'Going Digital: The Future of Work for Women' (2017) Policy Brief on the Future of Work <www.oecd.org/employment/Going-Digital-the-Future-of-Work-for-Women.pdf> accessed 8 May 2022.

'Making Trade Work for All' (2017) OECD Trade Policy Papers No. 202 <http://dx.doi.org/10.1787/6e27effd-en> accessed 8 May 2022.

Statistics Canada, 'North American Industry Classification System (NAICS) Canada 2012, All Demographics' <www.statcan.gc.ca/en/subjects/standard/naics/2012/index> accessed 8 May 2022.

UNCTAD, 'Trade and Gender – Assessing the Impact of Trade Agreements on Gender Equality: Canada–EU Comprehensive Economic and Trade Agreement' <https://unctad.org/system/files/official-document/UNWomen_2020d1_en.pdf> accessed 8 May 2022.

World Bank, 'Women, Business and the Law 2019' <http://pubdocs.worldbank.org/en/702301554216687135/WBL-DECADE-OF-REFORM-2019-WEB-04-01.pdf> accessed 8 May 2022.

WTO, 'Buenos Aires Declaration on Women and Trade Outlines Actions to Empower Women' (12 December 2017) <www.wto.org/english/news_e/news17_e/mc11_12dec17_e.htm> accessed 8 May 2022.

'Joint Declaration on Trade and Women's Economic Empowerment on the Occasion of the WTO Ministerial Conference in Buenos Aires in December 2017' (2017) <www.wto.org/english/thewto_e/minist_e/mc11_e/genderdeclarationmc11_e.pdf> accessed 8 May 2022.

REPORTS AND STUDIES

Bélanger Baur AA, 'Women-Owned Exporting Small and Medium Enterprises – Descriptive and Comparative Analysis' (2019) <www.international.gc.ca/trade-commerce/economist-economiste/analysis-analyse/women_owned-export-entreprises_femmes.aspx?lang=eng> accessed 8 May 2022.

WEBSITES, BLOGS AND NEWS ARTICLES

BMO Financial Group, 'BMO Women's Day Study: Majority of Canadian Women Would Start Their Own Business' (2 March 2012) <https://newsroom.bmo.com/2012-03-02-BMO-Womens-Day-Study-Majority-of-Canadian-Women-Would-Start-Their-Own-Business> accessed 8 May 2022.

Cooper L, 'Canadian Women Grabbing the Baton' (RBC Economics Research, October 2013) <www.rbc.com/economics/economic-reports/pdf/other-reports/canadianwomengrabbingthebaton.pdf> accessed 8 May 2022.

Index

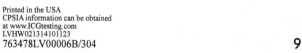

Printed in the USA
CPSIA information can be obtained
at www.ICGtesting.com
LVHW021314101123
763478LV00006B/304